Additional Praise for *The ART of Risk Management*

"Finally, a book that gets the fundamentals of alternative risk transfer down and, at the same time, explores the current innovations in the real world used by real risk managers, CFOs and insurers. I highly recommend it."

—Tom Skwarek
Principal, Swiss Re

"Culp shows us that there is, after all, a captivating way to explain corporate finance, risk management, and alternative risk strategy. Everyone involved in creating value or managing risk, from apprentice to Chairman, should read this book."

—Norbert G. Johanning
Managing Director, DaimlerChrysler Capital Services

"By integrating capital theory and risk management into the orthodox theory of corporate finance, Christopher Culp has created a new, more comprehensive theory of corporate finance. This innovative treatise allows us to understand why the capital and insurance markets are converging at record speed. More importantly, it sheds a great deal of light on how new products can be used to effectively play the alternative risk management game."

—Steve H. Hanke
Professor of Applied Economics, The Johns Hopkins University,
and Chairman, The Friedberg Mercantile Group, Inc.

"A very comprehensive and pedagogical analysis of alternative risk transfer products. This book will be highly valuable to anyone involved with decision-making involving the convergence between risk management and corporation finance."

—Rajna Gibson
Professor of Finance, University of Zurich

"An excellent insight into the history, theory, evolution and practical implementation of the risk management process. In an uncertain economic and legal environment, senior managers and directors should read this book if they are concerned about delivering shareholder value."

—Richard Bassett
CEO, Risktoolz

"This book provides a rigorous application of corporate finance and capital market theory to the fascinating field of alternative risk transfer. Most other books in this field are about instruments and techniques—Dr. Culp's new book is about management and economics. The book excellently integrates the investment banking, insurance, and corporate perspectives, in a way accessible for a broad audience."

—Professor Heinz Zimmermann
Wirtschaftswissenschaftliches Zentrum WWZ
Universität Basel, Switzerland

John Wiley & Sons

Founded in 1807, John Wiley & Sons is the oldest independent publishing company in the United States. With offices in North America, Europe, Australia, and Asia, Wiley is globally committed to developing and marketing print and electronic products and services for our customers' professional and personal knowledge and understanding.

The Wiley Finance series contains books written specifically for finance and investment professionals as well as sophisticated individual investors and their financial advisors. Book topics range from portfolio management to e-commerce, risk management, financial engineering, valuation and financial instrument analysis, as well as much more.

For a list of available titles, please visir our website at *www.Wiley Finance.com*.

The ART of Risk
management

Alternative Risk Transfer,
Capital Structure, and the Convergence of
Insurance and Capital Markets

CHRISTOPHER L. CULP

John Wiley & Sons, Inc.

Published by John Wiley & Sons, Inc.
Published simultaneously in Canada.

This publication is designed to provide accurate and authoritative information in
regard to the subject matter covered. It is sold with the understanding that the
publisher is not engaged in rendering legal, accounting, or other professional services.
If legal advice or other expert assistance is required, the services of a competent
professional person should be sought.

Chapter 24 is reprinted by permission of the *Journal of Risk Finance* (Winter 2001).

ISBN 0-471-12495-8

Printed in the United States of America

10 9 8 7 6 5 4 3 2 1

contents

ACKNOWLEDGMENTS   ix

PREFACE: COMPREHENSIVE APPROACH TO CORPORATION FINANCE   xi

PART I

THE QUEST FOR OPTIMAL CAPITAL STRUCTURE   1

CHAPTER 1

The Nature of Financial Capital   3
Appendix 1-1: A Brief Introduction to Capital Theory   19
Appendix 1-2: A Review of Basic Option Concepts   26

CHAPTER 2

A Securities Perspective on Capital Structure   36

CHAPTER 3

When Is Capital Structure Irrelevant?   72

CHAPTER 4

Benefits and Costs of Debt and the "Trade-off Theory" of Optimal Capital Structure   85

CHAPTER 5

Asymmetric Information, Adverse Selection, and the "Pecking Order Theory" of Optimal Capital Structure   116

CHAPTER 6

Distinguishing between Capital Structure Theories   127

CHAPTER 7

Risk and Signaling Capital   133

CHAPTER 8

Regulatory Capital   168

PART II
CAPITAL STRUCTURE AND RISK MANAGEMENT   183

CHAPTER 9
A Vocabulary of Risk   185

CHAPTER 10
Risk Management as a Process   199

CHAPTER 11
Risk Management and Capital Structure   218

PART III
CLASSICAL RISK TRANSFORMATION PRODUCTS   243

CHAPTER 12
Commercial Banking Products   245

CHAPTER 13
Derivatives   263

CHAPTER 14
Asset Disposition and Securitized Products   294

CHAPTER 15
Insurance   311

CHAPTER 16
Reinsurance   333

PART IV
ALTERNATIVE RISK TRANSFER PRODUCTS   349

CHAPTER 17
Alternative Risk Finance vs. Alternative Risk Transfer   351

CHAPTER 18
Alternative Risk Finance: Self-Insurance, Captives, and Captivelike Structures   362

CHAPTER 19
Alternative Risk Finance: Finite Risk Products and Solutions   380

CHAPTER 20
Integrated Multiline and Multitrigger Alternative Risk Transfer Products   401

CHAPTER 21
Committed Capital and Guarantees   427

CHAPTER 22
Alternative Risk Securitizations and Securitized Products   452

PART V

PRACTICAL CONSIDERATIONS FOR WOULD-BE ARTISTS   489

CHAPTER 23
USAA Prime: Choice Cats for Diversifying Investors   491
by Morton N. Lane

CHAPTER 24
Emerging Role of Patent Law in Risk Finance   503
by J. B. Heaton

CHAPTER 25
Weather Derivatives or Insurance? Considerations for Energy Companies   520
by Andrea S. Kramer

CHAPTER 26
Convergence of Insurance and Investment Banking: Representations and
Warranties Insurance and Other Insurance Products Designed to
Facilitate Corporate Transactions   532
by Theodore A. Boundas and Teri Lee Ferro

BIBLIOGRAPHY   545

INDEX   559

acknowledgments

The success of any book dealing with both the theory and the practice of a new and rapidly evolving market depends critically on the willingness of numerous individuals to help the author learn, assimilate, and critically assess the subject matter. I have been very fortunate in that regard to have received invaluable assistance in many different forms from many people. Space precludes me from mentioning each person's unique contribution, but that does not diminish my gratitude to them all. Accordingly, my thanks to Keith Bockus, Colleen Brennan, Mark Brickell, Ray Brown, Thomas Bründler, Christoph Bürer, Don Chew, Kevin Dages, Charles Davidson, Ken French, Roger Garrison, Steve Hanke, Roger Hickey, Brian Houghlin, Timo Ihamuotila, Norbert Johanning, Barb Kavanagh, Robert Korajczyk, Jason Kravitt, Martin Lasance, Alastair Laurie-Walker, Claudio Loderer, Stuart McCrary, Beatrix Münger, Stefan Müller, Jim Nelson, Greg Niehaus, Andrea Neves, Mike Onak, Paul Palmer, Pascal Perritaz, Philippe Planchat, William Rendall, Eric Ricknell, Angelika Schöchlin (whose timely comments on each and every chapter of the manuscript proved especially valuable), Astrid Schornick, Willi Schürch, Prakash Shimpi, Tom Skwarek, Fred L. Smith, Jr., Jürg Steiger, Giles Stockton, John Szobocsan, Jacques Tierny, Wally Turbeville, Domenica Ulrich, Carol Wakefield, Edith Wolfram, Paul Wöhrmann, Bertrand Wollner, Erwin Zimmerman, Heinz Zimmermann, and Mark Zmijewski.

I am particularly grateful to those who contributed the guest chapters that appear in Part IV of this book—Ted Boundas, Teri Lee Ferro, J. B. Heaton, Andie Kramer, and Mort Lane. Their expertise and insights have certainly increased my knowledge of the field, and their contributions make the book much stronger than had it been my effort alone.

Bill Falloon again served as an excellent editor. Now our third time at bat, he is always more willing than he should be to lend a helping hand—a task for which his combination of editing skills and content expertise make him uniquely well qualified. Both he and Melissa Scuereb at Wiley were more than patient with me in my effort to complete the book on time, especially following the disruptions created by the tragic events of September 11, 2001.

For serving as guinea pigs on early versions of this material, I thank the students in my MBA classes at The University of Chicago's Graduate School of Business in both Barcelona and Chicago during the Summer and Autumn 2002 quarters, respectively. I am also grateful to Claudio Lodver for giving me the first occasion to teach this book at the Institut für Finanzmanagement of Universität Bern, Switzerland in January 2002.

Writing two books in the space of two years is a good way to test the patience of those around you, and I am lucky to have so much support in that regard. I am especially grateful to Willie Doolie and Roger Plummer, past and current chairpersons of the Executive Committee of the Governing Members of the Chicago Symphony Orchestra, who both bailed me out more than once as I futilely attempted to serve my term on the Executive Committee as its Vice Chairman of Finance. Similar thanks to the staff at the Chicago Symphony for their understanding and tolerance—especially Jennifer Moran, Allison Szafranski, and Lisa McDaniel.

Most of this book was written from late July to early September in Vitznau, Switzerland. Although a self-imposed writer's exile on the shores of Lake Luzern can be both pleasant and productive, it also can get overwhelming and isolated at times. My Swiss friends and neighbors had more than enough hospitality to temper the bad days—Gerry Stähli, Eddi Schild, and Bruno Zimmermann, in particular. Kamaryn Tanner also deserves thanks in that regard—not just for trekking to Europe twice during my writing exile to give me a few badly needed breaks in Switzerland and in the Austrian heurigan, but more generally for her unfailing friendship and support over the past 15 years.

Finally, I am very blessed by a family whose love and tolerance seem to know literally no bounds. My wonderful parents, Johnny and Lindalu Lovier, are always at the top of that list, but I am also appreciative of the years of support I have received from Steve Anne Stockstill; Dan and Tee Ann Culp and their daughters Connie, Keri, and Danielle; S. S. Montgomery; Cathy and Mack Veach and their children Scott, Chad, Katie, and Josh; Stephanie Roe; Shelley Odgen; and Robert, Ann, and Mark Dennison. And posthumous thanks to my father, V. Cary Culp, without whom none of this would have been possible. A former senior captain for American Airlines, I can still hear his voice from the cockpit every time I am on a plane that has just taken off: "It sure is good to be back in the sky again."

Of course, the usual disclaimer applies. The views and positions expressed herein along with any remaining errors are mine alone and are not necessarily those of any institution with which I am affiliated, any clients of those institutions, or anyone thanked here.

preface
a comprehensive approach
to corporation finance

Capital and insurance markets are converging in both product offerings and institutional participation. Consider some examples. At the product level, asset assurance can be obtained through either (re-)insurance guarantees or credit derivatives, and foreign exchange or commodity price hedging now can be done with futures, forwards, options, and swaps or with a multiline insurance contract. At the institutional level, investment banks like Goldman Sachs and Lehman Brothers now have licensed reinsurance subsidiaries, and reinsurers like Swiss Re now directly place the functional equivalent of new debt and equity with their corporate customers.

The recent trend toward convergence in insurance and capital markets is much more fundamental than just increasing product or institutional similarities. The real convergence is between corporation finance and risk management. No longer is it possible to consider seriously how a firm will manage its risk without simultaneously considering how that firm raises capital. And conversely.

At the center of this convergence maelstrom is alternative risk transfer (ART), or contracts, structures, and solutions provided by insurance and/or reinsurance companies that enable firms either to finance or to transfer some of the risks to which they are exposed in a nontraditional way, thereby functioning as synthetic debt or equity (or a hybrid) in a firm's capital structure. In short, ART forms represent the foray of the (re-)insurance industry into the corporation financing and capital formation processes.

Today providers of risk control products like derivatives also are integrally involved in the capital formation process, although many participants in this area may not realize this. To discuss risk management in a corporate finance context is still considered odd by some. And yet, increasingly, to discuss one without considering the other is quite likely to lead to serious inefficiencies in either how a firm manages risk or how it raises funds—if not both.

A comprehensive approach to corporate finance must take into account both risk finance and risk transfer alternatives, both capital and insurance market solutions, and both risk management and classical treasury decision-making processes. Companies like Michelin, United Grain Growers, and

British Aerospace that have adopted this comprehensive approach to corporate finance have met with tremendous success and provide us with very useful examples of the kinds of efficiencies that can all too easily be left on the table when a more compartmentalized approach is adopted.

The objective of this book is to explore the theoretical foundations underlying a comprehensive approach to corporation finance and the practical solutions and structures available to corporate treasurers for turning this theory into practice.

TWO FACES OF RISK MANAGEMENT

Risk management remains a divided world. In one camp are the classical insurance types who speak using terms like "retrocessionaires" and "funded retentions" and "attachment points." In another camp are the financial risk managers who focus on concepts like value at risk, credit limits, and hedge ratios. Despite the fundamental similarities between what members of the two camps are trying to do for their companies, often it is impossible to hold a conversation with both groups at the same time without a translator.

The difference is not simply one of vocabulary, although that is surely still a major source of disparity between the insurance and capital markets worlds. The disparate nature of the two worlds of risk management, however, is more fundamentally a difference in perspective. Derivatives and financial instruments are considered the domain of asset pricers and financial engineers. And insurance is widely regarded as the playground of actuaries and brokers bent on finding the right attachment points for the hundreds of perils and hazards they can identify. Not helping things, most college and graduate insurance texts today pay little more than cursory attention to financial products. And even worse are the best-selling financial instrument texts, in which insurance concepts are virtually never mentioned.

The rise of "enterprise-wide risk management" in the 1990s has helped heighten awareness to the basic similarities between the two risk management camps. As companies increasingly seek to identify, measure, monitor, and control their risks in a holistic, top-down, integrated, and comprehensive manner, the basic complementarities between the financial and insurance risk management worlds have become more obvious.

The common ground underlying a comprehensive and integrated risk management program is one of *capital structure optimization*—that is, how to maximize firm value by choosing the mixture of securities and risk management products and solutions that gives the company access to capital at the lowest possible weighted cost. The questions a corporate treasurer must ask today thus now go well beyond questions like "What should be our dividend policy?" and "Should we have a target leverage ratio?" The questions today now include "How much excess capital should we hold for risk and signaling purposes?" and "What form should that capital take?"

We are taught, of course, that a firm's financing decisions do not affect its value under certain assumptions. And even when those assumptions are violated, there is no single empirically valid theory that delivers any clear notion of "optimal capital structure." Nevertheless, in some situations certain sources of capital simply make less sense for particular companies than others. And similarly, risk management products and solutions can impact the value of firms quite differently depending on the circumstances and business objectives surrounding those firms. The lack of any empirically supported theory of optimal capital structure thus does not appear to stop firms from searching for one, and in many cases value-enhancing decisions are the result. As such, there can be little doubt that the era of a comprehensive approach to corporation finance has arrived.

TARGET AUDIENCE AND OUTLINE OF THE BOOK

This book is aimed at participants in both the capital markets (derivatives and securities alike) and (re-)insurance industries as well as—if not more so—at corporate treasurers and financial officers responsible for deciding how their firms should finance themselves. Risk managers also should find the work relevant, as should university students seeking a graduate course on relations between risk management (both worlds) and corporate finance.

My 2001 book *The Risk Management Process: Business Strategy and Tactics* does have a few similarities to this book, but not many. That book was concerned principally with examining the organizational process of risk management, including risk identification, measurement, and control. This book, by contrast, focuses almost entirely on risk control, or the various products and solutions firms can use to maximize their value by closing gaps between actual risk exposures and the risk exposures security holders want their firms to have. With the exception of some overlap in Chapters 3, 9, and 10, the books are basically different.

Those familiar with my prior book will detect some similarities in the themes of Part I in each book, both of which seek to lay down a solid corporate finance foundation for what follows. Although similar in spirit, the actual groundwork laid is quite different. Part I of my 2001 book dealt mainly with how risk management can increase the value of the firm in a corporate finance framework. Part I here focuses much more on corporate finance itself and the process by which firms strive to find the holy grail of an optimal capital structure.

Specifically, Part I of this book begins by discussing the nature of capital (Chapter 1) and how the investment banking process enables firms to raise capital by issuing traditional securities (Chapter 2). We develop in these two chapters two fundamental concepts that will be used throughout the book. The first is a perspective on capital structure that allows us to view different sources of capital through a common lens—the lens of options theory, through which similarities between securities, derivatives, and ART forms will be very easy to see. The second concept is the notion of an economic balance sheet, or a way of viewing a firm's assets and liabilities from an economic perspective—without the constraining limitations of accounting rules.

Chapters 3 through 6 introduce the notion of optimal capital structure. We begin with a review of the assumptions under which a firm has no optimal capital structure—when its cost of capital and capital structure do not affect its investment decisions or value. In Chapters 4 and 5, we consider two competing theories of when and how a firm's capital structure does affect its value. Chapter 6 provides a summary of the empirical evidence for and against these theories. In Chapters 7 and 8, we consider a world where investment and financing decisions are not independent of one another and how that world can lead firms to want to hold capital for nontraditional reasons. Chapter 7 explores the role of risk capital and signaling capital, and Chapter 8 reviews various issues concerning regulatory capital.

Part II relates the corporate financing and capital structure issues explored in Part I to a firm's risk management decisions. The risks to which a firm may be subject through its primary business activities are reviewed in Chapter 9, and the process by which firms engage in the enterprise-wide management of those risks is summarized in Chapter 10. Chapter 11 explicitly explores the link between risk management and capital structure decisions.

In Part III, we review the traditional methods available to firms for controlling their risks and altering their effective economic balance sheet leverage in the process. Chapters 12 to 16 present an overview of the risk control and capital structure functions provided by banking products (Chapter 12), derivatives targeted at market and credit risk (Chapter 13), asset divestitures and securitizations (Chapter 14), insurance (Chapter 15), and reinsurance (Chapter 16).

Part IV examines the emerging market for ART forms based on their type and function. Chapter 17 introduces the ART world and distinguishes between two distinct parts of that world: risk finance and risk transfer. Chapters 18 and 19 review the major alternative risk financing structures, including funded self-insurance programs and captives (Chapter 18) and finite risk products (Chapter 19). Chapter 20 presents some recent developments in risk transfer products, including integrated risk management products that have emerged as a response to the heightened awareness of the benefits of enterprise-wide risk management. Multiline and multitrigger products are reviewed, especially in the context of some fairly prominent failures in the former category. Chapter 21 reviews contingent capital in the form of committed capital (i.e., synthetic debt) and guarantees (i.e., synthetic equity). Finally, Chapter 22 reviews some of the more important recent developments in alternative risk securitization and securitized products.

Part V presents some practical issues that potential users of ART products will want to take into consideration. To accomplish this, it made sense to seek out the advice of the experts themselves. Accordingly, the four chapters are written by guest contributors. In Chapter 23, Morton Lane presents a comparison of two catastrophic insurance structures to illustrate specifically some important distinctions between catastrophic insurance products and to show more generally the difference between catastrophic insurance derivatives and securitized products. In Chapter 24, J. B. Heaton provides some important background on the increasingly important role of patent law on financial innovations, relying on a number of specific ART examples to make his points. Chapter 25 by Andrea Kramer discusses the distinctions between derivatives and insurance in the area of weather risk management and presents some important issues for energy companies to take into account in choosing between these products. Part V concludes with an extensive review by Theodore Boundas and Teri Lee Ferro of the numerous ART forms available to facilitate corporate transactions such as mergers and acquisitions.

a guide for readers

Having summarized the outline of the book, a few comments are now in order on how to *read* the book. Importantly, the book is *written* in a way to develop the theory before getting into the products and applications. All case studies, for example, appear in Parts IV and V of the book so that readers might have an understanding of the theory behind these cases before getting embroiled in their details.

For academics and students seeking an understanding of both the theory and practice of ART in the context of modern corporate finance, it probably makes sense to read the book from start to finish. Similarly, practitioners directly involved in this market who already know how ART forms work may find a sequential reading of the book most beneficial.

For those readers, however, whose main interest is on understanding ART as a type of product—how ART forms work and how they have been used—skipping direclty to Parts IV and V (possibly with a review of existing risk management products in Part III) may make more sense than reading the book in order. Part I, in particular, admittedly requires a reasonable investment of time to get through, and it is *not* essential if your objective is just to get an overview of the market. If, having read about the mechanics of these products, readers want to learn about how ART fits into the theory and practice of corporate finance, returning to Parts I and II for a subsequent read is certainly still possible.

The Quest for Optimal Capital Structure

CHAPTER 1

The Nature of Financial Capital

Many of the financial products offered by insurance and derivatives industry participants today are increasingly similar to one another. Commentators on this phenomenon call it "convergence." The interesting question is not really whether convergence is occurring in these two markets—it is—but rather toward what are the markets converging?

The common theme underlying many of the new financial structures in insurance and capital markets is that of capital structure optimization. In short, insurance and capital market products are increasingly similar because they are increasingly designed to help firms reduce their cost of capital or to allocate their capital across business lines more efficiently on a risk-adjusted basis.

We thus must begin with a discussion of capital itself: What is the nature of capital? What is a firm's capital structure, and how does it relate to a firm's cost of capital? When and why can the capital structure of a firm affect the value of a firm? And how are capital structure, firm value, and risk management interrelated? These are the questions that are explored in Part I of this book.

This chapter tackles the first of these questions. An especially important part of our initial exploration of capital is the development of a common perspective we can use to evaluate different sources of capital and their costs. The perspective we adopt is to view capital, capital structure, and sources of capital from an options perspective. Specifically, we attempt in this chapter to provide answers to the following questions:

- What is capital, and, in particular, what is the difference between real capital and financial capital?
- How do firms utilize financial capital?
- What are the fundamental building blocks firms can use to create financial capital claims or claims on their real capital assets?

3

■ How can the fundamental building blocks of capital structure be viewed through an options framework?

■ How does the mixture of the types of claims issued by a firm define the company's capital structure?

WHAT IS CAPITAL?

To define "capital" properly would involve a heavier dose of economic theory and philosophy than space or time permits here. Appendix 1-1 at the end of this chapter provides a brief survey of capital theory from an economic history perspective. For our purposes here, it is sufficient to draw a critical distinction between what we may call "real" and "financial" capital.

Specifically, what firms do is act as organic production transformation functions, turning capital into a sequence of goods. How firms finance that process is where the crucial distinction between what we shall call "real capital" versus "financial capital" comes into play.[1]

In their classic work *The Theory of Finance* (1972), Fama and Miller define "total net investment" as "the value in money units of the net change in the stock of [real] capital," thus providing us with a bridge to link real and financial capital. In short, real capital is what gives firms their productive role in the economy, but financial capital is what is required to fund the acquisition and maintenance of real capital.

The following equation expresses the relation between financial capital and real capital at any one point in time algebraically as follows:

$$[E_{t-1}(t) + \delta(t)] + [D_{t-1}(t) + \rho(t)] = X(t) - I(t) + V(t) \qquad (1.1)$$

where $E_{t-1}(t)$ = time t market value of the firm's stock outstanding at time t−1
$D_{t-1}(t)$ = time t market value of the firm's debt outstanding at time t−1
$\delta(t)$ = dividends paid at time t to stockholders
$\rho(t)$ = interest paid at time t to bondholders
$X(t)$ = time t earnings on prior investments in real capital
$I(t)$ = time t investments in new real capital
$V(t)$ = discounted expected present value of future net cash flows

The left-hand side of equation 1.1 above is the value of the financial capital of the firm, and the right-hand side is the value of its real capital expressed as current earnings, current investment spending, and the discounted future income the firm's capital assets are expected to generate over time.

Modigliani and Miller (1958) showed, among other things, that the right rate to use in discounting the uncertain future input values and output values of a project is the cost to the investing firm of raising the investment capital—that is, the *financial* capital—required to support such a project.

Referring to the liabilities that firms issue to fund their acquisitions of real capital as another form of capital may seem a bit confusing. But there is good reason for this use of terminology. Namely, financial economists like to refer to financial capital assets such as stocks and bonds as "capital" because they are capital to investors. Indeed, the celebrated "capital asset pricing model" was developed not to explain how the value of televisions and drills are determined in equilibrium but rather how the value of stocks and bonds as claims on televisions and drills are determined in equilibrium. But if the model works for stocks and bonds, it should also work for plants and equipment—hence the use of the term "capital" to describe both.

To avoid confusion, however, when we subsequently refer to "capital" without any modifying adjectives, readers should assume that we are talking about financial capital. References to real or physical capital will be qualified accordingly. Similarly, terms like "capital structure" also are used here in the financial context—the structure of claims issued by a corporation to finance its net investment spending. This is at odds with the use of the same phrase in macroeconomics, where "capital structure" often refers to the relation between the productive real capital stock, other factors of production, and total output.[2]

CORPORATE UTILIZATION OF FINANCIAL CAPITAL

Financial capital can be defined quite broadly as the collection of contracts and claims that the firm needs to raise cash required for the operation of its business as an ongoing enterprise. Operating a business as an ongoing enterprise, however, often—if not usually—involves more than just raising money to pay employees and finance current investment expenditures. It also includes keeping the business going, and doing so efficiently.

Firms may need financial capital for at least five reasons, each of which is discussed briefly below. These sections are included mainly as a preview to the rest of Part I. We will return to all of the issues raised here later and in much more detail.

Investment Capital

In Chapters 2 through 5, we focus on the primary reason that firms are thought to need financial capital—to fund their investment activities. Accordingly, we call this *investment capital*.[3]

Fama and French (1999) find that an average of about 70 percent of all spending on new investments by publicly traded nonfinancial U.S. firms from 1951 to 1996 was financed out of those firms' net cash earnings (i.e., retained earnings plus depreciation).[4] Accordingly, a large bulk of most firms' investment capital comes in the form of *internal* funds—"internal" because the firm's need not go to outsiders to raise the money.

Despite the dominance of internal finance as a source of investment capital, the 30 percent average shortfall of net cash earnings below investment spending had to come from somewhere. To generate the funds required to close such deficits between net cash earnings and investment, firms issue "claims." In exchange for providing firms with current funds, "investors" in those financial capital claims receive certain rights to the cash flows arising from the firm's investments. In other words, by issuing financial capital claims, corporations can fund their investments and get cash today by promising a repayment in the future that will depend on how the firm's investments turn out. In this sense, financial capital claims issued by firms to generate investment capital are direct claims on the firm's real capital.

Note that investment capital as we define it is actually not strictly limited to investments but also includes operating expenses such as salaries, rent, coffee for employees, jet fuel for the company plane, and the like. Unless specifically indicated otherwise, in this chapter all of those operating expenses are lumped into the term "investment spending."

Ownership and Control

Financial capital claims also serve as a method by which the ownership of a firm—or, more specifically, ownership of the real capital assets that define the firm—can be transferred efficiently. In lieu of selling individual plants, machines, and employees, firms can sell claims on those real assets.

In turn, financial capital assets convey some form of control rights and governance responsibilities on the holders of those claims. By receiving a financial claim on the firm's real capital, investors naturally want some say in how the firm uses that real capital—including its acquisition of new real capital through its investment decisions.

For the most part, we will not deal with the connections between the existence of financial capital claims sold to investors and the governance issues those claims create.[5]

Risk Capital

As noted, Chapters 2 to 5 will focus on investment capital, because all firms need investment capital. Even if the financial capital used to fund investments is internal, all firms invest. Otherwise, they would not be engaged in production activities.

In Chapters 7 and 8, we explore three other reasons why firms might need financial capital. But unlike investment capital, these reasons do not hold true at all firms. The discussions in Chapters 4 and 5 lay the foundation for us to see when firms also might need capital for reasons beyond investment.

The first reason, discussed in Chapter 7, is risk capital. In order to operate its business as a going concern, some firms must carefully avoid the dangerous territory known as financial distress. Especially if financial distress costs increase disproportionately as a firm gets closer to insolvency, the more likely it is that the firm may need to use financial capital as a buffer against incurring those distress costs. When some firms find it necessary to raise risk capital, this capital is virtually always capital held in excess of that required to finance investment in order to avoid going bust.

Although the basic concept of risk capital is developed in Chapter 7, we will revisit the notion of risk capital repeatedly throughout Parts II to IV. In particular, we will see that risk capital is capital held by firms either to absorb or to fund losses that the firm elects to retain. Risk capital also can be acquired "synthetically" when a firm decides not to retain all of its risks, but rather to transfer some of its risks to other capital market participants. Although we review in detail different methods by which firms can access such synthetic capital in Parts III and IV, a very early understanding of the distinction between capital used for risk financing and capital obtained directly or *de facto* through risk transfer is fundamental.

Signaling Capital

A second reason that some firms might wish to hold financial capital over and above that required to fund current operations and investments occurs when managers have better information about the true quality of their investment decisions and growth opportunities than external investors. In this situation, firms often have significant trouble communicating the value of their investment decisions and their financial integrity to public security holders—trouble that ultimately can prevent firms from undertaking all the investment projects they would otherwise choose to make if everyone had access to the same information. The nature of these sorts of problems is the subject of Chapter 5.

For many years, people have conjectured that firms can use their financial capital in order to signal certain things about the information managers possess that investors do not. Quite often the issuance of financial capital claims is itself a signal. The Miller and Rock (1985) model, for example, says that firms issue financial claims only when they have information that future profits will be lower than expected. Conversely, firms pay dividends only when they perceive higher future profits than investors expect. Consequently, the issuance of financial claims and the dividend payout policy of the firm are both signals of the firm's future profits.

In the Miller and Rock world, issuing certain types of financial claims is a negative signal to the market about future profits. But especially in recent years, some contend that the signal sent to the market by issuing a financial claim depends on what the claim is and who holds it. Issuing new stocks through seasoned equity offerings or exchange offerings is widely considered to signal bad news at a firm, whereas taking out a bank loan is usually a positive signal.

Apart from the signal sent by the issuance of new financial capital, some also believe that the funds generated by issuing new claims can have benefits that exceed the costs of obtaining additional external finance. As will be explained in Chapter 7, signaling capital can provide firms with a means of indirectly communicating the value of their investment decisions to market participants, thereby reducing the firm's cost of raising new capital and, in particular, helping the firm to avoid situations in which positive net present value investment projects might have to be forgone because of an inability to convince investors that the investment makes sense.

Regulatory Capital

A final reason why some firms issue financial capital is because they have no choice if they wish to comply with the regulations to which they are subject. Banks, insurance companies, securities broker/dealers, savings institutions, and other firms are all subject to minimum capital requirements.

Unfortunately, regulation does not always define financial capital in the same way as corporate treasurers. Consequently, as we will see in Chapter 8, many firms are forced to issue specific kinds of financial capital in order to satisfy regulatory requirements. Regulatory capital is what we call the financial capital firms must hold for this reason.

FUNDAMENTAL BUILDING BLOCKS OF INVESTMENT CAPITAL

Investment capital is the financial capital that virtually every firm needs in order to do what firms do—"produce" something. As mentioned, the bulk of investment capital comes in the form of retained earnings and depreciation. But when firms need to go beyond these sources of funds to pay for current investment expenditures, they can offer two fundamental types of claims in exchange for cash:

1. Residual claims
2. Fixed claims

When a firm raises cash by promising investors a claim whose value rises as the net cash flows of the business rise, the firm has created a residual claim. When a firm raises cash today and promises to repay investors in the future a specific amount of cash plus some "interest"—that is, an amount that does not increase when the firm's cash flows or asset values increase—the firm has created a fixed claim. Both types of financial capital can be viewed by invoking some basic concepts of options theory.

Residual Claims

A residual claim gives its holder a claim on the net cash flows of a firm. As long as the firm remains in business, this claim represents a claim on the net cash flows on the firm's assets (i.e., real capital investments). If the firm shuts down, the residual claim is a claim on the net cash flows obtained from the liquidation of the firm's real capital assets. In return for this residual claim on the firm's net cash flows, the holder of this claim gives the company cash that it can use to fund its assets, service its investments, and the like. Residual claims are more commonly known as equity.

Exhibit 1.1 depicts the economic balance sheet of a firm that issues only equity in order to fund its acquisition of some assets. Suppose the firm otherwise has no liabilities and no internal funds. At any time t, the assets have a market value of A(t). The market value of the firm's equity, E(t), is thus exactly equal to the market value of its assets.

Suppose the firm whose balance sheet is depicted in Exhibit 1.1 liquidates its assets at time T for a total value of A(T). The time T value of the total distribution to equity holders of the firm would be equal to E(T). This liquidation payoff is shown in Exhibit 1.2 and varies dollar for dollar with the

Assets	Liabilities and Equity
Assets: A(t)	Equity: E(t)

EXHIBIT 1.1   Economic Balance Sheet of a Firm with Only Equity Claims

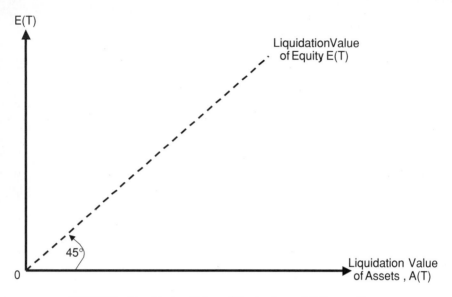

EXHIBIT 1.2   Liquidation Value of Equity in an All-Equity Firm

liquidation value of the firm's assets. Note that the figure assumes that equity holders have limited liability; equity holders can *at worst* have a claim worth zero and cannot be called upon to make an additional payment to the firm or its liquidator.

We can express the value of equity at time T in an all-equity firm more formally as

$$E(T) = \max[A(T), 0]$$

At any given time, a corporation can fund the acquisition of new assets or the assumption of new investment projects by issuing new equity claims. If the value of new equities issued at any time t is denoted $e(t)$ and the time t market value of equity claims outstanding from prior period t–1 is now denoted $E_{t-1}(t)$, then the time t value of the firm can be expressed as

$$V(t) = A(t) = E_{t-1}(t) + e(t) \qquad (1.2)$$

Equity holders of a firm can earn income from their claims even if the firm does not liquidate its assets. Some equity holders can generate income by selling their claims to others and pocketing any capital gain that may have occurred over the holding period. Other equity holders can obtain income through dividends, if the firm in question both has the cash flows to pay dividends and decides to do so.

A firm's ability to pay dividends to its equity claimants is dictated by its "cash flow constraint." (We shall return to the firm's *willingness* to pay dividends later.) At time t, the firm earns a total gross cash inflow from its assets of $X(t)$ and may invest a total of $I(t)$ in new investment projects or assets. Recall also that we include in $I(t)$ operating expenses such as salary and overhead.

The sum of dividends paid to equity holders at time t, $\delta(t)$, can be no greater than the net cash flow of the firm *plus* the proceeds from any new security issues. Assuming the firm retains no net cash flows and distributes all excess cash flows to equity holders in the form of dividends, the following relation holds:

$$\delta(t) = X(t) - I(t) + e(t) \qquad (1.3)$$

Substituting the firm's cash flow constraint in equation 1.3 into the value of the firm given in equation 1.2 allows us to express the total wealth of all equity holders as follows:

$$E_{t-1}(t) + \delta(t) = X(t) - I(t) + V(t) \qquad (1.4)$$

If the firm winds up its operations and liquidates its assets at some time T, the resulting distribution to equity holders can be viewed as a liquidating dividend, such that

$$E_{T-1}(T) = X(T) + A(T) \qquad (1.5)$$

where the left-hand side of equation 1.5 is the liquidating dividend.

Fixed Claims

The second way that a firm can raise cash is by issuing claims whose maximum payoff does not rise as the net cash flows of the firm increase. The value of such claims still depends on the firm's net cash flows because they must be adequate to make the promised payoff. But because that payoff is fixed and does not rise with the firm's profitability, this second type of claim is called a *fixed claim* and is more commonly known as *debt*.

Exhibit 1.3 depicts the economic balance sheet of a firm that has both debt and equity in its capital structure. The market value of the firm is equal to the market value of its assets at any time t, which in turn is equal to the sum of the market values of the firm's debt and equity, or

Assets	Liabilities and Equity
Assets: A(t)	Liabilities: D(t)
	Equity: E(t)

EXHIBIT 1.3   Economic Balance Sheet of a Firm Equity and Debt Claims

$$V(t) = A(t) = D(t) + E(t)$$

Suppose the total amount borrowed by the firm through the issuance of debt instruments is denoted FV, for the "face value" of all its fixed claims. Suppose further that the debt pays FV on some date T and nothing before then. If the firm liquidates its assets on that date T for A(T), debt holders will receive *at most* FV. If the liquidation value of assets exceeds the face value of debt, equity holders, in turn, receive the residual—that is, A(T) – FV. But if the liquidation of the firm's assets generates insufficient cash to pay off debt holders, the creditors to the firm as a group will receive only A(T) < FV. Accordingly, the liquidation value of all debt claims issued by the firm at time T is equal to

$$D(T) = \min[FV, A(T)]$$

This liquidation payoff is shown in Exhibit 1.4. When the market value of assets exceeds the promised debt repayment of FV, the payment to debt holders is constant at FV. When assets are below total debt liabilities, the payment to debt holders declines dollar for dollar with the liquidation value of the firm's assets. As in Exhibit 1.2, we continue to assume limited liability so that debt holders can never be called on to make an additional payment to the firm or its liquidator.

The issuance of fixed claims by the firm also affects the payoff of residual claim holders, because, as the term "residual claim" implies, residual claimants

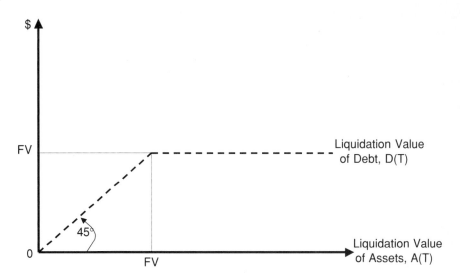

EXHIBIT 1.4 Liquidation Value of Debt in an Equity-and-Debt–Financed Firm

are entitled only to what is left after the firm has honored its other obligations—which now include debt. To see this, consider the distribution of proceeds obtained by liquidating the assets of a firm whose payoff to debt claimants was shown in Exhibit 1.4. Exhibit 1.5 now shows the market value of the residual claimants of this firm upon liquidation. Clearly, equity holders as residual claimants receive nothing until the total face value of outstanding debt has been paid off. But at that point, the residual claimants enjoy a dollar-for-dollar gain for every dollar of asset value above the debt obligation.

A corporation that issues both debt and equity claims can fund the acquisition of new assets or the assumption of investment projects either by issuing new equity claims or by borrowing through debt contracts. If the value of new debt issued at any time t is denoted d(t) and the time t market value of debt claims outstanding from prior period t–1 is denoted $D_{t-1}(t)$, then the time t value of the firm at any time t can now be expressed as

$$V(t) = A(t) = [E_{t-1}(t) + e(t)] + [D_{t-1}(t) + d(t)] \qquad (1.6)$$

Like equity holders, debt holders of a firm can earn income from their claims before the claims are due or before the firm wraps up and liquidates its assets, either by selling their claims or through receiving "interest payments" on the debt. Although we assumed in the example above that debt holders received a single payment—FV—only on date T, that need not be and often is not the case.

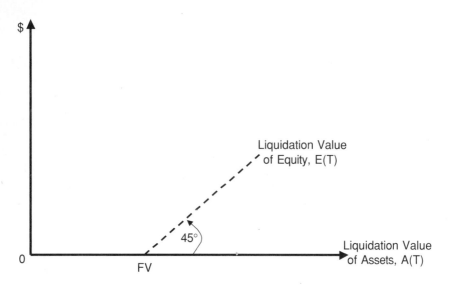

EXHIBIT 1.5 Liquidation Value of Equity in an Equity-and-Debt–Financed Firm

Interest paid to holders of debt securities is similar to dividends paid to equity holders—although, unlike dividends, interest on debt is defined in advance for the whole term of the debt contract. Consequently, interest payments are again restricted by the firm's cash flow constraint. At time t, a firm financed with both debt and equity capital that distributes all its excess net cash flows (i.e., $X(t) - I(t)$) to security holders must abide by the following cash flow constraint:

$$\delta(t) + \rho(t) = X(t) - I(t) + e(t) + d(t) \qquad (1.7)$$

where $\rho(t)$ is the interest paid to existing debt holders at time t. Substituting the new debt-and-equity cash flow constraint given in equation 1.7 into the value of the firm shown in equation 1.6 allows us to express the total wealth of all security holders as follows:

$$[E_{t-1}(t) + \delta(t)] + [D_{t-1}(t) + \rho(t)] = X(t) - I(t) + V(t) \qquad (1.8)$$

VIEWING THE FUNDAMENTAL BUILDING BLOCKS AS "OPTIONS"

Readers already familiar with the basics of option markets will recognize Exhibits 1.4 and 1.5 as the payoffs at maturity to the holders of financial products known as options. Indeed, one of the most versatile and insightful ways of viewing corporate financing strategies is from an options perspective. (Appendix 1-2 provides a brief survey of the essentials of options.)

If we return to Exhibit 1.2, we can see that the payoff to the residual claimants of a firm that issues no debt is equivalent to a call option on the value of the firm's assets with a strike price of zero. Or consulting Exhibit 1.5, the payoff to residual claimants of a firm that issues debt with face value FV is equivalent to a long call option on the firm's assets with a strike price equal to the face value of the outstanding debt issued by the corporation. Turning back to Exhibit 1.4, the debt issued by the firm with face value FV is equivalent to a short put option on the assets of the firm with a strike price of FV plus a riskless loan in the amount FV.

At the maturity date of the firm's debt T, we know that the value of the firm V(T) must equal the value of the firm's assets A(T). In turn, the value of the firm's assets is equal to the sum of the market values of the firm's debt and equity. We thus can express the value of the firm as

$$V(T) = A(T) = C(T) - P(T) + FV \qquad (1.9)$$

Expression 1.9 is a restatement of what is known in the options world as put-call parity. (Appendix 1.2 provides a more detailed discussion of this concept.)

Let us consider only the debt component of the firm for a moment. Residual claimants have a call option on the firm's assets. Subtracting that value from the market value of the firm's assets allows us to rewrite equation 1.9 as

$$A(T) - C(T) = FV - P(T) \qquad (1.10)$$

where the total value of debt is now the right-hand side of expression 1.10. The total debt position is thus equivalent to a risk-free bond with face value FV and an option written to residual claimants to accept the assets of the firm in exchange for the debt. At time T, debt holders thus get FV but then also have given shareholders the right to demand the FV back and give debtors A(T) instead. When A(T) < FV, shareholders will exercise that option. The time T payoff of this position is

$$FV - \max[FV - A(T), 0] = FV + \min[A(T) - FV, 0] = \min[A(T), FV]$$

The above expression is the payoff at maturity for a special type of option called an option to exchange the better asset for the worse, or a type of what is called an "exchange option." Exhibit 1.6 illustrates.

In Exhibit 1.7, we can now put the pieces together to express the whole firm as a portfolio of options. When the firm's assets are worth A(T) and

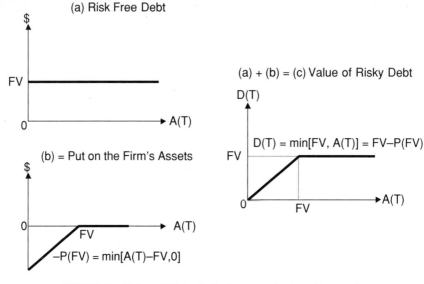

EXHIBIT 1.6 Value of Risky Debt from an Options Perspective

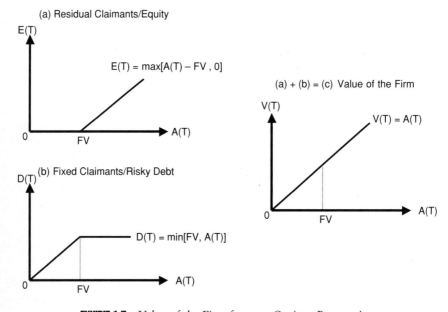

EXHIBIT 1.7 Value of the Firm from an Options Perspective

that amount is less than the face value of the debt, the firm is worth only the value of the assets. Debt holders then receive a pro rata distribution of those assets, and residual claimants receive nothing. When A(T) has a market value greater than FV, debt holders receive FV, equity holders receive a pro rata distribution of the surplus in asset value above FV, and the firm is again worth A(T). In either case, the value of the firm is equal to the value of its assets. The nature of the two types of claims issued by the firm to obtain capital to acquire those assets does not change the nature or value of the assets themselves.

A FIRST LOOK AT "CAPITAL STRUCTURE"

If we assume that all types of claims issued by a firm can be classified as either residual or fixed claims, then we can define a very basic notion of *capital structure*. The capital structure of a corporation is, very simply, the relative mixture of fixed and residual claims that a firm issues.

An easy way to characterize the capital structure of a firm at this most primitive level is through a "leverage ratio," or the proportion of fixed claims the firm issues relative to its total external financial capital outstanding:

$$\text{Leverage Ratio} = \xi(t) = \frac{D(t)}{D(t) + E(t)} = \frac{D(t)}{V(t)}$$

A leverage ratio of .30, for example, means that 30 percent of the capital structure of the firm is comprised of debt, or that 30 percent of the capital of the firm is in the form of fixed income obligations.

Note that the above expression is defined in terms of the variables with which we have been working—*market values* of debt and equity. Some also like to characterize this ratio in terms of *book values*, depending on the purpose of the analysis.

A firm's dividend payout policy is also often considered to be part of its capital structure.

NOTES

1. Real capital is traditionally studied in a macroeconomic context. See Garrison (2001).
2. See Lewin (1999) and Garrison (2001).
3. See, for example, Brealey and Myers (2000).

4. This finding is consistent with statistics reported in Eckbo and Masulis (1995), Brealey and Myers (2000), and elsewhere.

5. Closer to the topics we do address here is the belief held by some that the "value" of the control rights and governance responsibilities conveyed by the financial capital claims issued by a firm are directly related to the value of the firm. Harris and Raviv (1991) provide a useful survey of the academic literature on this subject.

A Brief Introduction to Capital Theory

Historically, capital and labor are the two principal factors of production in an economy. In neoclassical economic theory, some *production function* is presumed to exist that describes the physical transformation of inputs like capital and labor into final products. Solow (1956) posits most generally that aggregate output Y can be expressed as

$$Y = A(t)f(K,L)$$

where A(t) captures "technical change," K is capital, L is labor, and the ubiquitous f is a production function—Cobb-Douglas, constant elasticity of substitution, and the like.

Dating back to John Locke and Adam Smith, the value and meaning of the *labor* input to production as depicted by this function has generally been well-understood. But *capital* is a different story entirely. The road to this "production function" view of how capital is related to output has been a long and rocky one—and, some would say, one that has taken us more than once in the wrong direction, if not also deposited us in the wrong place.[1]

ADAM SMITH ON CAPITAL

As in much of economics, the earliest serious treatment of capital comes from Adam Smith. In his *Inquiry into the Nature and Causes of the Wealth of Nations* (1776), Smith depicted the capital stock of a country as including "fixed" and "circulating" capital, where the former includes plants, equipment, machines, and the like—largely things that did not really exist in Smith's time—and the latter includes goods in the making, inventory, and other "goods in the pipeline." Both ultimately result in produced goods that in turn make consumption possible.

Smith's conception of capital owed much to the context in which he was writing—an agrarian economy. To Smith, the "capital stock" was mainly circulating capital; indeed it was even vaguely synonymous with a harvest that might be used to feed laborers, feed animals used in other productive activities, and create seeds to be used for reinvestment in next year's crop. For Smith, capital thus was basically the same thing as "output" or "production."

In this sense, Smith's notion of capital was almost a "subsistence" notion—capital was the thing that sustained workers from one harvest to the next, and the main benefit to the owner of the capital was that it created the ability to continue employing laborers. At the same time, savings and accumulation were clearly important to Smith, who also believed that owners of capital did indeed earn a profit on their capital, one economic purpose of which was reinvestment that would continue and extend the division of labor. Smith's hypothesis about how capitalists earned a profit was an early instance of what was to become a significant question in the history of capital theory: What is it about capital exactly that makes it "valuable" and allows capitalists to earn a profit on it?

On this issue, Smith actually had two somewhat different—and contradictory—views. First, Smith simply asserts that capital "creates" value over and above the labor expended on the production of the capital good, and this surplus is the profit on capital. Second, Smith also seems to believe that the return on capital (i.e., "interest") is just a deduction made by capitalists from the value of the good defined by the value of labor expended on production of the good. In this sense, the return on capital kept as profit by the capitalist thus is really a return on labor, simply held back by the capitalist.

Not surprisingly, Smith's own apparently contradictory views of capital gave rise to decades of argument over what is meant by the term "capital." Some argue that capital is synonymous with a capital *stock* or a capital *good*. So capital is a physical "thing." Others have argued that capital is itself a concept of productivity and value that results from but is not the same as the capital stock. Lachmann (1956) summarizes this latter perspective nicely:

> Beer barrels and blast furnaces, harbour installations and hotel room furniture are capital not by their physical properties but by virtue of their economic functions. Something is capital because the market, the consensus of entrepreneurial minds, regards it as capable of yielding an income. . . .

Smith's two views of capital also spurred a century of debate on what gives capital its value. Because this line of thinking is what will ultimately bring us to the meaning we ascribe to capital in this book, the conflicts over capital value are worth reviewing.[2]

PRODUCTIVITY AND USE THEORIES OF CAPITAL

Smith's first view of capital became the basis for what would later be called "productivity" theories of capital. First developed by J. B. Say in 1803, productivity theories of capital argue that capital is "productive" in the sense that it is used to produce consumption goods that will satisfy future needs rather than current needs. Specifically, capital can be viewed as productive in four senses:

1. It is required for the production of goods.
2. It allows the production of more goods than could be produced without it.
3. It facilitates the production of more *value* than would be created in its absence.
4. It has the capability of producing more value than it has in and of itself.[3]

Unfortunately, many of the early productivity theories offer no reason for *why* capital is productive in these four senses. Some seemed to conjecture that "from capital springs value" in an almost mystical way, providing little economic intuition for their reasoning. Others argued that capital was valuable simply because it allowed the owners of that capital to appropriate the wages of the labor displaced by the use of capital.

Thomas Malthus was perhaps the first to add teeth to the productivity theory of capital. In his *Principles of Political Economy* (1820), he argued that the value of capital itself was the value of what was produced with that capital.

From this notion sprang the "use theories" of capital, which embraced the concept that there is a causal link between the value of products and the value of the production process for those products. But whereas pure productivity theories posited a direct link between the value of goods produced and the value of production, use theories argued that the value of capital also was driven by the fact that the *use* of capital was sacrificed to a production process during the time in which the capital was sacrificed to production. In other words, use theories developed a notion of the value of capital assets based on their *opportunity costs*.

A major proponent of the use theory was Austrian economist Carl Menger. In his *Principles of Economics* (1871), he developed a notion of capital in which production is viewed as a sequential process. "Higher-order" goods (i.e., capital goods) are transformed into "lower-order" goods (i.e., consumption goods) in this process. Menger also believed that the value of production was subjective and could not be measured by objective criteria like labor input—which, as we shall see below, is what labor theorists like Ricardo maintained. Menger (1871) states, "There is no necessary and direct connection between the value of a good and whether or in what quantities, labor or other goods of higher order were applied to its production." To Menger, the value of the capital stock was the sum of the subjective values of the consumption goods that would ultimately result (at different times) from the production process. And because production is time-consuming, the opportunity cost of not having those goods is the "use value" of capital.

LABOR THEORY OF CAPITAL

David Ricardo's *Principles of Political Economy and Taxation* (1817) contains numerous insights that impact the study of economics even today. Ricardo attempted to develop a labor theory of capital based on John Locke's notion that the natural right is the right to self-ownership of one's labor. Unfortunately, his theory was not well developed.

In Smith's time, assuming that capital was relatively homogeneous was at least plausible. But as Hicks (1965) put it, by Ricardo's time "it was no longer tolerable, even as an approximation, to assume that all capital was circulating capital; nor that, even in a metaphysical sense, all capital was 'corn.'" Nevertheless, Ricardo was reluctant to let go of the notion that all capital was circulating capital. When it came to complex capital such as machines, Ricardo simply believed that it was circulating "more slowly" than capital like corn.

To reduce all capital back to a homogenous concept, Ricardo thus embraced the labor theory of value that all productive outputs could be measured based on the labor inputs required for the production. In this manner, the return on capital was just the return on labor involved in the capital production process. Whether that production process involved a pig or a machine was of little consequence. A corn harvest this year could have its input value measured based on the number of hours it took to bring the corn to harvest, much as in Smith. But to Ricardo, a machine in production for 10 years involved an expenditure of labor hours in each of the 10 years. Part of the machine got "used up" in each year.[4]

Ricardo then developed his concept of a "uniform rate of profit" on capital. Simply put, he argued that all capital goods tended to earn the same rate of return in the long run. The distribution of wealth in society and the flows of capital to different activities of differing productivity was a result of this tendency toward a uniform rate of profit.

The Ricardian labor theory of capital value was filled with flaws. Despite the obvious one—that a uniform rate of profit does not exist and does not guide resource allocation—the analysis was also a completely static one. Indeed, many of Menger's efforts to emphasize the importance of a "time structure of production" in the use theory were a direct response to the completely static nature of the labor theory.

Despite its known logical flaws and clear empirical shortcomings, the labor theory of capital eventually was extended into a full argument that the value of capital was not simply the value of labor required to produce with capital but was rather the value to capitalists of *exploiting* labor to produce with capital. This theory, of course, owes its origins to Karl Marx (*Das Kapital*, 1859).

CONTRIBUTIONS OF HICKS

Because firms are productive intermediaries in the economy—they are the economic agents engaging in production, after all—the link between aggregate capital production at the macroeconomic level and firm-specific production decisions at the microeconomic level is fairly obvious. Indeed, it is hard to imagine how we would get to a theory of the former without first understanding the latter. Nevertheless, most of the early capital theorists paid very little attention to the role of "the firm" as a production transformation "function" in its own right.[5]

Over the years, a strong criticism of the neoclassical model has been leveled by members of the "Austrian" and "neo-Austrian" schools of economic thought, whose origins owe to Menger. One major flaw the Austrians emphasize with the traditional neoclassical production model is its inattention to the importance of time. Neoclassical economists typically have responded to such criticisms by arguing that the Austrian school has raised some legitimate issues—many of which are reflected in neoclassical growth theory—but that the so-called Austrian school is too loose, nontechnical, and informal to be considered a serious alternative to the neoclassical paradigm.

One of the few economists to win at least some considerable respect in both camps was John Hicks, who, on one hand, was a formalistic and well-respected neoclassical economist but who, on the other hand, also held fast to certain Austrian critiques of the neoclassical model, including its inattentiveness to the "time structure of capital."

Hicks considered the capital stock to encompass a wide range of capital assets, including fixed and circulating capital, or "goods in the pipeline." He embraced the productivity theorists' notion that the value of capital was not the value of the capital assets themselves but rather the value of the goods produced by those capital assets. At the same time, however, he also emphasized the need to retain Menger's important insight that production is a sequence or process of inputs that give rise to a sequence of outputs.

By combining a productivity theorist's view that the value of capital is driven by the value of what capital produces with a use theorist's view that the opportunity cost of capital over a sequence of a time also must impact the value of a capital production plan, Hicks was able to shed tremendous light on capital at the microeconomic level. Perhaps most notably, he provided a number of insights on capital investment—or capital budgeting—

decisions in which corporations evaluate whether to undertake investments in new production technologies to find new ways of transforming fixed and circulating capital into a sequence of outputs that ultimately become consumer goods.[6]

Hicks was not the first economist to recognize the importance of concepts such as "interest" and "present value." But he was one of the first to develop an early version of what we now call the "net present value criterion"—a basic staple of any finance diet, and one to which we will return in more detail in Chapter 3. Hicks was keenly interested in developing some means by which a production process could be considered "viable" or not. To determine this, he advocated comparing the discounted flow of values of outputs from a production process to the discounted flow of values associated with the inputs to the process. In other words, firms should undertake and continue a project only so long as the discounted present value of remaining outputs exceeds the discounted present value of remaining inputs. We now restate this to say that a firm should invest in a capital project only if the discounted present value of the net cash inflows on a project is nonnegative—that is, the NPV (net present value) criterion.

Hicks also developed the concept of an internal rate of return (IRR), which he defined as the discount rate that equates the NPV of a project to zero. And Hicks was concerned not only with evaluating capital investments at the beginning of a project but at all points along its time path, as well—a distinction we now know as the difference between a NPV and a conditional expected NPV, which is critical in deciding when to discontinue a project.[7]

What Hicks did not solve was the problem of how to find the right rate at which to discount the input and output values in a project. On this score, earlier work was not much help. Böhm-Bawerk (1959) argued, for example, that the outputs of a project should be discounted at the "subjective rate of time preference" of each consumer buying the finished goods. Not very helpful as a practical matter, and also not necessarily correct. A much more concrete contribution was required.

Ironically, the issue of what discount rate or "cost of capital" to use in evaluating firms' production and investment decisions was settled in a paper that did not set out with that goal in mind. Indeed, it was the inadequacy of many of the neoclassical production models that led Franco Modigliani and Merton Miller to begin their pioneering work together. And in one of intellectual history's great ironies, despite the fact that their seminal article "The Cost of Capital, Corporation Finance, and the Theory of Investment" was primarily intended to integrate more microeconomic and financial analysis into the neoclassical theory of capital investment, they failed to have much influence on that score.[8] But they developed the concept of a corporate cost of capital and gave birth to the modern theory of finance in the process.

NOTES

I am especially grateful to Roger Garrison for his thoughtful comments and discussions with me on this subject. He is blameless, of course, for any errors.

1. For some excellent recent thoughts on capital that challenge the current thinking, see Garrison (2001).
2. The terminology for the various theories summarized is borrowed from Böhm-Bawerk (1959).
3. Ibid.
4. See Lewin (1999) for a further discussion of this issue and especially how Ricardo's view of time compares to Menger's.
5. The neoclassical model of Solow (1956) noted at the beginning of this section shows that macroeconomics has unfortunately not come too far in this regard.
6. See Lewin (1999) for a discussion.
7. Culp and Miller (1995).
8. Modigliani and Miller (1958).

A Review of Basic Option Concepts

This is not a text on options, nor do readers of this book necessarily need a full text on options. In particular, knowledge of option pricing models will not be required to understand the material presented in this book. Some familiarity with the concepts, however, is highly desirable given that the options perspective is used to depict claims and securities throughout the book. Accordingly, this section provides a brief introduction. Readers with more of an interest who have not had a formal course on the subject are directed to the excellent text by Hull (2000).

BASIC TYPES OF OPTIONS

A *call option* gives its holder the right but not the obligation to *buy* some underlying asset or portfolio of assets at a prespecified price on or before the option's maturity date. A *put option* gives its holder the right but not the obligation to *sell* some underlying asset or portfolio of assets at a prespecified price on or before the option's maturity date.

If the right to buy or sell can be "exercised" at any time on or before the maturity date of the option, the option is called American style. Options that can be exercised only on their maturity dates are called European style. The preagreed price at which the buyer of the option can exercise the right to buy (in the case of a call) or sell (in the case of a put) the underlying is called the option's "striking," "strike," or "exercise" price.

The buyer of an option, called the long, pays for the rights conveyed by the contract by giving a "premium" payment to the seller of the option, called the short or the option "writer." Option buyers own limited liability assets, whereas option sellers can incur losses up to the point where the asset(s) underlying the option become worthless.

Exhibit A1-2.1 summarizes the payoffs at maturity for European-style calls and puts from the perspectives of both buyers and sellers. Panels a and b

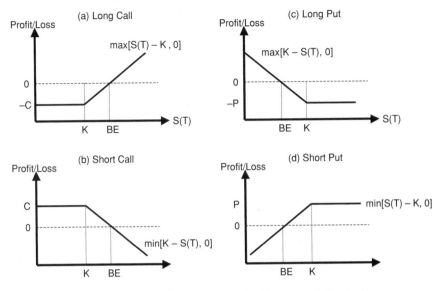

EXHIBIT A1.2.1   Payoffs at Maturity for European-Style Options

show the symmetric payoff obligations between the buyer and seller of a call option. In exchange for the limited liability right but not the obligation to buy some underlying asset at price K, the option buyer pays premium C to the option seller. (The concept of premium is an important one to which we shall return.) If the price at time T of the underlying asset, denoted S(T), is below the call strike price K, the option is said to be "out of the money." The buyer would lose money if she exercised the option and thus does not do so. The seller keeps the premium C and has no further obligations.

If the price at time T of the underlying asset is above the call strike price K, the option is said to be "in the money" and the buyer can exercise it for a payoff of S(T) – K. If the underlying price S(T) exactly equals the option strike price K, the option is said to be "at the money," but this does not guarantee the option buyer will make a profit from exercising the option. The option buyer breaks even only when the price S(T) has risen above the option strike K by enough to offset the premium paid for the option. This break-even point is labeled BE in the exhibit.

Because options would never be exercised at a loss by their holders, the values of purchased options at maturities are usually expressed using the maximand operator—max[X , Y]—which means the function returns the greater of X or Y. Accordingly, purchased calls and puts at maturity have values that can be expressed (respectively) as follows:

$$C(T) = \max[S(T) - K , 0]$$
$$P(T) = \max[K - S(T) , 0]$$

The seller of these options has the opposite exposure, and terminal values of a call and put on the same underlying with strike price K are thus

$$-C(T) = -\max[S(T) - K , 0] = \min[K - S(T) , 0]$$
$$-P(T) = -\max[K - S(T) , 0] = \min[S(T) - K , 0]$$

Let us illustrate the way these call options work with a numerical example. Suppose the options in question are options on one ounce of gold and the strike price of the call is set at $350 per ounce. Suppose the option buyer pays the seller a premium of $10 for the option contract. If the price of gold when the option matures is above $360, the buyer will make money—the net profit will equal S(T) less the strike price of $350, less again the premium of $10 paid. For prices between $350 and $360, the option is in the money but cannot be profitably exercised by the buyer. Or, equivalently, the seller does not make the maximum profit of C but manages to avoid an outright loss. And if the price is below $350, the seller collects the premium C happily and the buyer loses that premium exactly.

Panels c and d of the exhibit show that put options work in much the same way, except that the buyer benefits from price declines because the put conveys on the buyer a right to sell the underlying at a fixed strike price K. For underlying prices S(T) < BE (i.e., S(T) < K – P), the buyer of the put makes a net profit from exercising the option. For prices between BE and K, the option is in the money, but by less than the premium paid P. And for prices S(T) > K, the option is out of the money and the option seller wins.

Note in panels a and c that the liability of the option buyer is limited to the premium paid, regardless whether the option is a call or a put. No matter what happens to underlying prices, the option purchaser never has to make an additional payment. As panels b and d illustrate, however, the option writer, by contrast, assumes an essentially unlimited liability. A call writer has agreed to sell to the call buyer at price K, and as the price of underlying rises the call writer loses money dollar for dollar. In the gold option example, an option on gold struck at $350 per ounce could cost the writer an amount limited only by the maximum potential price of gold. If gold prices rise to $1,000 per ounce on date T, the writer must sell an asset for $350 that is actually worth $1,000. Similarly, the put writer depicted in panel d assumes a liability limited only by the decline in the price of the underlying asset to zero.

TIME VALUE VERSUS INTRINSIC VALUE

At expiration, any value the option has is said to be *intrinsic value*. The intrinsic value of a call at expiration thus is either zero or the difference between the expiration spot price S(T) and the option's strike price. Before expiration, the market value of an option is the sum of its intrinsic value *plus its time value.*

Time value reflects the fact that no matter what the intrinsic value of the option on any given date, that value could change again before the option matures if the underlying spot price changes. True, prices could move for or against the option holder, but because options are limited liability contracts, favorable price moves may increase the owner's final payout dollar for dollar whereas the maximum loss is zero. The longer the option has left during which time the price could move in favor of its holder, the more time value. And conversely for option sellers.

Exhibit A1-2.2 illustrates this principle graphically for a European call option. The y-axis shows the profit or loss on the call as in Exhibit A1-2.1 as a function of the maturity price of the underlying, S(T). A second y-axis shown on the right indicates the probability of S(T) being realized. Two possible distributions are shown from which the random value of S(T) may be drawn, denoted $f_{T-5}(S(T))$ and $f_{T-25}(S(T))$. The subscripts indicate the number of days away from maturity date T that we are.

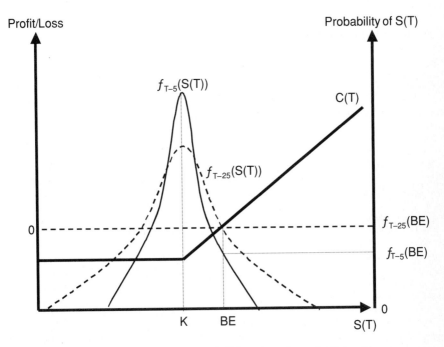

EXHIBIT A1.2.2   Value of European Call Based on Potential Price Changes

In this exhibit, the break-even point is labeled BE as before, which again represents the amount by which S(T) must rise above the option strike to recover the premium paid for the option and to start showing a profit. If the option has less than BE–K intrinsic value, the buyer will incur a net loss.

We can use this break-even point to show that a call with 25 days to maturity will be more valuable than an otherwise identical call with five days to maturity for the given underlying price of BE. Note that both probability distributions are centered around the strike price K, which also is presumed equal to the current price of the underlying. In both cases, the probability the option will expire in the money is 50 percent. But 25 days away from expiration, the potential still exists for the price to move a long way from its current and expected value. When we only have five days of price movements left to occur, the probability of a big upswing is lower. In other words, the volatility of $f_{T-25}(S)$ is higher than the volatility of $f_{T-5}(S)$.[1]

The area under the probability curve from 0 up to BE shows the cumulative probability that the call will break even. Exhibit A1-2.2 makes it clear that the longer-dated option—the option with the higher volatility probability distribution—has a greater probability of turning a profit, because $f_{T-25}(BE)$ lies above $f_{T-5}(BE)$, meaning that more area lies under the former curve at that point than the latter.

Exhibit A1-2.3 shows the same effect from a different perspective. The "hockey stick" payoff labeled C(T) is the value of the call at maturity—pure intrinsic value. Five days prior to maturity, the dashed line shows the value of the call C(T–5) as a function of the underlying price. And similarly for C(T–25). The two continuous curves relating the values of the five-day and 25-day options to the underlying price S(T) can be called "valuation curves."

The different time value of the two options is revealed by the vertical distance at any given point on the graph between the valuation curve and the option's intrinsic value. At the strike price K, for example, the distance between $C°(T – 25)$ and C^* is the time value of the 25-day option, whereas the smaller vertical distance from $C°(T – 5)$ to C^* reveals the shorter time value of the five-day call. As maturity approaches, the dashed line eventually converges to the pure intrinsic value hockey-stick line.

OPTION GREEKS

The sensitivities of an option's value to changes in different market variables often are easiest to understand from graphs. Typically defined in the colorful argot called "Fraternity Row," these sensitives include terms like *theta*—the change in the value of an option with the passage of time. Theta can be seen on Exhibit A1-2.3 as the gradual drop in the valuation curves toward intrinsic value as time to maturity shortens. The shorter the time to maturity, the lower the valuation curve, the less the time value, and the less the total option value.

ProfitLoss

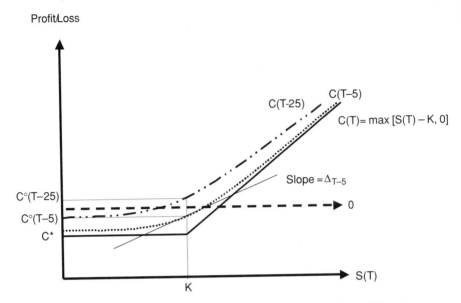

EXHIBIT A1.2.3 Payoff Profile of European Call Option Prior to Maturity

This is also known as time decay—because a purchased option loses time value as time passes, it is a wasting asset.

Similarly, *delta* is the sensitivity of the change in the value of an option to a small change in the value of the underlying. This can be seen on Exhibit A1-2.3 as the slope of the horizontal line tangent to the valuation curve for C(T – 15) drawn at the money. Notice that this slope changes depending on the underlying price at which the tangency point is being drawn. The change in delta as the underlying price changes is called *gamma*.

Finally, *vega* is the sensitivity of an option to a change in the volatility of the underlying. Exhibit A1-2.2 shows this effect, as the option on the asset whose distribution has a higher volatility has a greater probability of expiring deeply in the money. Because the buyer of an option has limited liability—the worst that can happen is a loss of premium—the higher volatility and higher change for a big price upswing is not accompanied by the equal risk of a major loss. Accordingly, options on more volatile assets tend to be more valuable. Although Exhibit A1-2.2 shows a situation where the volatility of the asset changes due to the passage of time, we could easily generalize the argument to options on different assets whose volatilities and probability distributions still look like those shown in this exhibit.

Exhibit A1-2.4 shows three of the Greeks as they vary with the price of the underlying S(T). Panels a and b show the delta of a call and put. Noticeably, delta is constrained to be between zero and one and often is used as a

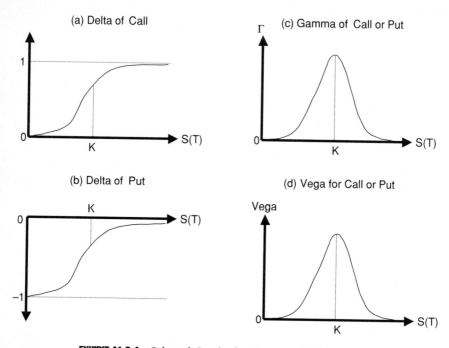

EXHIBIT A1.2.4   Selected Greeks for European-Style Options

measure of approximately how many units of the underlying the option is equivalent to. An at-the-money call option has a delta of 0.5, for example, and as it gets deeper and deeper in the money, it starts to look more and more like the underlying asset itself. The change in delta as S(T) changes is shown in panel c, which is quite similar to panel d showing vega and relating changes in volatility to the underlying price.

Examining how the Greeks change as a function of something other than the underlying price, such as time to maturity, can be equally interesting. Readers should see Hull (2000).

PUT-CALL PARITY

The values of calls and puts are related to one another through "put-call parity." For American options, put-call parity can be expressed as an inequality, whereas for European options the relation holds exactly subject to the transaction costs of arbitrage. In other words, deviations from this relation represent an exploitable arbitrage opportunity. We will rely strongly on the put-call parity relation to express the value of a firm using options.

To keep things simple here, suppose we are working with traded European options on some asset whose time t price is S(t) that does not pay dividends. Let r denote the riskless interest rate, K the strike price common between a call and put, and T denote the maturity date of the call and put. The basic put-call parity relation says that at any time before T, the price of a long call and a short put are related as follows:

$$C(t) - P(t) = S(t) - Ke^{-r(T-t)}$$

Buying a call and selling a put is synthetically equivalent to buying the underlying asset and borrowing K dollars at the riskless rate.

If we assume we hold a portfolio consisting of these four positions to maturity, the put-call parity relation at maturity tells us that

$$C(T) - P(T) = S(T) - K$$

from which one can immediately see that in the special case of at-the-money options, the price of a European call and put must be equivalent at maturity.

Exhibit A1-2.5 shows the put-call parity relation graphically at maturity by expressing the payoff of certain claims at maturity as a function of underlying price S(T). Note that these are *payoffs*, not profits and losses—that is, premium is not shown on these diagrams, just cash flows at time T. Panels a and b together are equivalent to panels (c) and (d), both of which are in turn equivalent to panel e. In other words, buying a call and selling a put at strike K reproduces the same payoff as buying the underlying asset for S(T) and borrowing K dollars without risk. Both of these are in turn equivalent to being long the asset at K. If the options are at the money, then S(T)=K and panels c and d become redundant.

SPREADS

The replication of the cash flows of a long position in the underlying asset is called a synthetic because options were used to replicate a position with a name of its own. When options are snapped together, they do not always yield payoffs equivalent to named instruments, however. Nevertheless, several particular combinations of options have received names of their own, both because they are so popular for trading purposes and because they establish particularly interesting exposure profiles.

The *straddle* and *strangle* are two popular types of spreads, primarily because the net of the multiple positions is a market position whose terminal payoff does not depend on the direction of asset prices but does depend on the movement of asset prices. Specifically, a straddle and strangle are called volatility plays because they are bets on changes in the volatility of the underlying asset price.

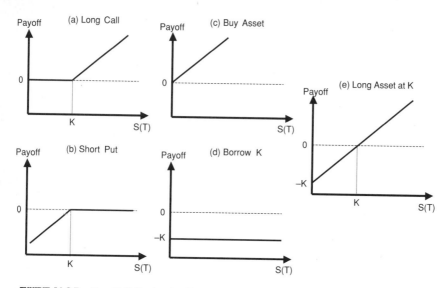

EXHIBIT A1.2.5   Put-Call Parity for European-Style Options (a) + (b) = (c) + (d) = (e)

Exhibit A1-2.6 shows short and long straddles and strangles. A long (short) straddle is constructing by buying (selling) a call and put at the same strike K. For the long, any large price movement results in a profit as long as the price moves enough to cover the two premiums paid. Conversely, the seller of a straddle benefits when prices remain close to K where the premium collected more than offsets the loss upon exercise of either the call or put.

A long strangle is essentially the same as a long straddle except that the range the price must move before the position pays off is greater.[2] The call strike M is higher than the put strike K, so the position is an outright loser if prices remain within K and M. But if prices fall below K or rise above M by more than the total premium outlay, the position is profitable. Conversely for the seller of a strangle.

A long straddle or strangle is a long volatility position. For increases in volatility, the position gains value, whereas it loses value in stable markets. Recently, products such as "variance" and "volatility swaps" have begun to offer nonoptions analogs of these products.

NOTES

1. In many options applications, it is convenient to assume the volatility is proportional to the square root of the number of days remaining in the life of the option.

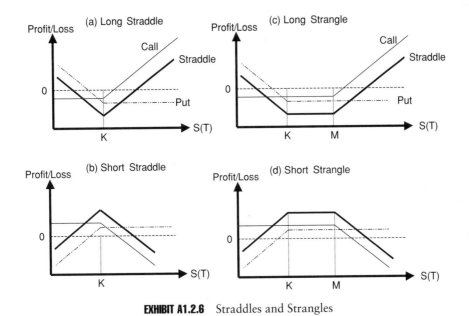

EXHIBIT A1.2.6   Straddles and Strangles

2. A strangle purportedly gets its name from the risk that when constructed with American options, the worst case occurs for a short when a major price decline is followed by a massive reversal. The put gets exercised against the short on the downswing, and the call may get exercised against the short on the upswing before the seller can hedge the remaining leg—thus "strangling" the seller from both sides.

CHAPTER 2

A Securities Perspective
on Capital Structure

To lend some practical relevance to the building block perspective of capital, we need to make the leap from theory to the world of financial practice—to how the basic building blocks are packaged and issued in the real world. In this chapter, we will spend more of our time on the major types of securities issued by firms as sources of paid-in investment capital—capital that results in an immediate cash inflow to the firm when the securities are issued. Accordingly, this chapter answers the following questions:

- What kinds securities do firms issue when they want to raise external investment capital?
- If the assets of the firm are insufficient to pay off all claim holders in full, what determines the order in which investment capital suppliers to the firm are repaid?
- What is the process by which securities actually are placed by corporations into the hands of investors and suppliers of investment capital?
- How do priority and security types work together to define a securities capital structure for a firm, or a capital structure based not just on the firm's leverage but also on the risk of its investment capital claims?
- What do capital structures of firms actually look like "in the real world"?
- What is the distinction between "paid-in" and "contingent" capital?

Notice that we pay no attention to the relation between the securities a firm issues and the value of the firm. Our focus in this chapter is solely on what alternatives are available to a firm for funding its investment activities. We will discuss how a firm chooses amongst those alternatives in Chapters 3, 4, and 5.

Before addressing the questions, however, we need to make a transition from broad economic concepts to the world of actual financial practice. One essential ingredient to that is developing a common vocabulary. We begin our discussion with a brief relation of the concepts we introduced last chapter to the actual world of financial statement analysis.

PRACTICAL CONSIDERATIONS

Many outsiders probably would be surprised to learn how differently accounting and corporation finance often treat essentially similar ideas. The concepts really are no different, but the languages spoken in the two worlds often hit in head-on conflict. Accordingly, it is worthwhile to discuss some of the differences in terminology.

Consider the year-end 2000 financial situation of DaimlerChrysler AG, whose year-end 2000 balance sheet is shown in Table 2.1. At year-end 2000, the book value of fixed investment capital at DaimlerChrysler was about €186 billion.

The current assets of the firm on December 31, 2000, included cash, accounts receivable, and other items. DaimlerChrysler's reported "financial liabilities" at year-end 2000 included both current liabilities (e.g., accounts payable) and both short- and long-term debt.

Exhibit 2.1 illustrates the economic balance sheet of the firm with terms used in the remainder of this book. The term "current assets and liabilities" includes short-term assets and liabilities, such as accounts receivable and payable. In addition, the cash and highly liquid marketable securities that a

TABLE 2.1 Balance Sheet for DaimlerChrysler AG, Year-End 2000 (amounts in €millions)

Assets		Liabilities and Shareholder Equity	
Current Assets:		*Liabilities:*	
Cash	7,127	Financial liabilities	84,783
Marketable Securities	5,378	Trade liabilities	15,257
Inventory	16,283	Other	9,621
Accounts Receivable	71,064	TOTAL LIABILITIES	109,661
TOTAL CURRENT ASSETS	99,852	Deferred Taxes	5,480
Fixed Assets:		Deferred Income	4,764
Intangibles	3,113	*Shareholder Equity:*	
Fixed Capital	85,966	Paid-in Capital	9,895
TOTAL FIXED ASSETS	89,079	Retained Earnings	29,461
Deferred Taxes	2,436	Accumulated Other Income	3,053
Prepaid Expenses	7,907	TOTAL NET WORTH	42,409
		Minority Interest	519
		TOTAL LIABILITIES AND	
TOTAL ASSETS	199,274	EQUITY	199,274

Assets	Liabilities and Equity
Current Assets	**Current Liabilities**
Investment Capital Real capital assets Long-term financial assets Real options/growth opportunities	**Financial Capital** Residual claims Fixed claims
Riskless Bonds Risk reserves Signaling reserves	**Excess Financial Capital** Claims issued above the amount prescribed by optimal capital structure

EXHIBIT 2.1   Economic Balance Sheet of a Firm

firm holds as assets show up as part of the firm's current assets—with the sole exception to be noted below.

On the right-hand side of the exhibit are the types of claims that firms issue as discussed in Chapter 1—residual and fixed claims. Later in this chapter we will discuss the specific types of securities firms can issue to populate this section of the balance sheet. In the exhibit, the term "fixed claims" essentially corresponds to any fixed liabilities the firm has issued for the purpose of raising money. The "shareholder equity" entry corresponds the value of what we call "residual claims," consisting on Table 2.1 mainly of paid-in capital and retained earnings. Retained earnings on the liability side of a balance sheet often correspond to an asset such as cash or marketable securities that the firm plans to use for future investment spending.

The slightly different definitions of equity as a residual claim in the sense of Chapter 1 and accounting shareholder equity often lead to a related source of confusion about the importance of earnings. In a finance context, equity is a residual claim whose value at any time t can be expressed per share as

$$P(t) = \sum_{j=1}^{\infty} \frac{E_t[\delta(t+j)]}{1+\lambda_{t,t+j}}$$

where $\delta(t+j)$ is the dividend per share paid to common stock holders at time t+j, $\lambda_{t,t+j}$ is the cost of capital for the firm (i.e., the appropriate rate at which to discount future cash flows), and $E_t[\cdot]$ is an expectation conditional on information available at time t. In other words, the price per share of a firm's equity is equal to the expected discounted cash flows (DCF) to equity holders. If the firm winds up its operations, the assets of the firm are liquidated and distributed as a liquidating dividend.

This DCF model is inherently at odds with the concept of accounting earnings, especially when used in an earnings-per-share context that often implicitly replaces dividends in the DCF equation above. But the two are not equivalent. Earnings are almost always higher than dividends, in part because of that portion of earnings held back as retained earnings. Accordingly, the value of a firm's equity is driven first and foremost by its expected future dividends—which should, in principle, equal the market value of the firm's assets in economic terms.[1] Indeed, corporate finance and accounting academics regularly debate whether earnings are even informative about how well a company is doing—see the survey by Lev (1989), for example.

The two types of claims issued by our firm on Exhibit 2.1 are what we call the financial capital claims of the firm. Chapters 3 to 5 discuss whether and how a firm determines the proportions and amount of these claims to issue. The last entry in the exhibit, "excess" financial capital, refers to fixed and residual claims issued above and beyond the amount required for investment purposes. In the context of capital utilization discussed in Chapter 1, these excess financial capital claims are used as risk or signaling capital—specifically, riskless bonds the firm holds in reserve for risk and signaling purposes as shown on the asset side of the balance sheet in Table 2.1.

From an accounting perspective, risk and signaling capital are essentially treated like any other current assets. The firm issues excess capital claims and uses the proceeds of that issue to finance the acquisition of riskless debt, which, as is explained in Chapter 7, the firm earmarks for signaling or risk mitigation purposes. Thus, as a management matter the firm distinguishes between riskless debt held for risk and signaling purposes and riskless debt held for the purpose of financing future investment or operating expenditures. But from an accounting perspective, these marketable securities likely will show up in the same place on a firm's balance sheet. Chapter 18 discusses exceptions to this.

Finally, the economic balance sheet in Exhibit 2.1 shows the assets held by the firm as investment capital, which typically correspond to "fixed assets" on Table 2.1.

Apart from the balance sheet, financial analysts also often focus on the firm's cash flows, either as presented in its cash flow statement or in a sources and uses of funds statement, such as that shown in Table 2.2 for Daimler-Chrysler. In this as in many accounting contexts, "funds" is a flow concept, referring to a change in cash or some other reporting variable over some period. In corporate finance, however, funds is often used as a synonym for cash in the bank—the stock of stuff with which one pays one's bills. Neither definition is wrong. They are simply different. When we use the term "funds" in

TABLE 2.2   Flow of Funds (Sources and Uses) for DaimlerChrysler AG in 2000 (amounts in € millions)

Uses of Funds		Sources of Funds	
Net fixed investment	26,765	Net income	7,894
Increased accounts receivable	8,582	Depreciation	13,618
Purchased marketable securities	(2,438)	Other	(5,495)
Repayment of short-term liabilities	3,238	New long-term debt issued	29,257
Repayment of long-term liabilities	9,152	New net equity issues	24
Dividends paid	2,379	Effect of FX changes on cash	501
Other	(200)		
TOTAL	47,478	TOTAL	45,799
NET DECREASE IN CASH	(1,679)		

this book, we usually use it as a synonym for "money in the bank." When we want to discuss funds as a flow, we use the phrase "flow of funds" to indicate a change in the balance of that money in the bank.

Just over half of DaimlerChrysler's total year 2000 cash usage was on new net fixed investment spending, and about 31 percent of Daimler-Chrysler's uses of funds went to debt and dividend payments on its outstanding investment capital fixed and residual claims. On the sources-of-funds side, about 47 percent of DaimlerChrysler's new cash funds were from internal sources—net income plus depreciation. The primary source of new cash during 2000, however, came from a net increase in the firm's long-term indebtedness. Net new issues of stock by the firm were trivial, which, for reasons we explore elsewhere, is neither surprising nor inconsistent with most other mature firms.

For comparison, Table 2.3 shows the sources of funds by U.S. nonfinancial, nonfarm corporate businesses from 1995 to 2000.[2] The uses of these funds are not shown here, but about 75 percent of total fund usage for this sample of firms went to new investment expenditures.

Comparing Tables 2.2 and 2.3, DaimlerChrysler evidently relied more heavily in 2000 on new debt issues than internal funds, whereas the broader U.S. sample shows a greater utilization of net income and depreciation to finance new investments. Nevertheless, in both cases the role for external financing is clear. With the need and role for such external financing now established, we can discuss more specifically the structure of such external financing.

The concept of cash flows is a crucial one in financial economics. The value of the firm is frequently expressed as the discounted net present value of the expected future cash flows on the firm's investments. But financial economics switches back and forth between cash flows and values quite frequently and sometimes without warning. The value of the firm, for example,

TABLE 2.3 Flow of Funds for U.S. Nonfarm Nonfinancial Corporate Businesses ($ Billions)

	1995	1996	1997	1998	1999	2000
Net Income and Depreciation	619.9	676	727.6	746.5	804.5	891.1
Net New Equity	-58.3	-69.5	-114.4	-267	-143.5	-166.6
Total New Debt	227.5	149.2	266.5	392.1	454.8	437.3

also is frequently expressed as the market value of the firm's assets. The DCF and asset views, of course, must yield the same value in an efficient capital market. The confusion arises because the market value of the firm's assets is the capitalized and discounted value of its cash flows. But asset value is a stock, and cash flows are a flow—hence, some confusion.

Another cash flow–related term that can be confusing is the notion of a firm's "free cash flow," or its cash flows in excess of the cash flow required to fund current operations and all positive-value investment opportunities the firm foresees. This concept is equivalent to the net of cash inflows and outflows on a firm's cash flow statement. A firm's internal funds, by contrast, are a balance sheet concept used to refer to a firm's retained earnings plus its depreciation.

The terms "free cash flows" and "internal funds" often are used in a loosely interchangeable way, and they are indeed related. Free cash flows can be invested by the firm in cash or marketable securities that become internal funds. When a firm spends money on investments by depleting its internal funds, it is essentially borrowing from its own equity holders to finance the investment opportunity. Nevertheless, free cash flow is a flow and internal funds represent a stock of assets.

BASIC TYPES OF SECURITIES

Now we turn to analyzing the specific claims that firms can issue to raise investment capital—"liabilities" and "shareholder equity" on Table 2.1 and "financial capital" on Exhibit 2.1 Here we limit ourselves to securities issued to raise *paid-in* capital. All the claims discussed result in a cash infusion for the issuing firm that occurs at the time of the new security issue. This cash appears as a current asset on the firm's balance sheet and is immediately available to the firm for investment financing purposes.

The securities that firms issue to raise external funds fall into essentially two categories—equity and debt. A third category of security—hybrid claims—enables firms to combine the features of both fixed and residual claims.

Equity Securities

Residual claims are often called shares, each of which represents a claim of some kind on the residual cash flows of the firm. The type of shares issued by the firm depends in large part on the type of firm in question.

Fama and Jensen (1983a, 1983b, 1985) define four types of organizations, distinguished principally by the nature of the residual claims they issue and the relation between the holders of those residual claims and the governance of the firm. An *open corporation* issues residual claims usually in the form of unrestricted common stock. Common stock entitles each shareholder to a proportional claim on the net cash flows or value of the assets of the firm. If the firm has issued N shares, each shareholder will receive $E_{T-1}(T)/N$ upon liquidation of the firm on date T or $\delta(t)/N$ in dividends in any period $t < T$ prior to liquidation (assuming the firm is a dividend payer).

Shares issued by open corporations can be freely bought and sold in a secondary market once they have been issued. Although the owner of a share is recorded at the securities registrar for the issuing company, the investor alone can decide when to buy or sell it. The company's permission usually is not required for a transfer of share ownership to occur.[3]

A *closed corporation* or *proprietorship* also issues residual claims in the form of equity shares, but the equity of a closed corporation usually cannot be bought and sold freely. In proprietorships, equity shares usually take the form of partnership shares or interests. These interests often are obtainable only by managers of the firm and usually cannot be sold or transferred to just anyone, unlike common stock, which can be freely bought and sold by anyone with the cash to buy it. In limited partnerships, equity shares may not be conditional on management responsibilities but still usually are bought and sold under highly restrictive conditions that tend to limit the number of potential partners to a prespecified group of investors with which the company wants to deal.

The third type of Fama/Jensen organization is a *financial mutual* or *syndicate*. The residual claimants in these types of firms are also the customers of the firms. Shares in an open-ended mutual fund or real estate investment trust (REIT), for example, represent pro rata claims on the assets in which the fund or trust invests the proceeds it receives from share sales. But the only reason the fund/trust has collected funds from investors in the first place is to reinvest these funds on behalf of investors in some specific asset class or investment program. This may seem like circular logic, when in fact it is merely evidence that the residual claimants of the firm are also its users.

Shares in some financial mutuals are listed for trading in organized markets, whereas others are available only through private negotiations or auctions. A share in a country club, for example, is a share in a mutual in which the share purchasers also use the club's facilities. In this case, the purchaser likely must obtain the membership share directly from the club and its governing members, must meet certain membership criteria, and may not necessarily sell the membership to the average person on the street without permission of the other governing members.

Finally, *nonprofits* are organizations that have no residual claimants per se. The closest thing are the donors and supporters who provide operating cash flows directly. Instead of receiving a residual claim on the net cash flows of the nonprofit, donors receive an "intangible" residual claim on the fruits of the nonprofit's labors.

Debt[4]

The most basic type of fixed claim a corporation can enter into to obtain funds is a loan, or a bilateral obligation of a borrower to repay a fixed amount, called principal, to a lender on some later date. The principal may be fixed, as in a traditional commercial and industrial (C&I) bank loan to a nonfinancial corporation, or it may amortize at some agreed-upon rate or the lender's discretion. A loan in which the principal is repaid on a single date is a bullet loan, whereas a loan with a sinking-fund provision has an amortizing principal.

Some loans also require the borrower to make periodic interest payments before the principal is repaid. For fixed-rate loans, those interest payments are based on a fixed interest rate expressed as a percentage of the principal value of the loan on which the borrower and lender agree. Variable-rate loans have interest payments that are periodically reset over time, and floating-rate loans have an interest rate that varies on each interest payment date, usually based on the value of some market-determined reference rate, such as prime or the London Interbank Offered Rate (LIBOR).

For a traditional loan, the borrower and lender negotiate all the terms individually. Loans are therefore nonfungible assets—that is, they are bilateral contracts that usually cannot be transferred by borrower or lender to another party without both parties' consent. Loans made by banks, finance companies, or nonfinancial corporates (e.g., trade credits), moreover, are typically not considered securities as such because the terms of the deal are completely bilateral and specific to the borrower and lender in question.

A debt security is essentially a fungible loan. Rather than borrower and lender negotiating the terms, a borrower simply predefines the terms of the loan in a security and issues the securities for anyone to purchase. Any investor in a debt security thus becomes lender to the issuer of the securities, the borrower. Because the terms of debt contracts are standardized, they can be transferred by the original purchaser to another agent.

The numerous types of debt securities that corporations issue today usually can be distinguished along several dimensions: principal repayment provisions; interest payment provisions; maturity or effective maturity; and security.

Principal Repayment Provisions

Principal-only debt securities, often called zero-coupon debt instruments, have a face value amount returned to investors at or before maturity. The face value of a security corresponds to the principal of a loan and in fact often is referred to as such.

Debt securities that pay no interest prior to maturity are often original issue discount (OID) instruments, because the price paid by investors for such securities when they are issued is less than (i.e., at a discount to) the face value of the instrument. The borrowing firm thus receives less cash than the face value of the bonds on the date they are issued but must repay the higher face value amount later when the bonds mature. The yield earned by investors in these claims, assuming no default, is the proportional discount to face value, or par value, at which the debt securities are issued.

Like loans, the principal on a debt security may be paid all at once (i.e., a bullet) or may amortize over time according to a sinking-fund provision. The principal of different debt instruments, moreover, also may be distinguished based on the currency in which the principal is denominated.

Interest Payment Provisions

A coupon-bearing debt security not only returns principal to the investor but also pays agreed-upon amounts to investors at periodic dates called coupon dates before the instrument matures. Coupon payments on such securities may be fixed for the whole life of the bond (e.g., level-coupon bonds), fixed for specific periods of time and then periodically reset (e.g., variable-rate bonds), or floating with some reference index (e.g., LIBOR-indexed floating-rate notes, or FRNs).

Maturity and Effective Maturity

Debt securities also differ in type based on their maturity. One of the most common forms of corporate debt, for example, is "commercial paper," or short-maturity debt issued by corporations to finance current operations or physical asset (e.g., plant and equipments) expenditures. Most commercial paper matures roughly 30 days after it is issued, and firms rarely issue commercial paper beyond 270 days to maturity.

Another popular type of corporate-issued debt security is the medium term note (MTN). Notes initially arose as an outgrowth of the commercial paper market, with an important difference being that debt with longer maturities often is regulated differently upon issuance. In the United States, debt beyond 270 days to maturity must be registered with the U.S. Securities and Exchange Commission (SEC). Commercial paper is thus exempt from such shelf registration requirements, whereas MTNs are not. Most MTNs extend from nine months through two to five years to maturity. Longer-dated MTNs also exist, however, sometimes extending as far as 30 to 40 years to maturity. As will be explained in more detail later, notes also are issued through the "private placement" process in which buyers for the securities are pre-arranged—usually by an investment bank—before the bonds are issued.

The maturity of a corporate debt security may be influenced by the degree of optionality in the security. A "callable" bond is one that can be redeemed by the borrower for a specific value (usually the face value of the security) after the occurrence of a specific event, such as an interest rate decline. In that case, the issuer might call its existing bonds in order to issue new fixed claims and effectively refinance its debt at a lower rate.

"Putable" bonds, by contrast, give the lender the right to demand repayment of the loan early, usually for a fixed amount and following a triggering event such as a rate increase that would allow the investor to relend in a different claim at a more favorable rate.

In either case, the effective maturity of the bond may be different from its stated maturity if the call or put option is exercised early. Noncallable and nonputable securities, by contrast, have absolutely fixed terms to maturity.

Security

A final way to distinguish between debt instruments is by their security. If one or more specific assets are pledged by the corporation as collateral to honor the interest and principal payments on a debt instrument, then the debt instrument is secured. If the payment obligations on the debt are backed only by the promise of the corporation, the debt is unsecured and is often called a debenture.

Note that not all fixed liabilities of a corporation constitute investment capital. Debt capital is a fixed claim issued for the purpose of obtaining funds (or for one of the other reasons explored in Chapter 7). Other types of fixed liabilities may be incurred by the firm for the purpose of obtaining services. A salary promised to an employee, for example, is a fixed claim in which the corporation promises to pay a specified amount over a defined period of time in return for services rendered by the employee. Care must be taken not to confuse such forms of fixed liabilities with debt capital per se.

Hybrid Claims

Equity and debt securities are the practical market analogs of the residual and fixed claim building blocks discussed earlier. In addition, the fixed and residual claim building blocks can be combined to form hybrid claims that have features of both debt and equity. Three typical hybrid securities are discussed below.

Convertible Debt or Debt-with-Warrants

Perhaps the most common example of a hybrid security is the convertible bond. A convertible bond is debt issued by a corporation that can be converted into equity by its holder under some prespecified conditions and at a specified conversion price. Such bonds frequently also contain call and put provisions designed to fine-tune the timing of any conversions, either on the part of the issuer or the buyer.

Suppose, for example, that Firm Brahms issues a zero-coupon, T-year convertible bond with face value FV. Suppose further that when the bond matures at time T, its owner may choose, instead of receiving a principal repayment of FV, to receive shares of Firm Brahms's common stock. For every dollar of assets Firm Brahms owns at time T, $A(T)$, the convertible thus is potentially a claim on $\alpha A(T)$, where α is the proportion of the firm's assets resulting from the conversion into shares. The payoff to the holder of this convertible bond at date T is shown in Exhibit 2.2.

The net value at time T to the holder of this bond is the maximum of the values of the two components. As before, the debt component is a put on the assets of the firm struck at the face value of the debt FV. The equity component is equivalent to a pro rata claim on α proportion of the firm's net cash flows or asset values $A(T)$. For values of the firm's assets $A(T) \leq X^*$, the bond holder would prefer to receive FV than the $\alpha A(T)$ resulting from a conversion into share equity. But for $A(T) > X^*$, the bond holder is better off surrender-

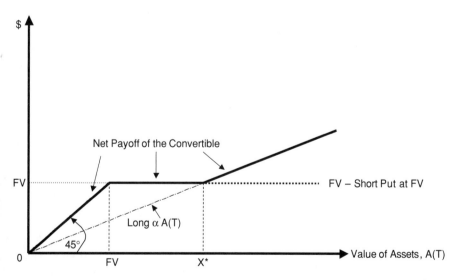

EXHIBIT 2.2   Value to Investor of a Firm Brahms Convertible Bond at Maturity

ing the repayment of FV in return for αA(T). The net position thus is equivalent to a short put on the assets of the firm struck at FV and α long calls on the firm's assets struck at X*.

Some forms of hybrid securities go even further and combine residual claims of the issuer with fixed claims on another firm, or vice versa. "Exchangeable debt," for example, is a debt instrument issued by a firm that entitles its holder to convert the debt into the common stock of some different firm after a major increase in the other firm's share price.

Other such examples of hybrid debt securities abound.[5] In addition, debt securities sometimes are issued alongside equity securities. Especially common is to issue debt-with-warrants, which amounts to the same thing economically as a convertible debt issue except that the warrants are detachable. This is especially common in mezzanine financing, which we discuss later in this chapter.

Preferred Stock

Preferred stock is classified as an equity security but pays its holders a dividend that usually is fixed and thus does not reflect a proportional claim on the firm's net free cash flows. The firm can choose not to pay the dividend on its preferred stock without being considered in default, whereas a failure to make a promised interest payment on a debt issue would constitute an event of default. (Payments to securities holders following defaults are discussed in more detail later in this chapter.) Apart from the nonpayment option, preferred stock is essentially perpetual debt. As long as the firm is financially viable, the interest remains fixed. Only when the firm runs into trouble do the equitylike features of these hybrid claims kick in.

Because some investors do not like truly perpetual securities, many preferred stock issues have optional or conditional redemption features. Some even have step-up provisions in which the interest paid resets to a much higher coupon rate after some specific period of time. Because the cost of borrowing in that manner will be quite high for the firm, the issuer will almost certainly exercise an early redemption option and retire the preferred shares. Although the instrument is technically perpetual, the step-up date provides investors with some notion of what the effective maturity of the shares may be—again with the result that the instrument looks more like debt than equity.

Companies sometimes issue preferred stock to investors indirectly out of a subsidiary rather than as a direct claim on the firm. The firm sets up a special-purpose vehicle (SPV) whose equity is wholly owned by the parent corporation—usually worth a nominal amount like $1. The SPV issues the preferred stock for some subscription price and then makes a loan to the parent corporation in an amount exactly equal to the total proceeds from the subscription. The parent corporation then pays interest to the SPV on the loan, from which interest is paid by the SPV to investors in the preferred stock. The cash flows are depicted in Exhibit 2.3.

Collateralized Preferred or Trust-Preferred Stock

Preferred stock also may be issued to investors through a trust rather than by the issuing firm or a wholly owned SPV of the issuer. In that case, investors hold a claim on the trust rather than the issuing firm's assets and cash flows, but the claim on the trust is essentially secured by an investment of zero-coupon preferred stock by the issuer in the trust itself. Exhibit 2.4 shows the mechanics of this issuance process.

As shown in the exhibit, the company raising capital by issuing claims issues those claims to a trust in the form of zero-coupon (i.e., zero-dividend) preferred stock. These shares are held by the trust as collateral against dividend-paying claims issued by the trust to investors for some subscription

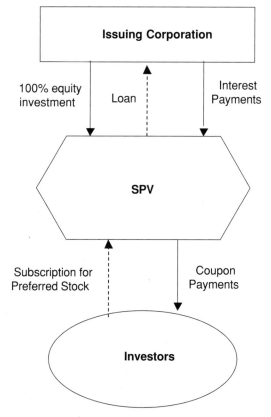

EXHIBIT 2.3   Preferred Stock Issued Indirectly by a SPV

amount. But because the preferred stock held by the trust does not pay dividends, the issuing corporation must get the funds to the trust in some other way to make the promised dividend payments to investors. To accomplish this, another trust maintained by the issuer or a wholly owned subsidiary or SPV of the issuer—the SPV is shown in Exhibit 2.4—makes a loan to the issuing corporation, and the interest it receives on that loan is paid by the SPV to the trust for payment to investors on their securities. From the investors' perspective, they are holding a preferred equity claim on the trust whose capital value is backed by the preferred stock of the issuing corporation and whose coupon payment is the coupon rate on a loan made by the trust to the issuing corporation via the SPV.

SECURITIES AND PRIORITY

We have shown that firms can enter into a variety of specific securities to raise capital and what the basic payoff profiles of those securities are. We have not examined what happens if there is not enough to go around—that is, when the firm becomes insolvent and the value of its assets (including internal funds) is below the value of the claims it has issued as liabilities. We address this issue by introducing the notion of the "priority" of specific claims. Priority refers to the preference given to certain claim holders when the firm becomes insolvent and the proceeds from the liquidation of a firm's assets must

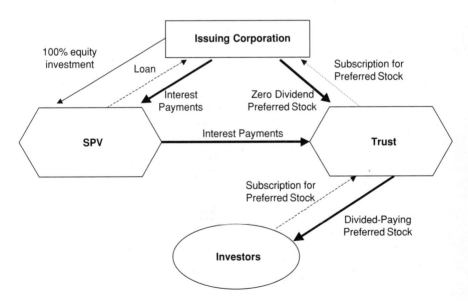

EXHIBIT 2.4   Collateralized Preferred or Trust-Preferred Stock

be distributed. "Seniority" is another way to refer to the priority of a claim in the securities capital structure.

To avoid unnecessary legal and accounting encumbrances, let us define insolvency here most simply as that situation when the market value of the firm's assets falls below the market value of its liabilities. This is not the definition usually used in actual insolvency laws around the world, which may instead rely on book accounting entries, cash flows, actual events of default on obligations, and the like. But for our purposes, the simple net asset value concept is adequate. In this case, equity is worthless and the debt holders of the firm cannot recover the total amount to which their fixed claims entitle them.[6] We *assume*, moreover, that the firm actually is liquidated at this point and the proceeds from its asset liquidation distributed to claim holders.[7]

Secured Claims and Priority

The securities issued by a corporation that receive the highest priority in the event of insolvency are those that are issued on secured terms. Secured borrowings, for example, involve debt instruments whose principal and interest payments are based on some underlying pool of assets or receivables on which the lender has a claim if the issuer goes bankrupt. In the event of insolvency, these assets are literally set aside to pay back the holders of securities backed by those assets as security. Consequently, those assets are inaccessible to all other claimants on the firm.

Equity Claims by Seniority

Equity claims are sometimes called soft claims because their seniority in the capital structure of the firm varies based on the other securities that the firm issues. In an all-equity firm, equity holders have a full claim on the assets of the firm. The only people standing in line ahead of equity holders if the firm goes bust are the holders of nondebt fixed liabilities the firm may have, such as pension liabilities or current accounts payable. Returning to the building blocks of Chapter 1, as the sole type of security holder in the firm, Exhibit 1.2 indicates clearly that equity is senior in capital structure. If a firm issues debt of any kind, however, equity slips behind debt in seniority, as shown clearly in Exhibit 1.5.

Given that equity holders as a group are "last in line" when the company is liquidated, in most types of corporations different levels of seniority may be assigned to the residual claimants within the equity category. In a financial mutual that takes the form of a limited partnership, for example, the managing partner may specify that his pro rata claim on the residual value of the assets of the firm are to be paid before claims of the other limited partners. Each partner still has a claim on an equal amount of the firm's assets, but the managing partner gets paid first. This can be important when the timing of an asset liquidation affects the value recovered.

Consider a hedge fund, for example, whose shareholders are all limited partners but whose managing partner receives priority in the event of an asset divestiture. For concreteness, suppose there are 10 partners and the total assets in the fund on date T are worth $1 million. For simplicity, assume—admittedly counterfactually—that the ownership of each partner is identical. Each partner has a claim worth $100,000. But suppose the market is moving when the fund is wound up and the assets are liquidated. The first 10 percent of the fund's assets are liquidated for $100,000, the next 10% of the fund's assets are liquidated for $90,000, and the remaining 80 percent of the fund's assets are sold for $700,000.

If all the partners in this fund enjoyed equal priority in the event of liquidation, then each partner would receive a prorated claim on the net liquidation value of all assets, or $890,000/10 = $89,000 each. But if the managing partner can get paid first, the managing partner will receive $100,000 and each of the other nine partners will receive only $790,000/9 = $87,777 each.

In open corporations, the usual way to create different priorities for equity holders is either to create different classes of common stock or to issue preferred stock. Classes of common stock often are defined based on the order in which the equity is issued, giving early investors in the firm a slight edge over subsequent investors. Preferred stock, in turn, is stock on which the dividend need not be paid by the firm if the issuer so chooses. But, dividends on common stock cannot be paid until dividends on preferred stock have been paid. In this sense, preferred stock has a higher priority than unrestricted common stock. In return for that higher seniority in the firm's capital structure, the holders of preferred stock usually receive a smaller dividend.

Debt Claims by Seniority

An unsecured senior creditor to a firm is the holder of an unsecured debt claim that is relatively senior in its capital structure—its holders get paid off first or nearly first in the event the firm is wound up. A junior creditor is a debt holder or creditor that stands farther back in the line when the firm liquidates its assets and distributes the proceeds. Typically, junior creditors are not paid off at all until senior creditors are paid off in full. Meanwhile, equity as a residual claim continues to slip to the end of the line.

"Senior debt" is a type of unsecured debt for which the lenders to a firm receive "me-first" treatment in the event the assets of a corporation are liquidated. Senior debt often comes in the form of bank loans made directly by commercial banks to corporations. "Subordinated debt" is debt in which the lenders receive a pro rata share of the cash proceeds from liquidated assets after senior lenders have been paid off. Extremely subordinated debt is often "junk."

Subordinated debt is sometimes called mezzanine finance. Firms commonly use mezzanine financing to facilitate corporate actions, such as management buy-outs or acquisitions, as well as for project finance. Popularized in the 1970s and again in the 1980s, mezzanine finance also is used frequently as seed capital for growth firms, especially if the equity portion of a deal or capital structure is too low for the firm to attract more conservative and senior creditors such as banks, which often require a higher debt/equity ratio than the borrowing firm has without the mezzanine layer.

Banks and insurance companies, in particular, have long viewed mezzanine finance as a hybrid or equitylike instrument for the purpose of their credit evaluations. Such perceptions arose for three somewhat different reasons.

1. The interest rate on mezzanine issues is usually closer to the equity return than the rate on senior debt. This does not, of course, make it a residual claim by our definitions, however.
2. Mezzanine debt often is accompanied by an issue of detachable warrants.[8] In this case, the mezzanine debt is still a fixed claim, but the total mezzanine package has features of both fixed and residual claims.
3. Mezzanine finance in some cases comes in the form of preferred stock rather than a debt issue, in which case it is a hybrid as we have defined it.

Mezzanine debt may be subordinated to senior debt either through "blanket" or "springing" subordination provisions. In the former case, mezzanine debt receives no principal or interest payments until senior creditors are fully paid off. In the springing subordination case, mezzanine debt holders can receive interest payments while the senior debt is outstanding, provided there is no event of default on the part of the issuer. If a default occurs, the subordination "springs up" and stops the payments on the mezzanine debt until senior debt has been made whole.[9]

Other Fixed Claims

As noted earlier, corporations often enter into fixed claims that are not intended to facilitate capital formation, such as employment contracts, independent contractor agreements, purchase or sale contracts, and capital market transactions like derivatives. In the event of insolvency, the unpaid fixed claims held by obligors to the firm generally receive a very low priority—that of the so-called general unsecured creditor to the firm.

A fixed claim holder that becomes a general unsecured creditor in the event of insolvency can in some cases be somewhere other than dead last in line. Some forms of highly subordinated junk or venture capital, for example, will fall behind general unsecured creditors of the firm. But typically, general unsecured creditors are close to the last in line.

SECURITIES UNDERWRITING AND PLACEMENT

The process by which a corporation supplies a financial claim on its real capital depends on the type of claim, the regulatory environment, and the intended market for the claim. There are essentially two ways for a company to "issue" an investment capital claim on its real capital in exchange for funds—through private negotiation and through public securities offerings.

Carow, Erwin, and McConnell (1999) examined the methods by which securities have been placed by U.S. firms for the last several decades. Table 2.4 reports their findings for U.S. firms issuing securities domestically from 1990 to 1997. It clearly illustrates the dominance of the public securities market.

Some of the particular details associated with each issuance method are discussed in the sections that follow. Note, however, that the private placements in the table above reflect only private *placements*, not privately negotiated debt contracts such as loans.

Privately Negotiated Capital

When a corporation or an agent of the corporation such as an investment bank does not feel the need to broadly market the investment capital claims issued by a firm, those claims can be created essentially by bilateral contracts between the firm issuing the claims and the party providing the capital. The cost of capital may vary based on the party supplying the capital, and the terms of bilateral capital contracts can be customized almost completely. Several popular types of bilateral contracts through which a firm can obtain investment capital are summarized below.

Private Placements

Until about 1985, most securities in the United States were issued publicly in a manner that will be described in the next section. But since 1985, the volume of "private placements" has grown explosively.[10] A private placement is

TABLE 2.4   Methods of Issuing U.S. Securities to Domestic Market ($ billions)

	'90	'91	'92	'93	'94	'95	'96	'97
Public	133.5	253.3	328.9	431.5	316.1	440.5	568.7	720.1
Private	56.8	51.8	48.5	62.7	32.6	40.6	70.4	134.9
Total	190.3	305.1	377.4	494.2	348.7	481.1	639.1	855.0

the placement of an investment claim on the real assets of a firm by its issuer directly to an end investor or a small group of end investors. Sometimes an investment bank is engaged to facilitate the matching of issuer to investor, but, importantly, a private placement does not usually involve the marketing of new securities to a dispersed and general audience. Private placements are also typically subject to fewer government regulations than public securities issues. Private placements are marketed, for example, using unregistered private placement memoranda (PPMs). Although common law obliges firms to adhere to basic contractual procedures (e.g., not defrauding potential investors in the PPM), no formal "shelf registration" of the PPM is required. Nevertheless, the degree of transparency and disclosure demanded by market participants often results in tighter self-regulation than the political regulations imposed on public issues.

When firms first start out, they often use venture capital as seed money in their early days of operation. Venture capitalists privately place cash with the start-up firm in exchange for either debt or equity claims on the firm's net cash flows.[11]

Start-up firms may go through several rounds of venture financing, usually beginning with private equity investments and then leading to private debt placements. Mezzanine finance often comes in late in the game, at the third stage or later, unless it is required very early to attract senior creditors to the deal.

Private placements also occur routinely on a nonventure basis—that is, to firms that have been around and viable long enough not to be classified as start-ups.

Partnership Agreements in Closed Corporations

As noted earlier, residual claims issued by closed corporations often are held by those who are also senior managers of the firm.[12] The ability to create partnership agreements bilaterally depends somewhat on the legal nature of the corporation.

In the United States, residual claims on the two most popular types of corporations—S and C corporations—cannot be created without the formal registration of shares. Even when the firm is owned by only one person, if it is a S or C corporation the firm must register shares and issue those shares to the manager/owner through a private placement or public security offering.

But if the firm is instead a limited liability company or partnership (LLC or LLP) or is a sole proprietorship, then partnership agreements can be created bilaterally without the registration of shares with a regulator like the Securities and Exchange Commission. In the United States LLCs have become especially popular recently. Now approved in most states, LLCs are companies that are essentially structured with the liability limitations of S or C corporations but are taxed as pure partnerships. Private placements are not even necessarily required to give force to such partnership agreements. In this sense, partnership agreements may well not be considered securities, but just commercial contracts between the firm and its managers.

Employee Compensation

Firms often use bilateral contracting to place contingent equity capital products. Employee and executive stock options, for example, are options on the stock of a firm that are granted bilaterally to employees and senior managers. The terms of these agreements are usually privately negotiated between the employee and the firm and may differ—sometimes materially—across specific employees. Similarly, employee dividend reinvestment programs are additional equity placement avenues. Deferred compensation schemes, by contrast, are a type of borrowing by the corporation.

Loans

As noted earlier, a loan is a nonfungible bilateral agreement between two parties to exchange cash now for cash later. Corporations can obtain cash in exchange for issuing fixed claims using several types of loan structures. The simplest loans are those made on a generally unrestricted basis by a credit union, savings institution, finance company, or bank to the corporation that is seeking cash to fund its investment activities.

Loans also may be targeted more specifically. Trade credit, for example, may be extended by one corporation to another to finance a specific trading activity. If Firm Wotan is a coffee producer, for example, it may be necessary for Wotan to borrow money to finance the export of its coffee—say, from the Ivory Coast in Africa to Switzerland. Firm Siegfried may lend Firm Wotan the money to secure transportation, storage, insurance, and the like required to ship the coffee. Typically the coffee itself will serve as security or collateral for the loan.

Project finance loans are popular types of specifically targeted capital structure claims negotiated bilaterally between the borrower and lender. In a project finance loan, a firm may borrow funds from a lender for the purpose of financing, say, a new construction or production project. The project itself (including any real capital assets dedicated to the project) then serves to collateralize the project finance credit extension.

Insurance and Reinsurance

Traditional and alternative risk transfer (ART) products offered by insurance industry participants may constitute important sources of financial capital for a firm. When a firm obtains contingent capital from an insurance company, the supplier of that capital is called an insurance company. When the firm that is seeking the contingent capital is itself an insurance company, the supplier of the contingent capital is called a reinsurance company.

Public Securities Offerings

All of the claims discussed in the prior section were targeted at specific individuals, institutions, or small groups of similar individuals and institutions. Closed corporations and small start-up firms often find it unnecessary to look further for their financing needs. But especially as companies grow and seek to diversify their capital supply base, public security offerings play an increasingly important role.

Public securities offerings can be distinguished from other types of security offerings in three ways.

1. They tend to be regulated. In the United States, for example, public securities must be registered with the SEC.
2. Public securities are usually assets that can be traded freely in a secondary market after their original issue.
3. Public securities offerings tend to involve the use of an intermediary known as an underwriter.

Popular Types of Public Securities Offerings

The initial public offering (IPO) is one of the most popular types of public equity securities offerings in which a new open corporation is set up or a closed corporation is transformed into an open corporation.[13]

In either case, the issuer's equity shares are marketed and sold as public securities for the first time in an IPO. In a primary offering, the issuing firm sells residual claims for cash. In a secondary offering, the original investors in the closed corporation (e.g., venture capitalists or limited partners) offer to sell their shares to the public.

In an IPO, the underwriter collects "indications of interest" and uses them to decide along with the issuing corporation what the original issue price will be. These periods often are called the premarketing and book-building periods.[14] Public securities offerings also may involve the determination of a price by a direct auction process.

Another common type of equity securities transaction is known as a seasoned public offering (SPO). This is a public offering of equity securities by a firm whose stock is already trading in a secondary market. IPO stocks usually lack a deep secondary market because, by definition, they are the issuer's first public securities offering. SPOs, by contrast, usually involve the offering of new equity into a market where the firm's existing equity is already trading.

Equity also may be sold—usually to the existing senior debt holders of a firm—by exchange offer, or an offer to exchange some amount of existing debt for equity shares in the firm. Such contracts are often associated with corporate actions such as mergers and acquisitions, in which the securities of a target are exchanged for securities of an acquiring firm. Exchange offers also may come in the form of bilateral contracts, depending mainly on whether the existing security holders are public security holders or not. These contracts may specify the exchange of equity for debt instead of the converse.

Investment Banking and the Role of the Underwriter

Investment banking is a process by which corporations raise investment capital by issuing claims on their real capital assets through an intermediary known as an investment bank. One of the principal functions of an investment bank is underwriting the issue of securities by a corporation and then engaging in the distribution and sale of that security to public security market participants.

Underwriters of public debt and equity issues typically have at least three roles in a deal: They advise the corporation on how to structure the transaction, buy the securities directly from the corporation, and then resell the securities (or some portion thereof) to the public.[15] Underwriters earn income from this process through a mixture of underwriting fees and a purchasing spread that usually allows them to purchase the securities at a discount to the public offering price.

The risk borne by underwriters of public securities depends on the nature of their contract with the corporation actually issuing the claim. In some cases, an underwriter simply agrees to purchase the whole security issue. In these *firm commitment* underwriting deals, the underwriter assumes the risk that the issue cannot be resold at a premium to the price paid by the underwriter. Conversely, the underwriter reaps the rewards of a successful IPO. Many IPOs include, for example, an overallotment option for the underwriter—called a green shoe—that allows the underwriter to sell additional shares of the offering at the IPO price.[16] If a green shoe is not exercised, the IPO likely was not a successful one.[17]

The underwriter also may choose to limit its price risk by prior agreement with the issuer of the claim. In a *best efforts* underwriting agreement, for example, the underwriter does not buy the security being issued from the company but instead simply acts as a marketing and distribution agent for the issuer. The underwriter guarantees only that it will use its best efforts to place the security, but bears neither price nor inventory risk if the issue cannot be fully placed—although the firm will still bear reputation risk. Similarly, in an *all-or-nothing* underwriting agreement, the underwriter and issuing firm agree that if the underwriter cannot place the entire issue at the offering price, the whole issue is called off.

All of these underwriting methods involve a cash offer to all prospective investors. In addition, underwriters may float the securities of a corporation using a rights offering. In a rights offering, existing shareholders of a firm are given warrants (i.e., types of call options on the firm's common stock)[18] on a pro rata basis—that is, options to buy new shares at a specific price. The strike price is usually 15 to 20 percent below the current market price of the firm's stock. If an existing shareholder does not exercise the right to acquire new stock, other existing shareholders may be given the chance to purchase more than their pro rata rights allocation originally entitled them—another version of the "green shoe."[19]

If the corporation issuing securities opts for a rights offer but is concerned that the rights offer will result in an undersubscription of the new issue, a rights offering can be combined with a cash offer using what is known as a stand-by. In a stand-by, an underwriter is engaged to offer a firm commitment to guarantee the purchase of any unsubscribed rights.

Eckbo and Masulis (1995) show that over the past 60 years, U.S. open corporations gradually have shifted their equity offerings from rights issues and stand-by issues to cash offers with firm commitments from underwriters. By 1990, rights issues had virtually disappeared in the United States. Firm commitment underwriting completely dominates as a method for issuing public debt securities.

SECURITIES CAPITAL STRUCTURE

We can now formulate a slightly more refined view of a corporation's capital structure than the simple leverage ratio discussed in Chapter 1. Now we also take into consideration the order in which claims are paid off. In other words, we now take a first cut at looking at capital structure based on the risk of the claims issued, with lower priority obviously implying higher risk to investors *ceteris paribus* (all else being equal).

Securities Capital Structure and Risk

The securities capital structure of a firm on liquidation date T is shown in Exhibit 2.5. The claims issued by the firm to external investors that show up on the liabilities and equity side of the balance sheet represent claims on the assets of the firm in descending order of priority. Recognize that this is not a balance sheet but rather a depiction of the external capital structure of the company.

The assets (net of nonsecurity liabilities) of the firm on date T are divided into two components. $A_0(T)$ represents the value of those assets that have been pledged as security for some secured claim issued by the firm. The corresponding secured issues on the claims side of the economic balance sheet are separated from the rest of the claims of the firm by a solid line, indicating that these assets and their associated claims are "walled off" from the rest of the capital structure. Whatever those pledged assets are worth on date T is used first to pay off the fixed secured claim holders. If FV_0 represents the value of all fixed secured claims issued by the firm, then the firm's secured creditors are

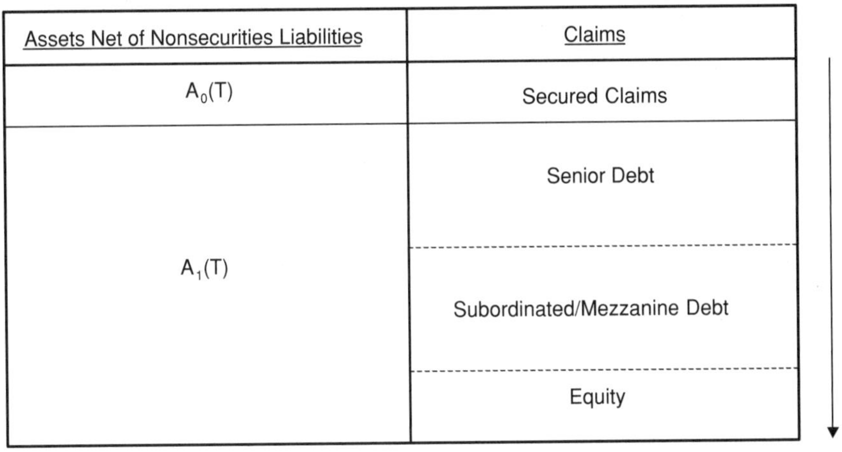

Assets Net of Nonsecurities Liabilities	Claims
$A_0(T)$	Secured Claims
$A_1(T)$	Senior Debt
	Subordinated/Mezzanine Debt
	Equity

Priority of Claim

EXHIBIT 2.5 Securities Capital Structure of a Firm by Priority

made whole in the event of insolvency as long as $FV \leq A_0(T)$. If $FV > A_0(T)$, then the secured creditors receive a pro rata claim on $A_0(T)$, unless otherwise specified in the debt covenants.

If the liquidated pledged assets generate a surplus—that is, $FV < A_0(T)$—the use of the surplus funds depends on whether or not there are any secured residual claims. A bank may lend in a project financing context, for example, with the assets pledged *in toto* to the bank as collateral. In this case, the bank's claim is more residual than fixed, as the bank may keep all the proceeds generated by the sale of the assets underlying the project. In other words, in return for taking the risk that the assets underlying the project are insufficient to cover the principal and interest due on a traditional loan, the firm makes the loan anyway but retains the rights to any surplus of asset values over what the terms of a fixed loan would have been.

A surplus of assets net of claims liabilities in the secured portion of the balance sheet is somewhat unusual. In most cases, a firm's inability to make secured creditors whole out of its own internal funds means that the secured creditors actually take possession of the collateral. If the collateral happens to be worth more than the securities, this is a windfall for the secured lenders. But this should not be the case for any length of time—a direct claim on a security should not be worth less than the security.

The priority of claim holders in Exhibit 2.5 is shown by the appearance of those claims in descending order. In the example, equity is a single group and is last in line next to the firm's mezzanine or subordinated creditors.[20] Each class of claim holder must be repaid *in full* before any funds generated from the liquidation of assets $A_1(T)$ are applied to the next class of claim holder in the seniority capital structure. In general, it is impossible for holders of mezzanine finance claims to receive anything unless senior debt holders have been paid everything they are due.

Securities Capital Structure from an Options Perspective

Now let us return again to the fundamental capital structure building blocks, with the goal of incorporating priority into them. When the capital structure of a firm is viewed most simply as comprised of residual and fixed claims, the value of the firm can be shown to equal the value of a long call option on the assets of the firm plus the value of a short put option on the assets of the firm—both of which have a strike price equal to the total face value of outstanding fixed claims and have a maturity date corresponding to the liquidation date of the firm or the maturity of its outstanding debt—plus the face value of the firm's debt. This simplistic perspective of capital structure and firm value is quite robust and can be generalized to take into account priority with little difficulty.

Consider a firm that issues unrestricted common stock as residual claims and then assumes two types of debt obligations with different priorities. Suppose the firm enters into senior bank loans with a total principal amounting to K_1 and issues subordinated debt with principal K_2. Suppose the firm has no secured claims and no additional general unsecured debt obligations. To keep things simple, further imagine that both the loans and bonds are zero-coupon and mature on date T, and that insolvency can only occur on that date T and not earlier. If insolvency can be triggered prior to the maturity date of the options that comprise the capital structure of the firm, the options should be viewed as types of barrier options. Equity, for example, becomes a down-and-out call that is knocked out once the firm becomes insolvent.

Equity

Equity is still a call on the value of the firm with a strike price equal to the sum of all outstanding fixed obligations—$K_1 + K_2$. Unless the value of the firm's assets upon liquidation exceeds this amount—that is, $A(T) > K_1 + K_2$—the firm's equity holders get nothing in insolvency.

Senior Debt

To model the debt using options, we really need only identify the options and strike prices to characterize each layer of fixed claims. Suppose the liquidation value of assets is exactly equal to the sum of the principal amounts of all debt types. In this case, all debt holders are made whole even though equity is worthless. But now suppose there is a shortfall of assets below the face values of all fixed claims. In this case, priority requires that senior debt be paid off first in its entirety. If $A(T) < K_1$, then clearly the bank creditors to the firm receive only a pro rata claim on $A(T)$ and the sub–debt holders receive nothing. But if $A(T) > K_1$, bank creditors are fully repaid. We know then that the exposure of the senior creditors is

$$\min[A(T), K_1]$$

which is equivalent to a short put option on the assets of the firm struck at K_1 plus a riskless loan with face value K_1:

$$K_1 + \min[A(T) - K_1, 0] = \min[A(T), K_1]$$

The senior debt position in isolation is shown in Exhibit 2.6.

Subordinated Debt

Now consider the subordinated debt. The face value of the debt is K_2, bringing the firm's total debt outstanding to $K_1 + K_2$. Because subordinated debt is junior in capital structure to senior debt, moreover, the assets of the firm must be worth at least K_1—the level at which senior debt is made whole—before sub-debt receives any principal repayment.

Let us write down explicitly what the sub–debt holders get in each of

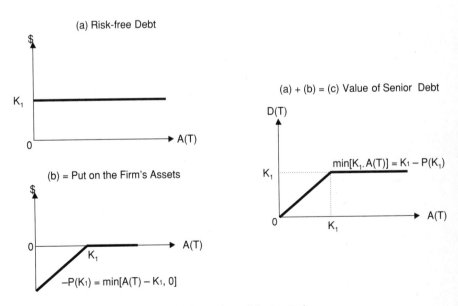

EXHIBIT 2.6 Value of Senior Debt

three scenarios, writing $D_m(T)$ to indicate the mezzanine debt holders' total recovery:

$$A(T) < K_1 < K_1 + K_2 \quad \rightarrow \quad D_m(T) = 0$$
$$K_1 < A(T) < K_1 + K_2 \quad \rightarrow \quad D_m(T) = A(T) - K_1$$
$$K_1 < K_1 + K_2 < A(T) \quad \rightarrow \quad D_m(T) = K_2$$

In the language of options, this is the payoff pattern at maturity for what is called a vertical spread, or a combination of two option positions written on the same underlying asset, having the same maturity date (e.g., the date that the fixed claims issued by the firm mature), and having different striking prices. A long vertical spread, or "bull spread," involves the combination of a long put with strike price K_1 and a short put with strike price $K_1 + K_2 > K_1$. The payoff on this position at maturity is

$$\max[K_1 - A(T), 0] + \min[A(T) - (K_1 + K_2), 0]$$

and is shown in Exhibit 2.7 as a function of some underlying asset value $A(T)$.

Just as senior debt can be viewed as a riskless loan and a put on the firm's assets struck at K_1, the subordinated debt also can be viewed as a combination of riskless bonds and a vertical spread. But what does the loan component look like?

In the senior debt case, the total position can be viewed as a riskless pay-

Profit/Loss

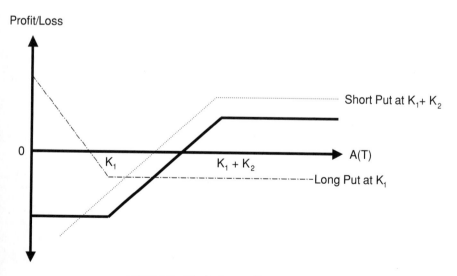

EXHIBIT 2.7　Vertical or Bull Put Spread

off of K_1 from shareholders and an agreement to give back that K_1 in exchange for the assets of the firm. Subordinated debt is no different. It is an agreement to receive K_2 risklessly, which shareholders can call back in exchange for the firm's assets. But this is true only for asset values above K_1.

Subordinated debt thus can be viewed as a riskless loan of K_2 plus a short put struck at $K_1 + K_2$ plus a long put struck at K_1. The long put prevents sub–debt holders from accessing funds until senior debt has been paid off, and the strike of the short put written by sub-debt is adjusted accordingly. The payoff of the sub-debt at maturity thus is

$$K_2 - \min[A(T) - (K_1 + K_2), 0] + \max[K_1 - A(T), 0]$$

and is shown in Exhibit 2.8.

Now let us take this characterization of subordinated debt as a vertical spread and snap this together with the other option building blocks to get a picture of this firm's total capital structure from a seniority perspective. Exhibit 2.9 depicts the value of each of the three types of claims as a function of the value of the firm's assets at liquidation date T. To sum up, senior debt can be viewed as a riskless loan of K_1 and a short put option on the firm's assets with a strike price of K_1, subordinated debt as a vertical spread on the firm's

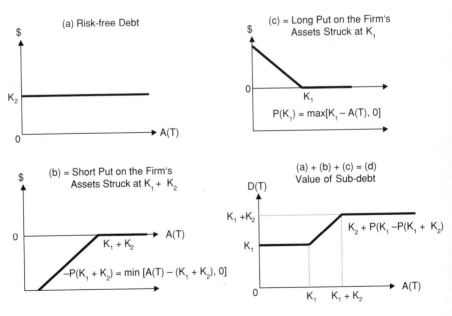

EXHIBIT 2.8   Value of Subordinated Debt

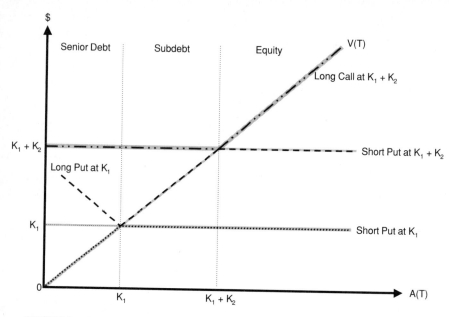

EXHIBIT 2.9 Option Components of the Securities Capital Structure with Priority

assets with strikes K_1 and $K_1 + K_2$ plus a riskless loan of K_2, and equity as a call on the firm's assets struck at $K_1 + K_2$.

EMPIRICAL EVIDENCE ON CAPITAL STRUCTURE

Various scholarly efforts have been undertaken to help us understand the securities capital structure of modern corporations. One recent such study by Fama and French (1999) confirms the results of prior studies and helps paint a useful picture of what the securities capital structures of firms tend to look like in the real world. Their study is based only on U.S. firms, although their findings are broadly consistent with the international evidence collected earlier by Rajan and Zingales (1995). Fama and French analyze all nonfinancial firms reporting to COMPUSTAT between 1974 and 1996—and in some cases, data permitting, between 1951 and 1996.

Table 2.5 summarizes the snapshot of capital structure taken by Fama and French of the types of securities firms issued over the 1974 to 1996 sample period. Percentages reported are based on the market value of each security type as a proportion of the total market value of the firm and are averages of annual data over the entire sample period. In this table, debt securities are classified by their maturity rather than their priority.

Fama and French examine the behavior of these numbers over time, and

TABLE 2.5 Average Proportion of Capital Structure by Security Type, 1974–1996

Type of Security Issued	Proportion of Total Market Value
Common stock	65.84%
Preferred stock	2.64%
Long-term debt	24.99%
Short-term debt	6.53%

the results of this analysis are shown in Exhibit 2.10. Evidently, the proportion of equity in U.S. corporate capital structures has declined since the 1970s, giving way to a higher proportion of mainly long-term debt. Consistent with prior evidence, however, the increase in leverage in the 1970s appears to have been a return of leverage to normal levels from unusual postwar lows. Notably, the so-called "decade of greed" of the 1980s does not show a particularly high amount of leverage relative to the other time periods, except the postwar period.

Fama and French also examine whether these capital structure snapshots

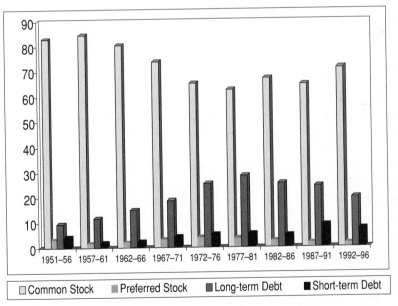

EXHIBIT 2.10 Trends in Capital Structure of U.S. Non-Financial Corporations, 1951–1996 (% of Total Market Value by Market Value of Security Type, Period Averages)
Source: Fama and French (1999).

differ for firms that enter and leave the sample. The former are mainly new firms, whereas the latter include firms that are acquired by other firms or experience financial distress and closure. Interestingly, firms exiting the sample (i.e., takeover targets or shutdowns) have capital structures nearly indistinguishable from the averages. Firms entering the sample, however, tend to be characterized by relatively higher amounts of equity.

Carow, Erwin, and McConnell (1999) provide a different perspective on capital structure by examining new issues by security type. The breakdown for types of securities issued domestically by U.S. corporations for the 1990 to 1997 period appears in Table 2.6.

Table 2.6 shows only new stock issues. But recall in Table 2.3 that for some of the same years, we already saw that stock repurchases and delevering exchange offers resulted in more stock being retired than issued. The proportion of new stock issued thus is clearly lower than the proportion of firms' capital structure accounted for by equity as shown in Table 2.5. This suggests that many firms may begin their lives with a heavy portion of equity, but that new issues tend toward other types of claims. In addition, Fama and French provide further information on how firms finance themselves. Specifically, internally generated funds (i.e., earnings plus depreciation) fell short of investment outlays in the period from 1951 to 1996 by an average of 4 percent of book capital—average annual internal funds were 15.11 percent of book capital, whereas average annual investment spending was 19.11 percent of book capital. So the average net inflow of external investment capital to firms was 4 percent of book capital—a fairly small number. Interestingly, a good portion of firms' internal funds was consumed on payments to security holders during the period—about 40 percent of cash earnings, in fact.

Given that there was an average annual shortfall of 4 percent that firms had to obtain by issuing external claims, how did firms structure these new security issues? By far the main preference for firms was to issue long-term debt, accounting for 57 percent of the net cash flow shortfall (or 2.26 percent of book capital). Equity was second place, accounting for about 26 percent of the shortfall (or 1.04 percent of book capital).

TABLE 2.6 Types of Securities Issued by U.S. Firms to Domestic Market ($ billions)

	'90	'91	'92	'93	'94	'95	'96	'97
Common Stock	21.0	54.3	69.7	95.4	53.9	73.3	99.0	102.1
Debt	104.4	171.9	203.8	258.0	140.2	254.2	283.7	444.9
Convertibles	1.4	4.5	6.3	6.4	3.1	1.7	10.3	11.3
Preferred Stock	7.0	18.1	32.2	29.1	14.7	14.7	50.4	55.4
Secured Debt	38.3	45.3	36.3	36.9	40.8	54.6	79.2	772.0

Using regression analysis, Fama and French provide a more detailed attribution of how firms funded their investment expenditures each year in the 1951 to 1996 period. On average, the sources of corporate investment capital were as follows: 69.5 percent from internal funds; 17.2 percent from new issues of long-term debt; 7.9 percent from new equity issues; and 5.3 percent from new issues of short-term debt. This is broadly consistent with the international findings of Rajan and Zingales (1995), who find that internal funds typically account for over 50 percent (and as much as 77 percent) of firms' annual investment capital raised between 1984 and 1991 in the United States, Germany, France, Italy, the United Kingdom, and Canada. Firms least reliant on internal finance were Japanese firms, which acquired only 44 percent of their investment capital from internal funds. Like Fama and French, Rajan and Zingales also find a strong bias toward debt finance vis-à-vis equity in all the aforementioned countries.

PAID-IN VERSUS CONTINGENT CAPITAL

As noted, debt, equity, and hybrid securities are all types of paid-in capital for which the firm receives funds upon the claims issue. In exchange for the funds the firm receives, it enters into either a fixed or residual obligation to the claim holder. Contingent capital, by contrast, usually involves the payment of a fee by the firm seeking capital to the capital supplier, in exchange for which the capital supplier agrees to stand ready to supply paid-in capital on fixed terms on some date in the future. Whereas paid-in capital claims are current obligations of the firm, contingent capital claims are rights and not obligations.

Contingent Capital as Options on Paid-in Capital

Contingent capital is essentially an option on paid-in capital. And just like a regular option, contingent capital can be characterized by its underlying, exercise style, tenor, strike price, and any "exercise triggers."

The underlying of a contingent capital facility is a fixed, residual, or hybrid capital claim. More specifically, a contingent capital facility is essentially a precommitment by a capital provider to provide paid-in capital on preagreed terms if the buyer of the facility chooses to exercise that right on or before the expiration of the contingent facility. Contingent capital thus may come in the form of contingent debt, contingent equity, or contingent hybrid capital. And, of course, sometimes contingent capital can supply the firm directly with cash, as in a classic (re-)insurance contract (see Chapters 15 and 16) or an in-the-money derivatives contract (see Chapter 13). The underlying of a contingent capital facility is defined up front as part of the contingent capital terms.

The exercise style of a contingent capital facility concerns the timing with which the purchaser of the contingent claim may convert that claim into paid-in capital. Like regular options, a contingent capital facility may entitle its buyer to utilize the facility and obtain paid-in capital only on a few specific dates (i.e., Bermuda exercise style), only when the contingent capital facility expires (i.e., European style), or on any date up to its expiration (i.e., American style). Most contingent capital facilities are American style.

The tenor of the contingent claim is the period during which the firm has access to the paid-in capital. Care must be taken not to confuse the tenor of the contingent claim with the tenor of the underlying. A contingent debt facility, for example, may have a tenor of a year but an underlying with five years to maturity. In this case, the firm buying the contingent capital has purchased a one-year American option on five-year debt—at any time over the next year, the capital provider has agreed to purchase five-year debt from the firm at a predefined price. A contingent equity facility, by contrast, may have a tenor of a year despite the fact that if exercised, the resulting paid-in claim is perpetual.

The contingent capital facility also includes the analog of a strike price, or the terms on which the paid-in capital will be transferred if the buyer exercises its right to draw upon that paid-in capital.

Finally, many contingent capital facilities include barriers or triggers that allow the buyer to access paid-in capital only in certain specific circumstances. Some of these triggers are relatively basic, such as contingent capital that comes in the form of a cash payment made to cover some or all of a firm's property losses arising from, say, a flood. In that case, the triggers that provide the firm access to flood-contingent cash are the occurrence of a flood *and* the loss of property value as a direct result of the flood.

Other triggers may be complex and/or unusual. Indeed, as we shall see in Part IV, many A.R.T. products are contingent capital facilities in which triggers play a crucially important role. Later we discuss a transaction in which the firm is able to convert its contingent claim into paid-in capital only if the gross domestic product of the countries in which the purchasing firm sells its goods has declined by a specified amount.

In sum, the basic distinction between paid-up and contingent capital, is that the former results when a company issues a claim on its net cash flows—fixed or residual—and receives funds for selling that claim at the time of sale. Contingent capital, by contrast, gives the firm the right but not the obligation to obtain funds on predefined terms on a later date. Although the claim is legally binding when issued, it does not result in an immediate infusion of funds.

Apart from the economic optionality of contingent capital that distinguishes it from firm paid-in capital, there is another important difference between the two types of capital. Namely, because contingent capital represents a right to obtain subsequent investment capital on fixed terms but does not obligate the firm to do so, contingent capital is usually off-balance-sheet. All the securities discussed in this chapter as sources of paid-in capital, by contrast, appear on the corporations' balance sheet.[21]

Contingent Capital Example: Letters of Credit

A common example of a contingent debt claim is a letter of credit (LOC), in which a lender—usually a bank—accepts a fee from a corporation and in return agrees to lend the corporation money at a subsequent time of the corporation's choosing, as long as the firm still meets certain criteria specified by the borrower.

If the corporation draws on the LOC, the contingent claim turns into an actual fixed claim in which the firm now owes interest and principal on the loan back to the bank. Before the LOC is drawn, however, the funds are not part of the company's economic balance sheet. Nevertheless, the right to those funds can be an important source of capital for the borrowing firm.

LOCs and other contingent capital often include a variety of restrictions that specify when funds actually will be available. In fact, LOCs are often criticized on the grounds that they are usually not available just when they are most needed. LOCs and other contingent debt instruments often contain restrictions known as MAC (material adverse change) clauses. A typical MAC clause states that a firm cannot draw on its letter of credit if it has experienced a material adverse change in its financial condition or credit quality subsequent to the execution of the original contingent capital agreement. Unfortunately, this means that LOCs tend to be available to firms as actual sources of funds only when the firms do not experience adverse events that eat away at their paid-in capital.

Contingent Capital and the Securities Capital Structure

Because contingent capital represents an option on paid-in capital, the claims capital structure of a firm with contingent capital will reflect the type of underlying the contingent facility contains. Whether the resulting paid-in capital claim will be debt or equity is known when the facility is first arranged. In other words, how the contingent capital will affect the firm's total leverage if the facility is drawn on is known. The question is whether it will be drawn.

How the contingent claim is treated in viewing the claims capital structure really depends on the purpose of the capital structure evaluation. If one is trying to value the company, for example, then the value of its contingent capital facilities is essentially the value of the options on paid-in capital, or the discounted net present value of the paid-in capital weighted by the *ex ante* probability that the firm will draw on some or all of the facility. But if one wishes to examine only the proportion of fixed to residual claims, then treating the contingent facility as if it either is fully undrawn or fully drawn—whichever is most conservative—can make sense.

NOTES

1. Given that not all firms pay dividends, the relation between expected future dividends and the value of the firm must include a potential liquidating dividend as well.
2. Eckbo and Masulis (1995) examine sources of funds for U.S. nonfarm nonfinancial corporate businesses from 1946 to 1991 (as reported by the Federal Reserve Board) and arrive at similar findings to those shown in Table 2.1.
3. Exceptions tend to be related to corporate actions or to regulations. As an example of the former, firms that amass more than a certain amount of an open corporation's stock must declare their intent to initiate a bid for control of the company if that is their goal. As an example of the latter, bank holding companies and their affiliates in the United States are not allowed to hold more than a certain percentage of the outstanding stock an open corporation has issued.
4. This section is based on Culp and Mackay (1997).
5. See Culp and Mackay (1997) for a review of some of the more creative types of these hybrid securities.
6. Many would argue that this definition of insolvency is far too simplistic. A firm can remain open for business, for example, as long as it can cover its operating cash flow needs or variable costs. This is sometimes possible when the value of the firm's assets is below its liabilities. Nevertheless, such a firm is indeed economically insolvent, and we stick to that definition based on market values of assets and liabilities to keep the analysis clean. See Merton (1974). In real-world bankruptcy litigation, of course, parties spend considerable time and money arguing about what it means to be "insolvent." See, for example, *In Re Trans World Airlines, Inc.*, 134 F.3d 188 (3rd Cir. 1998).
7. It is not always true that firms get liquidated when they are insolvent, even if perhaps they should. See, for example, Harris and Raviv (1990).
8. See Lerner (2000).
9. See, for example, Chapman Tripp (1998).
10. Eckbo and Masulis (1995).
11. Venture capital should not be confused with venture capitalists. In fact, most venture capital is privately placed with new firms by pension plans, endowments, and insurance companies. Such institutional investors almost always also have a wide range of investments in public securities or private placements in non–start-up firms. A venture capitalist, by contrast, is a firm that makes almost all of its investments in start-up firms. In

addition, a typical venture capitalist may not actually be investing its own funds. Often venture capitalists obtain funds from banks and other lenders and then immediately loan the proceeds of their borrowings to start-up firms—at a mark-up over what they paid.

12. General and limited partnerships often involve passive investors with no management role. This structure arises often for financial mutuals.

13. IPOs and their performance are surveyed in Ibbotson and Ritter (1995).

14. Brealey and Myers (2000) offer a good discussion of this process.

15. See Brealey and Myers (2000).

16. The term "green shoe" comes from the IPO of the Green Shoe Company, later Stride Rite.

17. If the extra shares were demanded, the exercise of this option eventually must be disclosed (usually within a few weeks of the IPO) to facilitate the final calculation of shares outstanding.

18. Warrants differ from regular call options mainly in that the firm is the writer of the option. Accordingly, the firm usually must issue new stock to honor the exercise of a warrant. In a regular call purchased, say, on the Chicago Board Options Exchange, the writer of the option need not be the firm that issued the stock. To honor an exercise by the long, the option writer simply needs to have the stock.

19. See Eckbo and Masulis (1995).

20. Technically, general unsecured creditors are also in line around here, but traditionally they are not included in the firm's capital structure for reasons explained earlier.

21. In the case of securities like trust-preferred stock, the preferred stock issued to the trust as collateral for the ultimate security issue will appear as the issuer's liability. Even though the liability of the company does not directly correspond to a legal claim held by investors, the economic implications are the same.

CHAPTER 3

When Is Capital Structure Irrelevant?

One of the great holy grails over the last several decades of corporate finance—in theory and practice—is the quest by firms to discover whether "an optimal capital structure" exists for any given firm. A unique optimal capital structure exists for a firm if some particular mixture of claims issued by the firm for capital maximizes the value of that firm. There are a number of obvious ways to restate this optimal capital structure question in more practical terms: What amount of leverage maximizes firm value? How much should a firm borrow? Does the maturity and priority mixture of the claims issued change the value of the firm? What kind of dividend policy should the firm adopt? How can a firm compute its cost of capital? How can a firm minimize its cost of capital?

We cannot meaningfully understand the statistics in Chapter 2 and the firm's quest for an optimal capital structure until we have first developed the baseline case in which the firm's value does not depend on the securities it issues or dividends that it pays. Thus, we develop some basic grounding in corporate finance theory by answering the following questions:

- In what situations does the mixture of claims issued by a firm to raise investment capital have no impact on the value of the firm?
- What criterion should firms use to ensure that the total wealth of their security holders (i.e., suppliers of external investment capital) is maximized, and what criterion should firms use to evaluate the desirability of new investments?
- How should a firm measure its cost of capital for the purpose of implementing its optimal investment criterion?

THE MOST RELEVANT IRRELEVANCIES OF FINANCE

The search for optimal capital structure predates the recognition of "finance" as a stand-alone intellectual and academic discipline. Ironically, the

72

article credited with beginning the scholarly study of finance showed not when firms could achieve an optimal capital structure but rather when they could not. We thus begin with a review of the implications of the now-classic M&M propositions, based on the seminal work of Franco Modigliani and Merton Miller (1958).

The propositions showed that under certain assumptions, a company's financial policy—that is, its decisions on how to raise financial capital to finance its real capital investments—cannot affect the firm's value. In other words, the total cost a firm pays to acquire its investment capital depends on what real capital the firm is acquiring, not on what financial capital is used to fund the acquisition. The M&M propositions, however, hold only under certain assumptions, and it is precisely these assumptions that make the propositions of practical use. As we will see in Chapters 4 and 5, violations of these assumptions are what can give rise to optimal capital structure. But for now, we remain interested in the base case.

These assumptions under which the M&M irrelevance propositions hold are as follows[1]:

- *Perfect Capital Markets*: Capital markets are perfect in the sense of no taxes, no transaction costs, no institutional frictions (e.g., short selling restrictions on securities), and no costs of bankruptcy or financial distress.
- *Symmetric Information*: All investors, firms, and firm managers have the same information about the quality of a firm's investments in real capital and have identical (as well as correct) perceptions concerning the impact of new information about such real investments on the prices of investment capital claims (i.e., securities) issued by the firm.
- *Given Investment Strategies*: Investment decisions by firms in real capital are taken as a given and as independent from financing decisions.
- *Equal Access*: Firms and individuals can issue the same securities in the capital markets on exactly the same terms.[2]

Now we turn to three implications of these assumptions.

Irrelevance of the Securities Capital Structure

The first M&M proposition tells us that the value of a company is independent of its securities capital structure. In other words, leverage does not affect the value of the firm—there is no such thing as the "right" amount to borrow.

To illustrate this proposition simply, consider Corporation Mozart, which has $100 of real assets. With no debt, the market value of Corporation Mozart at some time t is equal to the market value of its assets at that time t:

$$V(t)^M = A(t)^M = E(t)^M = \$100$$

where superscripts denote the company name—M for Mozart—and the argument in parentheses denotes time.

Now consider Corporation Berlioz, which invests in the same real assets as Mozart. The only difference between the firms is that Corporation Berlioz issues \$50 in fixed debt claims and Mozart does not. The value of Corporation Berlioz at time t is now equal to the sum of the market values of its fixed and residual claims at time t:

$$V(t)^B = E(t)^B + D(t)^B$$

In the absence of arbitrage, M&M's "Proposition I" tells us that value of Corporation Mozart must equal that of Corporation Berlioz. To see this, consider first an investment strategy in which the arbitrageur Mad Hatter buys 10 percent of the shares of Corporation Berlioz, which will cost Mad Hatter

$$0.10E(t)^B = 0.10[V(t)^B - D(t)^B]$$

In return for making this investment outlay, Mad Hatter earns 10 percent of the firm's profits each year after the interest on the debt is repaid. If the interest rate on the debt at time t is $R_D(t)$, the Hatter earns the following per year:

$$0.10[\pi - R_D(t)D(t)^B]$$

where π denotes the profits of the firm from its real assets.

Now consider a second investment strategy in which Mad Hatter borrows on his own in order to invest in Corporation Mozart. Remember that one assumption of M&M is equal access by individuals and firms to the capital market, which means they have the borrowing rate $R_D(t)$. Suppose further that the Mad Hatter borrows an amount exactly equal to 10% of the time t market value of debt issued by Corporation Berlioz, $0.10D(t)^B$, to invest in Corporation Mozart. Mad Hatter then has a net investment outlay of

$$0.10E(t)^M - 0.10D(t)^B = 0.10[V(t)^M - D(t)^B]$$

because $E(t)^M$ is the same as $V(t)^M$ for the unlevered firm Mozart. Mad Hatter then earns gross profits per year on his investment in Corporation Mozart:

$$0.10\pi$$

where π here is the same as it was for Corporation Berlioz because the firms are holding identical real assets. But Mad Hatter must subtract from this inflow of profits the cost of repaying the debt he incurred to make the investment. So, Mad Hatter's net profits per year are

$$0.10[\pi - R_D(t)D(t)^B]$$

Table 3.1 compares the costs and profits per annum of the two investment strategies.

Note from the table that the net profits of the two investments are exactly the same. In the first case, the Mad Hatter gets 10 percent of Corporation Berlioz's profits after the levered firm repays its debt, or $0.10[\pi - R_D(t)D(t)^B]$. In the second case, Mad Hatter earns 10 percent of profits from Corporation Mozart but then must repay his own debt. Because the gross profits of the two firms are equal and the borrowing rate for the Mad Hatter is equal to the borrowing rate for Corporation Berlioz, the net profits to the Mad Hatter are equivalent.

Because the net profits of the two strategies are identical, the costs also must be identical. To see why, just suppose otherwise and imagine that the value of Corporation Mozart exceeds the value of Corporation Berlioz, $V(t)^M > V(t)^B$. In that case, Mad Hatter could invest in Corporation Berlioz for less than Mozart and yet earn the same return as he would earn on Mozart for a lower initial outlay *and* for no additional risk. Other investors would behave likewise. With costless transacting, perfect capital markets, and symmetric information, no one would buy shares in the more expensive Corporation Mozart—or, more properly, investors would short the stock of Corporation Mozart and buy the stock of Corporation Berlioz. Eventually, the two values would equalize, so that $V(t)^M = V(t)^B$. This is the import of M&M Proposition I—the value of the firm is independent of its securities capital structure.

Irrelevance of Debt and Leverage

Some have been tempted to argue that the only implication of M&M Proposition I is that it does not matter whether the firm or the individual borrows. That does not mean that borrowing itself cannot be used to increase the value of the firm (or decrease its cost of investment capital). But, in fact, the M&M assumptions also imply the irrelevance of leverage on the firm's cost of capital.

TABLE 3.1 Comparison of Mad Hatter's Investments in Berlioz and Mozart

Strategy	Initial Cost	Net Profits
Invest 0.10 $E(t)^B$ in Berlioz:	$0.10E(t)^B = 0.10[V(t)^B - D(t)^B]$	$0.10[\pi - R_D(t)D(t)^B]$
Borrow $0.10D(t)^B$ and	$0.10E(t)^M - 0.10D(t)^B =$	$0.10[\pi - R_D(t)D(t)^B]$
Invest $0.10E(t)^M$ in	$0.10[V(t)^M - D(t)^B]$	
Mozart:		

We saw that Corporation Berlioz had a debt cost of capital of $R_D(t)$. That is Berlioz's *cost of debt capital* at time t. Now suppose we denote the expected return demanded by investors on Berlioz's equity as $R_E{}^B(t)$, where this is now the corporation's cost of equity capital. We can then usefully define Berlioz's weighted average cost of capital (WACC) as follows:

$$R_{WACC}^B(t) = \frac{D(t)^B}{D(t)^B + E(t)^B} R_D(t) + \frac{E(t)^B}{D(t)^B + E(t)^B} R_E^B(t) \qquad (3.1)$$

In other words, the overall cost of capital for Firm Berlioz is the interest rate paid on its debt weighted by the proportion of debt in Berlioz's capital structure plus the expected return demanded by equity holders weighted by the fraction of equity in the firm.

To illustrate M&M Proposition II, we need do little more than rearrange the firm's WACC in terms of its equity cost of capital:

$$R_E^B(t) = R_{WACC}^B(t) + \frac{D(t)^B}{E(t)^B}\left[R_{WACC}^B(t) - R_D(t)\right] \qquad (3.2)$$

With no taxes, the WACC for an all-equity corporation is equal to the cost of equity capital, or $R_{WACC}(t) = R_E(t)$. So, expression 3.2 tells us that expected return on equity can be viewed as the expected return on the whole firm if it were financed with all equity plus a "penalty" that increases as the leverage of the firm increases. Or in the language of Chapter 1, as debt increases, the strike on the equity option increases, equity becomes riskier, and the return demanded by investors to hold equity must rise.

Although debt may appear to be a cheaper source of financing for a firm, issuing debt increases the risk of holding equity, thereby leading investors to demand a higher expected return on equity. This increase in the cost of equity capital exactly offsets the benefit of the cheaper debt in the firm's capital structure, leaving the overall cost of capital unchanged.

Irrelevance of Dividend Payouts

Another important implication of the M&M assumptions is the irrelevance of a firm's dividend policy. Contrary to popular belief, companies with higher dividend rates are not necessarily "doing better" than companies with no dividends at all.

Recall from Chapter 1 that the cash flow constraint facing a firm that issues both residual and fixed claims was written as

$$\delta(t) + \rho(t) = X(t) - I(t) + e(t) + d(t) \qquad (3.3)$$

The cash flows of the firm $X(t)$ are the result of prior investment decisions and cannot be changed in the current period, and the investment decision for this period $I(t)$ is taken as given by the third M&M assumption. Denote this "net cash surplus"

$$Q(t) = X(t) - I(t)$$

so that the firm's cash flow constraint is now

$$\delta(t) + \rho(t) = Q(t) + e(t) + d(t) \qquad (3.4)$$

The interest payable on the debt $\rho(t)$ is fixed in the terms of the debt. So the firm can pay dividends only if it has a natural cash surplus in excess of its interest obligations—that is, $Q(t) - \rho(t) > 0$—*or* if the firm issues new debt or equity. The total welfare of residual and fixed claim holders of the firm can now be expressed using the notation in equation 3.4 as

$$[E_{t-1}(t) + \delta(t)] + [D_{t-1}(t) + \rho(t)] = Q(t) + V(t) \qquad (3.5)$$

Suppose first that a firm wants to increase its dividend without issuing any new debt and that its existing debt is riskless. The extra dividend payment thus must come from $e(t) = \delta(t)$, the issuance of new equity in an amount equal to the new dividend. But we know from Chapter 1 that the value of the firm is equal to the value of its real assets:

$$V(t) = A(t) = [E_{t-1}(t) + e(t)] + [D_{t-1}(t) + d(t)] \qquad (3.6)$$

Because increasing $e(t)$ has not changed the cash surplus $Q(t)$ or the assets of the firm $A(t)$, we know from equation 3.6 that the value of the firm $V(t)$ does not change, and, hence, an increase in $e(t)$ can be "paid for" only by a decline in $E_{t-1}(t)$. Looking back at equation 3.5, the value of outstanding equity must decline by an amount exactly equal to the higher dividend. The old shareholders are thus indifferent to the dividend increase because they pay for it with an offsetting capital loss resulting from the dilution the new shares cause.

Now suppose the firm decides to try to borrow more to finance a higher dividend. Once again, the higher dividend does not increase $Q(t)$ or $V(t)$ because the assets and investments of the firm are the same as before. If the debt outstanding at time $t-1$ was riskless, then the new debt will expose the firm to the risk of default, which will impact the new bond holders *and* the existing bond holders. Since the combined value of the securities cannot be affected by this financing decision, the decline in $D_{t-1}(t)$ that accompanies the issuance of new, risky debt results in an increase in $[E_{t-1}(t) + \delta(t)]$. Issuing new risky debt thus reduces the total market value of the firm's debt and increases the value of the firm's equity by the same amount. The increase in the value of equity comes first through the higher dividend. Whatever is left over shows up as a higher value of equity resulting from the new higher risk of the debt.

"MARKET VALUE" RULE AND NET PRESENT VALUE CRITERION

Saying that the value of a firm is independent of its capital structure is not quite equivalent to saying that the security holders of a firm are unaffected by all of the firm's investment financing decisions. The proof of the irrelevance of dividends shows that although a higher dividend cannot affect the total value of the firm, it can affect the relative distribution of wealth between equity and debt claimants.

In this section, we review what the M&M propositions tell us about when security holders are truly indifferent to a firm's financing choices. We then see how this leads us into criteria for maximizing the value of the firm and for evaluating prospective real investment opportunities. The analysis in the following sections closely follows Fma (1976).

Maximizing Security Holder Welfare

Suppose that the debt outstanding at a firm at time $t - 1$ is riskless and that the firm issues new debt at time t. The new debt will expose the firm to the risk of default, which will impact the new and existing bond holders just as it did in the case of dividends. But in this case, there is no increase in dividends to reflect the loss of value on the debt. The decline in the market value of existing debt $D_{t-1}(t)$ thus results solely in an increase in the current value of the firm's residual claims, $E_{t-1}(t)$. Issuing new debt thus reduces the total market value of the firm's old debt and raises the value of the firm's equity by the same amount.

Conversely, suppose the debt outstanding at time $t - 1$ was already subject to default risk and that the firm retires a portion of that existing debt at time t. If the firm subsequently goes bankrupt, the bond holders—assumed to have equal priority—each receive a pro rata claim on the firm's remaining assets. With fewer bond holders at time t after the partial debt retirement, each creditor to the firm would retrieve more in bankruptcy than before, resulting in a higher value of $D_{t-1}(t)$. This increase in the value of old debt does not change the value of the firm and hence must come from old equity holders. So, the rise in $D_{t-1}(t)$ is funded by a decline in $E_{t-1}(t)$.

The four M&M assumptions thus guarantee only that the value of the firm is independent of its financing decisions. To go one step further and say that the firm's financing decisions are truly irrelevant to the holders of both residual and fixed claims, an additional assumption is required. Specifically, we must assume that the bonds issued by the firm contain covenants that preserve what Fama and Miller (1972) call "me-first rules." Such rules require the firm to assign seniority to existing debt holders so that any new debt is junior in the securities capital structure. This protects current debt holders. In addition, any early retirements of debt would begin with the retirement of the most junior issues and end with the oldest, most senior issues. This protects equity holders. So, with properly defined priority of securities, the value of the firm is independent of its financing decisions and its security holders are indifferent to those decisions.[3]

We also can see that the firm's management should make its investment decisions in a manner that maximizes the current value of the firm V(t). Called the "market value rule," this investment objective alone guarantees that combined security holder welfare is maximized.

To see this more clearly, suppose the investment decisions that maximize the value of the firm result in current investment outlays of I*(t) and a current firm value of V*(t). But now suppose there is some investment policy I°(t) that results in firm value V°(t) < V*(t) *but* that makes equity holders better off than the optimal policy I*(t). From equation 3.5, we see that this can be possible only if equity holders are made better off at the expense of debt holders. And even though equity is better off, the firm's value V°(t) is less than the V*(t) that it could be. Under the M&M assumptions, the firm becomes an immediate takeover target. Existing debt holders will be willing to pay V°(t) to take over the firm and replace its management with a new management that pursues an optimal policy. The value of the firm will rise to V*(t), and debt holders will recover their loss.

Alternatively and equivalently, debt holders will be willing to pay off equity holders an amount equal to V*(t) – V°(t) to persuade them to push management to the optimal investment policy. Debt will rise in value by this amount, which will just offset the resulting decline in the value of equity. The proof works the same way in the event the firm's managers pursue an investment strategy aimed at maximizing the value of debt. Consequently, the only investment policy the firm's management can pursue that does not make the firm a takeover target is the optimal investment policy I*(t) that maximizes the value of the firm V*(t).

Maximizing Security Holder Welfare with the Market Value Rule

What is the optimal investment policy? Returning to equation 3.5, we can see that security holder welfare is maximized when the firm maximizes V(t) + X(t) – I(t). Let us now rewrite that equation to define the value of the firm as the discounted expected gross present value of all expected future cash flows on the firm's real assets:

$$\left[E_{t-1}(t) + \delta(t)\right] + \left[D_{t-1}(t)\right] = X(t) - I(t) + \sum_{j=1}^{T} \frac{E_t\left[E_t X(t+j)\right]}{1 + \lambda_{t,t+j}} \qquad (3.7)$$

where $\lambda_{t,t+j}$ is the firm's cost of capital through time j. Subtract aggregate current investment expenditures I(t) and add this period's aggregate cash flows X(t) arising from prior investment decisions and you have the combined total of security holder welfare. From equation 3.7, it is easy to see the firm's criterion for optimal investment decisions. Because X(t) was determined by prior investment decisions, this means the firm should maximize V(t) – I(t), the excess of the firm's market value over the investment expenditures required to generate that value at any time t.

Suppose that the two last terms in equation 3.7 reflecting aggregate current investment spending and the discounted expected present value of aggregate earnings can be split into K separate "projects" as follows:

$$\left[E_{t-1}(t) + \delta(t)\right] + \left[D_{t-1}(t) + \rho(t)\right] = X(t) + \sum_{k=1}^{K}\left(\sum_{j=1}^{T} \frac{E_t\left[X(t+j,k)\right]}{1+\lambda_{t,t+j}} - I(t,k)\right) \qquad (3.8)$$

The term in large parentheses in this equation is called the net present value (NPV) for any given project k.

The investment criterion by which real investments should be evaluated is one of the most important considerations facing any firm. The much-vaunted NPV criterion tells firms to accept only those investments with a nonnegative NPV and to reject all investments with a negative NPV. The reason this criterion is optimal—at least under M&M—should be obvious from equation 3.8. Any project with a negative NPV reduces the right-hand side of the equation, thereby reducing combined security holder welfare. Adhering to the NPV criterion for all new real capital investment projects thus guarantees that the firm is adhering to the market value rule and thus is maximizing the combined wealth of stock and bond holders.

WHAT DETERMINES A FIRM'S COST OF CAPITAL?

A crucial determinant for evaluating the financing choices of a firm or the NPV of a project is the firm's cost of financing investment capital. The cost of capital is the firm's cost of investment finance, and it also is used to discount expected future cash flows on real investment activity. When the M&M assumptions hold, the cost of capital for a firm is based solely on the "systematic risk" of the firm's assets. In other words, the firm's securities are like any other capital asset and subject to the prevailing method by which the market sets asset prices in equilibrium.

Theory

In an economy free from unexploited arbitrage opportunities populated with consumers who prefer more to less, the price of any asset—stocks, bonds, futures, forwards, options, swaps, insurance policies, refrigerators, beer—already reflects the risk of that asset in equilibrium. In a simple two-period world, the price of any asset is equal to the discounted net present value of the cash flows on that asset:

$$P_t = E_t[m_{t+1}X_{t+1}] \qquad (3.9)$$

where P_t is the current price of a security, E_t denotes an expected value conditional on the information investors have at time t, m_{t+1} is the discount rate used to discount risky cash flows at time t + 1, and X_{t+1} is the risky cash flow on the asset at time t + 1.

Finance theory guarantees us the existence of some discount rate—namely, the rate at which individuals are willing to substitute one unit of consumption tomorrow for a unit of edible consumption today.[4] In a M&M world, the unique "stochastic discount factor" is the intertemporal marginal rate of substitution (IMRS) of a representative investor or consumer.[5] Equation 3.9 also can be written in the form of returns

$$E_t[m_{t+1}R_{t+1}] = 1 \qquad (3.10)$$

As a matter of pure theory, the cost of equity capital for any firm should be the expected return that satisfies equation 3.10. Unfortunately, the model as stated often performs fairly poorly in empirical practice (i.e., just using consumption data to get the IMRS). Much of the challenge in cost of capital estimation is the challenge of finding something other than the IMRS to approximate m in a more estimable and practically useful way.

Perhaps the most common approach is the use of "factor models" to add structure to the stochastic discount factor, theoretically making it easier to estimate using real-world data. Factor models usually express the stochastic discount factor as a linear combination of one or more "risk factors" thought to influence all capital asset prices in equilibrium.

For N risk factors, the correspondence between the linear factor model and the stochastic discount factor in equations 3.9 and 3.10 is as follows:

$$m_{t+1} = a + b_1 f_{t+1}^1 + b_2 f_{t+1}^2 + \cdots + b_N f_{t+1}^N \tag{3.11}$$

where $a, b_1, \ldots, b_N$ are parameters to be estimated and where f^j is the jth systematic risk factor. As Cochrane (2001) explains: "By and large, the factors are just selected as plausible proxies for marginal utility: events that describe whether typical investors are happy or unhappy."

Capital Asset Pricing Model

Undoubtedly the most common way to estimate the equity cost of capital for a firm is using the capital asset pricing model (CAPM) in which a single factor—the excess return on the market portfolio of world wealth—prices all assets in equilibrium. In stochastic discount factor language, the CAPM implies

$$m_{t+1} = a + bR_{t+1,m}$$

where $R_{t+1,m}$ is the return on the market. In other words, the cost of equity capital for some firm k is the expected return of that firm as determined in equilibrium by the CAPM:

$$E(R_k = R_f + \beta_{k,m}[E(R_m) - R_f] \tag{3.12}$$

where

$$\beta_{k,m} = \frac{\mathrm{Cov}(R_k, R_m)}{\mathrm{Var}(R_m)}$$

Once an estimate is obtained, the WACC of the firm can be obtained by substituting $E(R_k)$ from equation 3.12 into R_E in equation 3.1.

Although still probably the method most often used by firms to estimate their equity costs of capital, the CAPM has been subjected to significant criticism as a poor approximation of the stochastic discount factor in equation 3.9. Fama and French (1992) provide a good survey of the shortcomings of the CAPM and of why, despite the simplicity of the model, it may not make sense to use it for true cost of capital estimation.

Multifactor Cost of Capital Models

The basic criticism of the CAPM as an estimate for a firm's equity cost of capital is that other risk factors apart from the market are known to provide explanatory power to expected returns. These factors include firm size (Banz [1981]) and the ratio of a firm's book-to-market equity (Fama and French

[1992, 1993, 1995, 1996]), labor income (Jagannathan and Wang [1996]), industrial production and inflation (Chen, Roll, and Ross [1986]), and investment growth (Cochrane [1991, 1996]).

That other factors apart from the market explain returns might not be very palatable in the absence of an alternative. But as equation 3.11 shows, multiple factors can correspond to the stochastic factor representation. Merton (1971a,b) recognized this early on in his multifactor Intertemporal CAPM (I-CAPM) model. It thus may make empirical sense to determine cost of capital using a multifactor model[6]:

$$E(R_k) = R_f + \sum_{j=1}^{N} \beta_{k,j} f_j \qquad (3.13)$$

where $\beta_{k,j}$ is the factor loading of risk factor j on firm k and where f_j is the jth factor risk premium.

Fama and French (1997) note that three problems complicate any efforts to extract a meaningful cost of equity from equation 3.13 by running the linear regression that the equation implies. The first and obvious problem is which model (i.e., what factors) to use.

A second problem is time variation in the parameter estimates $\beta_{k,j}$, even at the industry level—not to mention the firm level. Movement over time in these parameter estimates indicates changes in the "loadings" of various risk factors on expected returns. This makes the practical estimation of these parameters a real challenge. Fama and French (1997) study, for example, estimates of factor loadings in their own three-factor model consisting of the market portfolio, size, and book-to-market factors, as described in Fama and French (1992, 1993). They find that parameter estimates obtained from a full sample from 1963 to 1994 are no more reliable than estimates obtained from the last three years of data.

A third problem is imprecision in the statistical estimation of the factors or factor risk premiums themselves. Taking only the excess return on the market as a risk factor, Fama and French (1997) find that the 1963 to 1994 average excess market return is statistically indistinguishable from any number in the range from just under 0 percent to just over 10 percent.

So where does this leave today's corporate treasurer seeking a good estimate of the firm's cost of capital? Unfortunately, not anywhere particularly pleasant. Indeed, CAPM estimates of cost of capital are still widely used—not because graduate business schools have failed to communicate the failings of the model but rather because there is no good and obvious alternative available. Indeed, perhaps the main strength of the CAPM approach—and, more generally, an approach to WACC determination that adheres to the original M&M model—is its internal consistency with its assumptions. As most of the remainder of Part I of this book illustrates, the particular way that violations of M&M assumptions impact WACC can be so contentiously argued that a major case for using the CAPM is the very simplicity of its assumptions. In short, using CAPM and M&M approaches to WACC estimation allow us to avoid "my assumptions are better than yours" kind of arguments.

The CAPM and M&M framework remain the dominant—and probably the most tamper-proof—approaches for practical cost of capital estimation. With those models in hand, Fama and French (1997) rightly conclude, "[W]hatever the formal approach, two of the ubiquitous tools in capital budgeting are a wing and a prayer, and serendipity is an important force in outcomes."

NOTES

1. This particular representation of the Modigliani-Miller assumptions is based on the analysis in Fama (1976).
2. Fama (1976) shows that this assumption can be relaxed if it is replaced with the assumptions that no firm is a monopolistic supplier of any security and firms all maximize their total market value at whatever prices are given from a perfectly competitive securities market. We will work with the equal access assumption for simplicity.
3. Fama (1976); Fama and Miller (1972).
4. If and only if there are no arbitrage opportunities, m is positive. If markets are "complete," m > 0 is unique. See Cochrane (2001).
5. If $u(c_t)$ denotes the twice continuously differentiable concave von Neumann-Morgensten utility function of a representative investor for consumption at time t, then the IMRS can be expressed as $m_{t+1} = \beta u'(c_{t+1})/u'(c_t)$ where u' denotes the first derivative of the function and where β is the true rate of time preference of the investor.
6. It is important to recognize that the basic theory underlying the single-factor CAPM and the I-CAPM is essentially the same. Both are special cases of the stochastic discount factor representation shown in equations 3.9 and 3.10. We tend to gravitate toward an I-CAPM representation purely because of the empirical failings of the single-factor CAPM and the nearly undisputed fact (these days) that the market portfolio of world wealth is not a sufficient proxy of the stochastic discount factor. Unfortunately, many I-CAPM representations are also deficient along at least some empirical dimensions. We are thus left with a rather uncomfortable situation: We know as a matter of pure theory that as long as investors prefer more to less, a stochastic discount factor exists that prices all assets, but we really have no undisputed way to measure that stochastic discount factor for practical applications.

CHAPTER 4

Benefits and Costs of Debt and the "Trade-off Theory" of Optimal Capital Structure

We already have explained the assumptions under which capital structure does not matter. In Chapters 4 through 6, we turn to the more practical and relevant issue of when capital structure can or does matter. These chapters will pave the way for us to understand later why and when A.R.T. matters.

Two essentially mutually exclusive theories of optimal capital structure dominate the modern theory of finance.[1] The trade-off theory argues that firms choose some optimal leverage ratio that equates the benefits of debt (e.g., tax deductibility of interest) to its costs (e.g., higher expected costs of financial distress) at the margin. The pecking order theory implies that capital structure emerges as a response to the net cash flows to the firm from its investments in real capital. Specifically, when managers have information that security holders do not, firms issue securities based on a "pecking order" rather than in pursuit of an optimal leverage ratio.[2]

Not only are the rationales underlying these two theories different, but their implications are also different.[3] Most notably, the trade-off theory implies that any increase in the leverage of a firm should be associated with an increase in the value of the firm, whereas the pecking order theory implies that leverage is inversely related to the firm's profitability. Interestingly, both theories suggest that firms should, all else equal, avoid issuing new equity whenever possible.

Here we explore the trade-off theory and its implications for the types of claims the firm issues. We address the following specific questions:

■ What is the "static" trade-off theory that trades the tax benefits of debt off against the increase in financial distress costs associated with leverage?
■ How do "agency costs" change the static analysis by introducing underinvestment, overinvestment, and asset substitution problems?
■ What are the empirical implications of the trade-off theory?

"STATIC" TRADE-OFF THEORY OF OPTIMAL CAPITAL STRUCTURE

The basic premise of the trade-off theory of capital structure is that fixed claims have both costs and benefits to the issuing firm, and companies will achieve their optimal capital structure by choosing the leverage ratio that equates those costs and benefits at the margin. The simplest version of the trade-off theory is the "static" version, in which the only M&M assumption that is violated is the assumption of perfect capital markets. A more dynamic version of the theory also allows market participants to have different information. Before examining this more complete version of the theory, it will prove useful to develop the basics of the static theory first.

Benefit of Taxes

The impact of taxes on capital structure has been analyzed by Modigliani and Miller (1963), Miller (1977), Miller and Scholes (1978), DeAngelo and Masulis (1980), and many others.[4] Because many countries allow firms to deduct interest payments from their corporate taxes but do not allow a similar deduction for retained earnings or dividends paid, there would seem to be a natural bias, all else equal, toward debt.

Suppose a corporation's income or earnings are taxed at the rate of τ_c per annum. The firm's tax shield from debt is the present value of the tax savings generated by making interest payments on debt in lieu of dividend payments to equity holders or retained earnings. This present value typically is calculated with a discount rate equal to the firm's cost of debt capital, with the argument for this being that the risk associated with the tax shield is equivalent to the risk of the debt that generates that tax shield.

If all the M&M assumptions hold except for the existence of a corporate tax on income, the value of the firm at any time t can be redefined as follows:

$$V(t) = V^E(t) + T(t) \qquad (4.1)$$

where $V(t)$ is the value of the firm at t, $V^E(t)$ is the time t value of an otherwise identical firm financed only with equity, and $T(t)$ is the present value of the tax shield at time t.

In the special case of a firm that essentially issues "permanent debt" or that always has a core amount of debt outstanding, the present value of the tax shield is equivalent to an annuity. If a firm's cost of debt capital at time t is R_D, then the present value of a firm's tax shield from debt is

$$T(t) = \frac{\tau_c(D(t) \cdot R_D(t))}{R_D(t)} = \tau_c D(t) \tag{4.2}$$

Substituting equation 4.2 into equation 4.1 yields

$$V(t) = V^E(t) + \tau_c D(t) \tag{4.3}$$

which implies that the value of the firm is strictly increasing in the amount that the firm borrows. In other words, equation 4.3 taken in isolation implies an optimal capital structure of 100 percent debt.

This analysis, however, is incomplete. A corporation is essentially just a legal association between numerous parties, ranging from employees to residual and fixed claimants to customers. A corporation, in other words, does not have a mind of its own nor a purse of its own. The purse really belongs to the claimants on the firm. In this sense, the objective of a corporation should be to minimize not the corporate taxes it pays but rather the *total taxes paid* by bond and stock holders. These taxes include taxes the claimants pay indirectly through corporate taxes on earnings and personal taxes paid by claim holders directly on the cash flows generated by the securities they hold.

As the cash flow constraint of the firm reminds us, a firm with positive net earnings in a financial reporting and tax period may either retain those earnings or pay them out to investors in the form of dividends or interest payments. If profits are retained, they are taxed at the corporate tax rate τ_c. If profits are instead fully distributed to debt holders, the profits escape corporation taxation but are subject to personal taxation as income for holders of the debt securities. And if profits are paid to equity holders in the form of dividends or capital gains, they are subject to both the corporate tax rate and again to taxation as personal income of equity holders.

If the equity distribution comes entirely in the form of dividends, then the personal tax rate is the same whether the income is received as dividends or interest on debt. But if the equity distribution involves capital gains and there is a tax on such capital gains, then the personal tax rate paid by stock holders will differ from that paid by bond holders. Accordingly, we denote τ_p^E and τ_p^D to be the personal tax rates for equity and debt claimants, respectively.

Assume that annual net cash earnings $Q(t)$—that is, $X(t) - I(t)$—are fully retained or fully disbursed either to stock or bond holders—$Q(t)$ is not "split." Table 4.1 illustrates the tax consequences of these three scenarios.[5]

If the firm chooses a capital structure to minimize total taxes, the firm must choose the mixture of debt and equity that maximizes income net of all taxes. If debt is again assumed to be perpetual, Miller (1977) showed that the

TABLE 4.1   Corporate and Personal Taxation of Corporate Income

	Q(t) retained by firm as earnings	Q(t) paid as interest to bondholders	Q(t) paid as dividends to stockholders
Corporate Tax	$Q(t)\tau_c$	0	$Q(t)\tau_c$
Posttax Corporate Income	$Q(t)(1 - \tau_c)$	$Q(t)$	$Q(t)(1 - \tau_c)$
Personal Tax	0	$Q(t)\tau_{pD}$	$Q(t)(1 - \tau_c)\tau_{pE}$
Income Net of All Taxes	$Q(t)(1 - \tau_c)$	$Q(t)(1 - \tau_{pD})$	$Q(t)(1 - \tau_c)(1 - \tau_{pE})$

relative gain to the firm of choosing debt over equity—the gain from leverage—can be expressed as follows per dollar of earnings:

$$G_L(t) = \left[1 - \frac{(1 - \tau_c)(1 - \tau_{pE})}{(1 - \tau_{pD})} \right] D(t) \qquad (4.4)$$

Note that M&M is a special case of equation 4.4. When all taxes are zero, $G_L(t) = 0$. When capital gains taxes do not exist and $\tau_{pD} = \tau_{pE}$, equation 4.4 simplifies to an analog of equation 4.3 when only corporations were taxed—that is, $G_L = \tau_c D(t)$.

Unlike the earlier case with only corporate taxes, different personal tax rates now imply an "optimal" capital structure that is not 100 percent debt. Equation 4.4 together with the bottom row of Table 4.1 provide firms with a guideline for how to determine what that optimal capital structure is.

Miller (1977) argues, however, that this above situation cannot persist in equilibrium and that the original M&M result of capital structure irrelevance in fact still holds under taxation—at least when taxes on equity are well below taxes on debt and all firms face the same marginal corporate tax rate. To briefly summarize his argument, suppose personal taxes on stocks are zero and that all bonds are default-risk-free. With perfect capital markets, equilibrium in the debt market is shown in Exhibit 4.1, where the x-axis shows the aggregate amount of debt outstanding and the y-axis the interest rate on that debt.

The Miller model is based on the simple notion that as firms borrow, some investors must be encouraged to hold debt rather than equity. In the model, after all, the personal tax rate for stocks is zero, so the corporate tax rate prods firms to issue debt. Getting tax-exempt investors to hold debt is no problem since their personal tax rate is also zero. But eventually firms need to get taxable investors to hold taxable debt, as well, and this requires an extra payment to investors to cover their personal tax loss vis-à-vis holding equity.

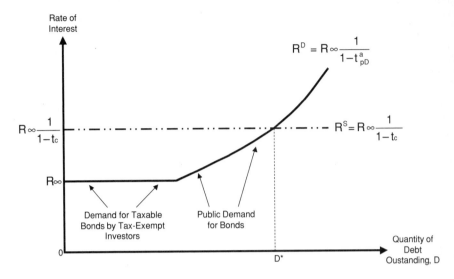

EXHIBIT 4.1   Miller (1977) Debt Market Equilibrium

As long as the tax loss that must be covered is below the corporate tax rate that hits profits before they are distributed to stock holders, this makes sense.

We can see Miller's point more easily by consulting Exhibit 4.1, where the line from $R°$ to $R°/(1 - \tau^{\alpha}_{pD})$ represents the demand curve for aggregate debt.[6] The demand curve intersects the y-axis at the interest rate $R°$, the equilibrium rate of interest on tax-exempt bonds (e.g., municipal bonds). The flat portion of the curve is then the demand for taxable corporate bonds by tax-exempt investors. And the rising portion of the demand curve is the public demand for bonds—the demand for taxable bonds by taxable investors as a function of the marginal tax rate paid by the marginal investor α, or τ^{α}_{pD}. The upward-sloping part of the demand curve in Exhibit 4.1 represents the tax-exempt rate $R°$ grossed up by an amount sufficient to cover the tax costs to taxable investors of holding taxable securities. This is the amount of inducement these investors require to hold bonds rather than stocks.

Equilibrium in the debt market occurs when D^* debt is issued at rate $R°[1/(1 - \tau_c)]$. If corporations borrow more than D^*, the interest rate would rise above $R°[1/(1 - \tau_c)]$. In this case, the inducement that taxable investors would require to hold taxable debt would exceed the corporate tax rate, and at least some firms would find issuing debt to be disadvantageous vis-à-vis issuing equity and just paying the corporate tax rate on dividends. Conversely, if aggregate borrowing is below D^*, the interest rate would be below $R°[1/(1 - \tau_c)]$. In that case, at least some unlevered firms would be driven to make the payment to bond holders and induce them to borrow so as to avoid the corporate tax on dividends. D would thus rise until it became *dis*advantageous to keep borrowing, which occurs at exactly point D*.

Note that the Miller model is all about aggregates. The quantity D* represents the optimal aggregate debt issue. This, in turn, implies an optimal debt/equity ratio for all firms in aggregate. But for any given firm, there is no optimal debt ratio. In the Miller equilibrium, firms with little or no leverage would find a market for their bonds in the high tax brackets, and highly levered firms would issue bonds that would appeal to tax-exempt investors. So, despite the existence of an optimal leverage ratio in aggregate, equilibrium in the debt market still guarantees that any given firm's value is independent of its capital structure.

Miller (1977) is often criticized as being plausible before the 1986 U.S. tax reform but less so afterward given the 1996 changes in U.S. tax laws.[7] Mackie-Mason (1990) and Graham (1996) find that firms with higher marginal corporate tax rates are more likely to issue debt. But as Fama and French (1998) remind us, this need not imply an increase in firm value. Proponents of Miller's model typically respond to criticisms by saying that the intuition and economic forces at work in the model still may be generally correct even if the results do not hold absolutely.

Fama and French (1998) find no evidence that debt produces tax benefits that result in an increase in firm value. They attribute this to either a "stretched" support for Miller (1977) or a failure of their approach to control adequately for the information contained in debt about profitability. (See the agency cost discussions later in this chapter.) Nevertheless, the result that debt does not produce an obvious increase in firm value for tax reasons is a strong one, whatever the explanation.

Costs of Financial Distress

Acting in opposition to any tax benefits of debt in the static trade-off theory is the expected cost of financial distress, or the costs of financial distress weighted by the probability the firm will incur such costs.

Financial distress costs can arise for many reasons, ranging from legal fees to the costs of liquidating assets and redistributing the proceeds. Actual insolvency (in the sense of the market value of assets falling below liabilities) need not occur for a firm to incur financial distress costs. Many firms incur distressed debt costs, for example, when they are nearing bankruptcy and perceived to be in trouble. Market participants' credit assessments of the firm deteriorate, and the firm's borrowing costs rise.

In some cases, perceptions that a firm is in distress can become self-fulfilling. When an art gallery has a fire, for example, it may be forced to sell undamaged paintings to generate enough cash to rebuild. But some people may not know the paintings for sale are truly undamaged. And even those who do know may take advantage of the gallery's need for fast cash and offer below-market prices.

Similar "fire sales" at banks can turn simple liquidity problems into solvency problems with frightening speed. A bank may have a balance sheet with assets more than sufficient to cover liabilities. But it may not have all of its assets in cash. If the bank experiences an unduly large number of redemption requests on its demand deposit accounts, it may be forced to start liquidating assets to generate enough cash to cover any deficit. If market participants know the bank needs to sell assets for cash quickly, the prices the bank will get on its assets may be well below market prices. In this case, a liquidity crisis can turn into a solvency crisis, forcing the bank to incur extreme financial distress costs in the form of depressed-value asset sales and extortionate borrowing costs.

The existence of debt in a capital structure does not necessarily increase the costs of financial distress, but it does affect the probability of distress, thus raising expected distress costs. Exhibit 4.2 depicts the securities capital structures for three firms—A, B, and C. The left-hand vertical axis shows how the value of the firm's claims varies with A(T), the value of the assets of each firm on date T, where T is the maturity date for the debt issued by Firms B and C. Firm A issues only equity, which can be viewed in aggregate as a call on the firm's time T assets with a strike price of zero. Firm B issues equity and senior

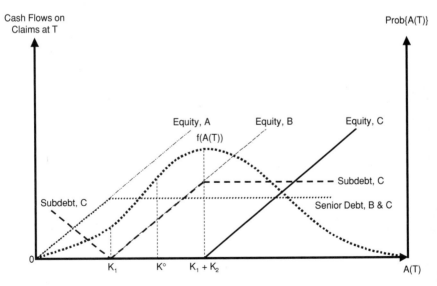

EXHIBIT 4.2 Leverage and the Probability of Incurring Financial Distress Costs

debt with a face value of K_1. Firm B's capital structure thus consists of debt as a short put on the firm's assets with strike price K_1 and equity as a long call, also struck at K_1. Finally, Firm C issues equity, senior debt with face value K_1, and subordinated debt with face value K_2. The claims capital structure of Firm C thus includes senior debt as a short put on the firm's assets with strike price K_1, subordinated debt as a short put struck at $K_1 + K_2$ plus a long put struck at K_1, and equity as a long call struck at $K_1 + K_2$.

Suppose, to keep things easy, that the firm incurs financial distress costs only when the value of its assets $A(T)$ is less than or equal to the face value of all its outstanding debt. Firm A thus never incurs such distress costs, whereas Firms B and C begin to experience distress costs at $A(T) \leq K_1$ and $A(T) \leq K_1 + K_2$, respectively.

Now suppose all three firms hold exactly the same assets. The right-hand vertical axis in Exhibit 4.2 shows the probability associated with a given value of these assets being realized at time T. This probability density function is labeled in Exhibit 4.2 as $f(A(T))$ and can be defined as the $f(A(T))$ that satisfies the following:

$$\mathrm{Prob}[A(T) \leq K^\circ] = \int_0^{K^\circ} f(A(T))dA(T) \tag{4.5}$$

for any given K°. In other words, the probability that market value of the firm's assets falls below some level K° on date T is the area under the curve $f(A(T))$ in Exhibit 4.2 to the left of the point K°.

Under the M&M assumptions, the market values of Firms A, B, and C are identical because the assets they hold are identical; capital structure alone does not affect the value of the firms. But if the M&M assumption of perfect capital markets is violated to allow financial distress costs,[8] these firms no longer have the same value. If the expected value of the firm is the expected value of the firm's assets less its expected costs of financial distress, Firm A is more valuable than Firm B, and Firm B is more valuable than Firm C. Despite the fact that the firms have identical assets, they have different expected financial distress costs.

If financial distress costs are constant and equal to Ω, the expected cost of financial distress to each firm is the probability that its assets are less than or equal to its debt obligation multiplied by the constant distress cost Ω. Clearly, the expected cost of distress is zero for Firm A because it never encounters distress. And Firm B clearly has a lower expected cost of distress than Firm C—that is:

$$\int_0^{K_1} \Omega \cdot f(A(T))dA(T) < \int_0^{K_1+K_2} \Omega \cdot f(A(T))dA(T) \tag{4.6}$$

If the mathematics of equation 4.6 are not clear, then you can still draw the same conclusion graphically from Exhibit 4.2. The area under curve $f(A(T))$ is clearly larger to the left of $K_1 + K_2$ than it is to the left of K_1. At point $K°$, for example, the call belonging to Firm B's equity holders is in the money—that is, the value of $A(T)$ is above the option strike price, and the call has value on date T. In other words, at asset value $K°$ Firm B can repay its debt holders the full amount K_1 and still has $K° - K_1$ left for equity holders. But at the same point $K°$, Firm C is insolvent. Because it has borrowed $K_1 + K_2 > K°$, Firm C's equity is worthless. Its senior creditors receive their entire loan principal K_1, but subordinated debt holders receive only a pro rata claim on $K° - K_1$.

Static Trade-off Optimal Leverage Ratio

The static trade-off theory of capital structure integrates the taxation benefits of debt with the costs of financial distress created by leverage. Under the theory, the value of a firm is equal to a modified version of equation 4.1 to add the financial distress cost dimension:

$$V(t) = V^E(t) + T(t) - \Omega(t) \tag{4.7}$$

where $V^E(t)$ is the value of an all-equity firm and $T(t)$ is the present value of the corporate tax shield, both as in equation 4.1, and $\Omega(t)$ is now the present value of the costs of financial distress.

Exhibit 4.3 illustrates the static trade-off theory of capital structure graphically, where the vertical axis is the value of the firm on some date t and the horizontal axis is the ratio of fixed claims (i.e., debt) to total firm capital—that is, the leverage ratio $\xi(t) = D(t)/V(t)$ as defined in Chapter 1.

The horizontal line in the exhibit at $V^E(t)$ is the value of an all-equity firm. The heavy dashed line at the top of the figure is the value of an all-equity firm grossed up by the present value of its tax shield for a given level of debt, $V^E(t) + T(t)$. The heavy solid line is then the value of the firm from equation 4.7—the all-equity value of the firm $V^E(t)$ plus the present value of the tax shield $T(t)$ and minus the present value of financial distress costs as a function of the firm's leverage ratio.

For small leverage ratios, the financial distress costs facing the firm are small. In fact, they remain small for a large range of leverage ratios, but past a certain point those distress costs rise quickly for even small increases in the firm's proportion of debt to total capital. The present value of the tax shield, by contrast, has value to the firm quickly for even small levels of debt. But the benefit of that tax shield begins to shrink for high levels of debt—at some point it simply no longer pays to issue debt from a tax standpoint.

The benefit of the tax shield starts to get overwhelmed by the costs of fi-

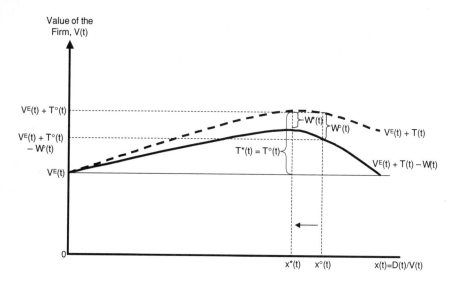

EXHIBIT 4.3   Static Trade-off Theory of Optimal Capital Structure

nancial distress when the firm's leverage ratio exceeds $\xi^*(t)$. In fact, the value of the firm is maximized at exactly point $\xi^*(t)$, so that is the firm's optimal capital structure.

To see why $\xi^*(t)$ is an optimum, consider first the leverage ratio $\xi^\circ(t)$. At that level of debt as a proportion of the value of the firm, the present value of the tax shield is $T^\circ(t)$ and the present value of financial distress costs is $\Omega^\circ(t)$. Now compare these levels to the optimum. At leverage ratio $\xi^*(t)$, the present value of the tax shield $T^*(t)$ is about the same as the present value of the tax shield $T^\circ(t)$ at leverage ratio $\xi^*(t)$. But the present value of the costs of financial distress $\Omega^\circ(t)$ are clearly higher with $D^\circ(t)$ debt outstanding than with $D^*(t)$ debt outstanding—$\Omega^\circ(t) > \Omega^*(t)$. A firm that issues $D^\circ(t)$ in debt thus is worth less than an otherwise identical firm that issues $D^*(t)$ in debt because it faces higher financial distress costs with no offsetting tax benefit from the debt.

One implication of this theory of capital structure is that new issues of debt by a firm will be undertaken only if they are value-enhancing. To see why, just suppose the firm is at leverage ratio $\xi^\circ(t) > \xi^*(t)$. As noted, the value of the firm $V^*(t)$ is greater than $V^\circ(t)$, and in order to realize this higher firm value, the firm must reduce its leverage. If the firm begins at some leverage ratio $\xi'(t) < \xi^*(t)$, then $V^*(t) > V'(t)$, but the firm can realize this higher value only by increasing its leverage. So the firm increases its leverage only when its current capital structure is suboptimally underlevered.

AGENCY COSTS OF EQUITY AND DEBT

The static trade-off model relies only on the violation of the M&M assumption of perfect capital markets. Now let us suppose further that all market participants are not equally well informed. With imperfect capital markets, the need for security holder "principals" to monitor their manager "agents" gives rise to costs, the most obvious type of which is the cost incurred by principals to monitor and measure agent behavior and to control that behavior through compensation, rules, policies, and the like. If the actions of agents can be only partially observed by principals, the potential for agents to pursue their own agendas at the expense of their principal masters is even greater.

A related agency cost is the cost that agents sometimes incur to demonstrate that they will not take certain actions adverse to principals' interests. Such bonding costs may be incurred either as a substitute for direct monitoring or as a way of paying principals back when the actual behavior of agents deviates from behavior consistent with the interests of residual claim holders.

A crucial concept in agency cost models is the distinction between internal and external financing. As noted in Chapter 1, a surplus of current cash flows over investment expenditures generates free cash flow that can be used to finance additional investments or that can be retained as earnings, often to finance future investments. Free cash flows thus are an example of internal financing, as is equity issued to managers of the firm, or corporate insiders. External or outside financing, by contrast, is financing obtained from the issuance of claims to those who are not managing the firm.

The proportion of internal financing to total funds raised does not necessarily tell us how bad the agency costs of a particular firm may be. As we shall see, free cash flows sometimes are thought to heighten agency costs when outsiders hold the firm's equity. But free cash flows together with inside ownership of equity can reduce agency costs. The impact that the proportion of internal financing has on the capital structure of the firm often depends on the specific firm in question.

In the Fama/Jenson taxonomy developed in Chapter 1, agency costs tend to be more severe in financial mutuals and nonprofits than in corporations because the costs to any one residual claimant of monitoring the actions of managers may be less than the benefits. Closed corporations usually have the fewest agency problems because the managers tend also to own residual claims on the net cash flows of the firm.

Let us now review how agency costs can put pressure on a firm to alter the optimum capital structure emerging from the static trade-off model. The result is a more dynamic trade-off model in which the frictional costs and benefits of debt are taken into consideration along with agency costs and benefits of debt.[9]

Agency Costs of Equity

One of the main benefits of debt from an agency cost standpoint is mitigating agency conflicts that can arise between residual claimants of the firm and managers of the firm. Debt can be a useful means of addressing these agency costs of equity, two of which are discussed below.

Perquisite Consumption by Managers and Agency Costs of External Equity

Jensen and Meckling (1976) argue that equity issued to outsiders can give rise to severe agency costs. The basis of the divergence between the interests of equity principals and manager agents lies in the ability of managers to divert the productive resources of the firm in order to accrue nonpecuniary benefits from employment that outside equity owners cannot enjoy. Such benefits include the quality of a physical office, the pleasure of collegial interaction, the development of personal and professional relationships in the office, plush carpets, and perhaps a corporate jet or two.

If the managers of a firm own 100 percent of the equity, their personal trade-offs between firm value and nonpecuniary benefits will lead them to pursue a level of production and pecuniary consumption that is optimal for them. With a portion of the firm's equity held by outsiders, however, the firm's managers reap all of the benefits of nonpecuniary consumption but do not bear all the costs. If, say, proportion $(1 - \alpha)$ of the firm's equity belongs to outsiders, the managers no longer bear the cost of nonpecuniary expenditures (e.g., a new coffee maker or plush carpets) dollar for dollar as in the case where they owned the whole firm. The managers alone benefit from the nonpecuniary spending, but each dollar spent now results in $(1 - \alpha)$ dollars being paid by the new equity holders.

The implications of this agency cost of outside equity can best be appreciated by imagining that 100 percent of a firm's equity is owned by insiders who then decide to sell a fraction of their equity to outsiders. If the managers/owners tried to sell the equity without also replacing themselves as managers, they would receive less than the maximum value of the firm. The new owners will assume, after all, that the old managers will continue to pursue a private optimum in the pursuit of activities in the firm's benefit and in their own interests.

The new equity holders of the firm also might decide to engage in the monitoring required to control the managers' nonpecuniary consumption (e.g., auditing, internal controls, policies, procedures, budget restrictions). But such monitoring is costly when the M&M perfect capital markets assumption is violated, and those costs tend be greater if new equity holders do not have the same information as managers about the firm's investment decision.

In fact, prospective external equity buyers of the $(1 - \alpha)$ of the firm should be indifferent between purchasing $(1 - \alpha)$ of the firm at a price that assumes managers will continue to abuse their privileges and $(1 - \alpha)$ of the firm priced without management abuses but with the costs of monitoring required to ensure that such abuses do not occur. In other words, the value of the firm to its new owners will be equal to the value of the firm less the costs of monitoring management whether those costs actually are incurred or not. The net result is that the value of the firm will be higher if the firm is owned by its management and not by external residual claimants.

"Overinvestment" and the Agency Costs of Free Cash Flows

In Jensen and Meckling (1976), the consumption of perquisites by managers is tied to production. Managers who wish to consume perquisites tend to overproduce. Jensen (1986) and Stulz (1990) argue that a similar problem arises over free cash flows, or cash flow in excess of current investment requirements assuming the firm accepted every positive NPV project. Managers are believed to like free cash flow because it enhances their consumption of perquisites.

Jensen (1986) and Stulz (1990) argue that a problematic "perquisite" managers may choose to pursue is the consumption value of making new investments, even when they may be in questionable projects with declining or negative NPVs. Whether a genuine mistake or a desire to flex their managerial muscles, this "overinvestment" in bad projects is a direct consequence of too much free cash flow and hence a direct agency cost of equity.

Overinvestment does not depend, moreover, on outside equity, as did the overproduction problem in Jensen and Meckling (1976). Stulz (1990) argues, for example, that managers always prefer to invest free cash flow rather than distribute it to shareholders. Jensen (1986) uses the oil industry in the 1970s to argue the same point. Unchecked, managers are simply presumed to prefer investing money than leaving it sitting "idle," even when idle money earns the risk-free rate and bad investments cost the firm.

Recall from Chapter 1 the cash flow constraint for a firm that issues only residual claims:

$$X(t) - I(t) = \delta(t) - e(t) \tag{4.8}$$

where $\delta(t)$ denotes dividends paid to equity holders at time t and $e(t)$ is new equity issued at t. $X(t)$ represents the cash flows accruing to projects associated with prior investment expenditures and thus is beyond the control of managers at time t.

To analyze the free cash flow problem, let us denote the current free cash flow at time t as

$$\Gamma(t) = X(t) - I^*(t)$$

where $I^*(t)$ denotes expenditures on zero- or positive-NPV projects. Let $I°(t)$ denote any manager spending in excess of the optimal level on negative-NPV growth projects. Assuming the free cash flows are simply retained by the firm, we can write the value of the firm as:

$$E_{t-1}(t) + \delta(t) = V(t) + \Gamma(t) = V^*(t) + X(t) - I^*(t) \tag{4.9}$$

where $V^*(t)$ is the value of the firm that would result if the only investment expenditures were the $I^*(t)$ payouts for positive-NPV projects—that is, $V^*(t)$ is the value of the firm if the market value rule is followed. In this case, the value of equity is unaffected by the excess cash. The only investment expenditures made are those that result in $V^*(t)$, thus guaranteeing that $V^*(t) - I^*(t)$ is positive—or, at least, not negative.

Now suppose the managers decide to invest the free cash flows $\Gamma(t)$ into new investments that are not associated with positive-NPV projects. Denote the negative-NPV investment expenditures as $I°(t)$ and let $I°(t)$ exactly equal $\Gamma(t)$ so that all the firm's free cash flows are disgorged into negative-NPV investments. The value of the firm is now

$$E_{t-1}(t) + \delta(t) = V(t) + \Gamma(t) - I°(t) = V(t) + X(t) - I^*(t) - I°(t) \tag{4.10}$$

Future cash flows are reflected in $V(t)$, which we can rewrite as

$$V(t) = V^*(t) + V°(t)$$

Equation 4.10 can be expressed as

$$E_{t-1}(t) + \delta(t) = [V^*(t) - I^*(t)] + [V°(t) - I°(t)] + X(t) \tag{4.11}$$

Because $I^*(t)$ is associated only with projects whose discounted expected cash flows meet or exceed this level of investment expenditure, $V^*(t) - I^*(t)$ thus is a positive number—or, at worst, zero. $V°(t) - I°(t)$, however, is by definition a negative number because $I°(t)$ is being invested in negative-NPV projects.

From expression 4.11, it is clear that the value of security holder wealth is not being maximized by management. Equity is worth $V°(t) - I°(t)$ less than it would be worth if the firm accepted only positive-NPV projects.

Debt as a Solution to the Agency Costs of External Equity and Free Cash Flows

Issuing fixed claims in the corporate capital structure is one way that firms can reduce the agency costs of equity, both arising from overproduction and overinvestment. Returning to equation 4.8, it is clear that free cash flow could have been used to pay a higher dividend to stock holders or to repurchase stock instead of being overinvested in bad projects. In this case, the negative-

NPV project is avoided and the cash is distributed to shareholders. The value of the firm is thus $V^*(t)$ and equity holders' welfare is maximized. And indeed in some situations dividends—as well as share repurchases—can work perfectly well to solve the free cash flow problem.

When monitoring costs are positive, information asymmetric, and agency conflicts acute, however, disgorging free cash in the form of dividends and share repurchases will not necessarily satisfy equity holders. Managers are, after all, still in control of any future free cash flows. They could announce a "permanent" dividend increase, but that creates problems of its own because the decision can later be reversed.

Jensen (1986) suggests a solution to the free cash flow problem that cannot be reversed by managers—*issuing debt*. Equation 4.8 then can be rewritten as

$$X(t) - I^*(t) = \Gamma(t) = \delta(t) - e(t) - d(t) \qquad (4.12)$$

and its value at time t + 1 can be written as

$$[E_t(t + 1) + \delta(t + 1)] + [D_t(t + 1) + \rho(t + 1)]$$
$$= V(t + 1) + X(t + 1) - I(t + 1) \qquad (4.13)$$

From equation 4.13, it is clear that *future* free cash flows will be constrained by the need to service the debt. Equation 4.8 seems to imply, however, that debt should be retired rather than issued because $d(t)$ is negative. If the firm did already have debt outstanding, retiring it early would be no different than repurchasing equity or paying a dividend. At best, it would be a temporary solution to a time t cash overage. At worst, it would remove the discipline on future free cash flows created by the debt service requirement.

In this example, the firm began as all equity and thus has no debt to retire. Equation 4.8 thus tells us that what needs to happen is an exchange offer of equity for debt, such that $\Gamma(t) = d(t) - e(t)$, so that

$$X(t) - I^*(t) = \Gamma(t) = \delta(t) - e(t) + d(t) = 0 \qquad (4.14)$$

If equation 4.14 holds, the mission has been accomplished. Debt has replaced some equity in the capital structure and created a disciplining mechanism for managers on their future investment decisions as well as the coffee maker purchases. And in the present time period where the cash surplus occurs, debt and equity have been swapped, thus leaving total security holder welfare unaffected.

Debt and the Firm's Liquidation Decision

Apart from the use of debt to mitigate the pursuit of managerial perquisites and overinvestment, Harris and Raviv (1990) also argue that debt has the benefit of forcing firms to make better liquidation decisions. If debt exists and a default occurs, then investors get to decide whether to keep the firm in operations or liquidate its assets. Without debt, managers make this decision, and will tend to err on the side of continued operations, even when the assets of the firm are more valuable if liquidated and placed into alternative use.

Agency Costs of Debt

If debt can help prevent managers from pursuing their own perquisites at the expense of outside shareholders, overinvesting in questionable projects, and choosing continued operations when liquidation is the right answer for security holders—all of which represent deviations from the market value rule—then why does the forgoing analysis not imply a firm should be financed with virtually all debt?

The static trade-off between tax and financial distress has not gone away, for one thing. Distress costs alone create costs of issuing debt that will prevent a firm even with severe agency costs from pursuing an all-debt securities capital structure.

Separate and apart from static trade-off issues, debt also has other costs associated with it, the most significant of which are discussed below.[10]

Asset Substitution

Fama and Miller (1972), Fama (1976), and Easterbrook (1984) explain how asset substitution problems can arise in firms with both fixed and residual claims in their capital structures. Asset substitution occurs when residual claimants substitute high-risk investment projects for lower-risk projects at the expense of fixed claimants. From Chapter 3, we know that the investment rule that maximizes the value of a firm is the market value rule, or the investment policy that maximizes total security holder welfare, the left-hand side of

$$[E_{t-1}(t) + \delta(t)] + [D_{t-1}(t) + \rho(t)] = V(t) + X(t) - I(t) \qquad (4.15)$$

Because $X(t)$ is based on prior investment decisions, the left-hand side of equation 4.8 is clearly maximized when $V(t) - I(t)$ is maximized. A firm that does not maximize $V(t) - I(t)$ is thus not maximizing *total* security holder welfare.

As argued in Chapter 3, the NPV criterion is one that should be adopted by both stock holders and bond holders; accepting a negative NPV project, after all, is bad for all security holders. But the NPV criterion tells us only whether the risk-adjusted expected value of the project is positive. It does not tell us about the variance or other aspects of the investment program, and it is on that subject—how variance can impact the attractiveness of a project—on which fixed and residual claim holders may disagree.

Exhibit 4.4 shows the value of equity as a call option written on the market value of the firm's real assets on some presumed debt maturity date T and struck at FV, the face value of all outstanding fixed claims. The y-axis shows the value of the equity, and the second y-axis on the right-hand side shows the probability of a given asset value being realized on date T. Two possible probability distributions are shown, $f_1(A(T))$ and $f_2(A(T))$. Both distributions are centered on the face value of the debt, making it essentially equally likely in both cases that the firm's assets fall below the face value of its debt and insolvency occurs.

The distribution f_2 has a higher variance than the distribution f_1—that is, $\sigma_2 > \sigma_1$. The cumulative probability of a given net asset value being realized is the area under the two curves. You can see that although both distributions have an equal probability of leaving equity holders in the money, the higher-variance distribution has a higher probability of reaching a high payoff, such as FV + k for some k. True, the probability they will end up with FV – k is also higher, but these probabilities do not change the fact that nothing is still nothing—provided, of course, that we still assume residual claimants have limited liability.

Equity holders thus will have a strong temptation to deviate from a simple NPV rule in order to pursue higher-variance projects. This does not necessarily mean equity holders will pursue negative-NPV projects, as in the overinvestment case discussed in the last section. Rather, equity prefers

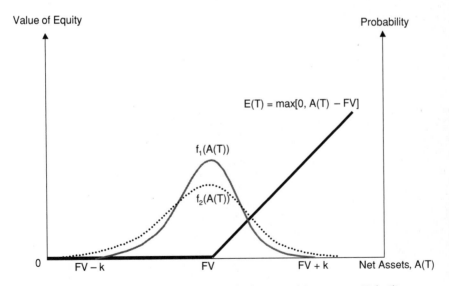

EXHIBIT 4.4   Relation between Residual Claims and Investment Volatility

positive-NPV projects that are also riskier projects. The benefit to equity holders of pursuing higher-volatility investments, moreover, rises as the value of the firm's assets approaches the face value of debt.

Debt holders have the opposite view of investment prospects, as Exhibit 4.5 illustrates. As writers of put options, debt holders benefit from volatility reductions. The best-case scenario for debt holders is to receive the face value of their loans back. If the firm does better, they do not benefit. But if the firm does worse, they pay the price in the form of a partial—or perhaps total—loss of principal. Because variance is symmetric, higher variance means more probability of either a decline to an asset value like FV − k or a rise in asset values to FV + k. Because rises cannot help debt and declines only hurt, anything that associates more probability with declines in net asset values is bad.

The timing of the investment decision vis-à-vis the financing decision is critical. If the investment decision is made before securities are issued, both debt and equity will simply reflect the distribution of the investment decision actually made. But if bonds can be issued before the investment decision is made, then equity holders have an opportunity to expropriate debt holders. Equity can agree to take the lower-variance project, sell bonds on that basis, and then actually pursue the higher-variance project, thus transferring wealth from debt to equity.

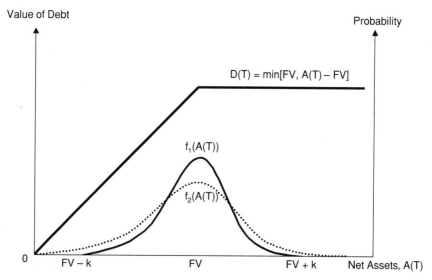

EXHIBIT 4.5   Relation Between Fixed Claims and Investment Volatility

To see this more clearly, consider another example where the firm has two investment opportunities. The distributions of the cash flows X on the projects, denoted $f_1(X)$ and $f_2(X)$, are shown in Exhibit 4.6. The expected value of the first project is slightly higher than the expected value of the second project—$\mu_1 > \mu_2$. The variance of the first project, however, is lower than the second—$\sigma_1 < \sigma_2$.

The value of the firm will be lower if the more volatile project is chosen because it has a lower expected value. If we denote the value of the firm given investment project 1 as $V(1)$ and similarly for $V(2)$, then $V(1) > V(2)$. Because the project with the lower expected value has a higher volatility, however, the value of equity could be higher if the lower expected value project is chosen. The net impact is not immediately obvious. The difference in the values of the firm for the two investment opportunities can be expressed as

$$V(1) - V(2) = [E(1) - E(2)] + [D(1) - D(2)] \qquad (4.16)$$

where the right-hand side of the equation represents the different market values of equity and debt, respectively, given the two possible investment projects.

If the difference in the expected values of projects 1 and 2 is small, then the difference between $V(1)$ and $V(2)$ is also small in equation 4.16. In this

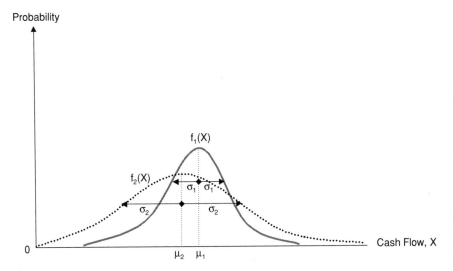

EXHIBIT 4.6 Asset Substitution in the Two Investment Project Case

case, it is quite possible that the value of the equity will increase. Rearranging the equation to show the change in the value of equity,

$$E(2) - E(1) = [D(1) - D(2)] - [V(1) - V(2)] \qquad (4.17)$$

The change in the value of equity thus can be expressed as the sum of the amount of wealth transferred from bond holders to stock holders $D(1) - D(2)$ less any reduction in overall firm value $V(1) - V(2)$, because $\sigma_1 < \sigma_2$, $D(1) > D(2)$ and because $\mu_1 > \mu_2$, $V(1) > V(2)$. The net impact on equity thus depends on the relative magnitudes. For two projects with extremely different volatilities and small differences in expected value, equity almost certainly will experience a net gain, despite the reduction in the value of the firm as a whole. Debt will lose more value from the increased volatility of the investment than the firm loses in value from the lower mean, resulting in a residual benefit to stockholders. Conversely, if the second project has a much lower expected value and only a trivially higher volatility than the first project, the reduction in the value of the firm will likely exceed the reduction in the value of its debt, so that both equity and debt are net losers.

Suppose stock holders control the firm and decide to pursue an investment strategy that maximizes equity holder welfare. This implies the firm is maximizing

$$[E_{t-1}(t) + \delta(t)] = V(t) + X(t) - I(t) - [D_{t-1}(t) + \rho(t)] \qquad (4.18)$$

rather than the left-hand side of equation 4.15. In this situation, the bond holders will take over the firm. Specifically, bond holders would buy out existing equity holders for the value that equity would have if the rule to maximize $V(t) - I(t)$ were being followed. In other words, if the rule to maximize the shareholder wealth is followed, the firm's bond holders will buy out the existing shareholders and adopt a rule to maximize total security holder welfare, which will raise the value of the firm by exactly the amount the bond holders paid for the buyout, as discussed in Chapter 3.

If we suppose bond holders control the firm and adopt a rule to maximize debt holder value instead of total security holder welfare, the same argument just used can be applied in reverse. The stock holders will buy out the debt holders, change the investment rule to maximizing $V(t) - I(t)$, and recover the costs of their buyout from an increase in the value of the firm exactly equal to the difference between the old and new debt prices.

As Fama (1976) explains, however, the dynamic aspect to this line of reasoning cannot be ignored, especially when violations of the M&M assumptions of perfect capital markets and symmetric information make monitoring costly. The market value of the firm at any time t depends on the probability distribution of $V(t + 1) + X(t + 1) - I(t + 1)$. $V(t)$ thus depends on the investment policy followed *at time t + 1*. Similarly, the value of the firm at time t – 1 depends on the investment policy pursued at time t. This logic can be carried back to the time 0 on which the firm is first set up. A firm's announcement at time 0 that it will pursue an investment policy of maximizing V(0) – I(0) is equivalent to the firm saying it will maximize security holder welfare in every period subsequent to 0.

Because of the inherent conflict between stock holders and bond holders, the value of the firm at any point in time t depends not just on the firm's commitment to adhere to the maximize V(t) – I(t) rule in all future periods but also on it's ability to convince stock holders and bond holders that commitment is credible. Fama (1976, pg. 42) states the problem succinctly:

> *[T]he essence of the potential problems surrounding conflicting stock-holder-bondholder interests is that once time 0 passes it will be difficult for the stockholders to resist the temptation to try to carry out an unexpected shift from a rule to maximize V(t) – I(t) to the rule that maximizes stockholder wealth. . . . To maximize V(0) – I(0), the wealth of its organizers, the firm must convince the market that it will always follow the investment strategy maximize V(t) – I(t). The market realizes that the firm might later try to shift to another strategy and it will take this into account in setting V(0). To get the market to set V(0) at the value appropriate to the strategy maximize V(t) – I(t), the firm will have to find some way to guarantee it will stay with this strategy.*
>
> *The important point is that the onus of providing this guarantee falls on the firm. In pricing a firm's securities, a well-functioning market will, on average, appropriately charge the firm in advance for future departures from currently declared decision rules. The firm can only avoid these discounts in the prices of its securities to the extent that it can provide concrete assurances of its forthrightness.*

A variety of mechanisms can be used to provide the market with assurances that expropriations will not occur on an ongoing basis. Covenants can be added to debt, for example, that commit the firm to an investment policy that does not expropriate debt holders, as suggested in Jensen and Meckling (1976) and as discussed and reviewed at length in Smith and Warner (1979).

Even without explicit covenants, reputation considerations alone may prompt firms to avoid investments that expropriate one class of security holders at the expense of another. Diamond (1989b) argues that the firm's reputation in the debt market affects its borrowing rate, and some firms—especially older, more established ones—can reduce their borrowing costs by not systematically choosing higher-risk projects (which presumably would lead to more defaults). Hirshleifer and Thakor (1989) propose that the reputation of managers is also an important mitigant of asset substitution problems.[11]

Corporate law, moreover, often requires managers to act in the interest of creditors rather than shareholders when the firm is near insolvency. The creditors of Rhythms NetConnections, Inc., for example, considered the firm to be in a "zone of insolvency" and thus asked the company to halt its cash drains and wind up its operations *before* a default occurred.[12] Similar actions occurred at other telecom firms in mid-2001 as creditors sought to get firms to pay them off prior to bankruptcy or to change their investment strategies to lower-risk initiatives.[13]

Underinvestment and Debt Overhang

We saw earlier that debt (and dividends or stock repurchases) can be a solution to the overinvestment problems associated with free cash flows. In this section we explore how the very same debt that mitigates *over*investment can lead to the opposite problem of *under*investment.

Myers (1977) argues that when a firm has too much debt, a "debt overhang" problem can discourage residual claimants from prodding management to take positive NPV investments because the benefits of the investments inure mainly to creditors and not shareholders. According to Myers (1977), the current value of a firm $V(t)$ can be expressed not just as the current market value of its assets—$A(t)$ as we have been calling it up to now—but rather as the sum of assets already in place and future growth opportunities:

$$V(t) = V_A(t) + V_G(t) = E(t) + D(t) \qquad (4.19)$$

where $V_A(t)$ and $V_G(t)$ denote current assets and growth opportunities, respectively, and where the sum of these two assets must equal the sum of the current market values of equity and debt, denoted $E(t)$ and $D(t)$, respectively. The main factor that separates $V_A(t)$ and $V_G(t)$ is that the former market value of current assets depends on investment expenditures that occurred either at some time before t or contemporaneously at time t.

Growth opportunities involve an investment expenditure in the future. Because the investment expenditure occurs in the future, the firm may or may not actually undertake the project on the decision date. Only on that future date can the project's NPV be determined. At some time t + k after time t, the firm will have the opportunity to spend $I(t + k)$ to generate cash flows $X(t + k + q)$ where q can be zero, some positive integer, or a vector of several integers. In other words, a growth opportunity is an opportunity for the firm to make a subsequent investment in a project that has one or more payoffs either at the time of the investment expenditure or in any periods after that. Myers called growth opportunities "real options," the term that has been adopted into modern use.[14]

To see how debt can create costs for a firm with a lot of real options, let us first return briefly to a firm that is all equity. Suppose this firm has no current assets—$V_A(t) = 0$—and one real option that gives the firm the right at time $t + 1$ to invest $I(t + 1)$ and obtain an asset worth $V_G(t + 1, s)$, where s is the "state of nature" that occurs at time $t + 1$. The state of nature can be anything that determines the value of the investment project and can include several different variables. A barbecue sauce factory that can be built at time $t + 1$, for example, has a NPV at time $t + 1$ that depends on the known investment cost $I(t + 1)$ and other factors, such as current demand for barbecue sauce, future expected sauce demand, the price of tomatoes and sugar as inputs, the price of sauce sold in foreign currency, the interest rate at which expected cash flows on the factors after time $t + 1$ are discounted, and so on. All these "other factors" are reflected in the state of nature.

If at time $t + 1$ the firm decides not to accept the project, then the real option expires worthless. The firm did not have to spend $I(t + 1)$, but nor does it have the asset worth $V_G(t+1,s)$. If the firm does accept the project, it invests $I(t + 1)$ in one period and receives an asset the same period worth $V_G(t + 1, s)$ given the state of nature s at time $t + 1$.

With no debt in its capital structure and no new equity issued at time t, the balance sheet at time t gives the initial market value of the firm and is shown in Table 4.2.

Now suppose time $t + 1$ arrives, and the firm must decide whether to accept the investment opportunity. If no investment is made, the firm acquires no assets and forfeits the real option. The firm and its existing equity are thus worthless. But if the investment is made, the firm spends $I(t + 1)$ and ends up with an asset worth $V_G(t + 1, s)$. Specifically, the real option value declines to zero, but the existing asset assumes a value equal to the value of the asset acquired at $t + 1$ as the "underlying" of the real option at time t. New equity must be issued to finance the investment expenditure, such that $e(t + 1) = I(t + 1)$. The time $t + 1$ balance sheet of the firm is shown in Table 4.3.

For simplicity, we can follow Myers (1977) and define the value of the newly acquired asset—and, from Table 4.3, the value of the firm—as an increasing function of our "states of nature." For $s_1 < s_2$, this implies that $V(t + 1, s_1) < V(t+1, s_2)$.[15] If the new asset is a new chemical and the states of nature represent the demand for the chemical, we are simply defining demand s_1 to

TABLE 4.2   Balance Sheet of All-Equity Firm at Time t

Assets		Liabilities and Equity	
Value of Real Option	$V_G(t)$	0	Value of debt
Value of Existing Assets	0	$E(t)$	Value of equity
Value of Firm	$V(t)$	$V(t)$	

TABLE 4.3   Balance Sheet of All-Equity Firm at Time t+1

Assets		Liabilities and Equity	
Value of Real Option	0	0	Value of debt
Value of Existing Assets	$V_G(t + 1,s)$	$E(t + 1)$	Value of equity
Value of Firm	$V(t + 1,s)$	$V(t + 1,s)$	

be lower than demand s_2, so that the value of the chemical is correspondingly higher for demand s_2 than demand s_1.

Exhibit 4.7 shows the investment decision faced by a Myers-like firm at time t + 1 graphically. Clearly, the firm invests only if s ≥ s*. Remember that I(t + 1) and s are known at t + 1. For the firm to invest in this project at s < s* would make no sense, because $V_G(t + 1,s)$ would clearly be negative. At s = s* the firm just breaks even, and for s > s* the firm acquires an asset with a positive value.

Exhibit 4.7 is, of course, just a restatement of the NPV criterion presented in Chapter 3. We see from the figure that the firm invests only if $V_G(t+1,s) - I(t + 1) \geq 0$.

Now is time to introduce debt back into the picture and see where the

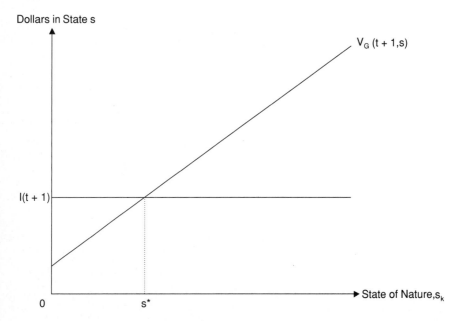

EXHIBIT 4.7   All-Equity Firm's Investment in a Growth Opportunity

problems come up. Because the firm is worthless when the state of nature is less than s*, the firm cannot issue riskless debt. If the firm issues debt and s < s*, the firm will be unable to pay the debt holders. But the firm can still issue *risky* debt. Let us now assume it does so at time t with a face value of FV and a maturity date of t + 1. Assume further the debt is used only to help fund the investment in the new asset at time t + 1—that is, to reduce the amount of new equity that must be issued to finance I(t + l).

Getting more particular about all the things going on at time t + 1, assume that the debt matures after the state of nature is realized but before the investment expenditure must be incurred at t + 1. If $V_G(t + 1,s) - I(t + 1) >$ FV, the shareholders of the firm will pay the debtors off. If instead $V_G(t+1,s) - I(t + 1) <$ FV, the bond holders will take over the firm. If $V_G(t + 1, s) - I(t + 1) \geq 0$, the bond holders will spend I(t + 1) and acquire the asset. If not, the firm is worthless and the bonds default. If the FV is set high enough that FV $> V_G(t + 1, s) - I(t + l)$ *for all states of nature s*, then equity is worthless and D(t) = V(t).

Now suppose that the debt matures at t + 1, *before* the state of nature is revealed. In other words, the firm's shareholders now must consider whether to pay off the debt before the true NPV of the growth opportunity is known—that is, while the growth opportunity is still a call option. In this situation, the time t balance sheet of the firm can be written as in Table 4.4.

If the firm decides not to invest in the project, existing assets are zero and there are no more growth opportunities. Debt and equity again are worthless, as is the firm. But if the firm invests I(t + 1) and acquires the new asset, the balance sheet of the firm at t + 1 then looks like Table 4.5.

Thus table 4.5 shows yet again that debt is an option on the worst of

TABLE 4.4 Balance Sheet of Levered Firm at Time t

Assets		Liabilities and Equity	
Value of Real Option	$V_G(t)$	D(t)	Value of debt
Value of Existing Assets	0	E(t)	Value of equity
Value of Firm	V(t)	V(t)	

TABLE 4.5 Balance Sheet of Levered Firm at Time t + 1

Assets		Liabilities and Equity	
Value of Real Option	0	$\min[V_G(t+1, s), FV]$	Value of debt
Value of Existing Assets	$V_G(t+1)$	$\max[0, V_G(t+1, s) - FV]$	Value of equity
Value of Firm	V(t)	V(t)	

two assets and equity is a purchased call on the firm's assets, both with striking prices equal to the face value of the debt.

The interesting problem arises when we consider the optimal exercise behavior for these options. As shown in Table 4.5, the equity call option is in
the money when $V_G(t+1,s) - FV > 0$. But because shareholders must decide
whether to pay off debt holders before the state of nature and the value of the
growth opportunity is revealed, this is *not* the criterion they use to decide
whether to exercise their option on the asset itself.

From Exhibit 4.8, it is clear that shareholders do not benefit from the in-
vestment project unless $V_G(t + 1,s) - FV - I(t + 1) > 0$, or, $V_G(t+1, s) > FV + I(t + 1)$. If $V_G(t+1, s) < FV + I(t + 1)$ and the investment is made at time $t + 1$, the
investment outlay will exceed the market value of the outstanding equity
shares even if the project has a positive NPV. In other words, shareholders
care about whether $V_G(t + 1, s) - FV - I(t + 1) > 0$ and not whether the project has a positive NPV—$V_G(t + 1, s) - I(t + 1) > 0$.

The point at which equity holders agree to undertake the investment
project is shown in Exhibit 4.8 as state of nature s°, such that s° > s*. At
the old break-even state of nature s*, equity is worthless. But at values of
s > s°, equity makes money on the project *and* can pay off debt. The size of
the triangle—hence, the value of the firm—depends on the face value of
debt outstanding.

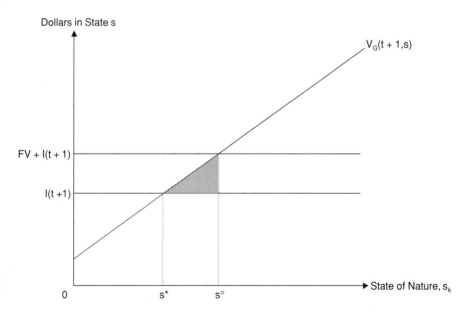

EXHIBIT 4.8   Levered Firm's Investment in a Growth Opportunity

Exhibit 4.9 shows the optimal capital structure of the firm in Myers (1977) model. At very low levels of debt, the equity holders' investment decision is not affected too significantly by the underinvestment problem, so the value of the firm V(t) is not dramatically below what its value would be in the absence of any debt, $V^E(t)$—although it is strictly lower. As the face value of debt rises, however, the loss in firm value begins to occur more rapidly. Myers (1977) calls this the debt overhang problem.

Exhibit 4.9 also shows that there is a definite amount that the firm should borrow, indicated by FV*. At this debt level, the firm is worth V*(t) and debt achieves its highest value, D*(t). Equity, however, is worth only $E^*(t) = V^*(t) - D^*(t)$, which is not the maximum market value for equity. Shareholder value is maximized only when the firm issues no debt—when FV = 0 and E(t) = V(t). Note that this is also where the combined value of debt and equity is maximized.

Underinvestment, Cash Flow Volatility, and Liquidity

Froot, Scharfstein, and Stein (1993) extend Myers's debt overhang story by arguing that external debt has liquidity costs associated with it that internal financing does not. These authors suppose the NPV of a firm is

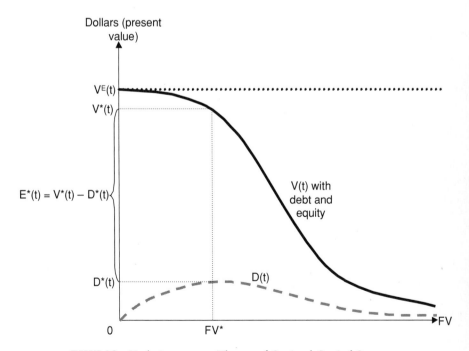

EXHIBIT 4.9   Underinvestment Theory of Optimal Capital Structure

$$F(I) = f(I) - I$$

where I is the investment expenditure and f(I) the subsequent level of production output, such that $f_I > 0$ and $f_{II} < 0$. When external debt has no agency costs, optimal investment occurs where $f_I = 1$—that is, the marginal product of the investment equals its marginal cost. This optimal investment expenditure can be denoted I*.

Now suppose, following Froot, Scharfstein, and Stein, that investment expenditures can be financed from internal funds, denoted w, and external funds, denoted ι:

$$I = w + \iota$$

If external financing is subject to agency costs, distress costs, and other costs in a fixed amount C, bonds issued by the firm earn C/ι over the riskless rate. Internal financing does not have these costs. So, the firm now chooses I to maximize $F(I) - C(\iota)$, where costs depend on the total amount of external financing $\iota = I - w$. The first-order condition for the firm now says that investment expenditures are optimal when

$$F_I - C_\iota = f_I - 1 - C_\iota = 0$$

or when $f_I - C_\iota = 1$. Because $f_I(I) > 0$ and $C_\iota(\iota) = C_\iota(I - w) > 0$, the optimal investment expenditure I is below the I* that satisfies the normal first-order condition $f_I = 1$. Thus, the firm invests too little because external debt is costly.

Froot, Scharfstein, and Stein go one step further than Myers, however, and argue that cash liquidity is an important determinant of the size of this problem. A firm that has low earnings volatility and a stable reserve of internal cash can avoid the agency costs of debt by relying mainly on internal funds. High earnings volatility, by contrast, make it more likely that the firm will have to borrow. In Myers's model, firms may walk away from positive NPV projects because the value of debt is so large that equity perceives no benefit from undertaking the project. But in Froot, Scharfstein, and Stein's model, firms also may walk away from positive NPV projects because they literally do not have the cash to fund them and raising external debt may simply be too expensive.

FINANCIAL IMPLICATIONS OF THE TRADE-OFF THEORY

Fama and French (2000) document the implications of the dynamic trade-off theory.[16] These implications are summarized in the following paragraphs, based on Chart 1 and the text of their paper. Note that in all the implications below save for one, references to leverage are to *book* leverage—that is, the book value debt, or the amount of outstanding debt under the firm's direct control.

1. *Firms with higher profitability have more leverage.* Because profitability is inversely related to expected financial distress costs, more profitability implies a lower probability of encountering financial distress and thus lower expected distress costs, which lowers the cost of debt.
2. *Higher earnings volatility is associated with less leverage.* Because earnings volatility is directly associated with the probability of encountering financial distress, higher volatility means higher expected distress costs and higher costs for debt. This also implies that small and/or ill-diversified firms tend toward less debt.
3. *Firms with higher profitability and lower earnings volatility have more leverage.* The impact of taxation on a firm's leverage choice depends on whether the marginal corporate tax saving is greater or less than the marginal corporate tax cost. A higher corporate tax rate with interest deductibility pushes the firm toward more leverage, whereas a higher personal tax rate—or a higher personal tax rate on debt relative to equity—encourages less leverage. But on net, firms with higher expected tax rates—that is, firms with higher profitability and lower earnings volatility—have a greater benefit to debt and thus tend toward more leverage.
4. *Firms with more profitable current assets have higher dividend payouts and greater leverage for a given investment opportunity set.* To mitigate managerial perquisites and overinvestment in low or negative NPV projects, firms disgorge excess free cash flows by committing a large proportion of their earnings to dividend and interest payments. Given a set of investment opportunities, this means that more profitable firms with larger free cash flows can be expected to disgorge more of those cash flows with higher dividends and larger outstanding debt obligations.
5. *Firms with a large number of positive NPV current investment opportunities or growth opportunities have lower dividend payouts and less leverage for a given level of profitability.* More sound investment opportunities mean that more free cash flow is absorbed in legitimate investment activities. For a given level of profitability, such firms have less need to disgorge free cash flows.
6. *Firms with higher leverage should have a lower dividend payout ratio; the converse also is true.* In the models of Jensen (1986) and Stulz (1990), dividends and debt are both viable mechanisms for firms to disgorge their free cash flows. We thus should expect an inverse relation between the two. In other words, a firm with a high dividend payout ratio need not also have a lot of debt to control its free cash flows.
7. *Companies with more investment and growth opportunities have less current leverage and lower dividend payout ratios.* Firms with a lot of

real options, in particular, will tend to keep free cash flows high enough to finance future profitable investment expenditures without running into the asset substitution problem (as in Fama and Miller [1972] and Easterbrook [1984]) or the underinvestment problem (as in Myers [1977] and Froot, Scharfstein, and Stein [1993]). Firms in this situation that already have a high dividend payout can be expected to have even less outstanding debt.

NOTES

1. Some authors argue for subdivisions of these two theories as well as for the inclusion of others. See, for example, Harris and Raviv (1991).
2. Harris and Raviv (1991) survey two other theories for why firms sometimes perceive an optimal capital structure—theories involving relations between product and input markets and capital structure, and theories of capital structure and corporate control. These theories are not addressed here for a mixture of reasons, which include mainly their lack of implications for the risk transfer and risk financing choices discussed later in this book. Nevertheless, the theories are well accepted and important. Interested readers are directed to Harris and Raviv (1991) for further details.
3. In fact, many of the implications of the two theories are the same. But where they differ, they do so in material ways.
4. For a summary, see Swoboda and Zechner (1995).
5. This analysis is based on the example given in Brealey and Myers (2000).
6. The demand curve is upward sloping because the y-axis shows the interest rate, not the price.
7. See, for example, Swoboda and Zechner (1995).
8. It also may help to imagine that the assumption of "symmetric information" is also violated. If information is perfectly symmetric, then a firm's creditors should be able to tell the difference between a "liquidity crisis and fire sale" and a genuine solvency problem. But if creditors do not have the same information that managers of the firm have, new bond holders may demand a higher return than old ones to compensate for a perceived increase in default risk.
9. The use of the term "dynamic" is a little misleading, because it has some implication of time playing a role. In fact, the dynamic trade-off theory differs from the static trade-off theory only in its inclusion of agency issues. But agency issues often are referred to as "dynamic" because timing often plays a role in determining the nature of the agency conflict. An example of this is Myers's (1977) underinvestment problem, explored later in this section.
10. Depending on the type of debt, various other costs—frictional or agency—may arise. See, for example, Rajan (1992).

11. Hirshleifer and Thakor (1989) argue that managers are perceived as either "succeeding" or "failing," and that managers benefit reputationally from success like fixed claimants and not like residual claimants (i.e., reputation is either "good" or "bad" and there are no "degrees of good"). Managers thus will choose investments that maximize the probability of success rather than returns, which discourages asset substitution and reduces the agency costs of debt.
12. Pacelle and Young, (2001).
13. See, for example, Davis and Pacelle, (2001).
14. See, for example, Sick (1995) and Trigeorgis (1995, 1996, 1999).
15. There is no economics behind this assumption; we simply are deliberately ordering states of nature from the "worst" to the "best" in terms of their impact on the value of the new asset. We also assume the function $V_G(t+1,s)$ is linear in s for simplicity, and again with no loss of generality.
16. See also Harris and Raviv (1991) for the implications of the agency cost-specific capital structure issues.

CHAPTER **5**

Asymmetric Information, Adverse Selection, and the "Pecking Order Theory" of Optimal Capital Structure

In the trade-off theory explored in Chapter 4, the firm's optimal capital structure emerged as an optimal leverage ratio equating the marginal benefits and costs of debt. In the theory we explore in this chapter—the pecking order theory of optimal capital structure—there is no optimal leverage ratio for firms. When the M&M assumption of symmetric information is violated and a firm's insiders (e.g., senior managers) have better information about the true quality of the firm's real investment decisions than external investors, however, the firm can suffer from adverse selection problems. The pecking order capital structure emerges in this world as a response to adverse selection and as a result of underinvestment and overinvestment as defined in the last chapter.

Here we review the pecking order model and some of its close cousins, seeking answers to the following questions:

- What is adverse selection and how does it relate to the sale of securities?
- Why does a pecking order in capital structure emerge under the presence of adverse selection, and what is that pecking order?
- Can a firm get around the pecking order and reduce its adverse selection costs by obtaining investment capital mainly from a small number of highly informed capital suppliers?
- What are the financial implications of the pecking order model?
- If the pecking order theory implies that capital structure is a solution to under- and overinvestment problems arising under adverse selection, what are the implications for capital structure decisions if we hold a firm's investment policy fixed?

ADVERSE SELECTION, THE MARKET FOR LEMONS, AND THE MARKET FOR SECURITIES

George Akerlof (1970), a winner of the 2001 Nobel Prize in economics, developed the notion of adverse selection in his study of the used car market. When information is asymmetric across car buyers and sellers, sellers know the true quality of the cars they are selling. Buyers do not.

Because used car buyers cannot ascertain whether they are buying "a lemon," they will demand a price discount based on the assumption that at least some of the used cars being marketed are lemons. This price discount, however, creates a disincentive for sellers of good used cars to come to the market. The discounted price buyers are willing to pay believing some cars to be lemons is below what the good cars are worth. Consequently, the only sellers that show up really do have a lot of lemons.

Buyers know this, too, of course. In what is known as a rational expectations equilibrium, buyers expect lemons, pay for lemons, and get lemons.

The securities sold by firms also can be perceived as lemons when insiders like the senior managers of a firm know the true quality of the firm's real investment decisions but outsiders do not. Investors will assume that insiders come to outsiders only when they have lemons to offer. External investors thus discount the price they are willing to pay for the firm's securities. In turn, firms with good information refuse to come to market because the price they will receive is too low. The result is that, indeed, securities are issued by firms only when they are lemons. As in the case of cars, securities investors expect lemons, pay for lemons, and thus get lemons.

But how does this possibly relate to a firm's capital structure?

ADVERSE SELECTION AND THE PECKING ORDER THEORY

Myers (1984) and Myers and Majluf (1984) argue that when managers and investors have different information, a capital structure emerges that conforms to the following pecking order of the securities capital structure[1]:

1. Firms always prefer internal finance to external finance.
2. Firms have target dividend payout ratios that are adapted to investment opportunities, but dividends are relatively "sticky"—that is, firms try to avoid sudden and large changes in their dividend policies.
3. Because of sticky dividend policies and unexpected changes in profitability and investment opportunities, internal cash flows may be greater or less than required investment outlays. When there is a net cash flow surplus, firms use the surplus to pay off debt or investment in liquid securities. When there is a net cash flow deficit, firms draw down

net cash balances and liquidate their investment portfolios of marketable securities.

4. If external financing is required, firms issue the lowest-risk security first. In other words, firms prefer to issue securities in the following order: senior or low-risk debt, mezzanine and subordinated (i.e., risky) debt, hybrid debt-equity securities, and equity.

This pecking order implies an optimal capital structure as a result of its requirements for external financing. Note that the theory does not imply a "target" debt-equity ratio because equity appears at both the bottom and the top of the pecking order—inside equity is a preferred source of funds, whereas outside equity is literally last on the list. Unlike the trade-off theory, in which capital structure emerges from the costs and benefits of debt, capital structure in the pecking order theory is based on the firm's net cash flows from its real investment decisions.

A Simple Rational Expectations Model

The pecking order theory is sufficiently important that we briefly reproduce Myers's (1984) simple model to understand the drivers of this capital structure model. Suppose a firm faces a positive NPV investment opportunity whose NPV is denoted Ψ, but that the firm must raise N additional dollars to undertake this activity. If the investment project is undertaken, the firm will be worth $V° + \Psi$ and is worth $V°$ otherwise. Finally, suppose all the M&M assumptions hold *except* informational symmetry.

Specifically, consider a situation where managers of the firm observe both Ψ and $V°$. Managers thus know what the firm will be worth—and, hence, what the securities issued by the firm should be worth—whether the investment is undertaken or is forgone. But investors in the firm's securities do not observe these two values; they see only a joint distribution of possible outcomes—say $f(\Psi,V°)$ for some joint density $f(\bullet)$.

If the firm issues stock to raise the N dollars it needs, the benefit to the firm is clearly that it can undertake the project. So, the benefit is Ψ, or the NPV of the project that cannot be undertaken if the N dollars are not raised. But as Myers (1984) explains, issuing stock in the amount of N dollars also has a cost when information is asymmetric. Namely, the true value of the stock may differ from the value of the stock sold to the less-informed investors because of the adverse selection or lemons problem described earlier. Specifically, let $N°$ denote the value of the company's stock after investors acquire the same information that managers have—that is, $N°$ reflects the "true information" about the value of the firm.

Managers seeking to maximize the true value of the firm's existing shares will issue the new stock and invest in the project *only when*

$$\Psi \geq N^\circ - N \equiv \Delta N \qquad (5.1)$$

If the manager's inside information is favorable—that is, ΔN is positive—then the issued shares may be undervalued. And if ΔN is positive and large relative to Ψ, the firm may pass up a positive NPV project because its securities are underpriced.

Conversely, if the manager has information that the project is bad and investors lack this information, ΔN is negative (i.e., shares issued are overpriced) and the firm always raises the funds. But because the project has a true NPV that is negative, managers do not use the N dollars raised for the project in question. They invest the dollars elsewhere.[2]

The problem becomes more complicated when we recognize that a new stock issue sends a "signal" to the market. Specifically, any decision to issue stock sends a negative signal to both current and new shareholders. To see this, recognize that the rational expectations equilibrium value of the firm—the market value from the investors' perspective, assuming they know that managers will act based on equation 5.1—is the expected value of the firm conditional on the signal sent by managers in deciding whether to issue N dollars worth of new stock:

$$V = E[V^\circ \mid \Psi < \Delta N] \qquad (5.2a)$$

$$V' = E[V^\circ + \Psi + N \mid \Psi \geq \Delta N] \qquad (5.2b)$$

For both V and V', the value of the firm is its price per share times the number of shares outstanding. N is a fixed dollar amount by assumption, but the number of shares required to raise this amount is endogenous to equation 5.2. In other words, ΔN depends on V'. If the managers decide to issue the new stock, the price per share for the new stock holders is N/V'. The manager can then see the true value of the stock upon issue as

$$N^\circ = \frac{N}{V'}(V^\circ + \Psi + N) \qquad (5.3)$$

Substituting equation 5.3 back into the decision criterion for managers in equation 5.1 yields

$$\Psi \geq \frac{N}{V'}(V^\circ + \Psi + N) - N$$

$$\Rightarrow \Psi \geq N\left(\frac{V^\circ + \Psi + N}{E[V^\circ + \Psi + N]} - 1\right) \qquad (5.4)$$

Because N, V°, and Ψ are given, the greater the price per share of the new issue, the less value is given up to new stock holders. When the market value of
the firm (i.e., the rational expectations expected value of the firm conditional
on the stock issue) is greater than what managers know to be the true value of
the firm, the right-hand side of equation 5.4 is negative and managers will always issue the new stock. But if the market expectation is below the true
value of the firm, it is possible the firm will not make the stock issue. In other
words, in a rational expectation equilibrium, the lemons problem occurs and
firms may well issue stock only when it is overpriced.

Myers (1984) argues that the immediate implications of this analysis are
twofold. First, the cost of external finance is not purely the cost of issuing securities (e.g., underwriting costs as described in Chapter 2). In addition, external finance can lead to underinvestment of the kind discussed in a different
context in Chapter 4. The obvious way to avoid such underinvestment is to
rely on internal cash balances to fund new investments before considering the
issue of new securities.

Second, if external finance is required, safer securities are preferred to
risky ones—the managers of the firm first prefer to issue riskless or low-risk
debt, then risky debt, then hybrids, and last of all outside equity. If the firm
lacks the internal funds to finance a positive-NPV investment with a present
value of Ψ, equations 5.1 and 5.4 tell us that managers will accept the project only if securities can be issued that are overvalued (i.e., $\Delta N < 0$) or that
are undervalued by an amount less than the marginal benefit of taking the
project, Ψ.

The only thing that managers really can influence at the point of security
issue is the size of ΔN. Following Myers's (1984) example, consider first a situation where managers have favorable information about a project and are
trying to avoid the underinvestment problem of not forgoing a legitimate (i.e.,
positive-NPV) investment.

Suppose the investment requires $10 million. If the shares the firm must
issue to fund the investment are really worth $12 million, the managers will
undertake the project only if its NPV is more than $2 million. If the project
has a net present value of $1.5 million, for example, the project is rejected.
The value of the firm is $1.5 million less because the positive-NPV project
worth $1.5 million was forgone, but old shareholders are $500,000 better off
than if the project had been accepted.

If managers could somehow reduce the size of ΔN to below the project
NPV of $1.5 million, then the project could be financed without making old
shareholders worse off.[3] Securities that are overvalued by only $500,000
upon issue (i.e., worth $10.5 million), for example, would make it possible
for managers to issue the securities, raise the $10 million required to under-
take the project, increase the value of the firm by $1.5 million, and not im-
pose a net loss on old shareholders.

The best way to finance a new investment project under conditions of adverse selection is to issue securities whose values are least sensitive to the ultimate revelation of information to the market, regardless what that information is. In other words, the safer the security, the less the price will change to incorporate the revelation of private information when that information is revelead. In the limiting case of riskless debt, the value of the debt will not change at all based on the revelation to the market of the true value of the investment project. ΔN is zero, and the firm will never forgo a positive NPV project.

What if the information managers have is not favorable, so that ΔN is negative? As equations 5.1 and 5.4 show, the managers will always issue new securities and always take the cash. They may not use it for its intended purpose, and may instead just put the cash in the bank. But they will undertake the security issue. The question in light of the preceding analysis is what securities they will issue.

Logically speaking, managers would seem to want to make ΔN as large as possible in absolute value terms—to maximize the overvaluation of the issue. This would lead to the opposite of the prior situation, where managers always prefer to issue securities whose sensitivity to the information they possess will be highest—that is, equity. But investors know this, too.

If investors realize that managers will issue equity only when it is overpriced and will issue debt otherwise, the immediate implication is that rational investors will not be willing to buy the equity. The only real situation in which investors would accept a new equity issue is if the firm has exhausted its debt capacity—that is, if it simply cannot issue any more debt without incurring extreme costs. Consequently, investors will essentially force the firm to follow the pecking order noted at the beginning of this section—financing new investments first through low-risk debt, next through subordinated and mezzanine finance, penultimately through hybrids, and last equity—and only then, as Fama and French (2000) put it, "under duress."

Myers (1984) notes that in some situations, firms may maintain a stock of external debt to keep enough cash in current assets to finance their investments, but in that case the firm does everything it can to make the debt as low risk as possible. He postulates that their rationale is both to avoid the costs of financial distress and to maintain "financial slack" in the form of "reserve borrowing power." In other words, issuing debt that is reasonably low risk or not issuing debt at all keeps the firm's debt capacity positive, especially for the subsequent issue of more low-risk debt.

This latter point is the basis for the model of Froot, Scharfstein, and Stein (1993) that we discussed earlier. Because external borrowing is costly, firms take actions that allow them to fund their investments internally or by keeping their capacity to issue low-risk debt high. The higher a firm's net cash flow volatility, the more it will need to dip into the debt market to cover internal funds deficits, and thus the more important it is that firms keep their low-risk debt capacity high.

Importance of the Information Asymmetry

In the trade-off theory, capital structure is a solution to the costs created by both underinvestment and overinvestment. In the pecking order model, underinvestment and overinvestment cannot occur at the same time for a given project. Either the project is positive NPV or it is negative NPV, but it cannot be both. The driver of the pecking order thus is the net cash flow of the project itself together with the assumption that managers of the firm, acting as agents of the firm's existing shareholders, know whether the project is positive or negative NPV, but investors do not.

Importantly, the nature of the information asymmetry dictates the degree to which the firm's securities are mispriced in the pecking order model. As Myers (1984) and Myers and Majluf (1984) argue, any source of external finance except riskless debt will change in value when the true information is revealed about the quality of the firm's investments. Those securities that change less in value for a given information release are preferred by the firm.

But what if the firm can address this problem by negotiating with certain classes of security holders?

DELEGATED MONITORING, INFORMED CAPITAL SOURCES, AND THE PECKING ORDER

That the managers of a firm may be able to reveal the true quality of its investments to certain creditors is plausible, especially if the creditors are small in number, have significant interest in incurring some costs to verify the true quality of a firm's investments, and have the internal capabilities to make such an evaluation.

Unsecured senior loans made to corporations by commercial banks have long been thought to help reduce the costs associated with asymmetric information. Commercial banks serve a role as "delegated monitors" of the investment activities of their borrowers. By providing borrowers with monitoring and outside discipline, banks encourage their borrowers to undertake only positive net present value projects.[4]

To understand delegated monitoring, consider each stage in the commercial lending process. Before extending a loan, a bank carefully evaluates the creditworthiness of the customer and signals its assessment by extending or declining the loan. If the loan is later rolled over, the bank then reevaluates the credit risk of the firm, thus giving the borrower an ongoing incentive to undertake only positive net present value projects and investments. Otherwise, the borrower risks the nonrenewal of the loan and the negative signal that nonrenewal would send to other investors. And when a loan is rolled over, the positive signal sent to the capital market tells other creditors to the firm that they need not undertake the same credit risk evaluations already conducted by the bank. In particular, the bank's scrutiny over a company's investment decisions abrogates the need for relatively less informed creditors (e.g., public bond holders) to undertake their own costly monitoring of the borrower's investments.

In that manner, "informed" bank funds make other sources of "uninformed" funds from public capital markets or venture capitalists viable as additional sources of credit.[5] Not surprisingly, as discussed by Diamond (1991), small firms and high-risk start-up ventures in particular build financial market reputation by first acquiring bank-monitored debt and only later move on to acquire arm's-length public or privately placed debt.

A natural question that arises, of course, is the following: Why, if bank debt is so valuable to firms for delegated monitoring purposes, do firms ever seek funds from institutions other than banks? The answer is twofold. First, delegated monitoring is costly. Obtaining bank finance can yield cost savings to borrowers through reduced agency costs of debt and through lower costs of nonbank debt finance—the cost of nonbank debt would be higher if delegated monitoring did not reduce adverse selection costs. Nevertheless, as described by Diamond (1984, 1989), firms will borrow from banks only up to the point at which those savings are equal to the marginal costs of delegated monitoring.

Second, although banks help ensure that a borrower undertakes only positive net present value investment projects, the borrower cedes bargaining power to the bank over ongoing projects in the process of purchasing delegated monitoring. Rajan (1992) argues that this can lead to bank-promulgated decisions that are too conservative. A project that originally has a positive NPV, for example, might be terminated early at the behest of a bank if the project NPV becomes negative at some point in the life of the project. To avoid ceding too much control to conservative bank lenders, firms diversify their borrowing sources across nonbanks with less incentive and capacity to monitor ongoing investment projects. In other words, borrowers often use less desirable forms of debt simply to avoid giving a bank total control over investment decisions.

Unfortunately, this analysis does not add much to the pecking order theory. Bank debt, after all, is already senior in capital structure and among the lowest-risk categories of debt. Indeed, consistent with Diamond (1993), one reason bank debt is senior and low-risk is because of the mutual desire of firms and banks to reduce the sensitivity of their claims to the revelation of private information.

As will be discussed later in this book, one of the more interesting developments in capital structure today is the replacement of banks as delegated monitors with well-informed insurance and reinsurance capital suppliers whose claims are not senior in capital structure. Despite the fact that many alternative risk transfer solutions may involve the supply of capital that is relatively junior in the securities capital structure, they are highly dependent on monitoring by the supplier of the capital. Although the junior nature of the claim makes it more sensitive to the revelation of private information, it also makes the claim riskier for the capital supplier. This makes (re-)insurers all the more inclined to gather additional information about borrowers—information that convinces the lenders to accept a junior position in the securities capital structure but that also reduces the sensitivity of the claim to the information asymmetry.

FINANCIAL IMPLICATIONS OF THE PECKING ORDER THEORY

Just as Fama and French (2000) summarized the practical implications of the trade-off theory, they do the same for the pecking order theory.[6] Again relying heavily on their work, these implications are as follows.

1. *Firms with higher profitability on assets in place for a given set of investment opportunities have higher dividend payments over the long term and less leverage (both book and market).* Because firms want to maximize their internal funds for investment purposes, dividends are less attractive for firms with low profitability on current assets, a large amount of current or anticipated investment spending, and high leverage. All else being equal, only firms with reasonably high profits have high dividend payouts.[7] And because dividends are a substitute for and hence inversely rated to leverage, such firms also tend to have less leverage on both a book and market basis.

2. *Firms with a lot of current or planned investments have lower dividend payouts over the long run, given profitability.* For a given level of profitability, firms that utilize their internal cash flows on investment decisions have little left over to fund high long-term dividend payouts.

3. *A firm concerned mainly with current borrowing costs will have a stock of debt that varies in size directly with its investment opportunity set, for a given level of profitability on current assets.* In the what Fama and French (2000) call the "simple version of the model," firms are concerned mainly with keeping current borrowing costs down. When the investment expenditures of such firms persistently exceed retained earnings, investments will be financed with larger amounts of debt. Conversely, firms whose retained earnings exceed their investments should have a declining stock of external debt.

4. *When a firm balances current and expected future borrowing costs, firms*

with more volatile net cash flows have a lower dividend payout rate and less current leverage. Cash flow volatility increases the risk that firms will have to issue securities to fund profitable investments. To avoid incurring these costs, firms with highly volatile cash flows may try to keep internal cash balances high in order to fund these future investments, which implies a lower dividend payout. Firms also may maintain a stock of low-risk debt for the same purpose.

5. *Because of assumed stickiness in dividend payout ratios, variations in earnings investments are absorbed primarily by changes in the firm's leverage.*

OTHER SIGNALING MODELS

In the pecking order theory, asymmetric information leads to over- and under-investment problems, and the firm's capital structure emerges as a means of addressing the costs associated with these problems. The net cash flows of the firm thus dictate its capital structure. Other models with asymmetric information at their root, by contrast, take the firm's net cash flows and real investments as given and then examine how capital structure decisions can be used to "signal" the quality of the firm's investments to a less informed capital market. These signaling theories are complementary to and not substitutes for the pecking order.

In an early model, Leland and Pyle (1977) consider a single entrepreneur seeking additional equity financing for a project about which the entrepreneur is better informed than the would-be investors. Although investors cannot observe the true value of the project, they can observe the amount of money the entrepreneur commits to the project. Not surprisingly, investors' willingness to pay more for their share of the project rises as the entrepreneur's investment in the project rises. The entrepreneur's insider investment decision thus sends a "signal" to less informed market participants about the unobservable investment project.

Miller and Rock (1985) develop a signaling model for dividends in which the investment expenditures and external financing of a firm are held fixed and external investors cannot accurately assess current and future expected operating cash flows of the firm. Recall that under M&M, dividend policy is irrelevant because, in the absence of surplus operating cash flows, new equity or debt must be issued to finance the higher dividend, which in turn depresses the value of outstanding securities by the amount of the increased dividend. Because operating cash flows cannot be observed by outsiders, the dividend paid by the firm can help reveal, or "signal." when a firm truly has a surplus operating cash flow.

In the Miller and Rock model, a higher-than-expected dividend signals higher-than-expected net operating cash flows. Conversely, a higher-than-expected external financing or new security issue signals lower-than-expected operating cash flows. In other words, announcements of higher-than-expected dividends are positive signals that should increase the value of outstanding residual claims, and announcements of new securities issues are negative signals that should depress stock prices. The empirical evidence is broadly consistent with these predictions.[8]

Ross (1977) develops a signaling model in which higher debt levels are a signal to the market of higher-quality investments. The intuition is simple enough. Firms with riskier investment projects have higher expected costs of financial distress than sound firms for any level of debt. Firms with safer investments can afford to issue more debt to distinguish themselves from bad firms as long as the increase in the marginal expected cost of financial distress associated with the higher debt level is more than offset by the adverse selection costs (i.e., the amount of underpricing of the firm's securities) that are avoided by sending an informative signal.[9]

NOTES

1. This list is adapted directly from Myers (1984).
2. Even investing in riskless Treasuries is a zero NPV project and thus better than the project at hand.
3. As Myers (1984) warns, the value of ΔN is endogenously determined in a rational expectations equilibrium, so it is not quite correct to say that ΔN can be "controlled" by managers. But to a first approximation, the order of magnitude of ΔN does indeed depend on the risk of the claims issued.
4. See Diamond (1984, 1991).
5. See James (1987).
6. See also Harris and Raviv (1991) for the implications of the agency cost-specific capital structure issues.
7. Myers (1984) notes, however, that short-term dividends are sticky. He offers no explanation for why. See Fama and French (2000).
8. See, for example, Smith (1986a).
9. A key assumption in Ross's analysis is that firms' return distributions are distinguished by "first order stochastic dominance." Otherwise, it would not necessarily be true that better firms have lower expected financial distress costs *at all debt levels*.

CHAPTER 6

Distinguishing between Capital Structure Theories

Here we consider how to distinguish between the two dominant theories of capital structure—the trade-off and pecking order theories. First we discuss how the theories differ, and then we review the empirical evidence for and against the theories. We conclude with a discussion of how these theories will prove useful in later parts of the book.

COMPARISON OF THE THEORIES

The dynamic trade-off theory of capital structure drives firms to choose a securities capital structure that equates the benefits and costs of debt at the margin. Taxes, financial distress costs, the agency costs of free cash flows (i.e. overinvestment), the agency costs of outside equity, and the agency costs of debt (i.e., asset substitution and underinvestment) all pull in different directions to drive the firm to a capital structure optimum—and a leverage optimum.

In the pecking order theory, by contrast, capital structure is driven by the net cash flows of the firm and the divergence in beliefs of market participants from the private information held by managers about those net cash flows. In the signaling equilibrium that Myers (1984) develops—and that Myers and Majluf (1984) develop in greater detail—the cost of securities is really an adverse selection cost. Firms will issue equity only when it is overpriced. Investors know this and force firms to resort to equity financing only as a last resort.

At their core, the theories have many important similarities and deliver very similar empirical predictions. Nevertheless, there are some important differences, especially at the theoretical level.

Stocks versus Flows

One significant feature distinguishing the two theories is the relative importance of stocks versus flows in each one. The trade-off theory is driven largely by stock concepts—the value of debt outstanding, the size of the stock of debt relative to the total financial capital stock, the total face value on a stock of debt (in the overhang context), and so on. The pecking order theory, by contrast, seems to rely more on flows, such as new securities issued, and, more important, the *timing* of those issues.

As noted in Chapter 2, stocks and flows are inherently related. Surprisingly little research has been done, however, relating these two theories at this level. Barclay and Smith (1999) argue that a practical solution to this problem is for corporate treasurers and chief financial officers to consider the stock issues first and then the flow issues. This means first carefully identifying the benefits and costs of different leverage ratios and then developing financial policies aimed at sustaining those leverage ratios.

For a variety of reasons, firms invariably need to consider new security issues, whether to fine-tune a capital structure target or to address problems like shortfalls in internal funds that necessitate external financing for subsequent investments. Financial professionals should again undertake a judicious comparison of the benefits and costs of issuing different mixtures of external claims, including pecking order costs.

Although Barclay and Smith's recipe is not a theoretical unification of the stock and flow issues, it does have the merit of forcing financial professionals to think clearly in two dimensions rather than just stocks or only flows.

Optimality of Investment Decisions in the Two Theories

Underinvestment and overinvestment were potential problems in both the trade-off and pecking order theories. But the cause and the manifestation of these problems is subtly different in the two.

Underinvestment in the Two Models

As discussed in Chapter 4, debt can result in underinvestment to the extent that a debt overhang prompts managers as the agents of shareholders to forgo positive NPV projects whose benefits will inure mainly to debt holders. This is just one cost of debt that must be traded off against other benefits of debt.

In the pecking order analysis, when the underpricing of a security issue is significant because managers know more than investors about the positive aspects of a project, the benefits of that project may accrue more to the new investors in the firm than the existing ones. So far, this seems similar to Myers (1977). But in the adverse selection model, all securities issued may be underpriced if managers have favorable private information.

In fact, debt engenders fewer underinvestment problems than equity in the pecking order model because it is less susceptible to underpricing. All risky external finance can lead to underinvestment when managers have favorable information about the firm's investments that investors lack—hence the clear prescription is for firms to use internal finance when possible.

The difference in these theories lies mainly in their underlying assumptions. In the debt overhang model, underinvestment would not occur if equity holders could observe the true value of an investment project before the debt matures. But in the debt overhang model, both debt and equity do not know the value of the project until after debt matures. When the debt matures before the value of the investment project is revealed, equity holders will undertake a positive NPV project only if the NPV of the project is positive after debt has been paid off. If the NPV of the project is positive but only covers the debt repayment, then equity holders may opt to forgo the project since they will not benefit from it.

Asymmetric information thus is not required in order to have underinvestment problems associated with debt overhang. Too much leverage in any situation will make equity holders question their investment decisions, if only because equity holders simply do not directly benefit from their investment decisions. But in the pecking order model, underinvestment can occur because the shareholders do not reap the gains of a new investment project—but this time the wealth transfer may be from old shareholders to new shareholders as well as from old shareholders to new creditors. The driver of the problem in this model is not the existence of a class of security like debt but rather the true cash flows on the firm's investments together with the fact that investors cannot see that true value.

Overinvestment in the Two Models

Overinvestment is a problem in the trade-off theory because overinvestment in questionable projects is a decision managers make in their own interests at the expense of security holders, often as a result of excess free cash flows. The driver of the overinvestment problem is thus the managers' desire to invest in low- or negative-NPV projects to "flex their muscles" and "build their empires" instead of to maximize the value of the firm.

Overinvestment occurs in the pecking order theory only when managers have unfavorable information about the firm's investments that results in an overpricing of the firm's securities on the open market. In this situation, managers always will opt to issue the securities, because the worst they can do with the new funds is put them in the bank. No pursuits of perquisites by managers is required here. The sole driver of the overinvestment is the true net cash flows to the firm on the investment project together with the unobservability of those cash flows to security holders.

EVIDENCE ON THE IMPACT OF CAPITAL STRUCTURE CHANGES

The empirical evidence on these two theories is for the most part mixed. In some cases, the models predict the same things, and on those issues the evidence is indeed consistent with both models. But when the theories differ in their predictions, each has at least one major "black eye" when tested on actual data (Fama and French [2000]).

Both theories clearly suggest that issuing new equity is not the best means of obtaining investment capital for open corporations. As is traditional in the empirical corporate finance literature, the impact of decisions like issuing new equity typically is examined by studying the abnormal returns of a firm's stock just after the announcement of a new security issue. The abnormal return on Firm Fido's stock, for example, is the firm-specific component of the total return on Firm Fido, or that portion of Firm Fido's stock returns that does not reflect broad market fluctuations that impact all stocks.[1]

The announcement of new equity issues tend to be followed by large negative abnormal returns.[2] Announcements of new preferred stock issues also result in stock price declines, and there is a strong negative effect for low-rated preferred stock.[3] Firms that repurchase their stock, as expected, tend to have stock price increases following the repurchase announcement.[4]

Exchange offers also adhere to the expected pattern. Exchanges of debt for equity yield higher stock prices, whereas exchange offers that increase outstanding equity yield lower stock prices.[5]

Evidence also suggests that convertible debt is viewed more as equity than debt. Consequently, convertible debt issues result in negative stock price responses,[6] with a highly rated convertibles engendering a larger negative reaction than low-rated ones.[7]

The evidence on increases in leverage is much more controversial and mixed. For the most part, increases in debt that do not involve reductions in equity produce weak stock price responses that generally are not distinguishable from zero.[8] In other words, issuing debt appears to have no real impact on firms' stock prices.

Consistent with the pecking order theory, Eckbo and Masulis (1995) find that commercial banks are a dominant source of external finance in all major industrialized countries. Smith (1986a) and James (1987) further find significant and positive stock price responses to the announcement of new bank loans—virtually the only security type that is viewed as "good" for firm value. But this is consistent with both models—with the trade-off theory because bank loans are debt, and with the pecking order theory because bank loans are the highest form of external finance in the pecking order and with the proper monitoring may not be susceptible to the information asymmetry that creates adverse selection problems for the issuance of public securities.

Apart from the classical event study literature, cross-sectional and time-series regression analysis has been applied more recently to the capital structure problem. Fama and French (1998) find, for example, that changes in leverage and dividend payouts do tend to convey valuable signals about profitability.[9] Rajan and Zingales (1995) and Fama and French (1998) also both conclude that high leverage and increases in leverage tend to be bad news for firm value, as the pecking order theory predicts in contrast to the trade-off theory. Fama and French (1998) also find that the negative relation between debt and firm value persist even after controlling for earnings, dividends, investment, and research and development.

But the evidence is hardly uncontroversial. Barclay and Smith (1996), for example, find that the relations between a firm's leverage and earnings increase is negative, suggesting that larger earnings increases are associated with firms that have relatively less debt. Similarly, Fama and French (1999) find that debt has more benefits for firms when they are mature and have established track records. This is consistent with the agency cost stories about debt in the trade-off theory more than with the pecking order theory.

Finally, Fama and French (2000) test all the "financial implications" noted for the two theories in Chapters 4 and 5. Consistent with both theories, firms with higher dividend payouts are firms with fewer investments and higher profitability. And also consistent with both theories, larger firms are more leveraged, which is sensible because larger firms tend to have less earnings volatility, which implies higher debt capacity in either model.

Consistent with the pecking order theory and contradicting the trade-off theory, Fama and French (2000) determine that more profitable firms have less debt. But at direct odds with the pecking order theory, they find that small, less-levered, growth firms have the largest new equity issues. These firms should have high low-risk debt capacity, so this is a troubling result for the pecking order.

WHAT DO WE DO WITH THESE THEORIES?

The purpose of presenting these theories of capital structure and the evidence associated with them is not to develop some "test" of the theories themselves. Rather, these theories provide us with a framework for analyzing the transactions and structures reviewed later in this book.

Many of the ART and innovative financial transactions that have evolved in recent years are difficult to explain without the backdrop of the theories presented here. Similarly, a number of transactions make sense in the context of either the trade-off theory or the pecking order theory, but not both. The purpose of exploring the theories is to provide plausible explanations for the transactions. If we can understand the theoretical underpinnings that may be consistent with certain of these transactions, then we can better understand the assumptions under which the transactions make sense and, accordingly, draw inferences for when and why firms might derive value from entering into these transactions.

NOTES

1. Thompson (1995) provides a useful survey of these methods.
2. See, for example, Masulis and Korwar (1986), Smith (1986a), and Eckbo and Masulis (1995).
3. See Linn and Pinegar (1988).
4. See, for example, Vermaelen (1981).
5. See Masulis (1980).
6. See, for example, Smith (1986a).
7. See, for example, Mikkelson and Partch (1986).
8. See, for example, Eckbo (1986), Smith (1986a), and Fama and French (1998).
9. This is at least one interpretation—and probably the most plausible—of the results in Fama and French (1998).

CHAPTER 7

Risk and Signaling Capital

We have defined a firm's free cash flows as its cash flows in excess of those required to fund every positive-NPV project and growth opportunity it faces and to finance current operating expenses. In a M&M world, firms will be indifferent to whether such free cash flows are retained inside the firm or paid out through higher dividends. And with me-first rules, security holders will be equally indifferent to the firm's distribution policy. But when one or more M&M assumptions are violated, the firm's "optimal" free cash flow is dictated by its optimal capital structure, as is the "optimal" stock of internal funds.

In discussing both the trade-off and pecking order theories of optimal capital structure, we clearly established that most firms have an incentive to hold some internal funds when capital markets are imperfect and information is asymmetric. Two of the reasons for firms to hold cash balances in these theories are for risk mitigation and signaling purposes.

Despite the fact that risk mitigation and signaling are already motives for holding internal funds, some contend that firms should hold even more cash for risk and signaling purposes than the level of funds dictated by the firm's optimal financial policy. This excess capital required for risk and signaling purposes either needs to be funded from surplus free cash flows—impossible in a pecking order world where free cash flow is always used to build up "unrestricted" internal funds—or raised by issuing new claims to external investors.

Especially if excess capital is to be obtained from external sources, it can be extremely costly. In order for an external claims issue to make any sense, the benefit of excess capital thus needs to be particularly clear and high. The balance of this chapter thus answers the following questions:

- What do we mean by "excess capital," and how does it relate to the management of reserves?
- What are the benefits to certain firms of holding excess capital as risk capital?

■ What are the benefits to certain firms of holding excess capital as signaling capital?

■ What are the costs of excess paid-in capital obtained from new securities issues?

■ How can contingent capital facilities be used to help firms manage the costs of excess capital when such capital is demanded?

■ How much risk capital should a firm hold in the form of contingent capital?

EXCESS CAPITAL AND RESERVE MANAGEMENT

Recall Exhibit 2.1 in Chapter 2, where we previewed the possibility that firms would want to issue excess financial capital to finance "reserves" consisting of cash or low-risk marketable securities to be earmarked as risk or signaling capital. Some of the firm's investment capital and/or current assets—as opposed to its excess capital—already includes internal funds in excess of those required to finance current operations and every positive NPV project. But that might not be enough for all firms.

In our discussion relating to Exhibit 2.1, we indicated that the proceeds obtained from issuing excess financial capital claims likely would be placed into reserves. As we will demonstrate, the reason is that most excess capital is raised prior to when it is actually needed. Accordingly, we can think of excess capital as funds that are placed into segregated company accounts, most likely in the form of riskless debt or extremely low-risk and highly marketable and liquid securities.[1]

When a firm does choose to issue external claims to raise excess capital, those claims are usually unsecured. Consequently, if an insolvency occurs, the claims issued to raise excess capital receive the same priority they would have received had they been issued for investment capital raising purposes. Even if the excess capital has been placed into special reserve accounts, such accounts are mainly for management purposes and are not truly segregated, as would be the case, say, for assets pledged as collateral or customer margin funds under management. Accordingly, whatever assets in which the excess capital has been invested are part of the firm's total unsecured assets and thus are available to pay off all claim holders based on the priority of their claims.

As a final note, not all reserves managed by a firm are excess financial capital. Some reserves are treated as prefunded losses by firms as an outright cost of investment.

BENEFITS OF EXCESS CAPITAL HELD AS "RISK CAPITAL"

One reason that firms may opt to hold excess capital is to provide an extra cushion in the face of risk. We discuss the types of risk facing a firm in Chapter 9, but such a breakdown is not relevant here because of the "bluntness" of capital as a risk mitigation tool. Holding excess capital, say, to absorb unexpectedly large losses usually does not allow the firm to pick the source of those losses to which its risk capital will be applied. Accordingly, risk capital as discussed below is held essentially without regard to what is causing the risk facing the firm.

A distinction that is important, however, is why a firm is holding risk capital. Specifically, is the risk capital intended to help a firm finance its losses when they occur, or is the risk capital intended to absorb those losses directly—that is, is risk capital debt or equity? As long as the firm has retained rather than transferred a risk, of course, equity holders ultimately will bear the brunt of any losses that arise from those retained risks. So the question is more whether the risk capital is intended to absorb losses when they occur or intended to help smooth those losses over a longer period of time. We will return to this issue again in Chapter 17 and repeatedly in Part IV.

Reducing Expected Costs of Financial Distress

As discussed in Chapter 4, financial distress can be costly. Risk capital of the proper form can provide a means by which some firms can reduce their expected costs of financial distress. Expected distress costs include both the costs of distress and the probability of encountering distress. When the two are independent, a firm's expected distress cost is, in fact, simply the product of the probability and cost of distress. Risk capital can, in certain circumstances, help reduce both.

Care must be taken to distinguish the capital a firm allocates to risks already versus excess capital. A firm that accepts a project that exposes it for the first time to the risk of financial distress, for example, should have taken that risk into consideration as a cost of the project in its NPV calculations. Accordingly, capital already should have been set aside for those risks in a type of "loss reserve." Loss reserves should not be confused with excess capital and risk reserves. Expected losses are part of the costs of investment, and firms frequently prefund those losses on their balance sheets by earmarking specific funds to cover such realized losses.

Nevertheless, in many situations there is indeed justification for the firm to go over its normal amount of capital for risk control purposes. Exhibit 7.1 shows the distribution of the losses that a firm may incur over a specific period of time (e.g., cumulative losses over one quarter), with loss on the x-axis and the probability of loss on the y-axis. For now, ignore the component risks that may give rise to these losses and consider only that this distribution reflects all losses the firm may incur over the next quarter, either tracing to a specific group of risks (e.g., interest rate risks) or in aggregate.

The cumulative loss on the x-axis labeled point E[L] in the exhibit

Probability of Loss

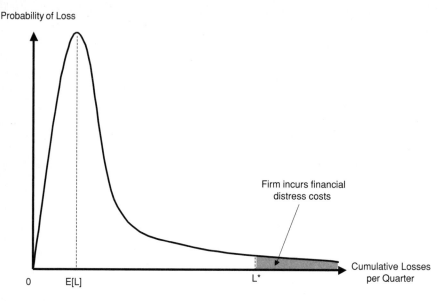

Firm incurs financial
distress costs

Cumulative Losses
per Quarter

0   E[L]   L*

EXHIBIT 7.1   Expected versus Unexpected Losses and Risk Capital

represents the expected losses the firm anticipates incurring over the next
quarter. Most firms that are actively involved in risky business lines routinely define some form of capital reserves to set aside for the purpose of
covering such expected losses. At a trading firm, for example, reserves frequently are defined to cover the following expected losses:

- Expected losses arising from the firm's inability to liquidate or hedge
  highly illiquid or exotic financial instruments in a timely fashion
- Expected accounting losses arising from the firm's purchase and sale of
  assets at bid and offer prices but its mark-to-market revaluation of positions at mid-market prices
- Expected losses arising from credit defaults by obligors to the firm
- Expected losses associated with the failure of internal controls, systems,
  and personnel (called "operational risk")
- Expected legal fees.

Similarly, banks routinely set aside capital for loan-loss reserves.

In all of these cases, the allocation of capital into a risk reserve to cover
expected losses is a normal cost of doing business. The quantity from the ori-
gin to level E[L] on Exhibit 7.1 thus should be the aggregate capital allocated
by the firm to its expected losses. Assuming the firm did its capital budgeting

homework correctly, this should be funded from the firm's investment capital. There is no role for excess capital in covering expected losses.

Now consider the cumulative loss on Exhibit 7.1 labeled L*. This may be the point at which the firm's losses become high enough that it starts to encounter financial distress costs. The cumulative loss reflected by the difference between point L* and point E[L] can be called the firm's unexpected loss. This quantity defines the firm's excess capital demand for the purpose of avoiding the costs of financial distress.[2]

Reducing Underinvestment Costs

Recall from Chapters 4 and 5 that in a firm with too little internal funds, underinvestment may occur when the firm is forced to reject positive NPV projects because funds are unavailable to make the required investment expenditures. Such problems are most likely to occur if the investment is required at a bad time for the firm, such as immediately following a large depletion of the firm's internal funds.[3]

Excess capital held to mitigate the potential for underivestment can be viewed as a type of *cash flow smoothing* device. When cash flows are abnormally high, funds flow into a risk capital reserve to cover losses when cash flows go into large deficits. When cash flows are too low relative to the investment opportunity set, the risk reserve can be tapped to replenish internal sources of funds for investment—somewhat like a firm making a loan to itself. Some call this "preloss financing," because the reserve was funded before the loss, and when the loss occurs the firm simply borrows from its own reserves to smooth its current performance.[4]

One clear potential benefit of preloss financing is avoiding the heightened costs of distressed debt financing—that is, issuing securities right after a large loss is expensive. But the bigger cost comes if the costs of external finance are so high following a depletion of funds that the firm has to curtail its spending on projects that it would otherwise certainly pursue.

To illustrate the benefit of a risk reserve in this context, consider a chemical firm—Firm Spock—that has three possible R&D projects for new chemical development that cost €100 million, €200 million, and €300 million, respectively.[5] Assume these are mutually exclusive projects that yield riskless discounted net cash flows of €200 million, €1,000 million, and €450 million, respectively. The resulting project NPVs are shown in Table 7.1.

From the table, Firm Spock clearly prefers Project 2, where a €200 million expenditure results in a €800 million NPV. Nevertheless, the NPVs of all three projects are positive, thus suggesting that Spock will undertake all three projects if it possibly can.

Now suppose that Spock has financed itself with debt and equity and that its debt is floating rate. Interest rate changes can cause Firm Spock's debt

TABLE 7.1 Capital Budget for Firm Spock's Chemical Production (€millions)

	Investment Expenditure	Discounted Cash Flows	NPV
Project 1	€100	€200	€100
Project 2	€200	€1,000	€800
Project 3	€400	€450	€50

service burden to fluctuate by as much as €150 million per annum. If Firm Spock's current net income plus depreciation plus retained earnings is €250 million, this means that interest rate changes can cause the free cash flows of the firm to fluctuate from €100 million to €400 million over the course of a year. Assume that Spock cannot issue new debt or equity following a rise in rates and an associated treasury loss.

Table 7.2 shows the net impact of the two interest rate scenarios on Spock's capital budget.

From the table, it is clear that the firm will be forced to choose a suboptimally low level of investment spending if interest rates rise and free cash flows fall to €100 million. The result is equivalent to the underinvestment problem, in which the firm essentially forgoes an additional €800 million in net present value terms purely because its free cash flows are too low to fund the project. A risk reserve would help the firm address this problem by providing a standby source of internal capital in the event of an unexpected loss due to interest rate increases.

Notice that this manifestation of the underinvestment problem is primarily a cash liquidity problem—a lack of internal funds that forces the market to reject risky but positive-NPV investments because of the costs of raising new liquid capital during periods of financial distress. Fluctuations in the firm's value or accounting earnings will not give rise to this problem unless also accompanied by a hit to internal cash funds.

BENEFITS OF EXCESS CAPITAL HELD AS "SIGNALING CAPITAL"

Asymmetric information can make it difficult for investors to distinguish "good" firms from "bad" ones along a variety of dimensions. As we saw in

TABLE 7.2 Firm Spock's Project Acceptance Decisions (€millions)

Interest Rates	Free Cash Flow	Project(s)	Investment	NPV
Down	€400	1 and 2	€300	€900
Flat	€250	2	€200	€800
Up	€100	1	€100	€100

Chapter 5, changes in a firm's capital structure often signal the true quality of the firm's investments when managers have information that investors do not have. In the Miller and Rock (1985) model, for example, higher dividends signal high-quality investments, whereas any public security issue signals low-quality investments.

Some argue that holding excess capital is itself a form of signaling. But care must be taken not to confuse signaling capital with the arguments that have already been presented for and against just having free cash flows. In addition, truly to send an informative signal to the capital market, it must be impossible for "bad" firms to imitate the signals that "good" firms send.[6]

Earnings Smoothing

2001 Economics Nobel Prize winner Michael Spence (1973) argues that a signal can be valuable for its sender when (1) the signaling action has some value to the firm apart from just the information it conveys, and (2) it is costly for "bad" firms to imitate "good" firms in sending this signal. Spence developed these criteria while analyzing job markets in which more talented individuals cannot easily distinguish themselves from less talented individuals. Talented workers thus are "pooled" with less talented ones for wage rate determination, resulting in good people being underpaid and bad people being overpaid—a "lemons in the labor market" problem.

This sort of a "pooling" equilibrium is what most signals are intended to break and to replace with a "separating" equilibrium in which each type of worker is properly paid. As a means of separating themselves from the less talented part of the workforce, individuals with more talent in the Spence model can incur the costs of acquiring more education. The higher the cost imposed on low-quality workers relative to the cost borne by high-quality workers, the more efficient—and likely the more effective—the signal will be. So highly talented members of the workforce will tend to acquire education in areas that are easiest for them *and* hardest for those with less talent to study.

Holding signaling capital also can help "good" firms separate themselves from "bad" ones. One common application of this actually involves good firms attempting to reverse the effects of incorrect or extremely noisy signals sent through mechanisms like accounting earnings that result in their being confused with genuine dogs. This signaling argument frequently is used as a justification for firms to engage in smoothing accounting information by using earnings volatility reserves, hidden reserves, and the like. Despite frequent criticisms of such reserves, they can make economic sense when used for this reason.

Consider a French telecommunications firm whose earnings are strongly influenced by, say, the U.S. dollar/French franc exchange rate. Specifically, the firm has "translation risk" arising from its need to reexpress its dollar earnings in francs on its U.S. operations. Adverse moves in the exchange rate may well not impose any economic losses on the firm because it has not repatriated dollar-denominated profits—and perhaps never will, using them instead to fund dollar investments or repay dollar-denominated debt—but the exchange rate move still will show up as a negative influence on earnings because the firm has dollar business but denominates its accounts in francs. In other words, the firm's earnings have a lot of "noise" in them about the investment activities of the firm; earnings are sensitive to factors other than the firm's true investments, thus making it quite hard for analysts and investors to interpret earnings as a signal of the firm's investment policies.

Now suppose the telecommunications sector experiences significant negative earnings shocks that are highly correlated across firms—as in 2000–2001—and more than one telecom firm is viewed as approaching financial distress. Imagine further that the dollar/franc exchange rate has moved against our French firm during the same period.

If the firm in question has made sound investments but still has high earnings volatility, there is a significant risk that investors will mistakenly include them in the category of firms whose investments have performed poorly. This could be costly for the firm in several ways. It could increase the firm's borrowing costs, cause a deterioration in its credit rating, or perhaps even deprive it of the ability to exploit large investment projects. A firm believed to be performing badly, for example, could have considerable trouble putting together the financing for a takeover.

Holding signaling capital can help firms attenuate the effects of these earnings swings that are not a result of an actual decline in profitability. In other words, our French firm has not taken any economic losses in the reporting period, but it has no real way of communicating that to investors. One possibility is simply for the French telecom to be so well capitalized that investors could not possibly mistake it for a firm about to encounter financial distress. Another is for the firm to use its signaling capital to make a dividend payment that is higher than expected, communicating (à la Miller and Rock) that its earnings are not revealing the firm's true financial performance. In either case, excess capital held by the firm prevents others from confusing it for a firm experiencing truly negative performance.

Project Finance

The signals sent by holding extra capital were informative mainly because "good" firms can send them at a much lower cost than "bad" firms. In this section, we consider a different type of signal, known as a "money-burning" signal. Unlike the Spence (1973) model, a money-burning signal is a signal that is equally costly for firms for all types. In addition, a money-burning signal has no independent value to the firm apart from the signal it sends.

Nelson (1970, 1974) argues that advertising is a type of money burning signal.[7] In his model, firms sell two types of products: "search goods" and "experience goods." The former is any good whose quality and product attributes can be ascertained by inspection, and the latter is any good that must be "used" in order to determine its characteristics and true value. Signaling is not required for the first type of good, but it can make a difference in the second case. Because a high-quality product is more likely to attract repeat purchases, an initial sale of an experience good is more valuable to a high-quality producer. Good firms thus are willing to spend money on advertising with essentially no informational content to separate themselves from bad firms. Milgrom and Roberts (1986) extend this analysis and show that the price of an experience good also can be a signal of its quality and that in equilibrium, firms will opt to signal using both price and advertising expenditures.

Money burning can make sense for firms as a way of addressing adverse selection problems, but Daniel and Titman (1995) argue convincingly that equity-financed money burning rarely makes sense. They show that issuing new equity and burning money is equivalent just to underpricing an equity issue deliberately—namely, issuing the equity to raise funds, but rebating the funds to investors instead of burning them.

Consider the case of an initial public offering (IPO).[8] Suppose there are two types of firms—good and bad—and the good type considers burning money to try to differentiate itself from the bad type. To accomplish this successfully, the firm would need to underprice its IPO to a level at or below the price of the IPO for the bad firm. But the good type also always has the alternative of not bothering to differentiate itself. The pooling equilibrium of good and bad types would result in an IPO price reflecting the average of the good and bad firms. Because this price would be higher than the price the good firm would need to set for its IPO to achieve a separating equilibrium, the good firm will prefer just to tolerate being pooled with bad types.

Welch (1989) considers an IPO done for project financing, in which a firm that issues equity also must take on a related project. If the project has a positive NPV for good firms and a negative-NPV for bad firms, a good firm may then differentiate itself successfully from the bad one by issuing stock. The bad firm will not mimic the good firm as long as the negative-NPV project imposes a cost on the bad firm that is higher than the amount by which the IPO is overpriced for that bad firm. If the NPV of the project is only slightly negative, then the bad firm may choose to mimic the good firm and accept the project, believing it will recover more from the overpricing of equity in a polling equilibrium than it will lose on the project. But in this case, the good firm can *under*price its IPO—just enough so that the costs to the bad firm of mimicking the good firm become just higher than the benefits.

Models like the one proposed by Welch (1989) may have some applicability to the incentives for firms to hold excess financial capital for signaling purposes. If we assume that firms sometimes want signaling capital associated with specific investment project opportunities, then the argument for issuing underpriced securities to raise signaling capital can make sense. Like Welch, suppose firms that issue securities for this reason also must accept the project in question, but suppose the project has a negative NPV for "bad" firms. Good firms may issue underpriced securities to raise capital that is above the amount required to invest in the project in question but that differentiates them from bad firms.

Consider an example of Firms Goldfinger and Blowfeld, where Goldfinger is a "good" firm and Blowfeld is a "bad" one. Goldfinger may want to differentiate itself from Blowfeld for a variety of reasons. The firms might be competitors, and Goldfinger believes being perceived as good will give it longer-term customer relationships.

It makes no sense for Goldfinger to try to differentiate itself by burning money. If Goldfinger issues new securities purely to raise signaling capital, the market will drop into normal pecking order behavior and assume Goldfinger has unfavorable private information and that its securities are overpriced, thus leading to an underpricing. Blowfeld can do the same thing and generate the same signaling capital, thus perfectly mimicking Goldfinger. The resulting capital raised thus conveys no useful information to investors and is expensive.

Now consider a third firm—a large dot-com called Bond. Suppose Goldfinger can realize substantial economies of scope and cost savings through the acquisition of Bond that Blowfeld cannot. Taking the cost of the acquisition into consideration, Goldfinger's acquisition of Bond is a positive-NPV project, and Blowfeld's is not.

Goldfinger has an incentive to acquire Bond anyway because the acquisition would represent a value-enhancing investment project. But Goldfinger also can use the acquisition as an opportunity to burn money and differentiate itself from Blowfeld. Money burning in a corporate action is not difficult. Goldfinger need only pay a lot of investment banking, advertising, public relations, and legal fees to cross over into the money-burning realm at some point. Blowfeld will not do this, because the acquisition of Bond is negative NPV. The costs to Blowfeld of imitating Goldfinger are thus too high.

Now consider the problem from an *ex ante* standpoint. Suppose Goldfinger issues securities to raise excess capital in order to fund as yet unidentified investment opportunities, like Myers's real options. Importantly, Goldfinger deliberately raises more funds than it needs specifically to discourage Blowfeld from imitating it. And indeed, to the extent that Blowfeld considers it likely that at least some of the investment projects that are valuable to Goldfinger will not be valuable to Blowfeld, maintaining a stock of signaling capital to fund future investments will be too costly for Blowfeld.

Admittedly these examples are fairly stylized. Holding signaling capital definitely seems more plausible when the firm in question has lower costs than its rivals, as in Spence (1973). Nevertheless, it is possible that a firm might deliberately issue underpriced securities in order to finance the acquisition of signaling capital even when the cost is the same to all of its rivals—but only because the total cost is lower due to the correlation of the firm's signaling capital and the pursuit of some future investment project.[9]

Risk versus Signaling Capital

The information asymmetry that gives rise to the pecking order and to most signaling problems is between investors and the firm's managers. But suppose that the customers of a firm are the less-informed parties. If the concern customers have is the creditworthiness of the firm, signaling capital can help avert such concerns.

Consider, for example, a financial clearinghouse whose primary business is the clearing and settlement of secondary market securities trades and derivatives transactions. If the clearinghouse acts as a "central counterparty," then it essentially guarantees performance on all transactions. Apart from prudential risk management guidelines to help a clearinghouse reduce the likelihood of a member's default, such clearinghouses usually also hold a "default reserve" funded by the clearinghouse, its users, or both—and, as we shall see in Chapters 20 and 21, often protected with financial guarantees.

A clearinghouse could hold default reserves either for risk or for signaling purposes. To see why, suppose Clearinghouse Kirk maintains a $200 million default reserve of its own funds and participant contributions to cover losses that could arise in the event of a user's failure to honor its trading and clearing obligations. Now suppose Kirk believes that the default of any large participant would indeed impose a loss on the clearinghouse of around $200 million. Accordingly, Kirk is considering adding another $100 million to that amount to bring the fund up to $300 million.

On one hand, the extra $100 million in capital can function as risk capital for any of the reasons noted earlier. A complete depletion of the fund could be tantamount to a forced shutdown of the clearinghouse the day after the loss, so Kirk may wish the additional $100 million to avoid the costs of financial distress. Similarly, Kirk might want the $100 million cushion to "buy time" to replenish the size of the fund gradually without having to incur distressed financing costs by borrowing new money the day after announcing a major loss.

On the other hand, the extra $100 million in capital could function as a signal of the clearinghouse's integrity to prospective customers. Just because Kirk's managers know the largest loss is unlikely to exceed $200 million, customers might not know that. Incurring the cost of raising an additional $100 million is a way for Kirk to signal its information to outsiders that it can weather a large loss. This $100 million might not ever be needed in a practical sense, but the fact that Kirk incurred the costs to raise it and allocate it to reserves may well give customers the confidence they need to continue clearing their transactions through Kirk.

Risk and signaling capital thus clearly may be related to one another. As an operational matter, however, distinguishing between risk and signaling capital does not much matter. Signaling capital appears on the economic balance sheet in Exhibit 2.1 in exactly the same way that risk capital does—as internal funds or external claims on the sources of funds side and as riskless assets held in reserves on the uses of funds side.

As an economic matter, there are situations where commingling risk and signaling will not matter. But there are also situations where it does matter. Specifically, if excess capital is held to signal financial strength but is perceived as being risk capital, the wrong signal may be sent. If Kirk raises excess capital in an effort to show its financial integrity to customers but its action is mistaken for engaging in preloss financing, for example, the value of the signal may be greatly reduced. Customers who do not know the potential size of a large loss may simply infer that the exposure of the clearinghouse is now $300 million.

COSTS OF EXTERNALLY RAISED EXCESS PAID-IN CAPITAL

A firm that seeks excess paid-in capital from external sources as either risk or signaling capital will have to issue new claims to raise cash, use that cash to acquire riskless bonds, and then lump those bonds into the rest of the firm's unsecured assets. Perhaps the firm will make a separate balance sheet entry declaring the bonds to be risk reserves of some kind, but they remain unsecured. Especially if the firm has issued low-priority claims like subdebt or equity, the net result is that the firm has issued highly risky and costly securities to raise funds that are essentially being parked in a risk-free investment fund.

As noted previously, one potential drawback of holding excess capital is avoiding the negative signal that the excess capital itself might send. Just imagine explaining the above process at a shareholder meeting—that your latest seasoned equity offering had been used solely to fund the acquisition of riskless debt. A firm in this situation runs the great risk of being confused for a Jensen (1986) or Jensen and Meckling (1976) overinvester that might be raising new money only to plow it into negative NPV projects.

Of course, if the benefits discussed in the two prior sections are high enough, then it makes sense to raise the excess capital—and perhaps hire a good public relations firm at the same time to handle the investor relations end of things. But the benefits of excess capital must be more than simply positive. They must be high enough to exceed the costs at the margin. Specifically, if a firm issues new securities at its cost of capital and invests the proceeds from the security issue in riskless bonds, the marginal benefits of additional reserves must at a minimum exceed the difference between the firm's cost of capital and the risk-free rate.

To examine these two costs of issuing external claims purely to invest in riskless bonds as a risk or signaling reserve, we consider the case of a debt financing and then an equity financing, followed by a brief discussion on combinations of the two.

Reserves Financed with New Risky Debt

Suppose first the firm issues new debt to finance the acquisition of riskless bonds to be placed in an excess capital reserve and that the new debt has the same priority as the outstanding debt. In this case, we can imagine that the firm is funding a risk capital reserve as a method of financing its risks over time. Equity holders eventually bear the risks as before, but issuing new debt to fund a risk capital reserve can help a firm prefund losses and smooth the timing of when the loss actually is borne by equity holders.

To avoid the complications of discounting, we compare two different firms, both on date T on which both firms' debt matures. Assume both firms have outstanding unrestricted common stock and risky debt.

Impact on the Value of the Firm

If the firm issues new risky debt to fund the acquisition of riskless debt that will be worth Z on date T, the firm's assets are no riskier than before. But there are more of them—by exactly amount Z raised from the debt issue. At the same time, however, there is now Z more debt that must be repaid.

Firms Ness and Capone can be presumed to hold identical risky assets. The material difference in the two firms is that Firm Capone also has issued extra debt to raise excess capital that has been placed into a risk or signaling reserve. Specifically, Firm Ness has FV in debt outstanding, whereas Firm Capone has FV + Z in debt outstanding to reflect the additional Z dollars Capone has borrowed to finance its excess capital. Capone has invested the proceeds Z entirely in riskless debt.

Remembering from Chapter 1 that the value of the firm is equal to the value of a call struck at FV less the value of a put struck at FV plus a riskless loan of FV, the market value of Firm Ness at time T is

$$V^N(T) = A(T) = C(A(T),FV,T) - P(A(T),FV,T) + FV \qquad (7.1)$$

where $C(A(T),FV,T)$ denotes the time T market value of the firm's total residual claims as a function of $A(T)$ given a debt stock of FV and where

P(A(T),FV,T) denotes the time T market value of the firm's risky debt obligations with face value FV as a function of A(T).

Firm Capone has FV + Z debt outstanding, but because the proceeds have been placed into a riskless reserve, Capone also has A(T) + Z in assets. In other words, because the risky assets of the two firms are the same, Capone also will have exactly Z dollars more than Ness, no matter what time T assets are actually worth. The T market value of Firm Capone thus is

$$V^C(T) = A(T) + Z = C(A(T) + Z, FV + Z,T)$$
$$- P(A(T) + Z,FV + Z,T) + FV + Z \qquad (7.2)$$

Comparing equation 7.2 with 7.1, we see that Firm Capone thus has a higher value than Firm Ness by Z dollars exactly—hardly surprising.

Note the differences between equations 7.2 and 7.1. First, the assets of Firm Capone are higher by Z to reflect the riskless bonds now held in reserves on the firm's balance sheet. Second, the face value of the debt on the right-hand side of 7.2 is also higher by Z to reflect the fact that those reserves essentially belong to bond holders. Finally, note two changes in the option-equivalent expressions for equity and debt's put. The increase in the face value of the firm's total debt has increased the strike price of the options from FV to FV + Z. In addition, the underlying of the options has now changed. Instead of being written on A(T), as in the case of Firm Ness, the options representing the financial capital claims of Firm Capone are now written on A(T) + Z.

Readers can verify the expression for the value of Firm Capone by recognizing that equation 7.2 can be rewritten as

$$V^C(T) = A(T) + Z = \max[A(T) + Z - FV - Z , 0]$$
$$+ \min[A(T) + Z - FV - Z , 0] + FV + Z$$

or

$$V^C(T) = A(T) + Z = A(T) + Z$$

Risk of Claims

Exhibit 7.2 shows the market value of the equity and debt claims issued by Firms Ness and Capone using the options framework developed in Chapter 1. The y-axis shows the value of the firm and the value of the two firm's debt and equity claims in date T dollars. The x-axis shows the possible value of the firm's assets A(T) at time T.

The market value of firm Ness's equity can be viewed as a long call struck at FV and its total debt as a short put struck at FV together with a riskless loan of amount FV. The underlying of Ness's option claims is the firm's assets A(T). For Capone, equity is valued as a long call at FV + Z and debt as a short

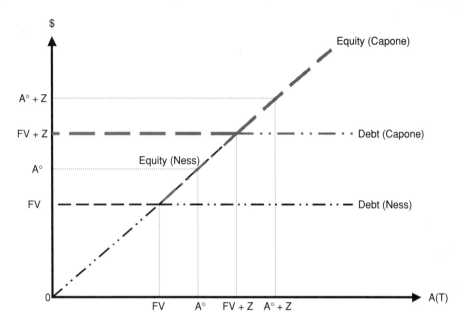

EXHIBIT 7.2   Values of Equity and Debt for Firms Ness and Capone after a New Debt Issue

put at FV + Z plus a loan of FV + Z. But the underlying of these options is now A(T) + Z to reflect the addition of riskless bonds to the firm's assets.

Some simple geometry allows us to verify that the value of equity for the two firms is the same. Choose any arbitrary asset value A°(T). At that asset value, Firm Ness's equity has a claim on date T on A°(T) in assets less the debt-servicing obligation of FV. For that same asset value, the equity of Firm Capone has a claim on A°(T) + Z, which is higher than the assets on which Firm Ness's shareholders have a claim. But Capone's debt-servicing obligations are also higher—by Z. Because Capone's assets have risen by exactly the same amount as its debt, the equity of Firm Capone is worth A°(T) + Z – FV – Z, or A°(T) – FV. For any A°(T), this relation will be true. Consequently, the value of total equity issued by Firm Ness is equal to the value of total equity issued by Firm Capone.

Exhibit 7.3 sheds some light on the market values of the two firms' debt. Unlike Exhibit 7.2, the y-axis of Exhibit 7.3 now shows the value of each claim separately rather than additively. The x-axis is still the terminal value of the firm's assets, and the probability associated with that asset value is now shown on the second y-axis on the right. The graph shows the terminal payoffs to the two firms' debt and equity claims as well as two probability distributions from which A(T) will be drawn.

Because Ness and Capone hold the same risky assets, the probability distribution $f(A)$ from which the time T asset value is drawn is the same for both firms. Specifically, the shape of the distribution is the same, as are its variance, skewness, and kurtosis. But the mean of the distribution is different. The distribution from which Capone's terminal asset value is drawn is to the right of the Ness asset distribution by exactly Z for every possible A(T)—that is, the distribution for Capone $f(A + Z)$ is equal to the distribution for Ness $f(A)$ plus the addition of the riskless Z dollars in assets that the proceeds of the new debt issue has funded. Note that $f(A + Z) = f(A) + Z$, so that the distribution of A + Z is equivalent to adding Z to whatever is drawn from the distribution $f(A)$ because Z is a constant.

To evaluate the risk of the debt of the two firms, consider the probability of a default. For Firm Ness, the probability of not receiving a full repayment of the debt is

$$\Pr[A(T) \le FV] = \int_0^{FV} f(A)dA \qquad (7.3)$$

The probability of default on the debt issued by Capone is given by

$$\Pr[A(T) + Z \le FV + Z] = \int_Z^{FV+Z} f(A + Z)dA \qquad (7.4)$$

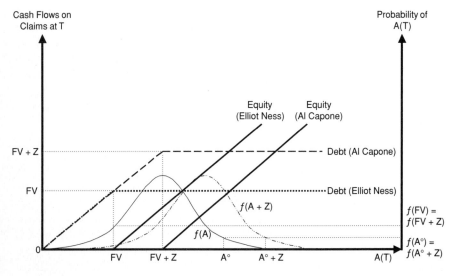

EXHIBIT 7.3   Securities Values of Firms Ness and Capone after a New Debt Issue

Although it should be obvious that adding the same constant to both sides of the probability distribution function leaves the original result unchanged, we can show this more formally. Starting with equation 7.3, we do a change of variables and let y = A + Z. The original interval over which we integrated was A ∈ [0, FV]. For the new variable y, the new limits of integration are y ∈ [Z,FV + Z]. Substituting the new limits of integration and transformed variable into 7.3 yields:

$$\int_0^{FV} f(A)dA = \int_Z^{FV+Z} f(y)dy = \int_Z^{FV+Z} f(A+Z)dA \qquad (7.5)$$

which is the same as equation 7.3. So, Ness and Capone debt have identical default probabilities. This is confirmed graphically on Exhibit 7.3.

Dilution

If the risk of the securities issued by the two firms is identical, the securities' values will be identical. But the value of Firm Capone is Z dollars higher than the value of Firm Ness. This extra Z does not mean there is an arbitrage opportunity here and that firms can make their security holders better off by issuing bonds and loading up on riskless debt. It simply means that the higher value of Capone had to come from somewhere other than a change in the value of total debt and equity.

The explanation, of course, is that the extra debt dilutes the debt holders of Capone. To see this, let us rewrite equations 7.1 and 7.2 using some new notation:

$$V^N(T) = A(T) = \eta^N c^N - \beta^N p^N + \beta^N q \qquad (7.6)$$

$$V^C(T) = A(T) + Z = \eta^C c^C - \beta^C p^C + \beta^C q \qquad (7.7)$$

where η is the number of shares of common stock outstanding, c is the price of the stock per share (i.e., each shareholder's call on a prorated portion of the firm's assets net of debt repayments), β is the number of bondholders, p is the price of the put component of the debt issue per bond, q is the face value of a single bond, and the superscripts N and C denote Ness and Capone, respectively. For ease of comparison, we can immediately rewrite 7.6 and 7.7 as

$$V^N(T) = A(T) = \eta^N c^N - \beta^N p^N + \beta^N q \qquad (7.8)$$

$$V^C(T) = A(T) + Z = (\eta^N + e)c^C + (\beta^N + d)(q - p^C) \qquad (7.9)$$

where we express the number of equity shares and bonds outstanding at Firm Capone as the number of shares and bonds outstanding at Ness plus a constant for each security type, so that $\eta^C = \eta^N + e$ and $\beta^C = \beta^N + d$, where e and d represent the number of shares and bonds Capone has issued in excess of Ness.

Capone is different from Ness only by the addition Z in assets and debt burden. This enables us to recognize that

$$Z = dq$$

so that equation 7.9 can be rewritten as

$$V^C(T) = A(T) + dq = (\eta^N + e)c^C + (\beta^N + d)(q - p^C) \qquad (7.10)$$

We know that the total value of Capone's residual claims is equal to the total value of Ness's residual claims. Because Capone has no additional shares outstanding—that is, $e = 0$—we also know that the per share prices of the two firms must be identical. Using this fact and equations 7.8 and 7.10, we can compare the price per bond of debt issued by Capone with debt issued by Ness:

$$p^N = p^C\left(1 + \frac{d}{\beta^N}\right) \qquad (7.11)$$

So the price per bond for debt issued by Ness is worth more than the price per bond for debt issued by a percentage equal to the proportion of additional bond holders in Capone. If Capone has 10 percent more bond holders than Ness, the price per bond for Ness debt will be 10 percent higher than the price per bond of Capone debt. It is easy to verify that the increased value of Capone relative to Ness by Z dollars comes entirely from this dilution effect.

Although our example has involved two separate firms, we can generalize the result to a single firm easily enough. Namely, the increase in the value of the firm resulting from the increase in assets by Z risklessly is financed entirely by old bond holders. The price paid by the new bond holders will fairly reflect the new asset value of the firm, but not so for existing bond holders.

Holding risk capital reserves may have benefits for the firm as a whole, but an issue of debt to finance the funding of these reserves is costly only for existing debt holders. To the extent those debt holders are not the sole beneficiaries of the excess capital, the funding of the reserve is not any different than the asset substitution problem discussed in Chapter 4.

Reserves Financed with New Equity

Now let us consider the case in which Firm Ness remains as before and Firm Capone finances a risk capital reserve with a new equity issue that will be worth Z risklessly on date T. In this case, the firm is simply augmenting the equity capital available to absorb losses arising from risks retained by the firm rather than spreading those losses over time through risk financing. The face value of the debt for Capone in this case is the same as Firm Ness at FV.

Impact on the Value of the Firm

The market value of Firm Ness at time T is still given as

$$V^N(T) = A(T) = C(A(T),FV,T) - P(A(T),FV,T) + FV \qquad (7.12)$$

Firm Capone has FV debt outstanding but now has A(T) + Z in assets. The T market value of Firm Capone thus is

$$V^C(T) = A(T) + Z = C(A(T) + Z,FV,T) - P(A(T) + Z,FV,T) + FV \quad (7.13)$$

Again note the difference in equations 7.13 and 7.12. Firm Capone evidently still has a higher asset value than Firm Ness by Z dollars—exactly the amount of additional assets. On the right-hand side, this is reflected by a change in the underlying asset on which the claims as options are based from A(T) to A(T) + Z. But unlike before, this time there is no change in the size of the riskless loan to debt holders and hence no change in the option strike prices.

Risk of Claims and Dilution

Exhibit 7.4 shows that without an increase in the firm's debt obligations, issuing equity to fund the acquisition of riskless bonds does not change the payoff diagrams for either debt or equity. But it does change their risks. Adding Z to current assets at every possible level of A(T) has the effect of making the equity call deeper in the money and the equity put deeper out of the money for A(T) > FV. For A(T) < FV, equity gets less out of the money or perhaps moves into the money, and conversely for debt. In either case, both equity and debt are better off than before. (Remember that debt is a riskless loan plus a written put that becomes more valuable when the underlying price rises.)

Subtracting equation 7.12 from 7.13 yields the following difference of values between Capone and Ness:

$$V^C(T) - V^N(T) = Z = [C(A(T) + Z,FV) - C(A(T),FV)]$$
$$- [P(A(T) + Z,FV) - P(A(T),FV)] \qquad (7.14)$$

Recognizing in this case that $\beta^C = \beta^N$, we can rewrite equation 7.14 as

$$\eta^C(c^C - c^N) + ec^C - \beta^C(p^C - p^N) = Z \qquad (7.15)$$

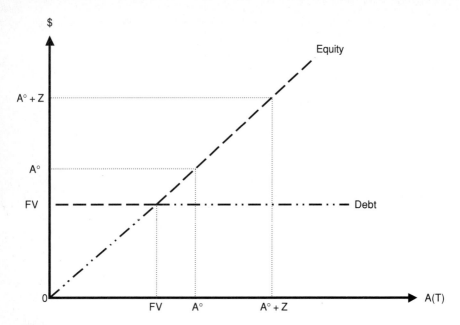

EXHIBIT 7.4   Values of Equity and Debt for Firms Ness and Capone after a New Equity Issue

Unfortunately, there is little else we can say about where the additional Z comes from. The pure risk component is ambiguous. Although $c^C > c^N$ and $p^C < p^N$, the relative magnitudes depend on the current market value of the firm's assets. Specifically, the more in the money an option, the greater the price difference will be for a given difference in the underlying asset distribution between $f(A)$ and $f(A + Z)$.

We can examine the situation in a couple of specific cases. If A(T) is extremely high, then the equity options are so deep in the money that they behave similarly to the underlying. The difference in the total equity value of Capone relative to Ness thus will be approximately Z, and the debt values of the two firms will be virtually the same. So

$$C(A(T) + Z, FV) - C(A(T), FV) \approx Z$$

and

$$P(A(T) + Z, FV) - P(A(T), FV) \approx 0$$

Because the number of bonds outstanding at the firms are equal, we can further see that

$$(p^C - p^N) \approx 0$$

so that the equity dilution is given by

$$c^N = c^C \left(1 + \frac{e}{\eta^N}\right) \tag{7.16}$$

So when the firm's assets are high relative to the face value of its debt, issuing new equity to fund a riskless bond capital reserve will be paid for almost entirely by equity through a dilution. Specifically, old equity shareholders pay for the increase in firm value by Z.

If the equity call option is close to at the money, though, then the value of debt will rise appreciably in response to a riskless stock of bonds being added to the assets of the firm; debt then has a higher likelihood of not defaulting. Equity values also still rise, but not by as much. And the dilution effect still hits equity. In this situation, debt thus unambiguously gains at the expense of equity because debt goes up in value with no dilution, whereas any increase in equity value is tempered by the dilutive effects of the new issue.

Importance of Me-First Rules

Both a new debt and a new equity issue give rise to the type of asset substitution problem mentioned in Chapter 4. Even if the benefits of holding excess capital are high, an all-debt or all-equity issue to finance the acquisition of that capital will have negative relative wealth effects. The benefits of the excess capital likely will accrue to both stock- and bond holders, but the dilutive costs are borne only by one class of claimants in the above examples. Apart from being impractical, such financing schemes also may well violate other protections the firm has in place against asset substitution (e.g., covenants). In addition, this will constitute a clear violation of the market value rule to maximize total security holder welfare rather than the oft-touted but nevertheless incorrect goal of maximizing shareholder welfare.

If the net benefits to the firm of holding excess capital are positive and the firm considers externally raised paid-in capital to be the best or only means of funding the acquisition of that capital, the firm should design the security issue to try to minimize the distortionary relative wealth effects discussed above. Otherwise, deviation from the market value rule will make the firm an immediate takeover target, as discussed in Chapter 3 and in Fama (1976). The obvious solution in either case is to establish me-first rules.

Or the firm could choose an alternative to paid-in capital as a source of its risk and signaling capital.

MANAGING THE COSTS OF EXCESS CAPITAL WITH CONTINGENT CAPITAL FACILITIES

Many firms do indeed utilize excess capital today, especially for the purpose of maintaining earnings volatility smoothing reserves, loan-loss reserves, liquidity reserves, and the like. Before incurring the significant costs of the former, firms should ensure that the benefits of holding excess capital are genuinely higher than the costs of raising it.

One way to tilt the benefit-cost calculus in favor of firms demanding excess capital is to reduce the costs of issuing new securities by utilizing contingent rather than paid-in capital. As we discussed in Chapter 2, contingent capital facilities are essentially options on the issuance of paid-in capital claims. Accordingly, they are likely to be more expensive than just issuing new securities because the option premium paid for the contingency option must be added to the cost of capital underlying the facility. But such facilities may more than pay for themselves by creating cost savings in other areas. We consider three examples.

Reducing Financial Distress Costs

A major opportunity for achieving cost savings through the use of contingent capital facilities—as well as for avoiding some of the nasty relative wealth effects just explored—is created by the presence of "triggers" in such facilities. Consider, for example, contingent risk capital used to reduce the expected cost of financial distress. Setting aside what the trigger actually would look like (see Chapter 21) assume it can be constructed to ensure that the firm receives a capital infusion early enough to avoid the costs of financial distress but nevertheless at a time when financial distress is on the horizon.

In this situation a contingent risk capital facility will be most highly valued when both debt and equity viewed as options are nearly at the money. A contingent risk capital facility would be virtually useless to both claimants if equity is deeply in the money and debt deeply out of the money. And if the converse is true, the facility likely will be too late to help. But if the facility can be drawn when the options comprising the firm's securities capital structure are nearly at the money, then both debt and equity will benefit from the infusion of funds, thereby at least partially mitigating any adverse relative wealth effects of dilution when the contingent facility becomes a real balance sheet claim.

The claim underlying the contingent capital facility also may, however, change the firm's risk profile. A capital supplier's commitment to purchase subordinated debt when a firm is nearing financial distress will likely exacerbate problems. If drawn, the net impact will be an increase in the firm's leverage. If the firm has been losing money, the value of its equity has been declining and the market leverage of the firm (as opposed to book leverage) already has been increasing. On one hand, this means the contingent capital will be quite valuable and will come at a time when the firm's debt capacity may be limited. But on the other hand, assuming new fixed obligations could push the firm over the edge, even if the debt is obtained on nondistress terms.

Consider instead an agreement by a capital supplier to purchase preferred stock from the issuer at a time when the firm is approaching financial distress. The firm's total indebtedness will not rise because the dividend on preferred stock can always be set to zero. Accordingly, the firm will not become riskier. But then we have the problem again that the major beneficiaries of this are senior debt holders, who then experience no dilution.

A solution is to allocate the premium paid for the contingent capital facility to the class of security holders the facility benefits most. In the last example, a contingent capital facility in which a capital supplier preagrees to purchase preferred stock from the firm when it is nearing financial distress will benefit equity holders through reducing financial distress costs and debt holders from a decreased probability of insolvency. Debt will benefit more, however, because it is a fixed claim. Consequently, the cost of the option to purchase preferred stock should be borne by the debt holders who would benefit most from the facility's subsequent exercise. Equity will pay for the facility through dilution, and debt will bear the cost of the facility in the event that it is not needed.

Reducing Underinvestment Costs

As in the financial distress case, paid-in capital may not be required to address underinvestment costs. Contingent capital whose terms are negotiated prior to a liquidity crunch can serve the purpose nicely. When a firm lacks the internal cash flows to exploit a positive NPV investment owing to a liquidity crunch, the contingent capital can be drawn and used to transfer investment funds into its capital investment account.

Unlike the scenario in which contingent capital is sought to reduce the expected costs of financial distress, however, the type of claim underlying the contingent facility designed to reduce underinvestment costs does not matter as much. The reason is that underinvestment problems are driven by liquidity considerations, not value considerations. The firm needs cash because it is short of cash, and its only alternatives are to sell assets—possibly at below-market prices—or forgo positive NPV projects. But just because the firm needs cash does not mean the firm is financially troubled. Consequently, the type of claim issued may well have little impact on the firm's risk.

Signaling Capital

As Spence (1973) reminds us, raising and holding excess capital purely as a signal makes sense only if the firm's rivals cannot do the same thing at the same cost. If a firm seeking to raise capital to smooth earnings is initially indistinguishable from its poorly performing rivals, the securities it issues to raise capital will be underpriced accordingly by virtue of the adverse selection problems discussed in Chapter 5. But its rivals can issue underpriced securities on the same terms. So the value of issuing securities purely to raise capital makes very little sense because all the rivals can imitate the good firm in raising excess capital by issuing underpriced securities, thus resulting in the signal being totally uninformative.

Where a firm might be able to distinguish itself is by raising capital from a capital provider that is less affected by the information asymmetry than public security holders. If a good firm with volatile earnings that are contaminated with a lot of noise can convince a bank or insurance company, for example, that its earnings volatility is primarily reflecting factors like exchange rate translation risk rather than bad investments, then the bank or insurance company may offer funds to the firm on much better terms than would be possible from a public securities issue.

If the firm seeking earnings smoothing capital is truly good and its rivals are truly bad, the rivals will not be able to obtain contingent capital on the same terms as the good firm. Reducing the amount of asymmetric information for the rivals, in fact, would actually expose them to worse financing terms as the pooling equilibrium collapses into a separating equilibrium. At least in the case of ignorance, the price paid for their securities will reflect the pooled good/bad firm assessment. But if a bank or insurer finds out that a bad firm is truly bad, then the resulting separating equilibrium will force bad firms to fund at their true risk-adjusted cost of capital.

Ironically, the fact that rivals cannot mimic good firms in this situation will lead to the same separating equilibrium anyway. If rivals cannot persuade banks and insurers that they are good, securing a contingent signaling capital source successfully is itself a differentiating and informative signal for a firm. The good firm will get contingent capital on good terms, and the bad firms will be revealed for what they are by their inability to do so. In that case, the benefits of the signal sent by the good firm in securing contingent capital are not limited to earnings smoothing. They also include the elimination of adverse selection costs from its subsequent public securities issues.

This view is a bit extreme, of course, as even banks and insurers are imperfectly informed. Nevertheless, the signaling capital may be available at a low enough cost at least to justify its use purely for earnings smoothing purposes, even if a full separating equilibrium does not result. More likely is a partial separating equilibrium in which some participants view the good firm properly as a good firm, but all other firms remain unclassified and pooled as a mixture of lemons and nonlemons.

The type of claim underlying the contingent facility in the case of earnings smoothing capital depends in part on the signal conveyed. Naturally, for an insurer or bank to agree to a contingent equity facility sends a stronger positive signal than if the outside firm agrees only to provide senior debt. But the cost issues raised earlier must be weighed against this additional benefit to determine which claim mixture is right for the demander in question.

DETERMINING THE AMOUNT OF CONTINGENT RISK CAPITAL TO HOLD

Here we consider the contingent risk capital needs of financial firms whose customers are also major liability holders. Whether holders of balance-sheet liabilities (e.g., demand deposit holders at commercial banks) or off-balance-sheet liabilities (e.g., swaps counterparties), customers of financial firms tend to place a very high value on the creditworthiness of the institutions on which they have claims. An a A-rated firm may be at a disadvantage to a AAA-rated firm in attracting customers. Risk capital can help mitigate that competitive disadvantage.

The advantage of considering financial firms here is that we can easily address the possibility that either the assets or the liabilities of the firm may need to be protected from risk with contingent capital facilities. As we shall see, the firm's net assets will be the sole driver of its need for risk capital. A nonfinancial firm may not need to worry about differences between gross and net asset values, but we can always consider this a special case of the analysis that follows.

Asset and Liability Insurance Providers and Claim Holders

Merton and Perold (1993), whose model and analysis is followed closely in this entire section, define the risk capital of a firm as "the smallest amount that can be invested to insure the value of the firm's net assets against a loss in value relative to a risk-free investment." In this context, the firm's net assets are its gross assets minus customer liabilities, assuming the customer liabilities are default risk-free.

Consider Bank Pascal, a wholly owned subsidiary of a default risk-free bank hold company. Bank Pascal has one deal—a one-year loan participation with face value $100 million and a single interest payment of 20 percent. The bank has no customer liabilities, and its net assets thus consist solely of the loan. Obviously, funding the loan requires $100 million in investment capital. But suppose the loan is risky—specifically, it returns the full $120 million in an "anticipated" scenario, defaults but has a 50 percent recovery rate in a "disaster" scenario, and defaults with no recovery in a "catastrophic" scenario.

In addition to the $100 million in investment capital, Bank Pascal needs risk capital to insure that any debt it issues is default risk-free. If the current risk-free rate is 10 percent, Bank Pascal thus could finance the loan with a $100 million one-year note issue resulting in a $110 million payment obligation in a year. The payments on the note can be guaranteed through the purchase of liability or asset insurance, both of which are contingent capital and both of which give rise to excess capital held by the firm as risk capital.

First suppose Bank Pascal buys asset insurance in the amount of $110 million for a total cost of $5 million. For any decline in the value of the loan below $110 million, the insurer makes a cash payment to Bank Pascal to make up the deficiency dollar for dollar. Accordingly, Bank Pascal always has adequate funds to repay the note holders fully, thus making the debt default risk-free.

The risk capital held by Bank Pascal as excess capital is equal to $5 million, or the price paid for the asset insurance. This insurance purchase is funded by shareholder equity. The accounting balance sheet of Bank Pascal is given in Table 7.3. In this example, the economic balance sheet—as shown earlier in Exhibit 2.1—is the same as the accounting balance sheet.

Table 7.4 shows the various payoffs in the three scenarios for the asset. In the anticipated scenario, the firm receives $120 million on the loan, $110 million of which goes to note holders and $10 million of which goes back to the parent corporation as the sole equity holder in Bank Pascal. In either the disaster or catastrophic scenario, the asset insurance pays off up to $110 million,

TABLE 7.3 Accounting Balance Sheet with Asset Insurance ($ millions)

Assets		Liabilities and Shareholder Equity	
Loan	$100	Note (default free)	$100
Asset insurance	$5	Shareholder equity	$5

TABLE 7.4 Payoffs After One Year ($ millions)

				Payoffs to Claimants	
Scenario	Loan	Insurance	Insured Loan	Note	Equity
Anticipated	$120	$0	$120	$110	$10
Disaster	$60	$50	$110	$110	$0
Catastrophe	$0	$110	$110	$110	$0

in which case note holders are always repaid but equity's residual claim is worthless. The risk capital also has been lost. So the insurance company bears the risk of the asset, and Bank Pascal's parent corporation as its sole equity holder bears the risk of loss of the risk capital.

Now suppose that instead of purchasing insurance from a third party for the loan asset, Bank Pascal instead seeks a parental guarantee for the repayment of its debt—another slightly different form of contingent capital. In this case, the parent corporation makes no equity investment in the firm. Table 7.5 shows the accounting balance sheet.

In this case, the risk of nonperformance on the asset is borne completely by the parent. In the disaster scenario, for example, the parent will have to make a cash infusion of $50 million to enable Bank Pascal to repay note holders in full. And in the catastrophe scenario, the cash payment from the parent will be the full $110 million required to pay off debt claimants. The risk capital thus in this case is an off-balance-sheet guarantee. Because the cash flows for the parent corporation on the loan guarantee are identical to the cash flows on the explicit asset insurance contract, the risk capital in this case must have the same value as in the explicit insurance case—$5 million. The economic balance sheet of the firm thus is now shown in Table 7.6.

Now suppose Bank Pascal is willing to issue debt that is subject to default risk. In this case, a 10 percent note with face value $100 million will no longer be riskless. To guarantee that the note returns more than the 10 percent riskless rate, the note thus will issue at a discount to par of, say, δ million. But this now implies that Bank Pascal raises $100 - \delta$ million in investment capital, despite needing $100 million to fund the loan. A cash equity investment by the parent of δ million is required to make up the

TABLE 7.5 Accounting Balance Sheet with Parent Guarantee of Debt ($ millions)

Assets		Liabilities and Shareholder Equity	
Loan	$100	Note (default free)	$100
		Shareholder equity	$0

TABLE 7.6 Economic Balance Sheet with Parent Guarantee of Debt ($ millions)

Assets		Liabilities and Shareholder Equity	
Loan	$100	Note (default free)	$100
Parent guarantee	$5	Risk capital	$5

investment capital shortfall. Table 7.7 shows the resulting accounting balance sheet at the beginning of the year.

In all three scenarios, Bank Pascal's parent has the same cash flows as the insurer in the asset insurance case and as it would have had in the parental debt guarantee case. Accordingly, the value of the equity must be $5 million initially, thus making the debt worth $95 million upon issue with an expected return of 15.8 percent or $15 million on $95 million.

Merton and Perold (1993) note that the position of risky debt holders can be viewed as the combination of a riskless loan plus a put on the assets of the firm. The put is equivalent to a type of asset insurance. The economic balance sheet of Bank Pascal in this case is now shown in Table 7.8.

Note in Table 7.8 that debt has an economic value of $100 million, as compared to a book value at the beginning of the period of $95 million. This additional $5 million arises from the fact that debt is now being shown as default free, and the default-free debt is equal to the value of the risky note plus the asset insurance put option value of $5 million. This additional $5 million shows up as risk capital on the asset side of the economic balance sheet, just as in Table 7.3 except that the note holders are now the sellers of the asset insurance—not a third-party insurance company.

The major point of this analysis is to recognize that the value of the risk capital in this case is driven *solely* by the need for risk capital associated with the asset Bank Pascal holds. This is why nonfinancial corporations holding risk capital may well not have the same analysis of risk capital; the need to provide a risk capital–backed asset to customers drives the result, and the source of the insurance is immaterial.

Risk Capital for Asset Risk

Still following Merton and Perold (1993), now consider more generally a firm with assets whose current market value is A(t). The firm has two types of lia-

TABLE 7.7   Accounting Balance Sheet with Risky Debt ($ millions)

Assets		Liabilities and Shareholder Equity	
Loan	$100	Note (risky)	$100 – δ
		Shareholder equity	$δ

TABLE 7.8   Economic Balance Sheet with Risky Debt ($ millions)

Assets		Liabilities and Shareholder Equity	
Loan	$100	Note (default free)	$100
Asset insurance	$5	Shareholder equity	$δ

bilities outstanding. The first are guaranteed investment contracts (GICs) with total face value K_1 that pay principal and interest to their holders in one period. The interest rate on the GICs is R, which is also the risk-free rate.

The firm has financed itself by issuing equity and debt capital, where the debt is junior in capital structure to the GICs. Suppose the face value of the firm's debt is K_2 and that the promised interest rate on the debt is R. For simplicity, let $K_1 = K_2 = K$.

Now assume that the firm can acquire asset insurance—a type of contingent capital—that allows the firm to finance its risky asset portfolio worth A(t) for one period. To keep things easy, let us express insurance costs as a fraction of the face value of the firm's debt (or, equivalently, GICs because we have assumed the two are equal). The total cost thus is presumed to be 0.5K. If the GICs and junior debt each have a face value of $1 billion, for example, the insurance has a total cost of $500 million.

Suppose it costs 0.2K to obtain some portion of this insurance from an insurer (or, if our firm in question is an insurance company, a reinsurer) such that the insurance covers the first W dollars of losses on the firm's asset portfolio. The insurance thus functions like a short vertical spread struck at A(t) – W and A(t) for a total net premium cost of K. When considered together with the assets of the firm, the payoff at time t + 1 to the firm is shown in Exhibit 7.5.

In the exhibit, note that we have drawn the short vertical spread using a long call option struck at A(t) and a short call option struck at A(t) – W. We could have constructed the short vertical spread using puts as we have done in

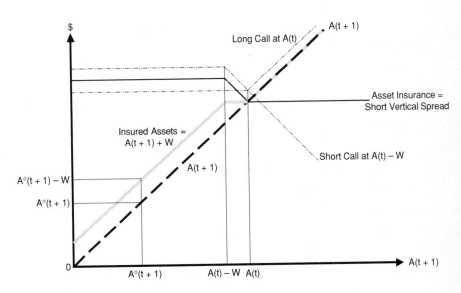

EXHIBIT 7.5   Asset Payoffs with Asset Insurance for the First W in Losses

earlier chapters—a short put struck at $A(t) - W$ and a long put struck at $A(t)$—but it is useful to see that calls work just as well.

The resulting payoff on the assets held by the firm is shown by the heavy gray line, equal to $A(t + 1)$ for values of $A(t + 1) > A(t) - W$ and equal to $A(t + 1) + W$ for values of $A(t + 1) \leq A(t) - W$. The insurance thus puts a ceiling on the value of the firm's assets at their time t market value. But because the insurance is capped to a maximum payout of W, asset values below $A(t) - W$ continue to decline, albeit with the extra W of protection provided by the insurance for asset values between $A(t) - W$ and $A(t)$. Consider time $t + 1$ asset value $A°(t + 1)$. Without insurance, this would be the value of the assets, shown as the corresponding point on the y-axis in Exhibit 7.5. But with asset insurance, an asset value of $A°(t + 1)$ leads to a liquidation value of the firm's assets of $A°(t + 1) + W$.

Now consider how the firm's liabilities enter into the picture. Both for the junior debt and the GICs, the purchase of the asset insurance de facto shifts the strike prices by W. Instead of defaulting when $A(t) < K_1(1 + R)$, GICs holders now receive a full repayment as long as $A(t) - W < K_1(1 + R)$. Similarly, junior debt holders receive a full repayment provided that $A(t) > K_2(1 + R) + W$ as compared to a default point of $A(t)=K_2(1 + R)$ before the insurance. And equity receives the residual claim on $A(t) - K_1(1 + R) - K_2(1 + R) + W$. The payoffs to claim holders are shown in Exhibit 7.6.

If we view each of the claimants on the firm as a provider of asset insurance, we can determine the amount of insurance each claimant supplies by examining the payoffs in Exhibit 7.6 more closely. These insurance payoffs are shown as a function of the firm's time $t + 1$ asset values in Exhibit 7.7.

The GICs can be viewed as providing a type of "catastrophic" insurance to the firm because the firm's total assets must fall below $K_1(1 + R) - W$ before the payment to GIC holders begins to erode. Following Merton and Perold (1993), assume the GICs thus trade only at a 1 percent discount to par, implying that the value of the insurance provided by the GIC holders is $.01K_1$ or $.01K$.

The junior notes are much riskier in Bank Pascal's senior capital structure. If the value of the loan falls below $K_1(1 + R) + K_2(1 + R) - W$, a portion of the junior debt's promised interest and principal payment will begin to erode. The worst case for junior debt occurs if the firm's assets fall in value to $K_1(1 + R) - W$, at which point junior debt receives nothing and there is just enough asset value (plus insurance) to pay off GIC holders. Accordingly, the $K_2(1 + R)$ in insurance provided by junior debt holders will be more expensive than the $K_1(1 + R) - W$ insurance provided by GIC holders. We let the price of this insurance equal 10 percent of the par value of the debt, or $0.10K$.

The total premiums paid in insurance thus far amount to $0.31K$ (= $0.2K$ from external insurance, $0.1K$ from junior debt, and $0.01K$ from GICs). The

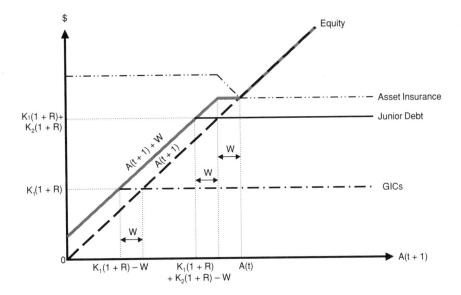

EXHIBIT 7.6   Value of Claims with Asset Insurance for the First W in Losses

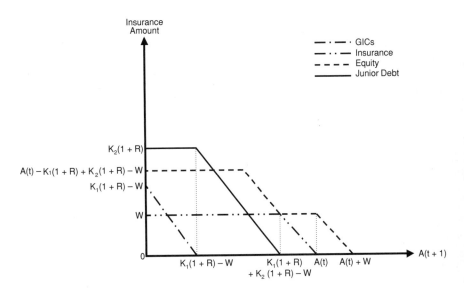

EXHIBIT 7.7   Value of Asset Insurance by Insurance Provider and Claimants

balance of the insurance premiums thus must be provided by equity holders in the total amount of

$$0.5K - 0.31K = 0.19K$$

If the face value of debt is $1 billion, this implies an insurance value for equity of $190 million.

Table 7.9 shows the accounting balance of the firm. Note that the value of shareholder equity on the balance sheet is, as usual, defined as the residual value. So if the par values of debt and the GICs are $1 billion each and the firm's current assets are worth $3 billion, for example, then shareholders' equity is worth $1.31 billion.

Now consider Table 7.10, in which the economic balance sheet of the firm is shown. The risk capital of the firm is the 0.5K in total insurance costs. Because this capital is all contingent capital, the entries on the asset side of the balance sheet for asset insurance are implied prices reflected in the value of the firm's contingent capital sources—in this case, synonymous with the claimants of the firm plus a single external insurance provider. Note also that the firm's financial capital is exactly the amount required to fund the investment portfolio worth A(t).

Consider the total investment by equity holders, which we see from Table

TABLE 7.9   Accounting Balance Sheet ($ millions)

Assets		Liabilities and Shareholder Equity	
Investment portfolio	A(t)	Junior Debt (par K_2)	$0.90K_2$
External insurance	0.20K	GICs (par K_1)	$0.99K_1$
		Shareholder Equity	A(t) − 1.69K
TOTAL	A(t) + 0.20K	TOTAL	A(t) + 0.20K

TABLE 7.10   Accounting Balance Sheet ($ millions)

Assets		Liabilities and Shareholder Equity	
Investment portfolio	A(t)	*Financial Capital:*	
Asset Insurance:		Junior Debt (riskless)	K_2
External insurance	0.20K	GICs (riskless)	K_1
Equity provided	0.19K	Equity (riskless)	A(t) − 2K
Debt provided	0.10K	*Total Financial Capital:*	A(t)
Customer provided	0.01K		
Total Insurance:	0.50K	*Risk Capital*	0.5K
TOTAL	A(t) + 0.50K	TOTAL	A(t) + 0.50K

7.9 is A(t) – 1.69K. As Merton and Perold (1993) argue, we can think of this as an investment that serves three separate functions:

1. It provides A(t) – K_1 – K_2 in investment capital that allows the firm to raise the cash it needs in excess of the cash raised from issuing debt and GICs in order to fund an asset portfolio worth A(t).
2. It provides 0.50K of risk capital to the firm to finance its acquisition of asset insurance.
3. It sells the firm a portion of that asset insurance for 0.19K. The net result is A(t) – 1.69K.

Three things are noteworthy from this analysis. First, all of the claimants on the firm are investment capital providers. Second, all of the claimants are also sellers of asset insurance. Customers provide the least insurance, kicking in only at catastrophic levels, whereas mezzanine debt holders provide a relatively large chunk. Third, notice that risk capital is provided by equity holders, as in all of the examples in the prior section. Other claimants will be suppliers of risk capital only if the market value of the firm's assets currently is below the value of the liabilities capitalized at the riskless rate.

These stylized facts lay a crucial foundation for our discussion in Part IV. Namely, we can see now that a firm's supply of risk capital is fundamentally tied to its capital structure. Not surprisingly, most of the risk financing and risk transfer ART forms we will encounter later thus are really synthetic debt, equity, or hybrid capital claims.

A comparison of the balance sheets in Tables 7.9 and 7.10 again is instructive. Note that the financial capital of the firm is driven entirely by the firm's need to raise cash to fund its investment capital acquisitions. Risk capital, by contrast, is determined by the riskiness of the firm's net assets.

Risk Capital for Liability Risks

In the preceding examples, the net asset risk was the same as the gross asset risk. The firm needed risk capital purely to address the risk of its asset portfolio, but its customer liabilities and financial claims had known payoffs. Now consider the reverse situation where the firm has contingent liabilities.

Suppose in particular that Bank Pascal now has contingent debt obligations in the form of commodity-indexed debt. Suppose the debt has face value $100 million and includes an embedded call option struck at the money at the time of the debt issuance on 100 kilograms of gold. Suppose further that the price of gold at the time of the debt issue is $350 per gram. If gold has gone up to $355 per gram when the debt matures, the firm owes $105 million to debt holders.

Table 7.11 shows the firm's accounting balance sheet at the time of the debt issue. The firm issues $100 million in debt and, in this case, puts the proceeds of the debt issue into the current asset account for cash. In this case, the firm's gross assets are riskless, because it has funded a risk-free risk capital reserve. But the net assets are risky. The parent corporation of Bank Pascal is short a gold option on 100 kilograms of gold struck at $350 per gram (plus the riskless interest earned on the $100 million in cash), and the value of this gold option is the firm's risk capital—the amount of capital required to make the net assets of the firm riskless.

The firm might have chosen instead to take the cash proceeds from its debt issue and invest in gold. In this case, the asset entry on the balance sheet in Table 7.11 would be a $100 million investment in gold. From a risk standpoint, the firm would be long gold at $350 in assets and short a gold call option at $350 on the liabilities side. Any increase in gold prices that would increase the firm's debt payments would be offset by an increase in the value of the firm's assets, but any decrease in the price of gold still would cause a loss. In this case, the net assets of the firm would be equivalent to a short put on gold—the synthetic equivalent of a long position plus a short call. The firm's risk capital thus would be equal to the value of a short put.

If the firm used the capital raised from its debt issue to buy gold call options, the firm's net assets would be invariant to price changes in gold, and the risk capital of the firm would be zero.

This example illustrates the important fact that the firm's net assets determine the amount of risk capital it should hold. Although we have been discussing this in a contingent capital sense, the same principle would apply if the firm wished to raise paid-in capital as risk capital as well.

These examples also have ignored the costs of contingent capital. Although contingent capital of the kind we have been discussing avoids the adverse selection costs of raising paid-in capital, adverse selection is still a problem in external insurance contracts, as will be discussed in Chapter 15. Accordingly, even a firm that uses contingent capital must seek to ensure that the benefits of the risk capital exceed its costs at the margin.

TABLE 7.11 Accounting Balance Sheet with Contingent Liabilities ($ millions)

Assets		Liabilities and Shareholder Equity	
Cash	$100	Commodity-indexed Debt	$100
		Shareholder Equity	$0

NOTES

1. Merton and Perold (1993).
2. The NPV calculation only admits expected values into the numerator. If a risk creates some expected cost for the firm, it belongs in the NPV calculation. But for very low probability events in the tail of a distribution that do not impact the cost of capital used by the firm to discount its expected cash flows, the costs associated with these events may not receive adequate weight from just an expected value and thus may have little if any impact on the NPV calculation—hence this rationale for holding excess capital.
3. The theoretical argument is advanced especially well by Froot, Scharfstein, Stein (1993), and an excellent practical version of the same argument can be found in Lewent and Kearney (1990).
4. See Doherty (2000).
5. This example is based on an analogous one presented in Froot, Scharfstein, and Stein (1994).
6. The sole exception to this is a "money-burning" signal. See Daniel and Titman (1995).
7. There are, of course, other rationalizations for advertising.
8. Money burning in the IPO process has been explored by Allen and Faulhaber (1989), Grinblatt and Hwang (1989), and Welch (1989).
9. This rationale is also consistent with the hypothesis of Daniel and Titman (1995) that money-burning signals can make sense when financed with project revenues rather than new equity issues. In this case, we are simply assuming the new equity issues are borrowings against future project revenues. The market must believe this, as well, of course. One or two bad investments by the firm will certainly end its ability to differentiate itself in this manner.

CHAPTER 8

Regulatory Capital

The M&M assumption of perfect capital markets can be violated by the existence of costly and/or distortionary taxes, subsidies, and regulations. Among those regulations that may affect the capital structure of a firm are the capital requirements imposed on certain types of firms by their regulators.

This chapter focuses mainly on capital requirements that affect the major suppliers of capital today, excluding individual and institutional (e.g., pension and mutual funds) investors in securities. Included are capital market intermediaries like securities broker/dealers and investment banks, over-the-counter derivatives dealers, and (re-)insurance companies.[1] At the end of the chapter we explore how demanders of capital can be affected by capital requirements imposed on suppliers of capital. Specifically, we address the following questions here in the order listed:

- To what kinds of capital requirements are commercial banks subject?
- To what kinds of capital requirements are securities broker/dealers subject?
- To what kinds of capital requirements and insurance and reinsurance companies subject?
- What is the impact of minimum capital requirements on a firm's value and its cost of capital?
- How do regulatory capital requirements on suppliers of capital affect the demanders of capital?

BANK CAPITAL REQUIREMENTS AND THE BASEL ACCORD

The Committee on Bank Supervision of the Bank for International Settlements (BIS) promulgated in 1988 the Basel Capital Accord (hereinafter accord or Basel I) primarily to strengthen bank safety and soundness and level the international playing field. Together with its five substantive amendments, the accord specifies minimum capital requirements for internationally active banks in the Group of Ten (G10) industrialized countries. Some other countries also have adopted the Basel requirements, and, although it is aimed exclusively at internationally active banks, some national banking regulators have chosen to apply it to all banks in their jurisdiction.

The accord essentially requires that banks hold enough capital at all times to weather losses related to certain types of risk that they might assume. We discuss the accord in brief in terms of what risks it covers, how banks can satisfy their capital requirements for those risks, and what changes in the Basel framework lay on the horizon. Readers desiring a more detailed account of the Basel Accord should see Matten (2000) or Crouhy, Galai, and Mark (2001), or should visit the BIS website for a listing of the bank's own extensive library of resources and reports at *www.bis.org*.

Scope of Basel I

In its current form, banks must hold enough capital to cover the risks of certain on- and off-balance-sheet assets and liabilities. Importantly, a bank's compliance with its capital requirements is aggregate, so that the bank either is or is not compliant at any given time. But compliance itself is determined by adding up the "risk weights" assigned to assets and liabilities with different risk characteristics.

On-Balance-Sheet Credit Risks

The main body of Basel I applies to the credit risk banks incur from their assets. The capital a bank must hold to cover its credit risk for most balance sheet assets is determined by multiplying the book value of the asset times by a predefined risk weight, where risk weights may be 0, 10, 20, 50, or 100 percent of the asset's value. Table 8.1 gives an example of the assignment of risk weights by asset type.

TABLE 8.1 Credit Risk Weights for Major Balance Sheet Assets Under Basel I

Asset Type	Risk Weight
• Cash	0%
• Sovereign debt issued by OECD[a] countries	
• Claims on government-sponsored enterprises	10%
• Claims on banks located in OECD countries	20%
• Claims on OECD securities firms with bank-like capital requirements	
• Claims on non-OECD banks with less than a year to maturity	
• Residential mortgages	50%
• All private nonbank lending	100%
• All claims on non-OECD banks with more than a year to maturity	
• All other assets	

[a]OECD = Organization for Economic Cooperation and Development

On-balance-sheet assets and liabilities sometimes can be netted for the purpose of calculating capital requirements, provided the netting is backed by a legal opinion concluding that netting is very likely to be legally enforceable. In addition, the maturity of the liability (e.g., term deposit) must be no less than the maturity of the asset (e.g., loan) against which it is netted, and the positions to be offset have the same currency denomination. Finally, the bank must manage the "net" position on a consolidated basis.

Off-Balance-Sheet Credit Risks

The credit risk of off-balance-sheet assets are also covered by Basel I. Such assets usually fall into one of two categories: contingent claims or derivatives. Contingent claims, such as those discussed at the end of Chapter 2, usually are assigned a risk weight based on their asset-equivalent position. To arrive at an asset equivalency, the BIS specifies "conversion factors" that amount to assumptions about how much of the contingent facility is presumed to be fully drawn. A conversion requirement of 100 percent for a letter of credit, for example, means that the bank must treat the LOC as if it were an existing loan. An undrawn standby credit facility made to a firm to support its trading operations, by contrast, has a 20 percent conversion requirement, which means that a $1 million contingent facility would be assessed the capital charge for the underlying loan but only on a $200,000 principal amount.

Table 8.2 summarizes the conversion weights used to transform some of the most popular contingent claims into asset equivalents.

Derivatives are assigned credit risk capital requirements based on current exposure of the transaction plus an add-on for potential exposure (reflecting maturity and type). If the transaction is out of the money, there is no credit exposure. But if it is in the money, the BIS requires a conversion of the position to an asset equivalent by adding the current market value (i.e., current re-

TABLE 8.2   Conversion Weights for Contingent Claims Under Basel I

Asset Type	Conversion
• Guarantees	100%
• Standby facilities and LOCs	
• Repurchase agreements	
• Forward agreements	
• Performance bonds	50%
• Transaction-specific contingencies	
• Note issuance facilities	
• Documentary credits	20%
• Standby facilities for trading with maturities over one year	
• Standby facilities for trading with maturities less than one year that may be canceled prior to drawdown	0%

placement cost in the event of a default today) and an add-on. The add-on reflects the potential exposure of the deal or the possibility that the asset may become a bigger asset in default at some point over its remaining life. The add-on amount is based on the notional size of the transaction and the add-on factors listed in Table 8.3.

After the asset-equivalent amount has been calculated as current exposure plus the add-on, the normal asset risk factor is used to compute the capital required on the deal. A six-month interest rate swap with a notional principal of $200 million and a current exposure of $100,000, for example, has a zero add-on and an asset-equivalent exposure of $100,000. An otherwise identical two-year swap is asset equivalent to $1.1 million (i.e., $100,000 current exposure plus 0.5% × $200,000,000). If the swap is with a non-OECD bank, the risk weight of 100 percent is applied the asset-equivalent amount to derive the total capital charge.

Some limited netting is allowed for derivatives following a 1995 amendment to the accord.

Market Risk

Apart from these capital requirements for credit risk, the "market risk amendments" to the accord of 1996 also require banks to hold additional capital against the risk of market price fluctuations in the values of certain assets, such as equities or derivatives. Banks can choose among several different methods to determine these risk weights.

Of particular significance in the market risk amendments was the decision by the BIS to let banks opt to use their own internal models to calculate their capital charges for market risk. The BIS still specifies the basic methodology, but its acknowledgment that internal models could be used for capital requirement calculations was a major step forward in modernizing the accord.

Compliance with Basel I

Bank capital is classified into three categories, or "tiers," by the BIS for the purpose of assessing capital adequacy. *Tier I* capital includes mainly fully

TABLE 8.3 Potential Exposure Add-On Factors for the Credit Risk of Derivatives

	≤ 1 year	> 1 year and ≤ 5 years	> 5 years
Interest rate	0%	0.5%	1.5%
Exchange rate and gold	1%	5%	7.5%
Equity	6%	8%	10%
Precious metals (not gold)	7%	7%	8%
Other commodities	10%	12%	15%

paid-up and issued equity, noncumulative perpetual preferred stock, disclosed reserves, and minority equity interests in subsidiaries that are consolidated on the bank holding company's balance sheet.[2] *Tier II* capital includes undisclosed and revaluation reserves, general loan-loss reserves, hybrid securities, and subordinated debt. Finally, *Tier III* capital includes debt with original maturities of at least two years that contains lock-in provisions allowing the bank to suspend interest and/or principal payments if its total capital falls below its required minimum.

A bank's total regulatory capital must equal at least 8 percent of the sum of its risk-weighted assets at all times (i.e., the sum of 8 percent of the values of the bank's assets), where risk weights are determined in the manner described earlier. At least 50 percent of the ratio of the bank's total regulatory capital to the sum of its risk-weighted assets—that is, the *total capital ratio*—must be in the form of Tier I capital. In addition, subordinated debt cannot exceed more than 50 percent of the Tier I capital amount. Tier III capital can be used only to meet the market risk requirement, and may not exceed 250 percent of the Tier I capital that is allocated to market risk.

Basel II[3]

International banking regulators announced in 1999 a plan to revise the accord, often referred to as Basel II. The proposed revision contains three "pillars," the first of which is risk-based capital requirements. The planned revision of the accord is a recognition of several major shortcomings with the original accord. Among other things, Basel II contemplates tightening the link between the credit risk of bank assets and the capital regulators require internationally active banks to hold against those assets. In particular, the current "standard model" for capital charges does little to distinguish between differences in credit quality. Capital held against corporate loans, for example, barely depends on the creditworthiness of the borrower; the distinction between OECD and non-OECD is widely regarded as excessively coarse.

Acknowledging the limitations of the accord, the BIS considered three alternative capital adequacy schemes in its concept release. The first, ultimately favored by the BIS, ties capital requirements when possible to ratings published by external credit assessment institutions or bodies like export insurance agencies. Transactions with relatively good credits generally will require less capital than before, and conversely for high-risk borrowers. Loans to corporations, for example, have a lower capital charge if the borrower is rated AAA to AA– and a higher charge if the borrower is rated below B–.

The second alternative would link capital charges to banks' internal credit ratings. A capital scheme based on banks' internal ratings would rely on information that banks themselves collect about borrower credit risk.

Banks always have been acknowledged to have comparative advantage in the acquisition and analysis of credit information about their own customers. Because external ratings tend to lag more than lead firms' actual financial conditions, an internal ratings approach thus may be preferable for promoting bank safety and soundness. Relying on internal ratings for capital charge calculations, moreover, would not penalize banks for dealing with firms that have chosen to remain unrated by external credit assessment institutions.

Internal ratings do not, however, allow banks to take into consideration portfolio effects arising from multiple credit exposures. Thus the BIS explored a third alternative that would allow banks to use internal portfolio-based credit evaluation models for capital measurement in the same spirit as the 1996 market risk amendments. Although only a handful of sophisticated banks would find this alternative palatable in the short run, those banks could benefit greatly from an internal model-driven approach.

Basel II also goes well beyond simply making marginal changes to the capital banks must hold against credit risk. Indeed, Basel II is intended to create a "whole capital charge" that reflects all the major risks facing banks, including the interest rate risk of the banking book and operational risk as well as the usual credit and market risk. Operational risk, in particular, has been contentiously debated—that is, little agreement exists on how the BIS should require firms to allocate capital to operational risks. Some argue for a "loss distributions" approach based on actual operational loss data, whereas others argue for more of a "basic indicators" approach or an "internal rating" approach. As of this writing, the implementation date for Basel II thus remains unspecified, having already been postponed once.

The second and third pillars of Basel II—apart from the first pillar of revised risk-based capital requirements—are "supervisory review" and "market discipline," respectively. The supervisory review pillar emphasizes the importance of examiner discretion in assessing a bank's total capital requirements. The market discipline pillar emphasizes the importance of enhanced risk disclosures and transparency by banks.

CAPITAL REQUIREMENTS FOR SECURITIES BROKER/DEALERS

The capital requirements to which international securities firms are subject are a bit different from the BIS risk-based capital standards for banks. The Basel Accord is concerned primarily with ensuring that banks have enough capital to absorb losses and remain in business, in large part to ensure that the failure of a major bank does not threaten "systemic stability." Capital requirements imposed on securities participants like broker/dealers take a very different approach and are intended not to prevent a failure, but rather to protect customers in the event of a failure. These requirements specify capital the firm must hold to ensure that it can be liquidated in an orderly and nondisruptive manner if the need arises.

Securities and Exchange Commission Net Capital Rule

Capital requirements imposed on securities firms are exemplified by the U.S. Securities and Exchange Commission "net capital rule" of 1975.[4] Under the net capital rule, firms are required to hold enough regulatory capital so that they can be liquidated in an orderly manner if they fall below minimum capital levels. Importantly and quite differently from the capital requirements imposed on banks, the net capital rule can be satisfied only with liquid capital, and the required minimum level is thus also aimed only at firms' liquid capital assets.

The actual minimum liquid asset requirement imposed on a broker/dealer depends on many factors—the size of the firm, whether it manages customer funds and/or issues securities, the other activities of the firm, and the like.

Despite the heterogeneity of the minimum capital requirement, the way that firms satisfy these requirements is the same across all firms. Specifically, to calculate minimum capital levels, securities firms take the market values of their current securities holdings and multiply them by asset-specific risk factors that are set by the SEC to reflect the credit, market, and liquidity risk of the securities. The resulting "haircuts" then are subtracted from the net worth of the institution for comparison to the firm's minimum capital level.

"Haircuts"

For equity securities, U.S. firms may choose between the "basic standard" and "alternative standard" approaches. The former specifies a 30 percent haircut and a requirement that aggregate indebtedness cannot exceed 15 times net capital. The latter requires firms to hold a capital cushion equal to 2 percent of customer and customer-related receivables and imposes a 15 percent haircut with some added complications. Almost all large firms today opt for the alternative standard method.

Under the alternative standard method, the net capital rule specifies a haircut based on the following calculation:

$$\text{Haircut} = 0.15\max[L,S] + 0.15\max\{0, \min[L,S] - 0.25\max[L,S]\}$$

where L and S denote the market values of the broker's long and short positions, respectively. This is confusing, so let us take an example. Suppose a broker/dealer has long positions in the common stock of Firm Dracula worth $200,000 and short positions in the same common stock worth $15,000. The long exposure is the greater of the two, so the haircut is

Haircut = 0.15($200,000) + 0.15max{0, $15,000 − 0.25($200,000)}

The last term is negative and thus vanishes, so the broker/dealer's haircut on its Dracula holdings is

Haircut = 0.15($200,000) = $30,000

Now suppose the long positions of the firm are worth $200,000 and the short positions worth $250,000. The short positions now represent the maximum exposure, and the haircut is now

Haircut = 0.15($250,000) + 0.15max{0, $200,000 − 0.25($250,000)}
= $37,500 + 0.15max{0, $200,000 − $62,500} = $37,500
+ 0.15($137,500)
= $37,500 + $20,625 = $58,125

In other words, if both positions are big enough, both enter the haircut calculation. The 25 percent multiplier in the last term reflects the fact that netting is only partially credited in this calculation—but that is still more than in the basic standard method.

Haircuts on debt securities are based on the credit quality of their issuer and the maturity of the claim, both of which materially impact the volatility of the security. Table 8.4 shows the current haircut amounts by issuer and maturity.

Derivatives Policy Group Voluntary Reporting Framework

In March 1995, the six largest U.S. securities participants in over-the-counter derivatives activity—Goldman Sachs, Crédit Suisse First Boston, Merrill Lynch, Morgan Stanley, Salomon Brothers, and Lehman Brothers—released a *Framework for Voluntary Oversight* intended to provide guidance for capital allocation to the risks of derivatives. Known as the Derivatives Policy Group (DPG), these six firms agreed to report their activities in derivatives to the SEC voluntarily.

In addition, the DPG members agreed to use proprietary statistical models to measure the capital at risk on their derivatives activities using a mutually agreed-on reporting framework.[5] The DPG participants calculate the risks of their interest rate, equity, foreign exchange, and commodity swaps, over-the-counter options, and foreign exchange forwards under two different scenarios—a large shock of a size to be determined by the member firms and a shock to several predefined "core risk factors" specified by the SEC.

The DPG participants report these results to the SEC but may not use these calculations as a substitute for the regular net capital requirements. The SEC appears to use the information mainly to monitor how a correlated shock to major risk factors would affect all firms at the same time.

TABLE 8.4   Haircuts for Debt Instruments Under the SEC Net Capital Rule

Issuer: / Maturity:	Government[a]	Municipal[b]		High-Grade Debt[c]	Others (Liquid)[d]	Others (Illiquid)[e]
0–1 months	0%		0%			
1–3 months			1/8%			
3–6 months	0.50%	1%	1/4%	2%		
6–9 months	0.75%		3/8%			
9–12 months	1%		1/2%			
			3/4%			
1–2 years	1.50%	2%		3%	30%	40%
			1%		(15%)[f]	
2–3 years	2%	3%		5%		
3–5 years	3%	4%		6%		
5–7 years	4%	5%		7%		
7–10 years		5.5%				
10–15 years	4.50%	6%		7.5%		
15–20 years	5%	6.5%		8%		
20–25 years	5.50%	7%		8.5%		
Over 25 years	6%			9%		

[a]Includes securities issued or guaranteed by the U.S. government, government-sponsored enterprises, or the Canadian government.
[b]The second column applies to municipal securities with less than 732 days to maturity at issue, and the first column applies to all other municipal securities.
[c]The debt must be nonconvertible and have a rating in one of the top four rating categories of a recognized rating agency.
[d]Three or more market makers.
[e]One or two market makers.
[f]Alternate method in parentheses.

Internal Models

The SEC has shown much greater reluctance than the BIS in allowing firms to use their own internal models for capital requirement calculation purposes. In February 1997 the SEC took its first step in this direction by agreeing to let broker/dealers calculate the haircut on their listed equity, equity index, and currency options positions using models.

Broker/dealers must report their positions to a "third-party source" that maintains generally accepted option pricing models and that is subject to supervision by a Designated Examining Authority. The third party revalues the broker's options under 10 specified valuation scenarios. The broker then downloads the change in option values under these scenarios and applies these changes to its own proprietary and market maker positions. The maximum loss at each of the 10 scenarios is the haircut.

The SEC is currently considering an approach more similar to the one embodied in Basel II, especially with respect to allowing large derivatives participants to rely on internal models for the calculation of their haircuts.

International Guidance

Securities regulation can differ quite a lot across international borders. The International Organisation of Securities Commissions (IOSCO) has attempted to promulgate some cross-border uniformity, and one area of particular interest to IOSCO has been the harmonization of international minimum capital requirements on securities broker/dealers. The Technical Committee of IOSCO worked on a document articulating its views on minimum capital requirements from July 1987 to June 1989.

The resulting *Capital Adequacy Standards for Securities Firms* sets forth a framework that is broadly similar to the SEC's net capital rule. Firms are expected to have sufficient liquid assets to meet their obligations given the risks to which they are subject. The liquid capital of broker/dealers is expected to exceed the sum of risk-based requirements imposed on assets in a manner analogous to SEC haircuts.

CAPITAL REQUIREMENTS FOR INSURERS AND REINSURERS

The regulation of insurance and reinsurance suppliers is complicated and disparate. Some countries are much more lenient than others, and some countries—including the United States—leave regulation to individual state insurance commissions and chartering agents.

Nevertheless, most countries do specify minimum capital requirements for insurance underwriters and sometimes for reinsurers. Some examples of these capital requirements are detailed below, but readers should keep in mind that, unlike the BIS, which applies to all internationally active G10 banks, insurance capital requirements can vary widely by jurisdiction.

Risk-Based Capital Standards for Insurers

Although American states ultimately are allowed a large amount of discretion in their implementation of minimum capital requirements, the National Association of Insurance Commissioners (NAIC) has developed a set of risk-based capital (RBC) standards in an effort to promote conformity. The NAIC RBC standards attempt to require insurers to hold an amount of capital deemed adequate to cover most of their major risks. Like the Basel Accord, risk weights are defined for all risky assets, liabilities, and premium writings. The size of the exposure is adjusted with a risk weighting factor, and the aggregate weighted risk exposure defines an insurer's authorized control level (ACL).

The total adjusted capital (TAC) of insurers is then compared to their ACLs to determine capital adequacy. Insurers may satisfy their TAC requirement with statutory capital, voluntary reserves, and certain premium surpluses. Companies with a TAC-to-ACL ratio of 200 percent or more typically are left alone. Insurers with a TAC-ACL ratio of between 150 percent and 200 percent often must submit a RBC Plan to their home state regulators proposing the corrective actions they will take to move their ratio in the right direction. Table 8.5 summarizes the usual implications for insurance writers based on their TAC-ACL ratios.

Solvency Margins in the European Union for Insurers

In the European Union (EU), capital requirements for insurance underwriters usually are based on a *solvency margin*, defined broadly as the minimum relation required between capital (called surplus) and premiums written and either claims incurred (non-life) or mathematical reserves (life). As early as 1946, for example, the United Kingdom required that the total assets of a nonlife insurer should exceed total liabilities by 20 percent of the premiums written.[6]

Note that we encounter here for the first time an important industry distinction that will arise repeatedly later in the book—the distinction between life and nonlife insurance lines. Nonlife may include property and casualty, professional indemnity, directors and officers, and other types of insurance. The two types of insurance lines have been separated by historical convention for many years, because the nature of the liabilities and the actuarial models required to manage the liabilities are inherently different. Most specifically, nonlife policies may never result in claims, whereas life policies always will because everyone dies eventually.

An EU directive sets forth minimum solvency margins based on the general type of insurance line. Nonlife lines, for example, must have capital that is equal to the greater of (1) 18 percent of written premiums, or (2) 26 percent

TABLE 8.5   NAIC RBC TAC-ACL Minimum Capital Ratio Triggers

Ratio of TAC to ACL	Action
≥ 200%	No action
≥ 150% and < 200%	RBC Plan must be submitted to state proposing specific corrective actions
≥ 100% and < 150%	RBC Plan as above *plus* regulatory agency-mandated corrective actions
≥ 70% and < 100%	Discretionary seizure of firm *allowed*
< 70%	Closure and seizure of firm *required*

of average net claims paid over the prior three to seven years. Adjustments are allowed in both cases for reinsurance.

Capital Requirements for Reinsurers[7]

As is the case with insurance companies, capital requirements on reinsurers can vary widely across countries and legal jurisdictions. Unlike insurers, however, solvency concerns with reinsurers are widely regarded as less of a "public policy" problem for the simple reason that insurers deal directly with members of the public and reinsurers do not. Accordingly, the solvency of a reinsurer typically is regarded as a concern only to the extent that it might affect the solvency of an insurer.

Reinsurance capital requirements may target companies' technical reserves and/or solvency margins. In the United States, for example, reinsurers must maintain the same technical reserves as insurers for similar lines. Other countries, such as the United Kingdom, rely on surplus margins in excess of reserves instead of just absolute reserves.

Whether credit is given to primary insurers for reinsurance in the calculation of their own capital and reserve requirements depends in part on how the reinsurers are regulated. In the United States and within Lloyd's, for example, there is no real distinction between insurers and reinsurers, and any firm purchasing insurance from another firm can deduct that cover from its own capital requirement. In France, by contrast, no reserve requirement is imposed on reinsurers, but primary insurers are not allowed to deduct reinsurance from their own technical reserve requirements. In other words, France enforces a "gross reserving" environment in which reinsurers are essentially unregulated, but insurers are not allowed to show the benefits of reinsurance in their own capital regulations.

IMPLICATIONS FOR CAPITAL STRUCTURE AND THE COST OF CAPITAL

What practical implication do capital requirements have on the capital structure and cost of capital of a firm? There are two possibilities. First, capital requirements can reduce a firm's expected cash flows owing to the costs of the regulation itself. Such costs can include the costs of compliance and reporting, the costs of administration (including any new personnel costs arising as a direct result of regulation), and ancillary expenditures (e.g., costs of systems required to facilitate compliance).

The second avenue—and, as we know from Chapter 3, the only other means by which the value of the firm can be affected—is a higher cost of capital. In this context, capital requirements can affect a firm's cost of capital both directly and indirectly.

The direct increase in costs occurs if capital requirements force firms to hold "too much capital." The cost associated with forcing a firm to hold excess capital, however, is probably not that high for several reasons. First, most of the industries discussed here—especially banking—already hold well above their minimum required levels. Second, the rationales for holding excess capital discussed in Chapter 7 may apply to the firms in question, in which case they might hold excess capital anyway. Nevertheless, for some firms, regulatory capital requirements may increase their cost of capital by simply forcing them to hold "too much" relative to their optimum.

The indirect upward pressure that capital regulations can put on a firm's cost of capital occurs not because of the requirements that firms hold a certain amount of capital but instead because of the specific claims firms often must use to meet capital requirements. In other words, to the extent that regulation forces firms to hold a mixture of claims that causes them to depart from their optimal capital structure, their cost of capital may be increased as a direct result of the regulatory distortion in the capital structure optimum.

Under the M&M assumptions in which capital structure is irrelevant, regulations that affect the relative distribution of claims should not impact the value of the firm. But when one or more M&M assumptions are violated, even firms with excess capital can experience distortions in their decisions about optimal capital structure.

By defining regulatory capital in a manner different from how firms define their own capital, companies may be induced to hold different types of capital that departs from what they might otherwise define as a private optimum. Recall, for example, that Basel I requires that banks hold at least 50 percent of their required capital in Tier I capital and further requires that of the remaining amount of Tier II capital, no more than 50 percent of the Tier I amount can be held as subordinated debt.

Consider a firm that has a required minimum capital level of $100 million that it can satisfy solely with external claims. The accord requires that the firm satisfy this requirement with at least $50 million of equity and, consequently, no more than $25 million of subordinated debt. The firm in question, however, might be a pecking order firm and thus prefer to raise significantly less of this capital with equity. If the firm has excess capital or retained earnings, there is no problem. But if the firm is forced to meet this requirement through public security issues, the capital requirements could force the firm to bear disproportionately higher adverse selection costs than necessary.

Apart from creating distortionary incentives that can impose costs on a firm by pulling it away from an optimal capital structure, capital requirements also can encourage firms to spend often-significant resources to engage in regulatory capital "arbitrage." The benefits of successful regulatory arbitrage often are reduced costs of capital or reduced distortions in the relative capital structure. But at the margin, a firm may spend up to its entire savings on just getting the arbitrage done.

Matten (2000) describes three types of regulatory capital arbitrage that occur specifically under the Basel Accord, all of which also can apply to many insurance regimes, as well. First, the accord may induce cherry picking, in which firms simply avoid exposures that may be positive NPV projects but that receive a higher capital charge. Consider, for example, a bank that considers a loan to an OECD bank and a non-OECD bank, and suppose the NPV of the loan to the latter is slightly higher. But further suppose the higher risk weight on the non-OECD bank is actually enough to tip the bank away from its pecking order capital structure optimum. If the costs of deviating from the pecking order optimum exceed the amount by which the NPV of the non-OECD loan exceeds the OECD loan, the bank may opt for the lower-NPV project. Other types of cherry picking are discussed in later chapters—see especially Chapter 22 on securitization.

The Accord also can prod banks to engage in asset transformation and risk transfer transactions purely to convert on-balance-sheet assets or liabilities to off-balance-sheet claims. As we shall see in Chapters 13, 14, and 22, securitized product vehicles, certain ART forms, and some credit derivatives can be used for this purpose.

Finally, the accord allows banks greater flexibility in assessing the capital they must hold against assets in their trading portfolio than assets associated with their traditional commercial banking operations. Specifically, the classical risk weights approach is required for banking book assets, whereas banks are already allowed to use the "internal models" approach for many capital issues arising in the trading book. As a result of banks' preference for the latter, transactions like "bistro swaps" and "zigzig securitizations" have arisen to exploit the regulatory arbitrage opportunity. See Chapter 22 for a more complete discussion of these types of deals.

CAPITAL REQUIREMENTS AND THE SUPPLY OF CAPITAL

In most cases, the institutions demanding risk management products on which we focus in this book are nonfinancial corporations and some smaller financial institutions. Although some small financial institutions may be subject to minimum capital regulations, most nonfinancial corporations are not. Nevertheless, this does not mean that capital requirements are irrelevant to such firms. On the contrary, capital requirements on suppliers of capital can also adversely affect demanders of capital.

The type of capital regulation to which suppliers of financial capital may be subject can influence the availability, type, and price of the financial capital they are willing to supply. An insurance company required to hold capital against a classical insurance product, for example, may not be required to hold capital against an undrawn contingent capital facility, thereby increasing the insurance company's capacity to write the latter kind of capital product lines. Alternatively, a bank that assists a firm by providing a credit enhancement to an SPV that issues securitized products may face a lower capital requirement than if it engaged in a credit derivatives transaction of fundamentally the same nature.

We have not really discussed any of these products yet, nor how some of them can even be viewed as capital or substitutes for capital. Nevertheless, it is important to explain the regulatory distortions that can influence the supply of capital. We will return to particulars as cases warrant later.

NOTES

1. Henceforth we use the term "(re-)insurance" to refer to insurance and reinsurance companies in the same group.
2. Disclosed reserves must meet certain criteria for their inclusion. In addition, Tier I capital also requires the deduction by the bank of "unamortized goodwill," such as the goodwill capital created for some U.S. banks during the savings and loan crisis of the 1980s.
3. This section is based largely on Culp (1999).
4. 17 C.F.R. 240.15c3-1 (U.S. Code)
5. The methodology was value at risk with a 99 percent confidence level and two-week risk horizon. See Chapter 10 for a further discussion of value at risk, as well as Culp (2001).
6. See Skipper (1998).
7. See Kiln (1991).

Capital Structure and Risk Management

CHAPTER 9

A Vocabulary of Risk

In Part II, we take a closer look at how firms view and manage specific types of risks and how the management of those risks relates to the concepts about capital structure that we developed in Part I. A natural starting point—rather, a requisite beginning—is to establish a clear "vocabulary" of risk. This task is made more complex by the different risk terminologies adopted in insurance and capital market circles. Although risk management products may be converging in these worlds, risk management definitions are certainly not. Accordingly, we address the following questions in this chapter:

- How do firms distinguish between risk types using a consistent "risk vocabulary"?
- How should firms differentiate between the risks they are in the business of bearing from those they are not?

BASIC PRIMER ON THE VOCABULARY OF RISK

Risk can be defined as any source of randomness that may have an adverse impact on the market value of a corporation's assets net of liabilities, on its earnings, and/or on its raw cash flows. Developing a common understanding of what is meant by the term "risk" at the conceptual level is no trivial task. Simply listing the ways a firm can lose money actually is not hard—but also is not helpful. We need instead to make a list of risks in a way that helps the firm manage those risks.

To begin with, let us set forth some important distinctions between "risks" that we will address here[1]:

- *Financial risk:* a financial event that can give rise to unexpected reductions in a firm's cash flows, value, or earnings, the amount of which is determined by the movement in one or more financial asset prices
- *Peril:* a natural, man-made, or economic situation that may cause a personal or property loss

■ *Accident:* an unexpected loss of resources arising from a peril
■ *Hazard:* something that increases the probability of a loss arising from a peril

We discuss each of these concepts in turn.

Financial Risks

A financial risk is a source of potential unexpected losses for a firm that will arise because of some adverse change in market conditions, the financial condition of an obligor to the firm, or the financial condition of the firm itself. Financial risk can impact a company's cash flows, accounting earnings, and/or value (i.e., asset and liability market values). Importantly, the amount of money a firm loses from financial risks that are realized usually depends on the behavior of one or more "market-determined" prices. Five specific types of financial risk are discussed below[2]:

1. Market risk
2. Funding risk
3. Market liquidity risk
4. Credit risk
5. Legal risk

Market Risk

Market risk arises from the event of a change in some market-determined asset price, reference rate (e.g., LIBOR), or index, usually classified based on the asset class whose price changes are impacting the exposure in question. Common forms of asset class-based market risk include interest rate risk, exchange rate risk, commodity price risk (through input purchases or output sales), and equity price risk.

Apart from the market risk factors that influence the value of an exposure, the market risk of an exposure also can be characterized based on how those risk factors impact its value. In this context, market risk generally is classified by using a colorful argot known as "fraternity row" that was reviewed in Appendix 1.2. Trade practitioners and academics alike tend to refer to five types of market risk by using Greek or Greek-sounding letters.

Delta is the risk that the value of an exposure will deteriorate as the price or value of some underlying risk factor changes, all else being equal. A bond is affected by changes in interest rates, so the interest rate is the risk factor. When interest rates rise, bond prices fall. In the bond world, this delta is called "duration." Other examples of delta include the sensitivity of a forward purchase/sale of foreign exchange to a small change in the exchange rate, the sensitivity of a commodity delivery contract to the change in the underlying commodity price, and the variability of a futures or options contract on the S&P 500 stock index to a small change in the prices of any S&P 500 stocks.

Gamma is the risk that delta will change when the value of an underlying risk factor changes. It is sometimes referred to as "convexity risk" or "rate of change" risk. Returning to the bond example, bond prices fall as interest rates rise, but the amount of the price change depends on the level of interest rates. Large interest rate increases may cause larger bond price declines than small interest rate increases.

The risk that volatility changes in the underlying risk factor will cause a change in the value of an exposure goes by many names. *Vega*, *lambda*, *kappa*, and *tau* are among them. For purchased options (longs), declines in volatility pose the risk. Less volatility means there is a smaller chance that the option held will expire profitably. For options written (short), lower volatility increases the odds for profits by reducing the opportunities for unprofitable exercise against the short to occur.

Theta measures the risk to certain exposures due only to the passage of time. Insurance, for example, is an asset that "decays" or "wastes" over time. For every day that passes on an unused insurance policy, there is one less day for the insurance contract to become valuable.

Finally, *rho* is the risk that the interest rates which are used to discount future cash flows in present value calculations will change and impose unexpected losses on the firm. For many exposures, the discount rate is the borrowing or lending rate that corresponds to the maturity of the contract. For other contracts, such as swaps, a yield curve is used to discount cash flows, and hence any shifts in the level of any of several interest rates may affect cash flows.

Yet another market risk—correlation risk—is the risk of an unexpected change in the correlation of two factors affecting the value of a contract. We must be careful here to distinguish between basis risk, or correlation risk arising from the combination of a derivatives contract with another asset or portfolio, and correlation risk affecting a single asset held in isolation or in a portfolio.

Funding Risk

Funding risk occurs in the event that cash inflows and current balances are insufficient to cover cash outflow requirements, often necessitating costly asset liquidation to generate temporary cash inflows. Most firms, both financial and nonfinancial, have liquidity plans designed to manage funding risks. The well-publicized failures of firms like Drexel Burnham Lambert Group, Inc., and MG Refining & Marketing, Inc. (a subsidiary of the German giant Metallgesellschaft AG), and SAir Group (parent company of Swissair and Sabena) occurred largely due to funding problems and have increased corporations' attention to this risk.

The distinctions between pure funding risk and market risk are subtle, as the two are clearly related. Market risk can be viewed as the risk of changes in the value of a bundle of cash flows when adverse market events occur. But value is just defined as the discounted NPV of future cash flows. Funding risk is based on the risk of cash flows when they occur in time. For the purpose of comparing liquidity risk at one time to liquidity risk at another, discounting to an NPV serves no purpose. On the contrary, all that is relevant is cash balances per period. Market risk, by contrast, deals with cash flow risks in any period, because all future cash flows ultimately affect the current NPV of the asset or liability in question.

Despite the distinction, market price fluctuations almost always characterize the exposure associated with funding risk. Although the "triggering event" is a cash funding shortfall, the amount of the shortfall itself and the economic consequences of the shortfall usually are determined by movements in market prices.

Market Liquidity Risk

Market liquidity risk is the risk that volatile markets will inhibit the liquidation of losing transactions and/or the establishment of new transactions to hedge existing market risk exposures. Suppose a firm has negotiated an agreement with a bank to purchase British pounds for Deutsche marks (Dmark) three months from now. If the British pound experiences a massive and rapid depreciation vis-à-vis the Dmark—as happened in September 1992 when the European Monetary System's exchange rate mechanism imploded on "Black Wednesday"—the currency purchase agreement will decline rapidly in value.

The firm in this case may attempt to neutralize its original agreement or enter into an offsetting contract. If the agreement is left unhedged or the counterparty to any offsetting contract defaults, volatility may be so high that a new hedge cannot be initiated at a favorable price, even using liquid exchange-traded futures on pounds and Dmarks. The firm's market risk is thus exacerbated by market liquidity risk.

As in the two prior cases, moreover, the exposure the firm faces—the size of its potential loss—will be based on the amount of the market-driven change in the sterling/Dmark rate.

Credit Risk

Credit risk is the risk of the actual or possible nonperformance by an obligor to the firm. Credit risk usually comes in four forms:

1. *Presettlement credit risk* arises from the potential for an obligor to default on a transaction prior to the initiation of the settlement of that transaction.

2. *Settlement risk* is specifically associated with the failure of a firm during the settlement window, or the time period between the confirmation of a transaction and the final settlement of that transaction.
3. *Migration* or *downgrade risk* is the risk that the increase in the market's perception of a default at a firm causes a decline in the value of the claims issued by that firm.
4. *Spread risk* is the risk that deteriorations in general corporate credit quality will affect the claim issued by a given firm.

The distinctions are best illustrated by a simple example. Suppose Wolfram owns a lyre and issues a claim that entitles its holder to receive his lyre one month hence for the prenegotiated price of 10 gold coins. Assume moreover that at the time the claim is issued, everyone agrees that Wolfram has no possibility of being unable to deliver his lyre. Suppose the value of this claim is worth one gold coin today and that the current market price of lyres is 10 gold coins.

Consider now that Tannhäuser buys the claim from Wolfram and that both payment and delivery are to occur in a month. If Wolfram informs Tannhäuser that he cannot deliver the lyre one hour before the exchange is due to occur, Tannhäuser may experience a presettlement loss. Specifically, suppose the market price of lyres has risen to 15 gold coins, and Wolfram informs Tannhäuser that there is no more lyre and gives Tannhäuser his one gold coin back. But if Tannhäuser still wants a lyre, he must now enter into a new lyre purchase agreement at the new and higher price. Tannhäuser thus incurs a five gold coin replacement cost presettlement credit loss.

Settlement risk, by contrast, arises after the transaction has entered the settlement process and one party defaults. Suppose a month has passed and Tannhäuser pays Wolfram the 10 gold coins, but Wolfram then informs Tannhäuser that he has no lyre to sell. In that case, Tannhäuser incurs a settlement credit loss of 10 gold coins and has no lyre to show for it.[3]

Both presettlement and settlement risk as described above involve the actual default by Wolfram to Tannhäuser. But credit risk also may occur in the form of migration or downgrade risk arising not from an actual default but by an increase in the market's perception of the probability a default will occur. To continue the example, suppose Tannhäuser no longer wishes a lyre but that Venus is in need of one. Tannhäuser may sell the claim to Venus. But if Venus suspects that Wolfram may not be able to deliver the lyre when the full month passes, she likely will pay Tannhäuser less than he paid Wolfram for the original claim whose value was based on the market's original assessment of Wolfram's creditworthiness. In other words, Tannhäuser will experience a capital loss on the claim even though Wolfram has not actually defaulted. The mere increase in the market's perception that he might is enough to reduce the value of the claim.

Finally, Tannhäuser may receive less for the claim than he paid when he sells it to Venus if the market's perception of all corporate credit risks has gone up. This is sometimes called "spread risk" in reference to the default credit spread over the risk-free rate at which cash flows on risky corporate claims must be discounted. Spread risk may be affected by firm-specific credit concerns (i.e., migration risk) or by more systematic default risk premiums in the sense of Fama and French (1993).

Legal Risk

Legal risk is the risk that a firm will incur a loss if a contract it thought was enforceable actually is not. The Global Derivatives Study Group (1993) identified several sources of legal risk for innovative financial instruments that often are associated with risk management, including conflicts between oral contract formation and the statutes of frauds in certain countries and jurisdictions, the capacity of certain entities (e.g., municipalities) to enter into certain types of transactions, the enforceability of "close-out netting," and the legality of financial instruments. In addition, unexpected changes in laws and regulations can expose firms to potential losses as well.

Legal risk is classified here as a financial risk because this particular incarnation of risk results in losses that usually are driven in size and economic importance by changes in market prices. A netting agreement that is unenforceable in insolvency, for example, could lead to cherry-picking losses whose total amounts are based on market price movements. Suppose, for example, that Firm Wotan has an agreement with Firm Siegfried to swap a fixed cash flow of $10,000 quarterly in exchange for receiving from Siegfried a payment equal to the total interest that Siegfried, in turn, receives on a loan portfolio—currently equal to, say, $10,000. With a netting agreement in place, if Firm Siegfried fails, no cash flow occurs on the agreement. If a netting agreement is in place and is held to be unenforceable, Firm Siegfried may try to cherry pick Firm Wotan by demanding the $10,000 Wotan owes Siegfried while simultaneously refusing to pay the $10,000 Siegfried owes Wotan.

The amount of risk borne by Firm Wotan in this example depends on the value of Siegfried's own loan portfolio. If Siegfried's loans are floating rate and the interest rate rises, Seigfried may then owe Wotan $15,000. But without a binding netting agreement, Wotan might never see that money.

Perils, Accidents, and Hazards

A peril is a natural, man-made, or economic "situation" that can cause an unexpected loss for a firm, the size of which is usually not based on the realization of one or more financial variables. A peril thus is essentially a *nonfinancial risk*. An accident is a specific negative event arising from a peril that gives rise to a loss and is usually considered "unintentional." A hazard is something that increases the probability of a peril-related loss occurring, whether intentional or not.

The distinctions between these three concepts are perhaps best understood by way of an example. Consider the peril to a firm of having its employees sustain on-the-job injuries. A related accident would be the unintended opening of a valve on some storage tank at a firm. A hazard could be alcohol or drugs that make an employee more likely to open the value, the presence of corrosive chemicals in the tank that dissolve the valve seals, and the like.

Different types of perils that firms typically face in their business operations include the following[4]:

- *Production*—unexpected changes in the demand for products sold, increases in input costs, failures of marketing
- *Operational*—failures in processes, people, or systems
- *Social*—adverse changes in social policy (e.g., political incorrectness of a product sold), strained labor relations, changes in fashions and tastes, etc.
- *Political*—unexpected changes in government, nationalization of resources, war, etc.
- *Legal*—tort and product liability and other liabilities whose exposures are not driven by financial variables
- *Physical*—destruction or theft of assets in place, impairment of asset functionality, equipment or mechanical failure, chemical-related perils, energy-related perils
- *Environmental*—flood, fire, windstorm, hailstorm, earthquake, cyclone, etc.

Outreville (1998) provides some examples of hazards that increase the probability of loss for different perils:

- *Human*—fatigue, ingnorance, carelessness, smoking
- *Environmental*—weather, noise
- *Mechanical*—weight, stability, speed
- *Energy*—electrical, radiation
- *Chemical*—toxicity, flammability, combustability

It is impossible to list and classify all the different perils and related accidents or hazards that may face all firms. Nevertheless, some are significant enough that they warrant further discussion.

Production Perils

Production-related perils cover any perils that threaten a firm's ability to carry out its normal business activities as expected, usually resulting from changes to the supply or demand for the firm's product or to the physical production process. Shocks to a firm's cost or demand functions, for example, can precipitate a loss of value owing to production risks. Three other production-related perils include customer loss risk, supply chain risk, and reputation risk.

At the core of risks facing a business is the risk that the business loses its customers, either because a competitor attracts them away or because they no longer demand the products and services the firm is selling at the prices it is quoting. Customer loss risk thus encompasses pricing risk, or the risk that firms misestimate either the level or the structure of prices for their customers.

The importance of customer retention has been vividly illustrated by the recent boom in Internet commerce. To a start-up Web company, its ability to accurately assess customer value is everything. Only when those values can be compared accurately to the cost of customer acquisition can the business truly be valued. For this reason, attention to customer loss risk and customer valuation has perhaps never been higher.

Nevertheless, customer loss risk is just as important—perhaps the real core risk of operating a profitable business—for all types of firms. An airline must worry about customer loss just as much as an online bookstore. And a consulting firm must be as attentive as an airline. If either the demand curve shifts inward for exogenous reasons or available substitutes for the good or service being sold become relatively more attractive, the business is in trouble.

Many nonfinancial firms also face risks from adverse events that may occur at any point along a physical "supply chain" (the chain that connects inputs to the firm's production process to its outputs). Problems may arise at any juncture. Consider, for example, a firm that grows wheat, mills it into flour, and exports the flour to bread makers around the world. Problems could arise at origination from disease, bad weather, insects, vandalism, or any number of other factors that prevent the crop from being grown and brought in according to schedule (both time and quantity). At the transformation stage, equipment breakdowns could occur, contamination of the grain is a possibility, and losses of product during transportation are a consideration. And so on. In short, the firm faces some form of inventory or product risk at every stage here.

A third major production-related peril faced by virtually all firms is the risk of a loss to their brand name capital or reputation that can translate into reduced revenues, increased expenses, and fewer customers—hence its classification as a type of production peril. Reputation risk can arise when a firm acts negligently or is simply perceived to act negligently—as Exxon was perceived following the Valdez, Alaska, oil disaster.

Reputation risk also can arise from poor public relations management of external crises, whether or not the crises are the direct fault of the company. A plane crash due to bad weather, for example, can still impose major adverse reputation effects on both the airline and the aircraft manufacturer if the public relations dimension of the disaster is not handled properly.

Finally, reputation risk can arise when a firm simply fails to honor its commitments. An insurance company that regularly tries to avoid paying out claims even when the claims are unambiguous and legitimate, for example, will quickly find itself short of customers.

Operational Perils

Operational risk has been defined by the International Swaps and Derivatives Association, British Bankers' Association, and Risk Management Association as "the risk of loss resulting from inadequate or failed internal processes, people, and systems or from external events."[5] Examples of losses that can be attributed to operational risk include failed securities trades, settlement errors in funds transfers, stolen or damaged physical assets, damages awarded in court proceedings against the firm, penalties and fines assessed by member associations or regulators, irrecoverable or erroneous funds and asset transfers, unbudgeted personnel costs, and negligence or fraud.[6]

Operational perils also can sometimes be considered as a type of financial risk if the operational losses are driven by market, credit, or liquidity risks. The failure of Barings to catch the huge position buildup by rogue trader Nick Leeson was in some sense an operational risk management failure. It was a failure of processes (internal audit and control), people (Leeson was defrauding the firm and others), and systems (a consolidated global position-keeping system would have revealed Leeson's rogue positions). But in the end, Barings went bust because Leeson's positions went underwater as a result of their market risk. Operational risk management may have failed to catch the process, personnel, and systems problem, but market risk sank the firm.

CORE VERSUS NONCORE RISKS

The *core risks* facing a firm may be defined as those risks that the firm is in business to bear and manage so that it can earn returns in excess of the risk-free rate. *Noncore risks*, by contrast, are risks to which a firm's primary business exposes it but that the firm does not necessarily need to retain in order to engage in its primary business line. The firm may well be exposed to noncore risks, but it may not wish to remain exposed to those risks. Core risks, by contrast, are those risks the firm is literally in business not to get rid of.

What Risks Is a Firm in Business to Bear?

Core and noncore risks are sometimes today called "business" and "financial" risks, respectively. An even earlier distinction was proposed by Frank Knight (1921). Knight defined noncore risks as "risks," or situations in which the randomness facing a firm can be expressed in terms of specific, numerical probabilities. These probabilities may be objective (as in a lottery) or subjective (as in a horse race), but they must be quantifiable. Because they can be quantified, they can be managed.

Unlike risk, Knight defined "uncertainty" as situations when a firm faces some randomness that cannot be expressed in terms of the probabilities of alternative outcomes. This was "core risk" in Knight's eyes, or the risks about which only the firm in question had some perceived special insight. To Knight, uncertainty was the source of all major profits and losses to businesses. Lord J. M. Keynes agreed, choosing the term "animal spirits" to describe essentially the same phenomenon.

A major distinction between core and noncore risk—Knightian uncertainty and risk—is driven purely by information. Those factors about which a firm perceives itself as having some comparative informational advantage will be those factors on which the business concentrates for its core business cash flows. Risks about which the firm has comparatively less information will be those risks more likely to be hedged, diversified away, insured, or controlled in some other fashion.

The distinction between core and noncore risk clearly rests on a slippery slope. Not only does it vary from one firm to the next, but it also depends not on the quality of information the firm actually has but rather on the firm's perceived comparative advantage in digesting that information. Perceptions, of course, can be wrong. Businesses fail, after all, with an almost comforting degree of regularity. Without business failures, one might tend to suspect the market is not working quite right. Accordingly, the preponderance of actual business failures clearly means that some firms thought they had a better handle on information than they did, whether that information concerns market demand for their products, their competitors, or their costs.

Slippery though the slope may be, it must be traversed. As we shall see in Chapter 10, a major distinction between risk management products and risk capital is that the former can be tailored to specific types of risk whereas the latter cannot. But the ability to tailor specific products to specific risks is really meaningful only when the firm can distinguish those specific risks it is in business to retain versus those that might be cheaper to avoid.

When to Manage Core Risks

Every firm should identify the risks to which it is subject and then classify those risks as core or noncore. And this classification will differ firm by firm. Indeed, sometimes the same type of firm may classify the same risk in different ways. Not all airlines hedge their jet fuel price risk, for example. This is a tacit indication that those airlines that do hedge believe their core risks to include flying planes without crashing them, selling as many seats as possible, and the like. Nevertheless, other airlines that do not hedge their core risks clearly seem to believe that part of their business means bearing jet fuel price risks.

Although there is no one correct way to draw this distinction, several important variables do need to be taken into consideration by a firm's managers when defining risk as core or noncore. Some of the most important of these considerations include shareholder preferences and expected costs of financial distress.

Shareholder Preferences

Perhaps the most important thing for a company to ascertain in classifying its core and noncore risks is what its residual claimants have to say on the subject. To illustrate very clearly the importance of shareholder preferences, it is worth returning to Chapter 3 for a moment and assuming the M&M assumptions hold. Under the same four assumptions that guarantee independence between the value of the firm and its capital structure, the value of the firm is also independent of any deliberate actions taken by management to control risks through hedging or insurance purchasing. The reason is simple: Shareholders can and do manage risks themselves.

Consider the historical classic of a big corporate farm whose business is selling corn to grain elevators and millers. Residual claimants that own the farm will find that the value of their cash flows and the value of the farm's assets are strongly and directly related to corn prices. When the price of corn rises, the farm's revenues rise, all else being equal. The converse is also true.

Under the M&M assumption of symmetric information, shareholders know the impact of corn price risk on their pro rata claim on the farm just as well as the farm's managers do. And under the M&M assumption of equal access, any individual shareholders can engage in financial transactions on the same terms as the farm itself—terms that include zero transaction costs under the perfect capital markets assumption.

The final M&M assumption was that investment decisions are taken as given. So shareholders look at the firm's investment decisions and its product market exposure to corn prices and then determine *on their own* whether they want to bear corn price risk as a part of their investment portfolios. If not, shareholders can neutralize their corn price risk exposure quite easily by buying shares in a grain elevator or mill. Otherwise, they do nothing and diversify away their idiosyncratic risks as they normally would. In either case, the decision as to whether to manage the corn price risk was made by the shareholder.

Note that the M&M assumptions do not imply that the shareholders should be indifferent to bearing corn price risk. All the M&M assumptions say is that shareholders should be indifferent to whether corn price risk is managed by the farm's managers in the form of hedging or on their own in the form of do-it-yourself hedging (i.e., diversification).

For these reasons, a corporation cannot meaningfully classify the risks to which it is exposed as core or noncore without knowing how shareholders draw that distinction. And the answer may differ based on the shareholders in question, even for remarkably similar firms.

Tufano (1996) conducted a very thoughtful survey of risk management practices in the gold mining industry by studying about 50 firms whose core business was clearly viewed as being the sale of gold. Financial contracts that allow companies and individual investors alike to hedge their gold price risk, moreover, abound. Nevertheless, there is really no way ex ante to predict which firms will decide to classify gold price risk as part of their core business risks and which ones will classify gold price risk as noncore and hence ripe to be hedged.

Indeed, Tufano found a remarkable disparity across these otherwise similar firms. Somewhat surprisingly, over 85 percent of the firms he studied used some form of gold price risk management tools between 1990 and 1993. In addition, he argued that "firms have adopted very different risk management approaches, ranging from Homestake Mining, which sold all of its production at spot prices and made vigorous pronouncements against gold price management, to American Barrick, which featured its successful hedging program on the cover of its annual report."

In the end, each company must decide on its own what business it is in, and what risks that means the company is in business to bear—what risks the firm's shareholders *do not* want it to hedge away. Answering this question is not always easy, but it is critical for determining whether bearing any given source of risk should be considered part of the firm's core business or not.

Expected Costs of Financial Distress

In some situations, a firm may define a risk as a core risk it is in the business of bearing it most of the time but not all of the time. An electric utility, for example, may conclude that bearing power price risk is core to its business and thus not routinely neutralize the impact of electricity price changes on its value, cash flows, and earnings. Nevertheless, even a firm like this might be unprepared for events like the summer of 1998 in the United States, when prices in the Midwest for power rose from an average of about $35 per megawatt hour to a bid of nearly $7,500 per megawatt hour. Even a utility in the business of bearing power price risk may want to try to avoid the impact of that scenario.

Note that if a utility concludes that it is routinely exposed to high distress costs from being unhedged against power price risks—more so than its competitors and more so than its shareholders would like to bear—that fact strongly suggests the utility's core business is in generating power, maintaining lines and poles, running customer bills, and the like but may not include bearing power price risk. If the utility considers power price risk a core risk, then examples like the one above should occur extremely rarely, only in catastrophic situations, and should only involve a short duration for the hedge. In other words, firms hedge their core risks mainly for market timing reasons and not outright exposure management reasons.

RETAINED VERSUS TRANSFERRED RISKS

A major purpose of distinguishing between risk—especially core versus non-core risks—is to help a firm make its *retention decision*. The retained risk or retention of a firm is the agglomeration of risks—core and noncore—to which the firm is naturally exposed in the conduct of its business that the firm decides to bear rather than to shift to another market participant. Transferred risk, by contrast, is any risk to which a firm is exposed that a firm decides it is not in the business of bearing and decides to transfer to another market participant.

The decision whether to retain or transfer a given risk is essentially a determination by the firm's shareholders of whether they want to absorb any realized losses arising from the risk in question or whether they would prefer to have the equity holders of another firm absorb those losses. A core factor to firms in making this determination will, of course, be the benefit/cost trade-off—whether the benefit of transferring the risk is above the cost at the margin. The cost of risk transfer can include both the opportunity cost of forgone profits or positive returns, the pure transaction costs of the risk transfer, and/or the price that the firm may have to pay to induce the equity holders of another corporation to assume the risk the firm is trying to transfer away.

Issues that can affect a firm's retention decision are discussed in the remainder of Part II. In addition, we shall return to the retention decision in Chapter 17, where we reconsider the risk transfer decision and explore the need for firms to finance the risks that they do choose to retain.

NOTES

1. See Outreville (1998).
2. Our categorization of financial risk is based on the Global Derivatives Study Group (1993). See also Culp (2001).
3. Settlement risk is sometimes called "Herstatt risk," so named from the failure of Bankhaus Herstatt in Germany in 1974. The convention in most foreign currency markets is for settlement two days after a spot transaction is consummated or a forward contract matures. A number of New York

banks had initiated payments to Herstatt on their side of a group of spot and forward currency trades, and Herstatt failed *after* those payments were initiated from New York but *before* any reciprocal payments were initiated from Germany. The New York banks suffered considerable principal losses.

4. This list is a hybrid from several sources, but mainly Outreville (1998) and Doherty (2000).

5. ISDA/BBA/RMA (1999).

6. These examples are based on the sample data entry form for the British Bankers' Association operational risk and loss database.

CHAPTER 10

Risk Management as a Process

Risk management is the process by which organizations try to ensure that the risks to which they are exposed are the risks to which they think they are and need to be exposed to operate their primary business. Risk management is thus the process by which firms identify their risks and then take any ex ante or ex post actions required to control deviations of actual risk exposures from predefined tolerances to those risks.

Culp (2001) explored the risk management process in terms of both strategy (i.e., when risk management can add value to a business) and tactics (i.e., how actually to do risk management). Accordingly, the focus of this book is not on risk management as a process but rather on relations between capital structure and one specific part of the risk management process—risk *control*. Nevertheless, some introduction to risk management as a process is required to understand where risk control fits into the bigger picture of capital structure and risk. Accordingly, this chapter addresses the following questions[1]:

- What are the components of risk management as an organized business process?
- What different kinds of "risk cultures" describe how firms utilize their internal risk management process?
- What are the primary business processes that a firm must modify to implement its chosen risk culture?

RISK MANAGEMENT AS A BUSINESS PROCESS

The objective of risk management need not be the elimination of risk. Every time a man crosses the street, he faces the risk of being struck by car. To eliminate that risk completely would require that he never cross the street. Most people opt instead to find more palatable risk management solutions, such as looking both ways before crossing.

Corporations following the market value rule are not fundamentally different from the man crossing the street. Corporations, after all, are in business to take risks, without which their shareholders would simply earn the risk-free rate on capital invested.

Risk management as an organizational process can be separated into five general activities, depicted in Exhibit 10.1:

1. Identify risks and determine tolerances.
2. Measure risks.
3. Monitor and report risks.
4. Control risks
5. Oversee, audit, tune, and realign the risk management process.

Some firms structure this process with more formality and centralization than others, but all firms manage risk in this five-step process—whether they realize it or not.

Identify Core and Noncore Risks and Determine Tolerances

Risk identification is the process by which a company recognizes and, in some cases, detects the different financial risks to which it is exposed through the

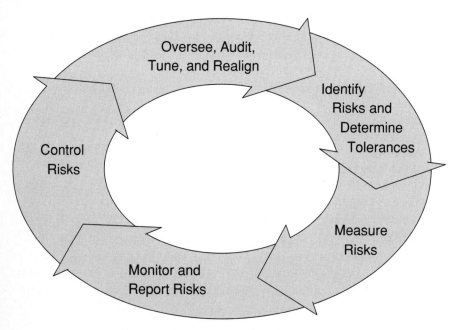

EXHIBIT 10.1   Internal Risk Management Process

normal course of conducting its business. Almost by definition, the risks that are most insidious for a company are those risks to which it is exposed that have not been identified.

Risks can be left unidentified for reasons ranging from poor internal controls that allow the unnoticed booking of risky financial transactions to basic oversight of fundamental exposures. The process by which members of a company review, analyze, and discuss their risk profiles is an indispensable means by which risks can be identified and hence managed.

Companies whose risk profiles do not change very frequently often feel that risk identification is not a crucial component of the risk management process. Nevertheless, numerous examples provide strong evidence to the contrary. Had Barings properly identified the huge long position on Japanese equities accumulated in Singapore by rogue trader Nick Leeson, the firm might not have gone bust. Had Procter & Gamble identified the massive interest rate risk affecting its treasury through a naked swap contract, the company might have avoided several hundred million dollars in losses.[2]

To take a simple example of the importance of risk identification, consider a hypothetical company called Airline FlyMe that transports passengers from the United States to Switzerland and back. The obvious core risks faced by the company include the risk of plane crashes, maintenance-related delays, equipment damage from fire, and a loss of customers. Less obvious but perhaps equally significant are risks such as rising jet fuel prices or fluctuations in the franc/dollar exchange rate. As noted in Chapter 9, without a systematic process to categorize these different risk exposures as core or noncore, Airline FlyMe's shareholders may never realize fully the different avenues through which the value of their capital can be adversely affected.

Given the risks a company has identified, senior managers and directors must agree on tolerable levels of those risks required for the operation of the firm's primary business. This determination should be made explicitly by the firm's key shareholders as well as senior managers and sometimes major creditors.

Enterprise-wide Absolute Risk Tolerance

A firm can express its tolerance for different risks in either absolute or relative terms. Firms that take the absolute approach may define risk across all exposures of the firm in terms of maximum loss amounts and frequencies of their occurrence. A firm might not wish its aggregate financial losses arising from noncore risks, for example, to exceed $10 million in more than five of the next 100 months. This $10 million loss tolerance is the firm's aggregate value at risk (VaR). Similar measures like earnings at risk (EaR) and cash flows at risk (CfaR) are also sometimes used with earnings and cash flow loss targets, respectively.[3]

For an enterprise-wide absolute risk tolerance to make sense, however, the company must be capable of measuring its actual exposure at any given time relative to that tolerance level, as the next section explains. Many firms find this intractable because all of the firm's exposures cannot be reliably aggregated. Most nonfinancial corporations, in particular, characterize their risk tolerances in relative terms instead.

Natural Risk Exposure-based Tolerances

A key concept in the definition of relative risk tolerance is the notion of a firm's "natural risk exposure," or the risk that the firm must take in order to meet its primary business (e.g., production) goals. Just because the risk is production-related does not mean it is a noncore production peril. On the contrary, we are discussing here by deliberate design risks that are not core, despite the fact they may still be entwined with the production process.

The determination of how much of a certain type of noncore risk is "too much" can be made relative to the corresponding natural risk exposure. In order for Airline FlyMe to meet its expected customer transit obligations, for example, the expected jet fuel requirement can be approximated, thereby defining a quantitative estimate of the natural jet fuel exposure the firm must incur in order to fly its planes. If its annual jet fuel requirement is X gallons per year, the airline may choose to be exposed to the risk of rising prices on no more than 50 percent of those X gallons. The firm then must use risk control mechanisms and risk management products to reduce its natural exposure to rising jet fuel prices in a manner discussed later.

How a firm decides the degree to which it wants to bear the risks of its natural business exposure is a decision that should rest with shareholders. At the same time Airline FlyMe determines that .5X gallons of fuel per year is its maximum tolerable exposure to rising jet fuel prices, shareholders of Airline BlueSky might quite rationally decide to hedge none of its natural exposure of, say, 100X gallons per year. The answer will differ for each firm, thus again underscoring the importance of involvement by key stakeholders in this determination.

Relative Exposure Tolerances

For some risks, the concept of a natural exposure is not well defined, in which case the company's relative risk tolerance must be compared to other yardsticks. Interest rate risk provides a good example. The degree to which a firm is subject to interest rate risk depends crucially on the firm's capital structure of the firm—the amount of debt the firm issues and the maturities of those debt instruments. If the firm has an optimal capital structure in the trade-off theory context, for example, the amount of debt the firm must issue—and, hence, its natural interest rate risk—will be based on the optimal leverage ratio that emerges from that capital structure model.

When natural exposure cannot be easily defined, other candidates for expressing the firm's risk tolerance are usually available. In the case of interest rate risk, for example, the firm may choose to define its tolerance by requiring its interest rate exposure to be no greater than the exposure on its issued debt instruments at any given time. That tolerance says nothing about what the outstanding level of debt should be, but it does preclude additional interest rate risk taking, as in the bet on interest rates made in the early 1990s by Procter & Gamble's treasury.[4]

Measure Risks

Risk measurement involves the quantification of certain risk exposures for the purpose of comparison to company-defined risk tolerances. The process by which different risks are quantified is a critical component in an organization's broad risk management program. Without a good measure of risk, a determination can be hard to reach about whether the company is taking "too much" of some types of risks or, conversely, "not enough" of another.

The proper tools for measuring financial risk depend both on the risk in question and the nature of the tolerable level of risk expressed by the company. In the cases of the two airlines, risk tolerances were expressed as the number of gallons to which the company is exposed on jet fuel price fluctuations. Measuring this is easy enough. But this risk tolerance says nothing about the potential losses the firm could incur on those gallons purchased at fluctuating market prices.

Market risks thus are most often quantified using measures such as VaR that reflect losses in terms of dollars and associate those losses with probabilities they will occur. Although harder to put in that framework, credit and operational risks are being increasingly measured in that fashion as well. Culp (2001) provides a summary of alternative methods for measuring market, credit, liquidity, and operational risks.

Monitor and Report Risk

A third component of the risk management process is risk monitoring and reporting. The risks to which a firm is subject can change for two reasons. The first is a change in the composition of a company's assets or liabilities. To monitor changes in risk arising for this reason, firms generally rely on simple tools, such as open position reports, statements of current payables and receivables, and the like. But the risks affecting a firm also may change simply because the factors affecting the cash flows on its assets or liabilities (or the discount rates for those cash flows) fluctuate. In Airline FlyMe's case, for example, the jet fuel risk profile could change either because additional fuel must be purchased above the company's baseline natural risk exposure estimate or because rising prices increase the cost of existing purchase requirements.

The frequency with which a firm monitors its current risk profile depends on the nature of the risks to which the firm is subject as well as the firm's ability to fine-tune its risk-taking activities. A trading firm in the business of selling options, for example, may monitor its market risk as often as intraday using tools like VaR to recalculate potential losses. Airline FlyMe, however, may monitor its jet fuel risks significantly less often. Not only does the risk profile of the airline change more slowly, but the firm may not be willing to incur the costs to control its risks more often than, say, monthly or quarterly.

Control Risks

Closely related to risk monitoring is risk control, or the actions a firm takes to keep its actual risk profile at or below its risk tolerance. Sound risk control decisions are possible only when the measurement and risk monitoring/reporting parts of the process are working properly. In other words, unless a firm can compare its actual risks to its risk tolerances, the firm cannot determine whether actions should be taken to reduce those risks except on a purely ad hoc basis.

Risk control is the part of the risk management process in which a firm determines whether to retain or transfer one or more of the risks to which it is naturally exposed. In some cases, a company's risk control response to a divergence between actual and desired risk exposures is to take no action. If the cost of closing the gap is larger than the gap, for example, hedging would end up costing shareholders, and retention will be the right decision. Consequently, a well-functioning risk management process does not always yield actions that change the risk profile of the company. But if the company's risk profile can be changed in a manner by which the marginal benefit of the change in exposure is equal to its marginal cost, risk transfer products—both traditional (see Part III) and alternative (see Part IV)—are means by which this is possible.

Risk control can be undertaken *ex ante* or *ex post*. The former usually involves internal controls on risk-taking activities that prevent actions from being taken *ex ante* that would increase the risk of a company beyond its tolerance. Internal controls may include market and credit risk limits and may require, for example, that traders seek advance approval before executing a contemplated deal that would push the firm's actual risks above its tolerance level. Risk management products such as position-keeping and monitoring systems are often essential support systems for a sound system of internal controls on financial risk.

Risk transfer or *risk transformation products* are also key components of the risk control process and can be used both *ex ante* and *ex post*. Such products may include traditional products such as insurance, reinsurance, and derivatives, and certain activities such as securitization (see Part III) and alternative risk transfer products (see Part IV). Risk transformation products are typically classified either as risk transfer or risk financing products. The former are used to change the risk profile of a firm, whereas the latter are more commonly associated with changing the firm's cash flow or funding profile without necessarily making a major change to the company's fundamental risk exposures. The relation between risk transfer versus risk finance and a firm's risk retention decision will be explored again in Chapter 17.

Oversee, Audit, Tune, and Realign

The final component of a properly functioning risk management process is risk audit and oversight and the fine-tuning of the risk management process itself. This component includes everything from external audits of risk management policies and procedures to internal reviews of quantitative exposure measurement models. In essence, risk audit and oversight is the process by which the firm addresses whether its risk management process is working properly and efficiently.

This final step in the risk management process, as Exhibit 10.1 demonstrates, feeds back into the first step of risk identification and determination of risk tolerances. In other words, the risk management process is a dynamic one, with each repeated iteration involving the incorporation of information obtained in previous implementation of the process.

The passage of time throughout the evolution of the risk management process is not instantaneous and can create significant differences between the expectations of senior managers and the actual implementation of the risk management process. Especially if the risk management process is time-consuming to implement initially, this stage of the process provides the critical opportunity for managers and directors to realign their goals and try to ensure that the design of the risk management process matches the current needs of the corporation.

RISK MANAGEMENT AND "RISK CULTURE"

The lens through which managers and directors of a company view its financial and business risks and organizationally manage those risks define the firm's "risk culture." In conventional corporate risk cultures, risk management is perceived as a cost center whose primary purpose is the reduction of financial risks that are seen to be undesirable virtually a priori. Risk reduction usually is achieved with the aid of expensive analytical systems and costly risk transformation products provided by swap dealers, insurance companies, exchanges, and clearinghouses. These products often appear to have little or no value to shareholders aside from helping companies avert catastrophic losses. In other words, the classical view of risk management is as a necessary evil.

Alternative risk cultures are increasingly observed in which firms leverage their internal risk management processes into potentially significant efficiency gains and new product development opportunities. In this new risk culture, financial risk is not a "problem" to be solved but rather a vital component of business and a critical source of innovation and growth. With proper attention to the business processes of governance, product management, customer management, and knowledge management, a well-designed risk management process thus can be viewed not as a cost center but as a business.

Corporations can utilize their internal risk management processes in at least three different ways, each of which leads to a different risk culture for the firm. As noted, many firms still rely on their risk management process solely for the purpose of internal risk control and policy compliance. Others leverage their own internal risk management expertise into the supply of risk management products that are demanded by their customers for risk control purposes. And still other firms utilize the risk management process to help identify and achieve efficiency gains in other business processes. Firms tend to evolve over time from one category to the next, as illustrated in Exhibit 10.2.

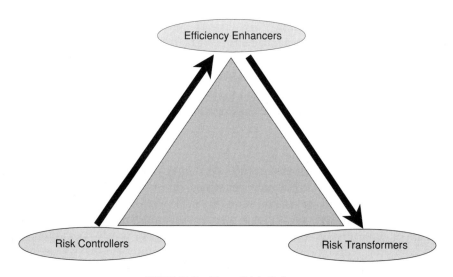

EXHIBIT 10.2   Three Risk Cultures

Risk Controllers

Risk controllers are those firms that allocate resources to a risk management process exclusively in order to avoid losses in excess of the firms' predefined risk tolerances. Firms of this type do not view risk management as a business at all. Instead, it is a cost center deemed necessary for the prevention of undesired losses in excess of stakeholder risk preferences.

For firms' whose business model is risk control, gaps between actual risk exposures and target risk exposures often must be closed with risk transformation products, such as those discussed in Part III. In addition, the internal risk management process at such firms usually emphasizes such concepts as VaR, EaR, CfaR, and downside risk calculations; policy and procedures reviews; evaluations of the effectiveness of hedging strategies; hedge ratio calculation and rebalancing; credit risk management and monitoring; collateral management; and cash management.

Efficiency Enhancers

Firms that leverage their risk management process into efficiency enhancements in other, non–risk-related business lines are, like firms that utilize risk management for pure risk control, concerned primarily with managing risk for their own internal purposes and not with providing risk management products to other firms in the marketplace. But the focus of firms with an efficiency enhancement business model is on the strategy of risk management rather than on the tactical implementation issues raised by firms with a risk control business model.

Firms adopting the efficiency enhancement model seek to use risk control tools not just for classical risk control but rather to operate their businesses more effectively. Firms that demand risk management services for efficiency enhancement purposes, moreover, often utilize risk management products that are quite distinct from those used by firms in the risk control category. Of paramount importance are strategic consulting services rather than precanned software solutions and overused policy and procedure templates.

In addition, specific systems tools also can prove useful for firms in this segment of the market, especially to the extent those tools facilitate enterprise-wide, efficiency-oriented risk calculations such as risk-adjusted return on capital, risk-adjusted capital budgeting, and earnings scenario analyses.

As an example, a common efficiency enhancement goal of companies is to enhance their utilization of capital and to analyze business opportunities with tools like capital budgeting and economic value added (EVA™) analysis. With the aid of analytical tools that calculate risk-adjusted return on capital as well as EVA™, firms can leverage the solutions adopted for risk control purposes into efficiency gains in other business lines. Traditional capital budgeting decisions, for example, can be augmented with "real options" valuation models that will better ration the investment of scarce capital. Alternatively, EVA™-type analyses can be augmented with a value-at-risk calculation to implement risk-adjusted return on capital (RAROC) calculations and allocation mechanisms.[5] Both of these types of calculations can, in principle, be done using the same basic analytical tools as are required in the pure risk control model, although the application of these calculations is fundamentally different.

Risk Transformers

Companies that pursue a risk transformation business model tend to view risk management primarily as a business opportunity. The design of new financial products was once largely the domain of investment and merchant banks, swap dealers, and insurance companies. An interesting feature of this market segment, however, is that it is increasingly being served by firms that have evolved from being demanders of risk management products for efficiency enhancement purposes into suppliers of financial innovations. Nonfinancial firms like ABB, Siemens, The Andre Group, Roche, and DaimlerChrysler are providing more traditional financial intermediaries with serious competition as they offer their clients more integrated, customer-driven risk management products and solutions. The other interesting feature of the market for the supply of risk transformation products is the theme of this book.

Although firms with this business model have moved away from using risk management purely for internal purposes, they also still need risk transformation products—perhaps to help offset any risks created by their entrance into "financial R&D."

Some firms supply risk transformation solutions as their core business. Swap dealers and insurance companies are obvious examples. But for nonfinancial firms that have migrated from the risk control and efficiency enhancement models to the risk transformation business model, an alternative implementation strategy may be required. Specifically, new risk management businesses often are set up on the periphery of a firm's existing business, challenging both the conventional business model and the status quo corporate culture. Accordingly, most new businesses should be set up as "incubators" outside the traditional business model and yet still under the control of the designer.

IMPLEMENTING THE APPROPRIATE RISK CULTURE

The position of any given firm in Exhibit 10.2 may well change over time. Firms like Siemens and ABB, for example, once focused more on risk control and efficiency enhancement than financial R&D and the provision of risk transformation products and services. Conversely, firms like Bank~Austria once actively supplied nontraditional risk transformation products like ART solutions but have increasingly backed away from such product offerings in favor of more traditional banking product offerings.

Where a company lies in this "cycle" and the degree to which a firm can utilize and leverage that risk management process to exploit commercial business opportunities depends on several key factors. One of the most important is the relative cost of providing capital and/or financial intermediation services. If a firm cannot provide risk transformation products at a lower cost than at least some of its competitors, for example, making the jump from efficiency enhancer to risk transformer does not make a lot of sense. Fundamentally, the choice of a firm's risk culture thus is a problem of corporate strategy and comparative advantage.

Once a firm has determined the risk culture appropriate to its business strategy, the risk culture must be implemented. This requires attention to four key factors or generalized business processes:

1. Governance
2. Product management
3. Customer management
4. Knowledge management.

The interaction between these generalized business processes and a firm's internal risk management process characterizes the company's risk culture.

Governance

The business process of governance is critical at each stage of the internal risk management process. Sound internal risk management requires independence of risk management decisions from risk-taking activities to preserve the integrity of the risk management process. Apart from the role of governance in the risk management process, however, governance as a more general business process also helps characterizes the relation between that internal risk management process and new business opportunities.

A sound governance process for a corporation should provide the proper organizational support for the design, implementation, evaluation, and tuning of a company's risk management strategy. For those firms wishing to limit their risk management activities to internal risk management, the key success factors for a sound governance process will include the following: independence between risk-taking and risk-controlling areas of the firm; clear determinations of risk tolerances by senior managers and directors; regular outside reviews of the process, and much more.

A firm that wishes to mobilize its internal risk management expertise into externally offered products, by contrast, faces some additional governance issues. First, the firm must ensure that the risks of supplying risk transformation products is managed in the internal risk management process. Second, governance processes should ensure consistency between the definition and treatment of risk internally and in externally supplied products. Finally, a critical role for governance is ensuring the separation of management responsibilities for the supply of risk management products and the implementation of the internal risk management process.

Whether a firm is restricting its attention to risk control issues or is leveraging its risk management process into efficiency gains and product development, sound governance also should try to ensure that resources are allocated to the risk management process in a responsible fashion—in a fashion that attempts to equate the benefits of risk management to its costs. For firms focused on risk control, governance often means avoiding the temptation to believe that the company has taken all the steps it needs for "due diligence" by investing a fortune in a piece of risk management software. And conversely. The functionality of the software purchased to assist internal risk managers should be adequate and yet not include too many redundant features, and sound governance processes are necessary to help organizations draw that distinction.

Product Management

Companies that wish to transform internal risk management processes, tools, and expertise into customer-vended products must be extremely attentive to their customer product mix. This mix may include a combination of risk transformation vehicles such as insurance solutions, risk advisory services, and systems-based risk management customer solutions.

Financial risk management products come in essentially three varieties. The first is the risk transformation product, or any financial product that allows a firm to alter its financial risk profile. Risk transformation products include trading and clearing products (e.g., securities, futures, and listed options), over-the-counter derivatives (e.g., forwards and swaps), and insurance contracts. Such products are especially important to firms in the risk control component of the risk management process shown in Exhibit 10.1.

A second type of risk management product is advisory services. Advisory services include consulting services provided concerning any aspect of a risk management process as well as transaction structuring advisory services that may play a role in selecting any risk transformation products acquired by a company.

Finally, risk management products include decision-support systems that can have a wide range of applications to the risk management process.

Designing Products for Customers

Rarely is the design and marketing of financial products viewed as the same type of problem as the design and marketing of, say, chemicals or razor blades, in which customer demand dictates the nature of the product mix. When the product innovation principles that apply to physical products are utilized in the financial engineering process, the outcome is tailored customer financial products and services delivered at a reasonable cost that help the offering firm secure wider market coverage and higher customer retention rates.

One principle of product design often overlooked in the marketing of financial products is the customer's risk profile and how much the customer is willing to pay for that risk profile. In certain competitive markets, the product mix is essentially given, thus precluding risk-based pricing. Consequently, nonprice mechanisms must be used to try to manage the risks of providing such products.

Companies can leverage their internal risk management expertise into new products by developing new customer-oriented products that allow those customers to price their own risk. When competitive forces dictate the pricing of the basic product, the company must use its own insights into the risk management process to provide new products that essentially price risk indirectly through the differences in the product mix, rather than observed differences in the pricing of the same product.

Customer Management

A key factor that drives firms away from using risk management processes solely for risk control is customer relationship management. "Economies of scope" are realized when the same input—such as information—can be used multiple times by a firm to reduce total costs. As noted in Chapter 2, banks, for example, have always been thought to enjoy economies of scope from their collection and analysis of information about their customers' credit risks.[6] Once information has been collected for a loan, that same information then reduces the bank's costs of providing the same customer with other services, such as capital markets intermediation or insurance solutions.

Increasingly, nonfinancial corporations face similar economies of scope and are enjoying the same informational advantage as banks through their multiproduct dealings with customers. As an example, consider a trade finance provider whose principal business is lending to customers to finance exports and imports. Through knowledge of its customers' total business portfolios, these firms are well positioned to leverage that customer information into the provision of risk management products and services. The trade financier might provide, for example, outsourced risk measurement to its trade finance clients, thereby both serving its clients' needs and helping ensure that its customers do not default or fail to hedge the collateral of their trade credits.

Banks can provide that sort of service as well and have done so for many years with little competition. But unlike a bank, trade financiers are also active in the physical markets in which its customers are operating. Accordingly, they have the same information about their customers as banks and the added knowledge of expertise in the specific product markets in which their clients are active. Not surprisingly, firms like Cargill Investor Services, Cargill Financial Services, and DaimlerChrysler Services have been extremely successful in making the leap from the efficiency enhancement model to the risk transformation model, at the expense of their classical bank and investment bank competitors.

Balancing Strategy with Operations

Utilizing risk management processes to serve customers requires a balanced alignment of corporate strategy, operations, and culture. On the strategic side, a company must address the following questions:

- To whom do we sell risk management products and services?
- What specific risk management products and services do we sell?
- With whom do we compete?
- How do we win?

Clearly and positively answering these strategic questions, however, is not enough. Equally important is a customer-focused organization and culture. For firms whose past experience with risk management is purely the risk control model, some shift in the corporate culture will be essential to leverage the internal risk management process to an external set of products and services. This shift requires the firm to organize itself for success, drive attitudes and behaviors within the firm toward a new strategic customer-centric vision, and fill any critical skill gaps.

Aside from aligning strategic goals with corporate culture, operational excellence in the risk management process is probably the key ingredient to sound customer management. To ensure excellence in this process, the firm should know those risk management activities in which it excels, how it interacts with customers, and how it leverages its risk technology, systems, and processes for competitive advantage.

Knowledge Management

A final business process that plays a critical role in determining how well a company can leverage its internal risk management process into efficiency gains and externally supplied risk transformation products is knowledge management. Many of the risk management tools, systems, and models used by a firm in its internal risk management can be used to develop financial products, as well as supply advisory services and systems solutions to customers. But doing this requires careful attention to the management of information and knowledge between the various parts of the company.

Returning to our trade finance company, the firm's internal risk management process will include models used for evaluating customer credit risk as well as models used to determine the effectiveness of customer hedging strategies. No matter how sound the models used by the internal risk managers for these purposes, they are only as good as the degree to which they are understood and utilized by line credit officers and account managers. The ability of credit officers to achieve maximum productivity gains from models and other tools, moreover, depends not just on the models themselves but also on the extent to which knowledge and information are being effectively communicated by the division of the company that maintains the models to the line credit officers.

A significant part of the challenge in optimizing the personnel-to-tools trade-off is ensuring that business line account managers and the risk management division are achieving the appropriate level of knowledge sharing. The ideal credit scoring model, for example, will be of limited use if business line managers do not understand its uses and applications. Similarly, a credit scoring model developed by an internal risk manager with no input from business line managers may lack many of the features that would enable the line approval process to become more standardized and automated.

In order to optimize the knowledge management issues related to risk management, a firm must address four dimensions simultaneously:

1. Content
2. Process
3. Culture
4. Infrastructure

Content

Any approach to enhancing knowledge management must start by asking which knowledge is relevant for strategy and ongoing operations. Which knowledge will be needed for the firm's activities in three to five years' time? In what form must lessons learned be documented in order to make an impact on future projects? The goal of knowledge management is not to create an encyclopedia but to determine the critical knowledge requirements for achieving strategic goals and improving operational efficiency. For our trade finance firm, the content might include the relevant models but also experiences about the different ways of applying those models and the lessons learned by line officers while using the models.

In many cases the existing sources of knowledge and experience do not provide the quality required in terms of content or form. Then the processes that deliver knowledge (e.g., the risk evaluation processes) have to be considered. Do they really ask the right questions to obtain findings that ultimately will lead to significant and sustainable improvement of the credit approval process? If not, how can they be changed accordingly?

Process

Knowledge management must be institutionalized. Processes like defining and redefining objectives, creating and updating knowledge, storing and disseminating knowledge, and applying knowledge thus must become part of the standard operating procedures of the organization. Knowledge management tasks and responsibilities also must be assigned, and, if necessary, new roles in the organization must be defined (e.g., knowledge sponsor, knowledge integrator or steward, knowledge base architect and knowledge base administrator). Recruitment and training for these new roles must be defined.

Culture

The definition and design of a knowledge base in terms of content and technology is often the easiest part in enhancing knowledge management. But how can a company ensure that the corporate culture supports the creation and exchange of knowledge? The barriers that oppose the exchange of knowledge in a company must be assessed, especially in the context of a firm's past experience. The corporate culture then must be evaluated and possibly reframed to ensure that the proposed exchange of knowledge can be supported.

In moving from a risk control business model to an efficiency enhancement or risk transformation business model, adopting a risk culture at the corporate level is arguably the most important key success factor for the firm. As noted earlier, the conventional interpretation of a risk culture is a focus on risk avoidance and risk reduction. An essential outcome of the knowledge management process at firms adopting the efficiency enhancement or risk transformation business models must be to ensure that different parties in the firm recognize this conventional interpretation is *not* the appropriate view of risk. Knowledge management must ingrain into the firm's culture the belief that risk is vital for business, innovation, and growth and that risk management is a source of opportunity as well as a means of maintaining the required internal controls.

Infrastructure

To facilitate easy access to knowledge, the appropriate media must be chosen, and this choice can differ radically across different companies and different company types. The overall purpose, the intended use, and the contents of the knowledge base define the requirements for the information technology (IT) infrastructure, and the integration of the knowledge management tools in the existing IT infrastructure is crucial. One of the goals of this step thus should be an assessment of the existing IT landscape and of the different technological options for the development of adequate knowledge management applications.

As noted in our discussion of governance, firms should exercise caution when identifying IT packages for support of the risk management process. When the firm is operating in the risk control model, the temptation to overspend on systems with a high degree of functionality is high. But overinvestment in the wrong system can have adverse consequences down the line if the firm finds that the high degree of functionality is not aimed at its particular business. An expensive VaR system, for example, may be functional for a swap dealer with a portfolio of exotic options, but, despite the price, it may lack basic tools, such as industry cost of capital calculations, that would be required for use by a nonfinancial corporation. While the expensive and sleek solution may appear better, it often is ill suited to the actual corporate strategy and thus makes little sense—especially when evaluated on a benefit/cost basis.

Differences across Firms

Depending on the type of firm in question and its business objectives, the four business processes will interact with the firm's internal risk management process to yield very different risk cultures. How a nonfinancial corporation leverages its risk management process, for example, may differ from how a financial intermediary views risk management as a business.

Consider first a nonfinancial corporation—say, a wholesale manufacturing firm that sells large machines to commercial customers. Exhibit 10.3 gives some examples of how the four business processes interact with internal risk management if the company's objective is to leverage its risk management expertise by turning the treasury function in a type of nonbank bank for external customers.

As the examples of the outcomes of each business process illustrate, a key challenge for a corporate treasury that wishes to provide financial management products and services to both internal business lines and external customers is establishing the risk control parameters for how much risk the treasury will take. The role of governance in this case thus is to ensure that by offering a wider range of products and services, the treasury does not assume interest rate risks that the company is unprepared to bear.

At the same time, attention to knowledge, customer, and product management is necessary if the treasury is to exploit its knowledge and systems in the risk management area to serve customers through enhanced relationship

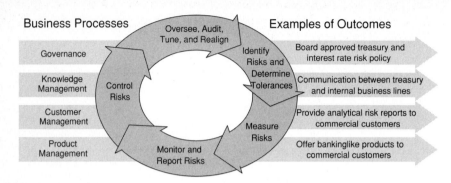

EXHIBIT 10.3   Nonbank Offering Banking Services to Customers

management and product offerings. In knowledge management, a key issue will be communication between treasury and both internal business line clients and external customers concerning the range of risk management products and services that are available and how those products and services can better help them accomplish their business goals. This is complemented by customer management, in which the treasury must learn enough about customers (e.g., the purchasers of the firm's machines) to provide the services they might need. And product management in turn requires the treasury to alter the financial services provided to commercial clients in a manner that exploits the firm's comparative advantage in risk and financial management by offering products that are tailored to the businesses in which the firm's customers are operating.

Now consider a different example of a financial agent. Although banks and insurance companies usually are considered the prototypical financial agents, consider instead our commodities trade financier from earlier that offers letters of credit and other structures to help customers finance their imports or exports. Exhibit 10.4 illustrates examples of the outcomes from interactions between business processes and internal risk management for such a financial agent.

Unlike the case in Exhibit 10.3 in which the nonfinancial corporate was setting up a nonbank bank, a firm mainly interested in trade finance and related services will have a governance process focus on policies like a clearly articulated *credit* policy. A knowledge management issue in this case, in turn, will involve how the firm manages information flows between line credit approval officers and the centralized credit risk management function. Customer management will likely focus on areas in which the firm can offer its customers new services that exploit economies of scope, such as the offering of cash management services to trade finance borrowers. And product management will involve the careful analysis by the trade financier of opportuni-

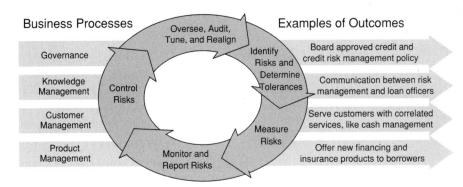

Business Processes

Examples of Outcomes

Oversee, Audit, Tune, and Realign

Governance

Knowledge Management

Customer Management

Product Management

Control Risks

Identify Risks and Determine Tolerances

Measure Risks

Monitor and Report Risks

Board approved credit and credit risk management policy

Communication between risk management and loan officers

Serve customers with correlated services, like cash management

Offer new financing and insurance products to borrowers

EXHIBIT 10.4   Trade Finiancier Offering New Financial Products

ties to expand its product mix to include products such as guarantees of performance in the supply chain.

The examples shown in Exhibits 10.3 and 10.4 illustrate how different the interactions between the four business processes and a firm's internal risk management process may be, depending on the business objectives of the firm and its relative sophistication in internal risk management.

NOTES

1. Most of this chapter is based on Culp and Planchat (2000) and Chapter 10 of Culp (2001). Although some of the language has been modified to suit the objectives of this book, readers familiar with either work may skip this chapter.
2. The social costs of these and other so-called derivatives disasters are discussed in Miller (1997).
3. For a discussion of these market risk measures, their uses, and their abuses, see Culp, Miller, and Neves (1998) and Culp (2001).
4. See Culp, Miller, and Neves (1998) and Culp, Hanke, and Neves (1999).
5. See Culp (2000, 2001).
6. See Culp and Neves (1998 a,b).

CHAPTER 11

Risk Management and Capital Structure

We now turn to see how the risk management process is related to a firm's capital structure decisions. In this chapter, we will see that many risk transformation products are actually substitutes for debt or equity. And even in the few cases when they are not, risk management products—as well as well-developed processes as discussed in Chapter 10—can still increase the value of a firm and affect its capital structure indirectly. Enterprise-wide risk management, for example, can help firms optimize their demand for raising costly risk capital.

In this chapter we answer the following questions:

■ When one or more of the M&M assumptions are violated, how can risk management enable firms to increase the welfare of their security holders?
■ How can risk management processes and products be used to increase a firm's expected cash flows?
■ How can risk management processes and products be used to decrease a firm's cost of capital?
■ What are the important distinctions between ordinary financial capital and risk transformation products?
■ How can we formulate a more comprehensive perspective of a firm's "risk-based capital structure" that integrates traditional capital structure concepts with risk transformation products?

RISK MANAGEMENT AND THE M&M IRRELEVANCE PROPOSITIONS

Under the same four assumptions that guarantee independence between the value of the firm and its capital structure, the value of the firm is also independent of any deliberate actions taken by management to control risks through hedging or insurance purchasing. The reason is simple: Shareholders can manage risks themselves. In order for risk management—either as a business process or as a set of risk transformation products—to add value to a firm, one or more of the M&M assumptions must be violated.

Irrelevance of Risk Management under M&M

Before considering the circumstances in which risk management can increase a firm's market value, let us first consider when it cannot. Assume the four M&M assumptions in Chapter 3—perfect markets, symmetric information, equal access, and given investment strategies—hold and that the firm's managers follow the market value rule and make decisions to maximize combined security holder welfare. In this situation, corporations should be indifferent to the active management of their risks. An example rather than a formal proof will suffice to get the point across.

Consider a corporate farm whose business is selling corn to grain elevators and millers. Residual claimants that own the farm will find that the value of their cash flows and the value of the farm's assets are strongly and directly related to corn prices. When the price of corn rises, the farm's revenues rise, all else being equal; the converse is also true.

Under the M&M assumption of symmetric information, shareholders know the impact of corn price risk on their pro rata claim on the farm just as well as the farm's managers do. And under the M&M assumption of equal access, any individual shareholders can engage in financial transactions on the same terms as the farm itself—terms that include zero transaction costs under the perfect capital markets assumption.

The final M&M assumption was that investment decisions are taken as given. So shareholders look at the firm's investment decisions and its product market exposure to corn prices and then determine *on their own* whether they want to bear corn price risk as a part of their investment portfolios. If not, shareholders can neutralize their corn price risk exposure quite easily by buying shares in a grain elevator or mill. Otherwise, they do nothing and diversify away their idiosyncratic risks as they normally would. In either case, the decision as to whether to manage the corn price risk was made by the shareholder.

Opportunities for Risk Management to Add Firm Value

When the parties whose mutual contractual interrelationships define "the firm" do not take actions that maximize the firm's value, under the M&M assumptions the firm will be taken over and replaced by decision makers who will maximize the value of the firm.[1] From Chapter 3, we know that the investment rule that maximizes the value of a firm is one that maximizes total security holder welfare, or the left-hand side of

$$[E_{t-1}(t) + \delta(t)] + [D_{t-1}(t) + \rho(t)] = V(t) + X(t) - I(t) \tag{11.1}$$

Maximizing security holder welfare is commensurate with maximizing the value of the firm—the market value rule. When this does not happen, the firm becomes a takeover target.

So the name of the game is maximizing the value of the firm in a M&M world, and the way to win the game is by maximizing the value of combined security holder welfare. Risk management, to the extent that it can be value enhancing for a firm, thus must somehow help the firm to play this game.

All opportunities for risk management to increase firm value require the violation of one or more M&M assumptions. But even when those assumptions are violated, a firm whose managers adhere to the market value rule can benefit from risk management only in certain circumstances, all of which come back to the V(t) in equation 11.1, which can be expanded as:

$$V(t) = \sum_{j=1}^{\infty} \frac{E_t[X(t+j) - I(t+j)]}{1 + \lambda_{t,t+j}} \tag{11.2}$$

where the firm's cost of capital is λ. In order for risk management to add value, either it must reduce the firm's cost of capital or it must increase its expected future net cash flows.[2] The next two sections explore these possibilities.

INCREASING EXPECTED NET CASH FLOWS

Risk management as a process and the use of risk transformation products, in particular, can be a means of increasing the firm's expected net cash flows either because they reduce the firm's expected or actual costs or because they actually increase the firm's revenues. We discuss a number of possible reasons that risk management can lead to this result in the subsections that follow.

Reducing Expected Corporate Taxes

One reason the M&M assumption of perfect capital markets may not hold is the presence of taxes. When a firm faces a *convex* corporate tax schedule, managing risk through the use of risk transformation products can reduce expected tax liabilities and thus increase the firm's expected net cash flows.

A convex tax schedule is one in which a firm's average tax rate rises as pretax income rises. Shown in Exhibit 11.1, panel a, a firm's tax schedule is convex if its tax liability rises *at an increasing rate* as the firm's earnings rise. This can occur because of progressivity in the corporate tax rate, the impact of the alternative minimum tax, tax carry-forwards and tax credits, and other tax shields that defer taxation.

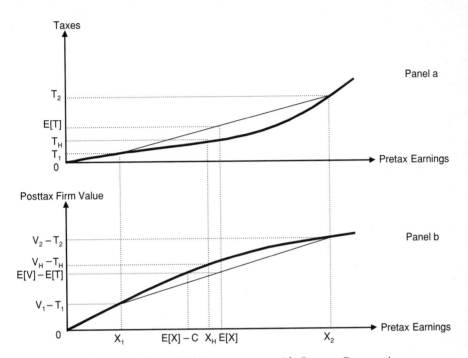

EXHIBIT 11.1   Value Added from Risk Management with Convex Corporation Taxation

Panel b of Exhibit 11.1 shows how the posttax value of the firm (shown on the y-axis) can be higher when risk transformation products are used to reduce fluctuations in the firm's pretax earnings.[3] Suppose that in the absence of a risk management strategy, a firm's earnings is susceptible to the impact of interest rate fluctuations that can lead to either a decrease in pretax earnings to X_1 or an increase in earnings to X_2, and suppose these occur with equal probability. At those levels of pretax income or earnings, the firm faces tax liabilities T_1 and T_2, respectively, as shown in panel a of the exhibit.

If the firm does not take any risk management actions, the expected pretax earnings of the firm is shown in the exhibit as

$$E[X] = \tfrac{1}{2}X_1 + \tfrac{1}{2}X_2$$

at which point the firm's expected tax liability is

$$E[T] = \tfrac{1}{2}T_1 + \tfrac{1}{2}T_2$$

The expected posttax value of the firm can be found as the value on the y-axis that corresponds to the firm's expected earnings less its expected tax liability, which is the y-value corresponding to the x-value that occurs at the bisection point of a straight line drawn from the firm's posttax value function between earnings levels X_1 and X_2.[4] The expected posttax value of the firm without hedging thus is $E[V] - E[T]$.

Now suppose the firm constructs a perfect hedge of its interest rate risk, so that the pretax earnings of the firm is locked in at X_H. Notice that this pretax earnings level is slightly below $E[V] - E[T]$, which we presume reflects the costs of hedging. At this value of the firm, the tax liability is known and indicated on the upper panel of Exhibit 11.1 as T_H. The posttax value of the firm is then also known and locked in as $V_H - T_H$.

As the exhibit shows, the posttax known value of the firm is higher than the posttax *expected* value of the firm. Although the probabilities of high and low earnings are equal, the high earnings value results in a more than proportional increase in taxes than the liability associated with the low earnings state. The firm thus will be willing to incur the costs of hedging in order to (all else being equal) avoid this high-earnings state. Indeed, the firm will be willing to spend up to C on the hedge. As Exhibit 11.1 shows, the posttax value of the firm at $E[X] - C$ if the firm hedges is the same as the posttax expected value of the firm at $E[X]$ if the firm does not hedge.

Reducing Expected Financial Distress Costs

Perhaps the most intuitive reason for firms to manage risk is to avoid the costs of financial distress that we explored in Chapters 4 and 5. In an M&M world, this would not matter; with perfect capital markets, bankruptcy merely results in the prorated redistribution of assets to the firm's claimants. But with costly financial distress, risk management can increase the firm's expected cash flows by reducing expected financial distress costs.

Suppose a corporation incurs costs of bankruptcy that are proportional to the shortfall of assets below liabilities. These costs are zero until the market value of the firm's assets falls below the face value of its debt, but then they begin to rise at an increasing rate the larger the net asset shortfall is.

Exhibit 11.2 shows the value of the firm on the y-axis, where the dashed line is the value of the firm before distress costs and where the solid line is the value of the firm after distress costs. The x-axis shows the market value of the firm's assets, and the second y-axis gives the probability of a given asset value being realized on the date the debt matures.

The distribution labeled f_U shows the distribution from which the firm's assets will be drawn if the firm does not hedge. The expected value of the firm is its expected asset value less its expected costs of financial distress, which

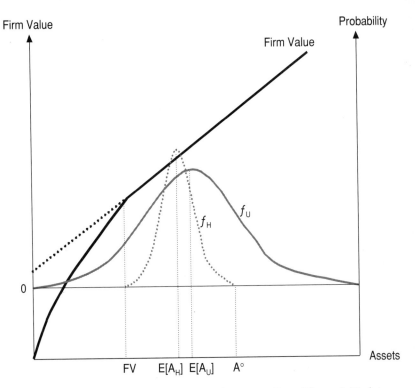

EXHIBIT 11.2 Reducing Expected Financial Distress Costs Through Hedging

can be denoted $\Omega(A)$ for any given asset value A. The expected value of the unhedged firm thus is

$$E[V_U] = \int_0^\infty A f_U(A) dA \qquad (11.3)$$

Now suppose that by using risk management products, the firm can reduce the variance of its asset value so that the terminal asset value is now drawn from distribution f_H. The hedge is costly, and it does not completely eliminate the asset risk of the firm, so the expected value of f_H is less than the expected value of f_U as shown in Exhibit 11.2.

Importantly, the risk management program has shrunk the support of the distribution of f_H. The possible values of the firm's assets without hedging were anywhere in the $A \in [0,\infty)$ interval, whereas hedging has now compacted the support of the distribution into $[FV,A°]$ for some $A°$. In other words, the probability that the firm's assets will fall in value below FV is now zero. The expected cost of financial distress thus is now zero, yielding the following expected value of the firm

$$E[V_H] = \int_{FV}^{A°} A f_H(A) dA \qquad (11.4)$$

Examining Exhibit 11.2 again will show more clearly what has been done. By hedging, the firm paid a small cost and reduced the expected value of its assets below what they would have been without the hedge, but it has in turn eliminated the risk of financial distress. The firm also has deprived itself of the large increases in asset value—in other words, asset values in the interval $A \in [A°,\infty)$ are now zero probability events.

Nevertheless, the firm may be willing to tolerate a smaller expected asset value and the elimination of large potential asset gains in order to avoid the costs of financial distress. Especially on an expected value basis, the hedged expected value of the firm given in equation 11.4 will almost certainly be greater than the unhedged expected value in equation 11.3; the reduction in expected asset value (see Exhibit 11.2) is small, but the expected distress costs that have been eliminated are large.

This analysis assumes that the trigger for financial distress is the value of the firm's assets. We could just as easily, of course, relabel the graph and repeat this analysis for risk management solutions aimed at reducing the volatility of a firm's pretax earnings instead of the market value of its assets.

Reducing Underinvestment

One major area in which risk management and the judicious use of risk transformation products can increase the firm's value by increasing its expected cash flows is by helping firms manage underinvestment problems. If a positive NPV project is rejected by the firm in the absence of a risk management program but accepted otherwise, then the benefit of risk management is fairly clear. Opportunities for risk management to add value in this manner come from several different possible sources.

Reducing Debt Overhang

We saw in Chapter 4 that a major cost of too much debt for a firm can be underinvestment arising from a "debt overhang." When the benefits of a positive NPV project accrue mainly to debt holders and the firm's managers act on behalf of shareholders, valuable investment opportunities can be forgone simply because too many of the benefits accrue to debt holders while leaving equity holders with all the risks.

Risk management can help solve this problem by increasing the debt capacity of a firm in the context of the trade-off theory of optimal capital structure. All else being equal, a higher stock of outstanding debt increases the probability that the firm will encounter financial distress. But as we have seen earlier, risk management products can be used to reduce the probability that the firm's assets fall below its debt servicing obligations and thus can reduce the probability that the firm encounters distress. When debt and risk management programs are properly combined, risk management can increase the firm's capacity to issue new debt without appreciably increasing its financial distress costs.

Reducing the Volatility of Cash Flows and Maintaining Adequate Internal Funds

We saw in Chapters 4 and 5 and again in Chapter 7 that underinvestment costs also can be incurred when a firm's cash flows are depleted below a certain level. If this occurs at a time when a firm is facing a positive NPV investment project, the depletion in cash either will force the firm to incur the costs of issuing new securities to finance the new project or may lead to the firm forgoing the project. In either case, the cost of a cash flow depletion is costly.

This led Froot, Scharfstein, and Stein (1993, 1994) to recommend cash flow–based hedging as a way to reduce a firm's expected underinvestment costs and thus raise firm value. The intuition behind this model is best seen from the example offered by Froot, Scharfstein, and Stein (1994), a similar version of which was presented in Chapter 7. To keep with their example and reproduce it as is, however, we now consider a hypothetical pharmaceutical company called Omega Pharmaceutical whose revenues are at risk from sales in Japan and Germany—specifically, from fluctuations in the mark/dollar and yen/dollar exchange rates. Omega is dollar-based and expects its net cash flows to be worth about $200 million per annum. Exchange rate swings, however, could change the dollar value of these revenues to either $100 million or $300 million per annum with equal likelihood.

As a pharmaceutical firm, the company's investment expenditures are heavily weighted toward R&D. As part of its normal capital budgeting exercises, Omega has forecast cash flows associated with different investment levels in new drugs. These investment expenditures, cost-of-capital-discounted cash flows, and NPVs are shown in Table 11.1. The firm's R&D budget was $180 million last year and will be $200 million next year assuming the firm chooses its R&D spending to maximize its project NPV.

Now suppose Omega does not have the ability to borrow funds to finance its R&D program and is unwilling to issue equity to do so. Internal cash funding thus is its only option. In this situation, Omega is quite vulnerable to exchange rate changes that can impact its net cash flows. If the dollar appreciates and Omega's net revenues decline in value to $100 million, only $100 million can be spent on new investment and R&D. By contrast, a dollar

TABLE 11.1   Omega Pharmaceutical's Capital Budget ($ millions)

R&D Expenditure	Discounted Cash Flows	NPV
100	160	60
200	290	90
300	360	60

depreciation would leave Omega with an extra $100 million above its planned $200 million spending level.

If Omega were to hedge its cash flows against exchange rate risk perfectly, the net revenue from its drug sales would be locked in at $200 million per annum. If the dollar appreciates and the dollar value of foreign sales declines from $200 million to $100 million, this means that the hedge will generate a cash inflow of $100 million. Conversely, a depreciation of the dollar that increases the dollar value of foreign sales by $100 million is offset with a $100 million loss on the hedge.

Ignoring the cost of the hedge, Table 11.2 shows the impact of the hedge on the available funds for R&D as compared to the no-hedging alternative. For a depreciating dollar, the hedge does not change anything because the cash outflow on the hedge just offsets the cash inflow on the foreign currency–denominated sales. But with an appreciating dollar, the cash inflow on the hedge that offsets the $100 million decline in foreign currency–denominated sales is just enough to finance the additional $100 million in investment that the firm decided to make. The increased investment expenditure from $100 million to $200 million increases future expected cash flows by $130 million. Because the $130 million gain exceeds the $100 million loss in a NPV sense, Omega Pharmaceutical can increase the value of the firm from hedging.

The Froot, Scharfstein, Stein story is all about using risk management to match the demand for internal funds with the supply of internal funds to avoid the presumed costs of issuing new debt to finance future investment projects. The demand/supply calculus is illustrated in Exhibit 11.3. The de-

TABLE 11.2   The Impact of Hedging on Omega Pharmaceutical's Investments ($ millions)

Dollar	Internal Funds	R&D without Hedging	Cash Flows on Hedge	Additional R&D with Hedging	Value from Hedging
Appreciates:	100	100	+100	100	+130
Stable:	200	200	0	0	0
Depreciates:	300	200	−100	0	−100

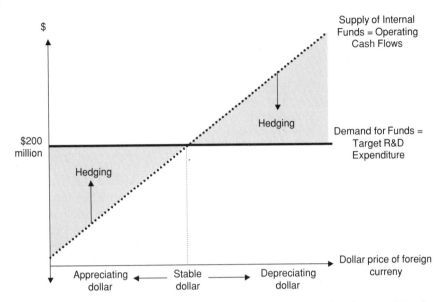

EXHIBIT 11.3   Using Hedging to Match the Demand for and Supply of Internal Funds at Omega Pharmaceutical

mand for R&D spending is shown at $200 million, the presumed target level. The supply of internal funds is represented by a 45° line that changes in value dollar for dollar with appreciations or depreciations in the dollar price of yen and Deutsche marks. The two are equalized at the point where the hedge perfectly locks in the current dollar value of foreign sales. The gain from hedging, in general, is indicated as anything that tilts the supply of internal funds curve close to the demand for those funds.

In this example, the demand for internal funds is presumed to be perfectly elastic with respect to exchange rate changes. In other words, the exchange rate ultimately may affect how the investment expenditure is *financed*, but the exchange rate does not affect the *demand for the investment.*

Froot, Scharfstein, and Stein (1994) offer another example to illustrate what happens when the investment itself depends on the value of a diversifiable risk, such as exchange rates. They describe a new company called Omega Oil whose supply of internal funds is clearly affected by oil prices. When prices rise, revenues rise—and conversely. But the authors then assume the demand for investments also is related to the price of oil. When prices are low, they posit that the demand for exploration and new reserves declines; the conversely also is true. Unlike revenues, which clearly depend on the price of oil in a one-for-one manner, however, investments are a bit less sensitive to oil price changes. Prices could, after all, recover before oil is pumped from the ground. Although the demand for and supply of internal funds both are affected by oil prices, they are not exactly matched. Exhibit 11.4 illustrates.

Comparing Figures 11.3 and 11.4 shows that the gains from hedging are higher for Omega Pharmaceutical than for Omega Oil. In the latter case, the firm's "natural exposure" to oil prices exists both in its investments and its sales, thereby providing a bit of a natural hedge. Nevertheless, as Exhibit 11.4 shows, there is still some room for the firm to protect its investment opportunities by hedging to ensure that cash flows always are adequate to fund new investment opportunities.

So the Froot, Scharfstein, and Stein model tells us that whenever the marginal cost of external finance is increasing in the amount of funds required and the marginal cost of internal finance is not, it makes sense for firms to reduce the volatility of their cash flows. Note that this is not the same as saying that firms should hedge their cash flows when external finance is "more expensive" than internal finance. If the rate a firm pays to bond holders is always 50 basil points (bps) higher than its shadow price of internal funds, then this model collapses. In that case the firm can always issue debt to finance investments, albeit at a cost of 50 bps.

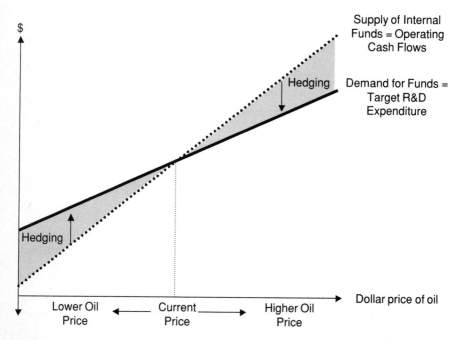

EXHIBIT 11.4 Hedging to Match the Demand for and Supply of Internal Funds at Omega Oil

Froot, Sharfstein, and Stein's argument for risk management really kicks in when the marginal cost of external finance is not a constant but the marginal cost of internal finance is. In this case, more funds required mean proportionally increasing costs of external funding vis-à-vis internal funding. Aside from firms near bankruptcy that encounter distressed debt problems as they lever up, external marginal financing costs also can increase with the level of debt if the pecking order world holds and the nature of the asymmetry dictates a disproportionately increasing adverse selection cost. When the capital market simply cannot perceive the quality of the firm's investment opportunities, investors may observe the increase in leverage and mistake it for a distressed debt situation, thus leading to a nonlinear increase in the cost of external funding.

Reducing Overinvestment

At odds with Froot, Sharfstein, and Stein's model is the possibility that too much internal cash will give rise to overinvestment costs, as in Jensen and Meckling (1976) and Jensen (1986). Suppose shareholders force managers to issue more debt to control free cash flows. This solves the free cash flow problem, but it creates other problems, such as a higher risk of incurring financial distress costs. These are precisely the sorts of benefits and costs of debt that led to the trade-off theory of optimal capital structure.

Risk management can be used in conjunction with the issuance of debt to reduce free cash flows while simultaneously helping ensure that the firm is not exposed to bankruptcy costs. In other words, utilizing selective risk management processes and risk transformation products can increase a firm's debt capacity. This, in turn, may enable the firm to achieve a new optimal leverage ratio by allowing the firm to exploit the benefits of debt without necessarily incurring higher financial distress costs.

Reducing Asset Substitution Monitoring Costs

If managers of the firm respond to shareholder incentives and costly monitoring mechanisms such as bond covenants are not used, managers may choose excessively risky projects to try to maximize the value of equity's call option on the firm's assets at the expense of fixed claimants. If the firm can utilize risk management products to reduce the volatility of net cash flows on projects with positive NPVs but with high risks, managers may be discouraged from taking on excessively risky projects.

Risk management could help creditors and shareholders address their asset substitution concerns by essentially eliminating most of the noncore risk of the investment project itself. Creditors, for example, might not agree to provide required bridge financing unless the hotel company agrees to hedge or insure all of the risks of operating the theme parks. In that case, the project's NPV becomes easier to observe and, if it is positive, easier to exploit by avoiding unnecessary risk taking along dimensions that the hotelier is not well qualified to control. In short, risk management can be used to eliminate the influence of variables that the hotel company knows little or nothing about in order to convince shareholders and creditors that the investment is genuinely a positive NPV expenditure.

Reducing the Costs of Managerial Risk Aversion[5]

In general, when too much of a manager's wealth is tied up in her compensation package, her expected utility starts to depend on the value of the firm where she works. If the manager faces capital market imperfections or does not have equal access to the market, she may not be able to diversify away enough of these risks.

As discussed in Chapter 3, any firm is subject to both systematic and idiosyncratic risk. Risk-averse managers with too much of their wealth tied to the value of the firm may have the incentive to hedge to reduce the idiosyncratic risks to which the firm is disproportionately exposed. Even then the managers may end up bearing too much systematic risk that they cannot eliminate through risk management programs; in this case the firm likely will lose managers without some adjustment to their compensation packages.

The nature of the risk management solution that is appropriate for the managers to pursue in this case depends on two variables: how the manager's own expected utility of wealth is linked to the value of the firm and how the manager is paid. Smith and Stulz (1985) explore this issue and ascertain that if a manager's expected utility of wealth is a concave function of the value of the firm, the manager's optimal solution is to hedge the firm completely. Unless the manager is compensated with higher expected income when the firm bears risk, she will choose not to bear risk.

Smith and Stulz (1985) explain that this situation is no longer true if the manager's expected utility is a concave function of her wealth but her wealth is a convex function of firm value. In this case, the manager's expected income is higher if the firm does not hedge because wealth is convex function of firm value. But because her utility is a concave function of wealth, she prefers certainty to uncertainty. In this situation, the manager is likely to hedge some but not all of the risks facing the firm. The trade-off between higher expected income from being unhedged and lower volatility from hedging leaves the manager somewhat in the middle.

Finally, if the manager's expected utility is a convex function of the value of the firm, the manager acts like a "risk lover" and opts not to hedge at all.

The important insight from the Smith and Stulz model is that the manager's compensation package can dictate her preference for bearing certain types of risk, and her preferences may or may not correspond to the risk tolerances of the firm's shareholders. By controlling whether the manager's expected utility is a concave or convex function of the value of the firm, the firm's security holders can determine its hedging policy. Many such compensation packages do not attempt to achieve uniformity across all firm values, moreover, but instead seek to achieve selective risk management—the management of noncore risks about which the firm has relatively no comparative informational advantages.

Recognize, however, that making a manager's expected utility a convex function of the value of the firm can have unintended consequences on the other side. Managers may be tempted to overhedge or reverse hedge in order to increase the risks faced by the company. Security holders might not benefit from this, even if they benefit from preventing the manager from hedging.

As an intermediate solution, many firms attempt to tie their managers' compensation packages to the value of the firm explicitly through the use of options. This alone is considered beneficial because it forces managers to focus only on those idiosyncratic risks that are priced into the firm's share value. Especially if we introduce asymmetric information and assume security holders cannot observe the distinction between systematic and idiosyncractic risk, this is the right way to go; you want managers to focus on idiosyncratic risks and ignore systematic risk.

If the firm successfully makes the manager's compensation a slightly concave function of firm value, then overhedging is discouraged but hedging is encouraged. As noted, managers will prefer less risky projects, other things being equal. Managers thus may tend to reject positive-NPV projects solely on the grounds that they create volatility. And this, in turn, can lead to the underinvestment problems we explored in Chapters 4 and 5. In this situation, it may make sense to allow managers to hedge in order to manage the volatility of their investments and prevent them from rejecting positive-NPV but high-variance projects.

Another important issue for the firm's security holders is to ensure that the manager's compensation package is tied to the appropriate decision variable. Many firms tie management compensation to accounting earnings rather than the value of the firm. But suppose the manager's expected utility of wealth is a concave function of accounting earnings and a convex function of firm value. Left alone, the manager would become a risk lover, because her wages and her long-term employment security depend not on market but on book values. But if the manager is paid based on accounting earnings, she will respond differently and choose to hedge accounting earnings. As explained in Culp (2001), a hedge that reduces volatility in accounting earnings may increase the volatility of the firm's value, thus making security holders worse off.

The main point of this section is to recognize that when monitoring managers is costly for security holders, managers may take risk management decisions designed to maximize their own expected utility—sometimes at the expense of security holders' welfare. The combination of an appropriately designed compensation package and an appropriate risk management program can prod managers to take actions that are consistent with security holders' wishes.

If managers have better information about the firm than security holders, the need for a carefully constructed compensation-cum-hedging policy becomes even more critical. Consider a firm that is owned by a collection of risk-neutral shareholders that appoint a risk-averse manager to make the financial and investment decisions on behalf of security holders. Managers can tell the difference between idiosyncratic risk and systematic risk, but shareholders cannot. In other words, shareholders can observe only the total volatility of the firm's value, not its various component risks.

In this situation, Diamond and Verrechia (1982) argue that it makes sense for managers to pursue a risk management policy. Specifically, if given the opportunity to hedge, managers will engage in the management of those risks that are under their control and within the purview of their own information. Managers will leave alone those risks about which they are as ill informed as shareholders. But by reducing risks that are under managers' control, the temptation for them to walk away from risky projects is reduced.

DECREASING THE FIRM'S COST OF CAPITAL

Risk management as a process and the use of risk management products also can increase firm value by decreasing its cost of capital. All of the situations in which companies may use risk management processes and products to increase security holder welfare share a common theme: Risk management processes and products can help reduce the firm's cost of capital because these processes and products are themselves capital structure products.

In some cases, risk transformation products are direct substitutes for traditional financial capital claims like debt or equity. In other cases, risk management processes and risk control products can change the firm's risk in a manner that also gives rise to a de facto change in its economic balance sheet, as shown in Table 7.1. In both cases, the firm's economic capital structure is affected by risk management decisions.

Risk Financing Products as Synthetic Debt

Risk transformation products come in essentially two forms—risk *transfer* and risk *finance* products. In the former, a firm actually offloads its risk to another participant in the capital market, whereas in the latter, the firm is using a risk management product to obtain pre- or postloss financing for its retained exposures.

Most risk financing products function as synthetic debt. Specific types of such products will be discussed in Chapters 12, 18, and 19 and include traditional banking products, formally funded self-insurance structures like captives and protected cell companies, and finite risk products as well as some types of derivatives.

In all risk finance products, the component of risk transfer is small relative to the component of risk finance. In other words, a risk financing instrument is typically a source of preloss or postloss funding for a firm but does not change the fact the company's equity holders eventually bear the cost of adverse realizations of risks to which the firm is exposed. In this sense, risk finance products are fixed rather than residual claims and present firms with an alternative source of borrowing to the traditional debt instruments discussed in Chapter 2. Some exceptions to this generalization are explored in Chapter 19.

Relations between the capital structure decisions of a firm and risk financing products can be identified at this point. An important feature of risk finance products, for example, is that they can be designed to help a firm smooth its cash flows, especially when used as a source of pre- or postloss funds. This can help the firm reduce underinvestment problems associated with excessive cash flow volatility (in the sense of Froot, Scharfstein, and Stein). A smoother cash flow profile also can increase a firm's ability to manage its internal funds and ensure an adequate degree of financial slack to avoid the pecking order problems of issuing new securities to finance investment capital spending. By smoothing cash flows, risk financing products also can facilitate earnings management and dividend signaling by increasing the ease of managing reserves allocated for those purposes.

Risk Transfer Products as Synthetic Equity

Risk transformation products such as futures, forwards, options, swaps, and classical insurance and reinsurance structures are risk *transfer* products. A firm entering into a risk transfer product literally pushes certain risks to which it is exposed out the door and into a new institution. The equity holders of the counterparty to a risk transfer transaction then become a type of residual claimant on the firm, bearing the costs *and* benefits of adverse realizations of risk.

Because risk transfer products can be used to reduce the risk exposure of a firm's net assets, cash flows, and/or earnings, risk transfer products can be viewed as a type of synthetic equity for a company (excluding, of course, governance and control issues). Reducing the risk of a firm through hedging, for example, can increase a firm's debt capacity. In other words, because the equity holders of the counterparty in a risk transfer product are now bearing certain risks that were facing the firm before, the firm's expected financial distress costs are usually lower after a risk transfer product is put into place. This in turn means that the firm can reduce its effective leverage or hold its old leverage ratio at a lower risk. Alternatively, if a firm wishes to increase its leverage, risk transfer products enable it to have a higher leverage ratio without experiencing heightened expected financial distress costs.

By allowing the firm to control and fine-tune its risk exposure, risk transfer products thus can help a firm mitigate the costs associated with debt overhang and reduce the expected costs of financial distress—both of which are functions that equity also plays in the securities capital structure. In addition, embedding risk transfer products into specific investment projects or portfolio management strategies can help firms mitigate the costs of risk-averse management as well as reduce the temptation for one class of security holder to try to prod management to engage in asset substitution.

Synthetic Diversification

As discussed in Chapter 3, a firm's cost of equity capital is determined in equilibrium by the expected return on the firm's equity, which in turn is driven by the systematic risk factors to which the firm is subject. In order for risk management to reduce an open corporation's equity cost of capital, the risk management program would have to somehow change the way that returns on the firm covary with systematic risk factors. This is highly unlikely. Virtually all of the risks discussed in Chapter 9 are diversifiable by open corporations, which means they do not matter anyway in determining the firm's equity cost of capital.

At a closed corporation whose owners are not be well diversified, however, shareholders may be incapable of holding diversified portfolios because so much of their wealth is tied up in their own firm. In this case, a risk management program adopted by the firm could reduce the impact of idiosyncratic risk on the firm's manager/owners—a reduction that cannot be accomplished in the private market given the nontradeability of the firm's shares and the proportion of managerial wealth tied up in the firm. Risk management thus can reduce the cost of capital for a firm by helping its managers "synthetically diversify" the risks that they cannot get rid of with their own portfolio management decisions.

Some obvious parallels can be seen in our discussion between the capital structure issues raised in Part I and the risk management processes and products reviewed in Chapters 9 and 10. This is not an accident. In fact, risk management is almost always a capital structure decision in disguise.

Risk Management as a Substitute for Risk Capital

Risk transformation products often can provide a cheaper source of risk capital to firms than can the traditional financial instruments explored in Part I of the book. To the extent this is possible, raising funds through risk transformation products rather than through the issuance of external claims simply might be cheaper for the firm.

We saw in Chapter 7 that the use of paid-up capital to finance risk capital reserves was both expensive and potentially dilutive. At the end of that chapter, we examined the implicit price of contingent capital provided by an external insurance company and claimants on the firm in the form of asset insurance. Importantly, we saw that the firm's net asset risk dictates its need for risk capital and the cost of that risk capital.

Risk transformation products can help reduce the demand by firms for costly risk capital. The risk capital required by a firm that issues gold-indexed bonds and invests the proceeds in cash is significantly greater than the risk capital required by a firm that takes some of the proceeds from issuing gold-indexed bonds and purchases call options on gold.

Even without acquiring new financial instruments, a sound enterprise-wide risk management process also can help firms reduce their need for risk capital by increasing "natural hedges" on the firm's economic balance sheet. Culp (2001) provides an explanation, for example, of how firms can identify "real-option" exposures that may well provide a natural risk mitigant to their net asset position. A petrochemical company, for example, may own oil in the ground and also may produce carpets using petroleum-based dyes. Recognizing that the oil in the ground is a type of call option on oil and that the firm's oil purchase requirements for carpet dyes is a natural short can go a long way to helping the firm recognize a lower demand for risk capital than it might otherwise have thought.

Reducing Adverse Selection Costs

As noted in Chapters 5 and 7, the adverse selection costs of raising paid-up capital are determined by the nature of the information asymmetry between the firm's managers and external investors. To the degree that a provider of external capital can be informed about the true quality of a firm's investment decisions, the cost of capital may be lower than that available in the public securities market.

Risk management can be used to help communicate information to external capital providers, and to help the firm's "bond" managers to take actions that will not adversely impact the ability of the firm to repay contingent debt obligations or to expropriate contingent equity investors. Consider a firm, for example, in the business of operating hotels that knows relatively little about amusement parks. Public investors in a pecking order world might impose a relatively high adverse selection penalty on the hotel company if it tried to raise funds to finance the acquisition of a theme park. A well-informed group of private capital suppliers, by contrast, might be willing to supply the firm with lower-cost funds provided that the firm agreed to use interest rate derivatives for the purpose of hedging its future debt servicing costs.

IMPORTANT DISTINCTIONS BETWEEN RISK TRANSFORMATION PRODUCTS AND CAPITAL

When risk management as a process or risk transformation products are undertaken as a capital structure decision, some important differences should be emphasized vis-à-vis traditional approaches to changing capital structure— issuing securities, changing a firm's dividend policy, and holding risk or signaling capital.

Benefits and Costs of Precision

Capital structure decisions tend to be "blunt" instruments whereas risk transformation products are more "surgical." A firm always can weather more losses simply by holding more equity and forcing those equity holders to bear the risk of greater losses. But in that case, the additional equity will absorb any losses, no matter what the source of risk causing them—core or noncore.

A risk transformation product, however, can allow the firm to manage its risk exposure profile selectively. Risk transformation products thus make it easier for firms to manage noncore risks, while still leaving core risks to be borne by equity holders. But this added precision of risk transformation products has costs vis-à-vis traditional capital structure products as well. Namely, if a risk transformation product is used on a risk that *ex post* ends up being of little problem for the firm, then the produce will be of limited use *ex post*. Simply holding more equity, by contrast, allows the firm to manage even risks it does not anticipate.

For the most part, capital structure decisions can be viewed as strategic risk management and corporate financing decisions, whereas the use of risk transformation products is tactical in nature.

Trading One Risk for Others

Issuing claims that result in immediate inflows of paid-in capital gives the firm cash today. Most risk transformation products, by contrast, are off-balance-sheet contingent capital sources, or options on paid-in capital. Consequently, a firm relying on risk transformation products as capital structure substitutes bears credit risk that firms holding paid-in capital do not. If the supplier of contingent capital is not financially viable at the time a firm wishes to draw on the facility, for example, the firm may be deprived of capital it could otherwise have raised by issuing new claims—perhaps at a particularly inconvenient time, moreover.

Apart from credit risk, some risk transformation products are subject to operational and/or legal risks, depending on the interpretation of the documentation and legal framework underlying the transaction—specifically with regard to when it can be used.

Consider the example of Metallgesellschaft AG (MG AG) and MG Refining and Marketing, Inc. (MGRM). In 1993 MGRM entered into contracts with their customers for the delivery of oil and refined oil products up to 10 years into the future. It hedged its primary exposure—the risk of changes in spot oil prices—by using futures contracts.[6] When oil prices plummeted in 1993, the margin calls on MGRM's futures hedge became significant, and the supervisory board of MG AG removed the management board and took over MGRM, liquidating first the futures hedge en masse and later the customer contracts. Culp and Miller (1995a) estimate that at the time the plug was pulled, the customer contracts were worth about $900 million.

MGRM let itself get into this situation in part because it believed it had a contingent capital facility designed to provide cash funds when required in an amount up to $1.3 billion in the event of a liquidity crisis. The bank-provided "guarantee" was designed to provide an infusion of capital in exchange for revolving senior debt—that is, synthetic debt—the proceeds of which would be used by MGRM to buy puts on oil futures. This would have converted MGRM's futures hedge into synthetic calls and completely terminated the huge margin outflows required to keep the hedge in place as oil prices fell.

The total cost of the puts that would have been required to totally halt the cash drain would have been about $126 million—a far cry from the $1.3 billion in the facility, and clearly worth it to preserve the $900 million of value locked up in the customer contracts. Unfortunately, the only person authorized to draw on the facility was the chairman of the MG AG management board, Heinz Schimmelbusch, who was removed by the MG AG supervisory board before he had the chance to invoke the facility.[7] The facility thus was not drawn, the margin calls continued unabated, and the forced liquidation of the program ultimately cost the shareholders of MG $1.3 billion—ironically the same amount as the contingent debt facility that sat idly by.

RISK-BASED CAPITAL STRUCTURE

Now that the relations between risk management and capital structure are clearer, we can reframe a corporation's capital structure in terms of the relation between financial capital claims and the risks facing the firm. In a capital budgetary context, Shimpi (2001) refers to this as his "insurative" model of capital structure.

Three-Dimensional View of Capital Structure

The risk-based capital structure of a firm—Shimpi's 2001 insurative model—is shown with three important dimensions in Exhibit 11.5.[8] The first dimension is the type of financial capital shown. As the arrows across the top indicate, capital is distinguished here based on whether it is paid-in (i.e., on balance sheet) or contingent. The latter may include risk finance products as well as classical risk transfer products like derivatives and insurance.[9]

The second dimension shown in the exhibit is the firm's risk retention. As in the traditional case explored in Chapter 2, securities like debt and equity represent retained risks, or risks the firm bears that have a direct impact on the value of its financial capital claims as shown here. But now we also allow for the possibility that the firm may choose to transfer certain types of risks. In order for a financial capital source to qualify as a form of risk transferral, any losses specified in the contract must be incurred by the holders of such capital claims and not by the firm's equity holders. Notice that this includes both risk transfer products and contingent liabilities, such as the gold-indexed bonds we explored in Chapter 7. Contingent capital and risk financing products, however, represent retained risks for the firm; these products provide funds to the firm but do not change the fact that ultimately risk-related losses are still borne by the firm's residual claimants.

Finally, the third dimension shown is the risk exposure of each claim, shown in increasing order moving from top to bottom. For our traditional paid-in capital securities, risk exposure here is analogous to the concept of

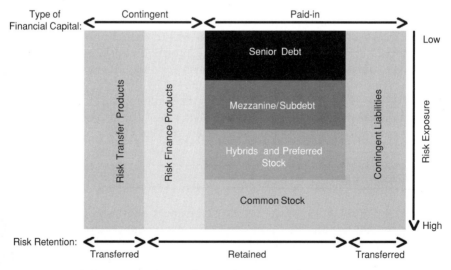

EXHIBIT 11.5   Risk-Based Capital Structure of a Corporation

priority that we developed for the securities capital structure in Chapter 2. If the market value of a firm's assets falls below its liabilities, the capital providers that appear toward the top of the diagram are paid off first.

For those capital suppliers whose positions in the figure cut across all risk exposures, any concept of "priority" will be defined in a manner specific to the claim. In addition, priority may be defined within the class of claims. Exhibit 11.6, for example, shows one possible way to see some additional detail within the risk transfer portion of the risk-based capital structure. In this figure, the specific types of risks the firm may be interested in transferring are listed along the horizontal axis. Note that funding risk does not appear here, as it presumably would be managed through risk financing and contingent capital products rather than risk transfer products.

As in Exhibit 11.5, the y-axis shows exposure to risk, increasing from the top to the bottom of the diagram. Contracts close to the bottom of the diagram are "near the money" and thus represent risk transfer products that compensate the firm for the first dollar loss owing to the specific risk shown. The height of the bar shown in each case then corresponds to the total exposure transferred for each risk type, with the top portion of the figure indicating "catastrophic" loss levels. Because these risk exposures are much farther out of the money than the first dollar loss, claims in this portion of the figure understandably have a lower risk. The bars as shown, moreover, indicate total coverage, but that coverage may well be provided by more than one type of contract and more than one risk transformation product supplier.

Consider in Exhibit 11.6 the specific example of the layer labeled "Property" appearing toward the top of the figure as an operational risk transfer device. Suppose this represents a classical insurance contract taken out by the firm in question. Specifically, this insurance contract will reimburse the firm for those property losses included in the policy up to loss level $B, but only for those losses in excess of $A. This is commonly called an excess-of-loss policy because it covers only those losses in excess of $A and only up to level $B. If $A is $1 million and $B is $5 million, we would say that this policy is a property insurance excess-of-loss policy for "$4 xs $1." Property losses below the $1 million mark are retained, as are losses in excess of $5 million. But the insurance company has agreed to absorb the $4 million of losses that may occur in between those "attachment points." We will discuss the mechanics of these and other typical insurance products again in Chapters 15 and 16.

Cost of Capital in the Risk-based Model

Shimpi (2001) suggests a framework for analyzing a firm's cost of capital when some of the capital is obtained through risk transfer and risk finance products. His concept ties closely into the concept of an economic balance sheet that we have already articulated, in which the economic value of the

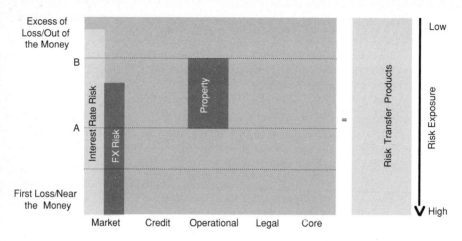

EXHIBIT 11.6 Risk Exposure of Risk Transfer Products

firm is equal to the value of its assets, in turn equal to the value of the firm's claims. Now taking into consideration all of the firm's possible claims, we can write the value of the firm as follows:

$$V(t) = A(t) = [E_{t-1}(t) + e(t)] + [D_{t-1}(t) + d(t)] + [CC_{t-1}(t) + cc(t)] \quad (11.5)$$

where $CC_{t-1}(t)$ is the time t market value of the contingent capital sources committed to the firm at time $t-1$ and $cc(t)$ is any new commitments of contingent capital.

In equation 11.5, the values of the contingent capital facilities are the values of options on the claims underlying those facilities. In other words, they are presumed not to be drawn as of date t. Once drawn, the contingent capital shows up as either debt or equity, but until then it has only optionlike features.

Note also that despite our very broad use of the term "contingent capital," this category can include almost any off-balance-sheet capital that is supplied to the firm either on demand or on the occurrence of some triggering event(s). Sources of contingent capital may include derivatives, classical insurance, ART products, and the like.

Equation 11.5 can be rewritten more simply as follows:

$$V(t) = A(t) = \Phi(t) + \phi(t) \quad (11.6)$$

where the uppercase $\Phi(t)$ denotes the market value of the firm's paid-in capital at time t and where the lowercase $\phi(t)$ denotes the market value of the firm's options on paid-in capital (i.e., contingent capital) at time t.

Taking all the firm's sources of investment, risk, and signaling capital into consideration, we can now rewrite the firm's WACC—first seen in equation 3.1—as follows:

$$R_{WACC}(t) = \frac{D(t)}{V(t)} R_D(t) + \frac{E(t)}{V(t)} R_E(t) + \frac{\phi(t)}{V(t)} R_\phi(t) \qquad (11.7)$$

where $D(t) = D_{t-1}(t) + d(t)$ = market value of debt at t
$E(t) = E_{t-1}(t) + e(t)$ = market value of equity at t
$\phi(t) = CC_{t-1}(t) + cc(t)$ = market value of contingent claims at t
$V(t) = A(t) = D(t) + E(t) + \phi(t)$
$R_D(t)$ = cost of debt capital
$R_E(t)$ = cost of equity capital
$R_\phi(t)$ = cost of contingent capital

The cost of contingent capital is the price paid for the contingent capital resource—for example, the premium paid for insurance or purchased options, arrangement fees paid for risk financing products and facilities like standby LOCs, up-front costs fronted for off-market derivatives, and the like.

We explored how to determine the market value of a contingent capital claim at the end of Chapter 7 when we reviewed the model of Merton and Perold (1993). For the many contingent capital sources that can be viewed as options on paid-in capital, the theoretical value of these capital sources can be estimated using appropriate option pricing models when observable market prices are not available.

A major problem with the above analysis, however, is forward-based derivatives. Fairly priced and "at-market" forward-based derivatives positions can be established at zero cost. At their inception, moreover, such transactions usually have a zero value as well. Inevitably, equation 11.7 thus will prove useful for certain options and insurance applications but will collapse when firms turn toward derivatives and certain ART forms.

NOTES

1. The firm can be viewed as a "nexus of contracts" among claimants, managers, employees, contractors, suppliers, customers, and the like. See Jensen and Meckling (1976) and Culp (2001).
2. Part I of Culp (2001) provides a more detailed discussion.
3. This figure and many of the subsequent figures in this chapter are based on Smith and Stulz (1985).
4. We can use this trick because we assumed the two earnings levels would occur with equal probability.

5. This section is drawn largely from Chapter 5 of Culp (2001).
6. The "basis risk" of the hedge and its consistency with the overall business strategy of MGRM is reviewed in Culp and Miller (1995c). The MGRM debacle and the ensuing debate are reviewed in the essays contained in Culp and Miller (2000).
7. Some reasons why this happened are explored in Culp and Miller (1995b, 2000).
8. See Figure 3.4 in Shimpi (2001).
9. Note that Shimpi (2001) has a different and more specific definition of "contingent capital," which for him is actually a risk financing tool and a source of retained risk for the firm. In this book, we refer to essentially any sources of capital that are not paid-up as contingent.

Classical Risk Transformation Products

CHAPTER 12

Commercial Banking Products

As we have discussed elsewhere, risk transformation products can be classified as either risk *financing* or risk *transfer* products. In Part III we briefly review the basic types of traditional rather than alternative risk transformation products.

Here we concentrate specifically on risk finance products that are typically considered "banking products." Apart from reviewing the basic products that banks regularly supply as capital structure and risk transformation products, we also consider the importance of banks in facilitating flows of funds.

The banking products considered in this chapter should not be confused with the capital market products often supplied by banks, which are addressed in Chapter 13. Our focus here is on those products truly unique to commercial banks. Specifically, we answer the following questions in this chapter:

- What is a "commercial bank," and how are "commercial banks" distinguished from one another and from "investment" or "merchant banks"?
- What types of products are offered by banks, and what is the relation between those products and the bank's assets and liabilities?
- What is the role played by commercial banks in the provision of payment and settlement services for funds transfers?

WHAT IS A BANK?

"Banks" have been historically considered somewhat unique and special institutions because they offer transaction accounts, serve as liquidity providers of last resort, act as transmission mechanisms for monetary policy, and serve as "delegated monitors" of the credit risk of their customers.[1] A bank was simply any institution that did all of these things.

With the modernization of the global financial system and the disintermediation of the retail financial services sector, however, no longer are any of these roles unique to banks. Nonbank clearing organizations participate in transaction intermediation, payments, and settlement. Backup liquidity is provided routinely through nonbank entities like GE Capital Corp. Monetary policy is regularly implemented through nonbank primary government securities dealers and transmitted through nonbank avenues such as money market mutual fund accounts. Delegated monitoring is now performed by insurance companies and nonfinancial corporates. Clearly we need another definition of a bank.

Commercial versus Investment or Merchant Banks

For many years, the banking regulatory system in the United States was responsible for a highly artificial but very strong distinction between "commercial" and "investment" or "merchant" banks. Commercial banks are traditionally institutions that take deposits and make loans, whereas investment and merchant banks tend to focus instead on the intermediation of capital markets transactions and the supply of securities.

In countries like Germany, Switzerland, and Japan, which have long practiced universal banking, these functions are provided by the same institutions. Even before the recent deregulatory initiatives in the United States, however, the lines between these types of firms blurred. J.P. Morgan, for example, was a commercial bank despite taking no retail deposits and making no retail loans, whereas Merrill Lynch was an investment bank that routinely provided depository and lending services through its money market mutual fund and collateralized borrowing programs.

No doubt regulation has contributed much to the distinctions drawn between banks and other financial institutions. And in the end, regulation is an important driving factor of the financial landscape. Either a company has a banking charter or it does not. Even in countries like Germany, which do not differentiate between types of banks, a nonfinancial corporation cannot offer a banking product like a letter of credit without a banking charter. As discussed in Chapter 8, for example, banks are subject to BIS capital requirements and national bank supervision and regulation, whereas nonbanks are not.

Pedagogically simplistic though it may seem, we define a bank as any institution that happens to hold a banking charter. Here we focus on products and services that, although no longer unique, tend to be supplied primarily by institutions that would be considered commercial banks. Chapter 13 reviews capital market products often supplied by commercial as well as investment and merchant banks. When we use the term "bank," we include all types of banks; if we want to be specific, we use "commercial" versus "investment" banking for clarity's sake.

Retail-Funded versus Wholesale-Funded Commercial Banks

Commercial banks often are distinguished from one another based on the nature of the liabilities they incur to raise funds. *Retail-funded banks* rely principally on retail sources of funds raised from customers. *Wholesale-funded banks*, by contrast, rely more heavily on funds from other banks obtained from interbank markets.

The rate at which the liabilities of a commercial bank roll over is called the repricing speed of the bank's customer liabilities. A bank funding itself mainly with three-month retail liabilities, for example, has a three-month repricing speed on its customer liabilities. But for retail-funded banks with a large amount of liabilities redeemable by customers on demand, the repricing speed depends on depositor withdrawal behavior. Such banks typically estimate their repricing speeds by defining a level of core deposits that represent a stable supply of funds and then determine how frequently the holders of those deposits roll over their products (i.e., make withdrawals and new deposits). Repricing speeds of retail-funded banks' core deposits in the United States can range from a few months to many years, depending on the interest elasticity of demand and liquidity constraints facing the banks' depositors.

Relations between Commercial Banks

Another feature often used to differentiate among commercial banks is their role in the global bank product marketplace. In this sense, three types of commercial banks can be identified: money center banks, correspondent banks, and regional banks.

A money center bank (e.g., JP Morgan-Chase) is a multinational bank whose revenues depend as much or more on wholesale product lines (e.g., trade credit, trading, securities underwriting in Section 20 subsidiaries, securitized products, commodity lending) as retail product lines (e.g., deposit-taking). Such banks typically create and manage retail relations indirectly through correspondent banks. Universal banks in Europe, such as Deutsche Bank, UBS, and Crédit Suisse, are virtually always money center banks.

Correspondent banks are smaller but often "superregional" banks that maintain ties with money center banks. Their extensive business with local or regional banks ranges from providing complex transaction services to those banks (e.g., settlements) to assisting local banks in marketing and client development. They also do extensive business with money center banks, usually relating to some ultimate service provided for the local banks. In turn, regional/local banks are banks that rely almost entirely on retail product services, such as small-customer demand-deposit-taking and mortgage lending.

Correspondent banks are the "link" between money center banks and local banks. The correspondent banks develop strong ties to local institutions, so the local institutions turn to them as "lead banks" for almost any services they demand that they cannot themselves provide. These local-bank services either can represent services they provide to their customers or services they themselves demand. In turn, the money center banks rely on the correspondent banks for referrals concerning even more complex transactions or services. Correspondent banks, moreover, look to money center banks as "lead banks" for structuring, securitization, and syndicated operations. As will be explained later, perhaps the most important linkage among these three types of banks is the role correspondent banks play in intermediating reserve account balances between local banks and money center banks.

Typical correspondent banks include Wachovia and First Union in the United States, Raffeisenbank in Austria, and Abbey National in the United Kingdom. Local banks include banks like Hyde Park Bank and Oakbrook Bank in the American state of Illinois and most of the Kantonalbanks in Switzerland.

COMMERCIAL BANKING PRODUCTS

As noted in Chapter 7, commercial banks and other financial institutions are different from nonfinancial corporations in large part because their assets and liabilities are often customer products. Whereas most nonfinancial corporations borrow in order to raise investment capital, commercial banks borrow mainly in order to lend. With a positively sloped yield curve, the old adage of generating net interest income by "borrowing short and lending long" still tends to explain a lot of commercial bank business strategies.

The classical banking products discussed here are all risk-financing products. They do not involve a transfer of any material risk from a bank's customer to the bank, but they do represent an extension of credit by the bank that firms can, in some cases, use for risk financing. Banking products of this kind appear on both sides of a bank's balance sheet.

Commercial Bank Liabilities

Commercial banks generally have three sources of funds available: deposits, borrowings, and financial capital. The financial capital claims that banks may issue are no different from those of other firms and have been discussed earlier. Both deposits and borrowings can fall into wholesale and retail funds categories. Some of the more important types of deposits and borrowings are discussed below.

Deposits

Although numerous types of bank deposits exists, they generally fall into six categories:

1. Demand deposit accounts (DDAs)
2. Savings deposits
3. Nonnegotiable time deposits

4. Negotiable certificates of deposit (CDs)
5. Treasury tax and loan (TT&L) deposits
6. Eurodollar deposits.

Eurodollar deposits and some types of CDs are wholesale; the other instruments are primarily retail.

DDAs play a central role in financial intermediation as the primary retail product offered by almost all banks. A DDA is a deposit that can be withdrawn or transferred to a third party at any time with no notice. DDAs thus are not term deposits. Both retail-funded and wholesale-funded money center banks accept DDAs, as do correspondent and regional banks.

Certificates of deposit are term deposits that characteristically have larger denominations than funds deposited in a DDA. Their tenors usually range from 30 days to 180 days. As term deposits, moreover, they are fungible and traded in a secondary market. Banks may offer CDs either with fixed term rates or variable rates that are readjusted periodically. CDs, moreover, accrue interest and do not return a payment to their holders until maturity. Virtually all correspondent and money center banks actively participate in the primary and secondary CD markets.

Eurodeposits are large-size, wholesale, term, interbank certificates of deposit. Eurodeposits can be negotiated in any currency, however, making the term "Eurodeposit" somewhat misleading. The market remains dollar-driven. Euro*dollar* deposits originated to avoid a U.S. regulation on U.S.-based, dollar-denominated deposit rates.

Eurodeposits may be offered on fixed- or floating-rate terms. The most common Eurodeposit now is a fixed-rate CD negotiated between two banks. The fixed rate on those instruments is the Eurodeposit interbank rate, such as the London Interbank Offered Rate (LIBOR) for Eurodollar loans.

Eurodeposits are a primary source of funds for wholesale banks, and all money center banks (both retail- and wholesale-funded) actively participate in Eurodeposit markets by borrowing and lending. Maturities on Eurodeposits range from 24 hours to 360 days.

Borrowings

Apart from issuing financial capital claims such as commercial paper and bonds, commercial banks can borrow in three additional ways: through the central bank funds markets, through repurchase agreements, and from the central bank directly.

Central bank funds markets are markets in which banks can borrow and lend central bank reserves to one another. In the United States, Federal funds (Fed funds) are commercial bank balances at the Federal Reserve that banks lend to one another. Term Fed funds loans are any Fed funds loans of greater than one day to maturity, usually not longer than a year. Intraday or overnight Fed funds borrowings are not considered term borrowings, although such borrowings are extremely common, especially between money center banks.

Contrary to a widely held misconception, the Fed funds rate is not set by the Federal Reserve. The rate is a freely determined market rate for the most part but is quite sensitive to Federal Reserve open market operations for reasons to be explained later.

As in other countries with analogous markets for trading central bank reserves, the Fed funds market in the United States represents a primary link between money center banks and local banks via their common associations with correspondent banks. Money center banks usually are net buyers of Fed funds balances, whereas local banks usually are net sellers of Fed funds. Correspondent banks act as "brokers" of Fed funds balances, buying them from local banks and selling them to money center banks. Money center banks often buy Fed funds even when they do not need to do so, just to maintain relations with the local banks.

A second type of commercial bank borrowing is a repurchase agreement (repo). A repo is a type of colleralized securities lending. A borrower might engage in a repo to convert relatively illiquid securities held as assets into liquid funds. In such a repo, the borrower sells the securities and agrees to repurchase them later at a price fixed at the inception of the contract. In return, the borrower receives a money loan or bond over the life of the repo.

Repos are extremely popular with wholesale-funded banks. Small wholesale-funded banks, in fact, usually repo all their illiquid securities as soon as they are purchased as a matter of practice. Because repos are de facto collateralized loans (usually with high-quality and liquid government securities), the repo rate generally is below the rate at which funds can be borrowed in the central bank reserve funds market—for example, the repo rate on U.S. government securities repos is usually below the Fed funds rate. Money center banks are natural borrowers in the repo market because they usually have a surplus of government securities.

Two types of repos can be negotiated by banks: "classic" or "U.S.-style" repos and "buy/sell-back" repos. In a classic repo, formal documentation is executed that transfers the actual ownership of the repoed security to the lender for the term of the repo. Such transactions are commonly used as a pure substitute for securities lending or to transfer custody of an asset to a party for a specific term. In a "buy/sell-back" repo, the transaction involves a simultaneous purchase and forward sale of the security to the lender. Such transactions usually are not documented as secured lending, so ownership of the security remains with the original asset holder that repos the instrument out.

A third type of borrowing in which commercial banks can engage in most countries is borrowing from the central bank. U.S. commercial banks have the unique privilege of borrowing at a low interest rate from the Federal Reserve's discount window. Such loans are intended to provide "adjustment credit" or "extension credit," both of which pertain to situations in which liquidity is not available from another source at a reasonable cost.

Regulations on discount window borrowing are extreme, so commercial banks try to avoid too much discount window borrowing. The discount rate, moreover, is determined by the Federal Reserve. Situations in which significant discount window borrowing is observed, in fact, are times when the discount rate is at a substantial discount to the Fed funds rate. As noted earlier, the Federal Reserve does not control the Fed funds rate. Because the Fed does control the discount rate, however, arbitrage between the discount window and the Fed funds market keeps the Fed funds rate generally at a small premium over the discount rate except in extreme situations where all liquidity is scant.

Commercial Bank Assets

Banks typically use the funds raised from issuing liabilities to extend credit, either retail or wholesale. Wholesale banks often provide credit instruments to other wholesale banks seeking sources of funds. Accordingly, all of the wholesale *liabilities* discussed in the prior section frequently appear as wholesale assets. Wholesale bank assets may include, for example, time deposits and CDs, Eurodeposits, and Fed funds loans placed at other banks. In addition, a repo at one bank constitutes a reverse repo at another bank. Money center banks also use reverse repos (or "reverses") to obtain specific securities they want to sell short in exchange for a cash loan.

Loans extended by banks to the nonbank sector usually are classified by the type of borrower and/or the type of security underlying the loan, if indeed it is a loan for which the bank has demanded collateral. Typical loan assets include mortgage and residential real estate loans, commercial real estate loans, commercial and industrial (C&I) loans, consumer loans, small business loans, and mezzanine and venture financing loans.

Banks also often extend credit for specific purposes. Project finance loans, for example, are loans extended by banks to facilitate large capital expenditures, usually on a well-defined infrastructure project (e.g., building a new factory, developing an oil pipeline, etc.). The project itself often serves as collateral for the loan. Trade finance credit also may be extended by banks to exporters, importers, or other physical commodity market participants. A bank may loan a cocoa producer funds, for example, to finance the export of its cocoa beans from the Ivory Coast to Europe where Nestlé has agreed to buy the beans. In this case, the cocoa itself is the collateral for the loan. Because cocoa prices may fluctuate as the cocoa moves through the supply chain, banks are likely to require the cocoa producer to hedge the cocoa in order to preserve the value of the collateral as the beans make their way across the ocean.

Other specialized types of loans that are secured include accounts receivable financing and inventory loans. In the former, the bank extends credit to a firm awaiting collection on its accounts receivable, in return for which it receives a lien on the accounts receivable—and usually also receives recourse to the borrower in the event of a default by both the borrower and the obligors on the receivables. Similarly, banks may extend credit to firms against inventories it holds of physical goods.

Short-term loans and contingent capital facilities are popular sources of risk finance, many of which (e.g., LOCs) have been mentioned already. In addition, firms can obtain committed or uncommitted lines of credit from banks as short-term funding sources. An uncommitted line of credit is a short-term unsecured loan a bank offers to firms up to a prespecified limit that can be drawn essentially on demand. Uncommitted lines of credit are informal arrangements between banks and their customers, whereas committed lines are formal legal arrangements. The main difference is that firms tend to pay more for the former *when the line is drawn* but do not have to pay an upfront fee, whereas the latter have a lower rate when drawn but involve the payment of a commitment fee to the bank to secure the availability of the funds. In other words, an uncommitted line of credit is essentially a service provided by a bank to its customers, whereas a committed line is an option on loanable funds written by the bank to its customers.

Lines of credit—especially uncommitted lines—often involve requirements set by banks that customers maintain "compensating balances" with the bank. A compensating balance is a deposit a borrower must keep with the bank, usually in a low- or zero-interest account, during the time the credit line is active. Compensating balances usually must be 5 percent to 10 percent of the amount of the total credit line.

Closely related to lines of credit are *revolving* lines of credit (or "revolvers"). Whereas traditional letters and lines of credit are for terms of a year or less and are subject to review upon request for renewal, revolvers automatically renew unless the firm experiences a material adverse change in its financial condition, as described in Chapter 2.

Yet another source of short-term financial capital supplied by banks is a *banker's acceptance*. Like letters and lines of credit, this is a contingent capital facility in which the bank agrees to remit payment to some other bank on behalf of the customer. If a corporation buys apple juice, for example, it can present the bill directly to the bank, and the bank will pay it. In this manner, companies can conserve their internal funds and better manage operating cash flows by passing vendor bills directly to their bankers.

PAYMENTS AND SETTLEMENT SERVICES[2]

Perhaps the only "unique" role left for banks—and only in certain countries—is their direct access to central banks. In most countries, only banks are allowed (or required) to hold reserves with the central bank, and this gives rise to several activities in which only banks can engage. Two such activities include banks borrowing from and lending to one another using central bank reserve funds markets and borrowing directly from the central bank. Quite apart from borrowing activities, however, the direct access of commercial banks to central bank money also secures for them a unique role in funds payments and settlement.

The intermediation of funds transfers between nonbanks is a major "product line" provided by commercial banks to their customers. In this sense, virtually any risk finance or risk transformation product that involves a flow of funds likely will involve a bank. As we will see in Part IV, the failure to include a bank in certain risk financing and risk transfer products often causes significant delays in the drawdown of contingent capital facilities in particular.

Mechanics of a Funds Transfer

Any funds transfer contains two components—the transfer of information and the final transfer of funds between two banks. The funds transfer process is initiated when one bank issues a payment order or instruction to the other bank. The transmission of a payment order essentially amounts to an electronic request for payment. The bank that sends the initiating payment request message is called the *payee*, and the bank receiving the request for payment is the *payer*.

Most modern payment systems are credit transfer systems. This means that both the payment messages and the funds move from the payer to the payee. After the initial request for payment from the payee, all messages thus are sent by the payer and received by the payee. These messages are typically electronic and consist of verifications of the transaction, identification authentications, reconciliations of payment instructions, and so forth.

The information exchange between two banks pertains only to the instructions for the funds transfer. The funds transfer itself usually is accomplished electronically and is independent of the information exchanges. Specifically, a funds transfer is said to have achieved *final settlement* when two conditions are met: the funds transfer is *irrevocable*, and the funds transfer is *final*. Revocability concerns the capacity of the payer or, in some cases, a third party to rescind payment after a payment instruction has been issued. Any funds transfer that can be rescinded is known as a *revocable transfer*, whereas *irrevocable transfers* are irreversible by any party once initiated.

In general, finality in a funds transfer is achieved only when central bank money has been transferred from the payer to the payee. Commercial banks in virtually all countries around the world maintain balances with the central bank. These balances are held in "nostro" accounts, meaning that the funds are on deposit with the central bank but still belong to the commercial bank. Finality in funds transfers usually is achieved through debits and credits to banks' nostro accounts with the central bank. Specifically, a funds transfer is final when the nostro account of the payer with the central bank has been debited and the nostro account of the payee with the central bank has been credited.[3] So, finality in a funds transfer occurs when central bank money has been used to settle the transaction.

Role of Commercial Banks in Payment Systems

Virtually all modern payment systems around the world are "bank-centric"— nonbanks usually must settle their funds transfers through banks, which, in turn, can usually only achieve payments finality through the local central bank. The hierarchy of the payments system thus has been referred to as an inverted pyramid, as depicted in Exhibit 12.1.[4] At the top of the inverted pyramid are the nonbanks that use the payments services of commercial banks. Whether financial or nonfinancial corporations, nonprofits, or even households, all nonbanks have payment obligations and rely on banks to effect the settlement of those obligations.

The second level of the pyramid consists of commercial banks themselves. Commercial banks engage in numerous activities relating to funds transfers. On this level, funds settlements occur between banks, through a payments clearinghouse, or through the central bank directly. Interbank funds can be transferred in essentially four ways:

1. Transfers of central bank money
2. Bilateral transfers between banks
3. Transfers of correspondent bank balances
4. Large-value transfer systems and clearinghouses

Transfers of Central Bank Money

Funds can be transferred between banks by the transfer of central bank liabilities to banks—that is, banks' reserve balances in nostro accounts with the central bank. As noted, in most countries this is the only way to truly establish finality in a funds transfer. As will become clear shortly, other types of funds transfers represent debits and credits to banks' balance sheets. All of these balance sheet transfers eventually can become final transfers of central bank money, but they themselves do not represent final flows of funds.

Finality achieved through the transfer of central bank money is usually

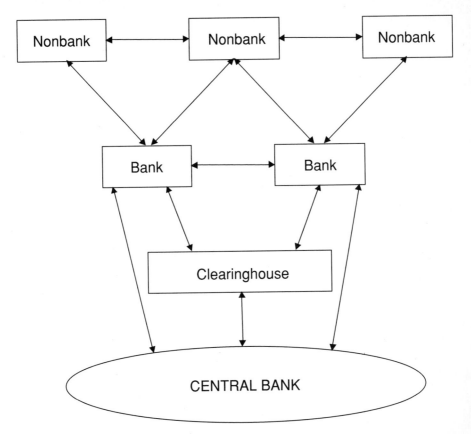

EXHIBIT 12.1 Inverted Pyramid of the Payment System

important only when some risk is perceived that one of the counterparties to a transaction will fail. If central bank money has been used to settle a funds transfer, the failure of the payee would not affect the payer. With other methods of funds transfers, complications can arise—a payee may end up with a claim on the failed payer rather than with hard cash. Nevertheless, finality achieved through central bank money transfers is not always a necessary ingredient to funds transfers. Indeed, because many central banks do not pay interest on reserve deposits, banks often do not maintain enough funds with the central bank to discharge all their payment obligations through central bank money transfers. Even though debits and credits to banks' nostro accounts at the central bank are the only means by which finality can be assured in a funds transfer, other means of funds transfers are routinely used, as described below.

Bilateral Transfers between Banks' Nostro and Vostro Accounts

When a bank maintains a deposit with another bank in a nostro account, the depositing bank is called the nostro bank. From the perspective of the bank accepting the deposit, the funds on deposit are held in what is called a vostro account and the bank taking the deposit is the vostro bank. If Bank A deposits funds at Bank B, Bank A is the nostro bank and Bank B is the vostro bank. The deposit is a nostro deposit for Bank A and a vostro deposit for Bank B.[5] Nostro and vostro deposits may arise either from transactions between the banks (e.g., money market transactions) or from transactions by banks on behalf of nonbank customers (e.g., the settlement of securities transactions).

We have already explained that funds transfers can be effected by banks through transfers between their nostro accounts with the central bank. In that case, the central bank is the only relevant vostro bank. In addition, funds transfers can be effected by direct debits and credits to banks' nostro and vostro accounts arising from bilateral interbank funds transfer obligations. Suppose, for example, that Bank N maintains a nostro account with Bank V with a current balance of $100. Then suppose that a nonbank customer of Bank V instructs Bank V to transfer $50 to Bank N—say, to settle a security purchase made by a broker who maintains a settlement account at Bank N. Rather than transferring central bank balances, the banks may simply agree that Bank V will credit the vostro account held for Bank N with $50. To Bank N, the value of its nostro account has risen by $50, and this represents a tangible balance sheet asset. If Bank N wishes to withdraw those funds permanently, a central bank balance transfer still will be required, but banks often are quite willing just to settle their transactions only using these sorts of book-entry debits and credits to nostro and vostro accounts with one another for operational simplicity, especially when the payer is a creditworthy institution.

Transfers of Correspondent Bank Balances

Not every bank has a nostro and/or vostro relationship with every other bank. Yet virtually all banks do maintain relationships with correspondent banks, or third-party banks whose primary services include the intermediation of interbank funds transfers. Suppose, to take an example, Bank A and Bank B both have nostro deposits at Correspondent Bank C with current balances of $100 and $500, respectively. Now imagine that two brokers engage in a securities transaction obligating one broker to deliver a share of stock in Company XYZ and the other broker to pay $100. Assume the selling broker has an account at Bank A and the purchasing broker has an account at Bank B. The securities sale will give rise to an obligation for the purchasing broker to pay the selling broker $100, and this obligation will be discharged through the banks of the two brokers.

If Bank A and Bank B do not have deposits with one another and do not wish to settle the transaction using their central bank reserve balances, they can settle the funds transfer through their common correspondent bank.[6] Bank B will issue a payment order to Correspondent Bank C instructing Bank C to debit $100 from Bank B's nostro account held by Bank C and then to credit Bank A with $100. To effect the transfer, Bank C will debit its vostro account held for Bank B by $100 and credit its vostro account held for Bank A by the same amount.

Large-Value Transfer Systems and Clearinghouses

In Exhibit 12.1, banks not only have relationships with one another and with the central bank, but they also often have relationships with clearinghouse organizations. Most countries have two types of funds transfer systems: large-value transfer systems (LVTSs) and retail transfer systems.

LVTSs support all interbank payments and thus comprise the backbone of any national payments system.[7] All major funds transfers occur through LVTS in the industrialized countries of the world. In essence, an LVTS acts as a funds clearinghouse, or a central counterparty standing in between individual banks and the central bank. Members settle their transactions with one another through the LVTS, and the LVTS then "links" these individual settlements with final settlements discharged in central bank money. Quite often LVTSs are provided and maintained by the central bank itself to facilitate transfers in nostro account balances of their members. For this reason, however, participation in LVTSs usually is restricted to institutions that do indeed maintain reserve balances with the central bank—that is, to banks.

Characteristics of Large-Value Transfer Systems

LVTSs are distinguished from one another by three primary features:

1. The manner in which multiple funds transfer instructions are "aggregated" over a specific period of time
2. The frequency and timing of funds transfers
3. The extension of intraday credit by the central bank

Net versus Gross Settlement

When a bank engages in a funds transfer on behalf of a customer, that bank is said to be operating as a settlement bank for that customer. Between settlement banking and their own interbank activities, commercial banks tend to have numerous single-currency transactions with one another through the course of a day. Clearance and settlement in national payments systems can occur on either a net or a gross basis to address those multiple funds transfer instructions.

In a gross settlement LVT system, all funds transfers are settled separately and independently. In a net settlement LVT system, by contrast, funds transfers are based on the net payables and receivables of a bank—either to other banks or to the central bank. A bilateral net settlement system involves separate debits and credits of a bank's nostro account with the central bank for each bank with which the original bank has transacted. If Bank A has 50 transfers with Bank B resulting in a $10 net debit to Bank B, and has 13 transfers with Bank C resulting in a net credit with Bank C of $5, in a bilateral netting system the debit with Bank A would be settled with a $10 debit to Bank A's nostro account at the central bank and a $10 credit to Bank B's nostro account, and the credit with Bank C would be settled by a $5 debit to Bank C's nostro account and a $5 credit to Bank A's nostro account.

In a multilateral net settlement system, the central bank or LVTS computes the net-net obligation of each bank—the net debit or credit of each bank to the central bank based on the net of all its net debits and net credits to other banks. In the above example, Bank A's transactions with both Bank B and Bank C would result in a net debit to Bank A's nostro account at the central bank—only one funds transfer, as compared to two in the case of bilateral netting.[8] Virtually all net settlement LVTS operating in industrialized countries rely on multilateral net settlement with the central bank.

Batched versus Continuous Settlement

LVTSs are either batched or continuous, depending on the frequency and timing of final funds transfers in the system. Batched settlement systems are LVTSs in which funds transfers occur only at designated times during the day. An end-of-day funds settlement system, for example, is a batched settlement system in which all funds transfers are processed in some predefined order at the end of the processing day. In such systems, like the Bank of England's system, payment messages may be transmitted throughout the day and on a transaction-by-transaction basis, but final settlement is achieved only at discrete settlement intervals. A continuous settlement system, by contrast, is a payments mechanism that can achieve the finality of funds transfers in real time throughout the day.

In practice, batched settlement systems may be either gross or net settlement systems. When considering both netting and the timing of settlement, four possible payment systems thus emerge: batched gross settlement, batched net settlement, Real Time Gross Settlement (RTGS), and Continuous Net Settlement (CNS).[9]

Daylight Overdrafts

An intraday loan is an extension of credit to a bank with a duration of a few hours—perhaps even just a few minutes. The extension of intraday credit by the central bank in a payments system can occur when a bank does not have adequate funds in its nostro account with the central bank to honor a payment order when that order is confirmed. In that case, the payer may incur a "daylight overdraft," or a payment obligation in excess of available funds constituting a loan from the payment system provider (i.e., the central bank) to the payer bank. Suppose, for example, that Bank A instructs the central bank to remit a $1 million payment to Bank B by debiting its nostro account and crediting the $1 million to the nostro account of Bank B. Suppose further that Bank A only has $600,000 on deposit with the central bank at the time the payment instruction is issued. In some systems, the central bank will allow the payment to occur by effectively extending Bank A a $400,000 loan to cover its overdraft.

In LVTSs for which intraday credit is extended by the central bank, the expectation is that any daylight overdrafts will be rectified by the end of the processing day. If not, LVTS providers typically impose heavy penalties on banks with net overnight debit positions in their nostro accounts with the central bank. When intraday credit is extended to banks in RTGS systems, in particular, the central bank usually charges interest on daylight overdrafts, at rates that often are subsidized.

Three Examples of Large-Value Transfer Systems

In this section, we provide three examples of actual LVTSs to illustrate the operation of various payment systems around the world.[10] The first two examples operate in the United States and together settle the vast majority of interbank funds transfers. The third example, in Switzerland, is offered as the "classic" example of a pure RTGS system with no intraday credit.

Fedwire

Fedwire is the payments system in the United States through which virtually all dollar interbank funds transfers are processed.[11] Fedwire is a RTGS large-value transfer system maintained by the Federal Reserve that settles large-value dollar-denominated transfers by debiting and crediting the nostro accounts maintained by Fedwire participants with the Federal Reserve. Debits and credits are accrued and settled in real time, and all funds transfers through Fedwire are irrevocable and final when a payment order is accepted for processing by Fedwire. Participants in Fedwire are subject to multilateral net debit limits (i.e., net-net limits) derived from self-assessments by participants of their capital adequacy. Members are not permitted to exceed the amount designated as the debit limit or cap.

Subject to participants' caps, however, the Federal Reserve does extend intraday credit by allowing daylight overdrafts in Fedwire. Suppose, for example, that a bank's Fedwire cap is $10 million. If that bank submits a payment order for $5 million but does not have $5 million on deposit with the

Fed, the payment order still will be processed. The result is an extension of intraday credit from the Fed to the bank in the amount of $5 million less whatever the bank has on deposit. The Fed began charging interest on such daylight overdrafts effective in April 1994. The expectation is that the overdraft will be rectified by the end of the processing day.[12] Daylight overdrafts are limited, however, by participants' net debit caps. If a payment order results in an overdraft in excess of the net debit cap, the payment instruction either is rejected or is booked as "pending" until the Fed receives adequate funds from the payer.

Because settlement is irrevocable and final in Fedwire when payment orders are processed, the extension of intraday credit by the Fed is also a form of "payment guarantee" to the payee on the other side of the $10 million transfer. If the bank fails during the day, the funds transfer has already occurred and the Fed assumes the loss, not the payee.[13]

Clearing House Interbank Payments System

The Clearing House Interbank Payments System (CHIPS) is an LVTS operated by the New York Clearing House that settles primarily the dollar side of multicurrency funds transfers. Unlike Fedwire, CHIPS is a batched net settlement system that settles only at the end of the day. The reason for this is that CHIPS is a private settlement system and thus cannot guarantee finality in funds transfers. Because finality really can be achieved in the United States only through transfers of balances between banks' nostro accounts at the Fed, finality in CHIPS transactions must be achieved at the end of the day through corresponding settlements on the Fedwire.

Because CHIPS is a batched net settlement system, no central bank credit is extended to participants during the processing day. Similarly, the batching of CHIPS instructions through the day implies that performance on intraday funds transfers are not guaranteed, as they are in Fedwire. For this reason, CHIPS imposes two types of limits on participants. First, all CHIPS participants must define bilateral net debit caps with respect to all other participants. These limits reflect the maximum net amount that can be payable from one participant to another during the processing day. In addition, CHIPS enforces total net debit caps that prevent any one participant from running a net debit in excess of 5 percent of the sum of all its bilateral net debit caps.

Swiss Interbank Clearing System

The Swiss Interbank Clearing system (SIC) is an RTGS large-value transfer system for interbank funds transfers in Switzerland denominated in either Swiss francs or Euros. Only banks can maintain accounts with the Swiss National Bank (SNB) for final settlements in central bank money (CHF) through the SIC. If the funds transfer is denominated in Euros, the bank may maintain an account at the Swiss Euro Clearing Bank (SECB) that settles through EuroSIC in a similar manner.

SIC is often considered unusual for three reasons. First, it achieves finality through transfers of central bank funds but does not involve any extensions of intraday credit by the SNB or SECB. The SIC thus is strictly a no-daylight-overdraft payment system. If funds are not available in the payee's SNB nostro account at the time a payment instruction is issued, the payment does not occur.

A second largely unique feature of the SIC is that it operates virtually continuously. If a funds transfer is originated on date T, the corresponding operating hours of the SIC *begin* at 6:00 P.M. Zurich time on date T and *end* at 4:15 P.M. Zurich time on date T+1. Payment orders can be originated at any time during this period. As long as the originating bank has funds in its SNB account to cover the transfer, the payment order immediately results in a debit of the payer's nostro account at the SNB and a credit of the payee's nostro account. If the payee does not have adequate funds on deposit with SNB when the payment order is submitted, the order is queued until the funds are on deposit. The payment order is left in that pending category until the end of the operating day—at 4:15 P.M. on the day after the order was submitted. If funds are still not on deposit at the SNB at that time, the payment order is canceled.

Banks that use the SIC typically engage in some intraday liquidity management by "managing the queue" of unprocessed payment orders. Payment orders may be canceled and may be assigned a priority of execution. Specifically, when funds are deposited by a bank with pending payment orders, the queued payment orders are processed first by priority level and second based on a first-in, first-out rule. Suppose, for example, that a Swiss bank with no funds on deposit at the SNB submits two high-priority payment orders—one for CHF10 million at noon and one for CHF7 million at 1:00 P.M. If the bank subsequently deposits CHF15 million with the SNB, only the first transaction for CHF10 million will settle because it was the "first in" among two equal-priority payment orders. If the bank wishes to process the CHF7 million transaction first, it must cancel the CHF10 million high-priority payment order.

Participants in SIC can monitor electronically all payment messages in real time. The payee on a given funds transfer receives two messages—one notifying it of a pending payment and one notifying it when payment has reached final settlement. At any time, a participant in the SIC can check on the status of all its pending payments by institution.

A third interesting feature of the Swiss payment system is virtually "straight-through" processing for capital market transactions. In countries such as the United States, securities and derivatives clearinghouses like the Options Clearing Corporation and Chicago Mercantile Exchange cannot directly access the national LVTS because they are not chartered as banks. But in the Swiss system, the securities clearinghouse SegaInterSettle (SIS), for example, is itself a bank, thereby enabling participants to avoid additional transactions between settlement banks and the securities exchange.

NOTES

1. See, for example, Corrigan (1982), Diamond (1984, 1991), and Fama (1985).
2. Most of this section is excerpted with minor modifications from Culp and Neves (1999).
3. See Blommenstein and Summers (1994) and Van den Bergh (1994).
4. See Corrigan (1990).
5. This rather difficult terminology is explained in more detail and illustrated in Blommenstein and Summers (1994).
6. Even if the banks have different correspondent banks, the two correspondent banks can settle with one another using any of the available interbank funds transfer options.
7. For a thorough discussion of LVTSs, see Horii and Summers (1994).
8. Note that the net-net balance for Banks B and C still works out. Bank A has had its nostro account debited by $5. Assuming Banks B and C have no other funds transfers, the central bank would still debit Bank C's account by $5. The net debit from Bank A of $5 and the debit from Bank C of $5 would exactly offset the required credit to Bank B's nostro account.
9. See Bank for International Settlements (1993, 1997).
10. These examples draw heavily from Horii and Summers (1994).
11. In practice, Fedwire operates as essentially two settlement systems—an LVTS and a securities settlement system—often called the cash Fedwire and securities Fedwire, respectively. All references in this section to "Fedwire" are to the cash Fedwire.
12. See Board of Governors of the Federal Reserve System (1995).
13. For more detailed discussions of Fedwire and its operations, see Board of Governors of the Federal Reserve System (1993, 1995) and Federal Reserve Bank of New York (1987).

CHAPTER 13

Derivatives

In this and the next chapter, we concentrate on risk finance and transfer products that are typically considered "capital market" products. Although certainly part of the global capital market, traditional securities such as those discussed in Chapter 2 are used mainly for capital formation purposes and not for risk transfer purposes. We thus do not discuss traditional securities again here. In this chapter, we focus our attention on financial contracts known as derivatives.

Just as most of the banking products discussed in Chapter 12 are used principally for risk finance, derivatives are used primarily for risk *transfer*. Perhaps more importantly, derivatives can be used to fine-tune the risk transfer process so that specific risks can be targeted for disposition by the firm. Most commonly associated with managing market risks like forex, interest rate, equity, and commodity price risk, the nearly $400 trillion in derivatives outstanding at year-end 2000 is a great testimonial to the effectiveness of these instruments.

This chapter is not intended to be an exhaustive introduction to these risk transfer instruments; plenty of entire books are dedicated to that subject.[1] Instead, our goal here is merely to introduce the basic kinds of derivatives and explore how they are supplied to customers. Specifically, we address the following questions:

■ What kinds of firms participate in derivatives activity, and how?
■ What types of risk transfer instruments fall under the term "derivatives"?
■ What are the basic building blocks and types of popular derivatives contracts, and how can they be used by firms to manage market risk?
■ What are the major types of derivatives used by hedgers to transfer credit risks to other market participants?
■ How do derivatives based on risks like operational risk function?
■ When can derivatives be used for risk finance rather than risk transfer?

WHAT ARE DERIVATIVES?[2]

The standard definition of a derivatives transaction is a bilateral contract whose value is derived from the value of some underlying asset, reference rate, or index.[3] This definition, however, is generally a bit too broad to be of much practical use. We have already seen, after all, that a share of common stock can be viewed as an option on the assets underlying the firm—a derivative.

In an effort to be a bit more formal, we might define a derivatives contract as a zero net supply, bilateral contract that derives most of its value from some underlying asset, reference rate, or index. This definition contains three distinct characteristics: zero net supply, based on some "underlying," and bilateral. "Zero net supply" simply means that for every "purchaser" of a derivatives contract, there is a "seller." If we view a purchaser of an asset as having a long position in the asset and a seller as having a short position, we can restate the zero net supply criterion as follows: For every long, there is a corresponding short.

An asset that exists in zero net supply is essentially created by the agreement of parties to establish corresponding long and short positions in the market. Prior to the agreement of buyer and seller to exchange the asset in the future, the contract defining the terms of future exchange for that asset did not exist. Derivatives, moreover, are not the only type of zero net supply asset. A more familiar example is a bank loan, which is literally created by agreement of a lender to transfer a cash balance temporarily to a borrower.

Derivatives contracts also must be based on at least one "underlying." An underlying is the asset price, reference rate, or index level from which a derivatives transaction inherits its principal source of value. In practice, derivatives cover a diverse spectrum of underlyings, including physical assets, exchange rates, interest rates, commodity prices, equity prices, and indexes. Practically nothing limits the assets, reference rates, or indexes that can serve as the underlying for a derivatives contract. Some derivatives, moreover, can cover more than one underlying.

Finally, derivatives are bilateral contracts. They represent an obligation by one party to the other party in the contract, and vice versa. The value of a bilateral contract thus depends not only on the value of its underlying but also on the performance of the two parties to the contract. The value of a contract in which one party sells a shoe to another party, for example, depends not just on the value of the shoe but also on the ability and intention of the seller actually to deliver the shoe to the buyer.

Even this seemingly detailed three-part definition of derivatives still has some serious drawbacks. Most of the problem comes from the term "underlying." Because a bond is just a fungible loan, debt securities could satisfy our definition of a derivatives contract.

In the end, although other definitions of derivatives exist, "definition by example" seems to be the most popular. People tend to define derivatives much as U.S. Justice Potter Stewart once defined pornography, quipping that he had no idea how to define it but would know it when he saw it. Accordingly, we tend to agree that futures, forwards, options, swaps, and combinations thereof are derivatives. We tend to agree that the securities discussed in Chapter 2 are not derivatives. And we tend to agree that mixtures of the two (e.g., structured notes) can basically be anything we want them to be.

As we have said several times before, what we call it is not as important as that we understand it.

PARTICIPANTS IN DERIVATIVES ACTIVITY

The broadest way to categorize derivatives activity is to distinguish between those transactions privately negotiated in an opaque, off-exchange environment and those conducted on organized financial exchanges. Exhibit 13.1 shows the explosive growth in privately negotiated derivatives activity over the last decade. At year-end 1999, for example, $58.3 trillion was outstanding in the world's major privately negotiated derivatives contracts.

Despite experiencing slower growth over the last decade, exchange-traded

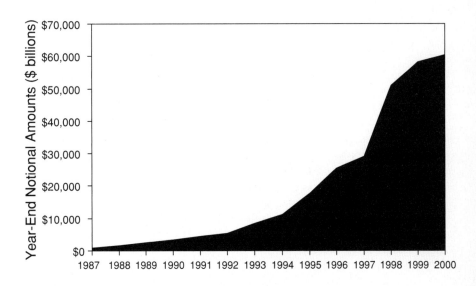

EXHIBIT 13.1 Outstanding Amounts of Privately Negotiated Derivatives
Source: International Swaps and Derivatives Association
Note: Outstanding derivatives for 2000 reported as of June 2000.

derivatives are also hugely popular. At year-end 1999, $317.7 trillion was outstanding in global interest rate, currency, and equity products.[4] Between the two markets, the global securities markets pale in size by comparison.[5]

Participants in Privately Negotiated Derivatives

There are two types of participants in privately negotiated derivatives: dealers and end users. Dealers act as agents for a variety of end-user principals in privately negotiated derivatives transactions, generally standing ready to accept both sides of a transaction (e.g., long or short) depending on which is demanded at the time. These dealers generally run close to a matched book, in which the cash flows on numerous transactions on both sides of a market net (it is hoped) to a relatively small risk exposure on one side of the market. When exact matching is not feasible, dealers typically lay off the residual risk of their dealing portfolio by using other (often exchange-traded) derivatives.

Because dealers act as financial intermediaries in privately negotiated derivatives, they typically must have a relatively strong credit standing, large relative capitalization, good access to information about a variety of end users, and relatively low costs of managing the residual risks of an unmatched portfolio of customer transactions. Firms already active as financial intermediaries are natural candidates to be dealers. Most dealers, in fact, are commercial banks, investment banks, and other financial enterprises, such as insurance company affiliates. The most active dealers in 2000 included ABN Amro, Bank of America, Barclays, Canadian Imperial Bank of Commerce, Citigroup, Crédit Suisse First Boston, Deutsche Bank, Dresdner Kleinwort Wasserstein, Goldman Sachs, HSBC, JP Morgan Chase, Royal Bank of Scotland, Lehman Brothers, Morgan Stanley, Société Générale, UBS Warburg, and Westdeustche Landesbank.

End users of privately negotiated derivatives are those institutions that engage in derivatives transactions as principals or for a purpose other than generating fee income, such as risk management. End users usually do not take both sides of a contract but instead enter into derivatives either as a long or a short to obtain or modify a particular risk exposure. End users of derivatives include commercial banks, investment banks, thrifts, insurance companies, manufacturing and other nonfinancial corporations, institutional funds (e.g., pension and mutual funds), and government-sponsored enterprises (e.g., Federal Home Loan Banks).

Dealers may use derivatives in an end-user capacity when they have their own demand for principal derivatives exposure. Bank dealers, for example, often have a portfolio of interest rate swaps separate from their dealing portfolio to manage the interest rate risk they incur in traditional banking.

Participants in Exchange-Traded Derivatives

The primary distinction between exchange-traded and privately negotiated derivatives is, not surprisingly, exchange trading. From an economic standpoint, in fact, exchange-traded derivatives such as futures and options on futures are essentially just standardized versions of privately negotiated derivatives for which the role of organized exchanges is of central importance. In fact, the role of all other participants in exchange-traded derivatives usually can be explained in terms of their relationship with an exchange.

Exchanges

There are two primary types of organized financial exchanges in the United States—securities exchanges and futures exchanges, with the distinction entirely due to regulation. The Commodity Exchange Act requires that futures contracts and options on futures contracts trade only on designated contract markets, which amounts to futures exchanges like the Chicago Board of Trade (CBOT) and the Chicago Mercantile Exchange (CME). Securities exchanges, such as the Chicago Board Options Exchange, Philadelphia Stock Exchange, and American Stock Exchange list for trading products such as options on individual stocks, options on cash equity indexes, and options on foreign currency. Futures exchanges are regulated by the Commodity Futures Trading Commission (CFTC), and securities exchanges are regulated by the Securities and Exchange Commission.

Clearinghouses

Two elements of credit risk are of potential concern to participants in forward-based derivatives: the probability of counterparty default and credit exposure (i.e., how much the company will lose if the counterparty does default). An important distinction between exchange-traded and privately negotiated derivatives is the means by which such credit risk is mitigated.

Credit risk in futures is addressed by exchanges in five ways.

1. After a futures trade is negotiated between a long and a short, the clearinghouse of the exchange on which the transaction occurred inserts itself as the central counterparty to both transactions. If Buyer Fig and Seller Grape consummate a transaction at a particular price, for example, the trade immediately becomes two legally enforceable contracts: a contract obligating Fig to buy from the clearinghouse at the negotiated price and a contract obligating Grape to sell to the clearinghouse at the negotiated price. Individual traders thus never have to engage in credit risk evaluation of other traders. All futures traders face the same credit risk—the risk of a clearinghouse default.

2. Clearinghouses engage in the netting of cash flows. "Bilateral netting" is the process by which the gross cash flows of all contracts between two parties (e.g., a trader and the clearinghouse) are netted to a single cash flow. Suppose at the end of a mark-to-market period Trader Erie owes $100 to the clearinghouse on one trading account, owes $25 to the clearinghouse on a second trading account, and is due $200 from the clearinghouse on a third account. Without bilateral netting, three gross cash flows occur. The trader bears credit risk from the clearinghouse on the $200 she is owed, and the clearinghouse bears credit risk from the trader for a total of the $125 it is owed. If Trader Erie and the clearinghouse bilaterally net their cash flows, the three gross cash flows are reduced to a single net cash flow of $75 by the clearinghouse to the trader (i.e., $200 less $100 less $25). The clearinghouse thus faces no credit risk, and Trader Erie's credit exposure to the clearinghouse is reduced by $125. Multilateral netting occurs when a futures clearinghouse bilaterally nets its obligations with all futures traders and then nets again all the gains and losses across traders, thereby further reducing the total cash flow credit exposure of the clearinghouse.
3. The distribution of daily profits and losses to futures traders ensures that the length of any relevant credit exposure is never longer than the time between mark to market times.
4. Futures clearinghouses typically specify stringent capital requirements for their members as well as conservative loss-sharing rules should a clearinghouse default occur.
5. Clearinghouses require all traders to post margin or performance bonds with the clearinghouse before trading, and the level of such initial deposits is generally set high enough to cover any loss that might reasonably occur before the next marking to market.

For privately negotiated derivatives, credit exposure and the probability of default often are managed separately. Part of the reason for this is that swaps and other privately negotiated derivatives can be very credit-sensitive instruments due to the often long-dated tenors of the transactions. Whereas daily marking to market limits the credit exposure on futures to the time between mark to markets, the credit exposure on a 10-year swap lasts 10 years.

To manage the credit exposure on a given transaction, companies typically set limits on their exposure to any one counterparty and try to ensure adequate capital is on hand to absorb a default if it occurs. To ensure that counterparty credit limits are not exceeded, participants must continually monitor the market value of their positions with each counterparty. In addition, cash flows on notional swaps negotiated with a single counterparty for the same product (e.g., interest rates) are virtually always bilaterally netted. Cross-product bilateral netting also is becoming more common as a means of reducing aggregate counterparty credit exposure.

The terms of the swap contract can be used to reduce the credit exposure of the transaction. Swap participants often use standard-form contracts called "master agreements," for example, to minimize risks such as the potential for ill-specified contract terms to inhibit netting if one of the parties goes bankrupt. "Credit enhancements" also are often required in swaps to reduce the exposure of the transactions. Collateral, for example, may be demanded by one or both swap counterparties at the inception of the transaction and/or after an adverse credit event, such as counterparty downgrade by a rating agency. Alternatively, some financial institutions act as credit support providers by guaranteeing all or part of the performance on a transaction in which they are not directly involved, thereby creating a third-party credit support.

Beyond just reducing credit exposures, some institutions mitigate credit risk by attempting to reduce the probability of a default. The simplest and most widely employed way to manage such default risk is to establish a cutoff level for credit quality below which the company will not do business. Many users of swaps, for example, deal only with AAA-rated counterparties. Firms that do not themselves have a AAA credit rating often set up separately capitalized affiliates with adequate capital and risk management systems to receive a AAA rating, thereby facilitating their ability to engage in swaps and other credit-sensitive derivatives.

Exchange Participants

Trading on exchanges is limited to exchange participants. To become an authorized trading participant, a firm or individual usually must meet certain criteria set forth by the exchange, such as minimum financial reporting requirements.

Exchange participants may trade for their own account, for the account of another participant, or for the account of an outside customer. Futures exchange participants that are primarily in business to act as agents, executing or clearing transactions for non-member customers, are called futures commission merchants. In securities markets, these participants are called broker/dealers. Unlike futures exchanges, however, securities exchanges often also have a specific designation for professional suppliers of liquidity, called market makers or specialists. One or several market makers on a securities exchange are obliged by exchange rules to buy or sell the listed contract at any time for a fair price, given demand for transactions by other members. Market makers can benefit from this privilege by earning profits on the bid-ask spread, but they in turn are generally expected to sell into a rising market and buy in a declining one.

All nonmember customer trades on securities exchanges go through a broker/dealer agent with an exchange membership, which in turn executes its trades on behalf of the customer through a market maker.

TRANSFERRING MARKET RISK USING DERIVATIVES

One reason for the tremendous success and popularity of derivatives over the last several decades is that they allow firms to tailor their risk profiles by facilitating the transfer of specific risk types. Most derivatives are aimed at helping firms manage market risk, but recently derivatives aimed at facilitating the transfer of credit, operational, and funding risks by firms have been developed.

The parallels between derivatives and the ART products discussed in Part IV of the book are sometimes striking. Derivatives and ART forms are in some instances nearly pure substitutes for one another. But perhaps more common is the use of derivatives by banks and (re-)insurers in the financial engineering process to create an ART structure. In that sense, derivatives and ART can be highly complementary products.

All derivatives are either constructed with or are one of two simple and fundamental financial building blocks: forwards and options.[6] A forward contract obligates one counterparty to buy and the other to sell an asset or its cash equivalent in the future for an agreed-upon price. In return for the payment of a premium, an option contract gives the buyer the right but not the obligation to buy or sell asset in the future at an agreed-upon price. Smithson (1987) refers to these two building blocks as the LEGOS® with which all derivatives contracts are built. Once these building blocks are defined, the cash flows on virtually any derivatives transaction can be viewed as the net cash flows on a portfolio comprised of some combination of these building blocks.

For the remainder of this section, we focus on the applications of derivatives for transferring market risk. The building blocks discussed below are the same ones that are used in derivatives aimed at credit or other risks.

Forward and Forwardlike Contracts

The most basic type of derivatives contract is a forward contract. A forward contract is a bilateral contract negotiated for the delivery of a physical asset (e.g., oil or gold) or its cash equivalent at a certain time in the future for a certain price fixed at the inception of the contract. No actual transfer of ownership occurs in the underlying asset when the contract is initiated. Instead, there is simply an agreement to transfer ownership of the underlying asset at some future delivery date. From the perspective of the buyer (seller), a forward transaction is thus actually the establishment of a long (short) position in the underlying commodity.

Forward Delivery Contracts

A simple forward delivery contract might specify the exchange of 100 troy ounces of gold one year in the future for a price agreed upon today, say $400 per ounce. If the discounted expected future price of gold in the future is equal to $400 per ounce today, the forward contract has no value to either party *ex ante* and thus involves no cash payments at inception. If the price of gold rises to $450 per ounce one year from now, the purchaser of this contract makes a profit equal to $450 minus $400 times 100, or $5,000, due entirely to the increase in the price of gold above its initial discounted expected present value. Suppose instead the price of gold in a year happened to be $350 per ounce. Then the purchaser of the forward contract loses $5,000, and she would prefer to have bought the gold at the lower spot price at the maturity date.

Algebraically, the payoff at maturity date T on a long forward contract based on one unit of some underlying is

$$S(T) - K$$

where K is the delivery price fixed at the contract's inception ($400 per ounce in our example) and S(T) is the spot price of the underlying (in this case gold) on the delivery date. For the long, every dollar increase in the price of gold above the price at which the contract is negotiated yields a $1 per ounce increase in the contract's maturity value, and every dollar decrease in the price of gold yields a $1 per ounce decrease in the contract's value at maturity. If the price of gold at maturity is exactly $400 per ounce, the forward purchaser is no better or worse off than if the contract had not been entered.[7]

The cash flow at maturity date T on a short position in a forward contract on one unit of the underlying asset is

$$K - S(T)$$

For the short, every dollar increase in the price of gold above the price at which the contract is negotiated causes a $1 per ounce loss on the contract at maturity. Every dollar decline in the price of gold yields a $1 per ounce increase in the contract's value at maturity. If the price of gold at maturity is exactly $400 per ounce, the forward seller is no better or worse off than if the contract had not been entered.

Combining the payoffs to the long and short on the forward contract also confirms that the transaction is zero net supply. Because (S(T) – K) + (K – S(T)) equals zero exactly, the creation of the forward contract by the agreement of the long and short has left the supply of the underlying asset unchanged and, all else being equal, has not affected any other market participants except the two that engaged in the forward transaction. This fact and the terminal payoffs of the two forwards are shown in Exhibit 13.2.

Forward contracts on foreign exchange and physical commodities are

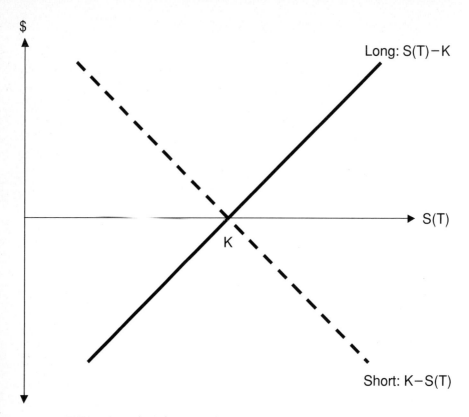

EXHIBIT 13.2   Value of Long and Short Forward Contracts at Maturity

commonly observed, and both involve physical settlement at maturity. A contract to purchase Japanese yen for Swiss francs three months hence, for example, involves a physical transfer of francs from the buyer to the seller, in return for which the buyer receives yen from the seller at the negotiated exchange rate. Many forward contracts, however, are cash settled rather than physically settled. At the maturity of such contracts, the long receives (makes) a cash payment if the spot price on the underlying prevailing at the maturity date of the contract is above (below) the prearranged fixed purchase price.

An especially popular cash-settled forward contract is the forward rate agreement, or FRA. An FRA is a cash-settled forward contract based on the LIBOR, or the rate on large-dollar, interbank term Eurodeposits. In a typical FRA, Firm Wells may agree to pay one year hence to Firm La Salle the then-prevailing three-month LIBOR based on an assumed principal value of $1 million, less a fixed interest rate of, say, 6 percent of the $1 million principal amount. If the three-month LIBOR one year hence turns out to be above 6 percent, Firm La Salle receives a net cash payment from Firm Wells. Firm La Salle thus gains at the expense of Firm Wells. If the three-month LIBOR is below 6 percent in a year, the opposite is true. Because the principal amount used to calculate the net cash flow is not actually exchanged, it is referred to as notional.

Forward contracts are sometimes "settled in arrears," meaning that the value date of the transaction (i.e., the date on which the value of the final payment is known) is prior to the settlement date (i.e., the date on which funds and/or assets are exchanged). A settled-in-arrears FRA is type of settled-in-arrears forward contract that pays the following to the long:

$$Z\left[(R_{T+m,T+m+d} - K)\frac{d}{D}\right] \qquad (13.1)$$

where Z is the notional principal amount of the transaction, K is a fixed rate, and $R_{T+m, T+m+d}$ is an annualized d-day interest rate paid on the Eurodeposit referenced by the FRA.

In the settled-in-arrears FRA, the trade, value, and settlement dates all can be spaced quite distantly in calendar time. The fixed-rate K is set on trade date T. The value of the FRA is not known to the short and the long, however, until the reference rate $R_{T+m, T+m+d}$ is set on date T + m. This rate is the rate paid on a CD placed at time T + m with a maturity date of T + m + d. Because the FRA is settled in arrears, the settlement date on the FRA is the same as the settlement date for the underlying CD—that is, date T + m + d.

Futures Contracts

Forward contracts are important not only because they play an important role as financial instruments in their own right but also because many other financial instruments embodying complex features can be decomposed into various combinations of long and short forward positions. Derivatives are "forward-based" if the contract can be decomposed into a forward contract or a portfolio of forward contracts.

Perhaps the most common forward-based derivatives contract is a futures contract, or a forward contract that is traded on an organized financial exchange such as the CME. Like forwards, futures can be based on a variety of underlyings and can be settled either physically or with cash. A popular cash-settled futures contract is the CME's Eurodollar futures contract, which has a value at expiration equal to 100 minus the then-prevailing three-month LIBOR. Eurodollar futures currently are listed with quarterly expiration dates and up to 10 years to maturity. The 10-year contract, for example, has an underlying of the three-month LIBOR prevailing 10 years hence.

Although exchange trading is the principal economic distinction between futures and forwards, that implies a lot.[8] A necessary condition for exchange trading, for example, is at least some degree of standardization in contract terms, such as the amount of the underlying on which the contract is based. In turn, standardization facilitates "offsetting," the process by which a long (short) position on an organized exchange may be neutralized or reversed when a trader takes a short (long) position in the same contract. Standardization and the ability to offset exchange-traded contracts usually results in relatively deeper liquidity for exchange-traded contract markets than in customized, off-exchange contracting.

Another feature typically associated with futures is the daily recognition of gains and losses. At least daily, futures exchanges mark the value of all futures accounts to current market-determined futures prices. Any gains in value from the previous mark-to-market period can be withdrawn by the winners, and those gains are financed by the losses of the losers over that period. The zero net supply feature of derivatives ensures that total gains will exactly offset total losses on any given day.

Swaps

A second popular forward-based derivative is the swap contract. Swaps are privately negotiated agreements between two parties to exchange (or swap) cash flows or assets at specified times in the future according to some specified payment formula. Interest rate swaps and currency swaps are the most widely used, although in principle swaps can be based on any underlying asset, reference rate, or index.

The basic building blocks underlying a swap are no different from those underlying forward delivery contracts. The cash flows on a simple swap contract, in fact, can always be decomposed into the cash flows on a portfolio of forward contracts. Equivalently, a forward contract is just a one-period swap with a single settlement date.

An interest rate swap obligates the counterparties to exchange interest payments periodically for a specified period of time. In the most common form of interest rate swap, called the "plain-vanilla" fixed-for-floating swap, one payment is based on a floating rate of interest that resets periodically (e.g., three-month LIBOR) and the other on a rate fixed at the inception of the contract. The actual amounts exchanged are calculated based on a notional principal amount. Like FRAs, the notional principal of interest rate swaps is not exchanged.

Currency swaps are similar to interest rate swaps in that one party makes a series of fixed or floating-rate payments to its counterparty in exchange for a series of fixed or floating receipts. In a currency swap, though, the payments and receipts are in different currencies, and the principal amounts of each currency are exchanged at the beginning of the swap and returned at its conclusion. The principal of a currency swap is therefore not notional.

To illustrate how the cash flows on a swap can be viewed as the cash flows on a portfolio of forward contracts, consider the following example. Suppose Firm La Salle enters into an interest rate swap with Firm Wells with a notional principal value of $10 million. La Salle may agree to pay a fixed 6 percent of the notional amount underlying the contract to Firm Wells semiannually for one year, in exchange for which Firm Wells will pay La Salle an amount equal to the six-month LIBOR percentage of the notional amount on the same dates. Firm La Salle thus has swapped a 6 percent fixed interest payment for the floating six-month LIBOR.

Now suppose that instead of entering into the interest rate swap, Firm La Salle had entered into a six-month FRA with a notional principal of $10 million that entitled it to receive the six-month LIBOR prevailing six months hence in exchange for paying 6 percent fixed. If Firm La Salle also entered a second FRA maturing in 12 months obligating it to exchange 6 percent fixed for the six-month LIBOR prevailing 12 months hence, the net cash flows on the portfolio of two FRAs would be exactly the same as the net cash flows on the single interest rate swap.

In addition to plain-vanilla interest rate swaps, many other types of swaps can be found, most of which are distinguished by differences in the key underlying economic terms of the swap. Even in fixed-for-floating interest rate swaps, numerous terms of the swap contract can be customized, including:

- The notional amount
- Whether the notional amount is subject to an amortization schedule, and if so what that schedule is
- Who pays and who receives fixed-rate payments
- The currency in which the interest and/or principal payments are to be made
- The holiday convention governing payments schedules
- The length of time the swap will be in effect (i.e., the swap's tenor)
- The level of the fixed rate
- The index to which the floating rate resets (e.g., six-month LIBOR)
- The spread (if any) to be added to the floating-rate index, reflecting considerations such as credit risk
- The frequency of cash flows
- The day-count convention for each payment stream
- The frequency and timing of the floating-rate reset
- Any terms affecting the credit risk of the settlements

Derivatives based on more than one underlying are also quite common. One of the most popular multifactor derivatives is a "basis" or "diff" swap in which both legs of the interest rate swap are floating. Like an ordinary interest rate swap, the transaction will have a notional principal amount used for calculating interest payments and will have scheduled payment and settlement dates that occur periodically over the life of the swap. But unlike a plain-vanilla swap in which one party always pays a rate fixed at the inception of the transaction, both parties in a basis swap pay an amount determined by a floating reference rate.

To see how such instruments can be used for risk transfer purposes, suppose a firm issued debt that pays quarterly interest equal to three-month LIBOR plus 75 basis points. Suppose further that the firm is concerned about excessive volatility in the LIBOR market arising from liquidity shocks and that it would prefer to pay a rate with lower variability. The firm might approach a swap dealer and enter into a LIBOR-for-Prime swap, in which the firm receives LIBOR from the swap dealer and pays the swap dealer the prime rate plus or minus a spread. If the dates, amounts, and reference rates are all chosen judiciously, the income on the swap will exactly offset the firm's interest obligations on its debt, and the firm has effectively swapped a LIBOR floating-rate obligation for a less-volatile prime-rate liability.

Options and Option-Based Derivatives

The basic payoff diagrams for European calls and puts and several combinations thereof were presented in Appendix 2 of Chapter 1, and the same chapter demonstrated how the securities issued by a corporation are themselves types of options. In this section, we briefly summarize several other types of options.

Barrier Options

A "knock-in" option is one that does not exist until the price of the underlying has crossed some barrier, whereas a "knock-out" option ceases to exist when some barrier is reached. A down-and-out call, for example, is a traditional call plus the additional feature that if prices ever fall below some "outstrike," the option disappears. If the outstrike is never reached, the terminal payoff on the option is the same as if the call were a traditional European option. But if the outstrike is reached, the option goes away. Similarly, if the *in*strike on a "down-and-in" put is X and the strike is K, the option pays nothing for $X < S(T) < K$, but when $S(T) < X$, the intrinsic value of the put is $K - S(T)$.

The outstrike on a barrier option does not affect the intrinsic value of the option, which still is determined solely by the relation between the terminal price of the underlying and the option's regular strike price. The outstrike is important, however, because it determines when the option is "live" or "dead." In this sense, the outstrike functions like a trigger mechanism. Until the trigger on a knock-in option is reached, the option may not be exercised, no matter how high its intrinsic value. Conversely, when the trigger on a knock-out option is reached, the option dies, again irrespective of its value to the long if exercised.

Binary or Digital Options

A binary or digital option is an option whose payoff upon exercise does not depend on how deep in the money the option is. The following is an example of a binary call option with strike price K:

$$C(T) = \max[0, S^\circ - K]$$

where S° is a fixed amount. The buyer either gets zero or $S^\circ - K$, and the latter amount does not vary with the degree to which the option is in the money. The payoff of this option at maturity (net of premium paid) is shown in Exhibit 13.3 and is contrasted with the payoff at maturity on a regular European call

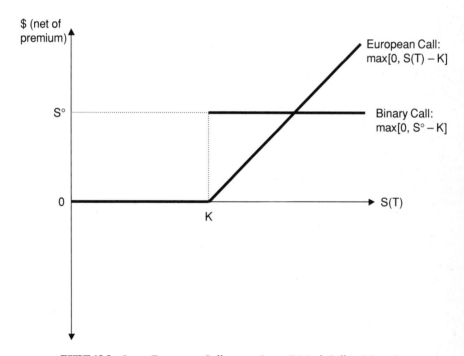

EXHIBIT 13.3 Long European Call versus Long Digital Call at Maturity

with the same strike price. It is evident that the binary option gives the long more money for any spot price $S(T) < S°$ but penalizes the holder relative to a European call for $S(T) > S°$.

Note that the underlying price still affects the welfare of the option buyer by defining when the option is in the money. The option's value to its buyer thus is not entirely independent of the price of the underlying at maturity or upon exercise. Only the *payoff* is independent of this price and is dependent instead on the parameter $S°$.

Quanto Options

Usually found in equity markets, a quanto option typically is an option on a foreign equity denominated in the local currency, where the currency conversion rate is fixed and embedded in the option payoff formula. At some maturity date T, the exercise value of a quanto option with strike price K (denominated in a foreign currency) on some underlying stock whose foreign currency-denominated value is denoted $S(T)$ is

$$C(T) = \max[0, XS(T) - XK]$$

where X is a fixed exchange conversion factor from the foreign currency into the local currency. The payoff formula thus can be rewritten as follows:

$$C(T) = X\max[0, S(T) - K]$$

so that the quanto is simply a traditional call with a fixed exchange rate conversion. The fixed exchange conversion factor X is a type of indexing parameter that, together with the traditional definition of intrinsic value, defines the payoff of the option upon exercise or at maturity.

Average Price and Average Strike Options

"Path-dependent" options are nontraditional options—usually over the counter—whose payoff upon exercise or at maturity depends not just on the underlying asset price at the time of exercise/maturity but rather on the *path* of underlying prices realized over some dates during the life of the option—perhaps back to the trade date. One popular type of path-dependent option is called an Asian or average price/strike option. For an Asian call option with maturity date T, the exercise value is

$$C(T) = \max[0, A(\tau_1,\tau_2) - K]$$

where K is the fixed strike price (as usual) and where $A(\tau_1,\tau_2)$ is the average price of the asset underlying the option from date τ_1 through date τ_2. The averaging period from τ_1 through τ_2 may include the trade date through the maturity date or anything in between, and the average itself may be geometric or arithmetic. Puts work the other way around, with the terminal payoff equal to the maximum of zero or the strike less the average price.

A similar type of Asian option is an average strike option. For a call with maturity date T, the payoff at expiration on an average strike call is

$$C(T) = \max[0 \, , \, S(T) - A(\tau_1, \tau_2)]$$

where $S(T)$ is the terminal price of the underlying and $A(\tau_1, \tau_2)$ is the average value of that underlying price over the period from τ_1 to τ_2.

Asian options tend to be quite popular for corporations wishing to smooth cash flows or earnings over relatively long periods of time. When the objective is to avoid spikes in cash flows or earnings, Asian options can be useful mechanisms for distributing the impact of such spikes over the chosen averaging period. At the same time, because the averaging effect in the payoffs of Asian options reduces the likelihood of extreme price movements, the probability of a large in-the-money move is lower with an Asian option than a traditional call or put. Consequently, Asian options tend to be cheaper—often significantly—than otherwise identical, traditional European calls and puts.

Lookback Options

Another popular type of path-dependent option is an option on an extremum, or a lookback option. At maturity or upon exercise, a lookback option gives its buyer the right to choose a strike price based on any price the underlying has realized either over its life or over some defined interval. A lookback call thus is equivalent to a call whose strike price is the minimum realized price over the indicated interval, whereas a lookback put is an option with a maximum price as strike. Payoffs of lookback calls and puts at maturity are shown below, respectively:

$$C(T) = \max[0, S(T) - S^{min}]$$
$$P(T) = \max[0, S^{max} - S(T)]$$

Ladder Options

A ladder option has a strike price that automatically changes when the underlying price moves through some predefined barrier. The buyer and seller can agree on multiple such "rungs" and a "ladder" of corresponding strike prices. Ladder options are popularly used to lock in some degree of in-the-moneyness of an option so that subsequent reversals before exercise or maturity do not deprive the holder of those gains.

A European ladder call option has the following payoff at maturity date T:

$$C(T) = \max\{0, S(T) - K, \max[0, L_k - K]\}$$

where L_k is the kth rung in the ladder of strike prices specified. The payoffs on a ladder call are shown for three different price paths in Exhibit 13.4 from Smithson (1998). Price path 1 generates a payoff equivalent to a traditional call because the terminal asset price $S(T)$ is above both ladder rungs. But for price path 2, the price path crossed ladder rungs L_1 and L_2, but the terminal price reversed and ended up below L_2. The ladder payoff thus is $L_2 - S(T)$ larger than it would have been for a traditional call. And for price path 3, the path crosses the first rung of the ladder and then slides downward so that $S(T)$ is well below L_1. Because the option is a ladder, the early appreciation in the underlying price above L_1, however, is locked in.

Shout Options

A shout option is a call or a put where the buyer can "shout" to the seller and define a ladder rung—just as in a ladder option—at one or more times over the life of the option. Usually the buyer can shout only once. In other words, a shout option is a ladder option where the rung is determined over the life of the option rather than in advance. When the buyer shouts to the seller, the intrinsic value of the option is locked in as a minimum terminal payoff. But if

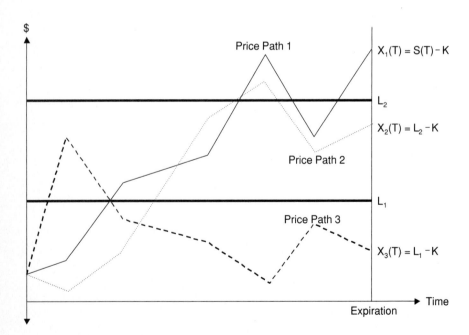

EXHIBIT 13.4   Payoffs for a Ladder Call Option at Maturity Date T

only one shout is allowed, the buyer may forgo other potentially more profitable shouting opportunities.

The payoff of European shout calls and puts on maturity date T are defined as follows for some buyer-chosen shout level K°:

$$C(T) = \max\{0, S(T) - K, K° - K]\}$$
$$P(T) = \max\{0, K - S(T), K - K°\}$$

Exhibit 13.5 shows price path 2 from Exhibit 13.4 and the predefined ladder rungs L_1 and L_2. If the buyer of the shout option shouts when prices reach ladder level L_2, the buyer of the shout option receives the same payoff as the buyer of the ladder option. If instead the buyer presciently shouts at Shout 1, the payoff is higher; if the option purchaser shorts at Shout 2, the terminal value of the call is less. The better a shout option buyer is at identifying trends and reversals, the more a shout option will resemble a lookback option.

Compound Options

A compound option is an option on an option. Upon exercise, the buyer receives another option rather than an actual physical asset, cash-equivalent, or forward-based derivatives contract. Examples include options on caps, collars,

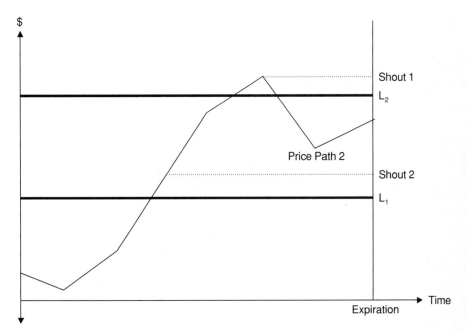

EXHIBIT 13.5 Payoffs for a Shout Call Option at Maturity Date T

floors, and a portfolio of options. Compound options can be calls or puts and can be written on calls or puts, leading to at least four combinations: a call on a call, a call on a put, a put on a call, and a put on a put.

Exchange, Rainbow, and Basket Options

Another type of option where the underlying is not a simple, single asset is an exchange asset, or an option to exchange one asset for another. A European exchange option has the following value at maturity

$$\max[S_1(T) - S_2(T), 0]$$

where $S_1(T)$ is the terminal price of asset 1 and $S_2(T)$ is the terminal price of asset 2.

Exchange options commonly are combined with a position in one of the two assets. When this is done, the net result is an option that allows the buyer to obtain the better or worse of two assets. An option that entitles its holder to obtain the better of two assets has a terminal payoff of

$$\max[S_1(T), S_2(T)] = S_1(T) - \max[S_1(T) - S_2(T), 0]$$

and an option that entitles its holder to obtain the worse of two assets has a terminal payoff of

$$\min[S_1(T), S_2(T)] = S_2(T) + \max[S_1(T) - S_2(T), 0]$$

The value of the debt issued by a corporation is an option on the worse of two assets—riskless debt equal to the face value of the debt plus a put struck at the face value of the debt.

The exchange option also is sometimes called a relative spread option or a rainbow option. Rainbow options can include two or more assets, and the assets may represent a basket of other assets.

Combinations of Derivatives

Forward and forward-based derivatives often are bundled together with explicit or embedded options or option-based derivatives to form combination derivatives. As a simple example, consider a putable swap in which one or both counterparties to a simple interest rate swap may terminate the swap early for a specified cash value if the underlying interest rate moves more than a specified amount. A fixed-rate payer, for example, may be allowed to terminate her pay fixed/receive floating swap if the underlying floating rate falls more than 200 basis points below the fixed swap rate. The cash flows on such a putable swap to the fixed-rate payor are the same as the cash flows on a portfolio comprised of a plain-vanilla swap and a floor.

What at first may seem like simple forward-based contracts are often combination derivatives due to the presence of embedded options, some of which may not be immediately obvious. Consider, for example, a forward contract requiring one party to sell 5,000 bushels of wheat to the forward purchaser in 90 days at a fixed price. Suppose also that the contract allows the seller to deliver either No. 2 Dark Northern Spring wheat or No. 1 Northern Spring wheat, one of which is likely to be cheaper than the other 90 days hence. The seller possesses a valuable option (written implicitly by the forward purchaser) to sell the cheapest of the two wheat grades. Such cheapest-to-deliver options are commonly embedded in commodity and some financial futures contracts.

Other popular combination derivatives include the following:

- A *forward-start swap*, or a swap contract whose terms are negotiated in advance of the period in which settlements occur—that is, a forward contract with a swap as its underlying
- A *swaption*, or an option on a swap
- A *fraption*, or an option on a FRA
- A *futures option*, or an option on a futures contract
- An *index amortizing swap*, or a swap whose notional principal value amortizes over time according to some schedule, often indexed to some reference rate like LIBOR; although viewed as a single product, many index amortizing swaps simply are combinations of caps or floors coupled with plain-vanilla interest rate swaps.

The process by which new financial contracts are built from the elemental forward and option building blocks is often referred to as financial engineering.

Structured Notes

Given the definition of derivatives set forth earlier, a structured note can be defined as a debt security whose cash flows can be decomposed into the cash flows on a traditional, straight debt security (e.g., a level-coupon or zero-coupon bond) and a derivatives contract. For that reason, structured notes also are sometimes called derivative securities.

Structured notes can contain embedded forward-based or option-based derivatives. Perhaps the simplest type of forward-based structured note is a floating rate note (FRN), or a note whose coupon payments are indexed to a floating interest rate such as LIBOR. The cash flows on a FRN can be decomposed into the cash flows on a straight fixed-rate, level-coupon bond and a fixed-for-floating interest rate swap whose notional principal is the same as the face value of the bond and whose settlement dates correspond to the bond's coupon dates.

The commodity-indexed debt discussed in Chapter 7 as an example of a contingent liability is also a type of structured note.

TRANSFERRING CREDIT RISK USING DERIVATIVES

As noted, all the options and forwardlike derivatives already discussed are used by firms to help fine-tune and tailor their exposures to market risk. But when the underlying is changed to capture some risk apart from market risk, derivatives of the types just discussed also may be used to manage nonmarket risks. The growth over the last decade in derivatives whose cash flows are based on credit events, in particular, has been staggering. In 1996, notional amounts outstanding in credit derivatives was reportedly around $40 billion. By 1997, some estimates put the market at $100 billion. And by year-end 2000, Goldman Sachs estimated the market's size at over $1 trillion.[9]

Among the types of credit risk discussed in Chapter 9 were default (settlement and presettlement) risk, migration/downgrade risk, and spread risk. Default risk is the risk of not getting a payment or asset when it was promised. Migration or downgrade risk arises from changes in market participants' perceptions about the probability of an actual default that cause a decline in the market value of the obligation. And spread risk is the risk that the excess yield on an asset over the riskless rate fluctuates, due either to migration risk or to fluctuations in the aggregate default premium. Popular credit derivatives exist for managing all three of these risks.

Transferring Default Risk with Credit Default Swaps and Options

A credit default swap is a contract whose payoff is based on default-related losses in the event of an adverse credit occurrence. In a credit default structure, the end user pays a fee to the counterparty and the counterparty agrees in turn to make a contingent payment to the end user in the event of a default on the underlying "reference asset." The reference asset is the asset whose default triggers a payment on the swap and may be an asset owned by the end user or not. A credit default swap based on a corporate bond held by the swap end user, for example, might guarantee a repayment of principal on that bond to the end user by the swap counterparty should the original bond issuer default. Or a credit default swap based on a loan portfolio held by the swap end user would ensure a payment equal to the default-related losses on the loan portfolio by the swap counterparty in the event the end user's original borrowers do not repay their loans.

As we saw in Chapter 7 and will see again in Chapter 15, credit default swaps function just like asset insurance. The concerned party pays premium to a swap dealer in exchange for asset protection. A typical credit default swap structure is shown in Exhibit 13.6. As shown, the reference asset—say, a bond or loan—is owned by the end user. In the absence of a default, interest and principal is paid to the end user, which pays a premium of xxx basis points for the credit default swap but never receives income on the swap. But if a default on the reference asset occurs, the default swap is triggered and the "contingent payment" will be equal to or close to the interest and principal forgone on the bond after the default. In some cases when the buyer of asset protection in the swap also owns the reference asset, the "contingent payment" actually may involve the transfer of the reference asset to the swap counterparty in exchange for a cash payment equal to the par value of the asset.

Like many derivatives, credit default swaps are called "swaps" in large part because of the benefits associated with documenting the transaction under a master netting agreement, known broadly as a swap under the U.S. Bankruptcy Code. Interest rate options like caps, collars, and floors are often called swaps for the same reason, and the term "swap dealer" is synonymous with "derivatives dealer." In addition, many credit default swaps require the party seeking asset protection to pay the premium periodically over the life of the transaction. To assist firms in managing the funding risk dimension of their asset portfolios, moreover, a LIBOR leg may be added to both sides of the transaction, so that the asset protection buyer pays LIBOR plus xxx basis

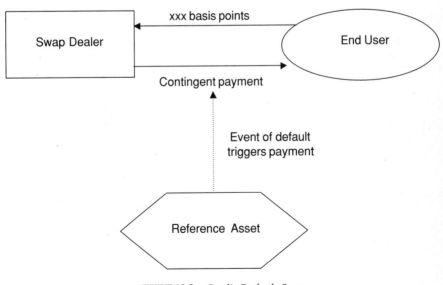

EXHIBIT 13.6 Credit Default Swap

points and receives LIBOR plus the contingent payment in the event of a default on the reference asset. These features clearly make an otherwise option-like product a bit more "swaplike."

A close cousin to the credit default swap structure is called a "first-to-default" structure. These derivatives have more than one reference asset and involve a payment by the swap dealer to the end user in the event of a first default on any of the assets. Suppose a small regional bank makes three commercial real estate loans and is concerned about the impact of a default on its net interest income and earnings. One possibility would be for the bank to enter a credit default swap on all three loans, so that any default would trigger at least a partial repayment of the loss by the swap dealer. But this is likely to be expensive.

Suppose further that the bank in question believes only one in three of its loans is likely to default. If it knew which one, it could use a traditional credit default swap to purchase asset protection for the loan in question. But if the bank knows only that one in three loans is likely to default and does not know which one will be the culprit, then a first-to-default structure makes sense. The payments of such a structure are shown in Exhibit 13.7. In this case, the bank pays a premium of yyy to the swap dealer for protection against losses arising from the first default of any of the three loans in the reference portfolio. If a default occurs on any of the three assets, the contingent

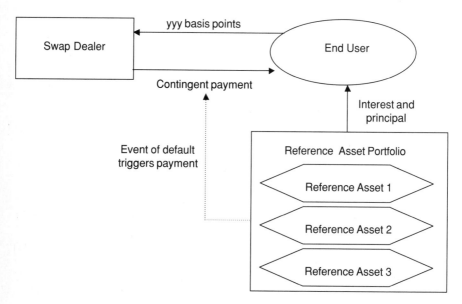

EXHIBIT 13.7　First-to-Default Default Swap

payment is triggered in the swap, but if there is another subsequent default, the bank is on its own.

A traditional credit default swap on a single loan will be cheaper than a first-to-default swap on a three-loan portfolio, and the first-to-default swap will be cheaper than a credit default swap covering all three loans. The one-loan swap has a lower probability of expiring in the money than a three-loan swap that includes the first loan unless the other nine loans are riskless. Thus, the former is cheaper than the latter. But because the first-to-default swap has a payout limited to the first default on a portfolio of three loans and the three-loan credit default swap potentially must pay out on all three loans if all three default, the latter will be more expensive.

Transferring Default and Migration Risk Using Total Return Swaps

As discussed in Chapter 9, credit risk can have several dimensions, only one of which is default risk. In fact, a major source of credit losses comes not from actual defaults but rather from changes in market perceptions of the probability a default will occur that result in larger discount rates and lower prices of claims. Especially for bonds, even the hint of a rating downgrade can precipitate a decrease in price. Recall that this type of credit risk is called migration or downgrade risk.

Classic credit default structures like those discussed in the previous section are in the money only when an actual event of default occurs. The documentation for these transactions usually spells out with great care what constitutes an event of default, such as the failure of an issuer to make a principal or interest payment on its claims. But because credit default swaps have "triggers" that allow payouts to end users only in the event of a default, these structures do not protect firms against downgrade risk.

A total return swap allows a firm to enter into an agreement with a swap dealer or some other counterparty and periodically receive LIBOR plus some spread in exchange for paying an income stream based directly on the performance of the reference asset. Importantly, a total return swap is much more of a swap than an option inasmuch as regular payments always should occur on the swap. An example will help illustrate.

Returning to our bank in the last section, suppose the bank has three loans in a loan portfolio and wants to get out of the business of bearing credit risk and focus on the fees it can earn from originating and servicing the loans. Each period—say, quarterly—the bank receives total interest R on the loan portfolio, which is equal to the interest due on all three loans less any defaulted interest payments. In the total return swap structure—shown in Exhibit 13.8—the bank agrees to pay the swap dealer LIBOR plus R each period. In other words, the bank passes on all interest it collects on the three

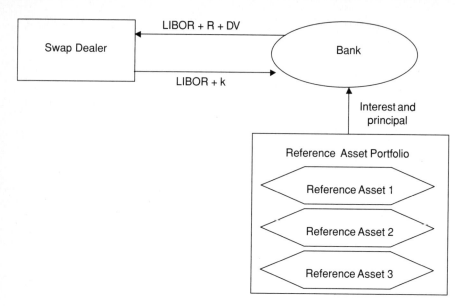

EXHIBIT 13.8   Total Return Swap

loans, including situations where interest collected is below interest due because of coupon defaults.

In addition, the swap dealer and the bank agree at the beginning of the swap transaction on a method for calculating the market price of the three-loan portfolio. This price may be calculated by a third-party calculation agent, by quoted prices of similar syndicated loans, or just about any other way provided the two firms agree to the calculation method *ex ante*. The bank then agrees to include in its periodic payment to the swap dealer an amount reflecting the change in value of the loan portfolio over the last period. If one of the borrowers is a gold mine and discovers a huge new mine, the perceived creditworthiness of that firm will rise and the value of the loan portfolio, ΔV, will be positive. In this case, the bank owes the swap dealer a larger payment to reflect the increase in the market value of the loan portfolio. But if the gold mine instead announces that its latest mine contains nothing but pyrite, this could cause a deterioration in the firm's ability to make remaining interest and principal payments, thus causing a decline in ΔV and a reduced payment by the bank to the swap dealer.

In exchange for making payments of LIBOR plus R plus ΔV to the swap dealer, the bank end user receives periodic payments from the dealer equal to LIBOR plus k, where k is a fixed spread over the life of the swap. From the bank's perspective, it has exchanged its credit risk on the loan portfolio for the credit risk that the swap dealer will not make its required fixed payment of k. In other words, the credit risk of the loan portfolio is now borne entirely by the swap dealer.

Transferring Spread Risk with Credit Spread Swaps and Options

As noted in Chapter 9, the excess yield on a risky asset above the riskless rate can fluctuate either because of migration risk endemic to the asset itself or because the aggregate default premium affecting the issuer's sector or industry fluctuates. The spread on BBB paper over AAA paper, for example, is counter-cyclical because more highly levered and less capitalized firms tend to get squeezed more in recessions. Accordingly, the spread risk on a BBB-rated bond may fluctuate even when the market's specific perceptions about that firm have not really changed; the deterioration in the class of BBB credits as a whole may simply take all such issues along for the ride.

When a firm wants to eliminate its spread risk without eliminating its realized default risk, credit spread swaps and options can be used. The swap functions like a classical interest rate swap in which periodic payments occur on both legs of the swap whose values are based on some notional principal amount and day-count convention. The net cash flows of the derivatives transaction are based on one or more credit spreads on one or more reference asset(s) that may or may not be owned by parties to the swap.

In a single-factor credit spread swap, the firm wishing to transfer away its spread risk on a specific asset or group of assets can exchange that risk for a fixed payment. Exhibit 13.9 illustrates the basic mechanics of such a transaction.

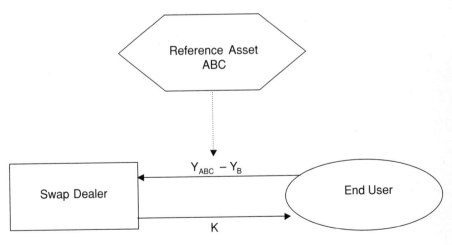

EXHIBIT 13.9   Single-Factor Credit Spread Swap

In this transaction, periodic payments are made by the swap dealer to the end user in the fixed amount K times the notional on the swap, where K is some fixed spread. In return, the end user pays $Y_{ABC} - Y_B$, where Y_{ABC} is the yield on some reference asset or portfolio of assets called ABC and where Y_B is the yield on a benchmark asset. The benchmark may be a Treasury or interbank rate, or it may be the yield on another risky asset. The documentation of the transaction must define carefully the method by which the yield is calculated for settlement purposes.

Exhibit 13.10 shows an alternative structure for a credit default swap in which the swap dealer and end user literally swap their spread risks. In such a multifactor credit spread swap, an end user pays the spread over a benchmark on some asset or portfolio ABC in return for receiving the spread over a benchmark on a different asset or portfolio XYZ. The benchmark is generally but not always the same on both legs of the swap.

Using a credit spread swap enables end users to transfer credit migration and spread risks—the former is a special case of the latter, after all—

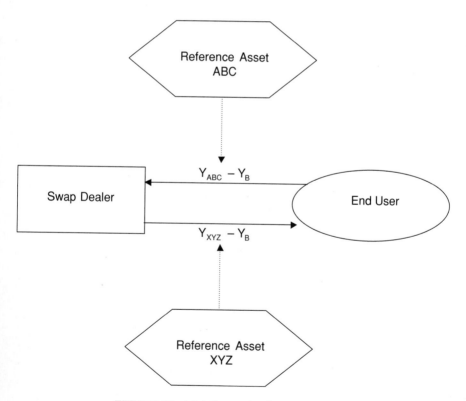

EXHIBIT 13.10   Multifactor Credit Spread Swap

without eliminating their exposure to the risk of an actual default if they own the reference asset. Credit spread options can be used to accomplish the same ends in a directional and limited liability manner. A credit spread call allows an end user to pay a premium in exchange for the right to "buy a spread" and thus participate in any reductions of the spread on a reference asset below some strike level. A credit spread put, by contrast, gives its owner the right to sell a credit spread when it rises above a strike rate. Note that the terms are reversed with respect to their normal meanings; a call (put) is essentially an option to go long (short) the credit risk of a firm by going short (long) its spread.

DERIVATIVES AND THE TRANSFER OF OTHER RISKS

In the wonderful world of derivatives, if you can document it, you can do it. In other words, a swap contract or other privately negotiated derivatives transaction can be constructed to pay off based on just about any kind of "triggering" event. Not surprisingly, swaps are being used increasingly to manage risks other than just market and credit risk.

As discussed in Chapter 8, Basel II places significant importance on the measurement and management of operational risk by internationally active banking institutions. Accordingly, the use of derivatives to try to address operational risks has become more common in the last few years. Operational risk derivatives have a form substantively similar to credit default swaps with payoffs like those shown in Exhibit 13.5. An end user pays a premium for operational risk protection to a swap dealer, in return for which the dealer agrees to make a contingent payment to the end user upon the occurrence of a triggering event. In this case, though, the triggering event is not a default on some reference asset but rather an operational risk–related loss.

Some swap structures of this sort arose around Y2K. If the Millennium Bug had caused operational failures and associated losses, a few swap dealers were prepared to bear this risk using operational swap structures. As we shall see in Part IV, however, such structures have been much more prevalent when offered under the banner of ART products by (re-)insurers.

DERIVATIVES, FUNDING RISK, AND RISK FINANCE

Despite the widespread popularity of derivatives for fine-tuning the risk profile of a firm—that is, for risk transfer purposes—some derivatives also can be used for risk financing purposes. In such cases, the end user is not really transferring the bulk of its market risk to a swap counterparty. Instead, often the firm is transferring the *timing risk*, or the risk that the cash flows on some asset portfolio it owns will not arrive exactly when they are needed. For the end user, an erratic cash flow pattern on its assets could cause all kinds of problems. It may be perfectly prepared to bear the risk of holding its assets, but it may not be prepared to deal with excessively volatile cash flows.

A popular derivatives transaction used for risk financing purposes is an asset swap. A plain-vanilla asset swap is usually just a simple interest rate swap whose cash flows are tied to a very specific asset rather than a general reference rate. Consider an investor who wants to own the bonds of Firm Tangerine. For his own cash flow or interest rate risk management purposes, however, the investor wants floating-rate exposure to Firm Tangerine at a time when Firm Tangerine has only fixed-rate debt outstanding. As a solution, the investor can buy the fixed-rate debt of Firm Tangerine and enter into an asset swap with a dealer to pay the fixed coupons on Firm Tangerine in exchange for receiving a floating-rate cash flow with a credit quality equivalent to Firm Tangerine's.

A typical asset swap is actually a risk transfer product and indeed is often considered a type of credit derivatives transaction. But a special type of asset swap—sometimes called an *income swap*—is a risk finance version of the classic asset swap. Consider a firm that is holding a portfolio of foreign bonds issued by numerous governments around the world. Suppose these bonds are all low risk and are being held as collateral on a secured liability—to guarantee the interest and principal on a claim the firm has issued. Suppose further that the claim being guaranteed by these foreign bonds has interest payable quarterly, but the foreign bonds pay interest semiannually and annually—and on different dates.

In this case, the firm could enter into an income swap with a swap dealer in which it pays all the income on its foreign bond portfolio to the dealer as it receives that income, in return for which the firm receives a stable and predictable payment each quarter on the swap of LIBOR plus a spread. The end user still bears all the risk of the asset portfolio, and the swap will no doubt contain covenants that guarantee as much. The purpose of the transaction is purely to allow the firm to borrow against the bond portfolio to smooth its cash flows and facilitate its timely interest payments on its secured liabilities.

Income swaps used for risk financing purposes are extremely common in securitized product structures of the kind we explore in Chapters 14 and 22.

NOTES

1. See, for example, Hull (2000).
2. Much of this section is adapted from Culp (1995a) and Culp and Overdahl (1996).
3. Global Derivatives Study Group (1993).
4. See the Bank for International Settlement's derivatives statistics reported in the statistical annex of the *BIS Quarterly Review*.
5. Some care must be used in interpreting these statistics. The principal un-

derlying most derivatives—both privately negotiated and exchange-traded—is used for calculation purposes but is never actually exchanged. The amounts reported in the text thus may be good indicators of the size and growth of the market, but they are not necessarily good measures of the capital at risk in these markets.

6. The "building block" approach was pioneered by Smithson (1987).

7. That a terminal price equal to the fixed price set at the contract's inception leaves both the long and short no better or worse off than if they had not entered the transaction is true by definition. The fixed price for future delivery is set precisely to ensure that both parties expect no gain or loss on the contract *ex ante*.

8. The legal distinctions between futures and forwards are much more complex and are not discussed here. See Culp (1995b).

9. See Kramer (2001).

CHAPTER 14

Asset Disposition and Securitized Products

In this chapter, we consider a second type of capital market product that has been used for the last several decades to facilitate both risk finance and risk transfer. The products in question are called securitized products, created by the process of securitization. Sometimes called synthetic asset divestiture, securitization is the process of unbundling the cash flows of balance-sheet assets and rebundling them into securities that can be placed with capital market participants.

Before getting into the basics of securitization and securitized products, however, we first need to understand the issues involved when an institution decides to transfer its risk by actually disposing of assets. Securitization, after all, is really just a particular means by which an asset disposition can be accomplished. This chapter addresses the following questions:

■ What variables may impact the asset divestiture decision of a firm?
■ How can derivatives be used to engage in "synthetic" asset divestitures?
■ What are the mechanics of a typical asset disposition accomplished through a securitization conduit?
■ What are some examples of common securitized products, and how do different structures involve differing roles for participating institutions?

ASSET DIVESTITURE[1]

If a company wishes to transfer the risk associated with a specific asset, one rather blunt way to accomplish this is through the sale of the asset. A Swiss chemical firm that funds a new production plant in Mexico, for example, is exposed to a wide variety of risks, including the interest rate risk on any project finance required, the operational risk of project-related problems, the core risks that the project itself will suffer production-related problems, the risk of fluctuations in the peso/franc exchange rate, and the like. If one or more of these risks exceeds the firm's risk tolerance, the project can simply be sold.

Asset divestiture gets rid of all the risks of an asset or project, but this may not reflect the company's problem. If the Swiss chemical firm is concerned only with the peso/franc exchange rate risk of the project, for example, then selling the whole factory project may be overkill. As discussed in Chapter 13, a much better solution may be to use transactions like derivatives to hedge the risk exposure that is causing the firm concern.

Asset Divestiture or "Abandonment" Option

The decision to abandon a project can be viewed as a type of option. Sometimes called a real option because it cannot be explicitly traded and represents more of a "strategic alternative" for the firm than a traded instrument, the option to abandon a current asset or project is the option to terminate all production and operations and sell the current asset for its market value, bearing in mind that the asset's market value represents what others are willing to pay for it—a value that may well be different from the value of the asset as it has been deployed in the selling firm's current project.

The abandonment decision is a permanent one. If a company divests itself of a balance sheet asset and subsequently regrets that decision, its only recourse is to repurchase the asset at then-prevailing market prices from the new owner. For highly specific capital assets, this can be tricky business. Accordingly, for capital-intensive projects in particular, the benefits of abandonment must be weighed carefully against its costs.

In capital-intensive industries, such as transportation and financial services, the capital intensity of investments is sufficiently high that even small declines in demand for the end product may imply a higher liquidation value of investments and assets than they would have if left in development or active production. Even excluding risk from the picture, abandonment thus can be attractive when fundamental shifts in costs or demand call into question the viability of the product that the project is intended to produce.

At the same time and as noted earlier, the value of an asset already committed to a project may differ widely across firms. To see how this can affect a firm's decision, consult Exhibit 14.1, which shows the value of the abandonment option for the Swiss chemical production facility in Mexico graphically. Suppose the figure includes all the assets in the production facility that is, say, half complete, and these assets include the machines in a factory, the factory building and real estate, the information technology support infrastructure, and the like. Of course the firm could unbundled these and sell the assets separately to the extent possible, but suppose for now the firm bundles the whole package of assets together.

The abandonment option is tied very specifically to the alternative use of

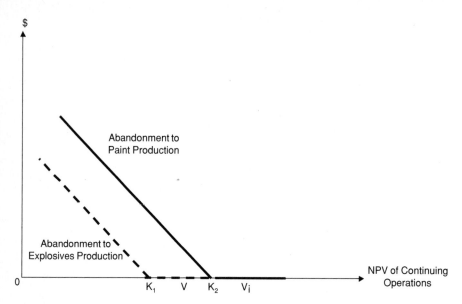

EXHIBIT 14.1   Option for a Swiss Chemical Producer to Abandon a Mexican Dye Production Facility

the assets in the project. If the Swiss chemical facility in Mexico is designed to produce chemicals that are sold primarily by its parent corporation—say, industrial dyes—it may be possible for the assets at the facility to be adapted to another firm's production needs for a different product line, but the adaptability depends on how similar that product line is to the intended dye production. Adapting a dye production facility that is half complete to a factory that will produce paint, for example, might not be too difficult. Suppose a different chemical firm is willing to pay K_2 for the project as a whole, where K_2 is the expected discounted net present value of cash flows on these assets if deployed into paint production. This NPV includes the additional investment costs the firm will have to incur to redeploy the dye production assets into paint production. The total NPV of the project for the acquiring firm thus is exactly zero—it will be willing to spend K_2 and no more to acquire a project whose NPV is just equal to K_2.

Now suppose in addition that a second firm also is willing to acquire the whole project from the Swiss chemical firm, but this second firm intends to redeploy the assets into the production of explosives. This is quite a long way from dyes and paints, so this potential acquirer will have to incur significant new investment expenditures to convert the facility into one suitable for its own purposes. Even if the gross present value of future expected revenues is the same for the explosives manufacturer as it is for the paint producer, the higher investment costs required for the former company means it will be willing to pay only $K_1 < K_2$ for the Swiss dye producer's Mexican project.

The x-axis shows the expected net present value of the Mexican production facility for the Swiss firm when it is due to be completed. This value essentially represents the discounted expected future cash flows from the factory assuming it goes into production less any additional investment expenditures required to bring the factory on line. The current expected NPV of the operation is shown in the exhibit as the point labeled V.

The two sales opportunities represent two put options for the Swiss firm. If the plant is kept and remains in operation, it will be worth V. If the only opportunity the firm has to sell the project is to the explosives producer for K_1, the abandonment option thus is out of the money at V and the Swiss firm is better off finishing the factory and putting it into use. But if the paint manufacturer offers K_2 to the Swiss firm for its Mexican facility, that abandonment option is in the money at V, so it pays for the Swiss firm to divest itself of the project.

Note that if the current NPV of the project is $V°$ instead of V, both abandonment options are out of the money and the firm is better off keeping the assets.

Other Real Options

Most firms in capital-intensive industries know the core production risks facing them when they undertake large capital projects. Accordingly, they often make capital budgeting and design decisions in a manner that maximizes their flexibility about what to do if the facility's terminal NPV ends up being called into question. In other words, knowing how costly abandonment is and how much it depends on the value of the assets in an alternative use, corporations undertaking large capital investment and infrastructure projects frequently try to increase the other real options to which they have access. Some examples of these are discussed below.

"Deferment" Option

The deferment option is an option to defer an investment expenditure to a later date. The underlying of this option is the gross present value of the project, and the strike price is the investment spending required. The option is more valuable for higher gross present values of project revenues, lower investment costs, more volatile project revenues (i.e., more chances for the project to pay off), and more time during which the investment can be delayed.

The deferment option is essentially an American call option on the underlying project, very similar to the growth opportunity encountered in Chapter 4. Exercising the option means spending $I(t)$ and getting a project or asset worth A(t), where A(t) is the discounted gross present value of cash flows expected on that asset. Not exercising the option means waiting to invest and possibly ultimately deciding not to invest if the option is out of the money.[2]

The option's value derives in large part from the possibility that waiting to invest will provide the firm with more information about whether the investment is positive NPV. The demand for dyes, for example, may be cyclical, but in the middle of a recession it may be difficult to tell whether demand will rise by enough in the next expansion to warrant the new production facility. Waiting until the business cycle turns can help a firm make a more informed decision about whether the project's expected NPV is positive.[3]

Another important factor that gives the deferment option value is the time value of the option—how long the firm can wait before it has to make the investment decision. Normally, American calls on non–dividend-paying assets should not be exercised early because it is always more valuable to sell the call than exercise it. And indeed, the option to abandon the project—sell the call—may be the correct solution. But situations may arise when the early exercise of the deferment option is sensible despite the project's American call–like features. Specifically, the time value of the deferment option is determined in large part by competitive considerations, or the degree to which competing firms also may be contemplating expanding dye production.

A "rivalous" real option is an option whose value to one firm depends on the behavior of other firms, whereas a "nonrivalrous" option can be exercised by multiple firms. Although the deferment of capital spending to build a dye factory is a decision that all dye producers can make, the value of the option clearly is driven in part by the timing of those decisions. If our Swiss firm waits too long and a German competitor builds a similar dye factory in Costa Rica, the gross present value of the Mexican subsidiary of the Swiss firm may be negatively affected through a shift outward in the industry supply curve. That also might affect the value of the abandonment option. Consequently, there are situations where a firm can wait too long to undertake a new project.

"Time to Build" Option

The time-to-build option combines the deferment option with the abandonment option by staging capital investment expenditures over time. Suppose the Swiss chemical firm can split the investment spending into two chunks, I(j) and I(m), where j and m > j denote the timing of the investment expenditures. The end result if both investment expenditures are made is a finished dye factory, expected to be completed on date T and yielding a discounted gross present value from date T through the end of the expected life of the factory of A(T). The value of the factory prior to date T—say, on date m—is denoted A(m), although that still reflects the expected discounted gross present value of the factory assuming it is on-line from date T onward.

By staging investment expenditures, the total project can be viewed as a compound option, or a call option on a call option. The first call option has strike price I(j) and an expiration date of j. If exercised, the firm ends up with another call option. The second call option is the deferment option, with strike price I(m) and expiration date m. If the firm decides not to spend I(j) on or before j and to let the first option expire worthless, the whole project is forfeit. But spending I(j) on or before date j allows the firm to wait and make its final investment decision up to date m. If the second call is in the money on (or for reasons of rivalry before) date m, the firm spends I(m) and ends up with the project. But at time m, the firm still can decide not to make the second expenditure and to forgo the project.

Terminating a project midway through its development, moreover, does not just result in the assets vanishing into thin air. On date m, the firm already has incurred investment costs I(j) and thus presumably has something to show for it. The firm thus has an abandonment option. Specifically, suppose the assets can be sold to another firm and redeployed into an alternative use worth K(m). At date m, the value of the project to the firm is

$$\max[K(m), A(m) - I(m)] = K(m) - \max[K(m) - A(m) + I(m), 0]$$

which we recognize from Chapter 13 as an option on the better of two assets or an "outperformance" option. The first option then can be viewed as a call option on the above outperformance option with strike price I(j):

$$\max\{\max[K(m), A(m) - I(m)] - I(j), 0\}$$

The time-to-build option is more valuable when the assets acquired through staged investment decisions can be resold, but the option has value even if this is not the case. If K(m) = 0, then the payoff to the second option is just a regular call rather than an outperformance option.

Staging investment expenditures in a time-to-build framework allows firms to get more information before irrevocably committing to a project. The more volatile the cash flows from the project are anticipated to be, the more value the option has. The deferment option gives its holders value for the same reason, but the difference is that it takes time to build—hence the name of this second option. If a project takes one year to complete, the deferment option alone gives companies the valuable option to wait before incurring any investment costs but in turn creates delays in the opening of the facility should it go forward. The incremental expenditures incurred in the time-to-build option, by contrast, allow the firm to pay a little bit for the option not to come in behind schedule. If the project is junked, the company has lost significantly less than its full investment outlay. But if it goes forward, it will go forward on time.

Option to Alter Operating Scale

Sometimes the abandonment or divestiture of an asset or project is a bit extreme, even if a contraction in demand for the product produced by an investment-intensive production process suggests a smaller scale from what was initially thought. Temporary shutdown decisions can make sense in this situation.

Conversely, suppose demand for the product being produced is much higher than expected. In that case, you might wish to incur additional investment expenditures in order to expand capacity and meet this newly arrived demand.

The option to expand or contract (including temporary shutdown and restart decisions) is known as the option to alter operating scale. Suppose our Swiss chemical producer can spend I(t) to build the Mexican dye factory worth A(t), where A(t) is the discounted expected net present value of cash flows on the new factory assuming it produces 1 million cubic liters of dye per annum for the rest of the life of the factory at a cost of C(q) per liter q. The I(t) is a fixed and sunk cost, whereas the cost C(q) subtracted from future expected revenues and discounted to get V(t) is a variable cost.

If p(q) denotes the demand curve for dyes, the Mexican factory reaches its productive optimum when $\partial p/\partial q = \partial C(q)/\partial q$—the usual optimality condition that marginal revenue equals marginal cost. Suppose the production optimum at time t is q^*, so the firm undertakes the project if

$$\sum_{j=1}^{\infty} \frac{E_t[p(q^*(t+j))q(t+j)] - C(q^*(t+j))}{1 + \lambda_{t,t+j}} - I(t) \geq 0$$

where λ is the firm's cost of capital as usual. In other words, the firm spends I(t) to undertake the project if the discounted expected net revenues from the project are at least as high as the investment spending required assuming optimal production.

Once the firm has incurred cost I(t), that cost is sunk, and the factory is under way or in production. At that point, if the demand curve or the cost curve shift, q^* may no longer represent the condition for optimal production. The option to be able to expand or contract operating scale and meet the optimality conditions for production is a valuable one.

Switching Option

The option to "switch" can refer either to switching inputs or outputs in a production process. Input switching is common in industries where production inputs are flexible, such as electric power and rotated-crop farming. In the former case, for example, power can be generated using natural gas turbines, hydroelectric and pump storage facilities, fossil fuels, nuclear fuels, and the like. If the price of natural gas rises significantly with respect to the price of fossil fuels like coal, the ability to switch generation from gas turbines to coal-fired plants is a valuable option.

Output switching is valuable and common in industries whose outputs are characterized by volatile demand. Rather than sell the Mexican plant to a German chemical concern that will use the dye facility to make explosives, the Swiss firm simply has the option of switching to explosives production itself. Just as in the case of abandonment, the output switching option has a payoff that is equivalent to an option on the better of two assets. In the abandonment case, the price the company could get for selling its assets to an explosives producer was K_2, presumed equal to the discounted expected future explosives revenues less the cost of converting the assets for a different use. The option to switch output from dye to explosives has exactly the same payoff as the abandonment option shown in Exhibit 14.1; switching outputs is equivalent to the abandonment of the factory to a new buyer, where this time the new buyer is just another (or possibly even the same) business unit of the Swiss firm.

Importance of Risk

We began this discussion by explaining how a firm could abandon a project or divest itself of assets in order to control its risks. We then reviewed several intermediate and less draconian ways to make the capital budgeting process more resilient to external factors so as to avoid the need of a full divestiture. In all of our subsequent discussion, however, we have paid little attention to the risk of the projects.

Discounting the expected future cash flows on a project at the firm's weighted average cost of capital already provides one "risk correction" in the above calculations. In other words, the value of the project itself will depend on the risk of that project in the firm's portfolio of exposures. If the project subjects the firm to any additional risks such as expected financial distress costs, those costs also must be subtracted in the NPV calculation. In other words, risk can be as strong a determinant of the abandonment and time to build and other real options discussed in the prior section as are shifts in costs or demand for the product.

"SYNTHETIC" ASSET DISPOSITION WITH DERIVATIVES

If the sole reason that a firm decides that the abandonment option is the one that makes the most sense, actually selling the asset(s) can be time consuming and expensive. Fortunately, derivatives sometimes can be used not just to transfer some of the risks of an asset, as we saw in Chapter 13, but to transfer all of the risks—and returns—of an asset to another party in the capital market. In this manner, derivatives can in some instances be used to facilitate "synthetic" asset divestitures.

Importantly, when a derivatives transaction is used to completely transfer the risk and return of an asset from the asset's owner to another firm, the ownership of the asset does not change. The asset remains on the accounting balance sheet of the original owner, even if the firm's risk or economic balance sheet is neutral with respect to the asset. But ownership can be important. If the firm is required to hold capital against a balance sheet asset and is not given a capital charge credit for an off-balance-sheet risk transfer contract, for example, then synthetic divestitures of assets can end up being more expensive than actual asset sales.

Synthetic asset divestitures tend to make sense for firms in lieu of actual asset sales in two situations: when the firm is more interested in a synthetic repurchase agreement than an actual sale and when the synthetic divestiture is simply cheaper than the alternatives.

Reversible Divestitures and Synthetic Asset Repos

If a company's desire to get rid of an asset is temporary, then the firm actually is best served by trying to engage in a synthetic asset repurchase agreement. In a traditional repo, as explained in Chapter 12, a firm sells a bond to a counterparty and simultaneously agrees to buy it back, usually a short time later. The firm thus "loans" the bond to a counterparty in exchange for cash. A repo of this sort is thus essentially a very short-term bond swap agreement.

Derivatives such as asset swaps and commodity swaps can be used to achieve the same effect as bond repos. As distinct from permanent asset divestiture or abandonment, derivatives can be used to divest synthetically an asset or project with an understanding that when the derivatives transaction matures or expires, the asset will revert to its original owner. We call this a "synthetic" divestiture because the asset itself has not moved. It is still in the same physical location and on the original firm's balance sheet. But the risks and return from that asset have been transferred temporarily to another firm.

Consider an example of a power company that has more than enough generation assets to meet both its normal (i.e., "baseload") demand and any reasonable demand during peak-load periods. In other words, the company has excess capacity in generation assets. Suppose, in particular, the utility owns a hydroelectric facility. All the fixed costs in the dam are sunk, and the variable cost of generating power is $K per megawatt hour. As power prices rise, the dam could be turned on to generate power for a net profit margin of $S(t) - K$ per megawatt hour, where $S(t)$ is the time t spot price. The payoff to power generation in that case is identical to the payoff on a call option on power struck at K.

By assumption, demand is not adequate in the utility's own area to re-quire the dam. The power company thus can sell the dam and recover at least some of the costs tied up in an otherwise wasting asset. But doing so also would deprive the power company of the dam in all future periods. If the firm believes baseload and peaking demand are on the rise, then keeping the dam would make sense in order to avoid having to build new generation assets at some point.

The firm can synthetically divest itself of the dam for the interim period of time during which the dam is not needed by entering into a swap transac-tion with another power supplier whose generation assets are not adequate to cover its demand. Suppose specifically that the cost of transmitting power generated by the hydrofacility to the other demand area is $T per megawatt hour. The power company that owns the dam could presell the power from the dam for $(K + T) per megawatt hour using a swap in which a firm com-mitment to deliver power is reached (say, for delivery during peak weekday periods). The combination of this short electricity sale at K + T plus the long call struck at K plus the transmission costs of T would result in the original utility being long a put on power at K + T.

Alternatively, the power company could sell calls, either to a specific counterparty or in the marketplace to a generic buyer (e.g., using options on electricity futures). The power company's other generation assets are being used to cover baseload and peaking demand, but because the dam is excess capacity and can be viewed as a call, any exercises of the options the firm writes can be honored by opening the dam's floodgates.

Note that the generator can be synthetically disposed of with a call sale or a swap in a relatively riskless manner only when the utility has excess capac-ity. Otherwise, the generator will be needed to meet peaking or baseload de-mand. And if a call has been sold against the generator in that case, the utility will have to go into the market and buy the excess power it needs—possibly at very high prices. Selling a call against a generation asset thus makes sense for a utility if its own demand area is covered.

The main advantage to the firm of this strategy over a sale of the dam is that the derivatives used to synthetically sell the dam expire after a certain amount of time, at which point the right to use the excess generating capacity reverts to the original firm. If the firm is genuinely convinced it will need the dam eventually, this strategy is far less costly than selling the generator and then either buying it back or building a new one.

Synthetic Divestitures Using Credit Derivatives

Just as asset or commodity swaps and options can be used to transfer synthet-ically the risk and return on a physical asset to another firm, total return swaps—as discussed in Chapter 13—can be used to transfer synthetically the risks and returns on a financial asset to another firm. Total return swaps are sometimes called "replication" products because they allow firms to replicate the risks and returns of asset ownership without actually owning the asset.[4]

Like the synthetic repurchase agreements just discussed, the synthetic divestiture of an asset using a total return swap is reversible. Total return swaps tend to have reasonably long tenors, however, and often can have maturity dates that match the maturity of the asset whose risk and returns are being swapped away. Synthetic divestitures accomplished with swaps thus are not always intended to be repurchaselike; rather they are intended to provide firms with a means of permanently divesting themselves of an asset without selling it.

Commercial banks have found total return swaps extremely popular for facilitating a shift away from credit risk–based income toward fee-based income. A bank may sell or syndicate a loan, but that means giving up its servicing role as well as its risk retention role. Many banks prefer to retain the fees associated with loan servicing without necessarily retaining all the credit risk of the transactions. Accordingly, they use total return swaps to transfer some or all of their credit exposure without taking themselves out of the servicing loop.

MECHANICS OF A TYPICAL SECURITIZATION

Securitization is the process by which the cash flows on an asset are repackaged and used as the basis for the creation of securities like those discussed in Chapter 2. Securitization is a type of asset divestiture decision, but it does not have quite the same draconian implications of a pure divestiture. Importantly, the firm divesting itself of the asset can choose to sell only part of the asset and even can choose the risk attributes of the part(s) to be sold to investors.

Assets that can be (and have been) securitized include virtually any form of loan (mortgages, home equity, auto, commercial and industrial, real estate, student, etc.), most forms of receivables (credit card receivables, computer leases, aircraft and marine leases, equipment leases), variable annuity fees, delinquent tax liens, utility stranded costs, and the like. More recently, credit and insurance risks have both become popular targets of securitization initiatives, although we will wait to discuss those until Chapter 22.

A typical securitization—say, of the trade receivables of a nonfinancial corporation—begins with one or more firms that have assets on their books that they wish to divest. A firm may accomplish this through a "conduit." Such conduits can take the form of single-seller or multiseller conduits. In a single-seller conduit, a single firm sells the assets it wishes to divest to a special-purpose vehicle (SPV), special-purpose entity (SPE), or special-purpose trust.

In the securitization context, an SPV is an entity created for the sole purpose of purchasing the assets to be securitized from their owner and issuing securities using those acquired assets as collateral. The owner of the SPV is usually not the original asset owner; otherwise, the SPV could potentially be consolidated up on the original owner's balance sheet, negating the asset disposition. Instead, the investment bank, a third party, or some other firm usually owns the SPV. Even then, "ownership" often consists of only a very nominal capital investment (e.g., one dollar) and extremely limited control rights.

Once the assets to be sold are conveyed to the SPV, it is responsible for the management of the collateral and the administration of cash receivables and payables. As part of those responsibilities, the SPV is responsible for the design of the asset-backed securities to be issued—that is, the manner in which the cash inflows on the new assets will be transformed into new assets in the form of securities. The principal and interest on the securities issued by the SPV are based on the principal and interest on the original assets (e.g., receivables). The securities themselves usually are issued to an investment bank, which then distributes them to end investors.

In a multiseller conduit like the one depicted in Exhibit 14.2, multiple sellers—Companies ABC and XYZ in the exhibit—convey their selected assets to a single SPV.[5] The cash flows on the multiple pools of assets then are combined as aggregate collateral for the securities issued by the SPV. In some cases, the SPV may issue different classes of securities whose collateral is

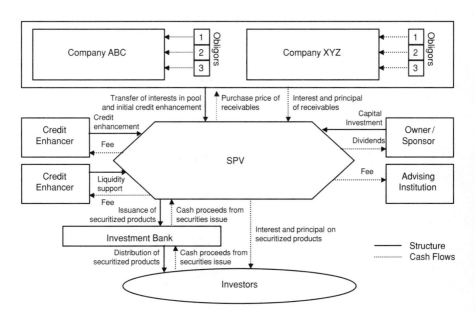

EXHIBIT 14.2 Typical Multiseller Securitization Conduit
Source: Kavanagh, Bohemio, and Edwards (1992).

based on the repackaged cash flows of the underlying asset pools. Mortgage-backed securities, for example, are issued based on pools of mortgage assets whose cash flows have been arranged into "tranches" based on prepayment speeds. The lower-risk securities issued by the SPV in that case would be backed by the tranche of mortgages that prepay earliest, whereas the riskier securities would be based on the principal and interest arriving last.

A major issue of concern to investors in many securitized products is the credit quality of the paper issued by the SPV. To enhance this credit quality, many securitizations involve at least two levels of credit enhancements. The initial credit enhancement is provided by the company conveying the assets and generally is the difference between the face value of the assets and the (discounted) price paid by the SPV to acquire those assets. Usually known as the holdback or overcollateralization of the assets, this amount usually is defined as a multiple of historical losses on the underlying asset pool and the relation between the credit quality of the asset pool and the rating the SPV desires on the paper it ultimately issues.

Usually a second layer of credit support provision is necessary both to make the new securities attractive to their holders and to stimulate trading in those securities. The SPV often engages a credit support provider for this purpose. In return for a fee, the credit support provider may provide a letter of credit, guarantee, senior subordinated debt, a pledged reserve account, or simply may sell puts on the conveyed assets and commit to purchase those assets at a specified price.

Closely related to the role of the credit support provider(s) is the liquidity support provider(s). Whereas credit support providers commit to making up any shortfall on the assets of the SPV below its liabilities, liquidity support providers commit instead to providing short-term financing for the servicing of the newly issued securities. Liquidity support is provided to ensure that mistimings in cash flows do not trigger defaults on the new securities. Liquidity support also can be provided—usually in the form of an income swap as discussed in Chapter 13—to smooth cash flows on any securities held as collateral to guarantee full or partial principal repayment on the securities issued by the SPV.

Finally, as Exhibit 14.2 illustrates, a typical conduit involves some participation by an advising institution. This institution may advise in the structuring of the conduit and also act as the sourcing or referral agent to identify the companies whose assets will be conveyed to the conduit.

COMMON SECURITIZED PRODUCTS AND THE ROLE OF PARTICIPATING INSTITUTIONS[6]

Depending on the type of securitized product issued by the SPV and the purpose of the conduit, different institutions may play different roles in the securitization process. The means by which cash flows are repackaged to form securities also depends on the type of product and structure. In this section, we discuss four common types of securitized products, leaving three others—credit-linked notes, collateralized debt obligations, and insurance-linked notes—for Chapter 18.

Mortgage-Backed Securities

Securitizations first began with the issuance of securities backed by mortgages in 1970 when the Government National Mortgage Association (GNMA) first issued mortgage-backed "pass-through" securities. The Federal Home Loan Mortgage Corporation (FHLMC or Freddie Mac) issued mortgage pass-through securities just a year later, and the Federal National Mortgage Association (FNMA or Fannie Mae) followed with a pass-through issue in 1981. In the mortgage-backed securities programs of three of these government-sponsored enterprises (GSEs), the GSE itself plays the role of the SPV, buying or sometimes originating mortgage loans and then pooling those loans to service the interest and principal payments on the pass-through securities they issue to investors.[7]

All three GSEs also act as credit enhancers to the securities they issue. GNMA pass-throughs are guaranteed directly by the U.S. Treasury, whereas Freddie Mac and Fannie Mae securities are agency securities and guaranteed only by the balance sheets of the GSEs. It is widely believed, however, that Freddie Mac and Fannie Mae would not be allowed to default and thus carry the implicit backing of the U.S. Treasury. Partly because of the already high quality the government and agency guarantees bring, pass-throughs generally do not involve any liquidity enhancement.

Collateralized Mortgage Obligations and Real Estate Mortgage Investment Conduits

Collateralized mortgage obligations (CMOs) and real estate mortgage investment conduits (REMICs) were developed as mortgage-based securitized products in which the prepayment risk can be separated so that the securitized products issued are affected in different ways by prepayments. A group of bonds issued in a CMO deal is called a tranche, and the collateral for these tranches may include original mortgage loans, mortgage-backed securities, or other CMOs and REMICs. Cash flows generated by the assets conveyed to the CMO issuer are used to pay first interest and then principal on the securitized products issued.

Mortgage-backed securities are called pass-throughs mainly because the cash flows on the underlying pool(s) of mortgages are used to fund the interest and principal payments on the securities on essentially a pro rata basis.

Consequently, prepayments on the underlying mortgage assets can strongly affect the timing and value of cash flows on the pass-through securities. For CMOs and CMO-like structures, tranches are distinguished by their principal prepayment risk. In a traditional "sequential" CMO, the tranches are assigned priority, and principal payments are made sequentially in that order of priority. In this manner, the bonds issued through a CMO structure have interest rate risk, prepayment risk, and effective maturities that vary by tranche, thus allowing investors a greater ability to pick and choose between risk/return profiles.

Credit enhancements are generally not used for CMO structures that rely primarily on agency mortgage-backed securities. For whole-loan-backed CMOs, the SPV issuer usually holds a reserve fund—equivalent to overcollateralization—to absorb some proportion of default-related losses before affecting cash distributions to investors. In addition, holders of the securities issued by the CMO often are given recourse to the underlying collateral. If the issuer of the securities defaults, the collateral reverts to the bond holders, thereby making the issuer's credit quality largely unimportant.

Liquidity enhancements are often accomplished either with a reserve fund similar to the credit default reserve fund or with an income swap. In either case, the liquidity enhancement usually is designed to convert the often-volatile income on the underlying mortgage asset pool(s) into a smooth (i.e., quarterly or semiannual) cash flow available for interest payments on the bonds the CMO has issued.

A variety of additional variations on this structure exist for CMO structures, including minimum sinking fund provisions, accrual or Z bonds, very accurately defined maturity (VADM) tranches, planned amortization class (PAC) bonds, strips, floaters, and the like. All such variations can change the risk/return features of the securities issued by the CMO structure by rearranging the type and order of application of cash income on the mortgage assets to the issued bonds, but the basic mechanical structure of the conduit remains largely the same in each case.

Nonmortgage Asset-Backed Securities

Mortgage-backed securities and CMOs are types of asset-backed securities. In addition to being collateralized by mortgage loans, asset-backed securities (ABSs) may also be collateralized by nonmortgage assets. The first such securitized product was issued in 1985 by First Boston and was a single-seller conduit whose securities were collateralized by computer leases originated by Sperry. ABSs are commonly based on leases or receivables, such as credit card receivables.

In a typical ABS structure, the single or multiple sellers convey a specific pool or pools of assets to the SPV that in turn issues securities based on the original asset pool(s). When the pool of assets either defaults or is fully repaid, the securities issued by the SPV are fully paid off and the SPV winds down. In other words, most ABS structures are "self-terminating" and have a finite life that depends on the life of the original assets conveyed. The maturity of most ABSs usually runs from two to five years.

The structure in Exhibit 14.2 is broadly representative of a traditional ABS conduit. In many ABS structures, the advising institution is also the firm selling the assets to be securitized. This means that the credit and liquidity support providers usually must be nonrelated third parties to ensure that, under accounting rules, the transaction can be treated by the seller/advisor as a legitimate asset disposition.

Asset-Backed Commercial Paper Programs

In the early 1980s, banks became concerned that they were increasingly unable to offer competitive financing to their corporate customers. As mentioned in Chapter 8, the Basel Accord also requires banks to allocate capital to balance sheet loans, and banks in the 1980s were concerned about pushing their regulatory capital utilization. As a solution, the banking community developed asset-backed commercial paper (ABCP) programs. These programs were conduits for banks' corporate clients to convert their receivables into short-term financing at highly competitive rates, but because the actual issuance of securities was through a conduit, banks could assist and participate in their corporate customers' capital formation process without inflating their balance sheets with new loans.

The structure of a typical multiseller ABCP conduit is well represented in Exhibit 14.2, as in our other examples. Some important differences between ABS and ABCP structures, however, can be illustrated using the diagram for assistance. First, the paper issued in an ABCP program by the SPV and through an investment bank to end investors is short-term commercial paper. Unlike ABSs, ABCP issues do not trade in an active secondary market; nor do they have long maturities. Instead, typically the paper is held to maturity by end investors for holding of often only a few months.

The short maturities of ABCP issues also imply a second difference between ABCP and ABS conduits. As noted, ABS conduits usually involve a one-time conveyance of assets to the SPV, and the SPV winds down after the receivables are repaid and the securities are fully paid off. In a typical ABCP program, by contrast, the SPV continually purchases new assets or receivables and rolls over outstanding commercial paper issues.

A third important distinction between ABS and ABCP programs is the role of the advising institution. In an ABS conduit, the banking institution is usually advisor and originator of the assets conveyed to the SPV, with third parties providing credit and liquidity support. In an ABCP program, by contrast, the advising bank is usually responsible for identifying and structuring the asset conveyance to the SPV, but the assets are owned by the customers of the bank and not the bank. Because the advising bank is not the original owner of the assets, however, it can and often does materially participate in the conduit also as a credit and/or liquidity support provider.

NOTES

1. Some parts of this discussion are similar to Chapter 14 in Culp (2001), although the presentation here is sufficiently different to warrant a review even by readers familiar with the other text.
2. See Ingersoll and Ross (1992).
3. Remember that the expectation in a typical NPV calculation is a conditional expectation. The conditional expected NPV of a project thus can change as new information arrives in the marketplace. This does not require, moreover, the assumption of asymmetric information. Everyone may well be equally ignorant and then become gradually more informed at the same rate as time passes.
4. See, for example, Das (1998).
5. Figure 14.2 is based on Kavanagh, Bohemio, and Edwards (1992).
6. This section draws from Kavanagh, Bohemio, and Edwards (1992).
7. Some of the distinctions between the pass-through securities issued by these government-sponsored enterprises are explored in Hayre, Mohebbi, and Zimmerman (1995).

CHAPTER 15

Insurance

We turn now to consider one of the oldest and most commonly used forms of risk transfer, insurance. Numerous parallels will quickly become obvious between insurance contracts and the risk transfer methods already examined—especially derivatives. Nevertheless, classical insurance and derivatives are indeed different forms of contracts. They often involve different types of risks, are regulated differently, and are supplied by different types of firms. As we shall see, moreover, insurance and derivatives also are separated by the important distinction between an insurable interest and an optionable interest.

When an insurance company buys insurance, the product used to accomplish a transfer of risk is called reinsurance. Some fundamental differences exist between primary insurance and reinsurance, however; we leave discussion of the latter to the Chapter 16. In this chapter, we focus on answering the following questions:

■ What are the mechanics of a risk transfer accomplished using a classical insurance contract?
■ When information is asymmetric between the insurance provider and purchaser, how does the insurance provider alter the design of insurance contracts to mitigate moral hazard and adverse selection problems?
■ How are insurance contracts distinguished by market or business line?
■ How are insurance companies organized?
■ How do insurance companies manage their liabilities using capital and reserves?

MECHANICS OF CLASSICAL INSURANCE

A typical insurance contract is a risk transfer mechanism enabling a firm to transfer the loss arising from some specific risk(s), peril(s), or hazard(s) from the equity holders of the insurance purchaser to the equity holders of the insurance provider. Insurance contracts can best be understood by first examining their distinguishing characteristics and then their mechanics, including the risks they are designed to cover.

Features of Insurance Contracts

Traditional insurance contracts are characterized by four important features[1]:

1. The purchaser of insurance must have an insurable interest.
2. Risk must exist at the inception of the contract.
3. The insurance contract must transfer some portion of the risk from the purchaser of the insurance to the provider or seller, in return for which some consideration (i.e., premium) must be conveyed to the seller by the purchaser.
4. The contract is "of utmost good faith."

The first three criteria differentiate the insurance contract from a gambling contract and often are required for the contract to be considered insurance for tax and accounting purposes. Of particular importance is the concept of an insurable interest, which also distinguishes insurance for otherwise similar nongambling capital market products. Having an insurable interest means that the purchaser of the insurance contract must be at risk to sustain some economic loss in order to receive compensation. A firm that has an insurable interest in property, for example, could sustain direct and material damage by the loss or degradation of the property asset. Or a firm with an insurable interest in professional liability must be capable of sustaining direct and material damage from the professional misconduct or negligence of its agents.

Insurable interest is required for a contract to be considered classical insurance as opposed to, say, a derivatives contract.[2] A derivatives transaction involves an optionable interest rather than an insurable interest. This means that the risks transferred in a derivatives contract need not be risks to which the derivatives counterparties are naturally exposed. In a typical pay fixed/receive LIBOR interest rate swap, for example, the end user need not have a natural exposure to rising LIBOR as a precondition of doing the swap. If LIBOR rises relative to the fixed swap rate, the fixed-rate payer is entitled to a net payment from the swap counterparty *regardless* of whether the fixed-rate payer has sustained any economic damage from the interest rate increase. This would impossible in a traditional insurance contract.

Another important feature of insurance contracts is that they are governed by the principle of utmost good faith. This means that the standard of honesty applied to an insurance contract is higher than the standard applied to ordinary commercial or capital market transactions. One important application of the utmost good faith principle concerns representations made by the party seeking insurance. If a material representation is made and turns out to be false, this is generally considered grounds for the insurance company to walk away from the contract.

The materiality of a representation, moreover, need not be tied to any actual damage incurred by the insurance purchaser. In order for the insurer to nullify the contract, it need be true only that the misrepresentation affects the risk of the contract to the insurer. Even if there is no *ex post* damage arising from the mispresentation, any representation that would have affected the insurer's risk assessment of the contract *ex ante* is considered material. To appreciate this distinction, suppose an auto insurer asks a customer if anyone in the family under the age of 25 is driving the car and the customer answers no. Then suppose one of the listed over-25 drivers has an accident. A subsequent determination during the accident investigation that there was an under-25 driver may void the auto insurance policy even though the under-25 driver was not behind the wheel when the accident occurred.

Utmost good faith also applies on the other side to warranties included by the insurance carrier. Although a misrepresentation must have a material impact on the risk to the insurer of underwriting the policy, a warranty included by the insurer creates a condition for the policy to be voided even if the condition is not material to the risk underlying the policy. If an insurer warrants that the policy shall not be effective if the triggering event occurs while it is raining, for example, then the insurer will not honor any claim made based on a triggering event that occurred on a rainy day. Common warranties often involve the exclusion of payments associated with acts of God, terrorism, seizure or capture, coup d'états, and the like.

Mechanics of Insurance

An insurance contract specifies very clearly the nature of the risk, hazard, or peril that can give rise to the contingent payment promised by the insurance company to the insurance purchaser. This is known as the trigger of the contract. Some insurance is highly specific to a certain enumerated risk, hazard, or peril. Examples include property damage insurance triggered by fire or flood, health insurance linked to particular medical problems (e.g., dental or opthomological coverage), or casualty insurance linked to injuries sustained in auto accidents. Other insurance structures may be more comprehensive in nature, such as a general homeowner's policy protecting property for essentially any damage not willfully imposed by the policy holder or general medical coverage applying to any treatments not arising from preinsurance health problems.

In some cases, a single risk is insured by more than one insurance company. Historically, the lead or primary insurance company would put its name at the top of a "slip" and then solicit other insurance companies to join in sharing the risk to be assumed. These firms would place their names underneath the lead insurer on the slip. The process by which an insurance company assumes risk thus came to be known as underwriting, and the lead insurer was called the lead underwriter.

In addition, an insurance contract will specify clearly the nature of the insurer's contingent liability payable to the insured party—sometimes called the benefit amount—in the event the triggering event occurs. Whether the benefit amount is fixed or variable depends on whether the insurance contract is a contract of value or a contract of indemnity.

A valued contract is an insurance contract that pays a fixed amount if the triggering event occurs. A regular life insurance contract, for example, pays a fixed amount following the triggering event of the death of the insured. A contract of indemnity, by contrast, has a contingent payment that is proportional to the economic loss incurred by the insured party. A small loss thus results in a small payment, whereas a large loss results in a large payment, subject to the important constraint that the insured cannot recover more on the insurance contract than the actual economic damage sustained. A full indemnity contract is one that restores the insurance purchaser to exactly the same condition as before the adverse triggering event.

Consider an example in which the insurance purchaser is a homeowner, the insurable interest is the value of the owner's house, and the insurance is tied to the specific triggering event of a fire. Suppose the value of the house is currently K. The homeowner can buy two insurance contracts. In the first—a valued contract—the insurance purchaser pays premium p_v for the right to receive Z in the event of a fire, where Z is a fixed amount. The second contract—an indemnity contract—pays the homeowner an amount equal to the damage sustained from the fire relative to the current price of the house K in return for receiving premium p_i. Exhibit 15.1 shows the payoffs to the value and indemnity contracts in the event of a fire.

Consider first the valued contract. If there is no fire, the value of the contract to the homeowner is $-p_v$, or the premium paid. In the event there is a fire, however, the homeowner receives Z from the insurer for a net gain of $Z - p_v$. As long as the damage caused by the fire does not cause the value of the house to fall below $V°$, the owner of the value contract actually receives more than the sustained damage. But for a decline in the value of the house to, say, level $V°°$, the net gain of $Z - p_v$ is not sufficient to compensate the owner for the damage sustained.

Now consider the indemnity contract. In the case of no fire, the homeowner is out the premium paid of p_i. But in the event of a fire, the value of the indemnity contract is exactly equal to the decline in the value of the house, $K - V$. Whether the house declines in value to $V°$ or $V°°$, the homeowner receives the difference in that value and the initial price of the house K less the premium paid. If the value of the house declines by less than $K - V°$, the

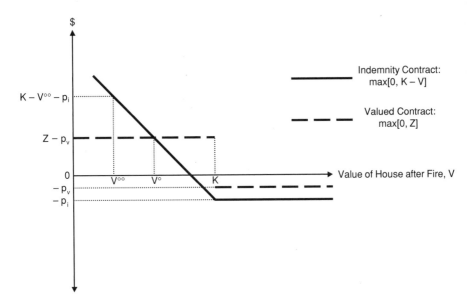

EXHIBIT 15.1 Property Insurance Contracts, Value versus Indemnity

homeowner would have been better off with the valued contract. But for declines in the property value below V°—say, to V°°—the indemnity contract provides better protection.

The value K in Exhibit 15.1 is called the *attachment point* of the insurance, and in the example it is equal to the value of the house. But this need not be the case. The fire insurance policy states that it will compensate the homeowner for a decline in the value of the house from its then-current market value, and this may be greater or less than the value of the house when the insurance contract was executed. Alternatively, some types of insurance specify that damages will paid relative to some predefined amount, such as K. In the former case, the insurance contract always compensates the homeowner with a payment equal to actual, current losses. In the latter case, whether the payment is adequate depends on whether the house has fallen in value relative to the attachment point at the time of the fire. In an indemnity contract, the converse—receiving more than the damage sustained—is not permitted, although practical problems of measuring losses may sometimes allow this to occur inadvertently.

Note in Exhibit 15.1 that the valued contract is equivalent to a binary put option on the house, as discussed in Chapter 13, whereas the indemnity contract is equivalent to a traditional put option on the property struck at K. Two important differences, however, separate the options discussed earlier and these insurance contracts. The first is the existence of an insurable interest; the insurance purchaser had to own the house and be at risk of sustaining actual damage from a fire in order to purchase either insurance contract shown in Exhibit 15.1. The second is that the exercise value of these options does not just depend on their intrinsic value but also on the occurrence of the triggering event. A decline in the value of the house arising from, say, a flood would send these options into the money, but in a nonexploitable way. In order for the insurance contracts to be "exercised," they must be in the money *and* a fire must have occurred.

MORAL HAZARD, ADVERSE SELECTION, AND INSURANCE CONTRACT DESIGN

An important practical consequence of the distinction between insurable and optionable interests is that insurance contracts, based on the former, tend to be associated with firm-specific risks, hazards, or perils. Indemnity contracts, moreover, have contingent payments based on firm-specific economic losses incurred. Because the purchaser of insurance must be at risk to suffer direct economic damage before engaging in an insurance transaction, insurance thus poses two potential problems to a classical insurer that are not found in markets for risk transfers involving optionable interests, such as derivatives.

These problems are called *moral hazard* and *adverse selection*. Both of these classical insurance problems are a result of asymmetric information between the insurer and insured. Moral hazard problems arise because insurers cannot perfectly observe the actions taken by insured parties to control (and sometimes to increase) their insurance risks and loss exposures. Adverse selection, by contrast, occurs when insurers cannot distinguish inherently "good" risks from "bad" ones. Moral hazard is sometimes called "hidden action," and adverse selection, "hidden risk."

Moral Hazard

When the purchaser of insurance can take actions that impact either the probability of incurring an insurable loss or the size of that loss *and* asymmetric information prevents the insurer form perfectly observing those actions of the insured, the problem of moral hazard can arise. Without fire insurance, for example, an individual may spend more on fire prevention. But with fire insurance coverage, the homeowner may not pay as much attention to fire prevention issues. Similarly, a corporation that insures the full value of a shipment of cargo crossing the ocean may be less inclined to invest in the safest ship around, knowing that the insurer will be there to pick up the loss.

In the extreme, full insurance with asymmetric information actually can create perverse incentives, such as the incentive of a fully insured homeowner to set fire to her own house. Or a fully insured owner of an auto that might be worth more insured than if resold might leave the keys in the car and then park the car in a bad part of town.

Insurers include several common features in their contracts to mitigate moral hazard problems. Moral hazard tends to be more problematic in contracts of indemnity than in valued contracts. For that reason, the following four features are most commonly observed in indemnity contracts:

1. Deductibles
2. Copayment provisions
3. Policy limits
4. Subrogation

Deductibles

The first mitigant against moral hazard used by insurers and included in most indemnity contracts is a *deductible*, or a requirement that some portion of any damages arising from the insured risk be paid by the insured before the insurance company makes a payment. To see how this works, return to the homeowner buying fire insurance as in Exhibit 15.1, and suppose the indemnity contract is chosen. We assumed before that the current value of the house was K and that the policy payoff was calculated relative to that amount. The policy thus paid K – V for any postfire value of the house V, and that amount was exactly equal to the loss of value sustained by the insured party.

Now suppose the current value of the house is V* and that the policy has a deductible of V* – K, shown on Exhibit 15.2, which now shows the value of an insurance contract excluding the cost of premium paid. For any postfire value of the house V, the policy still pays K – V. But because the current value of the house is V*, the loss of value sustained is V* – V. The first V* – K dollars of loss thus are absorbed by the homeowner. We refer to this first V* – K amount of loss exposure for the homeowner as a *retained exposure*. The policy still can be viewed as a put option on the value of the house, but one that is struck V* – K dollars out of the money at its inception.

With a large enough deductible, the insured party has some incentive to engage in protective actions, such as buying smoke detectors, fire extinguishers, and the like. In addition, the deductible lowers any return to arson on the part of the insured.

The above is an example of what is called a *straight deductible*—a flat amount applied on a per-loss basis. Other types of deductibles also may be included in insurance policies. Especially in liability policies, *aggregate deductibles* often are more common that straight deductibles. Aggregate deductibles are similar to straight deductibles in that they force the insurance purchaser to retain a fixed amount of a loss. But they differ by defining the loss and deductible *cumulatively*—usually over the course of a calendar year

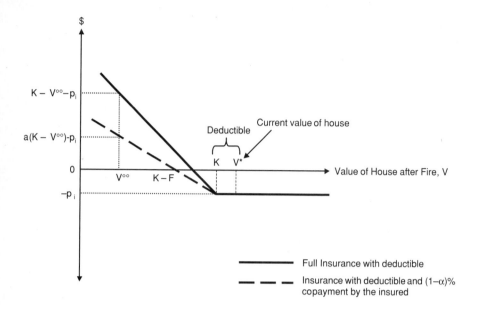

EXHIBIT 15.2 Deductibles and Copay Provisions in a Property Insurance Indemnity Contract

or the policy life—rather than per risk or per occurrence. A professional indemnity policy, for example, may require a firm to absorb the first $100,000 in losses, even if these losses are spread across several different claims.[3]

A *disappearing deductible* is yet another type of deductible that becomes smaller as the economic damage sustained becomes larger. Such a deductible results in the following contingent liability for the insurer following an occurrence of the triggering event underlying the policy:

$$(L - D)(1 + \zeta)$$

where L is the aggregate economic loss or damage sustained, D is a fixed deductible amount, and ζ is a "recapture factor" that turns the fixed deductible into a disappearing one. Consider, for example, a fixed deductible D of $10,000 and a recapture factor ζ of 10 percent. Suppose the aggregate loss is only $15,000. The insurance company then owes $5,500 (= ($15,000 – $10,000)(1.10)). The insurer retains the remaining $9,500 as a deductible. But for a much larger loss of $100,000, the insurance company then owes $99,000 (= ($100,000 – $10,000)(1.10)), which is almost the full amount.

Finally, a *franchise deductible*—which may be either a fixed or percentage number—specifies a minimum threshold for losses before any payments are made. When payments are made, however, the entire loss is payable by the insurer.

Return to our homeowner's example, and suppose the current value of the house is again K. Now suppose the franchise deductible is defined as F, shown in Exhibit 15.2. If the fire causes less than F dollars in damage to the house, the policy pays nothing. But if the fire causes the house to decline in value to any $V < K - F$, the policy holder receives $K - V$ as payment—not $K - F$, but $K - V$. In the vocabulary of Chapter 13, the fire insurance policy with a franchise deductible of F is equivalent to a down-and-in barrier put with a strike price of K and an instrike of $K - F$.

Copayment Provisions

A second way that insurers give policyholders an incentive to avoid moral hazard problems and take actions commensurate with risk reduction is by including *copayment* or *coinsurance* provisions in policies. A coinsurance provision requires an insurer to pay only some fraction of the total insured loss and leaves the remainder of the loss to be paid by the insured party. Indeed, coinsurance provisions often require that this uninsured portion of the exposure be retained to prevent the insured party from seeking cover for the coinsured amount under another policy from another insurance provider. The retention thus forces the policyholder to engage in some prudential risk management and discourages fraudulent or malicious claims.

Again consulting Exhibit 15.2, the heavy dashed line shows a fire indemnity policy with a deductible of $V^* - K$ and a copay provision of $(1 - \alpha)$percent. For every dollar of damage sustained to the house in excess of $V^* - K$ dollars, the insurance company pays the homeowner only α dollars. If the value of the house declines to $V^{\circ\circ}$, for example, the full insurance with deductible will yield a payment to the homeowner net of premium of $K - V^{\circ\circ} - p_i$ to be applied to the $V^* - V^{\circ\circ}$ in damage sustained. The insurance with a $(1 - \alpha)$ percent copay provision yields $\alpha(K - V^{\circ\circ}) - p_i$ payment. The latter thus is equivalent to α put options on the value of the home struck at K and initially out of the money by $V^* - K$.

Policy Limits

A third way to discourage moral hazard is for an insurer to limit its total liability to the insured party. Valued contracts are inherently limited by the fixed payment nature of the contract, and policy limits can be included in indemnity contracts for this purpose. It is rare to find an insurance contract without a policy limit of some kind.

Continuing with our fire insurance example, suppose the insurance company specifies a deductible of $V^* - K$ and sets a policy limit of Y. Exhibit 15.3 shows the payoff net of premium to the homeowner in this case. Under this

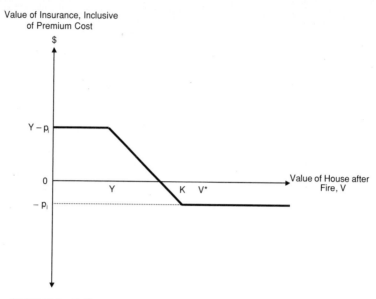

EXHIBIT 15.3   Policy Limits in a Property Insurance Indemnity Contract

policy, the homeowner's net retention is the first $V^* - K$ dollars of loss and any losses above Y.

Exhibit 15.3 should be familiar to readers as a short vertical spread in option parlance. In other words, a policy with a deductible of $V^* - K$ and a limit of Y written on a house currently valued at V^* is equivalent to a long put option struck at K and a short put option struck at Y, both of which have a maturity date equal to the policy term and an underlying defined as the postfire value of the house.

Subrogation

Insurance contracts also often include the right of *subrogation* for the insurer. Subrogation means that any right of recovery the insurance purchaser has to a third party for damage sustained is transferred to the insurer. Subrogation helps enforce the principle of indemnity that prevents the insured party from collecting more than one payment on a single economic loss.

Suppose, for example, that a homeowner purchases fire insurance as above and then experiences a major loss from a fire that is determined to be arson. Subrogation gives the insurer rather than the homeowner the exclusive right to pursue a claim on the arsonist for a recovery—at least up to the amount paid by the insurer on the claim.

In the absence of a subrogation right, it might be possible for the homeowner to collect twice on the fire—once from the insurer and once through a legal claim on the arsonist. This ability, in turn, can create a moral hazard, whereby the homeowner agrees to pay a large sum to the arsonist to torch her house—or simply agrees not to pursue the arsonist with a claim. Especially if the insured value of the house is above its market value at the time of the fire, then both the arsonist and the homeowner can make a substantial gain on such an arrangement in the absence of clearly defined subrogation rights for the insurance provider.

Adverse Selection

Informational asymmetries between parties seeking insurance and those providing it can give risk to adverse selection problems. In the insurance context, adverse selection occurs when the insurer cannot differentiate between good and bad insurance risks and thus inadvertently attracts more of the latter than the former. Specifically, when an insurer cannot distinguish between a good insurance risk and a "lemon," the premium assessed by insurers will be based on the assumption that it encounters both types of customers. But this pooled price will be too high for good risks and thus will guarantee that only bad risks want to buy insurance. The goal for the insurer is to develop a contract design or pricing mechanism that helps it to distinguish good from bad insurance risks, preferably by getting people to reveal their own types. A contracting or negotiation solution that induces insurance customers to reveal their true types to the insurance company is called a revelation mechanism.

More formally, consider health insurance and imagine two types of people—"sick" and "healthy." The insurer is presumed to know the true proportion of sick people in the market, but not whether any particular customer is sick or healthy. The premium the insurer will quote thus reflects the expected health quality of the people to be insured. As in Akerlof (1970), however, the higher the price of insurance, the fewer healthy people will want insurance. As the price approaches the true price that should be charged only to the sick, only sick people will buy insurance in the resulting equilibrium—hence the term "adverse selection."

To clarify the nature of the adverse selection problem, consider first a simple insurance model with no adverse selection. Suppose there are a large number of potential flood insurance purchasers and that these purchasers are risk-averse individuals with utility functions that are increasing and concave in wealth in the sense of Chapter 2. People are identical and have the same probability π of experiencing a loss L from flood damage. Assume all these individuals start with a wealth endowment W.

Exhibit 15.4 depicts equilibrium in the insurance market. The x-axis is wealth in the state of the world in which a flood does not occur, and the y-axis is wealth in the state of the world in which a flood does occur. The point marked O represents the base "no insurance" case. At this point, individual

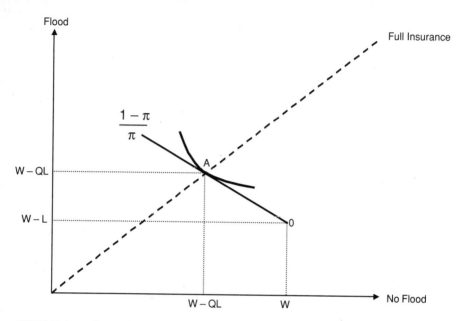

EXHIBIT 15.4 Full Insurance with Actuarially Fair Prices and Homogenous Consumers

wealth is W if no flood occurs and W − L in the event of a flood. The 45° line is the "full insurance" line in which the wealth of the individuals is the same regardless of whether a flood occurs or not.

The isolutility curve shown in Exhibit 15.4 indicates the trade-off the individual is willing to make between wealth in the no-flood state and wealth in the flood state. The slope of the indifference curve shown is negative and decreasing in wealth. The more wealth the person has, the less valuable a transfer of wealth from the no-flood state to the flood state. Conversely, people with relatively less wealth to begin with are presumed to suffer more severely from the flood damage in expected utility terms.[4]

An insurance policy is considered actuarially fair or fairly priced when the premium per unit of coverage equals the probability of a loss. With no transaction costs, the insurer thus breaks even at this price. The line in Exhibit 15.5 from endowment point O running through point A on the full insurance line is called the "fair odds" line. The slope of the line is $(1 - \pi)/\pi$, or the ratio of the probability of no flood to the probability of a flood. Points along this line represent all states where the trade-off between wealth in the no-flood and flood states is equal to the ratio of the probabilities of the no-flood and flood states. All insurance contracts offered along this fair odds line thus are actuarially fair or fairly priced and allow the insurer to break even on its policy offerings (ignoring transaction and administration costs).

Now suppose an insurance company sets a single price of insurance $Q = \pi$ and lets each consumer choose his own level of coverage z at that price. When a flood does not occur, the utility of the individual will be $U(W - Qz)$, where z is the amount of coverage purchased, Qz is the total cost of insurance, and U is the utility function. If a flood occurs, the individual realizes utility of $U(W - L - Qz + z)$—that is, his endowment minus his loss less the price paid for insurance coverage z *plus* the coverage level z. The consumer chooses z to maximize his expected utility of wealth:

$$\max_z [(1 - \pi)U(W - Qz) + \pi U(W - Qz + z - L)]$$

which yields the following first-order condition for optimum insurance coverage

$$\frac{U'(W - Qz + z - L)}{U'(W - Qz)} = \frac{(1 - \pi)Q}{\pi(1 - Q)} \tag{15.1}$$

Because the insurance is actuarially fair and lies along line OA somewhere, $Q = \pi$ and equation 15.1 becomes

$$U'(W - Qz + z - L) = U'(W - Qz) \tag{15.2}$$

Equation 15.2 is perfectly intuitive and says that the individual will choose an insurance coverage level that equates his marginal utility of wealth after a flood with his marginal utility wealth in the event a flood does not occur.

Clearly, the unique solution to equation 15.2 occurs when $z = L$. In other words, consumers purchase *full insurance*. This is shown in Exhibit 15.4 as the tangency point A between the indifference/isoutility curve and the fair odds line, which also lies on the full insurance line. When insurance is priced to be actuarially fair, risk-averse consumers thus always fully insure.

In practice, insurance companies typically charge an actuarially fair price *plus* a "load" to reflect the insurer's cost of writing the policy, managing its own risks, and administering the accounts. The insurance contracting line thus is no longer line OA with slope $(1 - \pi)/\pi$. As Exhibit 15.5 illustrates, the new insurance contract line OC has a slope $(1 - Q)/Q$. When $Q > \pi$, the slope of line OC is smaller than the slope of line OA. Now the consumers' indifference curve is tangent to the insurance contracting locus at point C, which is below the full insurance line. When insurers charge a price equal to the actuarial price plus a load designed to recover their costs of providing insurance, the equilibrium result is that risk-averse customers only partially insure themselves.

Suppose we again ignore transaction costs but assume that potential flood insurance buyers are divided into two groups—high risk and low risk.

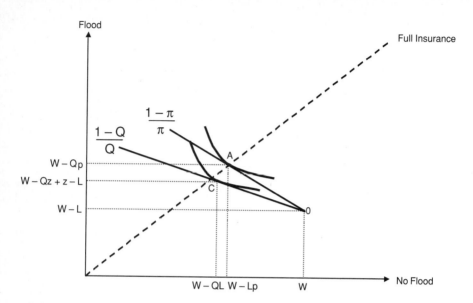

EXHIBIT 15.5   Insurance with Actuarially Unfair Prices and Homogenous Consumers

Within each group, people are identical and have the same probability of experiencing some loss L from flood damage. The probability of realizing flood damage is denoted π_L and π_H for the low- and high-risk groups, respectively. The insurer cannot distinguish between members of the two groups but is presumed to know the true proportion of the two types of customers in the market.[5]

Consider first an Akerlof-like model similar to the pecking order model presented in Chapter 5 in which the insurance company sets a single price of insurance Q and lets each consumer choose her own level of coverage at that price. The low-risk consumer chooses z to maximize her expected utility of wealth:

$$\max_z \ [(1 - \pi_L)U(W - Qz) + \pi_L U(W - Qz + z - L)]$$

which yields the following first-order condition for optimum insurance coverage

$$\frac{U'(W - Qz + z - L)}{U'(W - Qz)} = \frac{(1 - \pi_L)Q}{\pi_L(1 - Q)}$$

Similarly, for high-risk individuals the insurance coverage purchased is the z that satisifies

$$\frac{U'(W - Qz + z - L)}{U'(W - Q_z)} = \frac{(1 - \pi_H)Q}{\pi_H(1 - Q)}$$

Because $(1 - \pi_H)/\pi_H < (1 - \pi_L)/\pi_L$, $z_H > z_B$. This is illustrated graphically on Exhibit 15.6.

When the price of the insurance is set at $Q = \pi_L$, the low-risk individuals purchase full insurance at point A_L. But the high-risk consumers have indifference curves that are not as steep. The tangency between the high-risk consumer's indifference curve and the insurance contracting as at price $Q = \pi_L$ thus is point A_H. Because this point is above the full insurance line, high-risk customers buy more than full insurance. The insurance company breaks even on the low-risk customers but loses money on the high-risk customers and hence cannot offer this contract without expecting to go bankrupt.

Now consider instead a higher price Q such that $\pi_H > Q > \pi_L$. In this case, the low-risk customers buy less than full insurance at point B_L, which means the insurance company makes a profit on them. But high-risk customers continue to buy more than full insurance at point B_H. Whether the insurer makes enough on the low-risk customers to subsidize the high-risk customers is unclear. In at least some circumstances, the insurer will expect to lose more on

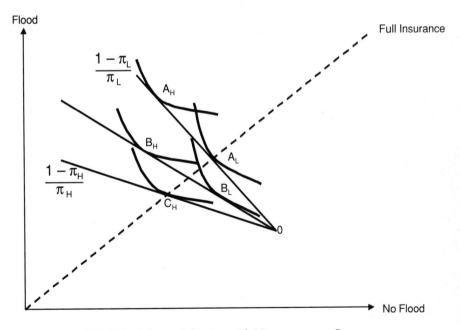

EXHIBIT 15.6 Adverse Selection with Heterogeneous Consumers

the high risks than it makes on the low risks and thus will expect to go out of business, so this contract does not represent a stable equilibrium.

Finally consider the price $Q = \pi_H$. In this situation, the low-risk consumers' indifference curve is never tangent to the insurance contracting line for levels of wealth below W. High-risk consumers fully insure at point C_H, low-risk consumers purchase no insurance and remain at point 0, and the insurer breaks even. Unlike the other two contracts, the insurer financially breaks even in all circumstances by offering this contract. This equilibrium thus is a stable one.

Unfortunately, the only one of the three contracts that represents a stable equilibrium (i.e., an equilibrium in which the insurer always at least breaks even in expected value terms) is the Akerlof outcome, as Exhibit 15.6 illustrates. When the insurer cannot distinguish between groups, the price eventually will be driven to the probability of flood damage being sustained by high-risk individuals, and low-risk individuals will be driven out of the market. In other words, the only contract the insurer is willing to offer in equilibrium is the contract that guarantees full adverse selection and attracts only bad risks to the market.

Rothschild and Stiglitz (1976) propose a solution to this conundrum. They argue that the key is in not offering consumers the choice of coverage. Instead, they propose a pair of insurance contracts to act as a revelation mechanism. One insurance contract gives high-risk individuals full insurance coverage at a high price, and the other gives low-risk people partial coverage at a low price. The result is a *separating equilibrium* that causes consumers to reveal their true type to the insurer through their choice of contract.

Exhibit 15.7 illustrates the Rothschild-Stiglitz separating equilibrium. The high-risk consumers will choose point C and fully insure, and the insurance company breaks even. The low-risk consumers will choose to insure partially at point E, where the indifference curve for the low-risk type is on line OA just below where the two indifference curves cross. The high-risk types prefer C to E, and the low-risk types prefer E to C.[6]

One problem with this solution to adverse selection proposed by Rothschild and Stiglitz is that theirs is a static model. Across multiple time periods, unstable behavior can result. In the first period, the high- and low-risk types reveal themselves in the separating equilibrium. In the next period, the insurer knows who is who and thus simply offers a fairly priced policy with full coverage to each group. But if people know that will happen in the second period, then high-risk types might choose the low-risk policy in the first period in the hope that they will be confused with the low-risk type.[7]

In a more practical context, insurers often choose a middle ground in which they offer a multiperiod contract to customers based on their voluntary disclosure of whether they are high or low risk. Over time, the insurer will gain more information about the insured parties. As a loss record accumu-

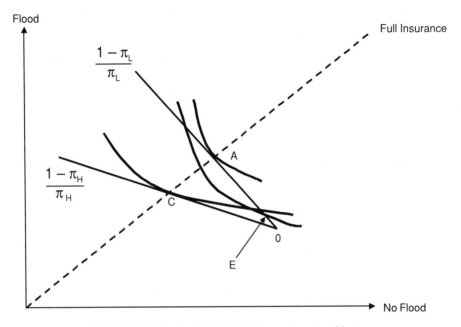

EXHIBIT 15.7   Rothschild-Stiglitz Separating Equilibrium

lates, the insurer eventually will know which type the consumer is. The contract might specify that if the insurer realizes the voluntary disclosure of type was not truthful and was instead a material mispresentation, the coverage is canceled.

INSURANCE MARKETPLACE

Strongly influenced by historical evolution, the insurance marketplace today is segmented along two dimensions. The first is the type of buyer and the risk, hazard, or peril covered by the insurance contract. The second is the range of coverage provided by the insurance company. Each of these is discussed below.

Insurance Product Lines

Historically, insurance has been divided into marine and nonmarine coverage lines. Ocean marine insurance includes hull, cargo, freight, and liability risks. Nonmarine insurance then can be divided into life and nonlife products. Life insurance provides financial protection to a beneficiary in the event of premature death and includes a wide range of products, such as term life, whole life, endowment life, variable life, and universal life. Nonlife, nonmarine lines often are separated based on the target population of insurance customers. One common division is as follows, along with examples of specific coverage offered to each group[8]:

- *Individual insurance* includes health and travel insurance.
- *Household insurance* includes home, renter's and auto insurance.
- *Business insurance* includes property, liability, credit, crime, and errors and omissions.
- *Employee benefits insurance* includes group health and life, disability, workers' compensation, and unemployment insurance.

Business insurance, in particular, has many different variations depending on the nature of the risk, hazard, or peril the firm wishes to transfer to an assuming insurer. Following are some of the most common types of business insurance and some examples of the risks, hazards, and perils these business insurance products typically cover:

- *Professional indemnity* (P/I)—liabilities arising from failures in business processes, negligent commercial conduct, and inaccurate information inadvertently supplied to customers
- *Crime and fidelity*—fraud, theft of firm resources, malicious damage and sabotage, and employee collusion
- *Directors and officers* (D&O)—failure to manage assets or finances of the firm responsibly, failure to maintain confidence or growth in the firm, negligent misstatements and accounting fraud, actions taken beyond the scope of authority, misappropriations of funds or property, and breach of statutory or fiduciary duty
- *Property damage* (PD)—physical damage to property and equipment, terrorism, and damage to information technology systems
- *Business interruption* (BI)—increasing working costs due to exogenous events, disruption of production, and interruption of service provision

Insurance Carriers and Lines

The insurance market is often described based on the product offerings of insurers. In this connection, insurance companies sometimes are called carriers because they "carry" certain types of insurance policy coverage, or *lines*. Within Lloyd's (which is explained in the next section), underwriters are separated according to whether their primary product offerings are marine, nonmarine, aviation, or motor. Non-Lloyd's commercial insurance companies usually are distinguished based on whether they are life or nonlife carriers, and, in the latter case, whether they are mainly property and casualty or liability carriers.

Another popular means of distinguishing insurers by product line is based on the number of fundamental risk types the firm underwrites. In particular, a *monoline* insurer is an insurance company that underwrites only a single type of risk, such as life or credit risk. A *multiline* (or *composite*) insurer, by contrast, offers products that cut across more than one type of risk, hazard, or peril.

INSURANCE COMPANY ORGANIZATIONAL STRUCTURES

Three types of companies typically provide insurance contracts to firms wishing to use insurance as a risk transfer mechanism.

1. Stock insurance companies are open corporations.
2. Mutual insurance companies are financial mutuals in the Fama/Jensen taxonomy discussed in Chapter 1. Here the policyholders insured by the company are also its owners.
3. Cooperative insurance companies are formed in conjunction with some cooperative movement, often in conjunction with organized labor or a trade association. Cooperatives may be organized as a stock or mutual and usually are distinguished from pure stock or mutual companies based on their mission statement and operating principles. A cooperative insurer might, for example, give policy preference to members of the trade union with which it is affiliated.

In only one forum are individuals allowed to supply commercial insurance, and that forum is Lloyd's, operating since it was founded by Edward Lloyd in 1688 as Lloyd's Coffee House. Lloyd's has more than 30,000 members, or "Names," that are grouped into nearly 500 "syndicates." Members are admitted as Names only if they deposit certain funds in trust and satisfy a minimum net worth requirement. Upon admission to membership, Lloyd's members are granted the right to underwrite insurance as individuals but face unlimited personal liability in any such underwritings.

Lloyd's is especially attractive to insurance purchasers wishing to underwrite an unusual or exotic risk exposure. Whether insurance for undiscovered environmental liabilities, kidnap and ransom (K&R), or an aborted treasure hunt in the South Pacific, Lloyd's has the reputation for offering coverage on just about anything that can be defined in insurance terms. To get coverage from Lloyd's, a firm brings its insurance need to a Lloyd's broker. The broker then declares the need of the insurance purchaser on a "slip" and solicits syndicate signatories to the slip to provide cover for the risk. Importantly, Names do not underwrite risks directly; syndicates underwrite slips and allow Names to underwrite only as a group through their syndicate.

RESERVE AND INVESTMENT MANAGEMENT BY INSURANCE COMPANIES

As noted in Chapter 12, a typical banking institution—including both commercial and investment banks—may rely on either retail or wholesale liabilities to fund the asset side of their balance sheet. Although retail-funded commercial banks, in particular, can generate fee income and customer relationships from their liabilities, banks for the most part are asset-driven firms, as are most nonfinancial corporations. Because most derivatives dealers are banks of some sort, derivatives dealers thus are also asset-driven organizations. In other words, the core business of banks and swap dealers are based on their investment and asset management decisions.

Insurance companies tend to operate in the opposite manner, because their liabilities represent their core business. Just as banks use liabilities as a way to fund their assets, insurance companies use assets mainly as a way of backing their liabilities. But the liabilities are the core focus.

In return for providing insurance contracts, insurance companies receive a premium. The total premium collected by an insurance company can be used to pay off claims arising from its contingent liabilities. But because claims do not necessarily arrive in the same time period (e.g., year) that premium is collected, insurance companies must utilize technical reserves, as briefly introduced in Chapter 8. How insurance companies manage their technical reserves is an important determinant for their demand for reinsurance as discussed in the next chapter, so some background discussion here is warranted.

Methods of Reserve Management

Technical reserves at an insurance company must be viewed differently from the concept of excess capital reserves discussed in Chapter 7. For an insurance company, its technical reserves are a liability. The premium an insurance company collects usually is invested in assets that back those technical reserve liabilities, and the technical reserves of the firm then represent the future claims expected on insurance contracts the company has offered.

Insurance companies utilize one of two reserve management methods for financing the claims arising from their liabilities[9]: the capitalization or compensation method. Under the capitalization method, an insurance company invests its premium collected in assets and then uses those assets plus the return on those assets to finance subsequent insurance claims. Firms using the capitalization method usually attempt to keep assets funded by premium collections linked to the technical reserves of the liabilities for which the premium was collected. If the premium is collected on a property damage line, for example, the assets acquired with that premium usually are earmarked to back the technical reserve liabilities of the property damage line. Technical reserves at firms using the capitalization method tend to be medium or long term, as are the assets invested to back the corresponding liabilities.

The compensation method, by contrast, is a pay-as-you-go system in which all premiums collected over the course of a year are used to pay any claims that year arising from any business lines. Under this method, no real attempt is made to connect assets with technical reserves. All premiums collected are used to fund mainly short-term assets, and those assets collectively back all technical reserves for all insurance lines.

The type and maturity of investments made by insurance companies of their technical reserves depends on the reserve management method and the nature of the claims for which reserves are held. In the compensation method, reserves usually are short term and thus usually are backed by money market–like assets. The capitalization method usually involves a longer gap between premium collection and claims payments. Firms adopting the capitalization method thus usually invest in assets like fixed income securities (government, corporate, and agency), securitized products, real estate, and common stocks.

Types of Technical Reserves

Whether using the capitalization or the compensation method, insurance companies writing nonlife business lines typically have two main types of reserves—unearned premium reserves and loss reserves.[10]

In most traditional nonlife insurance lines (e.g., liability and property), policy coverage lasts one year and the premium is payable at the beginning of the policy year. Although the premium is collected in advance, it is earned only as time passes if a claim has not occurred. Unearned premium is a premium that has been collected that still may need to be used to cover an as-yet unsubmitted claim. The unearned premium reserve is thus the proportion of premium that must be set aside to honor future expected claims.

Suppose, for example, that a firm writes a one-year fidelity policy on July 1 and collects $100,000 in premium for writing that policy, but the firm's financial reporting and fiscal year end on December 31. In this case, only $50,000 of the premium is considered earned at the end of the year. Unearned premium reserves may be calculated gross or net of commissions paid to insurance brokers and distributors and other expenses.

The technical reserves an insurance company maintains to honor any future claims—known or unknown—above the unearned premium are called the loss reserve. Loss reserves may be set aside for losses that have been reported and adjusted, reported but not adjusted, incurred but not reported (IBNR), or for loss adjustment expenses. Adjustment refers to the negotiation of claims amounts often required in liability lines, and reporting refers to the submission of claims to the insurer by the insured. Loss adjustment expenses (LAEs) are those expenses incurred in the process of determining exactly what the insurance company liability is on any given claim.

NOTES

1. See, for example, Williams, Smith, and Young (1995), Phifer (1996), and Outreville (1998).
2. An insurable interest is not always required for life insurance, provided the insured gives written consent to defining a different beneficiary.
3. Rather confusingly, the term "aggregate deductible" sometimes is used to define an aggregate policy limit over the calendar year—for example, an average deductible of $100,000 means that the total liability of the insurer is limited to $100,000.
4. For a review of expected utility theory in the context of risk management, see Culp (2001).
5. If you find this example implausible, you can switch back to our example of sick and healthy patients instead of high-flood-risk and low-flood-risk customers.
6. For completeness, one also should show that the separating equilibrium is not dominated by a "pooling" equilibrium. Although the proof is omitted, any standard reference on the economics of uncertainty includes the proof. See Laffont (1990), Chapter 8, on which the whole model in this section is loosely based.
7. Doherty (2000).
8. See Borch (1992) and Outreville (1998).
9. See Outreville (1998).
10. In life insurance, reserves are known as policy or mathematical reserves. Because the bulk of this book does not involve life products, readers are referred to Outreville (1998) for a discussion of life reserve management.

CHAPTER 16

Reinsurance

T he insurance structures explored in Chapter 15 all were directed at single policyholders wishing to purchase insurance on a specific risk from a single insurance carrier. When the assumptions underlying the M&M propositions hold, these sorts of contracts make sense only when sold by insurance companies to risk-averse individuals, and there is no role for the purchase of insurance by corporations—including insurance companies.[1] But when the assumptions underlying M&M do not hold, insurance companies themselves often wish to buy insurance—called *reinsurance*—to help them manage their risks and capital structures.

In this chapter we explore the basic principles of reinsurance, seeking to answer the following questions:

- When one or more M&M assumptions are violated, how can insurance companies increase their value by acquiring insurance for their own insurance underwriting activities?
- What are the different forms of reinsurance contracts?
- How are different types of reinsurance "treaties" distinguished from one another?
- How can "excess of loss reinsurance treaties" be viewed from an options perspective?

FUNCTIONS OF REINSURANCE

An insurance company that buys insurance is called a *cedant*. The outward transfer of risk by the cedant to the reinsurance company is called a *cession*, and the taking up or inward transfer of risk by the reinsurance company is called an *assumption*. In return for taking up the risk originally borne by the cedant, the reinsurance company receives a premium from the cedant.

When a reinsurance company buys insurance on a reinsured risk, the outward transfer of risk is called a *retrocession* and the reinsurance company buying the reinsurance protection called the *retrocedant*. The reinsurance company that assumes the risk in a retrocession is called the *retrocessionaire*. The reinsurance and retrocession process is shown in Exhibit 16.1.

Insurance companies can engage in reinsurance and retrocession for a wide variety of reasons, some of which are discussed below. Note that these structures would not make sense in an M&M world. But when capital markets are imperfect and information asymmetric, all can make sense in at least some circumstances. And in that context, the benefits of reinsurance should look extremely familiar. (See Chapter 11.)

Capacity

Perhaps the most obvious potential benefit of reinsurance is the creation of additional capacity for the cedant or retrocedant. In other words, reinsurance is a classic form of synthetic equity for insurance companies.

Capacity can be inadequate for a primary carrier or reinsurer along two dimensions. *Large-line capacity* is an insurer's ability to absorb an extremely large (i.e., catastrophic) loss on a single policy. In many situations, a policy may be attractive for an insurer but only up to a certain amount of losses (or, as we shall see later, only between certain loss layers). In order to underwrite

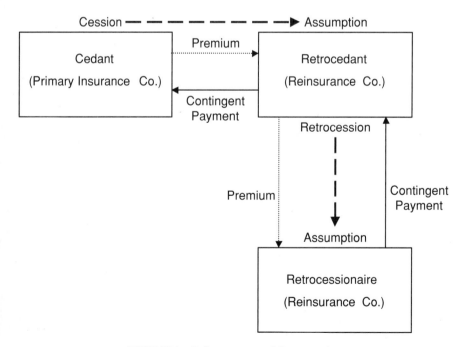

EXHIBIT 16.1   Reinsurance and Retrocession

the policy, the insurance company needs to know *ex ante* that it will not have to retain all of the underwriting risk. Reinsurance can provide insurers with precisely this assurance.[2]

Separately, some insurers lack *premium capacity*, or the ability to write a large volume of policies in the same business line. Of concern in this case is the insurer's ability to weather a large number of possibly small losses rather than a single massive claim. But the fundamental rationale for reinsurance is essentially the same as in the large-line capacity case—"renting the balance sheet" of another insurance company as synthetic equity so that the primary carrier or reinsurer can provide all the policies that it would like to write.

Reinsurance sought for capacity purposes can be viewed as a means of mitigating underinvestment and debt overhang problems in the sense of Myers (1977). If a single large policy or a business line of policies represents a positive NPV opportunity for the insurer but cannot be offered due to a lack of equity capital, reinsurance creates a synthetic equity infusion large enough to enable the firm to accept the positive NPV business opportunities.

Increased Surplus or Debt Capacity

As noted earlier, the total premiums written by a primary insurance carrier are constrained by the equity capital of the insurance company, sometimes called the firm's surplus. Reinsurance can provide synthetic equity capital to an insurance company if the firm might otherwise have to forgo positive NPV insurance lines because of capacity constraints. But reinsurance as synthetic equity also can be used to increase the firm's total debt capacity.

When premium is collected at the beginning of a policy term, the insurance company must establish an unearned premium reserve. Some types of reinsurance involve a cession of premium as well as loss exposure to the reinsurer. This in turn can reduce a firm's required unearned premium reserves, thereby increasing the firm's surplus and increasing its debt capacity.

Reduced Earnings and Cash Flow Volatility

When the diversification of risks in a policy line is too low, earnings and cash flows can be strongly influenced by underwriting losses. Like other firms, insurance companies may wish to reduce that volatility of earnings and/or cash flows to avoid underinvestment problems, to increase the signal-to-noise ratio in accounting signals, or just to facilitate their internal cash management operations and capital budgeting activities. Reinsurance thus can be used to effect "synthetic diversification" and reduce the vulnerability of earnings and cash flows to highly correlated adverse underwriting results.

Reduced Expected Financial Distress Costs

Volatility of earnings or cash flows in a particular policy line need not necessarily arise from a single massive claim on a single policy. Indeed, claims of a small to medium size whose arrival rates are highly correlated often can induce more volatility over time than just a single claim. The possibility of a single catastrophic loss thus tends to pose a different problem for insurers—the risk of incurring financial distress costs.

The need for some carriers to secure catastrophic protection usually arises from low-frequency, high-severity events such as natural disasters, major industrial accidents, multiple accidents arising from a single peril or hazard, and the like. As explained in Chapters 4 and 11, high-severity losses of this kind can cause the market value of a firm's assets to approach or perhaps fall below the face value of the firm's outstanding liabilities, both in a financial capital structure and technical loss reserves context.

Reinsurance can create an additional layer of synthetic equity capital that reduces the expected costs of financial distress by reducing the probability that the firm will encounter financial distress.

Information Acquisition

The reinsurance process is extremely information-intensive. Accordingly, the information acquired by a reinsurer during the underwriting process can be quite extensive—and valuable. Like banks doing credit checks on their customers, reinsurers engaging in due diligence of prospective cedants may acquire information that enables them to better serve their insurance company client again in the future. In addition, the reinsurer also may require valuable market intelligence, information about its competitors, pricing information, and the like.

Synthetic Liability Dispositions

Chapter 13 reviewed the various means by which derivatives and securitizations can be used to accomplish synthetic asset divestitures. In the same spirit, reinsurance can help primary carriers or reinsurers engage in synthetic *liability* divestitures.

Suppose, for example, that a primary carrier decides that the risks of providing marine coverage are too high and beyond its shareholders' risk tolerances. The firm really can only leave the business by terminating any new marine underwritings and then allowing its outstanding contracts to wind down. Or the carrier could purchase reinsurance, thereby synthetically eliminating the entire business line virtually overnight.

FORMS OF REINSURANCE

Reinsurance contracts can take one of two forms—*facultative* or *treaty*. A facultative reinsurance contract covers a single risk and insurance policy. In other words, the reinsurer and insurer negotiate separate facultative contracts for each policy the primary carrier wishes to reinsure. Consequently, facultative reinsurance is extremely flexible and can have terms fully customized by the two parties to the contract. Facultative reinsurance is commonly used for the reinsurance of extremely large or catastrophic risks, very unusual or exotic risks, or specific risks that are not core business line risks for the ceding insurance company.

Treaty reinsurance, by contrast, involves the reinsurance of a group of policies that fall within general guidelines defined by the cedant and reinsurer (or retrocedant and retrocessionaire). In treaty reinsurance, the reinsurer cannot refuse any specific risk or policy in the business line or policy group as long as that policy falls within the predefined parameters of the treaty itself. Because treaties have broad terms negotiated in advance, this type of reinsurance is popular for insurance carriers wishing to reinsure a large number of similar policies, a whole business line, or a fairly traditional set of risks.

Facultative reinsurance is generally subject to larger potential moral hazard and adverse selection problems than treaty reinsurance because the risk, hazard, or peril underlying a facultative reinsurance is defined very specifically. Accordingly, facultative reinsurance generally involves a more in-depth due diligence exercise on the part of the reinsurer. Facultative reinsurance is also more time-consuming to negotiate and more expensive than treaty reinsurance.

TYPES OF REINSURANCE TREATIES

Risk-sharing arrangements between the insurance provider and purchaser in classical insurance programs are defined on a policy-by-policy basis. Because reinsurance treaties involve the inclusion of more than one policy, however, the sharing of risk can be accomplished in a number of different ways. All risk-sharing arrangements in treaty reinsurance either fall under the proportional or excess of loss designation. Specific types of proportional and excess of loss (XOL) treaties are discussed in the sections below.

Proportional Reinsurance Treaties

Proportional reinsurance involves the sharing of risks between the cedant and reinsurer (or retrocedant and retrocessionaire) on a proportional basis. The proportionality may be defined in fixed or variable terms. The proportion of risk shared usually also acts as the proportion of premium collected that is divided between the two firms as well as the proportion of any loss adjustment expense (LAE) that must be allocated in the reinsurance program.

Quota Share Treaties

Reinsurance treaties that allocate risk, losses, premium, and loss adjustment expenses on a fixed-percentage basis are called *quota share reinsurance treaties*. A quota share treaty defines a common ratio when the original treaty is bound. This percentage is used immediately to cede a fixed proportion of premium collected from the cedant to the reinsurer, in return for which the reinsurer will bear the same proportion of subsequent claims and LAEs.[3] To compensate the cedant for the expenses incurred in originating the primary policies, the reinsurer also pays a ceding commission to the cedant.

Exhibit 16.2 shows a policy distribution diagram, which is common to the analysis of insurance and reinsurance structures. The x-axis represents the number of policies written by an insurance carrier in a single business line, and the y-axis represents the policy limit corresponding to each policy. Each point on the curve is a single policy. The symmetric nature of the diagram is indicative of a reasonably mature insurance portfolio that has a fairly large number of large-limit policies as well as a decent share of smaller ones.

From the exhibit, it can be seen that the quota share treaty simply in-

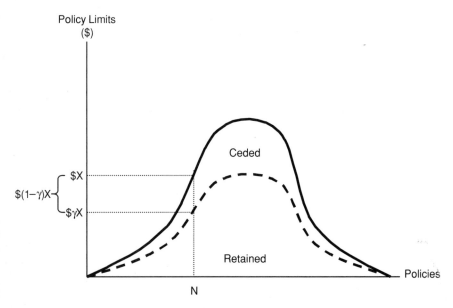

EXHIBIT 16.2 Quota Share Treaty Policy Distribution

volves the cession of a fixed percentage of each policy and premium to the reinsurer based on the policy limit. In other words, the reinsurance cession is based on the terms of the policy itself and not on the actual claims made.

Suppose the quota share treaty calls for a cession of $(1 - \gamma)\%$ of each policy in the policy class to the reinsurer. For any given policy—say, policy N, as shown in Exhibit 16.2—the policy limit is $X. Under the quota share treaty, the ceding insurance company retains γ for every dollar in the policy and the reinsurer assumes $(1 - \gamma)$ for every dollar in policy N. This proportion applies to the losses covered as well as the premium collected. If the policyholder files the maximum of $X in claims, the reinsurer pays $(1 - \gamma)X$ of these claims and the cedant retains a commitment to pay the remaining γX.

Quota share treaties are used frequently by insurance companies seeking either increased debt capacity through unearned premium reserve reduction or additional diversification to reduce cash flow and earnings volatility. As concerns the latter, *reciprocity* is a practice in which two primary insurers essentially exchange portions of their insurance portfolios with one another to increase the diversification of both firms' underwriting businesses. A quota share treaty can be a useful mechanism to accomplish a reciprocity cession.

In this connection, a quota share treaty used to facilitate a reciprocity cession can be viewed as a type of asset swap as discussed in Chapter 13.

Surplus Share Treaties

A reinsurance treaty that allocates risk, losses, and premium on a variable-percentage basis is called *surplus share treaty*. Although a treaty rather than a facultative reinsurance structure, the net retention of the cedant in a surplus share treaty is explicitly stated as a separate monetary amount for each policy or group of like policies. Because the dollar amount of the retention is fixed per policy or group, the percentage of each policy retained by the cedant varies from policy to policy or group to group.

Exhibit 16.3 shows a surplus share treaty with a retention level of $X across all policies.[4] Policy N, for example, would be 100 percent retained by the cedant under this surplus share treaty because its coverage limit is below $X. Policy M, by contrast, would involve a retention of $X by the primary carrier and a cession of $(Y - X)$ to the insurer.

Note that this is still a proportional reinsurance contract in which the cedant retains a proportion of all premium, losses, and adjustment expenses. The dollar value is chosen relative to a policy limit to define the proportion of risk to be ceded, but care should be taken not to assume that the reinsurer bears losses sequentially based on whether or not actual losses hit that fixed monetary amount. In other words, suppose a surplus share treaty defines a fixed cession based on $X of losses on Policy M. If a loss of exactly $X occurs on Policy M, the reinsurer does not have a zero liability. Instead, the reinsurer bears a proportion of those $X in losses equal to $(Y - X)/Y$. More generally,

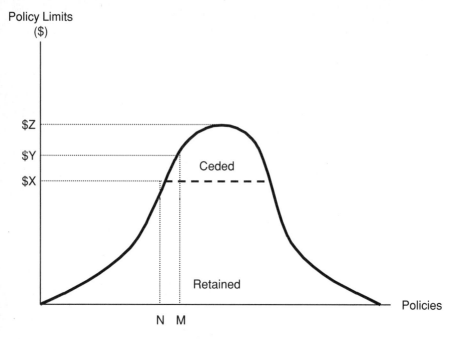

EXHIBIT 16.3   Surplus Share Treaty Policy Distribution

the reinsurer is ceded $(Y - X)/X$ dollars of each dollar of premium and bears $(Y - X)/X$ dollars of each dollar loss submitted in a claim. If X is $90,000 and Y is $100,000, the reinsurer thus receives 10 percent of the premium and bears 10 percent of any claims arising on the policy.

A surplus share treaty is effective in creating large-line capacity for the cedant, but it provides little unearned premium reserve relief because of the focus on large policy exposures. Note also that adverse selection problems can be significant with surplus treaties because the cedant can choose the retention on each policy. Accordingly, the cedant will tend to cede the bad business and retain the good business. Although the surplus share is a treaty, the moral hazard problems thus are more similar to a facultative reinsurance program than to a quota share treaty.

Excess-of-Loss Reinsurance

Proportional reinsurance like quota and surplus share treaties always involve some cession of premium and some allocation of losses to the reinsurer. In an *excess-of-loss treaty*, by contrast, the order in which the losses occur and the total amount of those losses affect the reinsurer's contingent liability. The reinsurer's obligations are based not on fixed or variable percentages of policy limits but rather on actual claims received. Small losses thus are retained by the cedant, and only losses over a certain amount are paid by the reinsurer.

A typical XOL structure involves the definition by the insurer and reinsurer of attachment points, or loss levels where the reinsurance treaty comes into effect and then subsequently terminates. Reinsurers usually abbreviate excess of loss as XS, X, or XOL. An excess-of-loss treaty that specifies $100,000 XS $50,000 would mean, for example, that the reinsurer is underwriting any losses above $50,000 and up to $150,000, or $100,000 in losses in excess of $50,000 in losses. The lower attachment point of such a treaty is thus $50,000. The number of zeros, moreover, usually is taken to be understood by the involved parties, so we would actually write the forgoing policy as $100 XS $50.

Different types of XOL treaties are available that are distinguished mainly in their triggers or in how losses are calculated, especially across multiple occurrences or risks. The most prevalent types of XOL reinsurance structures are summarized below.

Per Occurrence and Per Risk XOL Treaties

A *per occurrence* XOL treaty is a reinsurance structure in which losses are paid on each event causing damage to the insured party above the attachment point. Consider a casualty policy for workplace safety that specifies $50 XS $50 per occurrence. If a worker slips and falls and sustains $100,000 in total monetary damages, the cedant pays the first $50,000 of the claim, and the reinsurer pays the remaining $50,000. If the same worker—or, for that matter, a different one under the same policy—slips and falls again during the policy period and incurs $75,000 in medical expenses, the cedant again pays the first $50,000 and the reinsurer pays the remaining $25,000. As long as the occurrence is different, the reinsurer is liable for each excess of losses above the attachment point on all separate events.

Property claims often are defined *per risk* rather than per occurrence, where each separate piece of property is a single risk. Consider a blanket property damage reinsurance policy that covers $100 XS $500 per risk for a group of three buildings in a production facility, each of which is defined as a separate risk. If the policy period lasts a year and three buildings each sustain $550,000 in damage—from either the same or different events—the cedant will have a total liability of $1.5 million and the reinsurer a total payment obligation of $150,000, or $50,000 per building.

Now suppose the same building has two fires in the same policy year, one of which causes $400,000 in damage and the second of which causes $300,000 in damage. The reinsurer is liable only for the cumulative $100,000 loss, equal to its policy limit. Specifically, the reinsurer would owe nothing on the first loss because $400,000 is below the XOL reinsurance attachment point of $500,000. On the second loss, the reinsurer pays its full reinsurance policy limit of $100 XS $500.

Excess-of-loss policies commonly are structured to involve more than one insurer or reinsurance treaty. In the last example, the cedant retains the first $500,000 in losses per building plus any losses above $600,000 per building. If the cedant wants coverage for losses above $600,000, the insurer will need an additional XOL reinsurance treaty, this time with a new attachment point of $600,000.

Excess-of-loss reinsurance often is depicted using layer-cake diagrams, such as the one shown in Exhibit 16.4. Each "layer" represents the total losses insured per risk between attachment points, and the "cake"—the width of a given layer—represents the cession versus retention within each layer. This particular structure is a per risk excess-of-loss insurance pro-

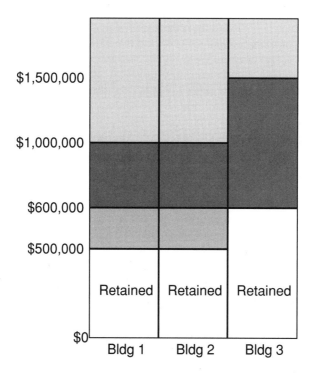

EXHIBIT 16.4 Per Risk Excess of Loss Treaties

gram with, say, a one-year duration and covering three risks or buildings. Each column of the diagram represents the loss exposure for a different building or risk. The different colors of the layers are chosen to indicate that different reinsurers have been engaged to reinsure different layers of losses on those buildings.

For Buildings 1 and 2, the cedant retains the first $500,000 in losses, whereas the first $600,000 are retained on Building 3. Both Buildings 1 and 2 then have three separate reinsurance treaties with attachment points of $500,000, $600,000, and $1 million. Building 3 then has its losses apportioned into three layers with attachment points of $600,000 and $1.5 million. The attachment points chosen by a cedant will depend both on the risk involved and the pricing quoted at different attachment points for the reinsurance.

The actual policy coverage could require that the cedant enter into up to eight different reinsurance treaties, perhaps with eight different reinsurers: $100 XS $500 on Building 1, $100 XS $500 on Building 2, $400 XS $600 on Building 1, $400 XS $600 on Building 2, $900 XS $500 on Building 3, $1,000 XS $1,000 on Building 1, $1,000 XS $1,000 on Building 2, and $500 XS $1,500 on Building 3. The cedant might identify many variations of this, though. For example, a single reinsurer could be engaged to reinsure both Buildings 1 and 2 between any two of the attachment points shown, which would be reasonably easy because the attachment points are identical on these two risks. Or perhaps a single reinsurer would be willing to take multiple layers per risk. For example, perhaps a single reinsurer is willing to reinsure $500 XS $500 on Building 1, thus underwriting the layers above both the $500,000 and $600,000 attachment points in a single treaty.

The top layer for each building is often called the *catastrophic layer* because it is the least likely to be reached and yet the most potentially costly (and likely to generate financial distress costs for the insurer). In the structure shown in Exhibit 16.4, the primary carrier may wish to retain the catastrophic layer, or the $1,000 XS $1,000 layers for Buildings 1 and 2 and the $500 XS $1,500 layer for Building 3.

Insurers (and reinsurers in retrocession) frequently use per risk and per occurrence XOL treaties for capacity enhancement as well as to stabilize earnings and cash flows and to increase debt capacity by reducing the unearned premium reserve. XOL treaty reinsurance thus is a classic form of contingent equity capital as discussed in Chapters 2 and 7. The pricing of such treaties is generally flat rate for the whole reinsurance treaty and usually involves some LAE sharing. Premium is allocated between the cedant and reinsurer both in terms of actual claims submitted and on a ratable basis over time.

Catastrophic Excess of Loss

Insurance losses arising from natural disasters such as windstorms, hail storms, earthquakes, tidal waves, tornados, and tropical cyclones are often extremely large. Accordingly, catastrophic excess-of-loss reinsurance treaties frequently are utilized by primary carriers to increase debt capacity, increase total underwriting capacity (i.e., reducing underinvestment by allowing the carrier to underwrite all positive NPV lines), and reduce expected financial distress costs.

Catastrophic XOL coverage functions in much the same manner as per risk or per occurrence XOL treaties, but with three differences.

1. The catastrophic coverage not only covers a catastrophic layer as in Exhibit 16.4, but the policy itself is almost always tied to a specific catastrophe as a triggering event. The excess-of-loss treaty shown in the exhibit was essentially a blanket property damage policy, whereas a true catastrophic XOL policy would pay claims only if the property damage was sustained as a direct result of some named catastrophic event like a tornado.
2. Catastrophic excess-of-loss reinsurance usually contains a coinsurance provision, rarely protecting more than 90 percent of the losses.
3. Catastrophic insurance of this sort also may involve a deductible.

Exhibit 16.5 shows a new layer-cake diagram for a revised coverage structure of the same three buildings as before. The coverage now includes a catastrophic excess-of-loss treaty overlaid on the per risk treaties acquired for lower-loss layers. The catastrophic XOL treaty has a 10 percent coinsurance provision in the $1,000 XS $1,000 layer and a $50,000 deductible. The fact that the "cake" portion of the catastrophic layer now cuts across all three buildings means that the policy is now a cover for the three buildings taken together. The deductible thus applies to catastrophic losses sustained on all three buildings *or* on any single building. Similarly, reinsured losses could come from any or all of the three risks.

Aggregate XOL or Stop-Loss Treaties

A third type of excess of loss treaty is an *aggregate excess-of-loss treaty* that applies to a predetermined aggregate loss arising from a policy portfolio. Aggregate excess-of-loss treaties are designed to cover a large number of small losses arising on multiple policies in the same policy year and thus are essentially the opposite of catastrophic XOL treaties.

Consider a primary carrier that writes homeowner's insurance and takes out per occurrence XOL reinsurance on its homeowner insurance portfolio for $1,000 XS $125. But suppose the policy year is characterized by a large number of $100,000 claims, all of which will fall below the

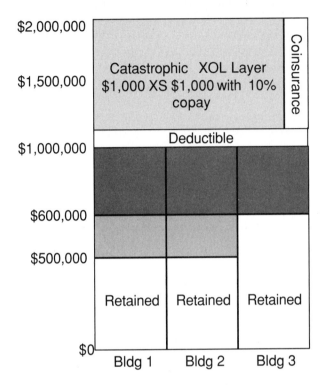

EXHIBIT 16.5   Per Risk XOL Treaties with Catastrophic XOL Overlay

$125,000 attachment point in the per occurrence reinsurance treaty. The carrier may wish to purchase aggregate excess-of-loss reinsurance for, say, $500 XS $500. Without the aggregate treaty, ten claims of $100,000 each would cost the carrier $1 million, because no single claim would be covered by the per occurrence treaty. But with the aggregate XOL reinsurance treaty in place, the cedant would be liable for only the first $500,000 in claims. The remaining five $100,000 claims would be covered by the aggregate treaty, even though no single claim is covered by any of the per occurrence treaties.

Aggregate XOL treaties usually do not specify risks or perils as triggers and thus can include any claims arising on a book of underwriting business. As such, aggregate treaties are a highly effective means by which insurers can reduce their earnings and cash flow volatilities by locking in a maximum loss amount.

The versatility of these treaties also makes them quite expensive. In addition, to prevent the underwriter from being inattentive to the risk of its book, aggregate treaties usually include reasonably significant coinsurance provisions.

Sixth Loss Excess

Insurers and reinsurers historically consider the number of very large claims per policy period to be limited. In particular, the belief is that the sixth largest claim in a typical insurance pool will be about the same value each year, with only the top five losses representing extraordinarily large or catastrophic events and varying dramatically from year to year. Six claims thus should define a reasonable expectation of a "worst-case payout" during a policy year for an insurer.

A *sixth loss excess* reinsurance treaty is a reinsurance treaty that covers the top six losses during the policy period. It is essentially a pure bulk-capacity vehicle used by some primary carriers to increase the depth of their underwriting lines and raise the policy limits they can offer.

EXCESS OF LOSS TREATIES FROM AN OPTIONS PERSPECTIVE

All XOL treaties can be viewed from an options perspective as vertical spreads with the strike prices of the options corresponding to the upper and lower attachment points. In Chapter 15 when we were dealing with single insurance policies, we found it useful to treat insurance as a put on the value of the insured asset. Now that we are working with reinsurance treaties whose value is based on actual losses on an underlying insurance policy portfolio, it will prove easier to work with options whose underlyings are insurance losses rather than asset values. What was a short spread on asset values before thus will become a long spread on losses now.

Consider an aggregate XOL reinsurance treaty covering all the property damage policies underwritten by an insurance company in a single policy year. Suppose the aggregate XOL treaty has a lower attachment point of A and an upper attachment point of B—that is, a (B − A) XS A treaty—no deductible, and no coinsurance provision. Exhibit 16.6 illustrates the payoff value of this reinsurance treaty assuming the treaty pays off at the end of the policy year as a function of aggregate property damage claims received.

For any losses below the lower attachment point A, the reinsurance does not pay off. For losses above A and up to B, however, the reinsurance fully reimburses the primary carrier for any claims. And for losses above B, the carrier remains exposed. In the absence of further reinsurance, the primary carrier thus has a net retention of losses from 0 to A and above B.

Value of Reinsurance
Treaty, Net of Premium

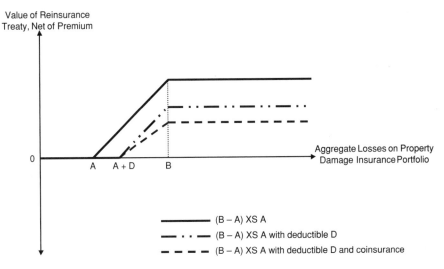

EXHIBIT 16.6   Aggregate Excess-of-Loss Treaty from an Options Perspective

The exhibit shows clearly that this treaty can be viewed as a long vertical spread consisting of a long call struck at A and a short call struck at B, both based on the underlying claims submitted on the property insurance portfolio.

Now suppose the aggregate XOL treaty involves a deductible of D. In this case, the reinsurance treaty has a payoff profile equivalent to a long vertical spread, but now with a lower strike price on the long call of A + D. The payoff on the reinsurance treaty is reduced by D at all insurance portfolio loss levels.

If we further add a coinsurance provision, the reinsurance does not pay off dollar for dollar for losses between A + D and B any longer. If the copayment percentage requires the cedant to pay γ dollars for every $(1 - \gamma)$ dollars paid by the reinsurer, the cedant gets only $1 - \gamma$ dollars for each dollar loss. The new position is now equivalent to $(1 - \gamma)$ long calls struck at A + D and $(1 - \gamma)$ short calls struck at B.

We could, of course, repeat this kind of analysis for all the types of XOL treaties examined in this chapter. The important point to recognize is that XOL treaty reinsurance is essentially similar to a portfolio of options whose values are based on reported insurance losses, again noting the important fact that this kind of risk transfer contract can be utilized only when an insurable interest exists. In addition, attention must be paid to any triggers contained in the XOL treaty. The aggregate XOL treaty shown in Exhibit 16.6 applies to any losses on the reference portfolio, but other types of XOL treaties may be conditional on a triggering event as well.

NOTES

1. See Culp (2001).
2. Indeed, reinsurance is sometimes called *reassurance*, and the purchaser of reinsurance called the re*assured*. See Kiln (1991).
3. The reinsurer in a quota share treaty usually also bears a fixed proportion of any loss adjustment expenses. See Kiln (1991) and Phifer (1996).
4. This is extremely unusual. One reason surplus treaties are used is to allow the retention to vary by policy.

Alternative Risk Transfer Products

CHAPTER 17

Alternative Risk Finance versus Alternative Risk Transfer

Having reviewed the traditional methods by which firms can accomplish the transfer of risk, we now turn to alternative risk transfer (ART) products and solutions. ART is a somewhat confusing term for several reasons, and thus we begin this chapter with a discussion of what we actually mean by ART forms.

ART forms in this book include both alternative risk finance and alternative risk transfer products. The former can usually—although not always—be viewed as synthetic debt products and the latter as synthetic equity. Central to this distinction is the concept of risk retention, which is the bridge that ties the risk finance versus risk transfer distinction back to the capital structure issues raised in Part I and the risk management issues raised in Part II. Accordingly, this chapter considers the following questions:

- What working definition of alternative risk transfer is used for the remainder of this text, and how does it differ from other popular definitions?
- How does risk retention provide an important link between a firm's capital structure and its risk financing and transfer decisions?
- What distinctions and issues are raised in considering risk financing versus risk transfer, and what are the basic types of options a firm has for securing preloss funding of its retained risks?

INTRODUCTION TO ART FORMS

ART is widely accepted to mean the set of insurance products that for the most part function more like capital market instruments than classical insurance and reinsurance structures. ART products are, quite simply, often taken to mean any products falling under the rubric of "convergence products" between capital and insurance markets, provided they are offered by the insurance market. In other words, ART products are the derivatives of the insurance industry.

But this definition is neither wholly accurate nor entirely satisfying. The operating definition that we will use for the remainder of the book is as follows:

> Alternative risk transfer products are contracts, structures, or solutions provided by insurance and/or reinsurance companies that enable firms either to finance or to transfer some of the risks to which they are exposed in a nontraditional way, thereby functioning as synthetic debt or equity in a customer's capital structure.

This definition can be split into a number of parts, each of which is discussed in more detail below.

Contracts, Structures, or Solutions

The first major component of our working definition of ART forms is that these so-called products can be contracts, structures, or solutions. Some ART forms are virtually indistinguishable from derivatives transactions; these fall plainly into the category of contracts.

Other ART forms, however, must be considered more broadly as structures rather than just bilateral contracts. Captive, rent-a-captive, and protected cell companies are discussed later and clearly are bundles of many contracts and relationships that together define a structure. Similarly, securitized products usually involve ART in the process by which those products are issued from a conduit or structure. The end product is not as interesting as the method by which an original risk exposure is transformed into that end product by a structure.

Yet a third type of ART form must be considered a solution more than a contract or structure. Specifically, some of the more innovative and recent synthetic contingent capital facilities are collections of contracts together with advisory services supplied to the customer, all of which result in an enterprise-wide risk management solution for the firm. These solutions are highly relationship intensive and tend to be dynamic, cooperative outcomes of combined efforts by (re-)insurers, customers, and sometimes banks to provide the customer with a total capital structure or balance sheet optimization.

Participation by a (Re-)Insurance Company

ART forms may be similar in structure and function to many types of derivatives and/or investment banking products, but they are fundamentally insurance or reinsurance structures. From tax, regulation, and accounting standpoints, ART forms are closer to insurance or reinsurance than to securities or derivatives. From an economic standpoint, however, they probably are somewhere directly in the middle of the two worlds.

We draw this important distinction mainly to emphasize who the capital providers are in ART structures. The involvement of an insurance company or a reinsurance company is essential for a transaction to be truly considered ART. This need not imply that a (re-)insurer is the only participant in an ART form. Indeed, many of the products we will review also involve banking organizations.

Requiring ART forms to involve at least one (re-)insurance company, moreover, need not imply that these transactions are unique to the (re-)insurance sector of the market. On the contrary, we require the involvement of a (re-)insurer precisely to differentiate ART forms from ordinary capital market solutions such as those discussed in Chapters 12 and 13.

Risk Finance versus Risk Transfer

Despite the clear use of the word "transfer" in the acronym, ART forms may be used for either risk finance or risk transfer. Perhaps a better definition of the "T" in ART would be *transformation*. Alternative risk transformation would then easily and logically include both alternative risk finance and alternative risk transfer.

One source of confusion arising from this definitional ambiguity is the fact that corporate customers of ART transactions may well not know where to look in a (re-)insurance company for the products they want. Some (re-)insurance companies have ART divisions or risk finance divisions, but not both. In such cases, it can be difficult to determine what the firm's product offerings are. A risk finance group may only offer alternative risk financing products. Zürich Financial's Risk Finance group, for example, primarily offers true risk financing solutions to corporate customers. But at firms like American International Group, the risk finance area provides both risk finance and risk transfer products.

Unfortunately, the distinctions are not always clear, not universal across firms, and not likely to improve in the near future. So those customers searching for ART solutions would be well served to ask who in a company is responsible for its ART forms and what ART forms are being sought out before jumping headlong into the first webpage that looks like a match. For the purposes of Part IV, however, we can simply agree that ART includes both risk finance and risk transfer.

Nontraditional Transfer Mechanism

Frequent confusion about terms of ART can be traced to confusion about what exactly the word "alternative" is presumed to modify. Is it alternative *risk* transfer, or alternative risk *transfer*? In other words, is the risk considered alternative, or is it the method by which a risk is transferred that is considered novel?

Our definition of ART says nothing at all about the risk being transferred or financed in an ART form. Accordingly, our definition implicitly assumes that the word "alternative" modifies the word "transfer." ART structures are alternative means by which firms can finance and transfer their risks. Whether the risks in question are plain vanilla or exotic is immaterial.

What exactly do we mean by "nontraditional"? Here the going gets tricky, especially because what is considered "alternative" or "nontraditional" in the reinsurance and insurance markets often is considered boilerplate in the capital markets community. Nevertheless, precisely this fact has led people to refer to ART products as convergence products—their dissimilarities to classical insurance are their similarities to capital market products. "Nontraditional" or "alternative" in the context of ART thus is defined specifically vis-à-vis classical insurance and reinsurance.

As we saw in Chapters 15 and 16, most classical insurance and reinsurance structures can already be viewed as optionlike agreements. So can ART products. What makes ART products nontraditional relative to classical insurance thus are the aspects of these products that go beyond simple payoff diagrams. Specifically, one or more of the following unusual or nontraditional features characterizes most ART products:

- The customer and (re-)insurance provider in an ART structure often participate in both the risk and the reward of the structure on nearly equal footing.
- ART forms generally involve several contracts, structures, and/or solutions packaged and priced as a single "product" for customers.
- Many ART forms do not give rise to loss adjustment expenses.
- Most ART forms pay their customers what is owed much faster than classical insurance or reinsurance and often involve an enbedded banking product or a relationship with a bank for this purpose.
- ART forms usually are designed so that the contingent payment is made automatically upon the occurrence of one or more triggering events; the submission of a "claim" is not required.
- ART forms often cover multiple risks, hazards, and perils and tend to provide coverage that crosses traditional insurance and reinsurance business line definitions.

Despite the last characteristic of most ART forms, the "alternative" in ART still refers to the transfer mechanism rather than the type of risk(s) being transferred or financed. In the course of researching this book, it became quite clear, however, that many people believe "alternative" modifies "risk" rather than "transfer." A normal insurance policy based on an exotic or unusual risk thus is usually interpreted to be an ART form. Insurance on representations and warranties made during a merger or acquisition, for example, has exploded in popularity in recent years and often is considered an ART form. Careful inspection of these programs, however, reveals nothing in them that is much different from a classic P/I or D&O insurance policy. They seem to be called ART because they are based on exotic risks. But this, in our vocabulary, is not enough. (See Chapter 26 for a discussion of the differences between M&A insurance products that are ART forms and those that are not.)

Novelty

A second misconception of ART forms is that they are all new. On the contrary, one of the most basic alternatives to direct insurance is the captive retention structure that will be discussed soon. Captives became reasonably popular in the 1970s, and some predate even that decade. To be sure, captives rely heavily on traditional insurance and reinsurance structures. But the structure taken as a whole is an alternative means of financing and transferring risk and thus is indeed an ART form. So "novelty" can no more be used to define ART forms than it can to define "derivatives," despite the frequency with which it is used to define both.

In the same connection, care must be taken not to limit our use of terms of ART to these older structures. Some insurance periodicals actually treated ART and captives as synonymous until just a few years ago, and this is equally wrong. In general, the length of time a particular risk financing or risk transfer contract, structure, or solution has been around should not in and of itself tell us anything about whether the transaction is an ART form.

Capital Structure Relevance

A last component of our working definition of ART forms is that they must impact the economic risk capital structure of a firm. Again, this is not a feature unique to ART forms. Capital structure relevance is thus a necessary but not a sufficient condition to be considered an ART product.

Most risk transfer and risk financing solutions ultimately influence a firm's capital structure. But not all. A firm's divestiture of a physical asset, for example, need not imply a change in the mix of financial claims issued by the firm. Similarly, a bank may securitize its credit card receivables as a way of terminating a business line just as easily as a way to raise funds. The latter is clearly a capital structure decision, whereas the former is an investment decision.

The products representing true "convergence" in capital and insurance markets, however, have the capital structure relevance characteristic in common. Some insurance market products still can be used for reasons other than optimizing the corporate capital structure, whereas ART forms have the clear intention of going directly to the issue of how a firm finances itself and/or manages its risk.

RETENTION, CAPITAL STRUCTURE, AND RISK TRANSFER VERSUS RISK FINANCE

Central to any discussion of risk transfer is the concept of retention, or the active decision to retain a risk rather than transfer it. Risk retention thus means that the equity holders of the company bear the risk, whereas risk transfer involves the shifting of a risk from the original firm to a new one—say, a (re-)insurer, futures or options counterparty, or swap dealer. As suggested throughout Parts I and II, a firm's retention decision is both a risk management and a capital structure decision.

Insurance industry participants differentiate between planned and unplanned retentions. The former involves a conscious, active decision by the firm's management not to shift a risk (usually a core risk) to the equity holders of an insurer, derivatives dealer, or some other enterprise. As shown in Exhibit 7.1, any portion of the expected plus maximum reasonable unexpected loss that a company deliberately decides not to transfer to another market participant for a given risk source is the firm's planned retention for that risk. The aggregate of those planned retentions across all risk types—core and noncore—is the company's aggregate planned retention.

Unplanned retentions, by contrast, occur when companies fail to transfer a risk whose full impact on the firm is unknown or incorrectly estimated. Unplanned retentions frequently occur because a firm experiences a failure in its risk identification process (see Chapter 9). If the firm does not know the risk is there *ex ante*, it cannot decide whether to retain or transfer it and thus retains it by default. If Corporation Albinoni has issued noncallable and callable bonds and simply omits the callable bonds from an interest rate risk exposure identification exercise, the firm easily could end up with an unplanned retention as a result of its omission.

Even if Firm Albinoni includes the callable bonds in its interest rate exposure analysis, the use of an inappropriate model to estimate potential exposure could also lead to an unplanned retention. Company Albinoni might, for example, generate a simulated loss distribution by using simulated changes in interest rates and the duration of its callable and noncallable bonds. The resulting approximation, however, will fail to capture any convexity in the bonds and the impact of volatility on the callable bonds in particular. In this case, the firm has identified the position but has not fully identified all the risks of the position.

Retention decisions based on any risk measurement models also will invariably be occasionally "wrong" *ex post*. Models are, after all, just that—*ap-*

proximations of reality. But reality quite regularly deviates from model-driven approximations. A firm that makes a risk transfer/retention decision based on a model *ex ante* and finds the model to be deficient *ex post* thus may end up with an unplanned retention—or, conversely, may have retained too little to match its shareholders' risk tolerances.

Factors Influencing the Retention Decision

As noted in Chapter 9, firms tend to prefer retaining their core risks, all else being equal. Because these risks are the risks firms believe themselves to be in business to take, core risk transfers tend to occur mainly when the core risk exposes the firm to a catastrophic loss potential and thus relatively high expected financial distress costs. Otherwise, most planned risk transfers will involve the noncore risks about which the firm's managers are comparatively less informed.

We have already reviewed the reasons why a firm may wish to transfer some of its risks to another participant: reducing expected taxes, expected financial distress costs, or underinvestment problems; mitigating asset substitution costs or countering the effects of managerial risk aversion; increasing debt capacity, internal funds available for investment spending, or the signal-to-noise ratio in noisy accounting aggregates; and so on.

Apart from these factors, the pure transaction cost of the administration of losses can affect a firm's retention decision. For some losses, such as payments owed on an out-of-the-money swap, administrative costs are negligible. But for other losses, such as operational, liability, or property damage losses, often the administration can be cumbersome. The process of loss recovery can include filing claims, investigating the losses, calculating damages, and other such issues. Especially a firm sustains a large number of small losses that are either insured or are related to the offering of insurance products, the costs of claims administration, loss adjustment expense calculations, damages calculations, and other such line items can become cumbersome quickly, thus raising the costs of retaining the risks that gave rise to those claims.

On the other side of the equation, of course, is the cost of risk transfer itself. Apart from the cost of any capital the firm may obtain through a risk transformation product, the transaction costs of risk transfer can be high, especially for highly customized risk transformation products. These costs can be manifest in the form of potentially wide bid-offer spreads on financial products, "arrangement fees" on ART solutions, structuring fees, credit and liquidity enhancement fees that some deals require, and so on.

Also affecting a firm's retention decision is the degree of precision with which expected losses arising from a particular risk, hazard, or peril can be estimated. As noted in Chapter 7, expected losses are a cost of doing business and should be factored into the capital budgeting decision. As those losses become more difficult to estimate, however, it becomes more difficult to plan the retention of those expected losses—not to mention unexpected ones.

Funded versus Unfunded Retentions and Risk Finance

Exhibit 17.1 generalizes the retention decision of a firm based on two risk criteria—magnitude and frequency of loss.[1] This figure excludes many of the issues discussed in Part I that we know to be important in helping a firm determine its retention decision. But the diagram is useful in the context of the predictability of losses and how that loss predictability may help a firm choose how to handle a group of noncore risks. In general, high-severity/low-frequency events like natural disasters, acts of terrorism, widespread and persistent information technology outages, and the like are much harder to model and predict than low-severity/high-frequency events like failed wire transfers, small physical property damage, and certain small financial risks. All else being equal, firms may prefer to transfer those risks that are relatively less stable and predictable and retain risks at the other extreme. In other words, firms are more likely to want to transfer those risks about which they

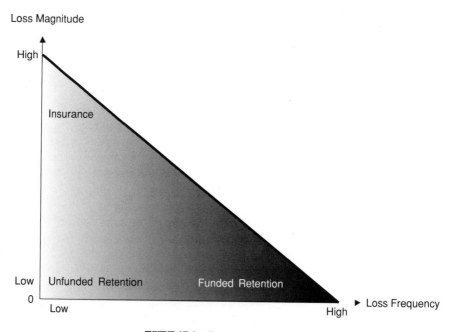

EXHIBIT 17.1   Retention Decision

have relatively less comparative informational advantage and retain those risks that are more easily and better understood.

Transferred risks are both financed and borne by the security holders of the firm to which the risk is shifted. The firm's equity holders ultimately will bear the costs associated with any realized losses arising from retained risks. But those losses must be financed somehow when they actually occur. *Unfunded retention* is the retained risk of a firm for which any losses are financed as they are incurred, whereas *funded retention* involves the allocation of specific funds to carrying particular losses. Earlier we referred to these same concepts as postloss financing and preloss financing, respectively.[2]

As shown in Exhibit 17.2, funded retention or preloss financing can be paid-in or contingent debt capital. As discussed in Chapter 7, issuing new securities to finance a risk capital reserve is equivalent to preloss funding. Issuing new equity to finance the risk reserve is equivalent to getting equity holders to prepay the losses they ultimately will bear, whereas issuing new debt is simply preloss borrowing to get the firm through any difficulties following the loss. Banking instruments like those discussed in Chapter 12 (e.g., letters of credit and revolvers) also can be used for this purpose.

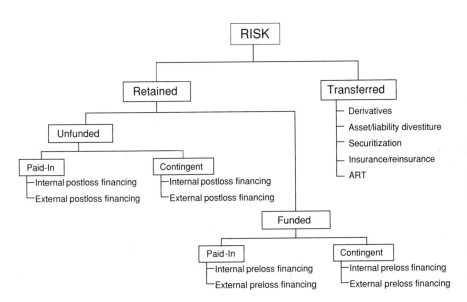

EXHIBIT 17.2   Risk Transfer versus Risk Finance

ALTERNATIVE RISK FINANCING CHOICES

Exhibit 17.3 provides a summary of the options available to a firm that de-cides to retain its risks. The firm depicted thus can be presumed to have es-chewed risk transfer, so the question remaining is how the firm will finance its retained risks.

Unfunded risks are subject to postloss financing, which can occur using any of the means for raising paid-in capital discussed in Part I, such as the is-suance of new securities or securing new borrowings from banks.

Retained risks resulting in actual losses can be prefunded using four types of structures. The first are contingent capital structures including cer-tain types of derivatives (e.g., the income swaps discussed in Chapter 13), certain types of securitizations (e.g., collateralized debt obligations) in which the sponsoring firm retains the equity tranche (see Chapter 22), con-tingent banking products (e.g., letters of credit), contingent liabilities (see Chapter 7), and contingent debt (see Chapter 21). Because several of these structures also can be used for risk transfer purposes, most are discussed elsewhere.

The remaining three means of securing preloss funding for retentions are self-insurance, captives and captivelike structures, and finite risk products. Self-insurance, captives, and related structures are all fairly similar and are discussed in Chapter 18; finite risk products are discussed in Chapter 19.

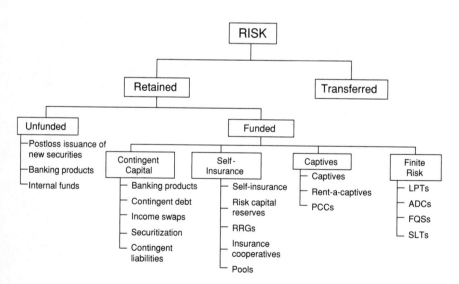

EXHIBIT 17.3   Risk Finance with Traditional and ART-istic Methods

NOTES

1. Although based loosely on Outreville (1998), this figure does have some important differences to Outreville's.
2. As Doherty (2000) explains, when asset substitution, dilution, and expected financial distress costs are taken into account, the situations where pre- and postloss risk finance lead to different values of the firm are more limited than might appear to be the case.

CHAPTER 18

Alternative Risk Finance: Self-Insurance, Captives, and Captivelike Structures

Exhibit 17.3 showed several ways by which companies could prefund their retentions, one of which involves the use of self-insurance and self-insurance–like structures. A second and related alternative risk financing source includes the use of a captive (re-)insurer. In this chapter we discuss the mechanics and benefits of both traditional self-insurance and captives. Note that because none of these risk financing methods involves traditional insurance structures, all of the methods discussed here are considered ART methods.

Our analysis concentrates on addressing the following questions:

- What different types of self-insurance programs can a firm adopt to realize certain benefits of preloss funding for retained risks?
- What is a captive insurance or reinsurance company?
- What different captive structures are available to firms seeking to fund their retain risks?
- How is the capitalization level for a captive determined?
- What are some of the benefits to firms of prefunding their retained losses through captives and captivelike structures?

SELF-INSURANCE

Retentions can be funded through self-insurance, or the process by which a firm establishes an internal insurance fund to cover specific losses. Self-insurance is essentially any organized form of prefunded retention that involves an insurancelike transfer pricing structure but does not require the firm to set up or rely on a separate organization to accomplish this. Self-insurance undertaken through a wholly owned subsidiary with an insurance license involves the use of captives; for now we discuss only *non*captive methods of self-insurance.

Types of Self-Insurance Mechanisms

Self-insurance can be accomplished using several different traditional insurance or insurancelike structures, shown on Exhibit 17.3. Not all of these structures are pure self-insurance, but all function like self-insurance.

Pure Self-Insurance

Classical self-insurance is the prefunding of risk internally using insurancelike internal contracting and transfer pricing methods. Pure self-insurance is generally an application of excess risk capital (as discussed in Chapter 7) with two additional features.

First, the risks that are insured in a self-insurance vehicle typically are sufficiently well specified that the funds raised to capitalize the self-insurance reserves can be earmarked for that purpose using mechanisms such as covenants. This mitigates investors' concerns that the funds will be used, say, to fund negative NPV projects. In a pecking order world, however, adverse selection remains a major cost to the funding of self-insurance reserves.

A second distinguishing feature of self-insurance programs is that the firm has enough homogenous risk exposures and loss opportunities that its aggregate expected losses are reasonably stable and predictable.[1] As noted in Chapter 7, the expected loss from any particular risk is a cost of doing business and should be factored into the firm's investment decision. Whether that expected loss is transferred or retained is immaterial, but it must be taken into account. When it is difficult to estimate such expected losses with any degree of precision, however, it is difficult to prefund any retention of those expected losses.

Reserves

Earmarked risk capital reserves are quite similar to pure self-insurance except that they lack the two key features of pure self-insurance—and thus are essentially identical to the risk capital concepts developed in Chapter 7. Specifically, (1) securities usually cannot be issued with covenants restricting the use of funds to cover only certain retained risks, and (2) the behavior of the losses for which reserves are held may not be predictable.

Risk capital thus is generally held to protect internal cash balances against unexpected large depletions arising from unexpected losses or unidentified risk factors. Risk capital reserves often are complementary to organized self-insurance programs as an extra degree of protection for the firm's internal funds. In other words, risk capital reserves can work together with pure self-insurance to help ensure that completely unplanned retentions are prefunded somehow on nondistressed financing terms.

Self-Insurance Pools

Despite its name, a self-insurance pool is not a vehicle in which companies can pool and self-insure their risks. Instead, self-insurance pools are means by which risk can be financed more effectively when firms pool their self-insurance funds.

As noted, one characteristic of self-insurance is a reasonably large base of losses from which expected losses can be predicted in a relatively stable manner. Self-insurance becomes difficult to fund when losses are large and arrive sporadically. In this situation, a larger pool of funds exposed to a different time pattern of losses can be beneficial—hence the rationale for a self-insurance pool.

Self-insurance pools are similar to mutual insurance companies (see Chapter 15), although they are not chartered as insurance companies per se. Participating entities contribute funds to the polled entity and then agree to "insure one another." As a practical consequence, this does not mean that the risks of each firm are transferred to the pool, but rather that the risk in the unfavorable timing in the arrival rate of claims or losses is transferred to the pool. If the loss exposures of the participants in the pool are diverse enough, the pool provides a way for the collective participants to smooth the timing of those losses so that expected losses over time are easier to predict and prefund than if all the loss exposures were left in constituent firms.

Benefits and Costs of Self-Insurance

Self-insurance has several benefits over traditional insurance purchased on the market, one of which is preferable pricing. A self-insurance structure not only avoids the load associated with traditional insurance but also is immune from any of the costs of asymmetric information typically associated with traditional insurance. In other words, the self-insuring firm can observe both its own risk management actions and its own risks and thus can avoid the adverse pricing or contract features included by traditional insurers to mitigate adverse selection and moral hazard.

Pure self-insurance and risk reserves also allow the self-insurer to retain the interest earnings on the premium, which is now retained within the company through a transfer pricing structure. Funds also are available in these two structures immediately to cover losses. Note that a self-insurance pool may not allow the same freedom of premium investment and the same speed of funds delivery as reserves or pure self-insurance, however, because a separate organization representing the interests of multiple firms is now in the picture.

Risk that is retained and self-insured is a risk financing and not a risk transfer solution, however, because the equity holders of the self-insuring firm still bear the ultimate cost associated with losses. Accordingly, a firm must weigh carefully the benefits of self-insurance against the benefits of risk transfer discussed earlier before choosing a self-insured planned retention.

CAPTIVES

A captive insurance or reinsurance company is a type of organized self-insurance program in which a firm actually sets up its own insurance company to fund and manage its retained risks. Captives became immensely popular in the late 1970s, but softening insurance and reinsurance premiums led to a decline in their usage through the 1980s. As the desire of firms to realize the benefits of captives especially regarding enterprise-wide risk management increased substantially in the 1990s, however, captives have once again become very popular tools for both financing retained risks and engaging in selective risk transfers.

To many, captives are the very embodiment of the alternative risk transfer market. In terms of the criteria we developed in Chapter 17, captives may be considered ART forms for the following reasons:

> *A captive is a risk management structures or solution involving the participation of insurance and/or reinsurance companies that enable firms either to finance or transfer some of the risks to which they are exposed in a nontraditional way (by relying on internal self-insurance combined in an innovative way with external reinsurance) thereby functioning as synthetic debt or equity in a corporate customer's capital structure.*

TYPES OF CAPTIVES AND CAPTIVELIKE STRUCTURES

Numerous types of captives exist in the world today. Generally, captives fall into two categories: single-parent and multiparent. Some of the major variations for each type are discussed in the subsections below.

Single-Parent Captives

A single-parent captive is the simplest captive structure in which a firm sets up a captive in order to manage its retained risks—and, in some cases, to manage the risks of the firm more generally. Single-parent captives can be set up as either insurance companies or reinsurance companies.

Single-Parent Captive Insurers

A single-parent captive insurance company, depicted in Exhibit 18.1, is a wholly owned subsidiary of the "sponsoring corporation," or the entity that is seeking to fund its retained risks.[2] To accomplish this, the sponsor capitalizes the captive by using either internal funds or the proceeds of externally is-

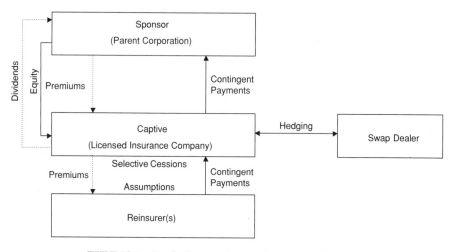

EXHIBIT 18.1   Single-Parent Captive Insurance Company

sued financial claims to purchase the captive's equity. The amount of equity required in the captive depends on the type of captive structure and is discussed later. The captive invests the proceeds of its equity sale to the sponsor in low-risk, marketable securities that function as excess risk capital reserves for the captive on behalf of the sponsoring corporation.

In addition to the equity infusion required to capitalize the captive initially, the sponsoring program then pays premiums to the captive for insurance against risks that the firm wishes to retain and self-insure. The captive, in turn, is licensed as an actual insurance company; it uses the premiums to fund unearned premium and loss reserves that, together with its equity, back the contingent payment obligations it accepts to the parent in return for receiving premium.

A captive can be managed by the sponsoring corporation, by the captive itself, or by a captive management firm. Companies active in captive management include large (re-)insurers like Zürich Financial and large insurance brokers like AON and Marsh.

Returning to Exhibit 17.1, retention is commonly associated with high-frequency, low-severity loss events. Captives thus usually retain these types of risks. To the extent that the sponsoring corporation may wish to seek insurance to manage its other low-frequency, high-severity exposures, the captive also assumes responsibility for managing such risks—including possibly transferring them to other participants. As the exhibit shows, the captive may utilize reinsurance to offload the risks to which the sponsoring firm is subject that it has elected not to retain. Note that this is *re*insurance because the captive itself is an insurer that has provided the sponsoring firm with primary coverage.

Similarly, swaps and other derivatives can be negotiated with the swap dealer for the same purpose. In either case, the sponsor prefunds not the expected loss but the cost of the risk transfer and then enters into some kind of contingency agreement with the captive that mimics the captive's risk transfer transactions.

Consider a specific example of sponsoring firm BigChip, a silicon chip manufacturer and distributor. Suppose BigChip is exposed to three risks: the risk of damage to chips in shipments BigChip has guaranteed, the risk of an earthquake causing significant damage to its California headquarters and main production facility, and the risk of fluctuations in the yen/dollar exchange rate arising from the fact that most of BigChip's chip sales are to Japan.

Firm BigChip may set up a captive insurer called BigChip Insurance Co., capitalized by BigChip through a purchase of 100 percent of BigChip Insurance Co.'s common stock. BigChip might then decide that the first risk—damage to chip shipments—constitutes a core business risk and is characterized by a high frequency of small losses. The earthquake and foreign exchange risk, however, are risks BigChip decides to transfer rather than retain and finance.

Accordingly, BigChip enters into three transactions with BigChip Insurance. The first is a per occurrence insurance contract with no deductible and no coinsurance that compensates BigChip for annual losses per occurrence on damaged chips in transit, in exchange for which BigChip pays an annual premium to BigChip Insurance. BigChip Insurance then retains 100 percent of this risk and finances any losses out of its equity (which must be at least as high as the expected losses on chip shipments) plus its allocation of premium into unearned premium and loss reserves (with corresponding investments in short-term interest-bearing assets to fund those liabilities).

In a second transaction, BigChip pays a premium to BigChip Insurance for a catastrophic XOL policy triggered by a California earthquake—say, with an attachment point of $100 million, no deductible, and no copay provision. Because this is a risk that BigChip does not wish to retain, BigChip then reinsurers the entire catastrophic loss layer with one or more reinsurers. If the reinsurer(s) request a deductible and/or coinsurance provision, BigChip Insurance will have a forced retention of that portion of its catastrophic risks on behalf of BigChip. The insurance policy between BigChip and BigChip Insurance likely will not reflect this deductible and copay, so that BigChip Insurance is the sole retention agent in the structure.

Finally, BigChip and BigChip Insurance execute a series of foreign exchange forwards, swaps, options, and/or cross-currency swaps on the dollar/yen rate to hedge the sponsor's currency risk. These derivatives will be "mirroring transactions" for whatever derivatives BigChip Insurance executes with one or more swap dealers.

Not uncommon today is for captives to play a role as outsourced enterprise-wide risk managers for their sponsoring firms. In this case, we might expect BigChip Insurance to have even greater responsibilities, including enterprise-wide risk identification, measurement, monitoring, and control. Especially with the potential synergies that can be created by combining some of the above transactions in single protective ART structures (see Chapter 20), vesting the captive with all risk control responsibilities is not unreasonable and may indeed be quite smart.

A major attraction of the captive structure—like pure self-insurance—is the retention of underwriting profits and investment income on assets held to back unearned premium and loss reserves. If the actual losses underwritten by the captive are lower than expected, the sponsor can repatriate those underwriting profits—plus any investment income—in the form of dividends paid by the captive to its sole equity holder, the sponsor.

Single-Parent Captive Reinsurers

A major issue for a sponsoring company to determine in setting up a captive structure is the domicile for the captive. Variables that can affect a firm's captive domicile choice include the following[3]:

- Restrictions on captive investments
- Reinsurance restrictions
- Financial reporting requirements
- Minimum capital requirements
- Premium and other taxes
- Underwriting restrictions
- Reserve requirements
- Tax relationship of domicile with home country of sponsoring corporation
- Domicile currency stability
- Privacy protections
- Local infrastructure and stability

Accordingly, firms often incorporate and charter their captives in jurisdictions other than the primary jurisdiction in which the sponsoring firm is incorporated. Exhibit 18.2 summarizes the number of captives by domicile in 2000.

When local laws, regulations, or tax requirements require sponsoring firms to obtain local insurance coverage, firms may opt for a captive structure in which the captive is incorporated and chartered as a *re*insurance company rather than an insurance company. The sponsoring corporation then gets a local insurers to "pass through" its premium and coverage to the captive reinsurer. Called a *fronting insurer*, the structure of a single-parent captive reinsurer with a fronting insurer is shown on Exhibit 18.3.

Licensing the captive as a reinsurer has certain advantages, but the draw-

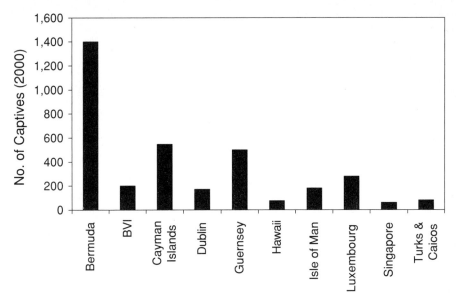

EXHIBIT 18.2   Captive Domiciles
Source: AMS Insurance Management Services Ltd. on *www.captive.com.*

backs of involving a fronting insurer usually more than offset those advantages. The fronting insurer will demand some arrangement fees. In addition, the presence of a fronting insurer can force the firm to bear certain administrative, compliance, regulation, and tax costs that it can otherwise avoid if the captive can be domiciled in a separate jurisdiction without the involvement of a fronting insurer. Kloman (1998) estimates that the costs of a fronting insurer range from 5 to 30 percent of total premiums.

Single-Parent Multibranch Captive Reinsurers

Some multinational conglomerates prefer to manage their risks on a local subsidiary basis rather than an enterprise-wide basis. Even if a firm prefers to centralize its risk management decision making, transactions executed for risk transfer or risk financing purposes still may require local insurers for multiple local jurisdictions. In this case, a firm can set up a single-parent multibranch captive reinsurance company.

Shown in Exhibit 18.4, a multibranch structure involves the separate payment of premium and insurance of risk by each branch (or, at least, by each branch in jurisdictions for which a fronting insurer is required) to a separate fronting company, all of which then cede to the captive reinsurer. The reinsurer then still may selectively retrocede or hedge certain risks that the sponsor does not wish to retain, as before.

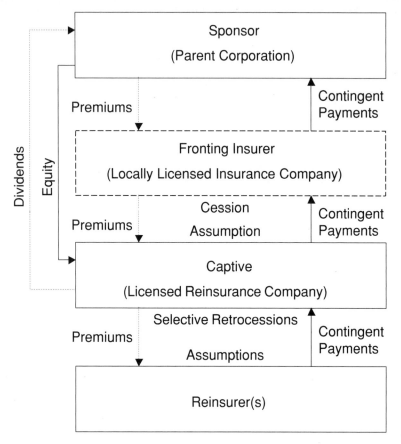

EXHIBIT 18.3   Single-Parent Captive Reinsurer with Fronting Insurer

Whether the individual branches or the sponsoring corporation holding company owns the captive's equity is essentially up to the sponsoring corporation. In either case, dividends arising from underwriting profits and investment income in the captive are paid back to the sponsoring company at some level.

Multiparent Captives

Some captive insurance and reinsurance companies are not wholly owned subsidiaries of single sponsoring firms. Such captives are called *multiparent captives* and facilitate some form of risk finance diversification across different firms. The most common such structures are summarized below.

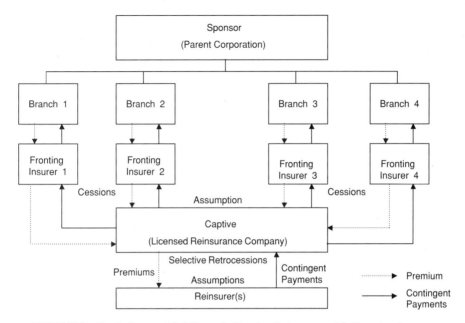

EXHIBIT 18.4   Single-Parent Multibranch Captive Reinsurer with Fronting Insurers

Group or Association Captives and Risk Retention Groups

A group or association captive has a structure essentially similar to the single-parent multibranch captive shown in Exhibit 18.4 but for the fact that the "branches" are now unrelated sponsoring corporations in the multiparent structure. In other words, a group captive is a captive insurance or reinsurance company that collects premiums from multiple sponsors and in turn agrees to underwrite certain risks of those sponsors. A multiparent captive structure with fronting insurers is shown in Exhibit 18.5. Note, however, that the presence of fronting insurers is not required and will be driven by the same domicile considerations as in the single-parent case.

Group captives are often set up by industry trade associations on behalf of their members. At its height, the International Air Transport Association's captive Airline Mutual Insurance (AMI), for example, had 44 active participants and offered hull liability and damage policies for 110 airlines.[4] Similarly, Energy Insurance and Mutual Limited is the group captive representing numerous U.S. electricity and gas utilities. When each member is too small to justify the expenses of having its own captive, this structure can make sense. Alternatively, situations in which self-insurance pools make sense also can explain

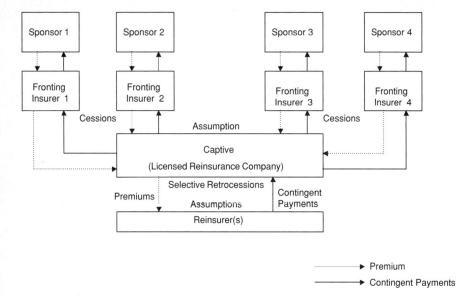

EXHIBIT 18.5 Multiparent Captive Reinsurer with Fronting Insurers

group or association captives—the benefits of pooling premiums and risks allow the group captive to achieve a smoother time profile of loss payouts than would be possible in any individual participant's situation. Similarly, risk retention groups are specific types of multiparent captives formed under U.S. liability law specifically for the purpose insuring certain liability risks.

The loss sharing regime in a multiparent captive structure is usually strictly proportional to the premiums paid into the captive. As noted in our discussion of self-insurance pooling, combining the resources of multiple firms is not intended to pool the actual risks, which each participant sponsor has chosen to retain or selectively reinsure. Instead, the sharing arrangement is designed purely to reduce cash flow risk of the combined firm and facilitate lower-cost funding for retained risks.

Rent-a-Captive

In recent years, the offering by (re-)insurance firms and insurance brokers of rent-a-captives has become another important ART solution for firms wishing to retain a large portion of their risks while seeking preloss financing for losses arising from those risks. A rent-a-captive structure is essentially similar to the multiparent structure for a group captive shown in Exhibit 18.5 except that the participating corporations relying on the captive for insurance do not actually own any part of the rent-a-captive. At least some of the participants thus own no equity in the captive and do not receive any dividends.

As shown in Exhibit 18.6, rent-a-captives are set up, maintained/managed, and owned by market participants like (re-)insurance companies or insurance brokers for the benefit and use of corporations that lack the equity capital to fund the creation of their own single-parent or group captive. Single- and multiparent captives must be subsidiaries of noninsurance companies, whereas rent-a-captives are usually insurance subsidiaries set up on behalf of their customers.

As Exhibit 18.6 illustrates, customers of a rent-a-captive remit premium payments to a fronting insurer that then cedes the premium to the rent-a-captive through facultative reinsurance to give the customer coverage for losses on the risks it wishes to retain. The rent-a-captive itself typically sets up "customer accounts" for participants. Premiums are credited to these accounts, and claims are booked against these premium reserves. In addition, investment and underwriting income are tracked and, unlike traditional insurance, may be returned to the participants, usually when the rent-a-captive contract is terminated. Participants thus can benefit in much the same way is if they had been owners of the captive, but the equity investment itself is not required. In return, however, rent-a-captive structures can be fairly expensive for participants.

Protected Cell Companies

Some people have expressed concerns about the fact that rent-a-captives commingle assets from different participants. Participants worry that the assets

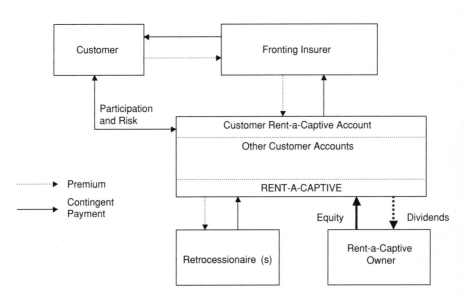

EXHIBIT 18.6 Rent-a-Captive
Source: Wöhrmann and Bürer (2001).

of the captive may be misinvested, yielding reserve losses, or that the loss of one firm could be applied to the account of another participant in situation of dire need.

As a result, captive management organizations have been offering protected cell companies (PCCs) since 1997.[5] A PCC is set up essentially like a rent-a-captive except that customers have "ring-fenced" segregated accounts. Premiums paid into a customer account and invested in assets that are used to fund subsequent losses are protected from liabilities that arise in other accounts through this segregation structure. In some cases, the PCC itself may even be set up as a SPV with each "account" representing a separate affiliated entity of the SPV. The mechanics of a typical PCC structure are shown in Exhibit 18.7.

CAPITALIZATION AND DIVIDENDS IN CAPTIVE STRUCTURES

The capitalization of a captive depends strongly on its type. In a single-parent structure, the equity capital issued depends largely on the expected losses the sponsor anticipates from any claims arising on its retained risks. In a multi-parent structure, the expected losses of each sponsor must be taken into account as well as the correlation in the arrival rate of claims that could cause temporary shocks to the captive's reserves.

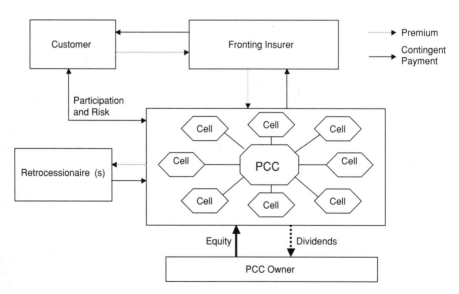

EXHIBIT 18.7 Protected Cell Company
Source: Wöhrmann and Bürer (2001).

In addition, captive capitalization levels also depend on the minimum capital requirements of the locality in which the captive is chartered, licensed, and domiciled, as suggested in Chapter 8. For the past few years, by far the largest number of captives are domiciled in Bermuda. Capital required for captives located in Bermuda depend on the type. For single-parent captives underwriting only the risk of the sponsor and any affiliates of the sponsor, $120,000 in capital and surplus is required at all times. If the captive underwrites the risk of multiple owners, the minimum capital required is $250,000. And if more than 20 percent of the risks underwritten by the captive are not for actual owners of the captive, the capital required is $1 million.

Some jurisdictions do not differentiate among types in assessing capital requirements. Guernsey, Channel Islands, for example, requires £100,000 plus a minimum solvency margin (see Chapter 8) of 18 percent on the first £5 million of net earned premiums and 16 percent thereafter. Every jurisdiction in which captives are recognized is usually unique.

BENEFITS OF CAPTIVES

Captive structures are not for every firm. As noted in the case of self-insurance, the benefits of a captive or captivelike structure are most likely to be realized when a firm has a good historical claims or loss experience so that expected losses can be estimated with reasonable precision and so that the ratio between claims incurred and premium paid is reasonably low. In addition, firms seeking to utilize a captive structure need adequate financial resources and cash flows to fund an annual premium payment large enough to justify the expenses of a captive. Minimum premium written in order for a single-parent captive to make sense is usually around $700,000, although using a rent-a-captive or PCC structure can reduce this amount to as little as $100,000 per annum.[6]

If a captive structure does make economic sense for a sponsoring (captive) or participating (PCC, rent-a-captive) firm, the potential benefits relative to traditional insurance can be substantial. Some of these benefits also apply to hedging programs run out of a captive rather than the sponsoring firm's treasury or risk management function.

Cost Savings

As discussed, any form of self-insurance can be cheaper than risk transfer because it allows the firm to avoid the adverse selection costs of issuing new financial claims to support losses externally. Especially if self-insurance reserves and premium can be funded internally, retention thus usually represents a cost savings vis-à-vis risk transfer.

Quite apart from the benefits of avoiding postloss external financing costs with self-insurance, the captive route specifically also can generate a cost savings for sponsors and participants for several reasons. First, *re*insurance obtained through a captive can be both cheaper and more flexible than primary insurance. Setting up a captive with a fronting insurer does require sometimes significant outlays to the fronting insurer, but these outlays may be significantly smaller than the cost savings associated with reinsurance. Similarly, any risks the sponsor or participant does not wish to retain can be retroceded by the captive, again at rates often preferable to those that could be obtained by direct insurance.

A major reason that reinsurance companies are willing to quote favorable rates to captives is that captive relationships with their reinsurers tend to be reasonably long term. A reinsurer dealing with a captive thus knows that there likely will be long-term relationship gains as well as potential advisory and servicing fees, and thus it may be more willing to aggressively price the reinsurance itself.

A second potential source of cost savings in a captive structure comes in the form of potentially reduced retrocession rates. If the captive can market the risks the sponsor does not wish to retain to several reinsurers, then reinsurers will be able more easily to assume specific risk layers with which they are most comfortable. "Optimal layering" through facultative or treaty excess-of-loss coverage often is cheaper than direct insurance or reinsurance in which the whole layer is forced onto a single retrocessionaire or reinsurer.

A third cost savings is the potential for lower reinsurance rates arising from diminished moral hazard problems. Because much of the risk is being retained by the sponsor, any insurers or reinsurers need not worry too much about hidden actions that might increase their exposure; the sponsor usually will be on the hook for the early losses.

Signaling

Some people argue that captives can be used as a signaling mechanism. Scordis and Portat (1998), for example, argue that captives are a "status symbol" for the managers that set them up and can be used to signal management's commitment to taking risk management seriously.

Similarly, Eva Air used its formation of a Singapore-domiciled captive as a competitive signaling tool against its primary competitor, Taiwan-based China Airlines. Eva claimed that its captive, Martinair Insurance, was proof of Eva's financial commitment to airline safety because it was literally putting its own money behind the risk.[7] Indeed, this is not an implausible interpretation of at least some captives.

Cash Flow Smoothing

Retained risks are essentially insured internally, and internal insurance premiums can be paid using transfer pricing. Classical insurance, by contrast, usually required prepayment of premiums annually. The ability for a firm that self-insures to choose the timing of its premium payments can create a valuable cash flow smoothing tool. Even within a captive structure, the sponsor usually can plan premium payments to occur at a time most advantageous to it.

Investment Income and Reserve Management

Users of self-insurance or captives retain the investment income generated by assets held to offset premium and loss reserves. By retaining this investment income, the cost of insurance capital is reduced, possibly creating a significant capital structure advantage for users of prefunded retention and captive programs.

Tax Considerations

Tax considerations alone should not drive the establishment of captives, but neither should the savings that tax deductions can generate in a captive structure be ignored. These tax savings depend strongly on both the domicile of the captive and the location of the sponsoring firm. But as long as the captive is set up as a legitimate insurance company in a recognized domicile, several home jurisdictions still allow at least some deductions for captive payments and expenses, such as certain realized losses and reported or incurred but not reported loss reserves. Many captive domiciles have tax laws designed to accord favorable treatment to captives in this manner. If the sponsor retains its risks internally without using a captive, not all of these tax savings can be realized.

Reduced Agency Costs of Overinvestment

Captives also can help firms reduce the agency costs of overinvestment discussed in Chapter 4.[8] By forcing the sponsor to disgorge internal funds to the captive in the form of premium payments, the management *of the captive* then becomes responsible for applying those funds to their specified purpose of controlling retained risks and associated losses. As noted elsewhere, simply earmarking funds in a risk capital reserve for loss retention may give rise to overinvestment concerns that the funds have been or might be suboptimally invested.

Agency cost reductions associated with the formation of a captive are likely to be higher for single-parent captives run either by their own management or by a third-party captive management firm. Although adding an additional layer of separation between the security holders of the sponsor and the management of the captive might seem to increase agency costs, the captive itself is such a transparent special-purpose company that monitoring its management is relatively easy. Relying on management whose incentives are limited just to managing the captive thus makes it more likely that overinvestment decisions could be observed and dealt with appropriately. This transparency is further rationale for vesting enterprise-wide risk management responsibilities in the captive as well.

Enhanced Funding Risk Management

One criticism of captives, in particular, is that they tie up the firm's internal funds. Although potentially mitigating overinvestment problems, this can lead to *under*investment problems by depleting the cash available for a firm to make its investment decisions.

One way around this problem is to opt for pure self-insurance or earmarked risk capital reserves instead of a captive. In this situation, the funds could be withdrawn from the reserve to fund investments if absolutely required, whereas the funds tied up in a captive are difficult to repatriate quickly. But in the pure self-insurance case, the funds earmarked as a risk reserve are no longer really playing that role. Either the funds have been set aside to cover retained risks or they have not.

Some captive domiciles recognize this problem and address it by allowing single-parent captives to make loans to the sponsoring parent corporation. Vermont and Hawaii, for example, allow captive lending to parents on a largely unrestricted basis, whereas otherwise-popular Bermuda heavily restricts such loans.[9] In Vermont and Hawaii, the firm can essentially engage in internal borrowing to finance investment decisions that might otherwise have to be forgone for purely cash flow reasons. Because the loan from the captive to the parent is an internal loan, the terms likely will be favorable and the cash transfer rapid. But in domiciles where such lending is restricted, potential underinvestment problems arising from depleted internal cash must be weighed against the benefits of allocating cash to prefunded retentions.

Risk Transformation Product Supply

As discussed in Chapter 10, three business models can be used to explain the way that firms can leverage their own internal risk management expertise from pure risk control, to efficiency enhancement, to risk transformation. In their most basic form, captives facilitate risk control for all the reasons explored earlier. But to the extent the captive also can be used, say, to enhance a firm's existing enterprise-wide risk management process, the firm is gaining efficiencies through the creative use of its captive.

Specifically, by centralizing a firm's risks in one place, a firm may realize numerous risk management process synergies. Not surprisingly, using captives as the center of enterprise-wide risk management processes has become increasingly popular over the past few years.

Indeed, as long as a sponsor is going to create a captive, it really makes very little sense to use the captive just for self-insurance purposes. Vesting the captive with all risk control authority on behalf of the sponsor can enhance the efficiency of the process, mitigate agency conflicts arising over which risks the firm should manage, and promote the firm-wide identification of risk exposure for both risk control and efficiency enhancement purposes as discussed in Chapter 10.

In addition, some firms even have moved toward using their captives to provide other firms a risk financing service. Whenever a (re-)insurer sets up a rent-a-captive or PCC, for example, that firm is leveraging its risk management expertise into a new product offering. Similarly, certain large banks now are providing explicit excess-layer private mortgage insurance to their customers through their single-parent captives.[10]

NOTES

1. See Outreville (1998) and Trieschmann, Gustavson, and Hoyt (2001).
2. All of the captive diagrams used here are based on those presented in the marketing materials prepared by Zürich Financial's Corporate Customer Financial and Risk Services (Zürich CH-8085, *www.zurich business.ch/art*). See also Wöhrmann (1998).
3. See Kloman (1998).
4. See Sullivan (1995).
5. See Wöhrmann and Bürer (2001) for a discussion of PCCs.
6. Zürich Financial, for example, requires a minimum premium payment of CHF250,000 per annum in its rent-a-captive program. See the previously cited marketing materials for Zürich Financial.
7. See Sullivan (1995).
8. Along slightly different lines, Scordis and Porat (1998) argue that captives can reduce manager-owner conflicts by increasing manager "status."
9. See Rogers, Sargeant, and Osborne (1996).
10. See Katz (1999).

CHAPTER 19

Alternative Risk Finance: Finite Risk Products and Solutions

We compare in this chapter various means by which firms can manage several different risks associated with contingent liabilities using finite risk products and solutions. The primary purpose of finite risk products is to help firms manage the risks associated with their loss development experience, or the rate at which losses on a known liability accrue. Finite risk products rarely address the underlying liability itself, focusing instead mainly on the timing and premium reinvestment risks associated with mismatches between the technical reserves allocated to a liability, the investment income earned on assets held to back those reserves, and the actual losses those assets are held to fund.

Finite risk contracts originally emerged as finite risk reinsurance, but we will see here that their applications as ART forms now transcends reinsurance and are commonly used by noninsurance corporations either directly as risk financing solutions or indirectly to obtain finite risk cover as reinsurance through captive (re-)insurers.

The questions we address in this chapter include the following:

- What distinguishes finite risk products and solutions from traditional (re-)insurance solutions?
- How do finite risk products function as a substitute for financial capital?
- What types of finite risk products can be used retrospectively to address liabilities that a firm has already incurred for which losses remain unrealized or incurred but not reported (IBNR)?
- What types of finite risk products can be used prospectively to address liabilities that a firm has not yet incurred?
- Can derivatives provide an alternative to finite risk products?

ALTERNATIVE NATURE OF FINITE RISK PRODUCTS

Finite risk products were originally developed and offered by Centre Re, later to become Centre Solutions.[1] Proponents of finite risk solutions typically eschew the description of these ART forms as "products," preferring instead to think of finite risk as a "philosophy" more than a one-time risk finance or transfer solution technique. Nevertheless, because finite risk solutions typically are implemented with specific contracting structures that strongly resemble reinsurance, the term "product" seems to fit well enough.

Finite risk products contain some elements of both risk finance and risk transfer, but the emphasis is usually on risk finance. Indeed, the fact that the insurer in the transaction typically assumes very little "underwriting risk" is what led to the name of these products as "finite" risk.

Finite risk contracts are sometimes also called financial reinsurance or financial insurance. The term "financial" in this context (and in contrast to the way we have used the term in earlier chapters) refers to the major risk that finite risk products are intended to address—the *timing risk* that losses occur faster than expected and thus accrue at a rate that exceeds the investment income on the firm's liability reserves. In financial reinsurance, the parties include a licensed insurance company as cedant or retrocedant and a reinsurer as the assuming firm or retrocessionaire. Financial insurance, however, can be negotiated between a noninsurance corporation and a (re-)insurer. In the context of finite risk, the cession by a single- or multiparent captive insurance company to a reinsurer usually is called financial insurance, although it is technically *re*insurance or even retrocession if a fronting insurer is involved (as explained in Chapter 18).

As we saw in Chapter 16, the benefits of reinsurance to the ceding firm include reduced earnings and/or cash flow volatility, increased debt capacity, increased underwriting capacity, diminished expected financial distress costs, information acquisition, and synthetic liability dispositions. Traditional reinsurance relies on the basic notion that certain risks can be retained or managed more cost effectively by reinsurers than cedants, usually because of risk pooling and diversification benefits enjoyed by the reinsurer.

Finite risk products deliver these same potential benefits to ceding firms, including both insurers using finite risk products as financial reinsurance and corporates using finite risk as a pure insurance solution. The primary distinction between traditional reinsurance and alternative finite risk products is that the latter typically convey value by helping cedants diversify their risks not across other risk types or sources but over time. Finite risk contracts thus are intertemporal risk tranformation products. Finite risk products rearrange the timing of losses over time (called the *loss development experience* on a given liability) but do not necessarily change who bears the ultimate risk. For this reason, finite risk products are risk financing vehicles more than they are risk transfer tools.

The distinctions between classical reinsurance and finite risk products are subtle but critically important in helping firms determine which risk transformation solution is the right one. These differences establish these products as a means of alternative risk transfer and thus differentiate them from classical (re-)insurance and define these ART forms as primarily alternative risk finance products rather than alternative risk transfer products. The main features that finite risk products possess collectively include the following[2]:

- *Risk:* The assuming party bears at least some amount of underwriting, investment, credit, and timing risk.
- *Profit and loss sharing:* The cedant and assuming party typically share in the net profits of the transaction.
- *Limited liability:* The assuming party's maximum payment obligation to the cedant is limited by the terms of the finite risk contract. For underwriting risk in particular, this limitation of liability is usually extremely conservative.
- *Multiyear:* Finite risk contracts are multiyear contracts.
- *Investment-based premium:* The premium calculation for finite risk contracts is based on expected investment income.

Each of these features is considered briefly below.

Financial versus Underwriting Risk

In general, most traditional and ART contracts are subject to four types of risk.

1. *Underwriting risk* is the risk that premiums collected are insufficient to cover realized losses.
2. *Credit risk*—a risk endemic to *all* insurance and reinsurance—is the risk that a (re-)insurer will not fully honor all of its obligations to its cedant customers.
3. *Investment* or *reinvestment risk* is the risk that the income generated by an insurer when a premium is collected is invested in assets is below the expected income reflected in the reinsurer's premium pricing.
4. *Timing risk* is the risk that actual loss claims occur at a faster rate than expected and therefore cause a deterioration in net investment income.

Investment, credit, and timing risk are called *financial* risks in insurance parlance not to be confused "financial risk" as we defined it in Chapter 9.

All insurance and reinsurance contracts involve the credit risk that the party assuming a risk through an insurance, reinsurance, or ART transaction will not honor its contingent obligations. Credit risk thus cannot be used to distinguish between the different types of transactions. Underwriting risk, however, is a risk that is borne mainly in classical insurance and reinsurance contracts, and much less so in finite risk deals. Finite risk contracts are exposed mainly to investment and timing risks.[3]

Partly because of regulations in certain jurisdictions—notably the United States—finite risk transactions must exhibit at least some of all four risk types in order to be considered a reinsurance contract. This is not the case, however, in the Lloyd's of London structure, where the earliest finite transactions originated. Called *time and distance policies*, these historical predecessors to modern finite risk ART contracts are essentially aggregate XOL reinsurance treaties that specifically limit an insurer's maximum exposure on future reinsurance recoveries arising from past policies.

Sometimes also called *retroactive cover*, time and distance policies specified a fixed schedule by which premiums were returned to the cedant by the reinsurer. This schedule, however, might not correspond to the actual timing of loss payments made by the ceding insurer on its original claims. Accordingly, there is no timing risk in a time and distance policy, whose main purpose seems to be pure cash flow smoothing. This lack of timing risk means that these policies are not considered financial reinsurance in the United States and other jurisdictions with similar risk requirements.

Despite the requirement that finite risk contracts exhibit all four risks just noted, such contracts usually emphasize financial risks over underwriting risks. Finite risk transactions thus commonly contain just enough underwriting risk to satisfy regulatory, tax, and accounting criteria for treating such contracts as (re-)insurance but are aimed more at firms wishing to manage their investment and timing risks by smoothing the cash flows and earnings of prefunded retained losses.[4]

Profit and Loss Sharing

Finite risk premiums often are quite high, but looking only at premiums on these ART contracts can be misleading. Unlike traditional insurance, reinsurance, and many capital market instruments, finite risk products almost always involve some profit-sharing provision so that the cedant and assuming (re-)insurer share the risks and returns of the transactions. Regardless of the quoted premium, the total cost to the cedant of a finite risk program is usually a function of the actual claims or loss experience.

The mechanics by which profit and loss sharing is accomplished in a finite risk transaction depend on the nature of the transaction and the particular counterparties to that transaction. In general, this sharing is accomplished through the use of an experience account that tracks the paper profits and losses on the actual underlying deal. Premiums paid by the cedant to the (re-)insurer are credited to the account, as is interest on invested premium reserves. Losses and various charges incurred by the (re-)insurer are debited to the account.

At the end of the term of the finite risk structure, the (re-)insurer and cedant essentially "split" the balance in the experience account, whether a net gain or net loss.

Limited Liability

As the name of this ART form implies, the risk to the (re-)insurer by assuming the responsibilities of a finite risk structure are limited. This limit usually is stated in the contract itself as a clear maximum liability of the (re-)insurer on the transaction. In finite risk transactions, the policy limit on coverage is sometimes called the sever limit. In addition to an aggregate sever limit, the terms of any given finite risk structure also may specify a maximum liability of the (re-)insurer per occurrence, per risk, per annum (in a multiyear structure), and so on.

The (re-)insurer also usually requires a deductible to limit its liability even further in a finite risk transaction. The deductible and the policy limit(s) of the transaction may involve the same or different loss calculation methods. A given finite risk policy may involve a $10 deductible per risk and a $100 maximum liability for the (re-)insurer. In this case, the cedant's retention would be any losses up to $10 and over $100, and it would not matter whether the $100 occurred per risk, per claim, or over the life of the policy. The policy could as easily be structured so that multiple policy limits apply to several different loss measures, such as a policy with a $10 deductible per risk, a $50 limit per risk, and a $100 aggregate policy limit.

The limitation of liability provisions in finite risk contracts do not reveal the differences between financial reinsurance and nonfinancial reinsurance. As Chapter 16 explained, virtually all excess of loss reinsurance involves some kind of liability limitation for the assuming reinsurer. To say that finite risk reinsurance involves limited liability thus is essentially to say that finite risk policies are neither surplus quota nor share quota treaties—that is, finite risk products are types of XOL reinsurance rather than proportional reinsurance.

Two features of finite risk products are noteworthy in this limited liability context. The first is that finite risk products can provide corporate customers with XOL treaty coverage on a primary insurance basis, despite the fact that an XOL treaty usually is considered a *re*insurance product. Second, the cedant usually is willing to limit the underwriting risks borne by the (re-)insurer fairly dramatically if the underwriter assumes more of the timing risk. As noted earlier, regulatory and accounting requirements do require some transfer of underwriting risk in finite risk structures, but the emphasis on liability limitation is usually still on underwriting risk. The timing risk of the products can be significant.

As noted, finite risk products usually achieve some sharing of profits and losses between the cedant and (re-)insurer through the use of an experience account. Because of the liability limitations on underwriting risks and the emphasis on timing risks, the degradation of loss experience below a certain threshold may force the cedant to have to increase premium payments to the fund either temporarily or perhaps even over the remaining life of the transaction.

Multiyear Coverage

As discussed in Chapters 15 and 16, most traditional (re-)insurance products have a single-year coverage term. Partly for operational reasons and to some degree because of convention, the (re-)insurance industry has long considered multiyear products "unusual" or, indeed, "alternative." Few today would consider only the fact that some contract has a multiyear tenor to be sufficient for deeming that contract an ART form, but, conversely, most contracts with other ART-like features are also multiyear.

Finite risk products, in particular, can have quite long tenors when compared even to other ART forms. Whereas some of the multiline products we discuss in Chapter 20 have three-year terms, it is not unusual to observe finite risk insurance and reinsurance with terms running a decade or more. Over this term, cedants can count on cover for long-term exposures, and (re-)insurers can count on a predictable and leveragable stream of premium income.

The longer the term of a finite risk product, the more the product will resemble a pure premium financing structure like a time and distance policy. Longer-term finite risk contracts thus usually have larger degrees of risk transfer.

Investment-based Premium

Both because of the length of some finite risk programs and the importance of timing risk, the present value of expected future investment income earned on premium reserves is taken into consideration by (re-)insurers when finite risk premiums are set. The assuming (re-)insurer usually credits the ceding firm with the expected investment income as an offset against the initial premium owed, thus reducing the total net premium obligation of the ceding firm.

FINITE RISK PRODUCTS AND CAPITAL STRUCTURE

Whether used by insurance companies or by corporations, finite risk products usually are designed to help cedants manage the timing risk of a liability. But because finite risk products require some material underwriting risk transfer, these products thus function as a synthetic hybrid security—synthetic debt issued for liability rather than asset management plus a synthetic equity component reflecting the transfer of residual underwriting risk. In other words, a finite risk product is not a perfect substitute for issuing new debt or for new equity. A firm would need to issue new debt to fund the acquisition of adequate reserves to cover timing risks and issue new equity to absorb underwriting losses in order to replicate a finite risk structure completely.

The main distinction between the types of finite risk ART forms available in the market today is whether the liability whose timing risk is being managed with a finite risk product has or has not already been incurred. Retrospective finite risk products are intended to help firms manage the timing risks of existing liabilities of the firm, whereas prospective finite risk solutions cover contingent liabilities that have not yet been formally assumed by the firm. In the case of an insurance company seeking financial reinsurance through finite risk products, retrospective finite risk products cover past underwriting years and prospective products cover current or future underwriting years. For a corporation, the distinction is essentially the same except that the liabilities being managed are not acquired through an underwriting process but are instead the result of some business decision(s) made by the firm that alter its natural risk profile.

RETROSPECTIVE FINITE RISK PRODUCTS

Retrospective finite risk products can help firms finance past liabilities that they still carry, thereby helping firms reduce the earnings and cash flow volatilities arising from those liabilities. Retrospective risk financing also can help firms optimize their funding costs by exploiting present value relationships that can be altered through changing the timing of losses arising from existing liabilities.

For an insurance company, retrospective finite risk products are appealing for managing the risks and costs of unrealized or incurred-but-not-reported losses on a line of insurance policies that already has been written. Similarly, insurance companies can use retrospective finite risk products to cleanly exit a line of business by dealing with as-yet-unrealized claims all at once.

Noninsurance corporations often find retrospective finite risk products useful in two situations.

1. Retrospective finite risk solutions can facilitate corporate transactions, such as mergers and acquisitions, that might otherwise be hampered by questions about the cost and size of prior liabilities that are unrealized or IBNR.
2. Finite risk can be useful in helping firms manage "run-off solutions," or programs by which certain past liabilities can be segregated away from other liabilities and separately managed. When the liabilities of a portfolio or business line are isolated from the rest of the firm, the process is

known as *ringfencing*. Liabilities may be ringfenced by segregation or transfer to a separate legal entity wholly owned by the original firm. Once segregated from the rest of the firm's assets and liabilities, often the risks of the liabilities in question can be managed more effectively.

Finite risk products allow firms to acquire risk financing for run-off solutions. In such cases, the firm with the liability still bears the ultimate brunt of the liability's cost but can use finite risk to manage the means by which that cost is spread over time.

Alternatively, firms can dispose of a liability using a risk transfer rather than risk finance solution by effecting a total transfer of the segregated liabilities to another firm. Total transfers of loss portfolios usually are accomplished most easily when the liabilities have been ringfenced in a separate company.[5]

Loss Portfolio Transfers

A loss portfolio transfer (LPT) is the cession by a firm of all remaining unclaimed losses associated with a previously incurred liability to a (re-)insurer. In addition to paying an arrangement fee, the cedant also typically pays a premium equal to the net present value of reserves it has set aside for the transferred liability plus a risk premium to compensate the (re-)insurer for the timing risks of the assumption. An LPT thus enables a firm to exchange an uncertain liability in the form of a stream of unrealized losses over time for a certain liability whose present value is equal to the expected NPV of the unrealized losses plus a risk premium and a fee.

Mechanics of a Typical Loss Portfolio Transfer

The principal risk that the cedant transfers to the (re-)insurer through an LPT is the risk that losses or claims arrive at a much faster rate than expected. In that case, the investment income on the reserves—and perhaps the reserves themselves—may be inadequate to fund the losses. A time series of losses that occurs more slowly than expected, by contrast, will represent an opportunity for a net gain that the (re-)insurer typically would share with the cedant. LPTs thus are risk financing mechanisms through which firms can address the timing risk of a liability.

LPTs usually include aggregate loss limits as well as exclusions for certain types of risks not arising directly from the ceded liabilities. Per loss deductibles sometimes are also included in LPTs by (re-)insurers.

Because the timing of losses ceded in an LPT sometimes can be extremely long term, the cedant also may demand some kind of surety from the assuming (re-)insurer. A cedant may request letters of credit, collateral, or bank guarantees to prove the financial integrity if the (re-)insurer has questionable credit quality.

Attractions of Loss Portfolio Transfers

LPTs can be attractive sources of risk finance for various reasons. For insurers, LPTs provide a low-cost means of synthetically exiting a business or an underwriting line very quickly. LPTs also can help primary carriers that are interested in converting future investment income earned on reserves into current underwriting income. Especially for United Kingdom insurance companies, tax and accounting rules allow the insurer to bring this whole investment gain forward into the current year and thus dramatically increase the current accounting value of equity.[6] LPTs also can strengthen the equity of the ceding insurer by increasing its ratio of equity to premium volume. This is possible because the premium paid to the reinsurer is the present value of current reserves, which is below the current value of those reserves that represents the ceded liability. The ceded liability thus exceeds the premium outlay.[7]

LPTs also can benefit noninsurance, corporate customers seeking to swap an uncertain liability stream for a fixed payment today. LPTs can help corporations with captives, for example, wind up certain self-insurance lines if the firm alters its retention decision for certain risks. LPTs are useful to nonfinancial corporations in securing risk financing for run-off solutions, especially in the area of environmental claims and clean-up cost allocation.

Example: The Iron Mountain Copper Mine Superfund Liability Loss Portfolio Transfer

The Iron Mountain Copper Mine is a Superfund site in Redding, California, owned by the Stauffer Management Co. of Wilmington, Delaware.[8] Stauffer Management is the sole potentially responsible party (PRP) under Superfund, which generally holds any PRP to a "Superfund site" jointly and severally liable for the entire cleanup costs of that site. Stauffer Management became the PRP to Iron Mountain because it manages the assets and liabilities of the former Stauffer Chemical Company, which acquired Mountain Copper Ltd. in the 1960s. It was Mountain Copper's mining operations above- and below-ground that fractured Iron Mountain, creating the Superfund liability by exposing the mountain's mineral deposits to oxygen, water, and bacteria and thereby generating substantial acidic runoff.

Mining operations ceased at Iron Mountain in 1963, at which time the federal government developed the Spring Creek Debris Dam to control the release of acidic water runoff from the mine. The Environmental Protection Agency (EPA) listed Iron Mountain as a Superfund site in 1983 with Stauffer as the sole PRP responsible for its cleanup. Eleven years later the State of California and the EPA concluded that the dam was not enough and ordered Stauffer to begin removing all the contaminants from the water.

In 2000, Stauffer Management settled its Superfund claim with the EPA and several other federal and California agencies for approximately $160 million.[9] Of that amount, $7.1 million was a settlement with the EPA, $10 million represented a mandatory contribution to other federal and California agencies for future regional environmental improvement projects, and $139.4 million was the premium Stauffer paid for a finite risk LPT obtained from American International Specialty Lines Insurance Co., a subsidiary of American International Group (AIG). The structure of the LPT is shown in Exhibit 19.1.

Under the LPT agreement, the parties have agreed to contract IT Corp. for the actual cleanup of the Iron Mountain site. The parties estimated the cost of cleanup to be about $4.1 million per annum over the next three decades for an inflation-adjusted total of about $201 million. Under the finite risk policy, Stauffer cedes all of its past, current, and future liabilities on the Iron Mountain site to AIG along with the finite risk premium. The premium payment of $139.4 million was funded by Stauffer out of its current cleanup reserves for the site, plus some insurance coverage under prior policies.

The LPT agreement then obliges AIG to reimburse IT Corp. for 90 percent its the actual cleanup costs incurred each year on the Iron Mountain site *up to a maximum* of $4.1 million per year. IT Corp. bears the risk of higher annual cleanup costs subject to two other protections. First, if inflation causes an increase in costs by up to $900,000 in a single year, IT Corp. can carry forward that additional cost into a subsequent year in which costs are below $4.1 million. Second, AIG also provides IT Corp. with $100 million in

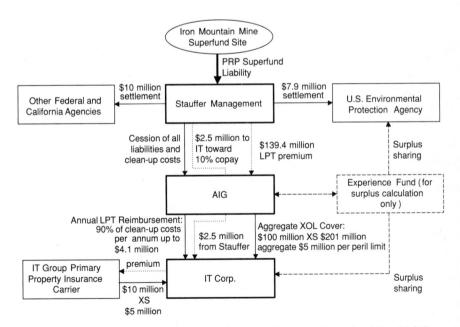

EXHIBIT 19.1 Stauffer Management LPT for Iron Mountain Superfund Site Liability

aggregate XOL coverage for cost overruns specifically triggered by catastrophic perils such as excessive rainfall or earthquakes, subject to a $5 mil-
lion limit per peril.

IT Corp. must finance the remaining 10 percent of its actual annual
cleanup costs as a copayment on the finite risk policy, although Stauffer
agreed to prepay in a lump sum approximately $2.5 million to IT Corp.
that it can use toward its 10 percent residual copay requirement. IT Corp.
bears all of the timing risk on how that additional 10 percent in costs is accrued as well as the timing risks on the clean-up costs themselves. In return,
the finite risk policy includes a type of experience account in which IT
Corp. retains some of the surplus if aggregate cleanup costs fall below
$201 million over the next 30 years. The EPA receives another portion of
that surplus, if it exists.

Adverse Development Covers

An adverse development cover (ADC) is a finite risk ART contract in which a
(re-)insurer agrees to provide excess-of-loss coverage for losses incurred on an
existing liability that exceed the cedant's current reserves. ADCs are commonly used by firms to manage their IBNR liabilities.

Mechanics of Adverse Development Covers

ADCs do not involve the cession of either a liability/loss portfolio or of reserves by the cedant to the (re-)insurer. Instead, the (re-)insurer simply agrees
to compensate the cedant for any losses above an attachment point set equal
to the loss reserves the cedant has allocated to the liability (perhaps plus a deductible). ADCs also may involve a policy limit, but a cedant is free to layer
ADCs in the same manner that traditional XOL reinsurance can be layered to
address concerns over catastrophic loss development layers. (See Chapter 16.)

Unlike LPTs, ADCs deal more with underwriting risk than with timing
risk. Timing risk is still important, however, as expected investment income
earned on reserves over time still can be credited to the cedant to reduce the
premium required. But beyond this credit, the risk premium charged by the
(re-)insurer will be higher than in the LPT because of the greater residual underwriting risk arising from the possibility that the cedant has underestimated
its reserves—perhaps badly. In this sense, although LPTs and ADCs are both
synthetic hybrid debt/equity securities, ADCs have a greater equity component than LPTs.

Exhibit 19.2, based on Shimpi (2001), shows the possible loss development for a portfolio of liabilities over time—that is, the value of losses as they
are incurred and reported over time to the firm bearing the contingent liability. The light gray triangle represents the expected development of losses over
time. The heavier gray triangle in the exhibit represents a possible time path

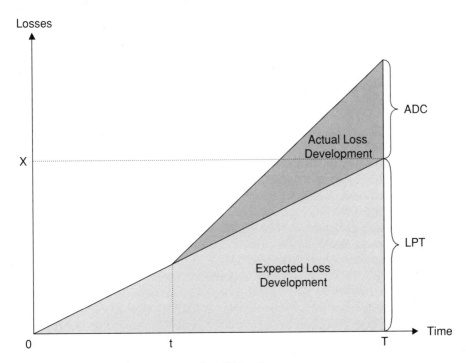

EXHIBIT 19.2 Retrospective Finite Risk ART Products
Source: Modified from Shimpi (2001).

of actual losses. Up through time t, actual losses are below or equal to expected losses. But from t through T, actual losses exceed expected losses.

The underwriting risk borne by the original cedant in the absence of a finite risk product can be seen by focusing on losses at time T. Current reserves at time 0 should grow to $X by date T. If actual losses are at or below $X, the cedant incurs no underwriting losses. If actual losses are above $X at time T, the cedant incurs an underwriting loss equal to the amount of the actual loss less the time T value of the reserves.

The timing risk can be seen by the relative positions of the two triangles over time. Through date t, the current value of reserves is adequate to cover actual losses. But beginning on date t, reserves are deficient. This may be because losses are unexpectedly high relative to reserves (i.e., reserves were underallocated) or because the investment income on the invested reserves accrues too slowly relative to the arrival rate of losses.

·If the firm uses an LPT, the contract likely will include a strict limit on underwriting losses to keep its maximum liability around $X at time T. The risk assumed by the (re-)insurer is thus mainly the risk that the time path of losses develops at a faster rate than implied by the investment income on the reserves—as is the case after time t. Focusing only on time T, the LPT likely will not extend to cover actual losses above X but rather will cover only timing problems that have occurred on all dates prior to X.

The ADC, by contrast, protects the firm against the risk of realized losses on an existing liability being higher than the terminal value of reserves. In this case the time smoothing is secondary to the insurance cover provided for the shortfall of reserves relative to actual losses.

Attractions of Adverse Development Covers

ADCs can be useful for firms in a variety of situations. ADCs commonly are used to cap old liabilities that are of concern in a merger or acquisition. When the acquiring firm or merger partner is concerned that a liability could be much greater than the target firm has planned for in its reserve holdings, the cession of XOL risk through an ADC can provide the target firm with a good remedy to such concerns on the part of its suitor.

In addition, ADCs are widely regarded as important devices for combating adverse selection problems through positive signaling. A firm that enters a charge-off against its earnings for a liability that has not been fully realized, for example, may be suspected of possessing superior information about the liability that leads to underreporting. A firm wishing to counter such fears by investors can take out an ADC to lock in its liability at the charge-off amount and thus signal its confidence that the charge-off was indeed correct.[10]

Finally, ADCs can improve the ability of cedants to find favorable pricing for catastrophic XOL layers with lower attachment points above the policy limit on the ADC itself.

Example: The Turner & Newall Signaling Adverse Development Covers

Turner & Newall, a United Kingdom motor components manufacturer, utilized an ADC for signaling purposes—to combat a concern among investors and analysts that it had inadequately reserved against a major liability.[11] The liability for Turner & Newall was a series of asbestos claims associated with some of its discontinued operations. Having paid over £350 million in claims from the mid-1980s through 1996, uncertainties over the size of potential future claims had grown high—hence, the ADC.[12]

Turner & Newall self-insured its asbestos claims by establishing a captive and then reinsured some of that underwriting risk with an ADC. The ADC had a 15-year tenor and, like other finite risk products, contained an agreement for a partial premium rebate if actual loss developments were favorable relative to its reserve holdings after the 15 years. Provided by Swiss Re, Munich Re, and Centre Re, the finite risk product gave Turner & Newall protection against any additional liabilities incurred above a retention of £373

million in additional claims in exchange for a one-time premium payment by
Turner & Newall of £92 million. Within 20 minutes of the announcement of
the ADC, Turner & Newall's stock price had risen by 23 percent, and ended
that week more than 40 percent up.[13]

Retrospective Aggregate Loss Covers

ADCs are sometimes called *retrospective excess of loss covers* (RXLs). A final
type of retrospective finite risk ART form is called a *retrospective aggregate
loss cover* (RAL). Despite the name similarity to ADCs, RALs actually are
more similar to LPTs than to ADCs mainly because they can be used to increase the balance sheet equity of the cedant by replacing the technical reserves allocated to an unknown liability with a fixed premium payment
whose value is less than the current technical reserves.

In a typical RAL, the cedant can finance existing and IBNR losses by paying a premium to a (re-)insurer equal to the current value of reserves and then
ceding the liability to the (re-)insurer, just like a LPT. But unlike an LPT, a
RAL also usually includes a provision that requires the cedant to pay for any
losses over a specified amount or above a defined loss ratio when they are actually incurred by the cedant. In the LPT, the risk of a very large claim arriving unexpectedly early in the loss development cycle is borne solely by the
(re-)insurer, perhaps subject only to an aggregate or per risk policy limit. But
the RAL specifically forces the cedant to retain some of this timing risk. The
RAL thus involves less timing risk for the (re-)insurer than an LPT.

At the same time, the RAL provides some excess of loss protection on the
underwriting risk that an ADC would provide but that a typical LPT would
not. A RAL thus makes sense for firms with a primary concern about timing
risk but that are willing to retain some of that timing risk in exchange for
some actual aggregate excess-of-loss underwriting risk transfer.

Bundling Retrospective Finite Risk Solutions:
The Frontier Insurance Example

The three retrospective finite risk programs just discussed are different primarily in the way they address underwriting and timing risks. The relation
between risk financing and risk transfer, synthetic debt and equity, and timing versus underwriting risk is illustrated in Exhibit 19.3 for each of these
three products.

The exhibit naturally begs the question: What if a firm wants to cover
more than one of the regions of this figure in the same policy?

RALs provide the middle ground of cover for a firm wishing to mix a bit
of XOL underwriting risk reinsurance with timing protection. But in a RAL, a
cedant limits the timing risk protection it receives in order to acquire some

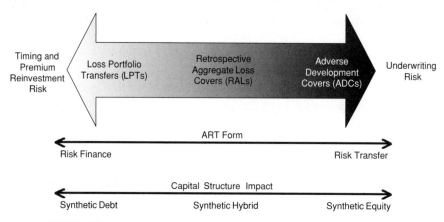

EXHIBIT 19.3   Retrospective Finite Risk Products and Synthetic Capital

adverse development protection on cumulative losses. We also can imagine a situation, however, when a firm wants both and may not be willing to trade off timing and underwriting risk in a manner as clear as that shown in the exhibit. In this case, the firm can bundle an ADC and an LPT into a single policy.

This is perhaps best illustrated by example. Frontier Insurance Company was a specialized property/casualty insurer that ran into financial problems in 2000.[14] It had $70 million in debt and had suffered significant losses on its physicians' malpractice insurance line. Frontier's losses were due both to inadequate reserves to cover total losses and to the unexpectedly rapid development of losses on the portfolio. Frontier had to replenish reserves several times to cover the time path of claims.

In the second quarter of 2000, Frontier entered into an option on a bundled finite risk agreement with Berkshire Hathaway's National Indemnity. If exercised, the option delivered $800 million in cover to Frontier, of which $514 million was an ADC that created XOL reinsurance for any aggregate losses in excess of Frontier's then-current reserves. The remaining $286 million in cover involved a cession of its current reserves to National Indemnity through an LPT, thus protecting Frontier from further unexpected accelerations in the timing of its claims submissions. National Indemnity thus allowed Frontier to transfer the underwriting risks and finance the timing risks of its existing physicians' malpractice line. In other words, National Indemnity allowed Frontier to finance its timing risks by replacing its reserves with synthetic debt and enabled the insurer to transfer its excess underwriting risks and replace those risks with synthetic equity.

Frontier exercised its option to obtain the $800 million in cover in late

2000. After ringfencing its liabilities in this manner, Frontier was able to cleanly exit this line of business and withdraw from the market in 2001.

PROSPECTIVE FINITE RISK PRODUCTS

All the finite risk products explored in the prior section are intended to help firms finance and/or transfer the risks associated with an *existing* liability. For an insurer, this may include unrealized or IBNR claims on a line of insurance policies already issued by the firm. For a corporation, existing liabilities may include contingent environmental cleanup costs, workers' compensation obligations, unrealized liability to hazards like asbestos in the workplace, and the like. The common denominator is that the firms in all these cases already have the liability.

Prospective finite risk products are designed to cover liabilities that a firm has not yet incurred, even on a contingent basis. For an insurer, this might include losses arising from a line of insurance policies that have yet to be written. A corporation, by contrast, could face this situation, for example, if it has an undetected Superfund chemical spill whose subsequent discovery will create a cleanup liability (as opposed to the identified Superfund site explored in the Iron Mountain example).

The basic structure of prospective finite risk products is similar to that of the restrospective products. Nevertheless, prospective finite risk products are different enough from retrospective finite risk solutions that some discussion is warranted.

Finite Quota Share Treaties

As discussed in Chapter 16, a quota share treaty is a form of proportional reinsurance rather than excess-of-loss reinsurance in which the assuming reinsurer agrees to pay a fixed or variable proportion of claims and loss adjustment expenses on a line of policies in return for receiving a proportion of the premium. In a traditional quota share agreement, the reinsurer's potential liability is limited only by the policy limits on the original policies ceded. If there are no policy limits, the reinsurer's liability is potentially unlimited.

The only real difference between a finite quota share treaty and a traditional quota share treaty is the explicit limitation of liability for the reinsurer in the former. Whether the ceded policies underlying the treaty have policy limits or not, the finite quota share imposes a contractual maximum obligation on the reinsurer.

Finite quota share treaties are useful mainly in the insurance market and have significantly less appeal to corporations. Their major function is to increase the accounting surplus of the cedant, usually for capital adequacy or regulatory purposes as discussed in Chapter 8.

In a finite quota share treaty, the primary insurer cedes part of its un-earned premium to the reinsurer along with the concomitant liabilities. In re-turn for this, the cedant receives a ceding commission. In this manner, the unearned premium is converted into current income. The finite quota share treaty thus is a pure risk financing product, converting an as-yet-unrealized stream of expected profits into a current income item.

The ceding commission together with the investment income on the un-earned premium reserves are expected to more than cover actual claims aris-ing on the new policy line. In the event that unexpected losses occur, the assuming reinsurer often is given the right to recover those losses from the ceding insurer over the term of the agreement.[15]

Just as the reinsurer wants to limit its loss exposure, the primary cedant also wants to retain the majority of profits on the underlying business line. To facilitate this, the ceding commission is often tied to a sliding scale that varies with the loss ratio—say, a 1 percent increase in commission paid for every 1 percent reduction in the actual loss ratio up to a maximum of 100 percent.[16] Alternatively, an experience fund can be established with a preagreed sharing rule for redistributing the profits between the cedant and reinsurer at the end of the life of the contract.[17]

Spread Loss Treaties

A second form of prospective finite risk product is called a spread loss treaty (SLT). Like finite quota share treaties, it represents a form of risk fi-nancing. In an SLT, the cedant pays an annual premium into an experience account over the multiyear term of the contract. Investment income on re-serves are credited to the experience account, and actual losses plus the reinsurer's arrangement fees are debited. If the fund goes into deficit, the primary insurer must pay increased premiums to restore the fund to bal-ance—including perhaps a final payment to ensure that the fund is in bal-ance when the SLT expires. But if the fund is in surplus, the fund's net investment income is distributed to the cedant. A surplus at the end of the life of the SLT results in a sharing of profits and thus a partial premium re-fund to the cedant.

The reinsurer's obligation is to make payments for claims as they occur, even if such claims create a deficit in the experience account. Any such losses are cumulated and then redistributed over the remaining term of the agreement, which can be quite long. The net effect from the cedant's per-spective is that the reinsurer is essentially prefunding losses and allowing the cedant to spread those losses out over a much longer period of time rather than incur them as they arise. The reinsurer does bear some underwriting risk in that structure, but usually subject to either an annual or an aggregate policy limit.

The SLT structure allows cedants to smooth the volatility of their claims payments and hence their earnings. In this sense, a SLT functions exactly like an earnings volatility or signaling capital reserve as discussed in Chapter 7. For this reason, SLTs are particularly popular for captives as a means by which the parent/sponsor of the captive can decrease its earnings volatility for all the possible reasons discussed in Part I.[18]

FINITE RISK VERSUS DERIVATIVES

As convergence products, finite risk ART forms can, not surprisingly, be offered directly by derivatives dealers. The degree to which corporations can look to swap dealers for the same sorts of protections afforded in finite risk products depends, however, on the specific risk management objective of the firm, as discussed in Chapter 10.

An LPT or SLT can be viewed as a type of income or asset swap of the kind discussed in Chapter 13. To illustrate this, suppose Firm Tangram has a retrospective liability with absolutely no prospect of adverse development—that is, the aggregate loss is essentially known. But the rate at which losses will arrive at Firm Tangram in the form of claims from claimants is not known, so the firm faces some cash flow timing risk and reserve reinvestment risk.

Exhibit 19.4 illustrates two ways that Firm Tangram can manage its timing and reinvestment risks, provided cash flow and value risk management (see Chapter 10) are its only concerns. In panel a, a LPT is shown in which Tangram cedes all of its liabilities to a reinsurer along with a premium of xxx basis points that will approximately equal its current technical reserves against the liability. The reinsurer assumes the liability and pays the claims when they arrive.

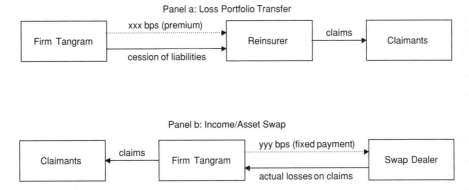

EXHIBIT 19.4 Loss Portfolio Transfer versus Income/Asset Swap

Panel b shows how a swap can be used to accomplish the same thing from a cash flow and value perspective. In the swap, Firm Tangram makes a regular payment to the swap dealer of yyy basis points. This payment may occur once at the beginning of the swap, as in a typical credit default swap, or can be made at regular intervals over the life of the swap, as in an income swap. (See Chapter 13.) The present value of the yyy basis points will be the same in either case. In exchange for making this payment to the swap dealer, the dealer agrees to pay Firm Tangram an amount equal to its realized losses on its claims when they occur. The income on the swap thus arrives at the same time as the payment Firm Tangram must make to the claimants.

As noted earlier, the equivalence of these transactions from a cash flow perspective does not imply equivalence in accounting earnings. If the firm does the LPT, the liabilities disappear from its balance sheet, whereas they do not in the case of a swap. Firms wishing to manage their earnings volatility thus cannot do so using the swap structure.

In general, provided that finite risk products satisfy certain criteria specified by tax and regulatory authorities, they are almost always considered insurance. And this can be a large part of their appeal for firms seeking protection primarily of their accounting earnings. The primary motivation underlying an SLT, for example, is to function as an earnings volatility reserve by swapping prospective losses that will occur with uncertain timing for a fixed "loss" in the form of a regular premium. Because an SLT does involve a material risk transfer, it is not pure premium financing, on which tax and accounting authorities tend to frown. But it is quite close. Derivatives rarely can achieve the same tax and accounting status and thus usually cannot be used for the specific purpose of earnings risk management in the context we have discussed it in this chapter.

Similarly, excess-of-loss reinsurance can be viewed as equivalent, from a cash flow or value perspective, to a vertical options spread. Adverse development covers thus can be constructed in the world of derivatives. And so on for the other finite risk products discussed here.

A major problem with using derivatives instead of finite risk products, however, is the need to customize the transaction to the specific liabilities of the firm seeking protection. For the most part, derivatives—even credit derivatives—tend to be cost effective only when their cash flows are based on products whose values and cash flows are fairly transparent—if not to the market at large, then at least to the swap dealer. But most firms seeking protection through finite risk products are interested in managing the risk of something extremely specific to their own balance sheets. More often than not, this may create a problem for derivatives dealers.

This situation brings up the distinction between an optionable and an insurable interest. Derivatives dealers tend to hedge their risk exposures rather than retain them. Reinsurers may either retain or hedge their exposures through retrocessions. In the case of finite risk products where timing risk is the major concern, however, reinsurers more often than not tend simply to retain the exposure. They ensure the transaction falls within their risk tolerances by virtue of the finite risk characteristics of the contracts themselves and thus do not assume more risk than they are prepared to retain. Accordingly, reinsurers do not really hedge these sorts of deals.

The problem, then, is that derivatives dealers cannot easily hedge products that are underlain by an insurable interest rather than an optionable interest. In order for a dealer to offer a product based on an insurable interest, the dealer essentially would also have to retain the risk. For a wide range of reasons, including capital requirements imposed on derivatives dealers that insurers do not face, in many cases dealers find the retention of these risks more costly than reinsurers do. We will run into some exceptions to this in Chapter 23, but for the most part, reinsurers are likely to provide corporations with a more cost-effective solution when the underlying liability whose risks need to be managed represents an insurable interest of the company without any traded market analogs.

NOTES

1. See Dyson (2001).
2. See Monti and Barile (1995) and Carter, Lucas, and Ralph (2000).
3. See, for example, Monti and Barile (1995), Phifer (1996), Carter, Lucas, and Ralph (2000), and Shimpi (2001).
4. Most finite risk products are designed to expose the assuming firm to a *reasonable potential* for a *significant loss*. See Phifer (1996).
5. Shimpi (2001) likens this sort of solution to the use of bridge banks in the United States following banking institution failures. A bridge bank receives the "good" parts of the failed firm and can be operated as a going concern, perhaps later to be sold to a new acquiring institution. The "bad" parts of the failed bank are left in the defunct receivership. Culp and Kavanagh (1994) discuss bridge bank and other run-off solutions for failed depository institutions involving significant amounts of over-the-counter derivatives.
6. See Carter, Lucas, and Ralph (2000).
7. See Shimpi (2001).
8. Background for this example was obtained from Lenckus (2000).
9. The settlement is still subject to a federal court approval.
10. Shimpi (2001) and Swiss Re, *Sigma* No. 5 (1997).
11. See Gerling Global Financial Products (2000).

12. See Buck and Riches (1999).
13. Ibid.
14. For a discussion of Frontier's situation and the finite structure it adopted, see "Frontier Gets a New Lifeline," *Reactions* (November 2000).
15. Monte and Barile (1995).
16. Carter, Lucas, and Ralph (2000).
17. Gerling Global Financial Products (2000).
18. See Carter, Lucas, and Ralph (2000), Gerling Global Financial Products (2000), and Shimpi (2001).

CHAPTER 20

Integrated Multiline and Multitrigger Alternative Risk Transfer Products

In this chapter we turn away from ART forms that are primarily intended to help firms finance their retained risks and begin to consider alternative risk transfer mechanisms—contracts, structures, and solutions that firms can use to transfer selectively some of their natural risk exposures to the equity holders of other firms. We saw in Part III that risk transfer can be accomplished through a variety of traditional avenues, including derivatives, securitization, asset divestiture, and (re-)insurance. Now our focus turns to nontraditional risk transfer methods.

Enterprise-wide risk management (EWRM) as a business process allows firms to exploit risk management and corporate financing efficiencies through more comprehensive risk identification, measurement, and control.[1] In response to the increasingly widespread recognition of the importance of EWRM as a management tool, many major players in the reinsurance world began to offer integrated risk management (IRM) products designed to provide enterprise-wide risk transfer solutions. The simultaneous coverage of multiple risks and the ability of firms seeking IRM solutions to participate with the capital provider in any *ex post* profits clearly establish these structures as *alternative*.

Some of the IRM products reviewed here have been remarkably successful at helping firms manage their overall cost of capital and optimize their balance sheets, whereas other IRM products have been dismal failures, culminating in the widely publicized dismantling of several IRM programs by such firms as Honeywell and Mobil Oil. In this chapter we explore the mechanics, benefits, and costs of the two primary types of IRM products—multiline comprehensive risk transfer products and multitrigger ART forms. In particular, we will attempt to distinguish between IRM ART forms that have come and gone as a passing fad versus those that seem to be here to stay and that genuinely can help firms revolutionize the way they finance themselves and manage their risks. The following questions are answered:

- What is the primary distinction between traditionally "layered" (re-)insurance risk transfer structures and integrated risk management ART products?
- What are multiline products, how do they work, and when do they make sense?
- What are multitrigger products, how do they work, and when do they make sense?
- How can IRM risk transfer products be combined with finite risk financing products to create synthetic hybrid securities?

LAYERED VERSUS INTEGRATED RISK TRANSFER

Risk transformation products often are distinguished from one another along three dimensions:

1. Length of coverage
2. Sequencing of losses borne by risk transfer counterparties
3. Types of risk resulting in potential losses

In this chapter we consider only multiyear contracts, which are prevalent in ART forms and derivatives and are increasingly common among traditional (re-)insurance structures.

The relation between the sequencing of losses borne by risk transfer counterparties and the types of risk giving rise to those losses is often different for traditional and alternative risk transfer products. The former are usually characterized by a "layered" approach in which individual risks are placed into silos and the risks are then transferred in layers—either "horizontal" or "vertical" layers or both. In several notable alternative risk transfer products, by contrast, risk and loss are combined into single "integrated" packages. Integration of risks across types within the same policy—multiline and multitrigger risk transfer solutions—is a sufficient condition for the solution to be considered an ART form, but it is not a necessary condition.

Layered Risk Transfer Products

Virtually all classical (re-)insurance products and many derivatives allow firms to manage their risks through an approach known as layering, which was introduced in Chapter 16. Because of the important distinctions between traditional layering and nontraditional integration, and the interactions between the two allocations of loss to different risk transfer counterparties, a thorough understanding of layering methods is requisite to our discussion of integrated risk products. Developing that understanding will prove easiest by example.

Consider a hypothetical nonfinancial corporation in Switzerland called Firm Wachau that buys coffee beans from Brazil and then sells ground coffee and coffee products in Europe and the United States. Suppose the firm has a financial capital structure consisting of common stock, senior bank debt, and junior subordinated bond debt. The three types of natural risks to which Firm Wachau is exposed include the following:

1. Production-related risks (e.g., supply chain risks, demand shock risks, etc.)
2. Financial risks
   a. Market risk
      (i) Interest rate risk on debt and other interest-sensitive assets and liabilities
      (ii) Exchange rate risk
      (iii) Commodity price risk on coffee purchases
   b. Credit risk on all assets
3. Operational and business risks
   a. Liability
   b. Property
   c. Casualty

The relation between the risk transfer product suppliers and the order in which those suppliers absorb losses incurred by Firm Wachau for the above risks is *layering*.

Vertical Layering

Classical insurance and reinsurance generally are considered "vertical" risk management products. The implication of this term can best be seen in a layer-cake diagram of the kind presented in Chapter 16. For each risk to which the firm is exposed, an insurance policy can be constructed to transfer some portion of that risk. Excess-of-loss reinsurance and classical insurance with both upper and lower attachment points (i.e., policy limits and deductibles, respectively) can be viewed in the context of loss layers that sit on top of each risk type like layers in a cake.

A vertical risk management program for Firm Wachau would involve a separate solution for each type of risk to which the firm is subject. For any given risk, a risk transfer solution might be adopted to limit the firm's exposure to at least some layers of that risk. Exhibit 20.1 provides one possible illustration of a vertical risk management program for a subset of the risks

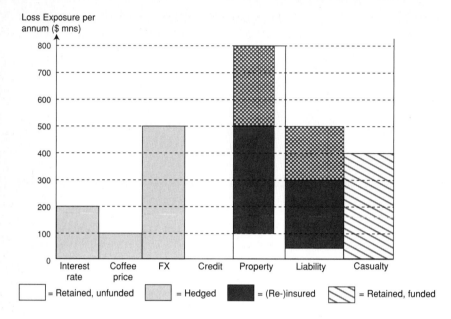

EXHIBIT 20.1   Vertical Risk Management Program

just mentioned. Note that the figure does not show the total potential exposure of the firm to each risk—for example, a 95th percentile annual VaR. We only know what the firm has hedged, not the proportion of its natural exposure or maximum reasonable loss that is hedged. As shown, in fact, all losses are presumed to be essentially unlimited (or, at least, greater than $800 million per annum).

The white and cross-hatched parts of the exhibit represent risks that the firm has retained. The former are retained and unfunded, whereas the latter—specifically, the first $400 million in casualty loss exposure—are prefunded. Suppose the prefunded casualty retention occurs through the use of either a formal self-insurance program or a rent-a-captive program. The unfunded retentions in the exhibit clearly include whole-risk types as well as certain layers for specific risks—namely, credit risk is left as an entirely unfounded retention, whereas unfounded retentions for the other risks are created by the presence of policy/derivatives coverage limits, deductibles, and the property copay requirement. To make it interesting, suppose credit risk is an unplanned retention and the others are planned but unfounded.

In Exhibit 20.1, the firm is presumed to hedge $200 million, $100 million, and $500 million of its annual exposure to changes in interest rates, coffee prices, and exchange rates. Assume these risks are hedged using derivatives negotiated with one swap dealer per risk or with exchange-traded futures.

Firm Wachau also is assumed to transfer some portion of its property, liability, and casualty risks using insurance contracts. For simplicity, suppose each risk is insured under a single blanket policy. The solid shaded area for each risk represents the coverage provided by the primary insurer on the first layer of potential losses (net of any deductible), and the dotted shaded areas represent additional layers of XOL insurance. As shown in Exhibit 20.1, the property insurance program involves a $100 million retention in the form of a deductible plus two insurance covers. The first cover is $400 million XS $100 mn policy limit with what appears to be a 10 percent copayment requirement. A second policy attaches to the firm's property loss exposure at the $500 mn attachment point and is an XOL policy for $300 mn XS $500 mn with the same 10 percent copayment provision. Liability risks are fully insured by a first-loss carrier for all losses above $50 million to a policy limit of $300 million, and a second carrier provides a $200 XS $300 XOL cover.

The reason that this program is referred to as a vertical risk management program is that each risk is managed independently of all the other risks facing the firm. Risks are put into "silos" and then managed one silo at a time based on the firm's tolerance to certain loss layers. Among other things, this means that the firm has at least one transaction or policy per risk, with all the premium and/or transaction costs that each individual transaction or policy might require. The vertical approach also means that one insurer's coverage is stacked vertically on top of another insurer's coverage.

Horizontal Layering

A risk management program also can be horizontally layered. Vertical layering implies that insurers cover different layers of risk within each silo, whereas horizontal layering involves multiple insurers participating alongside one another within a risk silo. Exhibit 20.2 depicts a horizontally layered program for Firm Wachau that provides the same risk transfer solution and leaves the firm with essentially the same ultimate risk profile as the vertical program shown in Exhibit 20.1.

In the horizontal program, Firm Wachau still has 90 percent of all property losses above $100 million covered up to $800 million, as before. In the vertical program, however, the first dollar of loss above $100 million. was covered 90 percent by a single insurer up to $500 million. A second insurer then covered 90% of additional losses from $500 million to $800 million. In the horizontal program, by contrast, property claims are split between two insurance companies from the first dollar loss (in excess of the $100 million deductible) up to the $800 million limit. Similarly, liability claims against Firm Wachau now are divided evenly between two different insurance companies for all losses in excess of $50 million and up to $500 million.

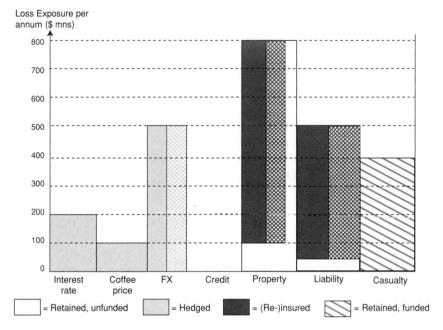

EXHIBIT 20.2   Horizontal Risk Management Program

Note in Exhibit 20.2 that the FX risk facing the firm also has been horizontally layered. This could be accomplished if Firm Wachau goes to one swap dealer for, say, its dollar/franc hedging and to another swap dealer for all other currency exposures.[2] Alternatively, Firm Wachau may partially hedge all of its currency exposures with multiple dealers.[3]

Vertical and Horizontal Layering by Risk Silo

Horizontal and vertical layering also may be combined within a particular risk silo. (They can also be combined *across* risk silos, but that will be discussed in the next section on integrated risk transfer structures.)

Exhibit 20.3 provides an example of both vertical and horizontal layering for specific risk silos—the property and liability risk silos for the firm, in particular. The checked pattern shown for each of these two risks indicates the involvement of a third insurer (possibly different for the two risks). In the liability risk silo, the first two insurers evenly divided the firm's liability claims above a $50 million deductible to a $300 million limit, and the third insurer then provides an XOL layer of $200 million in coverage with a $300 million attachment point.

Consider now the property risk silo. In this case, the first two insurers share 90 percent of the layer of losses from $100 million to $600 million. A

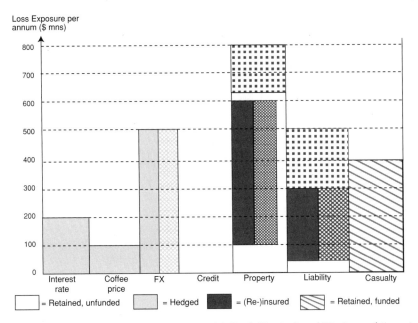

Loss Exposure per annum ($ mns)

□ = Retained, unfunded   ▨ = Hedged   ■ = (Re-)insured   ◨ = Retained, funded

EXHIBIT 20.3   Risk Management Program with Both Vertical and Horizontal Layering

third insurer then provides a $175 million XS $600 million layer of additional loss protection. Specifically, the third insurer appears to be providing $200 million of cover with a lower attachment point of $600 million but also with a deductible of $25 million. In addition, the third insurer provides a cover that does not contain a copayment provision.

Integrated Risk Transfer

When a single insurance company offers to underwrite losses arising from more than one source of risk (i.e., silo), the resulting risk transfer product is called an integrated risk management solution. IRM products arose in the 1990s as a response to the perceived need for EWRM. In particular, many people believed that the well-known efficiencies associated with identifying, measuring, and monitoring risk from an EWRM perspective (see Part II and Culp [2001]) could be repeated at the transactional level. IRM products thus arose as an explicit effort to reduce some of the inefficiencies known to be associated with classical silo-by-silo risk transfer products.

One major inefficiency often associated with layered (re-)insurance programs in particular is the overcommitment of capital such programs can engender. Consider again the layered program in Exhibits 20.1 to 20.3 in which at least one separate policy cover is taken out for each risk. Such a structure achieves a full risk transfer for each risk and over time. But if the occurrence of large losses across risks is not perfectly correlated, Firm Wachau will never actually need all of this insurance capacity at the same time. If forex and liability losses do not occur at the same time, for example, allocating capacity to the expected or worst-case loss on a silo basis overinsures the firm. On a correlation-adjusted portfolio basis, the total loss exposure of the firm is lower than the sum of the two individual risk silos.

IRM products can, in principle, help address this problem in two ways. First, firms can allocate less capital to their risks at a lower total cost when correlations across both time and risk types are factored into the premium charged for the policy. Second, firms can achieve a more customized, tailormade blanket of coverage that includes only those risks the firm is truly concerned about transferring to another party. At the same time, an IRM product also can be an effective way to catch "gaps" between silos or to cover unintended retentions, such as credit risk in the example of Firm Wachau.

The supposed benefits of a multiline IRM program do not just emphasize enhanced efficiency in capital utilization. In addition, most multiline policies are provided by a single carrier, thus reducing transaction costs and total arrangement fees. IRM products also are usually multiyear policies, thus simplifying renewals and/or reinstatements of policies.

MULTILINE PRODUCTS

"Integration" inevitably requires the inclusion of multiple risks in a single risk transfer product. In this section, we review multiline IRM products that achieve integration through an aggregate excess-of-loss structure designed to cover multiple sources of risk at the same time. Multiline policies may be created using either the attachment method or the single-text method.[4] If the attachment method is used, several individual monoline policies are grouped together, or "attached," using a single master agreement that creates the integrated risk policy. The single-text method, by contrast, involves the drafting of a new agreement that encompasses the terms of all the component monoline agreements. The former is generally cheaper but requires significant attention to conflicts and overlaps in definitions and policy terms.

Whatever mechanical method is chosen to draft the policy, it must contain at least one multiline trigger that clearly defines when the policy will be effective and can be invoked to cover actual losses sustained by the purchaser of the integrated coverage. In general, multiline policies created through the attachment method define insured events and losses according to the terms of the underlying monoline agreements, whereas single-text IRM policies usually explicitly enumerate the events and loss levels covered by the policy.

In and of itself, a multiline IRM program really contains nothing to separate it from traditional monoline insurance covers. What makes most multiline products ART forms is the multiple risks covered by the program. In addition, most IRM products include a feature that we encountered in Chapter 19 for finite risk products which allows the insured to participate alongside the insurer in certain profit circumstances. If the policy remains unused, a possible refund of some of the premium may be possible. Even if the policy is used, joint participation in excess investment income also may be possible.

Structures

Exhibit 20.4 depicts graphically how a multiline policy might work for Firm Wachau. The multiline product now provides combined coverage for all the risks shown up to an aggregate amount of $500 million and with a combined deductible of $50 million. Claims arising from any of the individual risks can be used to satisfy the deductible, and claims in excess of that $100 million deductible can be applied against the aggregate XOL policy limit of $500 million.

The exhibit superimposes the attachment points of the silo-specific program depicted in the earlier exhibits to show the apparent "gaps" in coverage that the multiline program creates. The light-shaded and cross-hatched bars

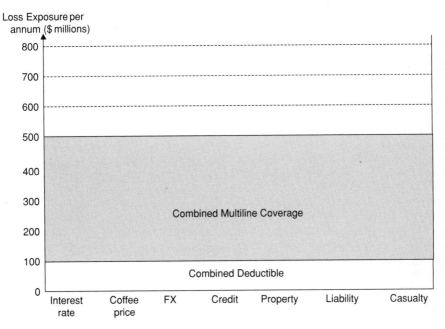

EXHIBIT 20.4 Integrated Multiline Risk Management Program

on Exhibit 20.5 indicate losses that would have been insured in the prior layered programs that now are not covered in the IRM policy.

Several of the coverage gaps appear around the first dollar loss and in the first layer. For interest rate, coffee price, and foreign exchange risk, the derivatives Firm Wachau was using before evidently covered the firm for its first dollar loss up to the limits of the hedging programs. Similarly, the $50 million deductible on the liability coverage is below the new $100 million deductible.

Before concluding these are true gaps in the multiline structure, however, it is important to consider how the aggregate deductible is set. In principle, the aggregate deductible level should be set to cover the firm's desired retention on a portfolio basis—that is, recognizing that all risks will not result in simultaneous losses. Firms offering IRM products assert that consider effort is undertaken to analyze their clients' actual loss experiences and to model financial risks—using both actuarial and financial modeling techniques—to arrive at an optimal retention level and lower attachment point (i.e., aggregate deductible). If indeed this modeling exercise yields the correct results, the so-called gaps in coverage for lower risk layers should not be gaps at all. Indeed,

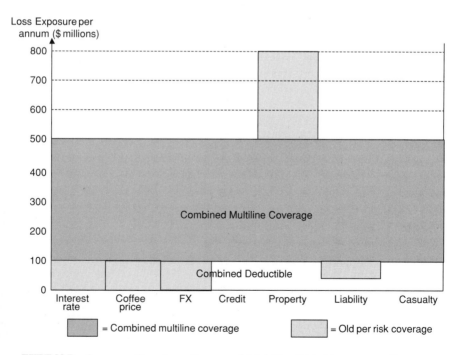

EXHIBIT 20.5 Coverage Gaps in an Integrated Multiline Risk Management Program

eliminating these coverages is one major supposed source of efficiency gains from integrated risk transfer solutions.

On the upper or catastrophic loss layers, firms usually can opt for supplemental risk/silo-specific XOL or catastrophic layer coverage. Firm Wachau had a policy limit of $800 million for its property exposures in the layered program, whereas the multiline program only provides total aggregate cover up to $500 million. As Exhibit 20.6 shows, however, a stand-alone policy providing $300 XS $500 XOL coverage for the catastrophic property loss layer can easily be added to the program.

Some IRM products also combine risk- or occurrence-specific limits with aggregate limits to help firms further customize their exposure. One such program is Swiss Re's Multiline Aggregated and Combined Risk Optimization (MACRO), a product aimed at nonfinancial corporations to help them bundle and tailor their exposure profiles and retention decisions. Depicted in Exhibit 20.7, the MACRO product is a multiline, multiyear structure that has a single annual aggregate deductible, a single aggregate exposure limit, and occurrence-specific catastrophic XOL supplements per risk silo at the customer's option. The program also may allow automatic or optional reinstatement if the customer wishes to simplify rollover decisions.

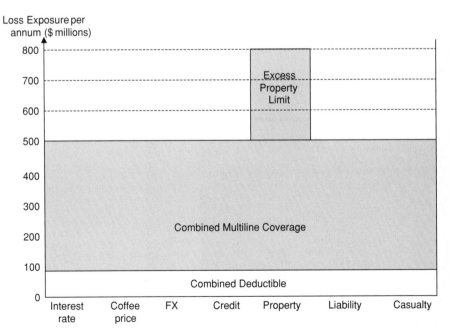

EXHIBIT 20.6 Multiline Cover with Optional Catastrophic XOL Coverage for Property

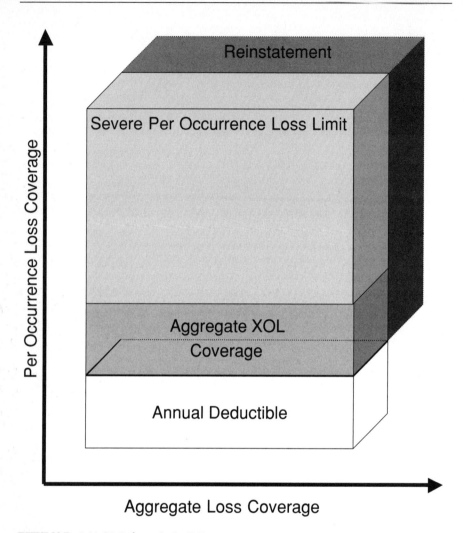

EXHIBIT 20.7 MACRO from Swiss RE
Source: Adapted from Swiss RE, *MACRO: A Holistic Approach to Multiple Risks*
(1997).

Range of Risks Covered

Many of the large reinsurance players have IRM product offerings. Some providers of these products include Centre Re Solutions (part of Zürich Financial), XL Capital, AIG, Munich-American Risk Partners, and Cigna. The risks covered by these programs ranges from two to virtually all.

Example: Cigna-XL Property/Casualty Twinpack

At the more focused end of the IRM spectrum are products now sometimes known as twinpacks that bundle only two related risks. A very popular such product was the joint offering by Cigna and XL Capital (an insurance provider that, along with ACE, gained prominence for being only catastrophic capital providers). The Cigna/XL twinpack covers high-layer property and casualty losses. Customers usually retain aggregate losses below about $2 million per annum and then either seek traditional insurance for the $8 XS $2 layer. (As will be discussed, some firms also use finite risk products in this layer to create a "bundled" program.)[5]

Exhibit 20.8 illustrates the distinction between the traditional separate-silo approach to property and casualty insurance and the ART multiline approach. In panel a, the traditional approach is shown in which a firm buys two separate policies for property and casualty coverage. Each policy has a

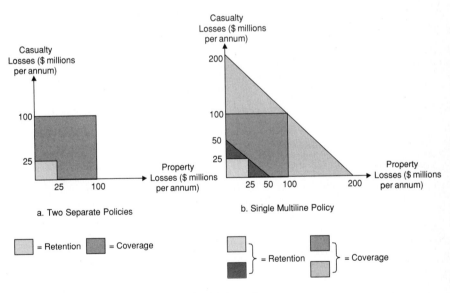

EXHIBIT 20.8   Typical Property/Casualty Twinpack
Source: Adapted from Shimpi (2001).

$25 million annual deductible, and each has a limit of $100 million. In panel b, the multiline version of the same policy is shown, where the aggregate deductible is now $50 million and the aggregate XOL cover is $200 million.

Panel b shows graphically the two major differences in coverage provided by the multiline policy. As the dotted region shows, the retention is now larger, so the multiline eliminates coverage for situations in which both property and casualty losses are low. Conversely, as the diagonally striped areas show relative to the old coverage square, high-severity losses of either type are now covered and were not before. The $200 million aggregate coverage thus might be spent on a single $200 million property or casualty loss, if required. This demonstrates the potential for such products to facilitate a better allocation of capital. Under the two separate policies, a $200 million property loss in the same year as zero casualty claims would leave the firm exposed to pay $100 million in property losses while leaving the $100 million in casualty unaccessible. The multiline policy allows capital to be applied wherever there is a loss.

Example: Insuring Earnings Per Share with AIG's COIN^sm and STORM^sm

The nature of multiline policies as synthetic equity that is not dedicated to a particular risk silo can best be seen by considering a multiline product at the opposite extreme from the twinpack. In the case of AIG's Commodity-Embedded Insurance (COIN^sm), the objective is to provide a product that delivers earnings per share (EPS) insurance. By including essentially all the major risk exposures that a firm might face, a multiline policy functions as a synthetic equity infusion for the firm that can be accessed any time total annual losses exceed the deductible. AIG's STORM^sm program is a similar EPS insurance structure with a bias toward helping firms manage adverse weather-related events. And Reliance Insurance Co.'s "Enterprise Earnings Protection Insurance" launched in 1999 offered indemnification against EPS shortfalls directly.

Multiline Successes and Failures

Some multiline policies have been very successful, whereas others have been dismal failures. In some cases, products marketed by large and reputable reinsurance firms were never bought and subsequently were taken off the market entirely, whereas in other cases the failures involved actually dismantling of multiline programs by their buyers. These failures have led many to question the viability of multiline policies.

Practitioners, commentators, and even providers of multiline products have given several reasons for the failure of such products to take off.[6] A major reason frequently cited is that some of the providers of early solutions emphasized multiline products as off-the-shelf products rather than tailor-made risk transfer solutions.[7] Similarly, many IRM products have met with little success because they tried to emphasize cost savings rather than optimal risk transfer. In particular, aggressive multiline policies approaching EPS insurance can create significant costs for the insurance provider that are difficult to recover if the product's main selling point is a lower premium.

Especially when the program includes financial risks, the (re-)insurer rarely will wish to retain 100 percent of the risk exposures in all categories. Consequently, the (re-)insurer is still faced with hedging, reinsuring, or retroceding the risks it is not prepared to retain. Integrating risks in the same policy allows the firm to charge a lower premium in principle because imperfect correlations across underwriting and timing risks allow better diversification. But unless the (re-)insurer can hedge or reinsure the risks it does not wish to retain using a similarly integrated product, its cost will essentially be the sum of the premiums of the risk transfer solutions for each risk managed separately.

In other words, many IRM products allow a (re-)insurer to offer an integrated solution but in turn merely push the unbundling problem back one level. Because a (re-)insurer will not offer policies at a loss, the load added to the original deal thus ultimately still must reflect the cost of risk transfer undertaken on a risk-by-risk basis.

A highly publicized illustration of this problem was the placement of an IRM solution with Honeywell that covered traditional insurance risks plus the foreign exchange risk facing the company. When Honeywell merged with Allied Signal, an assessment of the IRM program revealed that had Honeywell purchased separate insurance policies and engaged in classical hedging solutions to address its foreign exchange risk, it would have ended up with a cheaper risk transfer solution. Accordingly, the program was terminated and dismantled.

Mobil Oil also dismantled an IRM product—Swiss Re's BETA—in 1999 for the same reasons. And Utah-based petrochemical company Huntsman claims this was the reason it opted not to buy the risk solutions product offered by XL and Cigna in the first place, claiming that coverage with 30 different insurers was cheaper than the proposed combined policy.[8]

Nevertheless, some multiline policies do appear to have succeeded—at least as of this writing. Union Carbide recently renewed a major multiline IRM product,[9] and both Mead Corp. and Sun Microsystems claim to have saved over 20 percent by consolidating their numerous risk transfer policies into a single structure.[10]

While some firms claim to have achieved major cost reductions through multiline programs, many successful multiline structures have appealed to customers not because of the premium reduction they facilitate but rather because they allow customers to maximize capital efficiency and/or optimize coverage. Twinpack programs that couple somewhat related risks like property and casualty are an example of the former.

Example: The Marsh e-X Programme

A successful multiline program that shows the benefits of optimal packaging is the e-X Marsh Programme offered by Marsh Ltd., an MMC Company. The e-X program is a highly focused multiline product aimed at providing comprehensive insurance coverage for financial exchanges, clearinghouses, and settlement entities. The risks included in the most basic version of the e-X program include the following:

- *P/I*—failure of an exchange to maintain orderly markets, failure to monitor trading participants, noncompliance with regulation, inequitable application of rules, wrongful suspension of exchange trading members, etc.
- *Crime & Fidelity*—theft, fraudulent data input, manipulation of trading activity, fraudulent funds settlement instructions, sabotage, collusion, etc.
- *D & O*—breach of fiduciary management responsibilities, conflicts of interest, negligent misstatements of accounts, actions taken beyond scope of authority, unauthorized use of funds, etc.
- *Property & Business Interruption*—property damage, equipment damage, terrorism, IT failures leading to business interruptions.

A major appeal of this policy has been the use of a single underwriter to cover risks that are not only related but often are either duplicatively covered or inadvertently left out when single policies and multiple underwriters are used. Specifically, by integrating crime, fraud, negligence, and sometimes D & O and P/I in the same policy from the same underwriter, gaps are omitted and duplications avoided.

Although the e-X program may be cheaper than a number of separate policies, the major emphasis is on optimizing the coverage sought by exchanges and clearinghouses, not necessarily on reducing costs. In fact, costs *are* usually lower because Marsh is able to get the whole program underwritten by one or two (re-)insurers—usually Swiss Re or a panel of Lloyd's underwriters. But even were this not the case, the product likely will be successful anyway because of its packaging of risk transfer solutions in a highly tailored and hassle-free fashion.

Example: The United Grain Growers/Swiss Re Program

On a broader scale, most commentators are quick to admit that one clear-cut success of an IRM solution was the multiline program adopted by Winnipeg, Canada-based United Grain Growers (UGG).[11] Working together with Willis, UGG identified 47 risks affecting UGG's cash flows, earnings, and/or value. The most important of these was determined to be weather. Specifically, if UGG's grain volume falls, revenues can decline by as much as 20 percent—and the main reason for a decline in grain volume was determined to be the weather.[12]

After two years of work and deciding that neither weather derivatives nor stand-alone silo solutions made sense, UGG sought a multiline structure from Swiss Re. Although the specific retentions, limits, and premiums are not publicly available, it is known that the program is a three-year deal that combines credit, counterparty, weather, environmental, inventory, and grain price coverage with property/casualty cover. As concerns the grain volume component, UGG may make a claim for a loss based on differences in long-term grain volume averages and actual volume as measured by the Canadian wheat board.[13]

As with any EPS-like policy as comprehensive as UGG's, one risk for the (re-)insurer is the risk of significant moral hazard. A firm with EPS insurance can essentially kill itself and be sure that its financial results will be covered up to a point. In this manner, very comprehensive multiline programs function like put options on the earnings of the acquiring firm. With aggregate limits taken into account, the program is equivalent to a vertical spread on EPS, as discussed in Parts I and III.

In the case of UGG, Willis and Swiss Re agreed with the company that a good mitigant for the moral hazard problem would be to make the indemillionity of the policy contingent on declines in a grain volume index, whose value was not unduly influenced by UGG. That prevents UGG from pursuing a deliberately destructive strategy or from excessive underinvestment by tying the applicability of the claim to an index. Note that the grain volume index is not used to determine the economic loss sustained by UGG that Swiss Re has agreed to assume. Rather, the index is used as a second trigger for the activation of the policy.

MULTITRIGGER IRM PRODUCTS

With the exception of the UGG example, all of the discussion in the prior section involved IRM products with a single trigger. As long as aggregate losses on the different risk silos covered by a multiline policy exceed the deductible, the policy is triggered and an indemillionity payment can be sought for economic losses sustained. The single trigger is the condition that losses exceed the retention or deductible.

IRM products also may contain second triggers or, in the specific case of switching single triggers, a single trigger that acts like a double trigger. In this section we consider why such triggers can make sense for both the (re-)insurer and the purchaser of the ART form. We then examine alternative types of triggers.

Benefits of Multiple Triggers

The UGG case illustrates that a primary benefit of a second trigger is the mitigation of moral hazard problems. By making the policy conditional on a trigger or event whose outcome the risk transfer purchaser cannot influence, the (re-) insurer can be comfortable that losses have not been deliberately caused or loss mitigation mechanisms underutilized. Importantly, as noted above, second triggers of this sort affect the insured party's ability to make a claim but generally do not affect the amount of the claim itself.

A second reason for the recent proliferation in multitrigger structures is that they tend to be cheaper—often significantly so—than single-trigger solutions. The more conditions must be met in order for the policy to be drawn on, the cheaper will be the premium for the final solution.

Finally, multiple triggers can help (re-)insurers provide more tailored and better-optimized coverage to at least some of their customers, as some examples in the next section illustrate.

Mechanics of Multitrigger Structures

In an indemnity contract, at least one trigger is always that the insured party sustains economic losses arising from an insurable interest. Many traditional insurance products also include a second trigger tied to the occurrence of a discrete event, such as the realization of a hazard—for example, a flood occurs. In insurance parlance, the occurrence of the flood and the loss resulting from it are viewed together as a single trigger. It is a flood-related loss above the lower attachment point that triggers the policy.

In keeping with insurance jargon, we thus consider "discrete" triggers like the occurrence of an accident to be part of the terms of a policy and the definition of an insurable interest and not a trigger. Instead, we consider triggers specifically to include numerical conditions that must be satisfied in order for a policy to be effective.

Triggers and Moral Hazard

Doherty (2000) classifies triggers as either "internal" or "external," where the former is based on some variable specific to the cedant or corporate insurance purchases (e.g., bad earnings) and where the latter is outside the immediate control of the firm (e.g., exchange rate–related losses).

Although risk transfer solutions based only on internal triggers do exist, they are not very common. Such contracts expose the (re-)insurance capital provider to significant moral hazard, especially when the payment on the ART form is related to at least one of the triggers. Even when a firm's payment is based on an external index or is a nonindemnity value contract that pays a fixed amount to the insured, basing a trigger solely on variables under the firm's control can mitigate the firm's incentive to manage its risks effectively and can even create perverse incentives for fraud or deliberate underperformance.

Accordingly, double-trigger ART forms usually involve at least one external trigger.

Fixed versus Variable Triggers

A fixed trigger is a Boolean or binary operator that is either "on" or "off" based entirely on whether some numerical condition is satisfied. The fixed trigger in an indemillionity contract is almost always the development of economic losses at the cedant or corporate insurance purchaser in excess of the lower attachment point. For a multiline policy, the single flat trigger represents an aggregate loss in excess of the lower attachment point. In general, a fixed trigger is a completely exogenous numerical threshold that either is or is not satisfied.

Second and higher triggers also can be fixed. In the UGG example, the second trigger that must be "pulled" before the policy can pay out is a decline in the grain volume index by a prespecified amount. Because this amount is fixed and predefined as part of the policy, the second trigger is fixed.

A fixed first trigger is like a strike price in a traditional call or put option. If the option is not in the money, it cannot be exercised. A fixed second trigger resembles a type of barrier option, such as a knock-in option, where the instrike is just a fixed condition and usually is based on the same underlying variable as the first trigger.

A knock-in call option based on a share of common stock whose current price is $50 might have a strike price of $60 and an instrike of $100. The first trigger is pulled when the option moves into the money—that is, the price per share of the common stock goes above $60. But the option still cannot be exercised because the stock price is below the instrike—that is, the second trigger has not been pulled. When the stock price doubles relative to its current value, the second trigger is pulled and the option can be exercised for an immediate payment of $50.

As in the derivatives example, in insurance contracts with fixed triggers, usually the triggers do not affect the payout on the contract. The fixed triggers exist solely to limit the conditions under which the policy can be exercised but do not usually affect the value of the policy conditional on an exercise occurring.

A contract has a variable trigger if the trigger condition depends entirely on the realization of one or more random variables. First triggers are very rarely variable because they depend on the level of losses sustained relative to a fixed attachment point. But even a first trigger can be variable if the attachment point itself is variable.

Suppose a firm is concerned with "basis risk," or the risk that its specific loss development exposure will differ from "average losses" or "representative losses" reflected in some index. Take, for example, a catastrophe insurer that wants to reinsure the risk that its actual losses will exceed the losses on an index like the Property Claims Services (PCS) catastrophic loss index. In that case, the firm could buy insurance coverage with a lower attachment point equal to the current level of the PCS index plus a fixed deductible. If the firm's actual losses are below the reported index losses, the insurance does not pay. Conversely, the policy pays an amount equal to firm's excess loss over the index if such an excess exists. This type of insurance structure is equivalent in a capital markets context to an "outperformance" or "relative spread" option.

A second trigger may be added that also affects the insurance payout, but this need not always be the case. A second trigger added purely to mitigate moral hazard, for example, may dictate when the policy pays but not what the policy pays. To return to the previous example, the catastrophic insurer might reinsure its exposure using a standard XOL policy with a first trigger based solely on a fixed lower attachment point to which actual losses are compared. But the firm might add a second trigger that states it cannot make a claim unless its losses exceed losses reported in the PCS index.

If the first trigger is fixed, the second trigger variable, and the payout un-related to the second trigger condition, we have a structure that is virtually identical to a barrier option. In this case, the instrike is a variable condition that fluctuates with its index variable, but once the instrike has been crossed, the option is alive and the payout is based solely on the economic loss of the claimant relative to a fixed attachment point.

Switching Triggers

Multiline policies often have switching single triggers, or single triggers that vary based on some weighting scheme defined in the trigger definition across the multiple risks covered by the policy.

A switching single trigger often generates coverage that is more similar to a fixed double trigger than to a fixed single trigger. To see this, an example will help illustrate. The particular product, developed by Swiss Re, is aimed specifically at insurance companies that are concerned about joint underwriting losses and investment losses on the assets held to fund their technical reserves.[14]

Consider first a fixed single trigger that provides a fixed retention amount relative to an aggregate loss development experience arising from both invest-ment and underwriting losses. Exhibit 20.9 illustrates the coverage provided by such a policy with an aggregate limit of $Y million and a deductible of $X million, which is essentially the same as the capital provided through a twin-pack examined earlier in this chapter. The retention level is $X million per an-num, meaning that the first and only trigger requires that actual losses on the insurer's investments *or* its underwriting activities *or* both must exceed $X million before a claim can be made.[15]

Now consider a double trigger policy, where each trigger is fixed. To keep

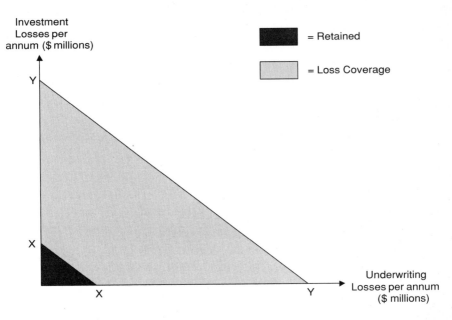

EXHIBIT 20.9   Multiline Policy with a Single Fixed Trigger

things interesting, suppose the triggers are not equal and that the insurer can make a claim only when annual investment losses exceed $X million *and* annual underwriting losses exceed $Z million. The aggregate policy limit remains $Y million as before. This type of structure provides a lower total coverage area than either two separate policies or a single-trigger policy. Accordingly, the coverage is cheaper. (See Exhibit 20.10.)

If assets invested to fund premium and loss reserves perform well, the double-trigger reinsurance will not activate even if underwriting losses are high. And if investments perform poorly but underwriting losses are low relative to premiums collected, the policy again will not activate. Such a double-trigger structure thus can be a very appealing low-cost source of protection for insurance companies that are concerned only with situations when both investment and underwriting losses are high.

Now consider the switching single trigger. Policies such as the Swiss Re investment and underwriting multiline policy often are designed to help firms optimize both their assets and liabilities (i.e., assets invested to fund premium and loss reserves and actual losses, respectively). A switching single trigger can help achieve that kind of optimization by allowing the trigger to be defined in

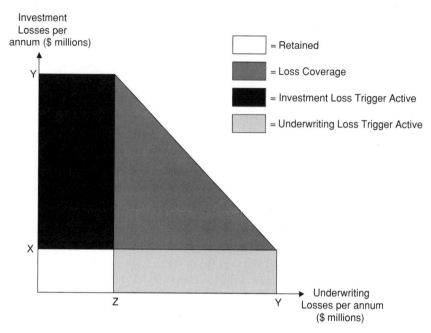

EXHIBIT 20.10   Multiline Policy with a Double Trigger, Both Triggers Fixed

terms of specific weights on the assets and liabilities in question—in this case, investments and underwriting claims.

An interesting version of the switching single trigger in the Swiss Re structure is designed to accommodate particularly strong investment or underwriting performance. The weights that define the trigger thus shift to allow cedants to bear more risk on one side of their balance sheet when the other side is enjoying very strong performance.[16]

Exhibit 20.11 shows the loss coverage area resulting from a single switching trigger centered at switching point S. The dashed line at $X provides a comparison to the comparable fixed single-trigger structure shown in Exhibit 20.9. To see how the switching trigger works, consider first a low underwriting loss level L°. Under the single fixed trigger, the policy is activated when investment losses rise to I*. But under the switching trigger, the investment loss trigger now kicks in at a higher loss level for good underwriting results. At loss level L°, the policy thus will not pay until investment losses reach I** > I*.

Similarly, consider a year when investment losses are low at I°. The single fixed trigger would make the policy active at underwriting loss level L*. But because the investment loss is low, the insurer does not necessarily require coverage unless underwriting losses are very large. So under the switching sin-

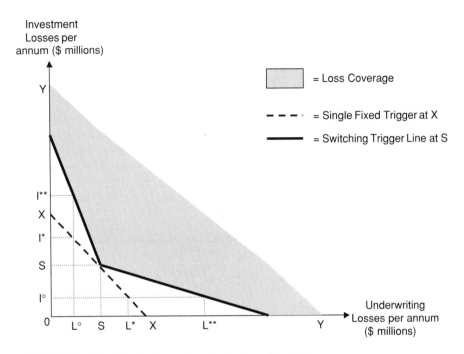

EXHIBIT 20.11   Multiline Policy with a Single Switching Trigger
Source: Based on Schön, Bochicchio, and Wolfram (1998).

gle trigger, the policy is activated only when underwriting losses exceed L** for investment loss level I°.

In general, the slope of the lines emanating from switching point S dictate the degree to which investment losses must be large for a given underwriting loss and vice versa. By this means, the insurer can reduce the cost of the policy relative to a single-trigger multiline aggregate excess of loss policy and can tailor its coverage to its net asset and liability position.[16]

In a capital structure context, this switching single-trigger multiline XOL policy resembles quite closely a synthetic equity issue that is engineered to be triggered only to supplement the equity of the firm following a very specific kind of asymmetry in the performance of the firm's insurance assets and liabilities.

Per Occurrence versus Cumulative Triggers

Care must be taken to determine whether a fixed trigger resets and/or has some lasting impact on the indemillionity of the contract. Some knock-in options are exercisable only when the underlying price is above the in-strike, whereas others are knocked in once and for all if the underlying price ever exceeds the instrike. Similarly, the nature of an insurance trigger must be examined carefully to determine whether the trigger is pulled once and for all or whether it has some kind of reset.

In general, multitrigger policies or single-trigger multiline policies (see below) are also multiyear policies. Accordingly, the triggers for these policies usually reset each policy year. Within a policy year, however, the triggers may take either of the above forms. Triggers based on cumulative underwriting losses of any kind are virtually always once-and-for-all triggers because of the cumulative nature of the triggering variable—that is, a firm cannot incur negative losses that reverse a cumulative underwriting loss number.[17] But triggers based on other variables, such as financial market indexes, can move around quite a lot, and the nature of coverage provided by the product can change substantially depending on the nature of the trigger.

Example: Swiss Re's Telecomm Business Interruption Protection

A good example of a creative double-trigger program can be found in Swiss Re's business interruption (BI) protection, a package specifically tailored to and aimed at the BI concerns of telecommunications firms.[18] The BI protection structure uses a fixed first trigger and a variable second trigger, and has a payment to the policyholder that is determined by the same variables underlying the second trigger.

The basic premise of the Swiss Re BI policy is that BI losses are most damaging to firms when they occur at the same time that a firm is experiencing worse-than-normal cash flows. The first trigger is a traditional fixed trigger that ensures the policy can be activated only if economic losses arise as a direct result of operational risks leading to business interruption. The hazards and risks included in the policy include large property damage, natural disasters, IT systems failures, billing problems, malicious computer sabotage, and the like. The second variable trigger is based on the cash flows of the firm relative to the cash flows of an industry peer group. Specifically, the firm's earnings before interest, tax, depreciation, and amortization (EBITDA) are compared to the EBITDA of its peers. When the firm's EBITDA growth rate falls to, say, more than three percentage points below the growth rate of an index of other telecom firms, the second trigger is activated. The value of the policy to the holder then is based on this EBITDA shortfall.

The four benefits of this particular transaction in the context of the issues explored in Part I are obvious.

1. The BI protection with an underperformance EBITDA second trigger creates access to preloss finance for the firm on preloss financing terms.
2. The product reduces cash flow volatility and will help its users mitigate underinvestment problems.

3. Managerial risk aversion or asset substitutions problems that could lead managers to pursue projects with excessively low volatility will be less likely with a BI protection cover triggered at times of cash and earnings shortfalls.
4. The cover will allow the firm to reduce paid-in capital reserves during normal business periods, thereby increasing debt capacity for users.

BLENDED COVERS

Multiline and multitrigger IRM products often are combined with finite risk products in what are called *blended covers*.[19] A blended cover ART supply product is essentially a mixture of risk transfer and risk financing.

Early multiline IRM products emphasized their ability to help firms avoid the practice known as trading dollars. Trading dollars occurs when a firm pays premiums for highly predictable risks and finds itself getting that premium back in the form of claims that could easily have been anticipated. An obvious way to avoid trading dollars in this fashion is through self-insurance or a planned retention. Multiline policies such as Swiss Re's BETA were designed to help firms address this problem, although such products were never particularly successful for reasons noted earlier.[20]

Multitrigger structures and multiline products that emphasize optimal risk packaging instead of premium reduction have enjoyed considerably more success than highly comprehensive (and hence extremely expensive to hedge) multiline programs aimed at essentially insuring a firm's EPS. To the degree the need for a pure financing component is still required, finite risk products like those discussed in Chapter 19 can be combined easily into a multitrigger or multiline aggregate XOL risk transfer program. On their own, multitrigger and multiline XOL policies as pure risk transfer devices essentially function as synthetic equity. When combined with finite risk products designed mainly to help firms prefund their losses and manage their reinvestment or timing risks, the result is a synthetic mezzaninelike structure or a synthetic hybrid security.

NOTES

1. Part II of Culp (2001) discusses the benefits and practices of EWRM.
2. Swap dealers do indeed specialize by currency, so this is not an implausible example.
3. We said nothing about the possibility for Firm Wachau to layer its FX risk *vertically*. This would require that one swap dealer be on the hook for the first $X in losses and another for the next $Y in excess of $X, and so on. It would be possible to construct such a "sequential loss" hedge using options with staggered striking prices; swaps and futures would not work.

4. This terminology and the ensuing discussion is based on Hoffman (1998).
5. See Young (1996).
6. See, for example, Lonkevich (1999).
7. See Banham (2000).
8. Ibid.
9. Ibid.
10. Gerling Global Financial Products (2000).
11. Compare Banham (2000), Gerling Global Financial Products (2000), and Green (2001). The UGG risk transfer program is discussed at length in the thoughtful paper by Harrington, Niehaus, and Risko (2002).
12. See Banham (2000).
13. See ibid. and Green (2001).
14. This example is based on Schön, Bochicchio, and Wolfram (1998).
15. In practice, the underwriting losses probably would be based on the loss ratio rather than actual dollar losses.
16. Schön, Bochicchio, and Wolfram (1998).
17. It is possible, of course, that losses will get revised based on recoveries, but loss triggers typically are based on final loss ratios net of recoveries and relative to premium.
18. For a description, see Imfeld (2000).
19. The term "blended cover" also sometimes is used to describe combinations of traditional reinsurance with finite risk products, understandably leading to some confusion.
20. In addition to being an early proponent of products like BETA, Swiss Re also has been an early proponent of moving beyond products like BETA. Swiss Re now emphasizes relationship-oriented solutions in which the reinsurer helps clients optimize their balance sheets on a long-term, ongoing basis rather than through a series of off-the-shelf product offerings. See, for example, Winston (2000).

CHAPTER 21

Committed Capital and Guarantees

This chapter examines the products that many consider to be the true state-of-the ART of risk transfer and risk finance. In the context of Part I, these products are the closest substitutes to the direct issuance of new financial capital claims by a firm that exist today in the ART world—and perhaps in the investment banking world as well.

Both contingent debt and equity are examined here as sources of risk finance and risk transfer that firms can access postloss, but on preloss financing terms. Committed capital is a debt substitute for risk finance, and guarantees are an equity substitute. We also review some of the synthetic equity products offered as pure capital market solutions, such as loss equity put options and reverse convertibles. All of these structures can be used for risk capital, signaling capital, preloss funding, or to reduce the firm's total cost of capital in a trade-off or pecking order world. These products make the most sense in the latter context as means by which firms can obtain new capital without incurring the adverse selection costs of going to the public capital market.

Specifically, this chapter addresses the following questions:

- What is committed capital, how is it a substitute for issuing new debt, and what are some concrete examples of these products?
- What is a guarantee, how is it a substitute for issuing new equity, and what are some of the successes and failures of recent guarantee structures?
- How have "residual value" guarantees been applied successfully in the area of aircraft finance?
- What are some of the primary capital market products that also can be used by corporations seeking to issue synthetic equity postloss on preloss terms?

RISK FINANCE WITH COMMITTED CAPITAL

A *committed capital* facility is an option on paid-in capital, as we explored in Chapters 2 and 7.[1] Usually (re-)insurance companies provide risk financing through committed capital.

Committed capital is usually contingent debt or a contingent hybrid. Accordingly, it is an ART form that usually does not directly relate to specific risk exposures of the acquiring firm. Committed capital is basically *unrestricted*, thereby making it a nearly pure substitute for the firm issuing new securities on its own.

Mechanics

In this section we review the significant terms of committed capital facilities that help characterize their mechanics. Viewing committed capital as an option, the terms of the committed capital facility include a definition of the triggering event(s), the terms of the underlying paid-in capital to which the purchaser has drawing rights, the expiration date of the contingent capital option, the price of the facility, covenants, redemption alternatives, and timing of payment.[2] Each of these is discussed briefly below.

Trigger(s)

Like the multitrigger products reviewed in Chapter 20, most committed capital products include a second trigger to mitigate moral hazard concerns. The first trigger is pulled when the option goes into the money. Interestingly, this first trigger condition is usually not defined as an explicit part of the committed capital agreement. Nevertheless, the firm that has bought an option on paid-in capital clearly will not exercise that option unless the intrinsic value is positive. In other words, if the firm can obtain equivalent capital more cheaply from some other source, the committed capital option will be out of the money and will expire worthless.

The second trigger in a committed capital facility, however, usually is designed to help ensure that the first trigger also will be pulled and that the capital is indeed available when the firm most needs it. But because the second trigger is a moral hazard mitigant, it usually is tied to a variable that is not under the direct control of the committed capital purchaser, even though the variable almost certainly will be highly correlated with a variable of direct interest to the firm. The UGG grain volume index trigger, for example, was outside the control of UGG but nevertheless highly correlated with its need for its multitrigger IRM facility.

Underlying Security

Committed capital usually gives a firm the option to issue paid-in debt or hybrid capital, where the latter may sometimes be in the form of fixed-term preferred stock. In virtually all cases, the security that is issued to the holder of the committed capital line when that line is drawn is issued on terms that are predefined at the beginning of the life of the contingent capital option—that is, before the security actually is issued. This helps ensure that committed capital facilities are negotiated on preloss financing terms.[3]

The debt or hybrid capital provided upon exercise of a committed capital facility almost always has a fixed maturity date. Whether the underlying security is technically debt or equity, the purpose of committed capital thus is virtually always risk finance rather than risk transfer.

Several early IRM and committed capital products resulted in the capital provider becoming a major shareholder of the firm to which it was providing capital. This is not usually the core business of the (re-)insurance capital provider, and the writer of a committed capital option often prefers to avoid this situation.

As long as the committed capital calls for the issuance of a straight debt security or private debt placement, redemption is not a major concern. The capital provider simply will be paid back when the debt matures. But if the committed capital calls for a hybrid or equitylike capital infusion, the facility may include alternative redemption methods for the capital provider. For example, the facility may contain a provision that allows the (re-)insurance provider to convert its financial capital claim on the borrowing firm into traded securities issued by the borrowing firm, thereby facilitating the sale of those securities if the (re-)insurer so desires.

Other elements of optionality may be included in the underlying capital claim, provided they do not give too many rights to the capital provider. The securities issued in a committed capital program usually are not putable by the security holder, for example. Including a put provision would make the capital less than fully committed and thus would not serve the purpose for which it is usually intended.

Expiration Style and Date

Committed capital facilities are American and usually have tenors less than the tenors of the underlying securities to be issued. For clarity, suppose the committed capital facility is negotiated on date t and expires on date τ. Suppose further that if exercised, the option writer provides committed capital in the form of debt securities that mature on date $T > \tau$.

If the triggering event does not occur in the interval from t to τ, the committed capital facility will expire worthless. But if it does occur, the firm has the right but not the obligation to acquire paid-in debt or hybrid capital on prenegotiated terms. Suppose the firm exercises this right on date $t + k$. The balance sheet of the firm then usually shows a new liability of the firm as of date $t + k$ that matures on date $T + k$.

Price

The price of a committed capital facility is essentially the option premium plus any loading the capital provider adds. The actual pricing can be structured like an option premium to be paid up front or like the commitment fee paid for a letter of credit. Especially if the committed capital facility contains an option for the buyer to terminate the facility early, some or all of the premium on the unused portion of the option may be returned.

In addition to the premium and the load, the price of a committed capital facility also may include a financing rate on the underlying security if the option is exercised. Shimpi (2001) explains that the financing rate can be fixed or floating and may be tied to the credit rating of the firm. Borrowers can opt for a higher option premium and a lower financing rate or vice versa, depending mainly on their view of whether the committed capital facility will move into the money and be drawn or not.

Covenants

Although the main deterrent to moral hazard is the second trigger, committed capital facilities also often include covenants that are further intended to protect the capital provider from the adverse consequences of asymmetric information. One such covenant is usually an *ex ante* due diligence process that is itself designed to eliminate as much of the information asymmetry as possible. If a prospective buyer of committed capital does not cooperate with and agree to a due diligence process, the facility may never be negotiated successfully. Similarly, if the due diligence process results in specific recommendations for the firm (e.g., appoint a chief risk officer), committed capital may include covenants to ensure those recommendations are followed.

Committed capital facilities are designed to be more readily available and less restrictive than traditional contingent capital vehicles such as bank-provided LOCs. Nevertheless, committed capital facilities usually also contain some form of MAC clause to ensure that the capital provider is not undertaking a new T-year credit risk with a firm that is days away from bankruptcy.

Other covenants found in committed capital facilities may include change-of-control covenants that allow for early exit if the firm changes hands, optional early redemption features, restrictions on the firm's investment decisions, specific targets for the firm's financial ratios (e.g., minimum net worth requirements), and the like.[4]

Timing of Payment

Once exercised, the capital provider writing the subject capital option can buy securities reasonably quickly. But for reasons noted in Chapter 12, non-banks may not always be able to send cash to borrowers fast enough to make them happy. When short-term funds are required, (re-)insurers can provide a bank wrap for the committed capital product that will ensure funds flow to the borrower almost immediately. For the right price, the facility even can be structured to ensure that the borrower receives firm paid-in capital within 24 hours of exercise of the option.

Swiss Re's Committed Long-term Capital Solutions

Swiss Re has successfully placed committed capital several times using its Committed Long-term Capital Solutions (CLOCS) product. Two of these CLOCS issues are particularly noteworthy and are summarized in the sections below.

Royal Bank of Canada

In October 2000 Swiss Re negotiated a committed capital facility with the Royal Bank of Canada (RBC) in which Swiss Re would provide C$200 million (US$133 million) to RBC in exchange for preferred stock in RBC at the spread prevailing on October 27, 2000—the date the CLOCS deal was negotiated. The triggering event is tied to RBC's loan portfolio and is activated when the bank incurs "exceptional" credit losses that are in high-loss layers but that are not so high as to expose the firm to default risk.[5] The C$200 million would result in Swiss Re owning about 1 percent of the firm's total equity if the facility is exercised, so Swiss Re did not need to worry about having to "run the company" one day.

Apart from the obvious advantage of helping RBC secure funding on preloss terms, the committed capital facility helps RBC in several other specific ways. First, it helps RBC lower the cost of funding its loan-loss reserves. As RBC executive David McKay indicated, "It costs the same to fund your reserves whether they're geared for the first amount of credit loss or the last amount of loss. . . . What is different is the probability of using the first loss amounts versus the last loss amounts. Keeping capital on the balance sheet for a last loss amount is not very efficient."[6]

By covering the upper layers of RBC's loan loss reserves, the CLOCS structure also helps RBC improve its financial ratios. Swapping balance sheet reserves for contingent capital increases RBC's return on equity, for example. In addition, early indications are that AAA-contingent capital provided by Swiss Re will be regarded as an acceptable substitute for Tier I capital under the Basel Accord by the BIS. (See Chapter 8.) Although the pricing terms of the deal were not disclosed, press accounts suggest it is far below the cost RBC would have incurred from issuing new Tier I capital directly, especially when costs like those explained in Chapter 5 are taken into consideration.

From Swiss Re's perspective, the risk of the deal includes the risk that a correlated shock to the Canadian economy could adversely impact loss developments on RBC's loans as well as moral hazard associated with RBC's lending behavior. To address the latter, Swiss Re undertook a massive due diligence and risk modeling effort until it was satisfied with the risk/pricing trade-off. Indeed, Swiss Re did not syndicate or reinsure any of the RBC deal; it retained 100 percent of the exposure.

Compagnie Financière Michelin

Together with Société Générale (SocGen), Swiss Re also placed a CLOCS facility with Switzerland's Compagnie Financière Michelin, the financial and holding company for French tire maker Michelin. The deal has been (rightly) heralded as one of the most innovative and successful corporate financing transactions of the last decade.

Michelin's deputy chief financial officer Jacques Tierny was known and well regarded as highly progressive on corporate financing matters well before the recent deal. Michelin, for example, is one of the few major nonfinancial corporations around the globe to employ a highly sophisticated and comprehensive risk-adjusted capital allocation model. In conjunction with a value-at-risk-based risk measurement system, Tierny has focused for several years on "unifying" corporate finance and risk management to optimize the firm's balance sheet and capital structure. CLOCS was another step in that direction.

The Michelin deal is actually part bank debt and part CLOCS. SocGen has granted Michelin the right to draw a bank credit facility up to 2005, and Swiss Re has given Michelin an option for five years to issue subordinated debt maturing in 2012.[7] The bank line is a classic banking product with no trigger, but the CLOCS option can be exercised only when the combined average growth rate of gross domestic product (GDP) across the European and U.S. markets in which Michelin is active falls below 1.5 percent from 2000 to 2003 or below 2 percent from 2004 to 2005. Michelin's earnings are highly correlated with GDP growth in these markets, but because GDP growth is a variable outside the direct control of Michelin management, moral hazard risks are mitigated.

The linking of the deal to low earnings is based on several ideas. The first is that the firm is more likely to restructure in a low-earnings environment, and additional capital would facilitate any such restructuring. In addition, the contingent capital will give Michelin access to adequate funds to exploit potential acquisition opportunities—that is, to avoid the cost and difficulty of having to issue new equity in a low-earnings environment in order to exploit positive NPV investment opportunities, just as in the classic rationale underinvestment scenarios explored in Part I.

The wish to avoid negotiating new financing around a potential acquisition is based in part on the history of the loan that the CLOCS replaces—a 15-year subordinated debt placement that was serving as bridge equity capital to help strengthen Michelin's balance sheet following its 1990 acquisition of Uniroyal Goodrich.[8] Rather than remarket the old loan, Tierny opted for the combined banking/CLOCS facility.

If drawn, Michelin pays an arrangement fee of 35 basis points per annum and 30 basis points for the banking and insurance facilities, respectively. The higher price on the banking facility owes to the absence of a triggering mechanism. Once drawn, the deals will be remarketed in years 6, 8, and 10. Tierny managed to cut costs on the original sub-debt bridge loan from 120 basis points to 60 basis points using the same remarketing strategy.[9]

Unlike the RBC deal, Swiss Re syndicated the Michelin deal, partnering with firms like Credit Suisse's Winterthur to spread the risk of the deal around. One advantage of syndicating the deal mainly across reinsurance companies is their lower capital requirements. The syndication fees and terms of the loan thus were reportedly significantly below those that would have been available either from a pure banking syndicate or from an investment bank.[10]

The SocGen banking side of the deal also was syndicated. Participants in the final structure apart from Swiss Re, SocGen, and Winterthur included BNP-Paribas, Crédit Lyonnais, Crédit Mutuael Banque Populaire, and others.[11]

RISK TRANSFER THROUGH GUARANTEES

A *guarantee* is an alternative risk transfer (as opposed to risk finance) form that functions as a nearly pure substitute for new equity. The British spelling of the noun is *guaranty*, which also is increasingly being used as an American spelling. Both should be interpreted to mean the same thing in this chapter. Not surprisingly, guarantees often are called simply *synthetic equity*.[12]

Mechanics and Benefits

The mechanics of a guarantee are simple. The capital provider and corporate customer agree to a trigger event and the terms of the underlying paid-in capital to be provided, and unless the corporate customer attempts to defraud the (re-)insurance company providing the capital, the corporation can access the capital unconditionally when the trigger is activated. Documentation for a true guarantee is short and to the point, contains very few covenants and restrictions, and generally does not involve any redemption issues. In short, if the trigger is active, the guarantor pays up, thus providing the buyer of the facility with cash in lieu of obtaining that cash through a new equity issue.

Guarantees fully transfer risk from their purchasers to the capital provider, although the guarantee itself is usually very broad in what risks are being assumed. The most prevalent guarantees observed to date have involved credit event triggers—specifically outright events of default. If a default occurs, the guarantor pays all the default-related losses up to the policy maximum.

Firms usually seek guarantees as signaling or risk capital. In the latter case, customers may need the funds quickly for liquidity risk management purposes following the occurrence of a triggering event. When funds are required within a few days of the triggering event, combining a guarantee provided by (re-)insurer with a bank wrap is not uncommon. Specifically, when a loss occurs that activates the trigger, a bank will accept a transfer of the payment obligation from the (re-)insurance company as collateral for a short-term loan. The bank then pays the claimant immediately and is repaid a few days later when the (re-)insurer settles up.

Guarantees may be placed directly or may be provided to SPVs or other entities issuing securities in a securitization. Indeed, perhaps the most basic and popular form of guarantee to date is bond insurance provided to SPV-issued asset-backed securities and equivalent credit enhancements provided to asset-backed commercial paper programs, both of which were discussed in Chapter 14. We discuss more alternative securitizations in Chapter 22, but that discussion is not necessary to understand the role played by guarantors. In short, SPVs issue securities that do not always warrant a AAA rating. A guarantee from an AAA insurer can solve that problem. Monoline insurers in the United States, in fact, specialize in offering such bond insurance guarantees.

Conditionality and Covenants

A true guarantee has only two real conditions: the trigger is active, and the claim is not fraudulent. If both conditions are met, the (re-)insurer is on the hook for any losses.

Nevertheless, some guarantees involve different degrees of *ex ante* scrutiny. All guarantees involve a significant amount of due diligence, of course, to help mitigate moral hazard problems. In turn, this due diligence helps eradicate asymmetric information problems that can lead to adverse selection costs, thereby usually implying much better pricing on guarantees than equivalent public securities issues. In a pecking order context, a guarantee provided by a single lead (re-)insurer is about as close to internal funding as a firm can get.

In addition to due diligence, some (re-)insurers include basic covenants or conditions concerning the nature of the risk being assumed. Monoline insurers usually condition their pricing and the guarantee itself to the external rating of the party seeking the guarantee—rather annoyingly often requiring parties to get rated if they are not already. Multilines tend to place less importance on external ratings but may instead condition their guarantees to a known population of credit risks. If the risk to which the trigger is tied changes materially, the guarantee may be invalid. Table 21.1 shows most active financial guarantors in 1999.

The more restrictions a guarantee contains, the more it resembles risk financing than risk transfer. And in some cases, guarantees can become so restrictive that they do not differ materially from traditional insurance. A very well publicized recent example of a guarantee gone bad, for example, has led many to question when a guarantee really is a guarantee.

TABLE 21.1 Active Financial Guarantors in 2000

Financial Guarantee Insurer	Premiums Ceded in 2000 ($ millions)
Munich Re/American Re	73.6
ACE	71.4
Enhance Re/Asset Guaranty	57.3
Tokio Marine and Fire	38.1
MBIA	36.8
Ambac	32.2
AXA Re	30.8
XL	20.7
RAM Re	17.7
Zürich Re	17.2
Partner Re	5.9
Swiss Re	2.9
Other	15.4
TOTAL	420.1

Source: Ballantine (2001b).

Example: The "Hollywood Funding" Debacle

Guarantees always have been viewed as particularly risky, especially for risks that are not well understood by the guarantor, for illiquid risks that are difficult for the guarantor to hedge or reinsure (retrocede), and for exotic risks subject to significant informational asymmetries and plagued by potential moral hazard and adverse selection problems. Until very recently, for example, Lloyd's syndicates were not even allowed to write guarantees. And even with a change of Lloyd's rules to allow syndicates to register for guarantee writing, Kiln is the only syndicate to have done so.

Despite the risks of guarantees, the stringent due diligence associated with them has delivered a reasonably good track record over time. In large part because of this good record of performance, the complete disaster in 2001 with Hollywood Funding has given several market participants a massive black eye and made would-be buyers of guarantees a bit wary.

Hollywood Funding was the name given to seven separate securitizations of private film financings.[13] The securitizations were structured by Crédit Suisse First Boston (CSFB), and the cash flows on the bonds issued in the securitizations were guaranteed by HIH Casualty & General Insurance and AIG's Lexington Insurance.

A U.K. firm called Flashpoint, run by an ex-Lloyd's underwriter, obtained the financing from these securitization conduits from 1996 to 1998 in order to finance the completion of several films whose revenue receivables were in turn transferred to the seven Hollywood Funding vehicles as backing for the bonds that each vehicle issued. HIH and AIG guaranteed the principal and interest payments on those bonds by agreeing to meet any cash shortfall in the event that film revenues were not adequate to pay off the noteholders. The existence of these guarantees was a condition of Flashpoint obtaining backing from Hollywood Funding. Exhibit 21.1 illustrates these relations graphically and indicates that HIH guaranteed Hollywood Funding 1 to 3 and Lexington guaranteed 4 to 7.

Hollywood Funding 1 and 2 had revenues that fell short of note obligations by $31 million. HIH then attempted to collect on the reinsurance it had secured for its guarantees. The reinsurance was an 80 percent quota share, and the reinsurance was led by AXA Re and also included New Hampshire Insurance and Independent Insurance. The reinsurers filed a claim in London against HIH on the grounds that HIH should not have paid the claim because the warranties to the policies required that six films per vehicle be made, and six films had not been made in each case. The Court of Appeals upheld the judgment by the High Court that the claims should not have been paid.

Meanwhile, AIG's Lexington subsidiary had already sued Flashpoint for failing to segregate film revenues in separate escrow accounts. Following the court decision in favor of HIH's reinsurers, Lexington refused to make pay-

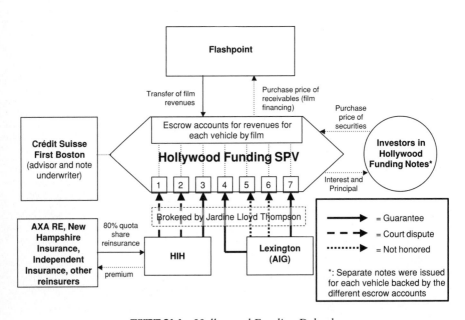

EXHIBIT 21.1   Hollywood Funding Debacle

ments on any claims arising on Hollywood Funding 5 and 6, citing the HIH judgment as evidence that it had no liability.

The notes issued by the Hollywood structures were rated AAA by Standard & Poor's (S&P). Following the Lexington revocation of its guarantee, notes issued by Hollywood 5 and 6 were downgraded to CCC– in February 2001. Hollywood 4, also guaranteed by Lexington, was downgraded to BB in March. Hollywood Funding 5 defaulted to its noteholders in May, and Hollywood Funding 6 defaulted in June.

The controversy that has surrounded this disaster primarily pertains to when a guarantee is a guarantee and who should know that. When S&P downgraded Hollywood 5 and 6, it issued the following statement: "After reviewing the insurance policies, Standard & Poor's believed that the policies were absolute and unconditional, that there were no conditions or warranties that needed to be satisfied in order to draw on the policies (other than the money in the escrow account being insufficient), that Lexington had waived all its defences to payment on the policies, and that the policies met the standards of the capital market for credit enhancement of financial market instruments."[14] S&P further explained, "The only exclusions to payment that appear on the face of the policies . . . are exclusions relating to war, civil insurrection, invasion of foreign enemies, revolution etc., and radioactive contamination."[15]

AIG has taken a different position, calling into question the competence of both CSFB and S&P. It issued the following statement in May 2001:

> *The issue here is not the refusal by an insurer to pay a claim under its policy. The real issue is whether CSFB understood what it was doing when it approached the insurance market to issue a property and casualty policy that was not drafted as the functional equivalent of a financial guarantee. Additionally, CSFB should be asked to address the standard of care and scope of liability that it undertook in organizing these transactions. . . . It may well be that the noteholders . . . expected that the policies in question were the functional equivalent of financial guarantees. But the purchaser of a note in such circumstances would rely on the efforts of others to fulfill the expectation."[16]*

The trustee of the Hollywood notes, Law Debenture Trust Corp. (Channel Islands) Ltd., has initiated legal proceedings against Lexington. One of the noteholders, Asset Backed Capital (ABC), a part of Quadrant Capital, has in turn filed suit against CSFB and Jardine Lloyd Thompson (JLT), the broker of the so-called guarantees. CSFB and JLT have been accused of failing to disclose information relevant to the deal. Additionally, CSFB has been charged with failing to understand the implications of structuring the transaction.[17]

Monoline providers of bond guarantees have said privately that this episode illustrates the tendency for multiline insurers to dispute claims more often than monolines and to offer guaranteelike products that are not really guarantees. At the same time, several multilines have not provided guarantees and reneged on them later. Indeed, as Table 21.1 shows, the multiline American Re subsidiary of Munich Re together with its German parent actually dominate the financial guarantee marketplace.

One clear lesson that does emerge from the Hollywood debacle is that the intent of a guarantee is to provide payment without question—as S&P describes it, guarantees are a "pay first, sue later practice."[18] But the reality may be quite different. Corporate customers should use caution.

Example: Exchange and Clearing House Guarantees

In Chapter 20, the Marsh e-X Programme was presented as an example of a successful, focused multiline structure whose appeal was primarily in helping financial exchanges and clearing organizations limit gaps in related coverage and tailor their total coverage. Brokered and offered through the Exchange and Clearing House (ECHO) unit of the Marsh Financial and Professional (Finpro) division, the e-X program also gives *exchanges* an option for a guarantee—many of which have chosen to take this option.

Financial exchanges and clearinghouses acting as central counterparties bear the credit risk that their members will default and that such a default will impose a loss on the clearing entity in excess of any collateral, margin, and/or capital pledged. Guarantees that provide synthetic equity in the event of a loss arising from a member default can be a very cost-effective means by which clearinghouses can ensure their ongoing operations following such a default as well as signal their integrity to the capital market. Note, moreover, that risk finance would not necessarily work in these situations. Depending on the assets the clearinghouse has of its own, a preloss loan might not stop the entity from becoming insolvent following a default. An equity infusion usually is required for that.

The provision of guarantees to exchanges and clearinghouses originated in the 1990s along two separate tracks. One track was paved by Paul Palmer, then of the AAA-rated monoline Asset Guaranty Insurance Co. and now Chief Executive Officer of Capital Credit, together with the developer of the Marsh ECHO practice, Alastair Laurie-Walker. Palmer and Laurie-Walker successfully created guarantees at such notable clearinghouses as the London Stock Exchange (prior to the cessation of its clearing function to the London Clearing House in 2001), the Sydney Futures Exchange, the Stock Exchange of Singapore, and Hong Kong Securities Clearing Corporation. Under the Asset Guaranty/Marsh program, Asset Guaranty was the sole guarantor, opting to reinsure the exposures selectively and on its own account.

About a year later, Diego Wauters began to market seemingly similar guarantees. Three successful placements included the Chicago Board of Trade Clearing Corporation, OM Gruppen AB in Stockholm, and the London Clearing House. Working with Michael March, then of Bank~Austria, the Lexington/AIG guarantee looked and worked differently from the Asset Guaranty structure. Specifically, AIG pushed almost all of the risk out the back door to a syndicate led by Bank~Austria, which then spread the risk around other market participants, such as the German Landesbanks and several other strong, creditworthy institutions.

The Asset Guaranty policies all remain in place today, but the AIG programs have not fared so well. In particular, AIG and Bank~Austria both essentially decided to stop providing these coverages, therefore leaving the existing customers to deal with a leaderless syndicate of banks that are essentially unfamiliar with the business of clearing and settlements. Although there has been absolutely no question about the integrity of the guarantees themselves, the problem has been more for the exchanges, which found themselves having to seek approval in advance for almost every new product offering or business decision from a group of bankers that seemed as unenthusiastic to engage in such reviews as the exchanges. All three of these policies are due to wind down in 2002, just after the publication of this book.

Since the pioneering work by Asset Guaranty/Palmer and Marsh/Laurie-Walker and by Wauters/AIG and March/Bank~Austria, other capital providers have entered the market for the provision of clearinghouse guarantees, as well. In September 1999 Clearnet—the clearinghouse for Paris Bourse transactions—acquired a guarantee covering €150 million in default-related losses in excess of €170 million in self-insurance capital for three years. The guarantee was placed by Société Générale, insured by Chubb, and reinsured by Swiss Re, Westdeustche Landesbank, Commerzbank, Banque Internationale a Luxembourg, and Royal Bank of Canada Insurance Co.

Similarly, in 2001 the Swiss Exchange acquired a guarantee from Zürich Financial for €30 million XS €1 million of default-related losses on its new joint venture with TradePoint called virt-x. Listing only securities and no derivatives, the Zürich coverage of virt-x is a substitute for implementing cash margin calls on open, unsettled positions.[19]

RESIDUAL VALUE GUARANTEES

The guarantees explored in the last section all concern credit risk. But this need not be the case. Indeed, another success story in the world of guarantees comes from the aircraft finance industry, where three deals have now been concluded. All three share the common element of providing residual value protection to their purchasers—that is, reimbursements for fluctuations in the value of capital assets relative to the income that those assets generate. The three notable deals discussed below all help very capital-intensive industries weather the risk of fluctuations in their sales and income generation cycles.

British Aerospace

British Aerospace (BAe) sought protection from losses arising from unexpectedly low lease income on about 600 of its regional aircraft. This risk included actual and contingent liability risk arising from the sales of aircraft to leasing organizations. Its direct lease commitments arise from BAe's aircraft sales to third-party lessors that lease the aircraft back to BAe, which then subleases it to an operator. Indirect lease commitments arise when aircraft sold to third parties have leasing and financing payments and residual values directly guaranteed by the aircraft maker.

At the end of 1997, BAe faced £1.02 billion in direct lease commitments, £1.53 billion in indirect exposure, and £420 million of residual value exposure. BAe also carried an expected income of £2.25 billion on its balance sheet to offset these risks. But the present value of the remaining recourse was still £536 million, equal to one-third of the firm's net assets.[20]

In 1998 BAe obtained a guarantee of its expected income through the Financial Risk Insurance Program (FRIP) brokered by Marsh. Underwriters includes monolines MBIA and Ambac as well as multilines Allianz, Swiss Re, Winterthur, and others. Under the FRIP, if lease income and sales fell below BAe's budgeted £2.9 billion over a 15-year period, the insurance policy provided £2.4 billion XS £500 million for a net pretax cost to BAe of £51 million.[21] The policy included two components. The lease portfolio cover protected BAe against the risk that actual lease income net of certain costs was less than the budgeted amount over the 15-year policy period. The option aircraft portfolio cover provided cover to BAe for leases in which BAe was obligated to buy the aircraft and lease income prior to the exercise of that put option by lessees was inadequate to cover the aircraft purchase price.

The FRIP used by BAe had no impact on its balance sheet, thus indicating that the firm was not seeking any kind of earnings protection. But what the deal did do was lock in the expected income of the firm, for which the recourse had been allocated. By the end of 1998, the recourse provision for aircraft financing stood at £490 million, but thanks to the FRIP, the net exposure was now less than £800 million, giving BAe significantly more comfort in the adequacy of the recourse provision.[22]

Saab

Swedish aircraft maker Saab concluded a deal extremely similar to BAe in November 2000.[23] The transaction locked in Saab's expected £1.7 billion in expected income from 203 Saab 340 leases and 2000 regional leases over a

15-year period—a smaller-scale version of BAe's FRIP. As in the BAe case, the Swedish aircraft maker retained about 10 percent of the policy coverage as a deductible.

The Saab deal was again brokered by Marsh. The insurers include Ambac, Mitsui Marine International, Swiss Re, and Winterthur. Saab paid about £43 million for the assurance that its leasing portfolio income was now safely insulated from future business fluctuations.

Rolls-Royce

U.K aircraft engine manufacturer Rolls-Royce concluded an ARTistic deal in 2001 involving the sale of its Trent engines to airlines for use in powering the giant Airbus 330 and Boeing 777 aircraft. The details and pricing of the deal are unknown, but the basic structure is.[24]

Under the insurance program, XL Capital offers Rolls-Royce residual value guarantees that the firm passes on to its customers. Unlike BAe and Saab, Rolls-Royce was not seeking any form of risk management but rather was firmly operating in the "efficiency enhancer" model (see Chapter 10) of using a risk transfer product to improve its customer relationship management. By guaranteeing the residual value of its engines, Rolls-Royce is providing its customers with a much more stable cost estimate for which they can seek external borrowings.

CAPITAL MARKETS SOURCES OF CONTINGENT CAPITAL

Committed capital and guarantees are primarily insurance solutions, although bank participation may be required to accelerate payments, through the use of bank wraps or through direct bank coparticipation in an ART structure. The Michelin deal illustrates that bank involvement can provide a useful means of providing short-term liquidity while also adding bulk capacity to the deal.

Many of the risk transfer solutions discussed also can be obtained directly from banks and swap dealers in the form of capital market products. Some of the credit derivatives discussed in Chapter 13, for example, can be used to construct synthetic financing.[25] A few other capital market products that can give firms postloss access to contingent debt or equity on a preloss funding basis are discussed below.

Put-Protected New Equity Issues

Firms can construct homemade contingent capital facilities by writing puts on their own securities. A firm concerned about raising postloss funds can, for example, buy puts on its own common stock. When a risk translates into a major unexpected loss—large enough to affect earnings perceptibly—the price per share of common stock likely will decline, leading to an increase in the value of the put option. The issuer of the put is also the issuer of the stock, resulting in a synthetic long call position as shown in Exhibit 21.2.

As shown, the put option is struck at K, which we can assume is a level at which the firm would be comfortable issuing new stock postloss. Suppose an adverse event precipitates a decline in the stock price by $-E°$ per share to $S° (= K - E°)$. Without the put, the postloss equity issue would be at a much lower price. But with the put, the postloss equity issue at $S°$ is now supplemented by a net gain on the put of $E° - p$, where p is the price paid by the firm for the protective put.

A major problem with using ordinary puts to protect a new equity issue from the adverse impact of an unexpected loss is the signal this can send to the market. For a company to buy traded puts on its own stock in any quantity—even if such a practice is legally permitted—can badly exacerbate adverse selection problems. In the extreme, a large put purchase by a firm could even create a self-fulfilling rundown in the firm's stock price if investors perceive the put purchase as indicative of some private negative information.

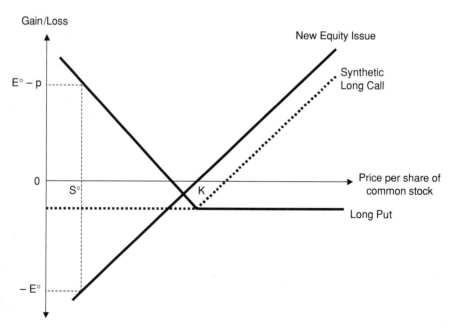

EXHIBIT 21.2   Protected Equity Issue

Loss Equity Put Options and "CatEPuts"

A variation on the above theme sometimes used by insurers to protect themselves against catastrophic losses is a *loss equity put*. The firm essentially prenegotiates an equity private placement with a single counterparty in the form of a put that allows the firm to directly issue and sell new stock to the counterparty at a fixed strike price. If an unexpected loss drives the actual stock price down, the issuer can exercise the put and issue new stock at the higher strike price, thus securing equity financing on preloss terms. To minimize dilution, moreover, firms often base these put options on preferred rather than common stock. A loss equity put option on preferred stock whose trigger is a natural disaster is known as a *CatEPut*, designed by Aon and issued mainly by insurance companies with catastrophic exposures.

To mitigate the moral hazard that such structures can create, loss equity put options often contain a double trigger so that the options are barrier options rather than traditional puts. The first trigger is the normal option trigger that requires the option be in the money in order to be exercised.[26] The second trigger usually defines a loss event for some risk or group of risks with which the firm is concerned, such as property losses arising following a natural disaster.

The loss event serving as the second trigger, moreover, usually is highly correlated with changes in stock prices. If a property loss following an earthquake is the second trigger, for example, it makes sense for the loss level that activates the loss put option to be sufficiently large that a decline in the stock price also can be expected. This helps ensure that the option is providing access to equity capital on favorable terms at a time when it is genuinely needed. To address moral hazard, the second trigger may be based on some index of losses rather than a firm's own loss exposure.

Some of the possible second triggers for loss put equity options are considered below. These triggers are similar to the types of triggers to which integrated multitrigger risk transfer products are linked, as discussed in Chapter 20.

Fixed Second Trigger

The second trigger may simply specify a minimum economic loss or damage level that the firm buying the loss equity put must sustain from a particular enumerated risk or group of risks. This minimum sustained loss usually can be associated with some expected decline in the stock price. Exhibit 21.3 shows a hypothetical functional relation between enumerated losses and expected declines in the per share price of the firm's stock arising as a direct result of losses incurred. As Doherty (2000) emphasizes, this function can have almost any form. As shown, for example, losses cause the stock price to decline at a decreasing rate, but this need not have been the case.

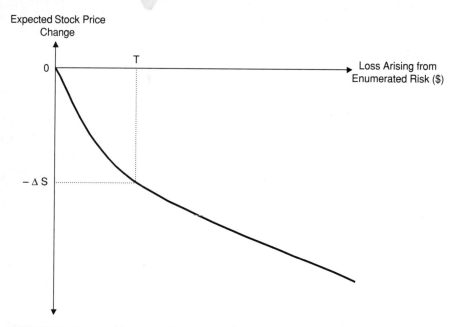

EXHIBIT 21.3 Expected Impact of Enumerated Loss Event on Stock Price
Source: Adapted from Doherty (2000).

For concreteness, suppose, following Doherty (2000), that the loss arising from the enumerated risk depicted in Exhibit 21.3 is a property loss arising from an earthquake. Suppose further that the loss equity put has a second trigger that is activated when $T in such property losses are incurred over a given period. The firm can issue new stock at some predefined strike price K per share if and only if the stock price is below K and an earthquake has occurred that gives rise to at least T in property losses.

For a property loss T, the firm's per share stock price is expected to fall by amount $-\Delta S$. This may be above or below the actual stock price change. But for this expected stock price decline, Exhibit 21.4 illustrates two different situations: one when both triggers are active and one when only the property loss trigger is pulled. The latter situation occurs when the initial stock price is S_1 per share. In that case, the expected decline in the stock price of $-\Delta S$ results in a new stock price $S_1 - \Delta S$ that is still above strike K. Loss T has occurred, but the option remains out of the money.

Now consider a situation where the option is closer to being at the money when the loss of T occurs. In that case, the expected stock price decline from S_2 to $S_2 - \Delta S$ causes the stock price per share to decline below the option

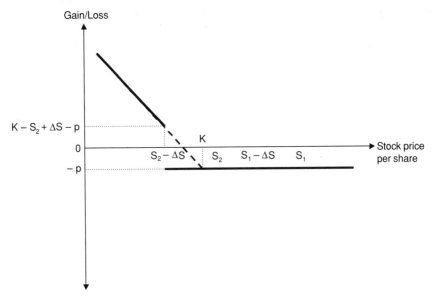

EXHIBIT 21.4 Loss Equity Put with Fixed Second Trigger

strike. Both triggers now are active, and the option can be exercised for $K - S_2$ + ΔS less the premium p paid for the loss equity put.

The heavy line in Exhibit 21.4 indicates the payoff on the option if it is exercised given a starting stock price of S_2. The dashed line is the payoff on a regular put for comparison. Notice that the knock-in aspect of the option gives rise to a discrete, discontinuous jump from a zero payout (excluding premium) to a positive payout because of the way the trigger works. If the stock price is exactly $K + \Delta S$ when the loss of T occurs and the actual stock price change is equal to the expected stock price change, the option will be just at the money, and further stock price declines will result in the usual dollar-for-dollar gain in the value of the put. For any stock price greater than $K + \Delta S$, the loss will be inadequate to knock the option in. For stock prices less than $K + \Delta S$, the option moves from zero intrinsic value to a positive intrinsic value by exactly the amount that the stock price is below $K + \Delta S$. The values in between zero and that number are never realized.

This "discontinuous gain," as Doherty (2000) calls it, can create moral hazard problems. If the stock price is just above $K + \Delta S$ when the loss occurs, the put owner has an incentive to overstate or exaggerate the effects of the loss in an effort to get the actual stock price decline to exceed ΔS and nudge the put into the money.

Fixed Range Second Trigger

Loss equity puts also may have a trigger that is active over a range of losses rather than at all losses above a single trigger amount. Exhibit 21.5 again shows the relation between losses—say, property losses from an earthquake, as before—and the expected stock price decline. Unlike Exhibit 21.3, Exhibit 21.5 now defines two loss trigger levels, T^{min} and T^{max}. In this case, the second trigger is active only when the property losses from the earthquake are above T^{min} and below T^{max}.

Exhibit 21.6 shows the value of this option at expiration assuming the relation between earthquake property losses and expected stock price changes holds *ex post*. The dashed line shows the payoff to a traditional put, and the heavy line shows the expiration value of the double trigger option for a starting stock price of S_1. The intrinsic value of this option is increasing in stock price declines for all prices below K, but the exercise value is increasing in stock price declines only for prices below $S_1 - \Delta S^{min}$ and above $S_1 - \Delta S^{min}$. Notice that the payment upon exercise is still relative to K, but the payment cannot be received unless the second trigger is active. If the option is deeply in the money after a stock price decline from S_1 to S', for

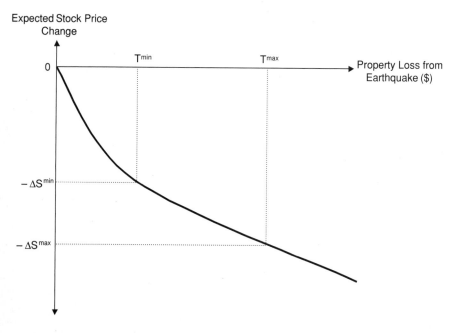

EXHIBIT 21.5   Expected Impact of Enumerated Loss Range on Stock Price

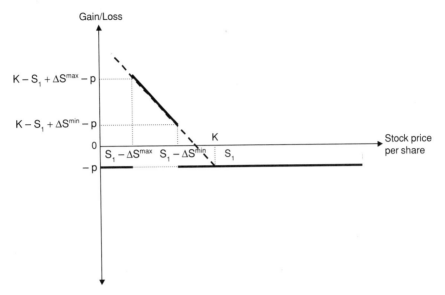

EXHIBIT 21.6 Loss Equity Put with Fixed Range Second Trigger

example, the intrinsic value of the option is $K - S'$, but this value cannot be realized because $S' < S_1 - \Delta S^{max}$.

A loss equity put with second trigger active when losses are within a fixed range is equivalent to a barrier option with both knock-in and knock-out provisions. Such products can lead to even more serious moral hazard problems than in the fixed lower trigger case provided the firm can influence its reported losses. For losses that are just under T^{min}, the firm may have an incentive to overreport or exaggerate the impact of losses in order to knock the put option in. But now, as losses approach the knock-out level of T^{max}, firms may be tempted to *under*report losses. The put owner thus has moral hazard problems on two sides.

The moral hazard associated with underreporting losses as the upper trigger is reached can be mitigated if the firm uses a capped payoff (i.e., vertical spread) rather than an upper-loss outstrike on the option.[27] Alternatively, the firm could opt for a trigger based on some variable correlated with the firm's losses but not under the direct control of the firm.

Variable Second Trigger

As an alternative to a fixed second trigger or range trigger, a firm also could use a variable second trigger (or range trigger) when it sees preloss equity financing through a loss equity put. As some of the examples in Chapter 20 illustrate for multitrigger IRM products, such variable triggers could include relative or outperformance triggers (e.g., the firm's property losses versus a catastrophic loss index). Triggers do not necessarily abrogate moral hazard problems, however, as the firm still could have an incentive to overreport losses relative to the chosen index in order to push its stock price below the instrike. In the case of a range-based trigger, underreporting relative to the index for the upper trigger to avoid a knock-out also could be a problem.

Indexed Trigger or Strike Price

The moral hazard risk of the firm overreporting losses to trip the lower trigger can be reduced by making the second trigger variable rather than fixed and based solely on a proxy for the firm's own losses. A catastrophic loss equity put, for example, might have a second trigger activated solely based on the amount of losses reported in an index like the PCS index mentioned in Chapter 20.

Doherty (2000) notes that an alternative mitigant to moral hazard problems would be the indexing of the option's first trigger (i.e., strike price) to the stock price of the company immediately prior to the loss event. The goal is to avoid situations where the option is in the money but has not knocked in because the loss event falls just short of the required amount, thus giving the holder of the put an incentive to nudge the reported loss upward.

Suppose we return to the property loss/expected stock price change relation shown in Exhibit 21.3. If the loss trigger is T, the stock price is expected to decline by $-\Delta S$ at that property loss level. Suppose the current stock price per share is S_1. The indexed strike price of the option K would then be set equal to $S_1 - \Delta S$, so that the option would be exactly at the money if the stock price falls by the amount expected following a loss of T. This is shown graphically in Exhibit 21.7.

By setting the option at the money assuming the actual stock price change equals the expected stock price change for loss T, the writer of the option can mitigate the owner's incentives to overstate the loss. Because the discontinuous gain has been eliminated, in many cases the put owner will be content to report the true loss. But the problem is not entirely eliminated. If the put owner can exaggerate the impact of the loss on the firm, the expected stock price decline will be less than the actual decline, thus tipping the option into the money.

Reverse Convertibles

A conversion of debt into equity also can help a firm achieve some relief for postloss funding by reducing the firm's leverage following a loss. (See Part I.) At market prices, however, this conversion would have no benefit because the debt and equity prices already will reflect the loss. Instead, the firm can issue a reverse convertible.

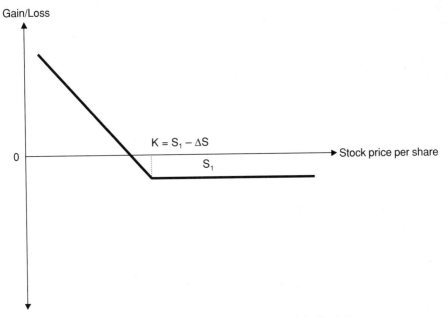

Gain/Loss

0

$K = S_1 - \Delta S$

S_1

Stock price per share

EXHIBIT 21.7 Loss Equity Put with Indexed Strike Price

A reverse convertible functions like a convertible bond by allowing debt to be switched for equity at a prespecified strike price. The important difference is that the issuing firm determines when the conversion occurs, not the bond holder. The firm will exercise this option when the value of its stock falls below a point where the shares offered have a lower value than the debt from which the shares have been converted.

Exercising a reverse convertible can make sense for an issuing firm following a large loss for two reasons. The first is that the optimal exercise policy involves converting only when the debt has a higher value than the equity. The conversion thus forces a shift in its capital structure toward a cheaper source of capital. The difference in the prices helps offset/fund the costs of the adverse loss. In addition, the conversion decreases the outstanding debt in the firm's capital structure and thus reduces the firm's leverage, thereby reducing expected distress costs and increasing effective debt capacity at a time when such shifts would have the highest benefit to the firm's security holders at the margin.

The option embedded in reverse convertibles often resembles those of the loss equity puts described earlier. Namely, the put option on the firm's equity embedded in the bond is often a barrier option with second triggers of the type described earlier.

NOTES

1. Shimpi (2001) and others refer to these products as *contingent* capital. We avoid that term because in the framework we developed in Part I, contingent capital may be either debt or equity. In Shimpi's terminology, contingent capital is always debt.
2. Shimpi (2001).
3. Doherty (2000) points out, however, that providers of committed capital will anticipate the exercise of such facilities on a postloss basis. Indeed, he argues that many committed capital facilities cannot really improve on postloss financing terms.
4. Shimpi (2001).
5. The RBC deal is discussed in Banham (2001).
6. Banham (2001).
7. The details of the Michelin deal are discussed in "Swiss Re and SocGen in $1 bn Loan," *Reactions* (September 2000); Schenk (2000), and Banham (2001).
8. The lead manager on the original loan was J.P. Morgan, where Tom Skwarek and Benoît de Font-Réaulx served as syndication and relationship manager, respectively. Mr. Skwarek is now a Swiss Re principal and the father of CLOCS, and Mr. Font-Réaulx is the senior banker at SG that negotiated the Michelin deal on the SG side.
9. See Schenk (2000).
10. Reinsurance firms allocate regulatory capital based on probability of draw-downs, whereas banks still are required to allocate regulatory capital based on notional exposures. Reinsurers are at a tremendous advantage to banks in this context.
11. Schenk (2000).
12. Swiss Re's CLOCS is so subordinated in capital structure that it also functions economically more like debt than equity, despite being a fixed claim.
13. The facts of this case are based on the excellent article by Ballantine (2001b).
14. Quoted in ibid., p. 29.
15. Lisa S. Howard, "Movie Bonds Get Bad Review After AIG Declines Coverage," *National Underwriter* Online News (February 9, 2001).
16. Quoted in Ballantine (2001b), p. 29.
17. See "CSFB and JLT Join Film Dispute," *Reactions* (September 2001).
18. Quoted in Howard, "Movie Bonds."
19. "Margin calls" on a securities exchange are designed to reduce the settlement risk on transactions that have been executed but have not settled. In a T + 3 settlement system, for example, margin calls would cover some of the replacement cost risk that could arise if the price of a stock rises (falls)

after a trade and the seller (buyer) defaults. The Zürich coverage is intended to substitute for such margin calls.

    Margin on futures exchanges like the Sydney Futures Exchange, by contrast, are performance bonds designed to mitigate the exposure in the event of a default on a futures or options transaction. Because of the different nature of the risk exposure of the clearinghouse, guarantees provided to futures and options exchanges usually supplement rather than replace margin requirements.

20. See Ballantine (2001a).
21. Gerling Global Financial Products (2000).
22. See Ballantine (2001a).
23. BAe holds a 35 percent stake in Saab.
24. See Ballantine (2001a).
25. For some examples of how credit derivatives can create financing opportunities, see Tavakoli (1998).
26. Traditional options do not necessarily preclude exercise when the option is out-of-the-money, but exercise in that circumstance makes little sense.
27. Doherty (2000).

CHAPTER 22

Alternative Risk Securitizations and Securitized Products

We encountered securitization as a synthetic asset and liability divestiture process in Chapter 14 and again (with Hollywood Funding) in Chapter 21. We also saw that derivatives can be used to facilitate synthetic securitizations and can be combined with securitizations or embedded directly into securities to yield structured notes. All of these risk transfer mechanisms present new alternatives for corporations attempting to optimize their economic capital structures.

One reason that securitized products are of so much interest in the ART world, however, is their appeal to investors. In many cases, securitized products and derivatives-based structured financing vehicles represent the first and/or most practical way for institutional investors to access alternative asset classes, like catastrophic insurance risk. The appeal of such instruments from a portfolio management perspective has been well documented.[1] But appeal to investors does not mean that these products are always suitable for those seeking risk transfer.

In this chapter we address several specific types of securization structures that are broadly considered to be ART forms. Admittedly, the line between a traditional secuiritization (e.g., mortgage-backed securities or asset-backed commercial paper) and an ARTistic securization is a fuzzy one. As such, we will relax our definition of ART a bit and focus mainly on products that most people consider ART forms. These include the securization of credit risk, insurance risk, capital asset value risk, and a few others. We also explore how derivatives can be used alongside, in addition to, inside of, or instead of structured financial products to take risk transfer one step further.

The specific questions we address are:

■ How can securitized products be used to manage credit risk through cash flow or synthetic collateralized debt obligations?

■ How can securitization be used to create synthetic insurance and reinsurance structures?

■ How have securitization structures improved the operation of catastrophic insurance and reinsurance markets?

■ What are some types of synthetic securitizations possible in catastrophic (re-)insurance?

COLLATERALIZED DEBT OBLIGATIONS

Collateralized debt obligations (CDOs), including collateralized loan obligations (CLOs) and collateralized bond obligations (CBOs), are probably the least ARTistic of the products considered in this chapter. These structures bundle credit risk and issue securities based on different exposures to credit risk, thus creating a risk transfer and financing conduit based on differential credit. We include them here instead of Chapter 14 not because they are true ART forms but because the structure of a typical CDO is the same structure used by most securitization conduits that are ART forms.

A CDO is a securitized product structure in which debt is acquired by a special purpose vehicle and held as collateral for the issuance of new securities based on the original (albeit perhaps "reengineered") cash flows on the portfolio of debt instruments. Prior to 1996, total CDO issues never exceeded $4 billion per year. The $5 billion R.O.S.E. Funding No. 1 Ltd. CLO sponsored by National Westminister Bank PLC introduced a period of explosive growth in these products. In the last three years alone, CDOs issued around the world have averaged about $137 billion per year.[2]

The assets held as collateral to back CDO bond issues can include bonds (in which case the structure is a CBO), bank loans (in which case the structure is a CLO), emerging market debt, asset-backed securities, or just about any other kind of debt obligation. When actual assets are conveyed to a conduit through the traditional securitization process, the resulting CDO is called a *cash flow* CDO. In addition, debt assets can be conveyed into a *synthetic CDO* structure using derivatives instead of actual asset divestiture. And in a very recent innovation, *equity* is now emerging as an asset on which a CDO's securities can be based. These three broad types of structures are explored below.

Cash Flow Collateralized Debt Obligations

Exhibit 22.1 shows the basic (and deliberately simplified) structure of a typical cash flow CDO, or a CDO in which actual asset ownership is conveyed to the SPV. The owner of the debt instruments used to collateralize the securities issued by the SPV first conveys them to the SPV for a purchase price. A collateral manager is engaged for a fee to select the securities that populate the

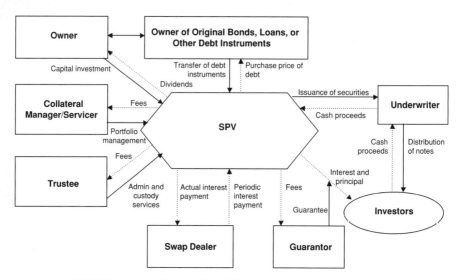

EXHIBIT 22.1 Simplified Collateralized Debt Obligation Structure

CDO, and in some cases this manager actively buys and sells securities or loans over some part of the life of the vehicle. A trustee acts as custodian of the assets and administrator of the SPV structure.

Mechanics

The notes issued by the SPV and distributed to investors through an investment bank underwriter typically fall into several classes. The classes essentially represent the priority of claims issued by the SPV in the capital structure of the SPV. As principal is repaid on the assets held by the SPV, it is repaid first to Class A security holders, then to Class B securities holders, and so on until the last class of note holder is repaid. The owner of the SPV—which may or may not own some or all of the debt instruments conveyed to the SPV—retains a residual value or equity interest on which dividends are paid after the note holder classes have all been paid off.

The senior notes issued by a CDO usually are wrapped in a guarantee like those discussed in Chapter 21. Indeed, bond insurance offered by monoline insurers is the dominant source of financial guarantees in the market today. Holders of lower-class securities, however, bear increasing credit risk that their principal will not be repaid in full. A typical CDO structure is shown in Exhibit 22.2 and is discussed further in Lucas (2001). The first two tranches involve both fixed and floating rate securities, whereas the third and fourth debt tranches are either one or the other. Representative credit ratings are shown for the notes that would be issued against each tranche.

Tranches	Rating

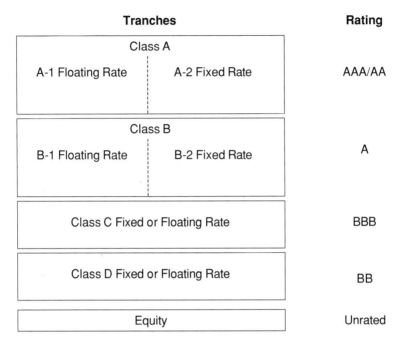

EXHIBIT 22.2 Typical CDO Tranche Structure

In addition, the structure may involve the participation of a swap dealer. Because the debt instruments held by the SPV likely will pay interest on an erratic and uneven basis over time, the swap dealer enters into an income swap (see Chapter 13) in which it receives the interest payments on the SPV's debt instruments as they occur and in return pays a more stable and regular stream of cash flows back to the SPV for the purpose of paying interest on some or all of its note classes. The swap dealer assumes timing risk but usually does not assume default risk on the underlying securities.

In the most basic CDO structure presented here, the notes are essentially credit instruments. As noted in Chapter 14, securitization conduits unbundle the cash flows of the assets they hold and repackage them based on some specific set of criteria designed to appeal to different groups of investors. The classical CDO apportions cash flows in tranches based on the credit risk of the assets in the pool. The size and number of tranches in a CDO depend on factors such as investor appetite for the end securities and funding costs for the structured product vehicle itself. In most CDOs, the senior tranche is the largest, with the riskiest equity tranche rarely representing more than 15 percent of the capital structure of the CDO.[3]

Purposes

CDOs are usually either balance sheet or arbitrage CDOs. The former structures usually are set up and owned by the institution conveying the debt assets to the conduit, such as a bank securitizing its loan portfolio through a CLO. The primary goal thus is asset (or sometimes liability) divestiture. In the case of banks, the more fundamental goal is usually to reduce the size of the balance sheet and/or regulatory capital requirements.

Balance sheet CDOs usually have a minimal role for the collateral manager/servicer because the bank is likely to retain the asset servicing rights. These types of CDOs, moreover, often wind down after the assets conveyed have been converted to capital market instruments.

Arbitrage CDOs, by contrast, involve the deliberate acquisition of assets and debt securities by the collateral manager. This usually occurs over a period of time called the *ramp-up period* as the assets in the CDO gradually are bought and tactically positioned. Whereas the equity or residual value portion of a balance sheet CDO is usually very nominal, the equity tranche of an arbitrage CDO is often the major appeal of the structure. The equity tranche offers investors a levered return between the postdefault yield of the assets and the funding costs on the debt tranches.

Apportionment of Funds

CDOs apportion funds to different classes of security holders in two different ways. The first is a *market value method* in which the assets held by the CDO are marked to market periodically. A haircut is applied to securities to account for potential future market risk in a fashion similar to the SEC risk-based capital rules discussed in Chapter 8. If the haircut value of the assets falls below the par value of a debt tranche, the collateral manager must sell assets and repay debt tranches until the haircut value is brought back above the SPV's debt obligations.

Nine out of 10 CDOs uses an alternative method of apportioning funds and credit risk to classes of note holders, called the *cash flow method*.[4] In this method, cash inflows on debt securities are used to pay off note holders of the structure as the cash flows occur. Subordination levels are chosen so that the expected cash flows on the securities cover the expected obligations to be paid to note holders. When the cash flows are insufficient to service all debt tranches, cash flow usually is diverted to the most senior tranche and on down through the capital structure in order of priority.

Synthetic Collateralized Debt Obligations

A synthetic CDO is one in which the actual assets are not conveyed to the SPV. The cash flows on a pool of underlying assets are transferred to the SPV through a mechanism other than asset divestiture. Synthetic CDOs are usually balance sheet CDOs done by banks. Because the risk of the bank redirecting the cash flows on its debt assets to the CDO's SPV is lower, the capital requirements on the bank are lower. But because the assets themselves remain on the bank's balance sheet, the size of the balance sheet does not shrink.

From 1997 to 2000, about 14 percent of all CDOs were synthetic.[5] And evidence suggests interest in synthetic CDOs is growing fast.[6] One reason may have to do with some of the signaling issues explored in Part I. Namely, when a bank syndicates its loans or sells them to a securitization conduit, the sale is public. The borrower, among others, will know the loan has been sold, and this knowledge could ameliorate some of the delegated monitoring signaling benefits that bank loans are held to deliver.

If a bank divests a loan asset synthetically, however, the mechanisms for accomplishing this explored below are not public. A loan can be sold without the borrower or other creditors relying on the bank ever knowing it has been sold. But if enough banks continue down this road, a pooling equilibrium could result in which borrowers and other creditors penalize bank loans in the delegated monitoring context because of the proportion of banks that are synthetically divesting those loan assets. In other words, if informational asymmetries preclude outside firms from determining whether any given loan has been securitized, those firms may conclude the loans of interest to them have been securitized. Even if they have not, the resulting pooling equilibrium could create adverse selection problems unless attentively managed by banks.

Mechanics

As we saw in Chapters 13 and 14, total return swaps can be used to facilitate a synthetic securitization. Accordingly, a total return swap can serve as the means by which the cash flows of debt assets are synthetically conveyed to a CDO conduit. The resulting structures are sometimes called *secured loan trusts* or *secured note trusts*. Exhibit 22.3 illustrates.

Note from the exhibit that the structure no longer involves a collateral manager. In this case, because the assets remain on the balance sheet of the bank owner of the loans being swapped into the SPV, the bank functions as the collateral manager. The bank may or may not also own the SPV, although ownership of the SPV sometimes can result in the SPV being consolidated back up on the bank's balance sheet, thereby mitigating the capital relief that the total return swap between the bank and SPV might otherwise provide.

The swap itself is a typical total return swap, as discussed in Chapter

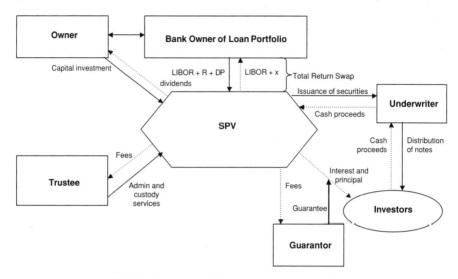

EXHIBIT 22.3 Secured Loan Trust Synthetic CDO

13, in which the bank pays LIBOR plus the interest received on its loan portfolio (R) plus any change in the value of its loan portfolio (ΔP). In return, the bank receives LIBOR plus x, where x is the swap's financing rate. LIBOR is included on both sides so that the bank still can fund the assets on its balance sheet.

Total return swaps usually are structured to make payments periodically rather than as interest is received. Accordingly, the income swap shown in the classical CDO structure in Exhibit 22.1 is no longer required here.

CDOs backed by total return swaps usually are called unfunded synthetic CDOs because the cash proceeds of the securities sale is used only to provide collateral to the swap counterparty. The notes are otherwise unfunded unless a guarantor provides protection through a financial guarantee.

A funded synthetic CDO, by contrast, involves the use of the proceeds from the note issue to fund assets of some kind acquired by the SPV that will either serve as collateral on the swap or as protection for the repayment of some or all of the notes. The SPV and bank both have credit risk on the total return swap. If the bank does not own the SPV, it also may require that the proceeds from the issue of securities by the SPV be used as collateral for the swap instead of to back the redemption of the notes.

Alternatively, the securities issued by the SPV may involve principal protection depending on the nature and purpose of the SPV and the investors to which the synthetic CDO is designed to appeal. If the proceeds from the security issue are used as collateral for the swap, they cannot be used simultaneously as collateral for the bonds. So a financial guarantee usually is required from an insurance company or reinsurer to guarantee principal repayment on the notes and bring them up to investment grade (or above).

Manufacturing Leverage: The Chase Secured Note Trust

Secured note trusts are leveraged very often to enhance their appeal to end investors. Leverage can be manufactured easily in a synthetic CDO by setting the notional principal on the total return swap to some multiple of the face value of securities issued by the SPV. The "Chase Secured Loan Trust Note^{sm}," sponsored by Chase Securities, provides a good example of how such leverage can be created. The underlying loan portfolio that Chase wanted to synthetically divest had a $150 million face value. The SPV that engaged in a total return swap with Chase with payments based on the $150 million loan portfolio and that had a notional principal of $150 million. Specifically, the trust periodically paid Chase LIBOR plus a financing spread of 125 bps, in return for which the trust received periodic payments equal to LIBOR plus the coupon rate on the loan portfolio of 365 bps plus the change in the price of the loans. Chase thus paid the trust a (possibly negative) net spread of 240 bps plus the loan price change.

The trust collected $50 million from investors as an initial subscription for the notes it issued. The ratio of this subscription amount to the notional principal of the swap (i.e., face value of the loan portfolio) thus was 3:1. After collecting its initial subscription to the notes, the trust invested the $50 million in Treasuries earning 6.4 percent per annum.

In return for their initial investment of $50 million, the investors in the notes received a leveraged coupon payment of 13.6 percent plus the loan price change, computed relative to the $50 million face value of the notes. The coupon yield of 13.6 percent was based on the 6.4 percent Treasury yield plus the leveraged net spread of 7.20 percent on the loan portfolio embedded in the swap—that is, the 240 bps net spread times the leverage factor of 3:1.

J.P. Morgan's Bistro Transactions

In 1997–1998, J.P. Morgan engaged in five synthetic securitizations of loans and other bank assets totaling $2.5 billion. These bistro transactions were called the "1998 Structured Finance Deal of the Year" by *Investment Dealers' Digest* and "Derivative Deal of the Year" by *Institutional Investor*.

In a bistro transaction, the proceeds of the note issue are used to fund the acquisition of a highly credit-worthy asset, such as asset-backed securities based on credit card receivables and credit-enhanced to AAA. The asset is held in trust by the SPV and is selected to have a maturity that corresponds to the tenor of the total return swap. When the two transactions mature, the proceeds on the asset's retirement held in trust may be used to pay the swap counterparty. Any residual value left over is allocated to security holders.

Credit-Linked Notes and SBC Warburg's Glacier Finance Transactions

A variation on the bistro theme was undertaken in 1997 by SBC Warburg. Instead of using the proceeds of the note issue to buy a high-quality asset posted as collateral on the total return swap, SBC Warburg embedded the swap into an asset to create a credit-linked note (CLN) and used these bonds as collateral for the CLO security issue.

The SBC Warburg vehicle was called SBC Glacier Finance Ltd. and issued five classes of securities based on a $1.7 billion portfolio of 130 loans made by SBC to investment-grade borrowers. Instead of conveying the loan assets to a trust or using a total return swap, SBC created a CLN. A CLN is created through an SPV structure of the kind shown in Exhibit 22.4. A trust or SPV is set that issues the CLNs. The proceeds of the note issue are placed in trust with a custodian and invested in highly rated marketable securities. The SPV also enters into a total return swap with a swap dealer or bank in which it pays LIBOR plus a financing rate and receives LIBOR plus the interest and change in market value on a reference asset or loan portfolio. In a simple CLN structure, the total return on the underlying reference asset(s) is passed through as the cash flows on the CLNs. The CLNs may or may not be principal protected.[7]

In the SBC Glacier Finance structure, the proceeds from the issue of the five classes of securities by the SPV were used to purchase 130 CLNs, each of which was based on each of the 130 loans in the SBC Warburg reference loan portfolio. The structure is shown in Exhibit 22.5.

As the exhibit shows, the Class A securities represented the bulk of the issue—$1,375 million—and was placed to public investors under a Aa1/AA+

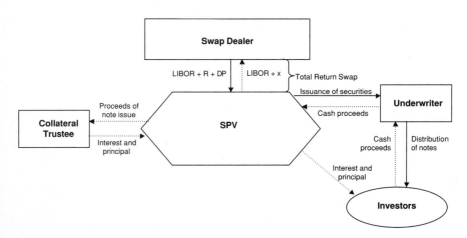

EXHIBIT 22.4   Credit-Linked Note

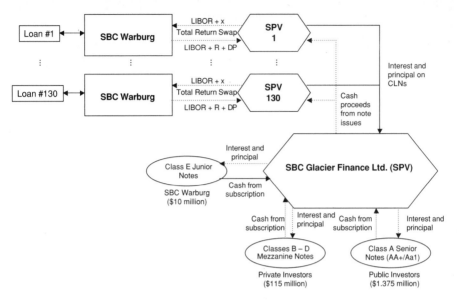

EXHIBIT 22.5   SBC Glacier Finance Funded Synthetic CLO

credit rating. The Class B, C, and D mezzanine notes represented $115 million of the issue, were placed privately, and were unrated. SBC Warburg retained the $10 million equity (i.e., Class E junior notes) tranche.[8]

As purchasers of the CLNs, Glacier Finance receives a spread over LIBOR to compensate for the credit risk of the underlying loans. If the original borrower defaults, SBC makes a payment to the SPV based on the market price of some liquid reference security. If the borrower's loans fall in value by 50 percent following a default, SBC makes a payment to the SPV equal to 50 percent of the notional principal on the corresponding CLN. If there is no public reference security available for this calculation, SBC pays 51 percent based on a historical analysis of comparable recovery rates undertaken by Moody's.

The Glacier Finance CDO is interesting for a few reasons. On one hand, the SPV purchases actual assets as backing for the five tranches of securities issued. On the other hand, those assets are CLNs that pay interest and principal based on the performance of underlying loans. But the CLNs themselves merely reference those loans by way of total return swaps. The vehicle thus is synthetic in the sense that the loans driving the performance of the CDO's securities are not owned by the SPV issuer of the securities. But the CDO is funded given that it purchases actual assets as collateral for the securities.

Equity-Backed Collateralized Debt Obligations

Both cash flow and synthetic CDOs can have much richer structures than those discussed in prior sections. One of the more novel such structures was introduced in 2001. The first CDO based entirely on private equity assets, the structure literally turns equity into debt.

The Prime Edge Capital PLC private equity CDO involved the issue of €150 million in three classes of notes. The proceeds from the issue were invested in a diversified pool of private equity funds of funds. The lead manager is the Swiss boutique Capital Dynamics, which, along with Rainer Marc Frey (RMF) and Hamilton Lane Advisors, will manage the structure's collateral selection, investment management process, and risk management.

Deutsche Bank arranged the structure and placed the securities, and Allianz Risk Transfer provided a guarantee to wrap the two classes of 12-year senior bonds (€72 million in Class A and €32 million in Class B) to get them an AA credit rating. The two senior classes of notes were priced at three-month Euribor plus a AA risk spread. The third and junior class of security accounted for the remaining €45 million. With 24 years to maturity, these junior notes act as equity and are unrated.[9]

The transactional appeal of this private equity-backed CDO was to offer the equity or junior note holders a leveraged private equity investment opportunity, but at the same time to retain a first loss position for the benefit of the senior debt. Allianz Risk Transfer facilitated a capital market execution of this new CDO asset class through the provision of its credit wrap.

SYNTHETIC (RE-)INSURANCE AND INSURANCE-LINKED SECURITIES

Lane (2000) explains that CDOs can be viewed as "self-contained reinsurance structures." Now that we have reviewed the robustness and mechanics of these products, his comment is more meaningful. After all, the holders of various classes of bonds issued by a CDO are, in effect, providing credit reinsurance. And to the extent that principal payments are made in reverse priority across classes of note holders, this credit insurance essentially is being supplied in vertical layers.

If CDOs are, in effect, synthetic credit reinsurance, can other similar securitized product structures synthetically replicate other kinds of insurance? The answer is yes. In this section we consider several structures in which insurance or reinsurance is provided directly by the capital market to the firm seeking some kind of insurance protection. The resulting securities often are called *insurance-linked securities* (ILSs) or *insurance-linked notes* (ILNs) because their payoff profile to investors depends in some part on the outcome of the (re-)insurance offered by the SPV that issues the notes.

Although there are a growing number of examples of risks that can be insured using a securitization conduit, we consider only a few particular risks and risk transfer vehicles: residual value insurance for capital assets, credit default insurance, bulk retrocession capacity for trade credit reinsurance, product liability insurance, and life insurance.

Residual Value Protection: Toyota Motor Credit Corporation

Like other automotive firms, the Toyota Motor Credit Corporation (TMCC) faces a risk that the residual value of a car that has been leased is below its market value. We saw in Chapter 21 that a guarantee is one way for firms facing residual value risk to address that risk, as three participants in the airline financing arena have done. As we shall see here, securitization provides another ART-istic alternative.

Most leases contain a provision allowing the lessee to purchase the vehicle at the end of a lease period. If the market price is below the residual value of the car, the lessee likely will exercise the option to buy the car. This means that most cars returned to TMCC result in an immediate loss equal to the difference between the residual value of the car and its resale value.

Grammercy Place Insurance Ltd. is a SPV and Cayman Islands–registered insurance company whose single purpose is to provide direct residual value insurance to TMCC. The underlying pool of assets was a predetermined pool of about 260,000 auto and light-duty truck leases originated by Toyota and Lexus dealers that were assigned to and serviced by TMCC.

Under the terms of the insurance contract between Grammercy and TMCC, TMCC paid a quarterly premium to Grammercy for the residual value insurance. In turn, Grammercy provides annual coverage to TMCC for three years for the risk of residual value losses. The multiyear coverage was structured as three separate insurance policies, each of which included a 10 percent copayment provision so that TMCC retained 10 percent of each year's annual residual value loss. In addition, each year's coverage involved a deductible equal to approximately 9 percent of the aggregate initial residual value of all the leases covered by the underlying policy.

Grammercy issued three classes of securities, all of which were floating rate notes paying interest quarterly equal to LIBOR plus a spread that depends on the class. The original issue amount called for about $60 million of senior Class A notes, $283 million of mezzanine Class B securities, and $222 million of highly subordinated Class C bonds. The total issue was planned for just over $566 million.

The proceeds from this security issue were placed in a trust collateral account managed by Chase. Chase used the cash subscription issue to acquire AAA-rated liquid securities. The interest on these securities was paid to Goldman Sachs Mitsui Marine Derivative Products LP through an income swap in exchange for a more stable LIBOR-based cash flow that Grammercy in turn paid out as interest to the note holders.

Because the insurance policy was annual with an October maturity, each October TMCC would submit its residual value claims—that is, losses in excess of the deductible for that year minus the 10 percent coinsurance requirement—to Grammercy. A portion of the collateral then would be liquidated (and the corresponding part of the swap unwound). Proceeds from the collateral liquidation would be used to pay any TMCC claims, with the remainder being used to make a scheduled principal repayment on the notes according to Table 22.1.

Principal repayments are made to each class of Grammercy note holder based on priority. If the value of the liquidated collateral less claims paid to TMCC is not enough to cover the scheduled principal repayments on all three classes for that year, the note holders bear the loss. If there is a surplus in years 1 or 2, it can be applied to a subsequent year's deficit.[10]

The Class A, B, and C notes had maturities of one, two, and three years, respectively. Principal on each class of note was at risk if sales prices on the reference portfolio fell by more than 23, 15, and 9 percent (respectively) below expectations. The notes were priced at 23, 45, and 325 basis points over three-month LIBOR, respectively, and were rated AA, A, and BB.

As Exhibit 22.6 shows, the TMCC Grammercy looks structurally a lot like a CDO, except that the event leading to a reduction in principle for the note holders is now a payment of a claim to TMCC on a three-year residual lease value insurance policy. In a CDO, principal reduction occurred because the funds were not paid in on the assets held by the SPV. In the TMCC issue, the SPV has the requisite assets, but it applies those to the insurance cover written to TMCC before repayment of principal on the securities Grammercy has issued.

The net result of this structure was TMCC obtaining a classical insurance cover through a highly nontraditional avenue. In essence, TMCC obtained residual value insurance from the capital market directly rather than from a (re-)insurance company.

Credit Default Insurance: Mortgage Default Recourse Notes

Morgan Stanley's Mortgage Default Recourse Notes (MODERNs) are notes issued through a SPV called G3 Mortgage Reinsurance Ltd. that allow the

TABLE 22.1 Principal Repayment Schedule on Grammercy TMCC Notes

	First Policy (October 1999)	Second Policy (October 2000)	Third Policy (October 2001)
Class A	$22,650,000	$23,230,000	$14,800,000
Class B	$105,690,000	$108,390,000	$69,050,000
Class C	$83,040,000	$85,170,000	$54,260,000
TOTAL	$211,380,000	$216,790,000	$138,110,000

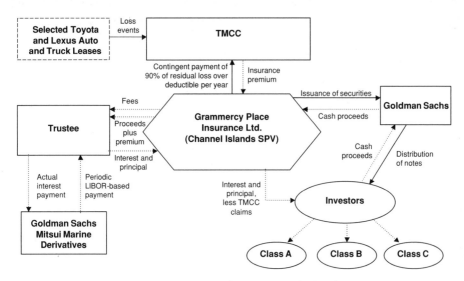

EXHIBIT 22.6   Toyota Motor Credit Corp. Residual Value Insurance

Federal Home Loan Mortgage Corporation (Freddie Mac) to obtain default insurance coverage through a securitization conduit rather than directly from a (re-)insurer. MODERNs include five classes of securities with 10 years to maturity that pay principal and interest based on the default record of an underlying $15 billion pool of fixed-rate, single-family 30-year mortgages originated in 1996.

MODERNs holders receive LIBOR plus a spread based on the outstanding principal amount. The principal is recalculated each period to include only the non-defaulted principal on the underlying mortgage assets. In the event of a mortgage default in the reference asset pool, the principal repayment to MODERNs holders is reduced accordingly.

Exhibit 22.7 shows the structure of MODERNs. They function very much like the TMCC Grammercy notes explored above. Proceeds from the sale of the five classes of notes are given to Chase, acting as the collateral manager and trustee. Chase invests the proceeds of the issue in marketable securities and then enters into an income swap with Morgan Stanley Capital Services to smooth the timing of the cash flows. The receivables on the swap are used to make interest payments on the notes issued by G3.

The insurance policy that G3 has written to Freddie Mac requires monthly premium payments by Freddie Mac that are added to the collateral account. In turn, the collateral account—including premium, the value of securities held, and income generated by those securities—is used to finance claims from Freddie Mac arising from defaults on its mortgage portfolio.

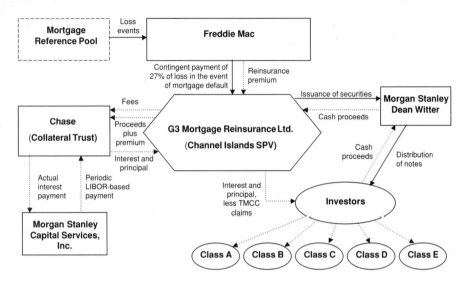

EXHIBIT 22.7 Mortgage Default Recourse Notes (MODERNs)

The remaining value of the assets in the collateral account are used to make scheduled principal repayments to the note holders based on the priority of their class.

Bulk Retrocession Capacity: Gerling Credit Insurance Group

The 1999 issue of Synthetic European Credit Tracking Securities (SECTRS) provides a good illustration of how securitized products can be used to create bulk capacity in the reinsurance area. Specifically, SECTRS were used to construct a synthetic retrocession for Gerling Credit Insurance Group's reinsurance of certain European trade credits.

Before analyzing SECTRS themselves, some background on the covered trade credit insurance is warranted. The ceding reinsurer in the SECTRS issue was Namur Re SA, a subsidiary of Gerling-Konzern Speziale Kreditverischerungs AG, in turn a subsidiary of Gerling Credit Insurance Group (GCIG) and Gerling-Konzern Globale Rückversicherungs AG. Namur Re provides trade credit reinsurance, and GCIG provides direct credit insurance.

The top portion of Exhibit 22.8 shows how trade credit insurance and reinsurance work in practice using the names of the firms involved with this transaction. A corporation extends trade credit to vendors, suppliers, and other obligors any time it renders services or makes a product delivery before it receives payment. Insurance on nonpayment following the provision of ser-

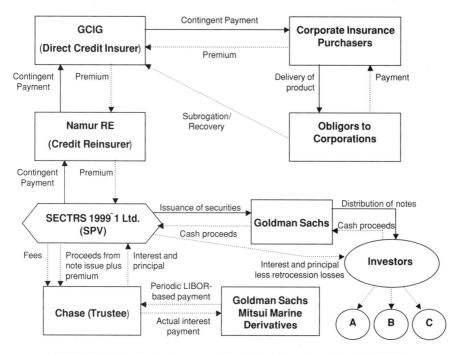

EXHIBIT 22.8 Synthetic European Credit Tracking Securities (SECTRS)

vices or delivery of goods is trade credit insurance. In the exhibit, the direct credit insurer GCIG makes a contingent payment to the corporation in the event of default by a trade credit obligor. As in any indemnity contract, GCIG retains subrogation rights to pursue the obligor for a recovery. Namur Re provides the reinsurance.

SECTRS were designed to provide €450 million in retrocession cover to Namur Re based on a portfolio of 92,000 businesses selected at random in the trade insurance market. To accomplish this, SECTRS 1999-1 Ltd. was set up in the Cayman Islands as a SPV and licensed reinsurer. Three classes of securities were issued for maturity three years after the issue date. Interest on the securities was payable quarterly in arrears and equal to LIBOR plus a spread, where the spread is higher the lower the priority of the claim on the SPV's capital structure.

As in the TMCC case and as shown in Exhibit 22.9, Chase acts as the trustee and is given both the proceeds of the security issue and the premium paid by Namur to the SPV. This is invested in marketable securities, and interest on the securities is swapped with Goldman Sachs Mitsui Marine Derivative Products LP for a LIBOR-based stable income stream that is used to pay interest on the notes.

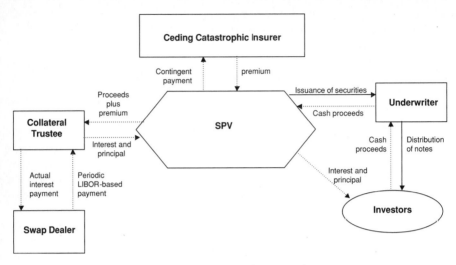

EXHIBIT 22.9 Typical Cat Bond

The SPV provides reinsurance to Namur Re on an XOL basis for three separate reference portfolios into which the 92,000 reference businesses are divided. To determine the retrocession payment structure, an annual count is made of the number of businesses in the reference portfolio that have experienced a trade credit default event in the prior annual period. In addition, a cumulative count is maintained for years 2 and 3 of the structure. The retrocession trigger is activated when either the annual count exceeds the annual attachment point for any of the three policies or when the cumulative count exceeds the cumulative attachment point. The payment due from the SPV to the ceding reinsurer then is determined by multiplying the excess of the annual or cumulative count above the lower attachment point by a predefined recovery rate. Each policy also includes an upper limit.

The end result is a series of three securities whose principal repayments are reduced based on the claims the SPV receives as retrocessionaire for Namur Re on the reference portfolio of trade credits. The ceding reinsurer, in turn, has successfully accessed significant bulk capacity directly from the capital market.

Product Liability Insurance: Capital Risk Strategies

Motivated by the size and severity of product liability claims—especially following Dow Corning's bankruptcy as a result of such claims—the insurance brokerage and investment banking firm Capital Risk Strategies (CRS) proposed in 1996 an ART form that creatively combines traditional risk transfer, finite risk, and securitization to provide up to $4 billion in cover for product liability claims.[11]

The program begins with collection of premiums from end corporate insurance purchasers—mainly pharmaceutical and medical device companies. The insured firms will commit to pay premiums for 10 years to a SPV based in Bermuda in return for a 10-year $4 billion product liability policy. The coverage will include a 5 percent copayment requirement for purchasers and will attach at $750 million in losses. The cover also includes a $1 billion per occurrence limit as well as a $2 billion per company limit.

The SPV will issue bonds—planned through Salomon Brothers—expected to generate $1.63 billion in initial subscriptions. With some supplementary capital, the SPV will have an initial capitalization of $1.75 billion, expected to grow to $4 billion over time. In addition, the premiums collected from the insured will be part of the SPV's assets. About 85 percent of those premiums written will be used as collateral for the bonds issued. From the remaining 15 percent, Centre Re will provide $3 billion in reinsurance for the SPV. The Centre Re policy is primarily a loss portfolio transfer designed to address the timing risk arising from the slow growth of the $1.75 billion in capital to the planned $4 billion, which would be jeopardized by large, early claims. But Centre Re also bears some underwriting risk on large losses that might occur early in the life of the program. The remaining $1 billion will be reinsured via quota share treaties with other large reinsurers.

The program was aimed at eight to 15 companies that would commit to the long-term plan and be willing to mutualize both their product liability losses and insurance coverage. As of this writing, the author was unable to ascertain if the product has been placed successfully.

Life Acquisition Costs and Mortality and Expense Fees

Very little in this book has addressed life insurance, but it remains one of the largest parts of the global (re-)insurance industry. And unlike almost all of the other risks discussed, life insurance is fundamentally different because it eventually will pay off. Excluding the odd disqualification of suicide or a lazy beneficiary, life insurance inevitably will result a claim.

One problem faced by life insurers is the cash strain they bear shortly after underwriting a life policy on policy acquisition costs. Every variable annuity or life policy sold generates a brokerage and/or distribution cost that the insurer must pay immediately, despite earning the cash flow back over the first three to five years of the policy life. This can create a drag on a life insurer's balance sheet.[12]

Three of the early and notable life insurance-related securitizations were aimed at securitizing these life policy acquisition costs.[13] In 1996 and 1997, American Skandia Life Assurance Corp. conducted a series of four transactions in which it conveyed to its parent 80 to 100 percent of its rights to receive future mortality and expense (M&E) charges and contingent deferred sales charges on a portion of its life program. The parent paid the insurance company an amount essentially equal to the present value of those expected future claims, much as in a loss portfolio transfer. The parent, in turn, securitized the future fees through an SPV backed with those receivables.

A second life securitization was undertaken by U.K. mutual insurer National Provident Institution (NPI). In a simpler structure, NPI securitized the future profits on a large block of its life policies. It established the SPV Mutual Securitisation PLC to issue two classes of limited recourse bonds, both of which received interest and principal based on the emerging surplus on NPI's block of life policies. The two classes of securities were separated by the dates of their principal repayments to amortize the expected surplus development over time. Class A repaid principal from 1998 to 2012, and Class B from 2012 to 2022. By securitizing its surplus, NPI was able to generate cash in 1998 for a surplus that would only emerge over many years. In many ways, the NPI securitization thus can be viewed more as a synthetic finite risk transaction than a classical risk transfer.

A third life transaction was conducted by Germany's reinsurance giant Hannover Re in conjunction with Rabobank. To finance the expansion of its life lines across Europe, Hannover and Rabo set up a Dublin-based SPV called Interpolis Re, owned by Rabo. Hannover retroceded 75 percent of its defined reinsurance treaties to Interpolis in a quota share treaty. In return, Rabo made a DM100 million loan to Interpolis, on which Hannover could draw for liquidity. Take out the SPV and the transaction is essentially just an asset swap. But with the SPV in the middle, Hannover received liquidity from Rabo. Interpolis absorbed the reinsurance risk, but Rabo in turn receives 75 percent of the profits on the future business.

SECURITIZED CATASTROPHIC (RE-)INSURANCE

The vast majority of ILNs that have been issued to date have been linked to catastrophic (re-)insurance and losses arising from natural disasters such as earthquakes, hail storms, tropical cyclones, windstorms, tornados, and the like. Often regarded as the most triumphant achievement of ARTists, the "Cat bond" industry actually is quite small compared to many of the other structures alaready explored. Nevertheless, Cat bonds certainly are among the most creative—and analyzed—ARTifacts in the market today.

Because of the volume of material available on Cat bonds, this section is brief and limited to a discussion of the most basic and prevalent structures.[14]

Mechanics

Most Cat bond issues emerge from a conduit that is fundamentally similar to the basic CDO structure explored at the beginning of the chapter. Once the nature of the protection desired by the reinsurer is defined, the reinsurer pays catastrophic reinsurance premiums to a single-purpose SPV, which then gives the premiums and the proceeds of its note issue to a collateral trustee. The investment income on the liquid assets acquired by the trustee for the SPV's collateral (including the proceeds from liquidations) usually is swapped for a more predictable and regular flow of income. The mechanics of the structure are shown in Exhibit 22.9.

As in the other structures we have examined, the collateral held in trust can be used to pay principal (and in some cases interest) on the securities issued by the SPV only after the SPV's contingent liabilities have been paid—in this case, claims on the cat reinsurance treaty negotiated between the ceding reinsurer and SPV.

This basic setup can be modified in a number of different ways. One variation involves the structuring of the conduit itself to allow for a reinsurer standing in between the ceding insurer and the SPV. Shown in Exhibit 22.10, this intermediary reinsurer can play two functions.

1. It can choose the risks to retrocede to the SPV so that the events on which the Cat bonds are based can be customized more easily than in a traditional insurance program.
2. The reinsurer might give the ceding insurer indemnity coverage but retrocede indexed cover to the SPV. This would increase the liquidity and

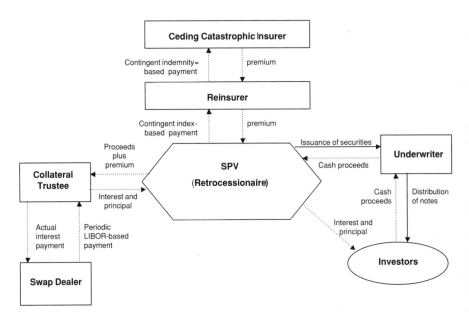

EXHIBIT 22.10   Cat Bond Structure with an Intermediary Reinsurer

transparency of the issue without forcing the ceding insurer to bear the basis risk of index/indemnity mismatches. The reinsurer, of course, would then have that basis risk with which to contend.

Other variations on the basic structure can involve changes in the payment provisions to end note holders. In the basic structure, cat claims result in principal reductions to holders of securities issued by SPV. If multiple classes of securities are issued, the principal reductions typically are applied to the securities in reverse order of their priority in the SPV's capital structure. Alternatively, a claim by the ceding (re-)insurer may result in a delay in principal repayment rather than a permanent forfeiture. Through the use of defeasance provisions, some proportion of the principal would be returned on schedule. The rest would be returned later and may be funded by the purchase of zero-coupon securities using the proceeds from the guaranteed portion of the original issue.

The maturity of the bonds is sometimes changed for reasons other than defeasance purposes. Losses on natural catastrophes often are reported gradually over a long period of time after the triggering event occurs. When a peril gives rise to a covered loss toward the end of the life of the bonds, the SPV often can optionally extend the maturity of the bonds to allow to include the full loss development period.

Yet another way to change the structure involves the wrapping of certain classes of securities issued by the SPV. In virtually all of the examples explored in the chapter thus far, the senior class of securities issued by an SPV is either funded or credit-wrapped to guarantee an investment-grade rating. The reason for this is that many institutional investors, such as U.S. commercial banks and pension plans, are precluded from holding below-investment-grade securities in any sizable quantities, if at all.

Most early Cat bond issues that were regarded as successful involved at least two tranches of securities, the senior of which was rated investment grade. The enhancement often was provided through a self-collateralization of the issue—that is, escrow investment of proceeds from the issue in Treasuries dedicated to back the principal repayment. A credit wrap was also a possibility.

More recently, however, the trend in Cat bond issues has been toward lower-rated securities. Even in the recent multitranche issues, the senior bonds may not be rated investment grade. As expected, participation in the issues has changed over time. Early issues were bought largely by money managers, mutual funds, and pension plans. But the more recent lower-rated issues have been placed mainly with hedge funds and insurance companies.

Events, Triggers, and Losses

The triggering event for a Cat bond may not necessarily be related to the bond holders' payments. The triggering event may be either single-peril (e.g., a single tropical cyclone damaging a specific firm) or multiperil (e.g., East Coast and West Coast earthquakes). If the specified events occur during the "risk period" specified in a Cat bond structure—which may or may not encompass the entire life of the bond—the event trigger is activated.

Cat bonds are often double-trigger instruments. The claims paid to the insurer seeking protection from a cat bond issue are generally loss based, although fixed-payment structures could be created. A loss-based insurance contract to which bond holders' payments are tied may either be indemnity based or index based. In the former, losses paid by the SPV's bond holders are actual business losses, whereas index-based loss claims are based on the loss development in one or more specific catastrophic loss indices (e.g., a PCS regional index). Index products are popular when there is a concern about moral hazard or adverse selection at the ceding (re-)insurer, but using an index introduces basis risk. Indemnity-based deals that are based on actual damages sustained by specific businesses result in coverage that matches a cedant's loss experience. Introducing an index of damages eliminates the cedant's ability to manipulate losses but at the same time increases the likelihood that the coverage will track the actual damages sustained poorly.

In addition to discouraging moral hazard, indexing the loss payments to which a Cat bond's interest and/or principal are tied can increase the bonds' liquidity and attractiveness to end investors. Indemnity-based losses are very opaque and difficult to monitor or anticipate, whereas loss developments in an index are usually more transparent and widely available to market participants. The easier it is for investors to analyze the risks and returns of the bonds, the more likely it is that they will identify portfolio benefits to holding them.

In any loss-based Cat bond, the second trigger is the lower attachment point specified in the insurance contract offered by the SPV and reflected in the bonds' interest and/or principal payment schedule. These products actually can be viewed as single-trigger products, where the trigger is defined as losses above the attachment point arising from the specifically enumerated peril(s).

Alternatively, some Cat bonds employ a physical trigger as the first trigger and a loss trigger above some lower attachment point as the second one. A physical trigger is activated by the occurrence of some specific physical events, such as an earthquake above 7.0 on the Richter scale.

Examples

Given the diversity of Cat bonds issued to date, the best way to get a feel for the wide degree of variance across these structures is to present a few examples. These examples are neither exhaustive nor necessarily representative. They simply demonstrate the range of what has been done.

Swiss Re/SR Earthquake Fund Ltd.

In 1997 the SR Earthquake Fund Ltd. SPV issued $137 million in four classes of notes whose repayment schedule was linked to the SPV's payment of claims to Swiss Re on a $111.9 million catastrophic retrocession cover. The triggering event was a California earthquake, and the SPV's contingent liability to Swiss Re was based on the largest insured loss from a single earthquake over a two-year period as determined by PCS. The SR Earthquake bonds thus were single-peril, indexed Cat bonds.

The SR Earthquake retrocession was a value contract, not a true indemnity contract. Depending on the size of the loss, the principal of the bonds is reduced by a fixed amount depending on the bonds' priority. The first two classes of SR Earthquake bonds were the first cat bonds to be rated investment grade—Baa3 by Moody's and BBB– by Fitch. A maximum of 60 percent of the principal was at risk, with the remaining amount self-collateralized by the SPV's acquisition of Treasuries. Class A-1 paid a fixed rate of 8.645 percent, and Class A-2 paid 255 bps over three-month LIBOR.

The third class had up to 100 percent principal at risk and paid 10.493 percent. Class B was rated Ba1/BB and had a principal risk tied to the PCS index losses arising from a California earthquake. The most subordinated issue, Class C, paid 11.952 percent and had no rating. Unlike the other three classes, principal losses were not based on the indemnity payments by the SPV. Instead, Class C bond holders forfeited 100 percent of their principal in the event that the largest California quake led to PCS-reported insured losses exceeding $12 billion.

Relative to original issue amounts of $62 million, $60 million, and $14.7 million for the Class A, B, and C notes, respectively, Exhibit 22.11 shows the various loss triggers and payment amounts (excluding any deductible) from each class of security as well as the total.

From a financial engineering standpoint, the exhibit illustrates that each bond in the SR Earthquake structure can be viewed as a coupon bond plus one or more binary options. Class C either returns full principal in the event of no quake resulting in over $12 billion in PCS index losses or returns nothing. From the SPV's perspective, this is equivalent to a coupon bond plus a digital call on PCS index losses (i.e., a put on PCS index-implied property values) struck at $12 billion with a fixed payout of $14.7 million, the total size of the Class C note issue.

The Class A and B bonds are synthetically equivalent to coupon bonds plus long vertical spreads consisting of digital options. In the Class B note case, for example, the SPV withholds no principal for losses under $18.5 billion, $12.4 million for losses above $18.5 billion, $24.8 million for losses above $21 billion, and $37.2 million for losses above $24 billion. The first piece of the binary vertical spread is a long call on PCS losses struck at $18.5 billion with a fixed payment of $12.4 million. The second component

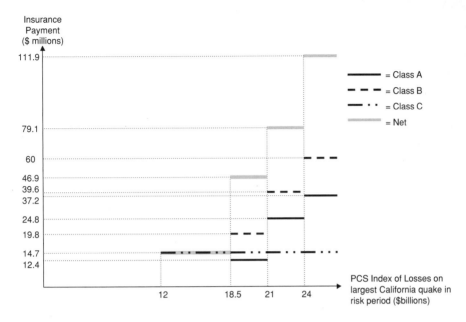

EXHIBIT 22.11 SR Earthquake Bond

is a long digital call struck at $21 billion with a fixed payout of $24.8 million. But without an additional leg, both options would be in the money at loss levels above $21 billion. To limit the total hold-back to $24.8 million, the spread thus also must include a short digital call on PCS losses struck at $21 billion with a fixed payout of $12.4 million. For loss levels above $21 billion, all three options are in the money, and the net is as follows: +$12.4 million on the long call struck at $18.5 billion, +24.8 million on the long call struck at $21 billion, and −$12.4 million on the short call struck at $21 billion. And so on for the rest of the loss trigger levels as well as for the Class A notes.

The SR Earthquake bonds included a one-year loss development period. A natural tension arises concerning scheduled principal repayments over loss development periods. (Re-)insurers prefer longer loss development periods, because reported losses only grow with time. The longer the period included in the retrocession agreement, the more Swiss Re would recover from bond holders. On the other side, investors clearly prefer a return of principal as quickly as possible. As a compromise, the SR Earthquake bonds require the regular comparison during the loss development period of estimated losses with a growing loss benchmark. If loss development is steadily growing, the trustee keeps the principal on reserve as a source of potential future claims by

Swiss Re for up to a year. But when loss development stabilizes below a predefined trigger relative to the benchmark, principal is returned.

Tokio Marine & Fire/Parametric Re

The Cayman Island SPV Parametric Re issued bonds in 1997 and simultaneously entered into a reinsurance agreement with Tokio Marine & Fire. Unlike the SR Earthquake bonds, where the trigger was index based, the Parametric Re issue involved a trigger based on the physical attributes of the event.

The insured event was an earthquake in or around Tokyo. The structure defined an "inner" and "outer" grid with Tokyo roughly at the geographic center. Upon the occurrence of an earthquake, the quake epicenter would serve as the basis for whether the event was deem to have occurred in the inner or outer grid. The location and magnitude of the quake then determined the required payment from Parametric Re to Tokio Marine on the reinsurance. A quake that registered 7.4 on the Japan Metereological Association scale, for example, would involve a hold-back by the SPV trustee of 44 percent of principal on the outstanding notes if the event occurred in the outer grid or a hold-back of 70 percent for quakes with inner-grid epicenters. These amounts held back from note holders then would be used to pay Tokio Marine in the reinsurance agreement between Tokio and Parametric Re.

The Parametric Re issue involved two classes of securities. "Notes" with a face value of $80 million were fully exposed to quake risk, whereas "units" were not. Units with a total issue value of $20 million included $10 million in defeasance certificates with no quake exposure and another $10 million in notes fully exposed to quake risk.

One advantage of a physical trigger like the one Parametric Re employed is the speed of payment. No loss development period is required, and claims can be funded by the trustee's investments of the proceeds from the original issue plus the premium received and any investment income generated on those investments. In addition, some users find physical trigger structures easier to hedge or reinsure. All that is required to virtually eliminate basis risk is another instrument that can be indexed to the same trigger.

Residential Re/USAA

One of the best-known Cat bond issues was undertaken in 1997 by the United States Automobile Association (USAA) based on a single peril—hurricanes on the eastern coast of the United States. Two classes of bonds were issued from which $477 million was raised—nearly four times the planned subscription amount. Class A1 securities in the amount of $87 million were issued with a coupon of LIBOR plus 273 bps. Class A2 bonds totaled about $313 million and had an interest rate of LIBOR plus 576 bps. The interest on both bonds was at risk. The Class A2 securities also had principal at risk, whereas $77 million of the $477 million collected from the issue was used to guarantee principal repayment on the Class A1 bonds. The A1 and A2 bonds were rated AAA and BB by Fitch, respectively.

Unlike the two prior structures, Residential Re's reinsurance contract of USAA was a true indemnity contract. In the event of a single hurricane hitting one or more of the 20 eastern states, the policy provided XOL cover to USAA with a copay—specifically, 80 percent of $500 mn XS $1 bn of actual USAA losses were covered by the policy.

Georgetown Re/St. Paul Companies

St. Paul companies undertook a $68.5 million securitization in 1996 to create additional retrocessional capacity for its reinsurance subsidiary, St. Paul Re, so that it could take advantage of a then-strong demand for catastrophic XOL reinsurance in North America.

Georgetown Re was capitalized by the issue of both notes ($44.5 million) and preferred stock ($23.2 million) with expirations in 2007 and 2000, respectively. The notes guaranteed a principal return through the investment of note issue proceeds by the SPV in zero-coupon marketable securities, thus leading to a AAA rating for the notes. The unrated preferred stock had no principal protection.

The Georgetown Re structure did not involve any specific definition of triggering events. Instead, St. Paul Re ceded part of its catastrophic XOL policy line to Georgetown Re in a classical proportional treaty lasting 10 years. The interest payments on the notes and shares and the principal repayment on the shares then was determined based on the overall performance of the ceded business lines. By including both the underwriting and the investment sides of its catastrophic XOL business, the resulting cession was well diversified and proved very attractive to investors.

SYNTHETIC CATASTROPHIC SECURITIZATION STRUCTURES

Just as CDOs can be cash flow or synthetic, catastrophic insurance products also have been undertaken on both an actual cash flow and a synthetic basis. The cash flow products described in the prior section have been a bit more prevalent than the synthetic structures, but synthetic securitizations of catastrophic insurance risk still accounts for a reasonable share of the catastrophic ART market. The best way to explore this range of products is again by example.

Allianz Risk Transfer/Gemini Re Options on Insurance-Linked Notes

Allianz Risk Transfer—the ART affiliate of the German insurance giant Allianz—developed a structure that allowed it to combine derivatives-like with insurance-linked notes in the issuance of an option on an ILN issue.[15] Concerned that a major catastrophic loss would lead to a hardening in the regular reinsurance market, Allianz sought to cap its future reinsurance costs by using the option on a ILN issue as a type of preloss funding.

The option was sold to investors in 1999 by SPV Gemini Re and gave Allianz three years during which that option could be exercised. If exercised, the writers of the option to Allianz agreed to purchase three-year notes whose principal and interest payments were linked to losses on European wind and hailstorms. Called *subscription agreements*, the options knock in when wind and hail losses reach a specified triggering amount. In exchange for preagreeing to purchase the notes at a specified price, the option writers receive a commitment fee.

The notes underlying the option were for an original principal of $150 million. If the options are exercised by Allianz and trigger a purchase of the notes, the structure functions much like the ones we have explored already. The note proceeds are placed in a collateral account in Gemini Re and are invested in reserve assets to fund insurance claims. As usual, Gemini Re engages in a total return or income swap to smooth the actual investment income on the investment portfolio into a LIBOR-based cash flow stream suitable for servicing the notes.

Gemini Re in turn entered into a retrocession agreement with Allianz Risk Transfer, itself a retrocessionaire for Allianz AG. The holders of the notes issued by Gemini Re receive a basic interest payment of LIBOR plus a risk spread unless the retrocession agreement between Gemini Re and Allianz Risk Transfer results in claims payments. In that case, both the interest and principal of the notes may not be paid off completely. The structure is shown in Exhibit 22.12.

Winterthur Hail Bonds

Eschewing securitization through an SPV structure, the Swiss primary insurance carrier Winterthur went directly to the capital market by issuing insurance-based structured notes—straight bonds plus embedded insurance derivatives. The bonds were three-year subordinated convertible debt instruments with face value CHF400 million.

In addition to a conversion provision, the bonds included what Winterthur called WinCat Coupons, or coupons indexed to a catastrophic triggering event. During the reference period, Winterthur would count the number of motor vehicle claims on which it had to pay out as a direct result of hail or storm damage. If the number was 6,000 or more, the WinCat Coupons were reset to zero. Otherwise, the WinCat coupons were set at a rate one-third higher than the interest rate on Winterthur's traditional convertibles. The conversion premium was 7 percent. Although the risk transfer provided to

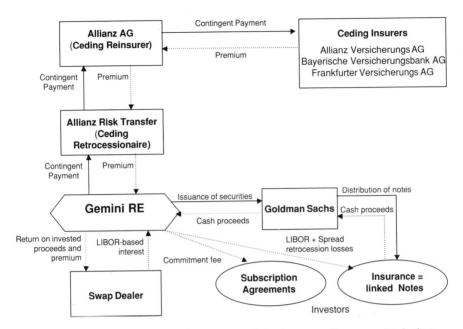

EXHIBIT 22.12   Allianz Risk Transfer/Gemini RE Option on an Insurance-Linked Note

Winterthur is estimated only to have been around CHF9 million, the issue is widely regarded as having been a success.[16]

From a financial engineering perspective, the subordinated WinCat convertibles can be viewed as subordinated convertible debt—itself a combination of straight coupon debt with warrants—plus a portfolio of knock-out options attached to the bond's normal coupons. The trigger on the knock-out options was the number of motor vehicle claims in the corresponding reference period. If the option was not knocked out, bond holders would receive their promised coupon rate. Therefore, the knock-out options were also binary.

Mitsui Marine/Swiss Re Cat Swap

The 1998 Mitsui Marine/Swiss Re Cat swap transaction is almost identical to the Tokio Marine/Parametric Re structure, except that Mitsui Marine accomplished a risk transfer similar to Tokio Marine using a swap rather than a securitization conduit. The trigger parameters underlying the swap were the same as those used in the Parametric Re bond deal.

Specifically, Mitsui agreed to periodically pay Swiss Re (i.e., the swap counterparty) LIBOR plus 375 bps for three years.[17] In return, Swiss Re agreed to make up to $30 million in contingent payments to Mitsui Marine in the event of an earthquake with an epicenter near Tokyo and a Richter scale rating of at least 7.1. The structure of this deal is shown in Exhibit 22.13.

Swiss Re/Tokio Marine Cat Basis Swap

Swiss Re and Tokio Marine completed a one-year $450 million swap agreement in 2001 that allows the reinsurers literally to swap catastrophic exposures with one another. The transaction involves three separate tranches, each of which is based on $150 million. The three tranches involve an exchange of Swiss Re's California earthquake exposures for Tokio Marine's Japanese earthquake exposures, Swiss Re's Florida hurricane risks for Tokio Marine's Japanese typhoon losses, and Swiss Re's French storm liabilities for Tokio Marine's Japanese cyclone liabilities.

The structure of the transaction, bundled under a single master swap agreement, is shown in Exhibit 22.14. Clearly the objective of the two insurance companies is to diversify their geographical catastrophic exposures.

Exchange-Traded Catastrophic Derivatives[18]

In 1992 the Chicago Board of Trade (CBOT) introduced exchange-traded derivatives contracts whose underlyings are based on catastrophic insurance losses.[19] In 2000 the contracts were delisted for trading. Although still a favorite subject for theoreticians to discuss, exchange-traded cat products have never passed the market test.

ISO Futures and Futures Options

In December 1992, the CBOT introduced catastrophe futures contracts (CATs). Separate contracts were listed for insured catastrophic losses by region. In addition to a national loss contract, the CBOT listed contracts covering catastrophic property losses in the eastern, midwestern, and western sections of the United States. These regional contracts were intended to track broadly insured losses arising from hurricanes, tornadoes, and earthquakes, respectively.

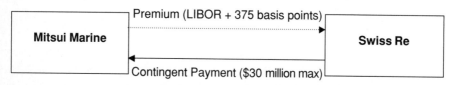

EXHIBIT 22.13   Mitsui Marine/Swiss RE Cat Swap

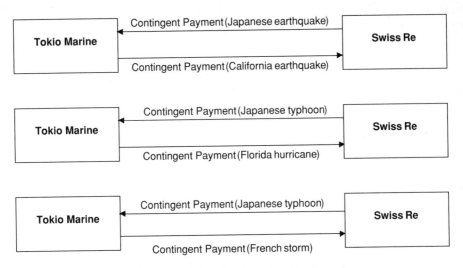

EXHIBIT 22.14 Tokio Marine/Swiss RE Cat Basis Swap

Because no "underlying" was readily identifiable for such contracts, the CBOT created an index that imparts values to the futures contracts by the contracts' reference to the index level at settlement. The index was based on losses reported quarterly to the independent Insurance Services Office (ISO), which collects information from about 100 insurance companies. The specific settlement value of the futures was based on a sample of companies selected by the ISO. The CBOT futures had a notional amount of $25,000.

A central concept for understanding Cat futures is the notion of an "event quarter." The event quarter is the quarter in which insured losses on which the futures are based occur. The CBOT listed four futures contracts for any particular year: March, June, September, and December. The listed contract months corresponded to the month in which the event quarter underlying the contract ended (e.g., March for the first quarter). Contracts were listed for trading four quarters before the beginning of event quarters.

To take a specific example, suppose the current time period is denoted as time t, and any increments to t are quarters. If time t denotes January, t + 1 is March, t + 2 is June, and so on. For a futures contract maturing at time t + 2, the CBOT defined the settlement value of the contract for the long as follows:

$$F_{t+2,t+2} = \$25,000 \min\left[2, \frac{L_{t,t+1}}{P_{t,t+1}}\right] \qquad (22.1)$$

where $F_{t+2,t+2}$ denotes the time t + 2 price of a contract maturing at time t + 2, $L_{t,t+1}$ denotes the reported losses incurred (based on the ISO index) from time t to t + 1, and $P_{t,t+1}$ denotes the value of the premiums collected by the companies in the ISO index for losses incurred between t and t + 1. The underlying of the contract was not the level of losses but rather the *loss ratio*, which was subject to a capped loss ratio of 2. If the ratio of losses to premiums collected exceeded 2, the long could receive only $50,000 per contract.

Calculations of the settlement value of the contract, losses, and premiums collected were based on aggregate figures reported to and estimated by the ISO. The value of the contract thus was based on a loss ratio for the pool of companies in the ISO index. The ISO announced that pool of companies when the futures contract was listed. At that time, the ISO also announced the estimated value of the premium pool collected by those companies for the relevant event quarter. Premiums thus were constant and known for the life of a futures contract, theoretically making their value a function of expected loss liabilities only.

Although the contract described in equation 22.1 settles at time t + 2, losses and premiums alike are indexed by a t,t + 1 subscript. Both losses and premiums on which the contract's settlement value were based on the event quarter starting at time t and ending at time t + 1. The quarter between time t + 1 to t + 2 was called the *runoff quarter* and was included to allow for a lag in the reporting of losses to the ISO. Although $L_{t,t+1}$ is an estimate of losses occurring between t and t + 1, losses continued to be reported on that quarter through settlement date t + 2. The settlement value of the contract thus was based on catastrophic losses incurred between t and t + 1 and reported between t and t + 2.

Cummins and Geman (1995) provide a simple illustrative example of how an insurer might have used the Cat futures contract to hedge catastrophic risk as an alternative to reinsurance. Suppose the insurer expects to collect premiums of $5 million and pay loss claims of $600,000 on catastrophic events that occur in the eastern United States between January and March. The loss ratio thus is expected to be 0.12, so the insurer is concerned about losses in excess of this ratio.

As an alternative to reinsurance, the insurer might go long at time t a number of eastern Cat futures determined as follows:

$$\Delta_{t,t+2} = \frac{P^*_{t,t+1}}{\$25,000} \left(\frac{\delta}{\rho_{t,t+2}} \right) \tag{22.2}$$

where $\Delta_{t,t+2}$ is the number of contracts held long at time t maturing at time t + 2, $P^*_{t,t+1}$ is the premium collected by the insurer, δ is the proportion of the expected loss the insurer wants to hedge, and $\rho_{t,t+2}$ is the proportion of total losses expected to be reported to the ISO between t and t + 2.

Suppose the hedger expects 80 percent of all losses reported to both itself and the ISO to be reported by June, when the March contract settles, so that $\rho_{t,t+2}=0.80$. If the insurer wants to hedge all its underwriting risk, $\delta = 1.0$. Substituting the values of $\rho_{t,t+2}$, δ, and $P^*_{t,t+1} = \$5,000,000$ into equation 22.2, the insurer evidently goes long 250 futures contracts at time t—that is, ($\$5$ million/$\$25,000$) $\times$ $(1/0.8) = 250$.

When the contract matures at time t + 2, suppose the actual losses on which the insurer must pay claims are $\$630,000$, or 5 percent higher than expected. The actual loss ratio thus would be 0.126. As a percentage of premium collected, the insurer has unexpectedly lost 5 percent, or $\$250,000$.

Assume for this example that the losses reflected in the ISO index are perfectly correlated with the losses the insurer actually experienced. In that case, the futures price will have increased by 5 percent relative to whatever its initial price was.[20] For each contract the insurer is long, the company will gain $\$1,000$ on its futures transaction—($\$25,000$/contract) $\times$ (0.05) $\times$ $(0.80) = \$1,000$. For $\Delta_{t,t+2} = 250$, the insurer thus makes $\$250,000$ on its futures hedge, exactly offsetting the unexpected loss (as a proportion of premium collected) due to the unanticipated higher loss liability.

In mid-1993 the CBOT augmented the Cat futures by listing options on Cat futures. At maturity, the holder of a Cat call thus had the option of entering into a long Cat futures contract at the strike price. For a Cat put, the option purchaser had the option at maturity of entering into a short futures contract at the strike price.

At the time they were introduced, Cat futures and options on futures seemed like a good idea. Most market participants never agreed, however. The National Cat options volume in November 1993, six months after the options first were listed, was 3,650 contracts traded for the month. By comparison, the CBOT's successful futures contract on long-term U.S. Treasury bonds had a daily volume on November 1, 1993, of 407,202 contracts. By June 1994, the product's one-year anniversary, volume had fallen to 98 contracts traded for the month. And in June 1995, no such contracts were traded. From their original listing in June 1993 through October 1995, the total volume of National Cat options traded was only 5,668 contracts. Total cumulative volumes for the eastern, midwestern, and western Cats from their introduction through October 1995 were 12,742 contracts, 60 contracts, and 44 contracts, respectively. The number of bond futures traded in one day was an order of magnitude greater than the volume of the most successful of the Cat contracts over the entire life of the contract. Cat futures and options died a slow, quiet death.

PCS Options

Rather than try to salvage catastrophic futures, the CBOT decided in 1995 that options had the most promising prospects as insurance derivatives. The

CBOT dispensed with the Cat contracts altogether and introduced options based on PCS indexes. Unlike the Cat options, the PCS options were cash-settled options with an underlying cash value determined by a new index. PCS options did not call for delivery of a futures contract; the CBOT did not even list PCS futures for trading.

PCS provides estimates of nine catastrophic loss indexes on a daily basis. These indexes are geographical and track PCS-estimated insured catastrophe losses nationally, by region (eastern, northeastern, southeastern, midwestern, western), and by state (Florida, Texas, and California).

Unlike the ISO index, the PCS index measures a loss, not a loss ratio. The PCS index value for any region is PCS's loss estimate divided by $100 million. To arrive at those catastrophic loss index values, PCS surveys at least 70 percent of companies, agents, and adjusters involved with catastrophic insurance. PCS's industry loss estimates are based on this survey, adjusted for nonsurveyed market share and adjusted again to take into account PCS's "National Insurance Risk Profile."

For each of the nine PCS indexes, the CBOT listed PCS options, available in both large-cap and small-cap forms. Large-cap PCS options track estimated catastrophic losses ranging from $20 billion to $50 billion, whereas small-cap PCS options track only losses of less than $20 billion.

As with the earlier Cat options, PCS options had settlement values based on an event period plus a runoff period. All but the western and California PCS options had quarterly event periods, and options thus were listed corresponding to the end of those four event quarters: March, June, September, and December. For the western and California indexes, the event period was annual.

Many people felt that the one-quarter runoff period for Cat futures had been inadequate for a large enough proportion of losses to be reported, so PCS option purchasers had a choice between two loss development periods: six or 12 months. The options traded until the last day of the development period.

The settlement value for PCS options was based on the settlement value for the relevant PCS index or the PCS loss estimate divided by $100 million. For convenience, the index value is rounded to the nearest first decimal. An estimated loss of $53 million, for example, has a true index value of 0.53. Rounded to 0.50, it implies an "industry loss equivalent" of $50 million.

PCS options were defined so that each index point was worth $200. A PCS loss index value of 0.50, for example, had a cash-equivalent option value of $100—(0.50) × ($200) = $100. Strike prices for PCS options were listed in integer multiples of 5 index points. For large-cap options, strikes of 200 to 495 were available, and for small-cap options, strikes from 5 to 195 were listed.

On the settlement date, the exercise value of a small-cap PCS call option with an event period from t to t + 1 (e.g., first quarter) and a six-month development period (e.g., second and third quarters) was as follows:

$$C_{t+3}^{sc} = \$200 \max\{\min[I_{t,t+1},200]-K,0 \qquad (22.3)$$

where C_{t+3} denotes the settlement value of the call at the end of the development period, $I_{t,t+1}$ is the value of the underlying PCS index based on losses incurred from t to t + 1 and reported from t to t + 3, and K is the strike price. The minimand reflects the definition of the option as a small-cap option—that is, gains on the option are capped at an index level of 200 or an industry loss equivalent of $20 billion. The maximand reflects the option's financial trigger—the exercise value of the option cannot be negative. For an otherwise identical large-cap call, the exercise value of the option was

$$C_{t+3}^{sc} = \$200 \max\{\max[\min(I_{t,t+1},500),200]-K,0\} \qquad (22.4)$$

The minimand reflects a cap on the index level at 500. Unlike equation 22.3, equation 22.4 contains two maximands. The first reflects the definition of the contract as a large-cap option, on which the index value is always at least 200. This extra maximand was not present in equation 22.3 only because the lower bound of losses covered by the small-cap options was $0. The outermost maximand, as before, reflects the limited liability of calls.

One reason why supporters of PCS products expected them to succeed was the synthetic equivalence between a vertical spread and XOL reinsurance. A long vertical spread strikes of 100 and 120, for example, locks in a vertical layer of protection between index levels of 100 and 120 and thus is synthetically equivalent to catastrophic XOL coverage at those levels.

The products also created an opportunity for reinsurers to design new, tailored types of structures. Lane (1998a) suggests how to use PCS options to construct synthetic accelerated quota shares, for example, in which the share of losses that the option user is hedging increases as the penetration of the loss layer gets larger.

Failure or Bad Timing?

Despite all efforts to construct a superior catastrophic insurance derivatives contract, ultimately the PCS options succumbed to the same fate as their ISO predecessors. Why?

One problem clearly was the absence of natural hedgers on both sides of the market. The appeal of buying a vertical spread makes sense only if there is a party willing to write it. Although reinsurance and retrocession are both common enough practices that one might have expected a two-sided market to emerge, it never did. Perhaps one reason was simply the concern of competition from the relatively concentrated reinsurance sector.

Another possible explanation for the failures of the two contracts concerns the sequencing of the evolution of substitutes and complements in derivatives activity. Exchange-traded derivatives typically are part of a process called "commodization" in which customized transactions negotiated in opaque, bilateral settings evolve toward more standardized transactions negotiated on formal markets.

Culp (1995a) summarizes the process by which cash-market and forward transactions have been commodized into exchange-traded derivaties such as futures. Like securitized products, however, exchange-traded derivatives did not replace privately negotiated cash and derivatives transactions. Instead, exchange-traded products evolved alongside their off-exchange and cash-market cousins.

A strategic planning issue faced by every futures exchange concerns the sequencing of listing a standardized product that is in the midst of the commodization process. Specifically, it is possible to list an exchange-traded product too early in the commodization cycle for the product to be demanded. Mortgage-backed securities, for example, likely would have been very unpopular had FNMA not begun issuing pass-through securities first.

A possible hindrance to the evolution of exchange-traded catastrophic loss derivatives was simply the lack of well-developed privately negotiated derivatives and securitization activity in the underlying catastrophic insurance pools first. Standardized contracts thus may not have been demanded—not until more customized off-exchange transactions evolve from the primary and reinsurance contracts responsible for the pool of capital at risk.

If this is true, then some day the success of exchange-traded catastrophic derivatives might still be successful. If the ever-present problem of basis risk can be kept to a minimum and both buyers and writers of products can be attracted to the market, the success of these products may only be a matter of timing.

NOTES

1. See, for example, Lane (1998b), Parkin (1998), and Canter, Cole, and Sandor (1999).
2. Lucas (2001).
3. Ibid.
4. Ibid.
5. Lucas (2001).
6. Compare Peterson (2001).
7. For more information on CLNs, see Cifuentes, Efrat, Gluck, and Murphy (1998).

8. See Thompson and Yun (1998).
9. See Hay (2001) and Walters (2001).
10. The trustee also has a reserve requirement to which surpluses must be applied in the event the collateral account becomes deficient relative to claims obligations to TMCC.
11. The information about this product is based on Sclafane (1996).
12. See Bernero (1998).
13. The details of these transactions are discussed in ibid.
14. Readers interested in additional information on these structures are referred to the excellent compilations of essays by Himick (1998) and Geman (1999) and to the web-published essays (regularly updated) by cat bond guru Morton Lane at www.lanefinancialllc.com. For a more complete look at the economics of catastrophic insurance as a whole, see Froot (1999).
15. Several other transactions like this one have also been done. For a discussion of the 1998 Reliance III Optionable Note, see Lane (1999).
16. See, for example, Gerling Global Financial Products (2000).
17. Bernero (1998).
18. Most of this section is based on Culp (1996), a small portion also appeared in Culp (2001).
19. Over time, the CBOT has considered a number of such insurance-based derivatives contracts. See Cox and Schwebach (1992), D'Arcy and France (1992), and Niehaus and Mann (1992).
20. Recall that because the premium pool for the ISO index is known at time t, the change in the loss index is the only factor that affects the settlement price of the futures contract. A 5 percent increase in the loss index results in a 5 percent increase in the value of the futures contract.

Practical Considerations for Would-be ARTists

CHAPTER 23

USAA Prime: Choice Cats for Diversifying Investors

Morton N. Lane

In November 2000 Munich Re entered into a financial swap transaction with a special-purpose vehicle, PRIME Capital Hurricane Ltd. (PRIME), to protect itself against losses resulting from severe hurricanes hitting defined areas of New York and Miami. PRIME in turn funded its swap (or counterparty) obligation by issuing securities to capital market investors. It issued $6 million Class B preference shares and $159 million Floating Rate Notes. PRIME agreed to pay its note purchasers an interest rate of LIBOR plus 650 basis points quarterly for the next three years. At the end of the three years the investors would receive return of their principal only if no hurricanes of the requisite intensity had blown in the designated areas of New York and Miami. If an adverse wind had blown, investors could lose all or part of their principal.

Six months later, in May 2001, United Services Automobile Association (USAA), a Texas-based insurer, entered into a similar transaction with a special-purpose vehicle, Residential Reinsurance 2001 Ltd. (Residential). Residential entered into a traditional excess-of-loss reinsurance treaty with USAA for three years. It funded this reinsurance obligation by issuing $150 million floating rate notes that promised investors an interest rate of LIBOR plus 499 basis points. By purchasing the notes, investors accepted the risk that they would have to pay USAA's losses, if USAA incurred those losses as a result of category 3 (or greater) hurricane affecting any of the Atlantic and Gulf coast seaboard states. If that happened investors could lose all or part of their principal. (See Exhibit 23.1.)

Casual inspection of these facts and a glance at the covered territories in the exhibit may prompt one to ask why the investor exposed to hurricanes anywhere on the whole U.S. East and Gulf coast receives only 499 basis points

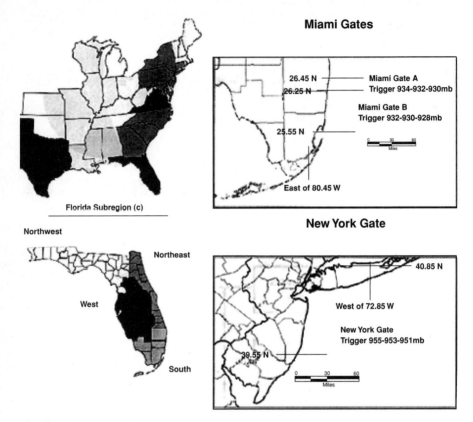

Miami Gates

26.45 N — Miami Gate A
26.25 N — Trigger 934-932-930mb

Miami Gate B
Trigger 932-930-928mb

25.55 N

East of 80.45 W

Florida Subregion (c)

Northwest

New York Gate

Northeast

West

40.85 N

West of 72.85 W

New York Gate
Trigger 955-953-951mb

39.55 N

South

EXHIBIT 23.1 Covered Territories
Note: This detailed representation of the Florida sub-region of USAA's coverage indicates that there is not a perfect correlation between USAA's Florida exposure and PRIME's.
Source: Private Placement Memorandum for Residential Reinsurance 2001 Limited, May 2001; Courtesy Goldman Sachs & Co., Lehman Brothers, and Merrill Lynch & Co.; Private Placement Memoranda for PRIME Capital Limited, December 2000; Courtesy Goldman Sachs & Co., Lehman Brothers, and American Re Securities Corporation.

over LIBOR while the investor exposed to small geographical "gates" around New York and Miami gets 650 basis points. But this may not be the most interesting question.

Munich Re is the one of the largest, oldest (1880), and most solid reinsurance companies in the world. It is rated AAA with shareholder equity of €18,454 million in 1999 when it wrote gross premiums of €27,413 million. The $10.7 million it will have to pay annually for the PRIME swap seems small, as does the potential recovery. Why do it?

USAA is not an international reinsurer, but as a domestic insurer it is no slouch either. It is also a AAA-rated credit. Furthermore, A.M. Best rates it

A⁺⁺ (superior), and it ranks respectively seventh and sixth largest among auto-mobile and homeowner property writers in the United States. USAA has is-sued catastrophe notes every year since 1996.

What benefit does each of these companies receive from securitization, and why do they choose the structures they do? This chapter explores these questions by contrasting the choices made by each cedant (USAA and Mu-nich), thereby exposing the issues most important to other potential users of the market.

INDEMNITY VERSUS INDEX

The single most important contrast between the two transactions is whether the losses to be recovered are to be exactly those of the cedant or just ap-proximately equal to the cedants' losses. USAA chose the former, Munich the latter. USAA's transaction is based on a fundamental principle of insurance: indemnity. Under this principle, insurance is defined as restoring a cedant to its preloss position. The cedant receives no more or no less than the losses experienced. Insurance provides downside protection and no possibility of gain. From this indemnity principle much of the organization and practice of the insurance and reinsurance market evolves. So do the consequences of is-suing cat bonds.

USAA wrote a reinsurance treaty with Residential and thereby was able to get reinsurance accounting treatment of its premium payments and any re-coveries. This is important since payments to a swap arrangement (as in PRIME) in the United States would cause the payments to be handled in the investment account. Furthermore, under Financial Accounting Standards Board SFAS 13 they may be required to mark such a transaction to market, essentially defeating the volatility reducing aspects of reinsurance.

Munich Re, on the other hand, chose to base its notes on a meteorologi-cal model. If the appropriate wind blows, Munich Re may or may not suffer actual losses in the defined geographical area. Its recovery under the notes could be more or less than those actual losses. Munich is said to experience a "basis risk." Now, presumably, Munich drew up the definition of its model with some precision. After all, why pay premium for protection unless there is something to protect? Skilled design can minimize basis risk, and we presume that is what has been done here. Still, the possibility of a mismatch between loss and recovery exists, and so the agreement between Munich and PRIME is not considered "insurance." There are accounting consequences to this for Munich in its home jurisdiction, which it presumably found to be acceptable.

There are other implications. In the case of PRIME's notes investors can examine the meteorological model and decide whether the inherent risk is worth taking at the price offered. It is of no concern to them whether Munich has exposure in the defined regions or what the exposure might be. All they care about is the premium and the risk. And typically, investment bankers engage third-party risk-evaluation firms to help investors assess the risk. PRIME engaged Risk Management Services. It is also of no concern to investors if Munich changes its exposure during the three years—it does not affect the model or the premium. Munich therefore has no obligation to reveal its subject business to investors and the world at large. It can keep its competitive edge in the area.

Investors in Residential, on the other hand, will want to know exactly (or be assured by third parties) what USAA is writing. What if USAA were to secure the protection of the investor, based on good past performance, then make a quick killing by changing its underwriting practice to write poor but high-paying risks all along the eastern seaboard? This is the "moral hazard" of assuming another's risk. If hurricanes hit, only the investor gets the loss if he has accepted all of USAA's losses. To prevent this, the reinsurance treaty and the notes are structured so that USAA stays on part of the risk, alongside the investor. This "retention" is integral to nearly all indemnity-structured notes.

With all such notes it is usual to show the mutuality of interest by way of a layer-cake diagram such as Exhibit 23.2.

The exhibit illustrates that USAA will retain 10 percent of the subject risk between $1.1 billion and $1.6 billion of actual losses (more precisely referred to as ultimate net losses). The diagram also shows that USAA will cede

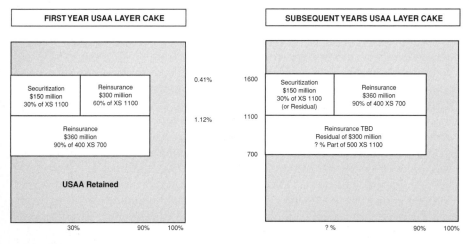

EXHIBIT 23.2 Layer Cake Diagram
Source: Private Placement Memorandum for Residential Re.

part of the risk to Residential (30 percent) and that a further 60 percent is to be placed in the traditional reinsurance market. There is also traditional reinsurance beneath the subject layer. The presence of both pieces of traditional reinsurance will be of some comfort to investors. In addition, the diagram shows that the components cannot be changed over time at least as far as Residential investors are concerned. Both the size of the risk and the attachment point probabilities must stay as originally defined over the three years. Any migration of USAA's book of business, for good or bad reasons, requires that the location of the risk layer be reset at its original probabilistic position. Resets are required annually and after losses are incurred. To assure investors that this exercise is done appropriately, a third-party risk-assessment firm—in this case Applied Insurance Research—has been assigned to perform the validation task.

Because USAA chose an indemnity structure, it has been forced to restrict its actions (as it would under a traditional treaty by many reinsurers) but, more important, it is forced to expose the nature of its book in some detail in the Private Placement Memorandum (PPM) of Residential. Accounting benefits and lack of basis risk evidently outweighed the disclosure requirements and restrictions in the mind of USAA. The firm is increasingly in the minority. Prior to 1998, 71 percent of cat bonds by dollar were in indemnity form; in 2000, only 32 percent were. Even by number of deals, which minimizes the USAA effect, the fraction of indemnity deals dropped from 86 percent in 1999 to 40 percent in 2001.

One final difference in the notes emanates from the indemnity choice. That involves final resolution of the notes. After a loss, a model's output can be calculated quickly. Final determination of ultimate net loss takes more time. The extension period for maturity of the notes on indemnity deals therefore is typically longer than in modeled or indexed deals. Here the difference is five months versus three months, although of course USAA is already way past the hurricane season at scheduled maturity. This is another reason for investors to prefer modeled deals.

TERM, LIMIT, AND OCCURRENCE

Both the PRIME and the Residential deals are for three years. Most recent securitization deals are for multiple years (60 percent longer than 12 months in 2001 compared to 29 percent prior to 1998). Some believe that this is due in part to the economics of issuance. As it is expensive to issue a cat bond, it is better, therefore, to spread the cost over a longer time period.

A more satisfying rationale is that reinsurance rates have been low, so there has been a tendency to extend maturities. It will be interesting to see if the next hard market produces a shortening of maturities.

USAA has been in the securitization market for five years. It has made different decisions about required coverage each year. Those decisions are captured in Table 23.1.

Clearly, at the beginning, 80 percent of USAA's subject coverage came from the cat bond market. Over time, investors have been put into price competition with the traditional market. The result is a declining share going to capital market investors. Of course, the cat bond prices are exposed to the markets' view. Reinsurance prices are not disclosed, but we presume they have been very competitive. Also noticeable is the rise in prices in 2001. This rise may be because USAA has switched to a three-year structure; more likely it is a reflection of a hardened market in 2001 (by about 20 percent) and the higher level of chosen attachment point.

Munich's inaugural effort was for three years without ambiguity.

Both PRIME and Residential notes contain a single limit that can be exhausted any time over the three years. It is possible to structure multiple-year deals where only part of the limit is exposed each year (see Toyota Motor Credit Corporation's transaction), and it is also possible to have multiple limits, but neither is the case here.

The way the limit can be exhausted is also important. Both notes allow for multiple occurrences, or events of loss, but each in a different way. Residential investors are restricted to one loss per year, at the discretion of USAA. This point is important. USAA's recovery depends on the size of its loss and is proportionate to remaining principal. If a hurricane only marginally affects the subject layer and the recovery otherwise would be small, USAA can decline to claim and keep its protection in place for later. Its ability to recover in later years is tied directly to remaining principal. It is best then in some cir-

TABLE 23.1 Required Coverage Decisions

	1997/8	1998/9	1999/00	2000/01	2001/02/03/04
AMOUNT	$477 million[a]	$500 million	$200 million	$200 million	$150 million
RETENTION	20%	10%	10%	10%	10%
REINSURANCE	0	0	50%	50%	60%
SECURITIZATION	80%	90%	40%	40%	30%
TERM	12 Months	12 months	12 months	12 months	36 months
COUPON or	A1:L1+250				
PREMIUM	A2:L1+576	L3 + 416	L3 + 366	L3 + 410	L3 + 499
EXPECTED LOSS	na	na	.44%	.54%	.68%
PFL	1.00%	.87%	.87%	.76%	1.12%

[a]The 1997/8 issue contained a "capital-protected" tranche that causes issuance size to be different from coverage.
Source: Private Placement Memoranda for Residential Reinsurance transactions 1997 to 2001; Courtesy Goldman Sachs & Co., Lehman Brothers, and Merrill Lynch & Co.

cumstances to defer, although USAA probably would make that election only in the early years of the transaction.

USAA also has the converse option. It has some ability to choose which event should be repaid in those years during which there are multiple events. When multiple events occur, it can, within limits, choose to claim on the larger event.

PRIME investors face a different potential loss pattern. They can experience multiple losses at any time during the three years. Investor losses are not tied to Munich's losses but to the intensity of eligible storms. And the loss is not proportional to intensity but is denominated in discrete pieces. An eligible meteorological event can cause PRIME bond holders to lose 20, 80, or 100 percent of their original principal. Theoretically it could lose five 20 percent events in one year or one 100 percent event at the end of year 3. Munich retains no options for choosing on which storms to claim.

In the case of both notes, interest is paid only on remaining outstanding principal.

Of course, in the vast majority of cases (95.59 percent and 97.76 percent, respectively) interest will be paid for the full three years and principal will be returned in full.

PAYOFF STRUCTURE AND EXCEEDENCE PROBABILITIES

In concluding that there will be no losses for PRIME and Residential investors in 95.59 percent and 97.75 percent of all cases, investors rely on the analysis of Risk Management Services and Applied Insurance Research. These risk assessment firms must take as their starting point the structure of the notes and the underlying risk of the book or model. Their analytic steps are perhaps best captured in Exhibit 23.3.

The upper panel shows the exceedence curve for the underlying book of business. The graph shows that USAA, for example, is gauged to have a 1.12 percent chance of ultimate net losses exceeding $1.1 billion and a 0.41 percent chance of losses exceeding $1.6 billion. Notice that the USAA curve is not smooth or straight line. That is because it represents an actual book of business, with all the consequences of concentrations and lumpiness that emanated from USAA's sales practices.

PRIME's exceedence curve, on the other hand, is smooth. It represents a meteorological model. It shows that the chance of a hurricane hitting the defined New York gate with a central pressure less than 955 millibars is 0.54 percent. The chance of hitting the Miami gates with central wind pressures of less than 932 or 936 millibars for A and B, respectively, is 0.17 and 0.76 percent. The chance of hitting any of the gates is 1.47 percent. All these statistics are given for annual periods (just like default percentages for various bond ratings). Actual probabilities depend on the term of the investment, in this

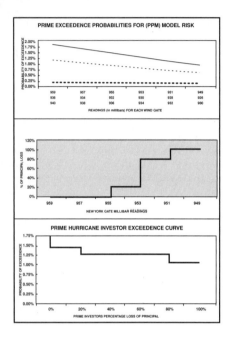
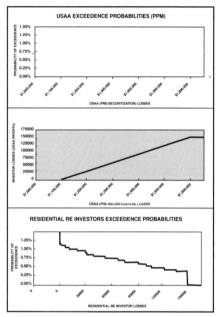

EXHIBIT 23.3   Risk Assessment

case three years. Three times 1.47 percent is 4.41 percent, hence the assertion that there is a 95.59 percent (= 100% − 4.41%) of no loss for PRIME investors.

What is noteworthy about the exceedence curve of PRIME is that it depends on millibars, not dollars of loss.

The features that turn millibars into dollars in the case of PRIME and USAA-dollars into investor-dollars in the case of Residential are the payoff functions illustrated in the middle panel of the exhibit. As we have already described, the payoff function for USAA investors is proportional to USAA losses, hence the straight line. PRIME, on the other hand, is a step function representing the fact that the investor can lose in amounts of 20, 80, or 100 percent. USAA's payoff is like that of a call option. PRIME's payoff is more like a collection of binary options.

The graphics represent annual exposures; for completeness, they also should be viewed over the three-year term of the investment.

The final panel in the set of charts is the exceedence curve for the investor. As we have seen, it is similar to that of the cedant in most cases, but not always. In USAA's case the Residential investor's curve is a truncated version of that of the underlying book. But with PRIME, the smooth model curve translates to a step function. Close examination of these investor curves shows why PRIME investors receive 650 basis points compared to the 499 of Residential. PRIME investors take an annual probability of one or more dollar of loss of 1.47 percent. This probability is 35 basis points higher than the probability experienced by Residential investors (1.12 percent). PRIME should pay a higher premium. It is not the geographical exposure that is important, it is the level of risk.

BENEFITS

Now that we understand the risks being transferred from cedant to special-purpose vehicle and then on to investors, we can see more clearly why such transactions are done. The reasons are basically no different from the reasons for doing reinsurance in the traditional market or, for that matter, for doing hedging in the capital markets. It is to purchase protection from adverse outcomes, which is another way of saying that all of these activities involve attempts to change the shape of the exceedence curve that arises in the normal course of business to one that is more desirable. The aim is to shift the curve in such a way as to make the probabilities of large losses lower.

We illustrate this shift in Exhibit 23.4. It starts with USAA's exceedence curve of ultimate net loss. Next we overlay the benefit (and cost) of protecting against large losses by issuing cat bonds. The curve, net of recoveries, is lower on the right-hand side of the graph, beyond the attachment point. It is higher on the left-hand side, below the attachment point, because protection must be paid for. The left-hand-side shift is equal to premium paid.

Also shown is the effect of the traditional program in addition to the

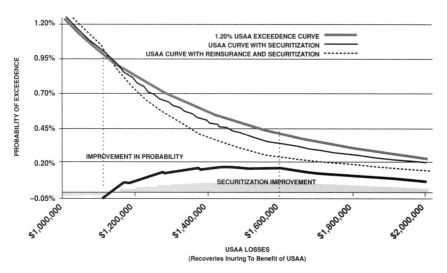

EXHIBIT 23.4   Shift in Exceedence Curves as a Result of Securitization and Reinsurance Program

securitization. Clearly the shift, both left and right, is more pronounced. (We assume that the traditional coverage is on comparable terms to the note issuance.) Is it worth it? Only the USAA members and shareholders can say for sure; evidently management thinks so. But here is one way to view the transaction.

Assume that USAA's point of insolvency is at an ultimate net loss of $1.6 billion. (Of course it is not.) Then if management did nothing, it would, according to Applied Insurance Research's analysis, have a probability of default of 0.41 percent. Other things being ignored for simplicity's sake, the rating agencies might view USAA as a BB insurance company. It would command less respect in the marketplace, may be forced to write less attractive risks, and would be vulnerable to severe storms at precisely the point when it might need new capital most. It may not even be viable in this example. Instead, by buying protection, it can call on dedicated loss-sharing capital (investors and reinsurers) as losses mount toward $1.6 billion. USAA has reduced its insolvency probability to 0.17 percent, the equivalent in ratings terms of going from BB to BBB+, from junk to investment grade. In credit markets the differential in the price of credit between BB and BBB+ is as much as 200 to 250 basis points, a considerable benefit.

Of course it is not a net benefit. To calculate that, one must add back the cost of the protection. In this example, the securitization and reinsurance cost 499 basis points for $450 million of protection, the equivalent of a premium of $22.46 million per year. Spread over the written premium base of $5.6 billion, this is a reduction in profit potential of 40 basis points. Not a bad trade-off, a 40-basis-point reduction in profit potential in exchange for an improvement in borrowing ability or market valuation of around 250 basis points. An economist or equally well-trained professional might suggest that management should buy more protection, right up to the point where the marginal benefits just outweigh the marginal costs. But that is further than we need go here. To repeat, $1.6 billion is not the insolvency point of USAA, and furthermore USAA is rated AAA, not BB. We have used the data available to us to illustrate how management may have approached their decision, not to quantify their exact calculation.

The folks in Munich will have gone through a similar analysis. Their task is slightly more difficult because basis risk must be added to the analysis. This aside, the same principles apply.

Other factors come into play in deciding to securitize. First and foremost is where the cheapest venue lies, capital markets or traditional reinsurance markets. Beyond that there are nonmonetary factors. What is the relative creditworthiness of the counterparty? Are the sources of coverage diversified? Are they stable through the price cycle? The most important task, however, is to conduct an analysis of the possibilities and design a program that is optimal in terms of levels of protection and structure of payoff.

PRIME Hurricane vs. Residential Re 2001

	PRIME Capital Hurricane Ltd.	Residential Re 2001 Ltd.
Issuer	PRIME Capital Hurricane Ltd.	Residential Re 2001 Ltd.
Ceding Insurer	Munich Re	USAA
Issue Date	November-00	May-01
Amount	$165 million	$150 million
Composition	$159 million FRN	
	$6 million Class B Shares	$150 million FRN
Maturity-Initial	January 7, 2004	June 1, 2004
Maturity-Extended	April 7, 2004	November 30, 2004
Extn. Notice Date	January 5, 2004	5 days prior to May 31, 2004
Risk Period To:	December 31, 2003	5/31/2002, 2003 and 2004
Capital Exposed	100%	100%
Cedant Retention		10% (may be less in years 2 & 3)
Covered Events	NY Hurricane	Category 3 (or greater) Hurricane loss in 20
	Miami Hurricane	Gulf and Atlantic coastal states and
		Washington DC*
Cover Form	Counterparty Agreement	Reinsurance
Coverage		30% of $500 million XS $1.1 billion
Indemnity or Index	Index	Indemnity
Occurrence	Multiple	Single in each Risk Period (at discretion of
		USAA)
Interest Rate - pa	Notes: L3 + 650bps	L3 + 499bps
	Shares: L3 +	
Interest Pay Date	January, April, July and October 7	March 1, June 1, Sept. 1, December 1
SPV	PRIME Capital Hurricane Ltd.	Residential Reinsurance 2001 Ltd.
SPV Location	Cayman Islands	Cayman Islands
SPV Capitalization	Class A: $1,000	$5000 common
	Class B: $6 million	
Charitable Trust	yes	yes
Charitable Trustee		HSBC Fin'l. Services (Cayman) Ltd.
Administrator	QSPV Ltd. (Maples & Calder)	HSBC Fin'l. Services (Cayman) Ltd.
Fiscal Agent	Deutsche Bank AG London	None
Indenture Trustee	Bankers Trust	Chase Manhattan Bank
Reinsurance Trust		yes
Reinsurance Trustee		Bankers Trust Company
Claims Review		KPMG (Cayman)
Attorney-Placement Agent	Cadwalader, Wickersham & Taft (NY)	
	Maples & Calder (Cayman)	Skadden, Arps
Attorney-SPV	Maples & Clader	Skadden, Arps
		Maples & Calder (Bermuda)
Acc't.-Principal		KPMG
Acc't-SPV Loc.		KPMG (Cayman)
Rated	S&P / Moody / Fitch	S&P / Moody / Fitch
	BB+ Ba3 BB	BB+ Ba2
Loss Estimates	RMS	AIR
Placement Agent/ Underwriter	Goldman Sachs	Goldman Sachs; Merrill Lynch
	Lehman Brothers	Lehman Brothers
	American Re Securities	
Comments	Landfall gates for NY and Miami areas.	Refinancing of Residential Re IV but for lower
		amount and for a three year term.
	Notes: Payouts of 20%, 80% or 100% of	
	original principal; multiple events until	AIR will remodel layer, trigger and exhaustion
	exhaustion. Shares:	amounts for years 2 and 3 using updated
Notable Features	100% loss at attachment.	USAA data and fixed probabilities (below).
Attachment Prob.	1.46%	1.12%
Exhaustion Prob.	1.08%	0.41%
Expected Loss	1.27%	0.68%

EXHIBIT 23.5 PRIME Hurricane versus Residential Re 2001

Source: Private Placement Memorandum for Residential Reinsurance for Residential Reinsurance 2001 Limited, May 2001; Courtesy Goldman Sachs & Co., Lehman Brothers, and Merrill Lynch & Co.; Private Placement Memoranda for PRIME Capital Limited, December 2000; Courtesy Goldman Sachs & Co., Lehman Brothers, and American Re Securities Corporation.

CONCLUDING REMARKS

The comparison of recent issues by two of the most prestigious insurers and reinsurers in the world today has been remarkably revealing. It has shown the decisions made by these two cedants and revealed the variety of choices available to others. (See Exhibit 23.5.) Securitization of insurance is new to capital markets. The market is at best five years old. However, it promises to grow and expand. Most important, it brings the technology of sophisticated analysis of difficult risks from the world of reinsurance to a more public market. Over time we will see risk analysis expand beyond its present coherent borders of mean-variance to a much wider universe. That is a most exciting prospect.

NOTE

Dr. Morton N. Lane is President of Lane Financial LLC, Kenilworth, IL, a broker dealer specializing in the convergence of the insurance and capital markets. Lane Financial has been involved in the issuance and analysis of risk-linked securities from the earliest days of this market.

CHAPTER 24

Emerging Role of Patent Law in Risk Finance

J. B. Heaton

To the Founding Fathers borrowing from English patent law, extending patent protection to financial innovations would have seemed quite strange. As one leading scholar has noted:

> [I]t would have been seen as absurd for an entrepreneur to file a patent on a new finance technique such as publicly traded corporate shares, techniques for obtaining private financing for a bridge to compete with an existing bridge, or a security interest in uncut timber. These were the earmarks of commerce, of enterprise; laudable surely, but something altogether distinct from the realm of "invention" and the "useful arts."[1]

Nevertheless, 200 years later, few can doubt that new finance techniques are patentable subject matter.

This chapter explores the potential implications of patent law for risk finance. As Christopher L. Culp notes in his risk management text, "perhaps nowhere are the opportunities for structured risk management solutions more interesting . . . than in the [alternative risk transfer] area of insurance—an area that has quite rapidly come to include total risk and integrated insurance, securitized products, and derivatives."[2] While few can question the important role that continuing financial innovation will have on traditional financial and insurance products, little concern has been focused on the possible effects of intellectual property law—especially patent law—on the alternative risk transfer field. Trends in patent law and litigation, combined with increased patenting activity in insurance, securitized products, and derivatives, suggests that alternative risk transfer professionals should take seriously the changing legal landscape.

It is difficult to overestimate the potential effects of a valid patent on any field of commercial endeavor. Patents are enormously powerful legal devices. The owner of a U.S. patent has the legal right to exclude others from making, using, offering to sell, or selling the patented invention for a term of 20 years. The patent owner may license these rights to others, granting them the right (on an exclusive or nonexclusive basis) to make, use, or sell the patented invention. In addition—and perhaps more visibly—patent owners can enforce their patent rights in a federal civil lawsuit. If victorious in a patent infringement lawsuit, patent owners can recover damages and/or permanent injunctions forbidding the acts that infringe the patent. For companies whose existence rests on patentable technologies, patent litigation can be all-out legal warfare. For that company's customers, patent litigation can determine whether products or services it has purchased in the past will be available in the future, and at what price and quality. More ominously, customers themselves can face liability for infringement.

The arcane world of patents and patent law is emerging as an important business concern to risk professionals. *Risk* magazine recently reported on widespread criticism of a patent awarded to Columbia University for a quasi-Monte Carlo method (U.S. Patent No. 5,940,810: "Estimation Method and System for Complex Securities Using Low-Discrepancy Deterministic Sequences"). A recent *Wall Street Journal* article reports on an emerging legal battle between the American Stock Exchange and two inventors over a patented process related to exchange-traded funds (U.S. Patent No. 5,806,048: "Open End Mutual Fund Securitization Process"). In August 2000 Amex filed a complaint in U.S. District Court (patent cases must be brought in federal court, not state court), seeking a declaration that the patent is invalid, while the patent's owner, Mopex, Inc., filed its own patent infringement lawsuit against Amex only days later. The litigation is pending as of this writing.

Applications for new financial and insurance patents are now surely but secretly in process at the United States Patent and Trademark Office. (Patent applications are now held secret by the Patent and Trademark Office for the first 18 months after filing.) The increase in financial patenting activity is attributable mainly to changes in the legal landscape. In particular, both the federal courts and Congress have signaled that financial inventions, once previously thought to be outside the scope of strong patent protection, will be treated by the patent laws as on par with inventions in more traditional fields like bioengineering and manufacturing machines. The changing legal landscape may have a significant effect on future development and sale of cutting-edge financial and insurance products.

Already, it is clear that financial patents are proliferating. Lerner (2000b) estimates that hundreds of financial and insurance patent applications are in process at the United States Patent and Trademark Office. The main effect of recent legal developments has been to increase confidence that these patents— if granted by the Patent and Trademark Office—will be upheld by the federal courts in later litigation. It is also clear that some owners of these patents will assert them aggressively against alleged infringers. Visible examples of patent lawsuits—such as Amazon.com, Inc.'s successful effort to enjoin Barnesand- Noble.com, Inc. from using "one-click" technology[3]—are likely to embolden financial patent holders in their discussions with potential infringers. Bottom line: The proliferation of financial patenting and the aggressive assertion of patent rights against alleged infringers may lead to high-stakes litigation over intellectual property rights in the alternative risk transfer field.

BASICS OF PATENTABILITY

The essence of patent protection is the right to exclude others from making, using, and selling the claimed invention. The congressional authority to enact patent legislation derives from Article I, Section 8, Clause 8 of the United States Constitution, granting the power "To promote the progress of science and useful arts, by securing for limited times to authors and inventors the ex- clusive right to their respective writings and discoveries." Pursuant to this au- thority, Congress has enacted several patent laws through the years. While even a basic introduction to patent law is beyond the scope of this chapter, the conditions for patentability are important to an understanding of the emerg- ing role of patent law in risk finance.

In general, an inventor wishing to obtain a patent must comply with four legal requirements for patentability. A patentable invention is (1) of patentable subject matter; (2) useful; (3) new; and (4) nonobvious.

Not everything is patentable. Some inventions are outside the scope of patent law, no matter how useful, new, or nonobvious they might be. For ex- ample, a printed book is not patentable subject matter (but may be pro- tectable under copyright law) despite the fact that its teachings might be useful, new, and not at all obvious to any reader. Typically, patentable subject matter was thought to include machines and manufactures, with later accep- tance of processes, chemical compositions, and bioengineered products. Out- side of the patentable subject matter category were laws of nature, natural phenomena, and abstract ideas.

Only "useful" products or processes are patentable: the patented prod- uct or process must "work" to produce some result of some benefit. It need not work well, however, and (and least on its own) the usefulness require- ment does not require that the patented product or process work better than anything preceding it does. A patent application on a "time machine" claiming the invention of allowing travel back to a prespecified date would likely be rejected as impossible and thus not useful. Further, a chemical compound with no known use to humanity also would likely be rejected on these grounds. However, a chocolate-powered automobile that traveled at speeds up to 2 miles per hour might very well pass the usefulness test.

A patentable invention must be "new." The patent laws test the novelty of an invention by reference to the relevant "prior art" in the field of the patent's invention. In general terms, fleshed out by particular statutes and case law, an invention is not new if the elements of the claim are contained in a single piece of relevant prior art. For example, suppose a relevant published journal article contained each element—either expressly or inherently—of a patent "claim." (Patent claims are statutorily required [35 U.S.C. §112] statements "particularly pointing out and distinctly claiming the subject matter which the applicant regards as his invention.") That claim would be "anticipated" by the prior art. Put simply, an anticipated invention is not new and is not patentable.

Finally, an invention is not patentable if it is "obvious." Obviousness differs from anticipation in the sense that no single piece of relevant prior art must contain (either expressly or inherently) all the teachings of a particular claim. Instead, the test is whether the invention would have been obvious to a person of ordinary skill in the art. The "person of ordinary skill in the art" is a legal construct, a hypothetical individual assumed to be aware of all of the pertinent prior art, but not necessarily a genius in the field.

While the conditions of patentability must be satisfied first at the patent application stage, each of these matters can be (and usually is) revisited in litigation. That is, although an issued patent enjoys a legal presumption of validity (35 U.S.C. §282), the alleged infringer during the course of litigation may rebut that presumption. Because of the unique challenges of overcoming this presumption, and because of the typically high stakes involved, patent litigation is typically highly complex and costly civil litigation that requires the skills of top trial teams and technical experts.

ILLUSTRATION: METHOD OF EXERCISING A CAT (U.S. PAT. NO. 5,443,036)

In litigation, financial patent holders will face intense scrutiny of, among many other things, their satisfaction of the legal requirements for patentability described above and summarized in Exhibit 24.1. To fix ideas about the four requirements, is useful to examine a short, easily understood patent. Exhibit 24.2 provides excerpts from U.S. Patent No. 5,443,036, "Method of Exercising a Cat." Despite the topic of this chapter, the "cat" exercised in the method of the patent is an animal, not a financial instrument related to catastrophic risk. Putting aside the pun, the patent reveals some of the issues that

EXHIBIT 24.1   Legal Requirements of Patentability Under U.S. Law

Requirement	Explanation
Patentable Subject Matter	The invention must fall into a category eligible for patent protection; not everything can be patented.
Useful	The invention must have some utility, although it need not work well and need not be superior to preexisting products or processes.
New	The invention must not have been described in a relevant piece of prior art (e.g., in a prior patent or published article).
Nonobvious	The invention must not have been obvious to a hypothetical person of ordinary skill in the art, assumed to be knowledgeable of all the relevant prior art.

might arise in risk finance patent litigation, without delving into the complex factual matters likely to arise in real finance patents.

Consider first the patent's "abstract" appearing on the front page of the patent as a matter of course. The abstract provides a summary of the patent:

A method for inducing cats to exercise consists of directing a beam of invisible light produced by a hand-held laser apparatus onto the floor or wall or other opaque surface in the vicinity of the cat, then moving the laser so as to cause the bright pattern of light to move in an irregular way fascinating to cats, and to any other animal with a chase instinct.

In other words, the patent concerns a method for causing a cat to exercise by using a laser pointer to create a point of light that will evoke the chase instinct of the cat.

The '036 patent (practitioners typically refer to a patent by its last three numbers) has four claims:

What is claimed is:

1. A method of inducing aerobic exercise in an unrestrained cat comprising the steps of:
   (a) directing an intense coherent beam of invisible light produced by a hand-held laser apparatus to produce a bright highly focused pattern of light at the intersection of the beam and an opaque surface, said pattern being of visual interest to a cat; and
   (b) selectively redirecting said beam out of the cat's immediate reach to induce said cat to run and chase said beam and pattern of light around an exercise area.

EXHIBIT 24.2 U.S. Patent No. 5,443,036, Method of Exercising a Cat

Title	Method of Exercising a Cat
Number	5,443,036
Inventors	Kevin T. Amiss; Martin H. Abbott
Issued/Filed Dates	August 22, 1995/November 2, 1993
Abstract	A method for inducing cats to exercise consists of directing a beam of invisible light produced by a hand-held laser apparatus onto the floor or wall or other opaque surface in the vicinity of the cat, then moving the laser so as to cause the bright pattern of light to move in an irregular way fascinating to cats, and to any other animal with a chase instinct.
Background of the Invention	1. Technical Field The present invention relates to recreational and amusement devices for domestic animals and, more particularly, to a method for exercising and entertaining cats. 2. Discussion of the Prior Art Cats are not characteristically disposed toward voluntary aerobic exercise. It becomes the burden of the cat owner to create situations of sufficient interest to the feline to induce even short-lived and modest exertion for the health and well-being of the pet. Cats are, however, fascinated by light and enthralled by unpredictable jumpy movements, as for instance, by the bobbing end of a piece of hand-held string or yarn, or a ball rolling and bouncing across a floor. Intense sunlight reflected from a mirror or focused through a prism, if the room is sufficiently dark, will, when moved irregularly, cause even the more sedentary of cats to scamper after the lighted image in an amusing and therapeutic game of "cat and mouse." The disruption of having to darken a room to stage a cat workout and the uncertainty of collecting a convenient sunbeam in a lens or mirror render these approaches to establishing a regular life-enhancing cat exercise routine inconvenient at best.
Summary of the Invention	Accordingly, it is an object of the present invention to provide an improved method of exercising a cat in normal day and night lighting environments. It is a further object of the present invention to provide a method of providing amusing, entertaining and healthy exercise for a cat. It is yet another object of the present invention to teach a method of exercising a cat effortlessly at any time. In accordance with the present invention, a light amplification by stimulated emission of radiation (laser) device in a small hand-

(Continued)

EXHIBIT 24.2   Continued

held configuration is used to project and move a bright pattern of light around a room to amuse and exercise a cat.

The method is effective, simple, convenient and inexpensive to practice and provides healthy exercise for the cat and amusement and entertainment for both the cat and the owner.

These and other objects, features and advantages of the present invention will become apparent from the following description and accompanying drawings of one specific embodiment thereof.

Claims

What is claimed is:

1. A method of inducing aerobic exercise in an unrestrained cat comprising the steps of:

(a) directing an intense coherent beam of invisible light produced by a hand-held laser apparatus to produce a bright highly-focused pattern of light at the intersection of the beam and an opaque surface, said pattern being of visual interest to a cat; and

(b) selectively redirecting said beam out of the cat's immediate reach to induce said cat to run and chase said beam and pattern of light around an exercise area.

2. The method of claim 1 wherein said bright pattern of light is small in area relative to a paw of the cat.

3. The method of claim 1 wherein said beam remains invisible between said laser and said opaque surface until impinging on said opaque surface.

4. The method of claim 1 wherein step (b) includes sweeping said beam at an angular speed to cause said pattern to move along said opaque surface at a speed in the range of five to twenty-five feet per second.

2. The method of claim 1 wherein said bright pattern of light is small in area relative to a paw of the cat.

3. The method of claim 1 wherein said beam remains invisible between said laser and said opaque surface until impinging on said opaque surface.

4. The method of claim 1 wherein step (b) includes sweeping said beam at an angular speed to cause said pattern to move along said opaque surface at a speed in the range of 5 to 25 feet per second.

The '036 patent may appear ridiculous to some observers, and indeed the patent is a favorite of critics of the patent system and the review applied by the United States Patent and Trademark Office. Nevertheless, it is important to examine the issues raised by the '036 patent in legal terms. Doing so shows just how difficult can be the problem of dealing with an asserted U.S. patent.

Suppose, for example, that one wanted to challenge the validity of the

'036 patent on the basis of the four requirements of patentability discussed above. Consider first the requirement of patentable subject matter. To pass this requirement, the method of exercising a cat covered by the '036 claims must fall within the types of subject matter covered by patent law. A method for exercising a cat may very well do so. A "process" can be patented (35 U.S.C. §101): "Whoever invents or discovers any new and useful process, machine, manufacture, or composition of matter, or any new and useful improvement thereof, may obtain a patent therefor, subject to the conditions and requirements of this title." The patent statute (35 U.S.C. §100(b)) further defines the term "process" to include a "method": "The term 'process' means process, art or method, and includes a new use of a known process, machine, manufacture, composition of matter, or material."

But there are some interesting issues for litigation here. For example, what would be the effect of the necessity for human participation in the method? As a general rule, the requirement of human mental participation renders a process unpatentable.[4] As claim 1 states, the method requires that the individual engages in the action of "selectively redirecting said beam out of the cat's immediate reach." That sounds like a requirement for substantial human mental participation and may render the claim invalid.

Next, consider the requirement that the invention be "useful." Here, matters seems easy, as they often are in utility inquiries. The author of this chapter will attest that the method works. Using a laser pointed to create a pinpoint of light can induce the cat to chase the pinpoint, providing the intended exercise.

Determining whether the invention is new—that is, whether elements of the claim are contained in a single piece of relevant prior art—would require substantial research. The lawyer (or his/her expert) would scour publications in the field and past patents to determine if anyone had ever disclosed the method of exercising a cat using a laser pointer. Note that here it matters not whether anyone (including the author) had employed the method in secret prior to the application date (November 2, 1993). What matters is whether all the elements of the claimed invention appeared in a reference that could be available to a potential inventor. Suppose, counterfactually, that there was a published article in *Cat Fancy* magazine, titled "Exercise Your Cat with a Laser Pointer" dated January 1993 and disclosing the exact method taught by the '036 patent. In that case, the patent would be invalid because the invention would not be "new." Obviously, the search for prior art is an important part of any patent litigation effort.

Also important is the obviousness inquiry. To many, it is here where the '036 patent might have its most serious problem. The patent itself—in the section titled "Background of the Invention"—discloses the well-known fact that "[I]ntense sunlight reflected from a mirror or focused through a prism, if the room is sufficiently dark, will, when moved irregularly, cause even the more

sedentary of cats to scamper after the lighted image in an amusing and thera-
peutic game of 'cat and mouse.'" (The author of this chapter was once fond
of "exercising" his own cat by reflecting light off the back of a CD and onto
the walls of his apartment.) Is the use of a laser pointer obvious to anyone
who has employed these methods? If so, the patent could be invalid on these
obviousness grounds alone, even if the method was never written down in a
relevant piece of prior art.

In litigation, all these questions of patentability (and many other questions as well) are up for grabs, and juries will decide questions like anticipation. In many cases, expert analysis may help, but the task is not an easy one.
Consider the use of expert analysis to show that certain financial patents were
"obvious" in light of prior art. There must be some motivation to combine
the prior art references or practices in ways that render the invention obvious.
That motivation can come from the prior art references themselves, from the
knowledge of one of ordinary skill in the art, or even from the nature of the
problem to be solved, but the showing must be clear.

The road for an alleged infringer is not an easy one for another reason as
well. Patent cases typically are tried to juries. Juries are prone to form a
strong hypothesis that a patent issued by the Patent and Trademark Office is
valid, not knowing that most inventions are never tested by examiners, that
patent examiners often are overworked and sometimes are underqualified,
and that patent applications are secret and not subjected to any meaningful
adversary process unless litigated.

But alleged infringers are not the only ones with problems. The problem
of detecting infringement is substantial for patent holders, especially for
methods that can be practiced in relative secrecy. Consider again the '036
patent. How could the inventors know whether the author of this chapter had
ever given up the CD method for the (admittedly superior) laser pointer
method? If the infringer cannot be identified, the right to exclusive use is
worth little. A similar problem may face some current and future financial
patent holders.

A FEW EXAMPLES OF RISK FINANCE PATENTS

Moving beyond arguably silly patents, it is instructive to look at some real
risk finance patents. These are patents that on their face purport to claim
rights to inventions that have undoubted application to risk finance applications. Exhibit 24.3 presents brief descriptions of three such patents.[5]

The first patent (U.S. Pat. No. 5,940,810) is the controversial one issued
to Columbia University for quasi–Monte Carlo methods. Rather than covering a risk finance product per se, the Columbia University patent covers a tool
for pricing a financial instrument. Its subject matter is most easily grasped by
reference to its abstract. The abstract reads:

EXHIBIT 24.3   Examples of Risk Finance Patents

Title	Estimation Method and System for Complex Securities Using Low Discrepancy Deterministic Sequences	System and Method of Risk Transfer and Risk Diversification Including Means To Assure With Assurance of Timely Payment and Segregation of the Interests of Capital	System and method for replacing a liability with insurance and for analyzing data and generating documents pertaining to a premium financing mechanism paying for such insurance
U.S. Pat. No.	5,940,810	5,704,045	6,026,364
Issued/Filed Dates	August 17, 1999/ July 30, 1997	December 30, 1997/ January 9, 1995	February 15, 2000/ July 28, 1997
Inventors	Joseph F. Traub, Spassimir Paskov, Irwin F. Vanderhoof	Douglas L. King, Alasdair G. Barclay, Rockie C. Wellman	Brian L. Whitworth
Assignee	The Trustees of Columbia University in the City of New York	Investors Guaranty Fund, Ltd.	
Subject Matter	Quasi-Monte Carlo Derivatives Pricing.	Risk transfer.	Premium financing mechanism.

In securities trading, in setting the initial offering price of a financial instrument, or in later revaluation as financial parameters such as interest rates may change, an estimate of the value of the instrument may be represented as a multi-dimensional integral. For evaluation of the integral, numerical integration is preferred with the integrand being sampled at deterministic points having a low-discrepancy property. The technique produces approximate values at significant computational savings and with greater reliability as compared with the Monte Carlo technique.

To a lawyer, the real meat of a patent is its "claims." Claim 1 of the '810 patent provides a more technical description of the invention, using language meant to convey as precisely as possible what exactly the inventor intends to claim:

1. A method for one of buying, holding and selling a complex security, comprising:
   (i) deriving a multivariate integrand which, when integrated over a domain of integration having at least 50 dimensions, represents an estimated value of the security;

(ii) calculating, by computer, integrand values at points in the domain of integration which are obtained from a low-discrepancy deterministic sequence;

(iii) combining the integrand values, by computer, to approximate the estimated value; and

(iv) effecting, based on the estimated value, one of buying, holding and selling the security.

The '810 patent contains 21 additional claims, many of which relate to (or, in patent parlance, are "dependent" on) the claim recited above.

In simple terms, the '810 patent claims the exclusive right to use any method that contains all the elements of any of its claims. In this case, those claims relate to the use of what are more commonly known as "quasi–Monte Carlo" methods. To fall under Claim 1, for example, use of the method must be "by computer" since that is a recited limitation in element (ii). If, for example, it were possible to solve in one's head the integration problem presented in element (i), then that use would not infringe the '810 patent. The limitations of such a "design-around" are obvious to all but the most gifted mental calculators.

The second patent described in Exhibit 24.3—U.S. Pat. No. 5,704,045— purports to cover a "System and method of risk transfer and risk diversification including means to assure with assurance of timely payment and segregation of the interests of capital." Again, the abstract provides a snapshot of the patent's intended coverage:

> *A system and method of accepting risk through contractual obligations transfers a portion of the risk to investors and includes means for absolute assurance of timely payment to contract holders, and segregation, of the interests of particular investors to specifically identified risks in a risk to capital matching system. The system creates separate ledgers and segregated reserves to tailor particular products for specific needs including transferring difficult to place risks. The system creates agreements which promise payments, based on loss from risks including investment risks. Data processing provides legally segregated relationship management links, supervising and balancing the interests of professionals in a risk transfer and diversification system.*

The '045 patent has 74 claims. Claim 1 is as follows:

1. A method employing operatively interconnected, input, output and data processing means for facilitating through an entity, the transfer and acceptance of specifically defined risks through the entity from risk transferors to capital providers accepting the risk transferred, the method comprising:

creating an entity for facilitating the transfer of risk from one or more risk transferors through the entity to capital providers accepting the risk through the entity;

creating and maintaining a communications system for communications between risk transferors and capital providers through the entity;

creating within the entity a capital reserve system;

exchanging information between and among one or more risk transferors, one or more capital providers and the entity relating to the nature and character of the risk for the purpose of one or more willing risk transferors entering into a policy/contract with one or more willing capital providers having defined obligations including the maximum monetary exposure on the risk and the duration thereof; and

causing the capital provider(s) to transfer sufficient capital to the capital reserve system prior to the effective date of such contract which capital when combined with risk compensation and other income is sufficient to meet any and all such defined obligations during such contract period.

The '045 patent appears to be assigned to Investors Guaranty Fund, Ltd., as part of the intellectual property underlying an "insurance securitization" system.[6] Investors Guaranty Fund, Ltd. was involved in litigation with Morgan Stanley over some elements of a system for converting specific insurance risks into capital market securities.[7] That litigation, however, does not appear to have involved the '045 patent, which issued after the events at issue there.

The third patent in Exhibit 24.3—U.S. Pat. No. 6,026,364—covers a "System and method for replacing a liability with insurance and for analyzing data and generating documents pertaining to a premium financing mechanism paying for such insurance" and is the invention of Brian L. Whitworth, an individual entrepreneur from Malibu, California, with a background in insurance and financial product development.

The abstract of the '364 patent is as follows:

A system and method for replacing a self insurance with insurance, employing a premium financing mechanism with a payout pattern determined in consideration of an estimated payout of the self insurance to pay for the insurance, identifying employers for whom leaving self insurance may be desirable, and, in one preferred embodiment, analyzing data and generating documents and/or computer-readable data files pertaining to such a premium financing mechanism.

The '364 patent has 63 claims, starting with Claim 1:

1. A system for analyzing data and generating documents pertaining to a premium financing mechanism, the system comprising:

    a computer executable program or programs adapted to:

    access estimate data of a cost of self insurance, a cost of insurance, and savings realized by replacing self insurance with insurance;

    access risk data pertaining to a transaction wherein a bond is employed to pay for said insurance to replace said self insurance;

    process said estimate data to provide data usable by a printer to generate a document pertaining to a bond proposed to pay for said insurance; and

    process said risk data to provide data usable by a printer to generate documents pertaining to an issuance of said bond.

The '364 patent's inventor makes clear on his website that he is monitoring financial activity for possible infringement of his patents (emphasis in original):

> *Finally, if you are an investment banker, actuary, insurance carrier, insurance broker, self insured company or municipality, and you will be involved in a departure from self insurance which uses sophisticated analysis or long term financing, please contact us regarding our patents. We are happy to consult on these transactions. **We also will be happy to spend a small amount of time (at no charge) verifying whether your transaction or analysis is likely to infringe any of the patents' claims.** The patents have over 130 claims relating to these types of transactions, so the coverage is quite broad. We will do our best to prevent accidental infringement and prevent unnecessary worries regarding analysis or transactions which will not infringe.*[8]

EVOLUTION OF FINANCIAL PATENTS: A THUMBNAIL SKETCH

The United States Supreme Court has noted that Congress intended that patent protection might extend to "anything under the sun that is made by man."[9] Still, most readers will note that patents have played no significant role in the surge of financial innovation over past decades.[10]

Simplicity certainly cannot explain the paucity of financial patents. To the contrary, financial engineering is a highly technical and complex field, whose "inventions" are often beyond the grasp of those without strong training in mathematics, computer science, and modern financial economics. At a technical level, critical financial innovations may be every bit as "complex" as more traditional fields of patent law protection like biotechnology and electrical engineering.

Nor can the failure to employ patent law protection be ascribed to any obvious superiority of other forms of intellectual property protection. Consider the two alternative mechanisms traditionally employed by financial innovators to "protect" the fruits of financial invention: secrecy and first-mover advantages. Secrecy probably has been the predominant means of protection for financial inventions such as the computer code and financial mathematics underlying cutting-edge derivatives pricing models. Secrecy can facilitate significant nonpatent legal protection, including contractual nondisclosure agreements and state trade secrets law. First-mover advantages—getting to market first and exploiting the gains from doing so—have been more important for protecting the financial innovation embodied in new security designs.[11] Although few doubt the ability of competing investment banks to reverse-engineer widely offered products, first movers appear to gain something from being first out the door with an innovative new offering.

However, both secrecy and first-mover advantages possess inherent weaknesses. Secrecy is vulnerable to the constant risk of disclosure, and (with an important recent exception noted below) secret inventions are not protectable against subsequent patents on the same inventions. First-mover advantages are less susceptible to this problem since the invention is disclosed in the first use or sale, limiting its later patentability and enforcement against the first inventor.[12] But the first-mover advantage may leave significant value on the table for competitors. Tufano (1989), for example, found that rivals imitated 35 of 58 studied financial innovations within one year of introduction. In addition, the incrementalism so prevalent in financial engineering—where one financial innovation builds in small ways on an earlier one—means that an early patent might allow even greater returns from an important financial innovation than otherwise available from the first mover's nonlegal advantages alone.

Finally, the paucity of patent protection in the financial field cannot be explained by any general discomfort with legal and regulatory rules. Indeed, many observers link many important financial innovations directly to legal and regulatory rules, especially tax rules.[13]

The best explanation for the past rarity of financial patents is instead that few financial "inventors" believed that their financial innovations were patentable subject matter. Or, more accurately, the risks that a court would find that a given financial invention was not patentable subject matter were high enough that the value of the patent was low. What has been important in the evolution of financial patents is the development of greater certainty over the patentabilitty of computing methods and mathematical algorithms. Financial patents tend to implicate both areas.

Even a summary of the long and twisting legal history of the patentability of computing methods and mathematical algorithms is beyond the scope of this chapter. Suffice it to say, however, that legal standards eventually began to embrace the patentability of computer-implemented inventions and then to dismiss with the need for a computer implementation per se, so long as the mathematical algorithm was not simply a mathematical formula in the abstract.

In a series of important decisions, the Supreme Court first presented seemingly high hurdles to patentability, suggesting that computer programs might be simply unpatentable mathematical algorithms. The Court then appeared to soften this position for computer programs performing useful functions. The lower courts further developed tests to determine whether computer programs were patentable subject matter and the role that the presence of a "mathematical algorithm" might play in that determination.

An important application of this development occurred in a relatively early and important patent case surrounding a financial patent. In 1983 the U.S. District Court of Delaware held that a patent related to Merrill Lynch's Cash Management Account (CMA) claimed patentable subject matter because the claims covered the use of a computer to effectuate a business activity. Linking the computer to the business method of the CMA proved the key to Merrill Lynch's litigation success, and Dean Witter Reynolds eventually paid Merrill Lynch a license fee to offer its own CMA product.

By any measure, however, the concern with financial patents is related to a recent and highly influential opinion of the Court of Appeals for the Federal Circuit. The Federal Circuit has responsibility for patent law appeals in the United States. In 1998 it decided the case of *State Street Bank v. Signature Financial*, 47 U.S.P.Q.2d (BNA) 1596 (Fed. Cir. 1998). In that case, the district court (the lower court where the initial complaint was filed) ruled that subject matter claimed in the patent was not patentable subject matter. On appeal, the Federal Circuit reversed, holding that that Signature Financial's software system for managing a "Hub and Spoke" mutual fund pooling system was patentable subject matter.

Against the background of earlier case law, the *State Street* decision was influential because it laid to rest any continuing doubt as to the patentability of "business methods," made clear that computer programs were patentable subject matter, and eliminated substantial doubt over the patentability of mathematically derived inventions. In perhaps its most important holding for financial patenting, the court stated:

> *Today, we hold that the transformation of data, representing discrete dollar amounts, by a machine through a series of mathematical calculations into a final share price, constitutes a practical application of a mathematical algorithm, formula, or calculation, because it produces a useful, concrete and tangible result—a final share price momentarily fixed for recording and reporting purposes and even accepted and relied upon by regulatory authorities and in subsequent trades.*

In the later case of *AT&T Corp. v. Excel Communications, Inc.*, 50 U.S.P.Q.2d (BNA) 1447 (Fed. Cir. 1999), the Federal Circuit made clear that the presence of a "machine" was unimportant: The patentability of claims containing mathematical algorithms is the same regardless of the form, machine, or process in which a particular claim is drafted.

The general viability of the Federal Circuit's interpretation was confirmed when, on November 29, 1999, Congress amended 35 U.S.C. §273 to provide that an alleged infringer of a business method patent can assert as a defense that it reduced the subject matter to practice at least one year prior to the effective filing date of the patent and commercially used the subject matter before the effective filing date of the patent. The amendment was intended to protect users of business methods who had not patented their earlier inventions but now were being sued by those who had. The implicit acceptance by Congress of the business method patent suggests that the Federal Circuit is unlikely to change its position in the future.

Thus, the important legal changes leading to greater financial patenting concern clarification of subject matter requirement. Decisions like *State Street* and *AT&T v. Excel* make clear that the subject matter requirement is no longer going to prevent most interesting financial inventions from being patented. This means that other requirements of patentability—usefulness, novelty, and nonobviousness—will become the key focus, as is the case in patent litigation in more well-established fields. Since inventions that are not useful are typically of little financial value, this means that the real focus will be on novelty and nonobviousness.

CONCLUSION

This chapter has explored the emerging role that patent law will play in financial and insurance innovation. Given recent legal shifts, it seems likely that patent law will become increasingly important in controlling the sale and use of newly designed financial products and widely used pricing and risk management software (as opposed to proprietary models). The evolution of legal views of patentable subject matter, and an increasing willingness of small companies to leverage intellectual property rights, suggests that intellectual property law—the laws pertaining to patents, copyrights, trademarks, and trade secrets—will play an increasingly important role in the process of financial innovation.

It is also important, however, to keep patent law in its proper perspective. Many financial firms will continue to rely on first-mover advantages and trade secret law to protect their intellectual property investment. This may be particularly true in financial engineering. Trade secret law, in particular, offers substantial advantages in that it enables a company to keep its proprietary information secret. Considering that the technological life of pricing models and the like may be obsolete by the time a patent issues, secrecy will continue to be an important source of protection for inventions in the financial engineering field. Nevertheless, the message to alternative risk transfer professionals is that as innovation in the field continues, the once-ignored possibility of patent protection must be taken seriously from both offensive and defensive standpoints.

NOTES

This chapter is reprinted by permission from the *Journal of Risk Finance* (Winter 2001).

J.B. Heaton, J.D., Ph.D., is an attorney at Bartlit Beck Herman Palenchar & Scott in Chicago.

1. Merges (1999).
2. See Culp (2001), Chapter 26.
3. *Amazon.com, Inc. v. Barnesandnoble.com, Inc.*, 53 U.S.P.Q. 2d 1115 (W.D. Wash. 1999).
4. See, for example, *Johnson v. Duquesne Light Co.*, 29 F.2d 784 (W.D. Pa. 1928), *aff'd*, 34 F.2d 1020 (3d Cir. 1929).
5. See Heaton (2000) for detailed examples of several other financial patents.
6. The '045 patent is described at Investor Guaranty Fund, Ltd.'s home page at *styx.forgedesign.com/domains/igf/pages/home/home.html*.
7. See *Investors Guaranty Fund, Ltd. v. Morgan Stanley & Co.*, 50 U.S.P.Q.2d 1523 (S.D.N.Y. 1998).
8. The quoted language was found at *www.financialpatents.com/Whyus.html*.
9. *Diamond v. Diehr*, 450 U.S. 175, 182 (1981)(quoting a 1952 Senate Report).
10. See Lerner (2000).
11. See Tufano (1989).
12. The patent laws contain severe restrictions on the patentability of inventions that were in public use or on sale during times prior to application. For example, one U.S. District Court recently held that a company's demonstrations of its computer software to non-employees without assurances of confidentiality could be such a public use.
13. See Miller (1986) and Gergen and Schmitz (1997).

CHAPTER 25

Weather Derivatives or Insurance? Considerations for Energy Companies

Andrea S. Kramer

Electric utilities and distributors do not sell as much electricity during a cold summer as they do in a hot one. And heating oil distributors do not sell as much heating oil, just as gas utilities do not sell as much natural gas in a warm winter as in a cold one. To both energy suppliers and consumers, temperature variations and weather fronts mean money—lots of money. As such, weather risks[1] are carefully examined and evaluated by energy-related businesses.

Estimates range from $1 trillion to $2 trillion as the portion of the U.S. economy that is sensitive to weather conditions.[2] Weather derivatives and weather insurance products have developed to help weather-sensitive businesses protect themselves against weather-related risks. Prior to entering into a weather-related derivative or insurance contract, a company with a weather risk must evaluate the appropriateness of the product for its particular needs, the comfort level of its board of directors or senior management, its regulatory environment, and its tax situation.

Weather products, irrespective of whether structured as derivatives or insurance contracts, rely on weather-related factors, such as heating degree days (HDDs), cooling degree days (CDDs), perceived temperature or chill indices, snowfall and snow depth indices, precipitation and rainfall measures, humidity indices, water flow, and sunshine indices. Weather products can protect against reduced demand or sales for the company's products or services (often referred to as volume risk). Weather products also can protect against increased supply or sales costs (often referred to as price risk). And they can protect against volatility in a company's revenues or net income.

In this chapter, I first look at weather derivatives, describing what they are and who regulates them. Then I look at weather insurance contracts, focusing on the legal distinctions that are made between insurance and derivatives. I highlight some key differences in the way derivatives and insurance contracts are documented and finally discuss some key tax differences between weather derivatives and insurance contracts.

WHAT ARE WEATHER DERIVATIVES?

Weather derivatives are financial contracts between two parties, with contract values based on changes in specified weather conditions. They can be traded on exchanges (as futures contracts or options on futures),[3] or they can be entered into as bilateral contracts between two parties, which is referred to as having been entered into in the over-the-counter (OTC) market.

Popular OTC derivatives include options, caps, floors, collars, swaps, and cash-settled forward contracts. As a general rule, one party to a weather derivative is paid if the specified weather-related payment event results. With a derivatives contract, neither party needs to prove that it has incurred a financial loss in order to collect the specified payment.

The two parties to a weather derivatives contract agree, upon entering into the contract, to the specific payment calculations that are reflected in the confirmation of the trade. For example, payout terms can be tied to a specified dollar amount multiplied by the HDD (or CDD) level specified in the contract and the actual HDD (or CDD) level reported in the specified location, during the specified time period.[4] The payment calculation is made and payment is due, without regard to whether one party can show proof of a loss or that it has an insurable risk. A party to a derivatives contract does not have to be regulated as an insurance company.

Utilities with active energy trading operations (for physical energy products and derivatives) may find weather derivatives less intimidating than ones without a trading operation and without experience in derivatives. As a result, utilities with trading operations may be more willing to enter into derivatives than a utility without a trading operation in derivatives.

Who Has Jurisdiction over Weather Derivatives?

"Weather" is included within the definition of a "commodity" in the Commodities Exchange Act (CEA).[5] This means that weather derivatives are subject to the federal commodities laws unless an exemption or exclusion from the CEA is available with respect to a transaction.

For weather derivatives, an important exemption from federal regulation applies if the derivatives contract falls within the category of "excluded swap transactions" in CEA §2(g).[6] The CEA does not apply to "any agreement, contract, or transaction in a commodity other than an agricultural commodity" if the agreement, contract, or transaction meets three requirements.

1. The contract must be entered into by parties that meet the definition of "eligible contract participants" at the time they enter into the transaction. For these purposes, the definition of "eligible contract participants" tracks the former definition of "eligible swap participants" at Rule 35.1(b)(2) of the Commodity Futures Trading Commission (CFTC).[7]
2. The contract must be subject to individual negotiation by the parties. Bilateral derivatives contracts negotiated between two parties generally are viewed as contracts subject to individual negotiation, and they meet this requirement.
3. The contract cannot be executed or traded on a trading facility, such as an established commodities exchange or a centralized electronic market.

In addition to the excluded swap transactions exemption, another exclusion or exemption from the CEA might apply to a particular transaction. As a result, even if a derivative product or its parties fail to meet all of the requirements to qualify as an excluded swap transaction, another exemption, such as the exemption for so-called trade options, may be available.

WHAT IS INSURANCE?

Insurance contracts are defined, and individually regulated, by each of the 50 states in the United States as well as the District of Columbia. In addition, each state has it own requirements that must be met by insurers, insurance agents, and others who solicit insurance customers in that state.

With a broad range of insurance contracts now available to protect against a wide range of business and financial risks, a single definition of "insurance" cannot be applied to all contracts that are regulated as "insurance." As a result, the analysis of what qualifies as "insurance" becomes difficult. For example, defining an insurance contract as a contract that "transfers and distributes risk," in and of itself, is too broad. This definition improperly sweeps into the definition of "insurance" many financial market transactions (including derivatives) that are not thought of, regulated, documented, or taxed as insurance. Yet certain other contracts are viewed as insurance contracts even though they do not "transfer" risk but rather "finance" or mitigate specified business or financial risks.

In evaluating whether a particular contract should be treated as insurance, it can be useful to consider five conditions typically associated (in case law and most state regulatory frameworks) with insurance. Applying the following requirements to a contract provides a much better indication of whether the contract is "insurance" than any attempts to define insurance as a contract that "transfers and distributes risk."

1. The insured must have an "insurable risk" (i.e., the risk of a financial loss on the occurrence of a disaster, theft, or weather event) with respect to a "fortuitous event" that is capable of a financial estimate.
2. The insured must show that it was injured as a result of the "insured event" if its "insurable risk" is destroyed or otherwise impaired. It must demonstrate that it suffered an actual loss.
3. The insured must "transfer" its "risk of loss" to an insurance company (referred to as "risk shifting" or "underwriting") under a contract that provides the insured with an "indemnity" against the risk of a loss (with the indemnity limited to the insured's actual loss).
4. The insured must pay a "premium" to the insurance company for the insurance company to assume the insured's "insurable risk."
5. The insurance company typically assumes the risks covered in the insurance contract as part of a larger program to distribute losses among a pool of contracts covering similar risks. The pool established by an insurance company is often large enough so that actual losses are expected to fall within statistical benchmarks (referred to as risk distribution or risk spreading).

What these concepts all mean, when addressing weather-related risk, is that a weather insurance contract must cover the risk than an insured suffers an insured loss (as that term is defined in the insurance contract). In addition, the insured can collect under the insurance contract only after it has provided proof of its loss, and it can collect only the amount of loss covered in the contract.

DISTINCTIONS BETWEEN INSURANCE AND DERIVATIVES

Case law wrestles with the definition of "insurance,"[8] with insurance often so broadly defined that if additional requirements were not imposed on its definition, virtually any contract could be found to be insurance if one party indemnifies the other party against a specified economic risk. But even though case law often defines insurance quite broadly, this is not the way that insurance is defined for insurance regulatory purposes. Even though the demarcation between insurance products and other risk-shifting contracts has blurred in recent years, the bright-line distinctions between insurance contracts and derivatives that I set out herein are important.

Let us look at New York insurance law as an illustration of how an important U.S. jurisdiction determines whether a contract is treated as "insurance" subject to insurance regulation. Under New York law, an insurance contract is defined as an agreement where one party (the insurance company) is obligated to confer a benefit of pecuniary value to another party (the insured or beneficiary), depending on a fortuitous event (beyond the control of either party) in which the insured or beneficiary has, or is expected to have, a material interest that will be adversely affected if the fortuitous event occurs.[9] This definition is quite similar to the concepts that I have already laid out in this essay.

With this definition of insurance as our starting point, let's consider the distinction made by the State of New York Insurance Department (NYID) in a June 25, 1998, opinion letter (the Cat Options Opinion) with respect to catastrophe options (Cat Options).[10] The Cat Options Opinion addressed options that provided a specified amount (unrelated to losses actually incurred by the purchaser) would be payable to the purchaser if a specified catastrophic event (i.e., a hurricane or major storm) occurs. The purchaser did not need to be injured by the catastrophic event specified in the contract in order to collect the specified contract amount. Because the purchaser did not need to prove that it had suffered a loss, the NYID concluded that the Cat Options were not insurance contracts. The Cat Options issuer was obligated to pay the purchaser without regard to whether the purchaser actually suffered a loss because of the catastrophic event specified in the contract.

If the Cat Options had, instead, been structured to provide for a payment to the purchaser *only* if the purchaser had suffered a loss with respect to an insurable interest, the NYID would have treated the Cat Options as insurance contracts, requiring both licensure and compliance with New York insurance requirements.

In the Cat Options Opinion, the NYID essentially made the following distinction: A "derivative product" transfers risk *without regard to* whether its purchaser has actually suffered a loss. An "insurance contract," on the other hand, transfers the risk of the purchaser's own and actual fortuitous— but insurable—loss to the issuer of the contract.

On February 15, 2000, the NYID applied the Cat Option Opinion analysis to weather derivatives (Weather Derivatives Opinion). In the Weather Derivatives Opinion, NYID concluded that weather derivatives are not insurance contracts under New York insurance law. As previously stated in its Cat Option Opinion, NYID concluded that weather derivatives are not insurance contracts because payment to the purchaser does not depend on the purchaser having suffered a loss. In fact, neither the amount of the payment nor the triggering event of a derivative bears a relationship to the purchaser's loss.[11]

DOCUMENTATION CONSIDERATIONS

Given the possible overlap between weather-related derivatives and insurance contracts, the way in which the contract is documented is significant in determining whether the contract is a derivative or an insurance contract.

Derivatives Documentation

Derivatives transactions are typically documented pursuant to a standard "master agreement," issued by the International Swaps and Derivatives Association (ISDA).[12] The parties negotiate a customized Schedule, which typically accompanies the ISDA Master Agreement. The Schedule and the standard-form ISDA Master Agreement reflect general legal terms that apply to transactions between the parties (i.e., which party has the right to make the calculations, what the terms are for payments on early terminations, and applicable governing law). The parties will negotiate the terms of any credit support and the posting of collateral, if appropriate, usually along with the customized Schedule. Individual transactions are reflected on separate trade confirmations that include the economic terms of each individual transaction.[13]

Parties to derivatives transactions can obtain three important advantages if they document their derivatives contracts under a "Master Swap Agreement" (which is often composed of an ISDA Master Swap Agreement, the Schedule, and all trade confirmations).

1. A Master Swap Agreement typically provides for netting of payments to be made or received on multiple derivatives transactions entered into between the parties on the same day and in the same currency.
2. If one of the parties to the Master Swap Agreement becomes insolvent (or files a bankruptcy petition), the other party has special rights under the U.S. bankruptcy laws to terminate the Master Swap Agreement and to offset (or net out) any termination values or payments.[14]
3. Certain other types of derivatives contracts are excluded from the "automatic stay" provisions of the U.S. bankruptcy laws with respect to setoffs.[15] These protections can be quite valuable to the solvent party.

Insurance Contracts

Insurance contracts typically are documented under an insurance policy that consists of the actual insurance policy (as offered to all prospective purchasers), declarations (specifying the contractual terms applicable to the insured), the insurance application, and any schedules, exhibits, or endorsements that are attached to or accompany the actual insurance policy.

A Derivative Contract or an Insurance Contract?

A contract offered by a licensed insurance company to transfer a purchaser's weather risk to the insurance company is likely to be viewed as "insurance" if the purchaser must prove it has suffered a loss in order to receive a payment under the contract. A contract is likely to be viewed as a derivative, on the other hand, if the same weather risk is documented under an agreement between two parties (typically, under an ISDA Master Agreement) where a payment is based on a calculation specified in the contract, without regard to whether the party entitled to receive the payment has incurred a loss. To further refine this general rule for derivatives and insurance, a contract that includes the following points is more likely to be viewed as a derivative rather than an insurance contract.

- ■ *Form of Contract:* A weather risk should be documented with a contract typically used in the derivatives market to document derivatives transactions.
- ■ *Disclaimer:* To be viewed as a derivative, the contract could include a disclaimer that the weather derivative is not intended to be insurance; the contract is not suitable as a substitute for insurance; and the contract is not guaranteed by any "Property and Casualty Guaranty Fund or Association" under applicable state law.

One final point: Any marketing materials with respect to a weather derivatives transaction should not dwell on the similarities between the contract and insurance.

TAX DISTINCTIONS

Energy companies managing their weather-related risks must evaluate the tax treatment of the products (derivatives and insurance contracts) available to them.

TAXATION OF WEATHER DERIVATIVES

Weather derivatives are difficult to categorize under established tax rules that generally apply to derivative products. This tax uncertainty results because weather derivatives usually do not relate to an identifiable asset or property owned by the company that enters into a weather derivative. This is because U.S. tax laws attempt to distinguish between "capital" and "ordinary" gains and losses on the basis of the nature of an underlying asset or property in the taxpayer's hands.

Derivatives can be categorized in different ways for U.S. tax purposes.

For example, weather derivatives might be characterized as "notional principal contracts" (NPCs) under Treasury Regulation §1.446-3; as "options" subject to section 1234 of the Internal Revenue Code (Code); or as a "contract" governed by Code §1234A.[16]

Although a detailed discussion of the tax treatment of various types of derivative products is beyond the scope of this chapter, I would like to make the point that, while there may be legitimate policy reasons for taxing weather derivatives in the same manner as other derivatives, existing Code and regulatory provisions provide little assurance as to the tax treatment of weather derivatives. As a result, if a weather derivative does not qualify as a tax hedging transaction within the meaning of Code §§1221(a)(7) and 1221(b)(2) and Treasury Regulation §1.1221-2, the resulting character and timing of any gains and losses is unclear.

Tax Hedge Qualifications

Once a company identifies a weather derivative it believes can protect it from a weather-related risk, a key tax question it must address is whether the transaction meets the tax definition of a hedge. This is because gains and losses on derivatives transactions that meet the tax hedge definition are eligible for ordinary income and loss treatment. If the transaction is not a tax hedge, losses are treated as capital losses, even if the transaction protects the company from a business risk. Under general tax rules, capital losses can be deducted only to the extent the company has capital gains from other sources. If a company does not generate capital gains, it will find capital losses are worthless.

To obtain favorable tax hedge treatment for a transaction that meets the tax hedge definition, the company must be sure it meets the tax identification requirements set out in the Treasury regulations.

Tax Hedge Defined

A tax hedge is defined as a transaction entered into in the normal course of a company's trade or business primarily to "manage" its interest rate, price, or currency risks with respect to ordinary property, borrowings, or ordinary obligations. Certain anticipated risks can be hedged for tax purposes.

Under current tax law, the risk being hedged must be with respect to ordinary property, borrowings, or ordinary obligations. (The risk being hedged is referred to as the hedged item.) For tax purposes, ordinary property includes property that, if sold by the company, could not produce capital gain or loss. A dealer's inventory, such as natural gas or heating oil, is ordinary property that the dealer can hedge. Similarly, electricity sold by a utility or power marketer is ordinary property that it can hedge.

On the other hand, transactions that protect overall business profitability (i.e., volume or revenue risk) are not directly related to ordinary property, borrowings, or ordinary obligations. As a result, transactions that protect a company's revenue stream or its net income against volume or revenue risk are not tax hedges under current tax law.

Treasury Authority to Expand Tax Hedging Categories

The tax law requirement that a company must hedge ordinary property, borrowings, or obligations means that favorable tax hedging treatment is not available for many legitimate risk management activities.

To modernize the tax rules with respect to hedging, Congress, in December of 2000, specifically authorized the Treasury Department to issue regulations extending the hedging definition to the management of other risks that the Treasury prescribes in regulations.[17] I hope that the Treasury will soon issue regulations extending the benefits of tax hedging to weather-related volume and revenue risks that are not tied to ordinary property, borrowings, or ordinary obligations. Many weather derivatives manage weather-related volume or revenue risks resulting from reduced demand for, or sales of, a company's products or services.

I see no policy reasons for the U.S. tax laws to prohibit tax hedging in situations where a company—in the normal course of its business—seeks to manage its risks against reduced volume or revenue simply because those business risks cannot be attributed to ordinary property, ordinary obligations, or borrowings.

Identification Requirements

If a transaction qualifies as a tax hedge, the company must identify the hedge in accordance with the regulations. Ordinary loss treatment is not available automatically to a hedger. Rather, the transaction must be identified properly as a hedge on the day on which the company enters into the hedge. And the hedged item also must be identified on a "substantially contemporaneously" basis.

Whipsaw Rules

Under tax whipsaw rules, if a company does not identify a tax hedge properly, gains from the transaction are ordinary while losses are capital. A similar whipsaw rule applies to transactions improperly identified as hedges.

Hedge Timing

Treasury regulations require a company to account for any gains and losses on its hedges under a tax accounting method that clearly reflects the company's income. According to Treasury Regulation §1.446-4(b), a company has some flexibility to choose its tax accounting method if the tax accounting method clearly reflects its income.

TAXATION OF INSURANCE CONTRACTS

Insurance companies offering weather insurance contracts compete directly with weather derivatives. As discussed earlier, a weather insurance policy provides a company with insurance coverage if the weather conditions specified in the contracts result in an insurable loss that the company can prove it suffered.

For tax purposes, premiums paid to buy an insurance policy to protect against weather-related losses are deductible against the company's income, when paid as ordinary and necessary business expenses.[18] In addition, the insurance proceeds received from certain types of insurance generally are not taxed, unless the proceeds exceed the company's tax basis of the property lost or if the proceeds represent lost business profits.

If a U.S. company purchases insurance for casualty or accident insurance (with respect to hazards, risks, losses, or liabilities incurred in the United States) from a foreign insurance company, the insured party who pays the premium has the obligation to pay an excise tax to the Treasury. This excise tax is imposed on premiums paid by the U.S. company to the foreign insurance company.[19]

Special tax rules apply to companies that issue insurance contracts. One special rule is that insurance companies that issue insurance contracts are taxed as "corporations" under U.S. tax laws. Another special rule is that insurance companies receive certain exemptions from current taxation. Whether a contract is treated as "insurance" for U.S. tax purposes depends on whether the contract (1) is designated as insurance, (2) reflects terms generally associated with insurance, and (3) is treated as insurance by relevant state insurance regulators.[20]

With respect to a weather-related risk, assume a company pays a premium to an insurance company that, in turn, agrees to pay the company's losses or expenses from the triggering of the weather-related event specified in the contract. Let us also assume that the contract is written as an insurance policy; it relates to a fortuitous weather event; and it provides the company paying the premium with an indemnity against specified losses.

For tax purposes, such a contract should qualify as insurance *if* the insurance company pools the risks that it assumes similar contracts. If the insurance company does not pool these risks, the contract is not insurance for tax purposes. In fact, because of this pooling requirement for tax purposes, courts have found certain contracts that are regulated as insurance are not "insurance" for tax purposes.[21]

CONCLUSION

An energy company interested in protecting itself against weather-related risks must consider carefully the advantages and disadvantages of entering into either a weather derivative transaction or an insurance policy. There are no definitive rules as to which terms will qualify a contract as either a derivative or an insurance contract.

NOTES

Ms. Kramer is a partner in the international law firm of McDermott, Will & Emery, resident in its Chicago office. She is the author of *Financial Products: Taxation, Regulation, and Design* (Panel Publishers, 2000) and its annual supplements. Ms. Kramer can be reached at *akramer@mwe.com.*

1. Weather risks are based on daily fluctuations in the climate rather than unexpected events, such as hurricanes, major storms, or other catastrophes.
2. Many industries, in addition to energy utilities and distributors, are sensitive to weather conditions. In this chapter, however, I focus on energy companies because weather risk is often the single largest risk affecting their business.
3. Exchange traded weather futures and options on futures began trading at the Chicago Mercantile Exchange in September 1999. In October 2001, the London International Financial Futures and Options Exchange announced that it would offer exchange trading in weather futures.
4. When addressing temperature changes, HDDs and CDDs typically are used to measure how far a temperature varies from the designated baseline over the time period specified in the contract. Because many people set their thermostats at 65 degrees Fahrenheit, 65 degrees is usually the baseline used for HDDs and CDDs.
5. A commodity is defined in CEA §1(a)(4) as certain enumerated agricultural products and "all goods and articles . . . services, rights, and interests in which contracts for future delivery are presently or in the future dealt in."
6. New CEA §2(g) was enacted by the Commodity Futures Modernization Act of 2000, which was signed into law on December 21, 2000.
7. An eligible swap participant includes banks and certain financial institutions, insurance companies, certain employee benefit plans, certain entities registered with either the Securities and Exchange Commission or the CFTC, and corporations with total assets exceeding $10 million or with net worth of $1 million.
8. See, for example, *Union Labor Life Ins. Co. v. Pireno*, 458 U.S. 119, 128–29 (1982), *Group Life & Health Insurance Co. v. Royal Drug Co.*, 440 U.S. 205, 210–17 (1979).

9. NY *Ins Law* §1101(a)(1) (LEXIS through Chap. 221, August 29, 2001).
10. Although insurance commissioners of other states are not bound by decisions of the NYID, New York's view is instructive because it is an important insurance regulator, with jurisdiction over many U.S. insurance companies.
11. The Weather Derivatives Opinion points out that NYID has not ruled out the "possibility" that a contract or transaction might have unique circumstances (not addressed in this opinion) so that "NYID would deem certain weather derivatives to be insurance contracts."
12. ISDA has developed standard agreements that have been widely adopted by parties to derivative contracts. The ISDA website is at *www.isda.org*. ISDA Master Agreements that typically are used to document weather derivatives transactions include the 1992 Master Agreement (Multicurrency-Cross Border) and the 1992 ISDA Master Agreement (Local Currency-Single Jurisdiction). Use of an ISDA Master Agreement is not required, however, and the parties to derivatives contracts can enter into a customized (often referred to as "home grown") agreements.
13. Sample confirmations for weather derivatives can be found at the website for the Weather Risk Management Association at *www.wrma.org*.
14. 11 U.S.C. §§362(b)(17) and 560.
15. 11 U.S.C. §362(b)(6).
16. For a detailed discussion of possible tax treatments of weather derivatives, see Kramer (2001), at §§6.07, 35.03[D], and 80.05.
17. Code §1221(b)(2)(A)(iii).
18. Code §162.
19. Code §4371.
20. See *Helvering v. Le Gierse*, 312 U.S. 531, 539 (1941), *rev'g* 110 F.2d 734 (2nd Cir. 1940), 39 B.T.A. 1134 (1939).
21. See *Allied Fidelity Corp. v. Comm'r*, 66 T.C. 1068 (1976), *aff'd* 572 F.2d 1190 (7th Cir. 1978).

CHAPTER 26

Convergence of Insurance and Investment Banking: Representations and Warranties Insurance and Other Insurance Products Designed to Facilitate Corporate Transactions

Theodore A. Boundas and Teri Lee Ferro

INTRODUCTION

As the volume of corporate transactions surged in the 1990s, major insurance companies realized that risks inherent in corporate transactions called for innovative insurance solutions. Corporate transactions, including mergers and acquisitions (M&A), depend on the services of a variety of professionals, such as investment bankers, accountants, and lawyers, to assess the actual and potential exposures inherent in a transaction, orchestrate financing options for the transaction, and document the understanding of the parties and the terms of their agreement. Within the last few years, insurers actively entered the market for insurance products designed to facilitate business transactions. This chapter examines some of the insurance products designed to facilitate business transactions. Generally, these products are referred to as M&A insurance because they developed in response to the tremendous volume of merger and acquisition activity in the late 1990s. These products, however, are not limited to use in merger and acquisition transactions, and some of these products also are used to facilitate other types of transactions, such as financing arrangements. While insurance nomenclature is far from standard, most insurance professionals consider a variety of products, such as representation and warranty insurance (R&W insurance), tax opinion or tax indemnity insurance, aborted bid insurance and loss mitigation products (LMPs), as examples of M&A insurance products. Since these products all share the common purpose of facilitating business transactions, including but not always limited to mergers and acquisitions, we refer to them generally as transactional insurance products (TIPs).

Here we examine the most prevalent forms of TIPs and explore the market for them. In our exploration of the TIPs market, we consider whether TIPs are traditional insurance products or alternative risk transfer (ART) insurance products; discuss how TIPs represent the continued convergence of the insurance, banking, and finance industries; and examine the future prospects for TIPs.

PRODUCTS DESIGNED TO FACILITATE MERGERS AND ACQUISITIONS AND OTHER TRANSACTIONS

Essentially, TIPs transfer an unknown or unwanted exposure from the parties in a transaction or from a company's balance sheet to a third-party insurer for a price. It appears that TIPs originally were used by private equity partnerships and private businesses that wanted to eliminate or minimize postclosing problems, disputes, and liabilities. However, the market for TIPs has expanded to reach all types of businesses entities, including public corporations. The reality facing any public corporation is that bad news can severely impact the market valuation of its shares and ultimately its balance sheet. In fact, the failure to meet earnings projections or Wall Street's "whisper number" by even a nominal amount can have severe consequences for public corporations and their shareholders. A contingent tax liability or an actual or potential securities or environmental problem, for example, could cast a cloud over a company's stock price or impede its ability to obtain financing or capital. Likewise, such issues could drive down a purchase price or derail a merger or acquisition. A variety of TIPs, particularly R&W insurance, tax opinion or indemnity insurance, aborted bid cost policies, and LMPs, allow businesses to diminish the impact of an actual or potential exposure associated with a specific event or sequence of events by removing the liability from a company's balance sheet or guaranteeing the payment of an unrealized but actual or potential future risk.

Even after a transaction closes, TIPs can be useful where a party later recognizes a problem and decides to implement an insurance solution to manage an exposure that otherwise could present difficulties. Usually TIPs are tailored to defined risks and issues in the transaction and often require the insurer to conduct its own due diligence and risk assessment in consultation with its own lawyers, economists, and other experts. TIPs can be purchased by the buyers or sellers in a transaction and usually are based on negotiated issues, legal opinions, or representations and warranties involved in the transaction. The insured may not be the party paying the premium, and often the responsibility for financing the premium, much like the allocation of all other responsibilities in the transaction itself, is a negotiated item. Additionally, tax benefits may be gained by placing exposures into TIPs instead of holding reserves for them on a company's balance sheet or holding funds in an escrow after the closing of a transaction. Aside from potential tax benefits, the premiums for TIPs may be a cost-effective alternative to the usual mechanisms for dealing with the potential risks associated with representations and warranties in transactions, such as holding money in escrow or otherwise reflecting the risk in the purchase price.

The key to finding the right solutions for business risks is to help clients identify and evaluate complex business risks and create the most appropriate insurance or financial solutions that generate the most value for the insured while utilizing accurate pricing methodologies for the insurer. The placement of TIPs into corporate transactions is not as linear a process as that of traditional insurance products that are placed by insurers directly or through brokers and agents. The attorneys, bankers, accountants, and other professionals integral to the deal-making process and the parties to the transaction itself may not be aware of or open to the use of TIPs to facilitate the deal.[1] Some early industry observers commenting on TIPs noted concerns expressed by bankers and consultants that insurers could not be "responsive in the heat of the deal"[2] or that TIPs might be used to substitute for conducting sufficient due diligence.[3] Insurers and their advisors who are experienced in the use, placement, drafting, and pricing of TIPs, however, typically have a ready source of professionals, such as consultants, lawyers, and economists, ready to quickly assess and underwrite deals. As such, these concerns have diminished as the marketplace for TIPs has become defined and supported by professionals experienced in the underwriting and pricing of such insurance products. In order to craft a product that addresses specified risks, these professionals independently evaluate the specified risk in the transaction and often review and augment the due diligence conducted in connection with the transaction. Particularly in transactions involving intellectual property rights and environmental and securities exposures, insurers will utilize the services of expert consultants with substantial experience in both evaluating these specialized risks and designing insurance products for these risks. Experienced insurers and their advisors, working with other professionals integral to the deal, can add value by assisting with the process of articulating and addressing the risks inherent in the transaction.

The following sections discuss some of the most popular TIPs available in the market today. While these TIPs often are marketed as distinct products, they all are used to transfer identified risk to facilitate a transaction and may, in certain situations, be interchangeable solutions for a problem.

Representations and Warranties Insurance

R&W insurance insures specified representations and warranties, and corresponding indemnity obligations, in corporate transactions. It is "sleep" insurance for parties to a transaction who want to eliminate potential risk from future disputes arising out of representations or warranties in a transaction. Basically, sellers will represent and warrant a variety of things about the business, assets, or liabilities involved in a transaction to augment the due diligence and other information exchanged in connection with the transaction. Representations and warranties will vary depending on the type of transaction (e.g., a stock or asset sale) and the type of entities involved in the transaction. The representations may involve a variety of issues including but not limited to ownership in the business or its intellectual property, size of inventories, cash flows, tax issues, known litigation, and products liability or environmental concerns. Parties extensively negotiate the scope, breadth, and materiality of representations and warranties because these declarations often concern the assets, liabilities, and financial condition of the business and influence the purchase price. Additionally, broader representations and warranties benefit the buyer and allocate more risk and responsibilities to the seller. Therefore, the seller typically attempts to narrow the representations and warranties so future events not specifically addressed in the agreement cannot constitute a breach of a representation or warranty.

In connection with the representations and warranties, transactional agreements usually impose an indemnification obligation upon the seller to provide the buyer with recourse against the seller for liabilities or losses that occur after the transaction closes. The indemnification obligation also may require that a portion of the sale proceeds be set off or held back or otherwise placed into escrow to secure the seller's indemnification obligations in the event a representation or warranty later is found to be untrue. The seller usually negotiates limits on any indemnification agreement so that it is enforceable only for a set period of time and only up to an agreed upon amount.

Although R&W insurance can cover all representations and warranties in a corporate transaction, it is not uncommon for such policies to cover only very specific or narrowly defined risks, such as specified intellectual property rights, environmental issues, existing claims or litigation, and contingent tax liabilities. Any potential uncertainty that could impact the value of a transaction or require the seller to make certain representations and warranties about the state or condition of the potential risk or liability can be addressed in an R&W insurance policy. Of course, the price of the policy should reflect the nature and magnitude of the risk, and some risks may be too expensive or risky for the insured and/or the insurer. We suspect that R&W insurance and all TIPs in general are most effective and better priced when tailored to address narrowly defined risks.

R&W insurance products can cover either the buyer and/or seller as insureds. R&W insurance policies covering sellers offer third-party coverage to secure the sellers' indemnity obligations. In exchange for an insurance premium, a seller could avoid posting a portion of the sale proceeds in escrow and shift all or a portion of its indemnification obligation to a third-party insurer. A buyer could utilize R&W insurance where it does not want to accept the risk, cost, and expense of pursuing the seller if a breach of a representation or warranty occurs and where the buyer may be concerned about timing issues associated with a future pursuit of the seller in the event of such a breach. If the buyer does not have adequate resources to pursue the seller or the seller is not financially viable, indemnity obligations may not help the buyer timely recover its losses. A buyer's R&W insurance policy would operate as first-party insurance, much like a fidelity bond, in that the insured is both the policyholder and the claimant. Such a policy allows the buyer to recover the loss at issue from the insurer if it is unable to obtain recovery from other available sources, such as the seller. R&W insurance, particularly for a buyer, can limit uncertainties in the deal that necessitated the insured representations and warranties in the first place.

R&W insurance products are particularly useful in transactions involving companies in the high-technology industry because their values are usually very dependent on intellectual property rights that can be difficult to assess or may be subject to ownership disputes. We expect that R&W insurance will continue to play an important role in transactions involving intellectual property rights and that the value of intellectual property rights will continue to be an important component of the total value of many companies.[4] Two notable examples of this from our experience in assisting R&W insurers involved the multibillion-dollar acquisitions of an Internet professional services firm and a telecommunications technology firm. In both transactions, the buyers insisted on seller warranties concerning the ownership of certain intellectual property, particularly business methods patents, crucial to the economic viability of the involved businesses. The underwriting centered on an assessment of the actual warranties given and the potential scope and magnitude of the types of claims that could implicate the indemnity obligations associated with the representations and warranties and, ultimately, the R&W insurance policy.

Of course, representations and warranties are used in a variety of transactions, and often they are used to allocate risks and responsibilities between the parties. For example, in a transaction involving the sale of a theme park, the buyer did not want to assume the liability for the retention obligation in the seller's existing liability policy. Based on an analysis of the potential exposure from our firm and other consultants, the insurer decided to underwrite the buyer's exposure for the retention on the liability policy. Therefore, for a set premium, both the buyer and the seller were relieved of this obligation to pay the retention on the liability policy and that responsibility was no longer an issue that needed to be allocated between the parties. The matter of which party was obligated to pay the premium, however, remained an issue open for negotiation.

In one particularly novel transaction, a lender sought an insurance solution to secure a loan obligation to finance the multibillion-dollar acquisition of a business dependent on gambling revenues. As in the case of technology companies that have a substantial portion of their value tied to intellectual property, a substantial portion of the value of the company depended on its ability to continue to operate a certain type of gambling establishment in a jurisdiction with some noted opposition to the gambling industry. Essentially, the transaction rested in part on certain representations about the ability of the business to continue its gambling operations in the relevant jurisdiction. After investigation, we determined that the uncertainty the parties were trying to transfer to an insurance solution was legislative in nature, and we examined the likelihood of adverse legislative or governmental action that could impair or diminish the ability of the company to obtain sufficient revenue to service the debt that would be created by the acquisition. Contrary to the expectations of the parties, the analysis indicated that the potential risk was within a level the lender was willing to assume as part of the pricing structure for the loan obligation.

Many potential purchasers of R&W insurance question the utility of such coverage if most sellers and buyers already have a variety of insurance coverages in place, most notably directors and officers liability insurance and usually some other form of professional liability insurance. R&W insurance policies specifically cover representations and warranties and the parties making such representations and warranties. Therefore, the R&W insurance policy would be considered more specific, and therefore primary, if other coverage arguably was available under a more general coverage like a directors and officers policy. A typical directors and officers policy, however, may not cover a breach of a representation or warranty in a corporate transaction. Consider the situation where sellers breach representations and warranties and the buyer pursues a cause of action against the sellers. While many sellers may be directors, most sellers will be shareholders. The usual directors and officers policies will not cover directors acting in their capacities as shareholders. Therefore, the directors and officers policy should not extend coverage to shareholders, and to the extent the directors made the representations or warranties at issue, there could be an issue as to whether they did so in their capacities as directors or shareholders. Even if some other type of professional liability coverage was available, professional liability policies generally cover claims arising out of the insured's rendering of professional services to third parties in the regular course of conducting its business. As such, the sellers' professional liability policy would not cover claims against the sellers arising out of the sale of their business.

These same considerations apply to R&W insurance purchased by the buyer. No buyer's professional liability policy would provide first-party insurance to cover loss associated with the buyer's purchase of a business. Even if the buyer sued the seller and then sought to collect under the sellers' directors and officers liability or professional liability policies, as explained above, the sellers' policies probably would not cover the exposure arising from the breach of representations and warranties by the sellers in connection with the sale of its business. Therefore, R&W insurance creates more certainty for sellers and buyers because it specifically addresses this type of exposure; other coverages not otherwise designed for this purpose probably will not provide any coverage (or questionable coverage, if any) for these exposures.

Tax Opinion or Tax Indemnity Insurance

Tax contingencies are often the subject of representations and warranties and could be addressed in an R&W insurance policy. However, many companies separately offer tax opinion or tax indemnity insurance to insure against the adverse consequences that a particular tax treatment or position might be incorrect. These policies insure the risk of a successful Internal Revenue Service challenge of the intended tax consequences of a transaction as, for example, where a spin-off of a subsidiary is intended to be a tax-free event. Tax issues, similar to securities, antitrust, environmental, and intellectual property issues, can present a significant impediment in a transaction and may not be covered by other traditional insurance products. Even if the particular tax treatment has been approved in a formal legal opinion, a buyer may not be willing to sustain the financial impact resulting from incorrect tax treatment. If the questioned tax treatment might cause the buyer to lose interest in the deal, reduce the purchase price, or require the seller to place a portion of the sale proceeds in escrow, the buyer and/or the seller may find that transferring the uncertainty associated with the questioned tax treatment to a third-party insurer is worth the premium associated with such a policy. Tax opinion and tax indemnity insurance policies can insure the buyer and/or the seller, depending on how the parties address the tax issues in the transaction documents and who will bear the responsibility for any future adverse tax consequences.

Aborted Bid Insurance— Coverage for the Costs of the Uncompleted Transaction

Aborted bid insurance covers the external third-party fees and costs incurred in connection with a transaction that fails for reasons beyond the control of the insured company or a party. Merger attempts can be very costly and often involve the fees of a variety of professional advisors, including lawyers, accountants, investment bankers, stock brokers, management consultants, lobbyists, proxy solicitors, and public relations consultants. Typically, the policy defines the specific trigger for the coverage, such as loss of financing, failure to obtain regulatory approval, a failure to obtain shareholder approval, or the effective withdrawal of the other party to the transaction (not the insured). Such coverage generally does not apply to "breakup fees." Another similar product provides reimbursement for the third-party costs incurred in the defense of a hostile takeover bid and/or proxy contest. The existence of a policy to cover the costs of defending a hostile bid could be an effective negotiating tool for a company that is concerned that it could be a takeover target.

Loss Mitigation Products—Coverage for Existing Claims

LMPs are smoothing mechanisms similar in concept to the smoothing function of finite risk insurance products[5] except that finite risk finances exposure over time whereas LMPs effectuate the transfer of risk above certain levels of retained, insured, or financed risk. LMPs limit, or cap the uninsured, underinsured, or contingent exposure of a known claim by transferring the specified risk to a third-party insurer for a fixed price. LMPs transfer actual or contingent risk exposures associated with known claims. They are an effective tool for limiting a company's exposure to liability arising out of a significant claim, such as a securities class action lawsuit, antitrust litigation, or a long-tail environmental claim, because these types of exposures could fall outside of the parameters of a business entity's insurance program or the magnitude of the potential exposure may exceed available insurance program limits. To the extent an unresolved claim can dampen the financing and acquisition abilities and strategies of a business entity or impact its valuation, an LMP can limit the exposure presented by an unresolved claim to the self-insured portion of the risk (plus any insurance premiums for the LMP).

In the context of an acquisition, an LMP can allow the seller to avoid posting sale proceeds in escrow or retaining any liability or indemnity obligation to the buyer for a known claim. Even beyond the financial certainty the seller and buyer can obtain by using a LMP to limit the exposure arising out of a known claim, LMPs allow the parties to the transaction to define and limit the magnitude of the exposure associated with the known claim and reduce further transaction costs associated with that claim. Probably the most publicized LMP involved Oxford Health Plans. Oxford, a health maintenance organization, was a defendant in class action litigation involving patient billing practices. The program took the form of a LMP that would pay 90 percent of any adverse judgment over $175 million up to a $200 million cap in exchange for a premium in the amount of $24 million.[6]

DEVELOPMENT OF THE MARKET FOR
TRANSACTIONAL INSURANCE PRODUCTS

While an active market for TIPs is relatively new, insurance products that facilitate business transactions have been in existence for many years. In the early 1980s, for example, underwriters at Lloyd's of London offered tax insurance policies for risks associated with the legal uncertainty surrounding the tax treatment of certain equipment leasing transactions.[7] Although there is little statistical data tracking the volume and growth of TIPs in the insurance industry, an active market for such products developed over the past few years in connection with the increased volume of corporate transactions in the late 1990s.[8] For example, R&W insurance has been offered in the worldwide insurance market for many years. However, the market for this product in the United States is still in its incipient stage of development, and the vast majority of R&W policies underwritten have been placed within the last two years.[9] Likewise, the market for LMPs was nonexistent five years ago. Industry observers predict that premiums for these products should exceed $500 million in 2001.[10] Even though the increased activity in the TIPs market appears to coincide with the high volume of corporate transactions in the late 1990s, TIPs were utilized in a relatively small portion of the numerous corporate transactions conducted during that period.

Another factor limiting the development of the TIPs market was the reluctance of many insurers to underwrite very significant TIPs after the disastrous experience of insurers in the property and casualty markets in the 1980s. Over the past few years, insurers have become more open to underwriting these products because the TIPs market is more developed and insurance professionals have more experience assessing transactional exposures as well as drafting and pricing the appropriate policies to address such exposures. Of course, the ability of any insurer to underwrite an insurance product depends on the state of the insurance market and the availability of reinsurance. If the insurance market hardens, insurers have less access to the capital that supports their underwriting efforts. Additionally, the ability of insurers to market TIPs will depend on the level of corporate transactions sustainable by market conditions. During the first half of 2001, the volume of worldwide merger and acquisition activity decreased nearly 54 percent from levels reported the prior year.[11] Although a decrease in the volume of corporate transactions may limit the opportunities for insurance companies to place TIPs, the economic slowdown could well increase the demand and utility for such products. Weak economic conditions generally increase the risk associated with transactions and could provide the impetus for parties and their advisors to seek insurance solutions like TIPs.

Although the market for TIPs is becoming more established with each passing year, we suspect that the use of TIPs has not become more prevalent because many insurance practitioners and dealmakers are not familiar with these products. Indeed, within the insurance industry, there exists some confusion surrounding the classification of TIPs. Many insurers and insurance commentators categorize the various forms of TIPs as alternative risk transfer insurance products. Putting aside the issue of what properly should be considered under the rubric of ART, the insurance industry offers a variety of products and programs under the broad classification of ART, and there exists a divergence throughout the industry on the types of products classified as ART. The only apparent uniformity in the use of the acronym ART is that it is not used uniformly and may encompass almost any insurance product not defined as a traditional insurance product regardless of whether the product actually transfers risk or operates as a smoothing mechanism for financing retained risk and reducing the impact of losses on corporate results.[12] In their varied forms, many insurance products classified as ART represent the evolution of traditional insurance into a wide range of products that allow insurers greater and more direct participation in the goals and results of their clients. Many of these nontraditional insurance products, regardless of whether they are true ART products, finance rather than transfer risk and represent the convergence of the insurance, banking, and finance industries.

Of course, this begs the question of whether the TIPs described in this chapter are ART insurance products. They are not true ART insurance products because they do not contain a mechanism for profit or loss sharing between the insurer and the insured, an important hallmark of an ART product. Although one could characterize TIPs as traditional insurance contracts, they remain distinguishable from traditional insurance products. Quite simply, traditional insurance products are the commonly available insurance products that are well established in the industry by insurers, insureds, the public, and the legal system. The use, acceptance, and understanding of traditional insurance products, such as commercial general liability, employment liability, or directors and officers liability products, are built on years of underwriting, claims, and coverage experience. To the extent TIPs sometimes are treated as ART products, the TIPs discussed in this chapter have fallen into the ART rubric because they do not otherwise fall into the rubric of traditional insurance products common in the market. Therefore, they are not considered traditional because they are relatively new products covering nontraditional risks for a new market. Stripped of their novelty in this regard, these products otherwise function like traditional insurance contracts and their form of contract is often derivative of standard insurance contracts used for directors and officers liability insurance products. Even though they are basically traditional insurance products, TIPs can be distinguished from traditional insurance products because they not only transfer risk like a traditional insurance product but transfer risk for the explicit purpose of facilitating a business transaction. Viewed in this light, these products, much like many true ART insurance products, also represent the convergence of the insurance, banking, and finance industries.

Even outside the insurance industry, dealmakers have been slow to warm to the prospects offered by TIPs products. Throughout this chapter we explained how TIPs facilitate business transactions. Used to complement other banking and financing services, TIPs represent one of many crossroads in the financial services sector where the insurance, banking, and finance industries converge. This convergence of separate industries within the financial services sector has both limited and frustrated the development of a market for TIPs. Although the insurance, banking, and finance industries deal with similar concepts and goals, they developed along different paths and remain somewhat insular, in large part because of differences in terminology[13] and access to capital. As such, while the forms of a variety of insurance, banking, and finance products appear very different, substantively they may be very similar, and practitioners within these respective industries may not be aware of services and products in other industries that are identical or complementary to products and services in their own industries. Without common experience and terminology, dealmakers and insurers continue to face a learning curve as they become accustomed to the integration of insurance solutions into business transactions. Of course, the trend toward continued convergence among the insurance, banking, and financing industries is inescapable. Just consider the expansion of commercial banks into consumer insurance products and the expansion of investment banks into the business of transferring bundled insurance risks into the capital markets by issuing catastrophe bonds. In response to the competitive threat presented by the convergence of the insurance, banking, and finance industries, insurers became interested in leveraging their capital resources and knowledge to enter into markets traditionally serviced by the banking and finance industries and developed products to facilitate business transactions and operations. Insurers realized that offering products that transfer or finance risk, as a strategic business tool or as part of a risk management program, could help them remain competitive with the banking and finance segments of the financial services sector.[14]

The competition from banking and financial institutions is only one of the catalysts propelling insurers to expand into the types of business transactions traditionally serviced by commercial and investment banks. But whatever the impetus, insurers and their advisors are becoming more adept at assessing opportunities to utilize the capital of insurers to facilitate business opportunities for a price. The access to capital and risk evaluation services provided by insurers who underwrite TIPs usually complement the professional services provided by investment bankers and other professionals involved in corporate transactions. Insurers often use brokers, lawyers, economists, and other consultants to conduct independent due diligence assessing the risk exposure it may underwrite in connection with a transaction and to structure appropriate TIPs to address the specific nuances of transactions. It is not uncommon for insurers and their advisors to help recast a transaction because they may approach the risk or transaction from a different perspective or present options not otherwise contemplated by the parties. Therefore, TIPs are not a replacement for the professional services offered by investment bankers and other professionals. In this regard, the convergence of insurance, banking, and finance has increased competition as well as cooperation among insurers, bankers, and financiers.[15] This convergence should continue to foster opportunities for insurers to market TIPs as a mechanism for facilitating business transactions.

NOTES

Theodore A. Boundas and Teri Lee Ferro are with Peterson & Ross, a law firm internationally recognized as a leader in insurance law. Peterson & Ross provides sophisticated legal and consulting services worldwide, with a special emphasis on the risk management, insurance, and financial services industries.

1. M. J. Auer with J. Berke, "Risk Management-Insuring the Deal," *The Daily Deal.com*, April 28, 2000 (updated November 8, 2000).
2. Ibid.
3. Banham (1999).
4. Hansen (2001) observed that merger and acquisition activity has become riskier not only because of slowing economic conditions but also because of the increasing trend toward cross-border transactions involving intellectual property assets, as differences in laws, legal systems, and cultures increase the risk associated with such deals.
5. Generally, finite risk insurance is considered a smoothing mechanism that spreads losses over long periods, usually five to 10 years, to eliminate peaks and valleys from a company's earnings statements—thereby "smoothing" the financial impact of adverse developments.
6. R. G. Mullins, "Boxing the Unknown Exposure," January 24, 2001, at *www.erisk.com*.
7. Auer with Berke.
8. See, for example, ibid. (quoting estimates from AIG that premiums for M&A products written between 1998 and 1999 increased 50 percent from $400 million to $600 million).
9. Hansen (2001) and Auer with Berke.
10. Mullins.
11. Hansen (2001) (quoting Thomason Financial).
12. See, for example, Loh (2000).

13. See Booth (2001).
14. Sammer (1999).
15. Booth (2001). See also Bernstein (2000), (discussing the convergence among insurance, financial services, and finance and commenting that the statement that insurance companies transform "damaging consequences into manageable consequences" is an observation that is equally applicable to all hedging strategies.

bibliography

Akerlof, G. A. 1970. "The Market for 'Lemons:' Quality and the Market Mechanism." *Quarterly Journal of Economics* Vol. 84 (August).

Allen, F., and G. R. Faulhaber. 1989. "Signaling by Underpricing in the IPO Market." *Journal of Financial Economics*. Vol. 23.

Allen, F., and R. Michaely. 1995. "Dividend Policy." *Handbooks in OR & MS, Vol. 9.* Amsterdam: Elsevier.

Allen, F., and A. Winton. 1995. "Corporate Financial Structure, Incentives and Optimal Contracting." *Handbooks in OR & MS, Vol. 9.* Amsterdam: Elsevier.

Ballantine, R. 2001a. "Deals That Fly." *Reactions* (April).

Ballantine, R. 2001b. "Not Like It Is in the Movies." *Reactions* (August).

Banham, R. 1999. "Dealing with a Safety Net." *CFO Magazine* (December).

Banham, R. 2000. "Rethinking the Future." *Reactions* (April).

Banham, R. 2001. "Clocs Ticking to New Market." *Reactions* (April).

Bank for International Settlements. 1993. *Central Bank Payment and Settlement Services with Respect to Cross-Border and Multi-Currency Transactions.* Basel.

Bank for International Settlements. 1997. *Real-Time Gross Settlement Systems.* Basel.

Banz, R. W. 1981. "The Relationship Between Return and Market Value of Common Stocks." *Journal of Financial Economics*. Vol. 9.

Barclay, M. J., and C. W. Smith, Jr. 1996. "On Financial Architecture: Leverage, Maturity, and Priority." *Journal of Applied Corporate Finance*. Vol. 8, No. 4 (Winter).

Barclay, M. J., and C. W. Smith, Jr. 1999. "The Capital Structure Puzzle: Another Look at the Evidence." *Journal of Applied Corporate Finance*. Vol. 12, No. 1 (Spring).

Belonsky, G., D. Laster, and D. Durbin. 1999. "Insurance-Linked Securities." In *Insurance and Weather Derivatives*. H. Geman, ed. London: Risk Books.

Bernero, R. H. 1998. "Second-Generation OTC Derivatives and Structured Products: Catastrophe Bonds, Catastrophe Swaps, and Insurance Securitizations." In *Securitized Insurance Risk*. M. Himick, ed. Chicago, Ill.: Glenlake Publishing Company, Ltd.

Bernstein, P. C. 2000. "Hidden Linkages: Risk Management, Financial Markets, and Insurance," American Academy of Actuaries (November/December).

Blommestein, H. J., and B. J. Summers. 1994. "Banking and the Payment System." In *The Payment System: Design, Management, and Supervision*. B. J. Summers, ed. Washington, DC: International Monetary Fund.

Board of Governors of the Federal Reserve System. 1993. *Overview of the Federal Reserve's Payments System Risk Policy* (October).

Board of Governors of the Federal Reserve System. 1995. *Federal Reserve Policy Statement on Payments System Risk* (August).

Böhm-Bawerk, E. von. 1959. *Capital and Interest*. New York: Libertarian Press.

Bollen, Nicolas, and Robert Whaley. 1998. "Simulating Supply." *Risk* (September).

Booth, G. 2001. "Needed: A Common Language of Risk." *MMC Views* (November 1).

Borch, K. H. 1990. *Economics of Insurance*. Amsterdam: North-Holland.

Brealey, R. A., and S. C. Myers. 2000. *Principles of Corporate Finance*. 6th ed. New York: Irwin McGraw-Hill.

Buck, G., and P. Riches. 1999. *Risk Management: New Challenges and Solutions*. London: Reuters.

Canter, M. S., J. B. Cole, and R. L. Sandor. 1999. "Insurance Derivatives: A New Asset Class for the Capital Markets and a New Hedging Tool for the Insurance Industry." In *Insurance and Weather Derivatives*. H. Geman, ed. London: Risk Books.

Carow, K. A., G. R. Erwin, and J. J. McConnell. 1999. "A Survey of U.S. Corporate Financing Innovations: 1970–1997." *Journal of Applied Corporate Finance*. Vol. 12, No. 11 (Spring).

Carter, R., L. Lucas, and N. Ralph. 2000. *Reinsurance*. 4th ed. London: Reactions Publishing Group in association with Guy Carpenter & Company.

Chapman Tripp. 1998. "Mezzanine Finance: One Person's Ceiling is Another Person's Floor." *Finance Law Focus*. (November 11).

Chen, N., R. Roll, and S. Ross. 1986. "Economic Forces and the Stock Market." *Journal of Business*. Vol. 59.

Cifuentes, A., I. Efrat, J. Gluck, and E. Murphy. 1998. "Buying and Selling Credit Risk: A Perspective on Credit-Linked Obligations." *Credit Derivatives: Applications for Risk Management, Investment, and Portfolio Optimisation*. London: Risk Books.

Cochrane, J. H. 1991. "Production-Based Asset Pricing and the Link Between Stock Returns and Economic Fluctuations." *Journal of Finance*. Vol. 46.

Cochrane, J. H. 1996. "A Cross-Sectional Test of an Investment-Based Asset Pricing Model." *Journal of Political Economy*. Vol. 104.

Cochrane, J. H. 2001. *Asset Pricing*. Princeton, N.J.: Princeton University Press.

Corrigan, E. G. 1982. "Are Banks Special?" *Federal Reserve Bank of Minneapolis Annual Report*.

Corrigan, E. G. 1990. "Perspectives on Payment System Risk Reduction." In *The U.S. Payment System: Efficiency, Risk, and the Role of the Federal Reserve*. D. B. Humphrey, ed. Boston: Kluwer Academic Publishers.

Cox, S. H., and R. G. Schwebach. 1992. "Insurance Futures and Hedging Insurance Price Risk." *Journal of Risk and Insurance*. Vol. 59, No. 4.

Crouhy, M., D. Galai, and R. Mark. 2001. *Risk Management*. New York: McGraw-Hill.

Culp, C. L. 1995a. *A Primer on Derivatives*. Chicago, Ill., and Washington, D.C.: Board of Trade of the City of Chicago, and Competitive Enterprise Institute (July).

Culp, C. L. 1995b. "Regulatory Uncertainty and the Economics of Derivatives Regulation." *The Financier: Analysis of Capital and Money Market Transactions*. Vol. 2, No. 5 (December).

Culp, C. L. 1996. "Relations Between Insurance and Derivatives: Applications from Catastrophic Loss Insurance." In *Rethinking Insurance Regulation: Vol. I, Catastrophic Risks*. Y. B. McAleer and T. Miller, eds. Washington, D.C.: Competitive Enterprise Institute.

Culp, C. L. 1999. "Wettbewerbsnachteile für Schweizer Banken? Konsultativpapier des Basler Ausschusses mit Schwächen." Neue Zürcher Zeitung (October 15).

Culp, C. L. 2000. "Revisiting RAROC." *Journal of Lending and Credit Risk Management* (March).

Culp, C. L. 2001. *The Risk Management Process: Business Strategy and Tactics*. New York: John Wiley & Sons.

Culp, C. L., and B. T. Kavanagh. 1994. "Methods of Resolving Over-the-Counter Derivatives Contracts in Failed Depository Institutions: Restrictions on Regulators from Federal Banking Law." *Futures International Law Letter*. Vol. 14, Nos. 3–4 (May/June).

Culp, C. L., and R. J. Mackay. 1997. "An Introduction to Structured Notes." *Derivatives*. Vol. 2, No. 4 (March/April).

Culp, C. L., and M. H. Miller. 1995a. "Auditing the Auditors." *Risk*. Vol. 8, No. 4 (April).

Culp, C. L., and M. H. Miller. 1995b. "Blame Mismanagement, Not Speculation, for Metall's Woes." *European Wall Street Journal* (April 25).

Culp, C. L., and M. H. Miller. 1995c. "Metallgesellschaft and the Economics of Synthetic Storage." *Journal of Applied Corporate Finance*. Vol. 7, No. 4 (Winter).

Culp, C. L., and M. H. Miller. 1995d. "Hedging in the Theory of Corporate Finance." *Journal of Applied Corporate Finance*. Vol. 8, No. 1 (Spring).

Culp, C. L., and M. H. Miller. 2000. *Corporate Hedging in Theory and Practice: Lessons from Metallgesellschaft*. London: Risk Publications.

Culp, C. L., and A. M. P. Neves. 1998a. "Credit and Interest Rate Risk in the Business of Banking." *Derivatives Quarterly*. Vol. 4, No. 4 (Summer).

Culp, C. L., and A. M. P. Neves. 1998b. "Financial Innovations in Leveraged Commercial Loan Markets." *Journal of Applied Corporate Finance*. Vol. 11, No. 2 (Summer).

Culp, C. L., and A. M. P. Neves. 1999. *A Primer on Securities and Multi-Currency Settlement Systems: Systemic Risk and Risk Management*. Washington, D.C.: Competitive Enterprise Institute.

Culp, C. L., and J. A. Overdahl. 1996. "An Overview of Derivatives: Their Mechanics, Participants, Scope of Activity, and Benefits." In *The Financial Services Revolution*. C. Kirsch, ed. Chicago, Ill.: Irwin Professional Publishing.

Culp, C. L., and P. Planchat. 2000. "New Risk Culture: An Opportunity for Business Growth and Innovation." *Derivatives Quarterly*. Vol. 6, No. 4 (Summer).

Culp, C. L., S. H. Hanke, and A. M. P. Neves. 1999. "Derivatives Diagnosis." *The International Economy*. Vol. 13, No. 3 (May/June).

Culp, C. L., M. H. Miller, and A. M. P. Neves. 1998. "Value at Risk: Uses and Abuses." *Journal of Applied Corporate Finance*. Vol. 10, No. 4 (Winter).

Cummins, J. D., and H. Geman. 1995. "Pricing Catastrophe Insurance Futures and Call Spreads: An Arbitrage Approach." *Journal of Fixed Income* (March).

Daniel, K., and S. Titman. 1995. "Financing Investment Under Asymmetric Information." *Handbooks in OR & MS, Vol. 9*. Amsterdam: Elsevier.

D'Arcy, S. P., and V. G. France. 1992. "Catastrophe Futures: A Better Hedge for Insurers." *Journal of Risk and Insurance*. Vol. 59, No. 4.

Das, S. 1998. *Credit Derivatives*. New York: John Wiley & Sons.

Davis, A., and M. Pacelle. 2001. "Covad to Pay Its Bondholders Before Default." *Wall Street Journal* (August 8).

DeAngelo, H., and R. W. Masulis. 1980. "Optimal Capital Structure Under Corporate and Personal Taxation." *Journal of Financial Economics*. Vol. 8.

Diamond, D. 1984. "Financial Intermediation and Delegated Monitoring." *Review of Economic Studies*. Vol. 51.

Diamond, D. 1989a. "Asset Services and Financial Intermediation." In *Financial Markets and Incomplete Information: Frontiers of Modern Financial Theory, Vol. 2*. S. Bhattacharya and G. Constantinides, eds. Savage, Md.: Rowman & Littlefield Publishers, Inc.

Diamond, D. 1989b. "Reputation Acquisition in Debt Markets." *Journal of Political Economy*. Vol. 97.

Diamond, D. 1991. "Monitoring and Reputation: The Choice Between

Bank Loans and Directly Placed Debt." *Journal of Political Economy.* Vol. 99.

Diamond, D. 1993. "Seniority and Maturity of Debt Contracts." *Journal of Financial Economics.* Vol. 33.

Diamond, D., and R. Verrechia. 1982. "Optimal Managerial Contracts and Equilibrium Security Prices." *Journal of Finance.* Vol. 37.

Doherty, N. A. 2000. *Integrated Risk Management.* New York: McGraw-Hill.

Doherty, N. A., and C. W. Smith, Jr. 1993. "Corporate Insurance Strategy: The Case of British Petroleum." *Journal of Applied Corporate Finance.* Vol. 6, No. 3 (Fall).

Dyson, B. 2001. "Striking the Vital Balance." *Reactions* (January).

Easterbrook, F. H. 1984. "Two Agency-Cost Explanations of Dividends." *American Economic Review* Vol. 74, No. 4 (September).

Eckbo, B. E. 1986. "Valuation Effects and Corporate Debt Offerings." *Journal of Financial Economics.* Vol. 15.

Eckbo, B. E., and R. W. Masulis. 1995. "Seasoned Equity Offerings: A Survey." *Handbooks in OR & MS, Vol. 9.* Amsterdam: Elsevier.

Fama, E. F. 1976. "The Effects of a Firm's Investment and Financing Decisions on the Welfare of Its Security Holders." *American Economic Review.* Vol. 68, No. 3.

Fama, E. F. 1985. "What's Different About Banks?" *Journal of Monetary Economics.* Vol. 15.

Fama, E. F., and K. R. French. 1992. "The Cross-Section of Expected Stock Returns." *Journal of Finance.* Vol. 47.

Fama, E. F., and K. R. French. 1993. "Common Risk Factors in the Returns on Stocks and Bonds." *Journal of Financial Economics.* Vol. 33.

Fama, E. F., and K. R. French. 1995. "Size and Book-to-Market Factors in Earnings and Returns." *Journal of Finance.* Vol. 50.

Fama, E. F., and K. R. French. 1996. "Multifactor Explanations of Asset Pricing Anomalies." *Journal of Finance.* Vol. 51.

Fama, E. F., and K. R. French. 1997. "Industry Costs of Equity." *Journal of Financial Economics.* Vol. 43.

Fama, E. F., and K. R. French. 1998. "Taxes, Financing Decisions, and Firm Value." *Journal of Finance.* Vol. 43, No. 3.

Fama, E. F., and K. R. French. 1999. "The Corporate Cost of Capital and the Return on Corporate Investment." *Journal of Finance.* Vol. 54, No. 6.

Fama, E. F., and K. R. French. 2000. "Testing Tradeoff and Pecking Order Predictions About Dividends and Debt." Graduate School of Business, The University of Chicago, Center for Research in Security Prices, *Working Paper No. 506.*

Fama, E. F., and M. C. Jensen. 1983a. "Agency Problems and Residual Claims." *Journal of Law and Economics.* Vol.26.

Fama, E. F., and M. C. Jensen. 1983a. "Separation of Ownership and Control." *Journal of Law and Economics*. Vol. 26

Fama, E. F., and M. C. Jensen. 1985. "Organizational Forms and Investment Decisions." *Journal of Financial Economics*. Vol. 14.

Fama, E. F., and M. H. Miller. 1972. *The Theory of Finance*. Hinsdale, IL: Dryden Press.

Federal Reserve Bank of New York. 1987. *A Study of Large-Dollar Payment Flows Through CHIPS and Fedwire* (December).

Froot, K. A. 1999. *The Financing of Catastrophic Risk*. Chicago, Ill.: The University of Chicago Press.

Froot, K. A., D. S. Scharfstein, and J. C. Stein. 1993. "Risk Management: Coordinating Investment and Financing Policies." *Journal of Finance*. Vol. 48, No. 5.

Froot, K. A., D. S. Scharfstein, and J. C. Stein. 1994. "A Framework for Risk Management." *Harvard Business Review* (November-December).

Garrison, R. W. 1991. "Austrian Capital Theory and the Future of Macroeconomics." In *Austrian Economics: Perspectives on the Past and Prospects for the Future*. R. M. Ebeling, ed. Hillsdale, MI: Hillsdale College Press.

Garrison, R. W. 2001. *Time and Money: The Macroeconomics of Capital Structure*. London: Routledge.

Geman, H. 1999. *Insurance and Weather Derivatives*. London: Risk Books.

Gergen, M. P., and P. Schmitz. 1997. "The Influence of Tax Law on Securities Innovation in the United States, 1981–1997." *New York University Tax Review*.

Gerling Global Financial Products, Inc. 2000. *Modern ART Practice*. London: Euromoney Institutional Investor.

Global Derivatives Study Group. 1993. *Derivatives: Practices and Principles*. Washington, D.C.: The Group of Thirty.

Graham, J. R. 1996. "Debt and the Marginal Tax Rate." *Journal of Financial Economics*. Vol. 41.

Green, P. 2001. "Risk Management Covers Enterprise Exposures." *Global Finance* (January).

Grinblatt, M., and C. Y. Hwang. 1989. "Signaling and the Pricing of New Issues." *Journal of Finance*. Vol. 44.

Hansen, F. 2001. "The M&A Triple Threat." *Business Finance* (October).

Harrington, S., G. Niehaus, and K. Risko. 2002. "Enterprise Risk Management: The Case of United Grain Growers." *Journal of Applied Corporate Finance*. Vol. 25, No. 1 (Winter).

Harris, M., and A. Raviv. 1990. "Capital Structure and the Informational Role of Debt." *Journal of Finance*. Vol. 45.

Harris, M., and A. Raviv. 1991. "The Theory of Capital Structure." *Journal of Finance*. Vol. 46, No. 1.

Hart, O., and J. Moore. 1990. "A Theory of Corporate Financial Structure Based on the Seniority of Claims." NBER Working Paper 343 (September).

Hay, J. 2001. "Equity Turns Into Debt." *Structured Finance International* (May/June).

Hayre, L. S., C. Mohebbi, and T. A. Zimmerman. 1995. "Mortgage Pass-Through Securities." In *The Handbook of Fixed Income Securities.* F. J. Fabozzi and T. D. Fabozzi, eds. Chicago, Ill.: Irwin Professional Publishing.

Heaton, J. B. 2000. "Patent Law and Financial Engineering." *Derivatives Quarterly.* Vol. 7, No. 2.

Hicks, J. R. 1965. *Capital and Growth.* Oxford: Oxford University Press.

Himick, M., ed. 1998. *Securitized Insurane Risk.* Chicago, Ill.: Glenlake Publishing Company, Ltd.

Hirschleifer, D., and A. V. Thakor. 1989. "Managerial Reputation, Project Choice and Debt." Working Paper. Andersen Graduate School of Management, UCLA.

Hoffman, W. 1998. *Multiline Multiyear Agreements: A Guide for the Drafter and Negotiator.* Zürich: Swiss Re New Markets.

Horii, A., and B. J. Summers. 1994. "Large-Value Transfer Systems." In *The Payment System: Design, Management, and Supervision.* B. J. Summers, ed. Washington, D.C.: International Monetary Fund.

Howard, L. S. 2001. "Movie Bonds Get Bad Review After AIG Declines Coverage." *National Underwriter Online News* (February 9).

Hull, J. C. 2000. *Options, Futures, and Other Derivatives.* 4th ed. New York: Prentice-Hall.

Ibbotson, R. G., and J. R. Ritter. 1995. "Initial Public Offerings." *Handbooks in OR & MS, Vol. 9.* Amsterdam: Elsevier.

Imfeld, D. 2000. "Keeping an Eye on Interruption Risk." *Alternative Risk Strategies: Special Supplement to Risk Magazine* (December).

Ingersoll, J., and S. Ross. 1992. "Waiting to Invest: Investment and Uncertainty." *Journal of Business.* Vol. 65, No. 1 (January).

ISDA/BBA/RMA. 1999. *Operational Risk: The Next Frontier.* New York: International Swaps and Derivatives Association, Inc., British Bankers' Association, and Risk Management Association (December).

Jagannathan, R., and Z. Wang. 1996. "The Conditional CAPM and the Cross-Section of Expected Returns." *Journal of Finance.* Vol. 51.

James, C. 1987. "Some Evidence on the Uniqueness of Bank Loans." *Journal of Financial Economics.* Vol. 19.

Jensen, M. C. 1986. "Agency Costs of Free Cash Flows, Corporate Finance and Takeovers." *American Economic Review.* Vol. 76.

Jensen, M. C., and W. H. Meckling. 1976. "Theory of the Firm: Managerial Behavior, Agency Costs and Ownership Structure." *Journal of Financial Economics.* Vol. 3, No. 4.

Katz, D. M. 1999. "Banks Gain Entry into Insurance Via Captives." *National Underwriter* (March 15).

Kavanagh, B., T. R. Bohemio, and G. A. Edwards, Jr. 1992. "Asset-Backed Commercial Paper Programs." *Federal Reserve Bulletin* (February).

Kiln, R. 1991. *Reinsurance in Practice*. London: Witherby & Co. Ltd.

Kloman, H. F. 1998. "Captive Insurance Companies." In *International Risk and Insurance: An Environmental-Managerial Approach*. H. D. Skipper, ed. New York: Irwin McGraw-Hill.

Knight, F. H. 1921. *Risk, Uncertainty, and Profit*. New York: Houghton Mifflin Company.

Kramer, A. S. 2001. *Financial Products: Taxation, Regulation, and Design*. 3rd ed. New York: Aspen Publishers, Inc.

Lachmann, L. 1956 (1978). *Capital and Its Structure*. Kansas City, MO: Sheed Andrews and McMeel.

Laffont, J. J. 1990. *The Economics of Uncertainty and Information*. Cambridge, MA: The MIT Press.

Lane, M. N. 1998a. "AQS: Accelerated Quota Share." *Trade Notes*. Sedgwick Lane Financial (December 23).

Lane, M. N. 1998b. "Price, Risk, and Ratings for Insurance-Linked Notes: Evaluating Their Position in Your Portfolio." *Derivatives Quarterly*. Vol. 4, No. 4 (Summer).

Lane, M. N. 1999. "An Optionable Note: The Reliance III Case Study." *Trade Notes*. Lane Financial LLC (*www.lanefinancialllc.com*).

Lane, M. N. 2000. "CDOs as Self-Contained Reinsurance Structures." *Trade Notes*. Lane Financial LLC (*www.lanefinancialllc.com*) (December 10).

Leland, H. E., and D. H. Pyle. 1977. "Information Asymmetries, Financial Structure, and Financial Intermediation." *Journal of Finance*. Vol. 32, No. 2 (May).

Lenckus, D. 1997. "Self-Insurance Expanding Its Reach: Risk Management Takes Sophisticated Turn." *Business Insurance* (February 17).

Lenckus, D. 2000. "Finite Risk Superfund Deal Set." *Business Insurance* (November 6).

Lerner, J. 2000a. *Venture Capital*. New York: John Wiley & Sons.

Lerner, J. 2000b. "Where Does State Street Lead? A First Look At Finance Patents, 1971–2000." Harvard Business School Working Paper #01-005.

Lerner, J. 2000b. *Venture Capital*. New York: John Wiley & Sons.

Lev, B. 1989. "On the Usefulness of Earnings and Earnings Research: Lessons and Directions from Two Decades of Empirical Research." *Journal of Accounting Research*. Vol. 27, Supplement.

Lewent, J. C., and A. J. Kearney. 1990. "Identifying, Measuring, and Hedging Currency Risk at Merck." *Journal of Applied Corporate Finance*. Vol. 1.

Lewin, P. 1999. *Capital in Disequilibrium: The Role of Capital in a Changing World*. New York: Routledge.

Linn, S. C., and J. M. Pinegar. 1988. "The Effect of Issuing Preferred Stock on Common and Preferred Stockholder Wealth." *Journal of Financial Economics*. Vol. 22.

Loh, J. 2000. "Alternative Risk Transfers: What Managers Need to Know Separating Hype from Facts, and Is It Right for You?" *Asia Insurance Review* (December 5).

Lonkevich, D. 1999. "Integrated Risk Products Slow to Catch On." *National Underwriter* (April 12).

Lucas, D. 2001. *CDO Handbook*. New York: J.P. Morgan Securities, Inc.

Mackie-Mason, J. K. 1990. "Do Taxes Affect Corporate Financing Decisions?" *Journal of Finance*. Vol. 45.

Maksimoic, V. 1995. "Financial Structure and Product Market Competition." *Handbooks in OR & MS, Vol. 9*. Amsterdam: Elsevier.

Malthus, T. 1820 [1967]. *Principles of Political Economy*. Cambridge: Cambridge University Press.

Marx, K. 1859 [1967]. *Capital: A Critique of Political Economy*. New York: Modern Library.

Masulis, R. W. 1980. "The Effects of Capital Structure Changes on Security Prices: A Study of Exchange Offers." *Journal of Financial Economics*. Vol. 8.

Masulia, R. W., and A. W. Korwar. 1986. "Seasoned Equity Offerings: An Empirical Investigation." *Journal of Financial Economics*. Vol. 15.

Matten, C. 2000. *Managing Bank Capital*. 2nd ed. New York: John Wiley & Sons.

Menger, C. 1871 [1994]. *Principles of Economics*. New York: Libertarian Press.

Merges, R. P. 1999. "As Many As Six Impossible Patents Before Breakfast: Property Rights for Business Concepts and Patent System Reform." *Berkeley Technology Law Journal*. Vol. 14.

Merton, R. C. 1971a. "Optimum Consumption and Portfolio Rules in a Continuous Time Model." *Journal of Economic Theory*. Vol. 3.

Merton, R. C. 1971b. "An Intertemporal Capital Asset Pricing Model." *Econometrica*. Vol. 41.

Merton, R. C. 1974. "On the Pricing of Corporate Debt: The Risk Structure of Interest Rates." *Journal of Finance*. Vol. 29.

Merton, R. C., and A. F. Perold. 1993. "Management of Risk Capital in Financial Firms." In *Financial Services: Perspectives and Challenges*. Boston: Harvard Business School Press.

Milgrom, P., and J. Roberts. 1986. "Price and Advertising Signals of Product Quality." *Journal of Political Economy* Vol. 94.

Miller, M. H. 1977. "Debt and Taxes." *Journal of Finance* Vol. 32, No. 2.

Miller, M. H. 1986. "Financial Innovation: The Last Twenty Years and the Next." *Journal of Financial and Quantitative Analysis*. Vol. 21.

Miller, M. H. 1997. *Merton Miller on Derivatives*. New York: John Wiley & Sons.

Miller, M. H., and K. Rock. 1985. "Dividend Policy Under Asymmetric Information." *Journal of Finance*. Vol. 40, No. 4 (September).

Miller, M. H., and M. S. Scholes. 1978. "Dividends and Taxes." *Journal of Financial Economics*. Vol. 6.

Mikkelson, W. H., and M. M. Partch. 1986. "Valuation Effects of Security Offerings and the Issuance Process." *Journal of Financial Economis*. Vol. 15.

Modigliani, F., and Miller, M. H. 1958. "The Cost of Capital, Corporation Finance, and the Theory of Investment." *American Economic Review*. Vol. 47.

Modigliani, F., and Miller, M. H. 1963. "Corporate Income Taxes and the Cost of Capital: A Correction." *American Economic Review*. Vol. 53, No. 3.

Monti, R. G., and A. Barile. 1995. *A Practical Guide to Finite Risk Insurance and Reinsurance*. New York: John Wiley & Sons.

Myers, G. 2000. "The Alternative Insurance Market: A Primer." White Paper. Munich RE/America RE (June 30).

Myers, S. C. 1977. "The Determinants of Corporate Borrowing." *Journal of Financial Economics*. Vol. 5.

Myers, S. C. 1984. "The Capital Structure Puzzle." *Journal of Finance*. Vol. 39, No. 3.

Myers, S. C., and N. S. Majluf. 1984. "Corporate Financing and Investment Decisions When Firms Have Information That Investors Do Not Have." *Journal of Financial Economics*. Vol. 13.

Nelson, P. 1970. "Information and Consumer Behavior." *Journal of Political Economy*. Vol. 78.

Nelson, P. 1974. "Advertising as Information." *Journal of Political Economy*. Vol. 81.

Niehaus, G., and S. V. Mann. 1992. "The Trading of Underwriting Risk: An Analysis of Insurance Futures Contracts and Reinsurance." *Journal of Risk and Insurance* Vol. 59, No. 4.

Outreville, J. F. 1998. *Theory and Practice of Insurance*. Boston: Kluwer.

Pacelle, M., and S. Young. 2001. "Bondholders Press Telecom Firms to Halt Spending Sprees." *Wall Street Journal* (July 2).

Parkin, A. 1998. "Catastrophic Risk as an 'Alternative Investment.'" In *Securitized Insurance Risk*. M. Himick, ed. Chicago, Ill.: Glenlake Publishing Company, Ltd.

Peterson, M. 2001. "Master Chefs of the Credit Market." *Euromoney* (June).

Phifer, R. 1996. *Reinsurance Fundamentals: Treaty and Facultative*. New York: John Wiley & Sons.

Rajan, R. G. 1992. "Insiders and Outsiders: The Choice Between Informed and Arm's-Length Debt." *Journal of Finance*. Vol. 47.

Rajan, R. G., and K. Zingales. 1995. "What Do We Know About Capital Structure? Some Evidence from International Data." *Journal of Finance* Vol. 5, No. 5 (December).

Ricardo, D. 1817. [1962] *Principles of Political Economy and Taxation.* Cambridge: Cambridge University Press.

Rogers, M. T., A. Sargeant, and G. Osborne. 1996. "Insurance Captives Offer Buoyant Risk Financing." *Corporate Cashflow* (April).

Ross, S. A., 1977. "The Determination of Financial Structure: The Incentive-Signalling Approach." *Bell Journal of Economics* Vol. 8 (Spring).

Rothschild, M, and J. Stiglitz. 1976. "Equilibrium in Competitive Insurance Markets." *Quarterly Journal of Economics.* Vol. 90.

Sammer, J. 1999. "Brave New Business Risks." *Business Finance* (December 1999).

Say, J. B. 1803 [2001]. *A Treatise on Political Economy.* London: Transaction Publishers.

Schenk, C. 2000. "Michelin: Setting the Standard." *Alternative Risk Strategies: Special Supplement to Risk Magazine* (December).

Schön, E., V. Bochicchio, and E. Wolfram. 1998. *Integrated Risk Management Solutions.* Zürich: Swiss Re New Markets.

Sclafane, S. 1996. "Product Liability Plan Taps Capital Market." *National Underwriter* (April 22).

Scordis, N. A., and M. M. Porat. 1998. "Captive Insurance Companies and Manager-Owner Conflicts." *Journal of Risk and Insurance.* Vol. 65, No. 2.

Senbet, L. W., and J. K. Seward. 1995. "Financial Distress, Bankruptcy, and Reorganization." *Handbooks in OR & MS, Vol. 9.* Amsterdam: Elsevier.

Shimpi, P. 2001. *Integrating Corporate Risk Management.* New York: Texere.

Sick, G. 1995. "Real Options." *Handbooks in OR & MS, Vol. 9.* Amsterdam: Elsevier.

Skipper, H. D. 1998. "The Nature of Government Intervention into Insurance Markets: Regulation." In *International Risk and Insurance: An Environmental-Managerial Approach.* H. D. Skipper, ed. New York: Irwin McGraw-Hill.

Smith, A. 1776 [1994]. *An Inquiry Into the Nature and Causes of the Wealth of Nations.* New York: Modern Library.

Smith, C. W., Jr. 1986a. "Investment Banking and the Capital Acquisition Process." *Journal of Financial Economics.* Vol. 15.

Smith, C. W., Jr. 1986b. "On the Convergence of Insurance and Finance Research." *Journal of Risk and Insurance.* Vol. 53, No. 4.

Smith, C. W., Jr., and R. M. Stulz. 1985. "The Determinants of Firms' Hedging Policies." *Journal of Financial and Quantitative Analysis.* Vol. 20, No. 4.

Smith, C. W., Jr., and J. Warner. 1979. "On Financial Contracting: An Analysis of Bond Covenants." *Journal of Financial Economics.* Vol. 7.

Smithson, C. W. 1987. "A LEGO® Approach to Financial Engineering." *Midland Corporate Finance Journal*. Vol. 4.

Smithson, C. W. 1998. *Managing Financial Risk*. 3rd ed. New York: McGraw-Hill.

Solow, R. 1956. "A Contribution to the Theory of Economic Growth." *Quarterly Journal of Economics*. Vol. 70.

Spence, M. 1973. "Job Market Signaling." *Quarterly Journal of Economics*. Vol. 87.

Stulz, R. 1990. "Managerial Discretion and Optimal Financing Policies." *Journal of Financial Economics*. Vol. 26.

Sullivan, A. 1995. "A Sprung Trap." *Airfinance Journal* (July/August).

Swoboda, P., and J. Zechner. 1995. "Financial Structure and the Tax System." *Handbooks in OR & MS, Vol. 9*. Amsterdam: Elsevier.

Tavakoli, J. M. 1998. *Credit Derivatives*. New York: John Wiley & Sons.

Thompson, R. 1995. "Empirical Methods of Event Studies in Corporate Finance." *Handbooks in OR & MS, Vol. 9*. Amsterdam: Elsevier.

Thompson, R. E., Jr., and E. F. J. Yun. 1998. "Collateralized Loan and Bond Obligations: Creating Value Through Arbitrage." In *Handbook of Structured Financial Products*. F. J. Fabozzi, ed. New Hope, Pa.: Frank J. Fabozzi Associates.

Trieschmann, J. S., S. G. Gustavson, and R. E. Hoyt. 2001. *Risk Management and Insurance*. Cincinnati, Oh.: South-Western College Publishing.

Trigeorgis, L. 1995. "Real Options; An Overview." In *Real Options in Capital Investment: Models, Strategies, and Applications*. L. Trigeorgis, ed. New York: Praeger.

Trigeorgis, L. 1996. *Real Options: Managerial Flexibility and Strategy in Resource Allocation*. Cambridge, Mass.: The MIT Press.

Trigeorgis, L. 1999. *Real Options and Business Strategy*. London: Risk Books.

Tufano, P. 1989. "Financial Innovation and First-Mover Advantages." *Journal of Financial Economics*. Vol. 25.

Tufano, P. 1996. "Who Manages Risk? An Empirical Examination of Risk Management Practices in the Gold Mining Industry." *Journal of Finance* Vol. 52, No. 4 (September).

Van den Bergh, P. 1994. "Operational and Financial Structure of the Payment System." In *The Payment System: Design, Management, and Supervision*. B. J. Summers, ed. Washington, D.C.: International Monetary Fund, 1994.

Vermaelen, T. 1981. "Common Stock Repurchases and Market Signaling: An Empirical Study." *Journal of Financial Economics*. Vol. 9.

Walters, L. 2001. "Cutting Edge." *International Securitisation Report* (July/August).

Welch, I. 1989. "Seasoned Offerings, Imitation Costs, and the Underpricing of Initial Public Offerings." *Journal of Finance*. Vol. 44.

Williams, C. A., M. L. Smith, and P. C. Young. 1995. *Risk Management and Insurance.* 7th ed. New York: McGraw-Hill.

Winston, P. D. 2000. "Seeing Insurance as Capital Rather than Cost." *Business Insurance* (November 27).

Wörhmann, P. 1998. "Swiss Developments in Alternative Risk Financing Models." The European America Business Journal (Spring).

Wörhmann, P. 1999. "Finite Risk Solutions in Switzerland." *The European America Business Journal* (Spring).

Wörhmann, P. 2001. "Alternative Risk Financing—Developing the Market Potential of Small and Medium-Sized Companies." *European America Business Journal* (Spring).

Wörhmann, P., and C. Bürer. 2001. "Instrument der Alternativen Risikofinanzierung." *Schweizer Versicherung.* Vol. 7.

Young, J. B. 1996. "Alternative Risk Financing: The Calm Before the Storm." Manuscript, Alternative Risk Solutions, Inc.

index

ABB, 208
Abbey National, 248
ABN Amro, 266
Adverse development covers, 390–395
Adverse selection:
  costs, reducing, 235–236
  market for lemons, 117
  overview, 321–327
  pecking order theory, 117–122
Agency costs, 95–112
AIG. *See* American International Group (AIG)
Airline Mutual Insurance (AMI), 371
Airlines, 194–195
Akerlof, George, 117
Allianz Risk Transfer, 462, 477–478
Allied Signal, 415
Alternative risk transfer (ART):
  defined, xi
  financial theories and, 131
  financing options, 360
  guarantees, 433–439
  overview, 351–356
  products
    derivatives and, 270
    integrated, 402–407
    layered, 402–407
    (re)insurance, 55
  retention, 357–359
  risk finance, 358–359
Amazon.com, 505
American International Group (AIG), 389, 413, 414, 435, 439
American International Specialty Lines Insurance Co., 389
American Skandia Life Assurance Corp., 469–470
American Stock Exchange, 267
American style (options), 26
Andre Group, 208
AON, 366
Applied Insurance Research, 495, 500
Asset Backed Capital (ABC), 437
Asset divestiture:
  credit derivatives, 303–304
  deferment option, 297–298
  option to alter operating scale, 300
  overview, 294–297
  reversible, 302–303
  risk in, 301
  switching option, 300–301
  synthetic, 301–304
  synthetic asset repurchase agreement, 302–303
  time-to-build option, 298–299
Asset Guaranty Insurance Co., 438
Asset substitution, 100–106
Asset-backed commercial paper (ABCP) programs, 309–310
Asset-backed securities (ABSs), 308–309
Assumption, 333
Asymmetrical information:
  importance of, 122
  models based on, 125–126

*AT&T Corp. v. Excel
    Communications, Inc.*, 518
Authorized control level (ACL), 177
AXA RE, 436

Balance sheets:
    for DaimlerChrysler AG, 37
    economic, 38
    samples, 9, 12
Bank of America, 266
Bank Austria, 439
Bank for International Settlements
    (BIS), 168
Banker's acceptance, 252
Bankhaus Herstatt, 197–198n. 3
Banks:
    bridge, 399n. 5
    commercial, 246
        assets of, 251–252
        liabilities, 248–251
        relations among, 247–248
        retail-funded, 246–247
        role of, in payment system,
            254–257
        whole-sale funded, 246–247
    correspondent, 247–248
    defined, 245–246
    investment, 57, 246
    merchant, 246
    money center, 247
    nostro, 256–257
    vostro, 256–257
Barclays, 266
Barings, 193, 201
BarnesandNoble.com, 505
Basel Capital Accord:
    committed capital and, 431
    compliance with, 171–172
    overview, 168–169
    regulatory capital arbitrage and,
        181
    scope of, 169–171
    securities broker/dealers and, 173

Basel II, 172–173, 291
Berkshire Hathaway, 394
Black Wednesday, 188
BNO-Paribas, 433
Bonds:
    convertible, 46–47
    callable, 45
    planned amortization class (PAC),
        308
    putable, 45
Book values, 17
Borrowings, 249–251
British Aerospace, 440
British Bankers' Association, 193
Business interruption (BI) protection,
    424

Call option, 26
Canadian Imperial Bank of
    Commerce, 266
Capital:
    committed (*see* Committed
        capital)
    contingent, 67–70
    defined, 4–5
    excess (See Excess capital)
    financial (see Financial capital)
    investment (see Investment capital)
    vs. labor, 19
    paid in, 67–70, 144–153
    privately negotiated, 53–55
    real, 4–5, 17n. 1
    risk (*see* Risk capital)
    risk transformation products,
        236–237
    signaling, 7–8, 138–144, 156–157
    theory of, 19–25
*Capital Adequacy Standards for
    Securities Firms*, 177
Capital asset pricing model (CAPM),
    82, 84n. 6
Capital Credit, 438
Capital Dynamics, 462

Capital requirements:
  capital structure and, 179–181
  supply of capital and, 181–182
Capital Risk Strategies (CRS),
    468–469
Capital structure:
  average proportion of, by security,
    65
  defined, 17
  determining cost of capital, 80–84
  empirical evidence on, 64–67
  implications of capital
    requirements on, 179–181
  irrelevance of, 72–84
  risk-based, 237–241
  optimization, xii–xiii
  three-dimensional view of,
    238–239
  trends in nonfinancial U.S.
    corporations, 65
Captives:
  benefits of, 375–379
  capitalization of, 374–375
  dividends in, 374–375
  group/associative, 371–372
  multiparent, 370–374
  overinvestment and, 377
  overview, 365
  popularity of, 355
  protected cell companies, 373–374
  rent-a-captive, 372–373
  risk management and, 378
  risk retention groups, 371–372
  single-parent captive insurers,
    365–368
  single-parent captive reinsurers,
    368–369
  single-parent multibranch captive
    reinsurers, 369–370
  tax considerations for, 377
  types of, 365–374
Cargill Financial Services, 212
Cargill Investor Services, 212

Cash flows:
  captives and, 376–377
  importance of, 40–41
Cash Management Account (CMA),
    517
Catastrophe futures contracts
    (CATs), 480–486
CatEPuts, 443
Cedant, 333
Centre Re, 380, 392, 413, 469
Certificates of deposit (CDs), 249
Cession, 333
Chase:
  Secured Loan Trust NoteSM, 459
  Securities, 459
  Morgan Stanley Mortgage Default
    Recourse Notes and, 464
Chicago Board of Trade (CBOT):
  catastrophe futures contracts,
    480–486
  Clearing Corporation, 439
  derivatives and, 267
Chicago Board Options Exchange,
    267
Chicago Mercantile Exchange
    (CME), 261–262, 267
China Airlines, 376
Cigna, 413, 415
Citigroup, 266
Claims, 101, 102
Clearing House Interbank Payments
    System (CHIPS), 260
Clearinghouses, 267–269
Coinsurance, 319
Collateralized bond obligations
    (CBOs), 453
Collateralized debt obligations
    (CDOs):
  apportionment of funds, 456
  cash flow, 453–456
  equity-backed, 462
  mechanics of, 454–456
  overview, 453

CDOs (*Continued*)
  purpose of, 456
  reinsurance, 462–470
  synthetic, 457–461
Collateralized loan obligations
    (CLOs), 453
Collateralized mortgage obligations
    (CMOs), 307–308
Commercial and industrial (C&I)
    bank loans, 43
Commercial paper, 44
Committed capital:
  CatEPuts, 443
  covenants, 430
  expiration style and date, 429
  fixed range second trigger,
    446–447
  fixed second trigger, 443–446
  indexed trigger, 448
  loss equity put options, 443
  mechanics of, 428
  price of, 429–430
  put-protected new equity issues,
    441–442
  reverse convertibles, 448–449
  Swiss Re's solutions for, 431–433
  timing of payment, 430
  triggers and, 428
  underlying security and, 428–429
  variable second trigger, 447–448
Committed Long-Term Capital
    Solutions (CLOCS), 431–433
Committee on Bank Supervision,
    168–173
Commodities Exchange Act (CEA),
    267, 521–522
Commodity Futures Trading
    Commission (CFTC), 267
Commodity-Embedded Insurance
    (COIN^SM), 414
Compagnie Financière Michelin,
    432
Control, 6

Cooling degree days (CDDs),
    520–521, 530n. 4
Copayments, 319
Corporations:
  C, 54–55
  closed, 42
  S, 54–55
Cost of capital:
  decreasing, 232–236
  in risk-based model, 239–241
Crédit Lyonnais, 433
Crédit Mutuael Banque Populaire,
    433
Credit risks:
  off-balance-sheet, 170–171
  on-balance-sheet, 169–170
Crédit Suisse First Boston (CSFB),
    175, 247, 266, 433, 435, 437
Credit-linked note (CLN), 460–461

DaimlerChrysler AG, 37, 40, 208
DaimlerChrysler Services, 212
Das Kapital, 23
Debt:
  agency costs of, 100–112
  claims, 51–52
  exchangeable, 47
  irrelevance of, 75–76
  market equilibrium, 89
  overhang, 106–111
  overview, 11–14
  securities, 43–44
  senior
    defined, 51–52
    securities capital structure and,
      60–61
    value of, 61
  subordinated
    defined, 51–52
    securities capital structure and,
      61–64
    value of, 63
  synthetic, 232–233

Deductibles, 317–319
Delegated monitoring, 122–124
Delta, 31, 32, 186–187
Demand deposit accounts (DDAs), 249
Derivatives:
  combinations of, 282–283
  credit default swaps, 284–287
  credit risk, 284–291
  default and migration risk, 287–289
  defined, 264–265
  documentation for, 525–526
  exchange-traded, 267–269
  exchange-traded catastrophic, 480–486
  vs. finite risk, 397–399
  forward delivery contracts, 270–273
  futures contracts, 273–274
  vs. insurance, 523–524
  participants in, 265–269
  privately negotiated, 265, 266
  spread risk, 289–291
  structured notes, 283–284
  swaps, 274–276
  transfer of risks, 270–284, 291
  weather, 521–522, 526–529
Derivatives Policy Group (DPG), 175
Deutsche Bank, 247, 266, 462
Dilution, 149–150
Discounted cash flows (DCFs), 39
Divestiture. *See* Asset divestiture
Dividends, 76–78
Dow Corning, 468
Dresdner Kleinwort Wasserstein, 266
Drexel Burnham Lambert Group, Inc., 187

Earnings before interest, tax, depreciation, and amortization (EBITDA), 424–425

Earnings smoothing, 139–140
Economic value added (EVA), 207–208
Effective maturity, 44–45
Energy Insurance, 371
Enterprise Earnings Protection Insurance, 414
Enterprise-wide risk management (EWRM), 401
Environmental Protection Agency (EPA), 388
Equity:
  agency costs of, 96–100
  claims, by seniority, 50–51
  securities capital structure and, 60
  synthetic, 233–234
Eurodeposits, 249
European Monetary System, 188
European style (options), 26, 27
Eva Air, 376
Excess capital:
  held as risk capital, 134–138
  held as signaling capital, 138–144
  managing costs of, 154–157
  reducing underinvestment costs of, 137–138
Exchange and Clearing House (ECHO), 438
Exchanges, 267, 269
e-X Programme, 416

Fannie Mae. *See* Federal National Mortgage Association (FNMA)
Federal Home Loan Mortgage Corporation (FHLMC), 307, 464–465
Federal National Mortgage Association (FNMA), 307
Federal Reserve, 259–260
Fedwire, 259–260, 262n. 12

Financial capital:
  claims, 39
  corporate use of, 5–8
  vs. real, 4–5
Financial distress:
  costs of, 90–93, 135–137,
    154–155, 196–197
  reinsurance and, 336
Financial mutuals, 42
Financial Risk Insurance Program
    (FRIP), 440
Finite risk:
  adverse development covers, 390
  capital structure, 385–386
  vs. derivatives, 397–399
  finite quota share treaties,
    395–396
  investment-based premium, 385
  limited liability, 384–385
  loss portfolio transfers, 387–390
  multiyear coverage, 385
  products, 380–386
  profit/loss sharing, 383–384
  prospective products, 395–397
  retrospective products, 386–394
  spread loss treaties, 396–397
First Boston, 308
First Union, 248
Fixed claims, 11–14. *See also* Debt
Flashpoint, 435–436
Floating rate note (FRN), 283–284
Flows, 127–128
Font-Réaulx, Benoît de, 450n. 8
Forward rate agreement (FRA), 272
Framework for Voluntary Oversight,
    175
Fraternity Row, 30–32
Freddie Mac. *See* Federal Home
    Loan Mortgage Corporation
    (FHLMC)
Free cash flow, 41
Frontier Insurance Company,
    394–395

Fronting insurers, 368–369
Funds:
  defined, 39–40
  federal, 249–250
  internal, 41
  transfers, 253–254

Gamma, 31, 32, 187
Gemini Re, 478
Georgetown Re, 477
Gerling Credit Insurance Group
    (GCIG), 466–468
Global Derivatives Study Group,
    190
Goldman Sachs, 175, 266
  Mitsui Marine Derivative Products
    LP, 463, 467, 479–480
Government National Mortgage
    Association (GNMA), 307
Government sponsored enterprises
    (GSEs), 307
Grammercy Place Insurance Ltd.,
    463–464
Green shoe, 71n. 16
Guaranteed investment contracts
    (GICs), 160–165
Guarantees:
  benefits of, 433–434
  clearinghouses, 438–439
  conditionality/covenants, 434
  exchanges, 438–439
  mechanics of, 433–434
  residual value, 439–441

Haircuts, 174–175, 176
Hamilton Lane Advisors, 464
Hannover Re, 470
Heating degree days (HDDs),
    520–521, 530n. 4
Hedge funds, 51
Hicks, John, 23–24
HIH Casualty & General Insurance,
    435–437

Hollywood Funding, 435–438
Honeywell, 401, 415
HSBC, 266
Huntsman, 415

IBNR losses. *See* Losses, incurred
    but not reported (IBNR)
Independent Insurance, 436
Information technology (IT), 215
Initial public offerings (IPOs):
    money burning in, 167n. 8
    overview, 56
    project financing and, 141
Inquiry into the Nature and Causes
    of the Wealth of Nations, 19
Insolvency, 50, 70n. 6
Institutional Investor, 459
Insurance:
    contracts for, 312–313, 525–526,
      529
    defined, 522–523
    vs. derivatives, 523–524
    lines, 328–329
    marketplace for, 327–329
    mechanics of, 313–316
    overview, 311–312
    product lines, 327–328
    providers
      asset and liability, 157–160
      defined, 55
      management by, 330–332
      organization structures of,
        329
      risk-based capital standards for,
        177–178
      solvency margins in the
        European Union for, 178–179
Integrated risk management (IRM):
    overview, 401–402
    products
      multiline, 408–417
      multitrigger, 417–425
      range of risks covered, 413

Interest payment provisions, 44
Internal rate of return (IRR), 24
International Air Transport
    Association, 371
International Organisation of
    Securities Commissions
    (IOSCO), 177
International Swaps and Derivatives
    Association (ISDA), 193, 525
Intertemporal capital asset pricing
    model (i-CAPM), 83, 84n. 6
Intertemporal marginal rate of
    substitution (IMRS), 81
Intrinsic value, 28–30
Investment capital:
    building blocks of, 8–14
    fixed, 37
    overview, 5–6
    viewed as options, 14–17
Investment Dealers' Digest, 459
Iron Mountain Copper Mine, 388
IT Corp., 389–390

Jardine Lloyd Thompson (JLT), 437
JP Morgan Chase, 247, 266,
    459–460

Kappa, 187
Keynes, J. M., 194
Kiln, 435
Knight, Frank, 193–194

Labor, 19
Labor theory, 22–23
Lambda, 187
Lane, Morton, 487n. 14
Large-value transfer systems
    (LVTSs):
    batched, 258
    characteristics of, 257–259
    continuous, 258
    daylight overdrafts, 258–259
    examples of, 259–262

Laurie-Walker, Alastair, 438
Law Debenture Trust Corp. Ltd., 437
Layering, 403–407
Leeson, Nick, 193, 201
Lehman Brothers, 175, 266
Letters of credit (LOCs), 69
Leverage ratio, 17
Lexington Insurance, 435
Liability risks, 165–166
Life insurance, 469–470
Limited liability partnerships, 54–55
Liquidation, 99–100
Lloyd, Edward, 329
Lloyd's:
  finite risk transactions, 383
  Hollywood Funding and, 435
  transactional insurance products and, 540
  underwriting, 328, 416
Loans, 43–44, 55, 251–253
Locke, John, 22
London Clearing House, 439
London Interbank Offered Rate (LIBOR), 43, 249, 312, 458
Loss adjustment expenses (LAEs), 332
Losses, incurred but not reported (IBNR), 386, 390
Loss mitigation products (LMPs), 533–535, 539
Loss portfolio transfers (LPOs), 387–390

M&M propositions:
  assumptions of, 73
  capital requirements and, 180
  debt and, 75–76
  dividend payouts and, 76–78
  free cash flows and, 133
  irrelevance of risk management and, 219
  market value rule and, 78–80

net present value criterion and, 78–80
risk management and, 218–220
securities capital structure and, 73–75
shareholder preferences and, 195–196
static trade-off theory and, 86–94
Malthus, Thomas, 21
March, Michael, 439
Market risk, 171
Market values, 17, 78–80
Marsh, 366, 416
  Financial and Professional (Finpro) division, 438
Martinair Insurance, 376
Marx, Karl, 23
Material adverse chance (MAC) clauses, 69
Maturity, 44
McKay, David, 431
Mead Corp., 415
Medium term note (MTN), 44
Me-first rules, 153
Menger, Carl, 21–22
Mergers and acquisitions (M&A), 532–533
Merrill Lynch, 175, 517
Metallgesellschaft AG (MG AG), 187, 237
Mezzanine finance. See Debt, subordinated
MG Refining and Marketing, Inc. (MGRM), 187, 237
Miller, Merton, 24, 73
Mobil Oil, 401, 415
Modigliani, Franco, 24, 73
Money burning, 141
  in IPO process, 167n. 8
  signals, 167n. 9
Moral hazard:
  adverse selection, 321–327
  copayment provisions, 319

deductibles, 317–319
overview, 316–317
policy limits, 319
subrogation, 320–321
triggers and, 418–419
Morgan Stanley, 175, 266
Capital Services, 465
Mortgage Default Recourse
Notes (MODERNs),
464–466
Mortality and expense (M&E)
charges, 470
Mountain Copper Ltd., 388
Multifactor cost of capital models,
82–84
Multiline Aggregated and Combined
Risk Optimization
(MACRO), 411, 412
Munich-American Risk Partners,
413
Munich Re, 392, 491–502
Mutual Limited, 371

Namur Re SA, 466–468
National Association of Insurance
Commissioners (NAIC),
177
National Indemnity, 394–395
National Provident Institution (NPI),
470
National Westminister Bank, 453
Nestlé, 251–252
Net present value (NPV):
in asset divestiture, 296–297
calculation of, 167n. 2
early version of, 24
expectations in, 310n. 3
overview, 78–80
reducing underinvestment and,
224–226
New Hampshire Insurance, 436
New York Clearing House, 260
Nonprofits, 43

OM Gruppen AB, 439
Open corporation, 42
Opportunity costs, 21
Option, abandonment. *See* Asset
divestiture
Options Clearing Corporation,
261–262
Options:
American style, 26
Asian, 278–279
average price/strike, 278–279
barrier, 276–277
basket, 282
binary/digital, 277–278
compound, 281–282
European style, 26, 27
exchange, 282
Greeks, 30–32
investment capital as, 14–17
ladder, 279–280
lookback, 279
overview, 26–34
quanto, 278
rainbow, 282
shout, 280–281
value of firm, 16
value of risky debt, 16
Original issue discount (OID)
instruments, 44
Ownership, 6
Oxford Health Plans, 539

Palmer, Paul, 438
Parametric Re, 476
Patent law:
basics of, 505–506
evolution of financial patents,
515–518
"Method of Exercising a Cat,"
506–511
overview, 503–506
risk finance patents,
511–515

Pecking order theory:
adverse selection and, 117–122
vs. dynamic trade-off theory,
127–129
evidence on impact of capital
structure changes, 129–131
financial implications of, 124–125
overinvestment in, 129
underinvestment in, 128–129
Perils:
operational, 193
production, 191–193
Philadelphia Stock Exchange, 267
Placement, 53–58
Potentially responsible parties
(PRPs), 388
PRIME Capital Hurricane Ltd.,
491–502
Prime Edge Capital PLC, 462
Principal repayment provisions, 44
Principles of Economics, 21
*Principles of Political Economy and
Taxation*, 22
Principles of Political Economy, 21
Priority, 49–53
Private placement memoranda
(PPMs), 54
Procter & Gamble, 201
Productivity theories, 21
Project finance, 140–143
Property Claims Services (PCS)
index, 420, 483–486
Proprietorships, 42
Protected cell companies (PCCs),
373–374
Put option, 26
Put-call parity, 32–33

Quadrant Capital, 437

Rabobank, 470
Raffeisenbank, 248
Rainer Marc Frey (RMF), 424

Real estate investment trust (REIT),
42
Real estate mortgage investment
conduits (REMICs), 307–308
Real Time Gross Settlement (RTGS),
258
Reassurance. *See* Reinsurance
Regulatory capital, 8
Reinsurance:
aggregate XOL treaties, 344
capacity, 334–335
capital requirements for, 179
catastrophic XOL treaties, 344
defined, 55
excess-of-loss (XOL) treaties,
340–346
forms of, 337
functions of, 333–336
increased surplus or debt capacity,
335
information acquisition, 336
from options perspective, 346–348
per occurrence XOL treaties,
341–343
per risk XOL treaties, 341–343
proportional, 337–340
quota share treaties, 338–339
reduced earnings and cash flow
volatility, 335
reduced expected financial distress
costs, 336
surplus share treaties, 339–340
synthetic liability dispositions, 336
Reliance Insurance Co., 414
Representation and warranty
(R&W) insurance, 533–538
Repurchase agreements, 250
Reserve management:
captives and, 377
excess capital and, 134
methods of, 330–331
Reserves, default, 143
Residential Re, 477, 491

Residual claims, 9–11
Retention, 356–359
Retrocession, 333–334
Retrospective aggregate loss (RAL)
    covers, 393
Retrospective excess of loss (RXL)
    covers, 393
Rho, 187
Rhythms NetConnections, Inc., 106
Ricardo, David, 22
Ringfencing, 386–387
Risk:
  asset, 160–163
  in asset divestiture, 301
  control of, 204–205
  core, 193–197, 200–203
  credit, 188–190
  efficiency enhances, 207–208
  enterprise-wide absolute risk
      tolerance, 201–202
  excess capital and, 134–148
  financial, 186–190, 382–383
  finite (*see* Finite risk)
  funding, 187–188
  Herstatt, 197–198n. 3
  identification of, 200–203
  legal, 190
  market, 186–187
  market liquidity and, 188
  measurement of, 203
  monitoring of, 203–204
  natural risk exposure-based
      tolerance, 202
  noncore, 193–197, 200–203
  relative exposure tolerance,
      202–203
  reporting of, 203–204
  retained, 197
  securities capital structure and,
      58–60
  settlement, 197–198n. 3
  vs. signaling capital, 143–144
  silos, 306–308

transferred, 197
underwriting, 382–383
vocabulary of, 185–193
Risk-adjusted return on capital
    (RAROC), 208
Risk-based capital (RBC) standards,
    177
Risk capital:
  for asset risk, 160–165
  contingent, 157–166
  excess capital and, 134–138
  for liability risks, 165–166
  overview, 6–7
Risk controllers, 207
Risk culture:
  customer management, 211–212
  differences across firms, 215–217
  governance, 209–210
  implementation of, 208–217
  knowledge management and,
      212–215
  product management, 210–211
Risk management:
  adding firm value, 219–220
  as business process, 199–205
  captives and, 378
  M&M propositions and, 218–220
  reducing asset substitution
      monitoring costs, 229–230
  reducing costs of managerial risk
      aversion, 230–232
  reducing expected corporate taxes,
      220–222
  reducing financial distress costs,
      222–224
  reducing overinvestment, 229
  reducing underinvestment,
      224–229
  risk culture and, 205–208
  as substitute for risk capital, 235
Risk Management Association, 193
Risk transformers, 208
Roche, 208

Rolls-Royce, 441
Royal Bank of Canada, 431
Royal Bank of Scotland, 266

Saab, 440–441
Salomon Brothers, 175
Say, J. B., 21
SBC Glacier Finance Ltd., 460–461
SBC Warburg, 460–461
Schimmelbusch, Heinz, 237
Seasoned public offerings (SPOs), 56
Secured claims, 50
Securities:
  broker/dealers
    capital requirements for,
      173–177
    internal models, 176–177
  debt, 43–44
  equity, 42–43
  hybrid claims, 45–49
  priority and, 49–53
  public, 56–58
  types of, 41–49
Securities capital structure:
  contingent capital and, 69–70
  of a firm, by priority, 59
  irrelevance of, 73–75
  M&M propositions and, 73–75
  from options perspective, 60–64
  risk and, 58–60
Securitization:
  asset-backed commercial paper
    programs, 309
  collateralized mortgage
    obligations, 307–308
  mechanics of, 304–306
  mortgage-backed securities, 307
  nonmortgage asset-backed
    securities, 308–309
  participating institutions, 306–310
  products, 306–310
  real estate mortgage investment
    conduits, 307–308

Self-insurance:
  benefits of, 364–365, 375–376
  costs of, 364–365
  overview, 362–363
  pools, 364
  pure, 363
  reserves, 363
Shareholders, 195–196
Siemens, 208
Signaling, 376
SIS SegaInterSettle (SIS), 262
Skwarek, Tom, 450n. 8
Smith, Adam, 19–20
Société Générale, 266, 432
Solvency margins, 178–179
Special-purpose entity (SPE),
  304–306
Special-purpose trust, 304–306
Special-purpose vehicle (SPV):
  asset-backed commercial paper
    products and, 309–310
  collateralized debt obligations
    and, 453–456, 457–459
  preferred stock and, 47–48
  securitization and, 304–306
Spence, Michael, 139
Sperry, 308
Spreads, 33–34
SR Earthquake Fund Ltd., 474–476
St. Paul Re, 477
Standard & Poor's, 437–438
State of New York Insurance
  Department (NYID), 524
*State Street Bank v. Signature
  Financial*, 517–518
Stauffer Chemical Company, 388
Stauffer Management Co., 388
Stewart, Potter, 265
Stock:
  collateralized preferred, 48–49
  vs. flows, 127–128
  preferred, 47–48, 51
  trust-preferred, 48–49

STORMSM, 414
Straddles, 33–34, 35
Strangles, 33–34, 35
Subrogation, 320–321
Subscription agreements, 478
Sun Microsystems, 415
Swiss Euro Clearing Bank (SECB),
    261
Swiss Interbank Clearing (SIC)
    system, 260–262
Swiss National Bank (SNB), 260
Swiss Re, 392, 416, 417, 421–422,
    479–480
    Committed Long-Term Capital
        Solutions, 431–433
    double-trigger program in,
        424–425
    MACRO from, 411, 412
Sydney Futures Exchange, 451n. 19
Syndicates. *See* Financial mutuals
Synthetic European Credit Tracking
    Securities (SECTRS),
    466–468

Tau, 187
Tax hedges, 527–529
Taxes:
    benefits of, 86–90
    of corporate income, 88
Theory of Finance, The, 4
Theta, 30–31, 187
Tierny, Jacques, 432–433
Time value, 29–30
Tokio Marine & Fire, 476
Total adjusted capital (TAC), 178
Toyota Motor Credit Corporation
    (TMCC), 463–464
Trade-off theory:
    dynamic
        evidence on impact of capital
            structure changes, 129–131
        financial implications of,
            112–114

vs. pecking order theory,
    127–129
    underinvestment in, 128–129
static
    overview, 86–94
    optimal leverage ratio, 93–94
Transactional insurance products
    (TIPs), 533–535, 540–543
Triggers:
    blended covers, 425
    for cat bonds, 472–473
    committed capital and, 428
    example, 424–425
    fixed vs. variable, 419–420
    moral hazard and, 418–419
    multiple
        benefits of, 417–418
        mechanics of, 418–424
    per-occurence vs. cumulative,
        423–424
    switching, 420–423
Turner and Newall, 392–393

UBS Warburg, 247, 266
Underinvestment, 155
Underwriting, 53–58
Union Carbide, 415
Uniroyal Goodrich, 432
United Grain Growers (UGG),
    416–417, 419
United States Automobile
    Association (USAA),
    476–477, 491–502
United States Patent and
    Trademark Office,
    504–505
United States Securities and
    Exchange Commission
    (SEC):
    debt and, 44
    internal models, 176–177
    net capital rule, 174–177
Use theories, 21

Vega, 31, 32, 187
Venture capital, 70–71n. 11
Very accurately defined maturity
        (VADM), 308

Wachovia, 248
Wanters, Diego, 439
Web start-ups, 192
Weighted average cost of capital
        (WACC), 76

Westdeutsche Landesbank, 266
Whipshaw rules, 528
Willis, 416–417
WinCat Coupons, 478–479
Winterthur, 433, 478–479

XL Capital, 413

Zero-coupon debt instruments, 44
Zürich Financial, 366, 413